PERSONAL DATA

Name:

Home Address:

Business Address:

Telephone Numbers

Home: Business: Mobile:

Car: Fax: e-mail:

Website: ISDN: Other:

MEDICAL/ACCIDENT

Contact:

Address:

Telephone - Home: Business:

Doctor: Telephone:

Blood Group: Allergies:

USEFUL INFORMATION

Nat. Health Ins. no.: Driving Licence no.:

Passport no.: AA/RAC Memb. no.:

USEFUL CONTACT DETAILS

Name: Tel: Fax:

Address:

Name: Tel: Fax:

Address:

Name: Tel: Fax:

Address:

DAVID WELCH

IT was only a few years ago that a distinguished Telegraph editor accepted that sport sells newspapers and felt sufficiently moved to advise a possible successor that he would have to recognise its importance if he wanted to make a success of editing.

(Incidently, in common with many of his peers, the editor in question, had something less than a lifelong passion for sport himself.)

So, while enormous thanks are due to assistant sports editor, Martin Smith, and chief photographer, Russell Cheyne, for their work in helping to compile this first Telegraph Yearbook, the real credit for its debut on the bookshelves should go to all those enlightened editors who have had the courage and insight to help create the climate in which sports writing has been allowed to flourish as never before.

We may still be some way short of seeing the news section of a daily paper produced as a 12-page Supplement *inside* the sports pages. But we are getting there....thanks largely to the writers and photographers whose work is recorded on the pages which follow; our other talented contributors for whom space unfortunately ran out on this occasion; and all those working so hard behind the scenes to give the Telegraph sports pages their unique depth and edge on a daily basis.

For too long, much of the outstanding work to have emerged has been discarded almost as soon as it has been published. This Telegraph Yearbook ensures it will be available for reading and re-reading long after the crowds have gone home.

Thanks are also due to our raw material without which we could not function...the sportsmen and women who provide the scope for our writers to be witty, acerbic, enlightening, instructive, and, occasionally, it has to be said, downright rude.

MICHAEL PARKINSON

HE was our centre-half. He used to wait at the bus stop at the top of the lane with his boots knotted together by the laces and dangling round his neck. He was a famous son of Barnsley and took his fame seriously. In those days when players and fans travelled together on the bus to and from the ground on match days there was no room for prima donnas. Public transport was either a chariot or a hearse depending on how the team had played and respect was hard won.

On this particular journey to Oakwell, the only spare seat was next to me. I was paralysed with hero-worship as the player settled into his seat. I had just started work as a junior reporter on a local newspaper and imagined it wouldn't be too long before I would be in the press box writing about football and cricket. 'Off to t'match?' asked the centre-half. I gibbered something in reply, being struck dumb with adoration. 'Does tha' work?' he asked. 'I've just started a job as a reporter on the *South Yorkshire Times*. I want to be a sports reporter,' I said. 'Sports reporters are pillocks,' he said. 'Think on that and get thissen a decent job'. Since that time I have had a lifetime in which to test the veracity of his statement and come to the conclusion he was neither right nor wrong.

When I went for my interview on *The Manchester Guardian* in the late 1950s the editor asked if I wanted to be either a drama critic or a sports writer. I wanted to be both but I sensed hostility in his question. 'Neither,' I replied. 'Make sure it remains that way, for one is a dreamer and the other an oaf,' he said. This was an opinion vouchsafed by another editor of my acquaintance who christened the sports desk 'the toy department'. Most of my life I have written about sport as well as doing other jobs for radio and television which did not involve contact with muddied oafs and flannelled fools. Then, more than ever, I was made aware of the discrepancy in public perception between one and the other. It was most clearly defined when I found myself in Israel covering the Six Day War for BBC Television and writing a column about sport for the *Sunday Times*.

In a break from filming hostilities I wrote an article about my beloved Barnsley and the great Skinner Normanton. I took this along with my television script to the censor, a sardonic man who taught English at University. He passed my television script without much ado, but the article chronicling the exploits of a hard-tackling wing-half in the Third Division North seemed to completely baffle him. Moreover, excellent though his English was it did not encompass a knowledge of the way they speak in Barnsley. He became convinced 'Ayup' and 'Th'what' were encoded messages and I was cunningly passing on secret information to the *Sunday Times* news desk. Eventually I managed to convince him I really was writing a funny article about football in the middle of a war. As he handed back my article he said: 'How can a sports journalist cover a war?' It didn't occur to him to ask how a current affairs journalist could write a column about sport.

The fact is ever since I took up my trade, for some time before, and more than ever nowadays, some of the best reporting and most elegant and humorous writing has been found at the back of the paper. I have known this all my life ever since my father taught me the correct way to read a newspaper was backwards and my heroes were Arlott, Cardus, Robertson-Glasgow, H.D. 'Donny' Davies and many more.

Nowadays, because sport has become this glamorous, multi-million pound industry attractive to women as well as men, children as much as grown-ups and can be marketed as a soft drink or a T-shirt or cuddly toy and players are more pop stars than athletes, you might imagine the lot of the sports writer would have improved accordingly. Not a bit of it. He still finds himself in the bargain basement of journalism while the leader writers and the political analysts and those who write scholarly but incomprehensible articles about EMU walk tall in the knowledge they are employed in what is regarded as a respectable occupation. We sports journalists are still the poor bloody infantry of journalism. Let others wear the plumed hats, we are the footsloggers, the beetle-crushers. So why bother? Simple. It's the best job in the world. Don't tell anyone. They'll all want to do it.

CONTENTS

BEST CHRISTMAS PRESENT AND ALL WRAPPED IN AN IMMERSION SUIT by PETE GOSS

AS the engines of the Royal Australian Air Force plane fade into the distance, I sit down, take the weight of Raphael Dinelli's life and spend quite a few minutes contemplating round two as Aqua Quorum continues to bash her way to windward.

I must have a new, clear strategy, as the fight has changed. My opponent is wily and I need to adapt. More thought is required. Instinct and determination are not enough.

I have always believed that one of the most powerful tools that we possess is that of visualisation. I break the way ahead into clearly defined chunks and mentally walk the course a few times – this is in full colour and 3-D. I am actually there, each time throwing in a new scenario and coming up with a practical solution.

I have often used this and find it roots out most of the surprises so that, when something happens, I am able to deal with it quickly and efficiently as if I have already done it. Each run culminates with a successful rescue.

Phase 1 is a simple yacht race to Raphael's immediate location. Phase 2 will take a little more effort to crack. It's a big grey area and it will be like looking for a needle in a haystack, particularly as it will be getting dark. Phase 3 will be the pick-up. This could present all sorts of complications.

No worries, though, I have plenty of time for some more re-runs on this phase. First of all, I need information. I fax Philippe Jeantot and ask for a detailed 12-hour weather forecast for my area. I also ask if there have been any further updates from Raphael's ARGOS Beacon. Philippe is one of the world's top sailors and, amongst other things, has raced round the world singlehanded four times. He is a rock and plays a vital role throughout the operation.

Very soon, a special forecast comes through from Meteo France – a front will arrive in the afternoon, the wind will head me all day, visibility will reduce, and winds of 40 knots are expected. This will add a good four hours to the passage and make it very hard to find him. There's no room to manoeuvre. I'll just have to get on deck and sail like the devil.

THE rest of the day is spent on boat speed. Nothing dramatic, just sailing, and it is a relief apart from the frustration of being headed off the course by the hour. I get continual updates as to Raphael's position and drift – MRCC Australia confirm that a RAAF plane will aid the rescue in the morning. This gives me great comfort for we have a safety net if I can't find him during the dark hours.

Provided Raphael can cope with the cold I feel we have him. I am now 20 miles directly downwind of him and start short-tacking up his drift line. It starts to get dark. This could actually be a blessing if the raft has a light.

The wind just will not settle and, without the luxury of anticipation, the auto-pilot finds it hard to keep as close to the wind as I would like in the confused seas. So it is back to the helm. Some five hours later, we are five miles downwind of where Raphael should be given his drift. I slow Aqua Quorum down and start popping up to the first spreaders to catch a glimpse of him. It is readily apparent that, given the seas, we'll need a lot of luck.

On going below, I see another message has come in. It is a position update and it has changed considerably. We have overshot the mark by seven miles. I wonder where we would be without BT INMARSAT. Philippe also informs me that he has seen a picture from the RAAF plane. Algimouss has been

dismasted and is submerged. There is nothing to see apart from the life raft and he thinks he may have sunk by now, anyway. The needle gets smaller.

I sail back to the exact position I have been given and, being to windward, I drop the main and zigzag down his drift line under storm jib, keeping the speed down to between three and five knots.

It is very dark and the front has arrived. A sense of desperation sets in as the wind rises and the visibility falls. I stand on the bow, blasting the fog-horn and firing rocket flares. If only I can attract Raphael's attention, he will let off a flare and we've cracked it. 'Come on Raphael, wake up', I shout into the darkness. There is no response, just an all-enveloping greyness that cloaks any attempt to penetrate it.

I reach the end of his projected drift line. He is here, I know it. I can feel it and yet emptiness pervades. Come on, come on, we didn't tackle that storm for this. Give us a break Neptune, surely we deserve one now. I decide to carry on the run until I have doubled his drift. We have to conclude each avenue. Nothing.

Right. Turn round, get the main up and work back. We'll bloody well do this all night if we have to. You'll never grind us down, damn you. The main keeps jamming in the lazy jacks. My elbow aches and there is no strength. But be mechanical. Persistence pays.

I nip below and another position comes in. It has changed and the drift is different. All that for nothing. I start to re-plot the position but there are two charts now. As if I am drunk, I just can't work it out. The first plot puts him a crushing 50 miles away. Wow, hang on, that's not right. I go on deck and stick my head in a bucket of water. It's the first time I am thankful the Southern Ocean is cold. Back to the chart table and start again. It makes sense now. He's six miles away and the plot is quite recent.

Slowly, slowly. Concentrate, don't miss him. Come on, Raphael, bang off a flare or something. You have got to help yourself now. I am not enough. I try the Navico VHF in desperation. It is waterproof and I can use it on deck . . . 'Aqua Quorum. Aqua Quorum. This is rescue 252. We have started our descent and should be with you in four minutes.' Thanks, guys. The relief is heady. Soon the RAAF plane flies past. They've a visual. He is three miles away and they'll drop a smoke flare by him. They turn round and fly towards me. As they pass over Raphael, they flash their lights. I take the best bearing of my life. They inform me there are two rafts, Raphael is in the first and he has waved at them. Good lad, he must have the constitution of an ox. Phase 3 suddenly becomes simple.

I drop the main, feel the wind and, as the raft comes into sight, I judge the best approach. Port side. I have grab lines all round the boat and a long line with two fenders on it aft just in case I overshoot. Fifty, 40, 30, 20 metres. It's going to be a good one. Thank heavens for all the practice. Run forward and throw off the headsail halyard. Raphael grips the grab line. Got him!

Wow, got a true professional here. He insists on passing me three distress beacons and a box of stores. There's a bottle of champagne. 'Oh, go on then, seeing as you've brought a drink.' We both heave and he's on deck. Just like that. The best Christmas present I've ever had, all wrapped up in an immersion suit. ★ **02/01/97**

Flashback... Pete Goss, on Aqua Quorum, helps Raphael Dinelli from his life raft on Boxing Day Popperfoto/Reuters

DALGLISH READY TO ANSWER CALL

HENRY WINTER,

who collaborated with Kenny Dalglish on his autobiography, believes the Scot is the man to replace Kevin Keegan

ALL Newcastle eyes now train on Spain. Kevin Keegan has retreated to Marbella. In seeking his successor, Newcastle's board are linked with Barcelona's coach, Bobby Robson, and Deportivo La Coruna's John Toshack.

Yet the answer to Newcastle's managerial vacancy might be a man with property in Spain but currently back home in Southport. The feeling grows that if Sir John Hall offered the job to Kenny Dalglish he would accept.

A misconception exists in certain parts of St James' Park that Dalglish is unavailable because Rangers are grooming him for Walter Smith's managerial job. This could not be further from the truth. Dalglish, a boyhood Rangers fan but a celebrated captain of Celtic, surely has no intention of wishing to undermine, or step into, Smith's position. Besides, Dalglish is not employed by Rangers but by Carnegie, a subsidiary owned by David Murray, Ibrox's power-broker.

Dalglish's part-time role with Carnegie centres as much on making contacts for Murray's empire as scouting activities for Rangers. It does not preclude the former Liverpool and Blackburn manager's return to full-time management.

Suggestions that Dalglish lacks the requisite steel also angered him. Slightly disparaging comments by Jimmy Hill on the BBC last Friday were swiftly followed by a phone-call from someone close to Dalglish, demanding a retraction. The implication for this is clear: Dalglish is ready and waiting for Newcastle.

The critics' question is: if stress forced him out of Liverpool and Blackburn, how could Dalglish possibly handle the Newcastle job? Yet such theories, blithely trotted out over the airwaves by people who should look deeper, need addressing. After 14 successful years at Anfield, six of them as player-manager, Dalglish stood down to protect his health, which had deteriorated in the horrifying wake of Hillsborough.

AS a club and city mourned, Dalglish played the rock and comforter, once needing a police escort to carry him between a relentless procession of funerals. The pressure eventually told, Dalglish telling Liverpool he had to leave because he felt 'my head was about to explode'.

Soon refreshed, Dalglish was back, building another championship-winning team at Blackburn, where he became only the third manager to win titles with separate English clubs. Having achieved the grand prize, a year ahead of Jack Walker's hoped-for schedule, Dalglish removed himself from the day-to-day fray.

His eventual departure, after the growing distance between him and the Blackburn board, had nothing to do with stress. Dalglish was pushed more than he jumped, Rovers understandably feeling that he should have contributed more in his nebulous role of director of football.

Those who know this competitive Scotsman, whose hunger for footballing involvement remains undimmed, would wager that his appointment might just turn Newcastle's dreams into reality.

A glance at the records of Blackburn and Liverpool confirms Dalglish's credentials. He won the Double in his first season as Liverpool's player-manager, having changed half the team along the way. The success was unremitting, producing in the 1987–88 championship-winning side some of the most exhilarating football witnessed in modern times.

Newcastle's supporters relish verve. Dalglish's Liverpool sides, if not his Blackburn ones, certainly delivered thrills as well as trophies. Yet a streak of defensive intelligence, pragmatism and tactical solidity existed in Dalglish's teams. He would not have allowed the sort of defensive chaos that occasionally undermines Newcastle. He would have bought replacements. And any prima donna tendencies would quickly be stamped out; Dalglish is unimpressed by the star syndrome.

HIS effect on Newcastle would be instantaneous. Dalglish is close to Alan Shearer, such a pivotal figure at St James'. While at Blackburn, Dalglish also bought David Batty, now on Tyneside. Terry McDermott and Mark Lawrenson are old team-mates. He has also worked with Peter Beardsley, though their relationship is not thought to be close.

Dalglish inspires the respect of players like Shearer and Batty because of his reputation and his managerial style. Not a great training-ground coach, as he has admitted, Dalglish motivates his players by simple words and his own winner's attitude. Few people in the game read a match situation as well as him, and his vision is as sharp as during his playing days. As for Alex Ferguson's mind-games, Dalglish just plays a straight bat.

From Newcastle's perspective, and that of their financial backers, Dalglish is a proven winner, one who is also noted for developing youth, such a current *cause célébre*. It would hardly be the greatest of gambles to appoint him on an 18-month contract, with two shots at winning the League. As one Newcastle fan observed: 'I wouldn't mind if he cracked up again, so long as he won us the championship first.'

The fire still burns. If the right offer was made for Dalglish to dive into the managerial maelstrom again, his response is likely to be: Yes. ★ **14/01/97**

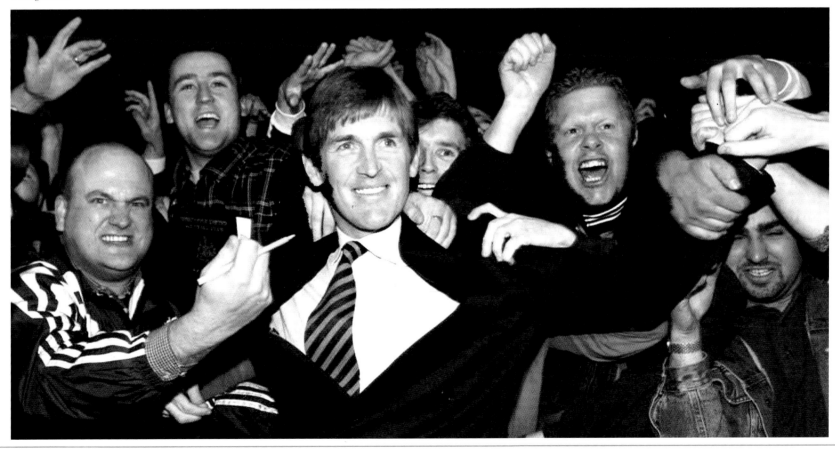

A warm welcome for Kenny Dalglish from Newcastle fans at St. James' Park Owen Humphreys, PA

THIS LOOKS LAST YEAR'S

NEW YEAR MET BY OLD FAILINGS

IT is probably debatable as to whether England were the worst team of 1996, but for the moment, anyway, there is not much argument about 1997. Frankly, this year's model looks suspiciously like last year's clapped-out old banger, and yesterday's defeat was yet another example of a side who go into mental paralysis whenever they come under pressure.

Zimbabwe have never before won a one-day international series, or indeed any series, but they now have an unbeatable 2-0 lead to take into the final game. The joint man of the match, John Crawley, wins a British Airways ticket to anywhere in the world provided he goes via Gatwick – which is a destination the entire team might be contemplating should they lose again tomorrow.

There was some confusion over the official margin of defeat, because of the new system of revising targets for weather interruptions. After poor England bowling had allowed Zimbabwe to recover from 38 for four and 126 for seven to 200 all out, rain reduced England's allocation to 42 overs, from which, under the old overall run-rate system, they would have required 169.

However, this one – so indecipherable that the Admiralty might be interested in it for a new secret code – is the brainchild of the Royal Statistical Society magazine's editor and a university mathematics boffin, and coughed up a revised target of 185.

When England fell short of this, many people thought that Zimbabwe had won on faster scoring rate, but as Zimbabwe actually scored their runs more slowly (4.0 as opposed to 4.3) this would have meant that England, bless them, would have invented a new way of losing.

The system is known as the Duckworth-Lewis plan, and while there is not yet any official name for England's batting formula, Heath-Robinson has a suitable ring to it. They are the great tinkerers of international cricket (more than 30 Tests have gone by without them fielding the same team twice in a row) and yesterday's masterplan involved the captain, Michael Atherton, coming in at No 5.

The bars open early on Zimbabwean cricket grounds and when Atherton came in at a slightly precarious 95 for three from 23 overs, an inebriated voice shouted: 'See you back here in a minute, Atherton.' In fact it was 38 minutes later, as the captain found some semblance of form before flat-batting a long hop to long-on, and by that time England were apparently well on course.

The key dismissal, however, was just around the corner. Crawley, who had taken over Atherton's No 3 position in the first one-dayer in Bulawayo, had made 73 well-crafted runs from 108 deliveries, and only had to bat through to the end to see his team home.

However, it was then that England's latent propensity for making poor decisions under pressure undermined them once again. Crawley jumped out of his crease to the leg spinner,

Bails Off! Michael Atherton, the England captain, loses his middle stump to Matabeleland's Henry Olonga Chris Turvey EMPICS

YEAR'S MODEL
SUSPICIOUSLY LIKE
CLAPPED-OUT OLD BANGER
by **MARTIN JOHNSON**

FINAL HUMILIATION AS BRANDES FINISHES OFF WOUNDED ENGLAND

Paul Strang, missed, and was stumped by Andy Flower.

Strang, having already dismissed Atherton, then made further progress towards his joint man-of-the-match award with Crawley when Ronnie Irani charged down the pitch and was stumped by such a margin that he was almost invisible in the side-on television replay.

England had made an awful start, losing Nick Knight to a reckless drive in the third over, only for Crawley, and Alec Stewart in particular, to put them back in charge with a second-wicket partnership of 66 in 10 overs.

Stewart's dismissal, however, when he got too thin a contact with an intended dab to third man off Guy Whittall, was the prelude to a period between the 16th and 33rd overs during which England were unable to muster a single boundary. So by the time Irani was sixth out at 165, England required 20 runs off the final 14 balls.

MICHAEL ATHERTON WAS

ACCOMPANIED BACK TO THE

DRESSING ROOM BY A BEERY OIK

WAVING A WHITE HANDKERCHIEF

It was the penultimate over which finally killed them off, Heath Streak conceding only three runs to leave Robert Croft and Darren Gough needing 16 from the final over. Croft's edged slog at John Rennie produced a first-ball four, another heave brought two off the next, but none of the final four deliveries yielded more than one run.

Zimbabwe, put in to bat on a pitch with much more pace than the Test wicket, slogged their way heartily to 38 for four from 10 overs, while England's bowlers, and Chris Silverwood in particular, were busy donating 13 extra deliveries from wides and no-balls. The fielding was not very special either, laughably so when Gough overran what should have been a simple catch on the square-leg boundary. That was an important miss, in that Andy Flower went on from 15 to make 63 from 114 balls before skying a catch off Alan Mullally. Streak then made an unbeaten 43 in the closing overs, leaving England with more to do than they had bargained for.

David Lloyd, the coach, kept his emotions admirably in check on this occasion – unlike Alistair Campbell, Andy Flower and Craig Evans, who were severely reprimanded by Hanumant Singh, the match referee, for excessive appealing – despite some provocative prodding from a Zimbabwean journalist hoping for a 'we murdered you' quote. Lloyd, however, returned a verdict of suicide, saying: 'The game was there to be won, and we weren't up to it.'

He also lightened the mood when he said: 'I have never taken Zimbabwe seriously....' breaking into a chuckle when he realised he had missed the word 'not' out of the sentence. That's how it is when you're the England coach. If you don't laugh once in a while, you'll spend all your time crying. ★ 02/01/97

THE uncomfortable parallel between certain southern African wildlife and England cricket victories - endangered species - was mirrored by a banner which summed up England's final Zimbabwean humiliation here yesterday: 'Forget The White Rhino, Save The Poms'.

There was also something symbolic in the way the drums beat on into the night, a reminder that the orchestra played on when the Titanic went down. However, any resemblance to an ocean-going liner has long since departed - replaced by a barnacle-hulled tub that wouldn't make it to the other side of a duck pond.

If the first two one-day internationals contained at least the odd glimmer of hope, this was not so much a defeat as a public flogging. The margin, 131 runs, was as appalling as England's overseas record in one-day internationals, 12 consecutive defeats against Test-playing nations. Their only victims during that sequence were the United Arab Emirates and Holland, and even now they must be shaking their heads in Dubai and Amsterdam, wondering how on earth they lost.

The last overseas one-day series England won, in fact, was in New Zealand in 1992, since when they have failed in India, Sri Lanka, the West Indies, Australia, South Africa, and now Zimbabwe. As for Zimbabwe-England one-day internationals, the score now stands at 5-1.

David Lloyd, the coach, had prayed that it would not rain yesterday, so that England would have the chance to leave here on a positive note, but if most of Harare remained dry, there might just have been some moisture on his handkerchief.

'If these players are professional, they'll really be up for this game,' Lloyd had said the previous evening. Well, they weren't, and they paid a well-deserved price in the ritual taunting they endured from the well-lubricated home supporters. Batsmen trailing from the field were variously advised to seek alternative employment, and Michael Atherton was accompanied back to the dressing-room by a beery oik waving a white handkerchief.

ENGLAND, having put Zimbabwe in to bat and been flogged around for 249, disintegrated to 118 all out in 30 overs on the back of the top order being decimated by an Eddo Brandes hat-trick, only the 10th in one-day internationals and - a little more surprisingly - the first against England.

Most one-day hat-tricks involve lower-order batsmen slogging, but this one cleaned up the cream (or maybe we should now be calling it the skimmed milk) of England's batting. None of England's bowlers managed to produce the late swing and away seam of Brandes, and it is hardly surprising the batsmen struggle against international-class bowling when county attacks are so mediocre.

Brandes's first victim, Nick Knight, could hardly be said to have got out to a lethal delivery, thin-edging a legside catch to the wicketkeeper - much as he did in the second Test - to the last ball of Brandes's second over. The first ball of Brandes's third over was not unplayable either, John Crawley playing across a more or less straight delivery, but the hat-trick ball was undeniably special.

The perfect length drew Nasser Hussain forward, the ball swung late to take the outside edge, and wicketkeeper

Andy Flower took a stunning full-length catch low down in front of first slip.

Brandes continued to bowl superbly, picking up Alec Stewart with another late outswinger and getting Michael Atherton (who had virtually resumed his opener's spot despite coming in at No 5) with one which lifted and left him.

From 54 for five there was no way back for England, and all that remained was to try to pass their previous lowest one-day score, 93 in the 1975 World Cup semi-final against Australia at Headingley. At 77 for eight they were odds against, but some desperate slogging finally lifted them past three figures before the last two wickets went down off consecutive balls. No fewer than five batsmen were out for a duck.

England's attack, by contrast, only picked up wickets through loose strokeplay as Zimbabwe looked to press on from a healthy 131 for one (and that to a run-out) from their opening 29 overs. Grant Flower, who used to be a dedicated blocker until he was weaned on to frisky strokeplay by England's bowlers, struck a rapid 62, and Alistair Campbell, the captain, batted through the last 35 overs of the innings for his 80 not out.

Ronnie Irani bowled steadily, but without looking as though his remodelled action will ever get him a Test wicket, and Alan Mullally also offered few free hits until Paul Strang hoiked him high over square leg - one of five sixes in the Zimbabwean innings - in his final over. The rest, frankly, were just ordinary.

ATHERTON and Lloyd declined to be interviewed on the players' balcony, which was understandable in view of the alcohol-fuelled taunting going on below, but both captain and coach managed to grit their way through private interviews with a wry good humour that was commendable given the circumstances.

What they were feeling inside, of course, would have been entirely different, but Atherton fended off the inevitable questions about resignation with a straighter bat than he has been using out on the field. 'Of course I'm upset and disappointed, but we're only halfway through the winter. Ask me again at the end of the tour.'

Lloyd insisted, as he has always done, that England would have won both Tests given better weather, but agreed that his side had 'not been up to it' in the one-dayers.

'They're totally different disciplines, and we'll probably have to re-think our one-day strategy in New Zealand. But we won't let ourselves get down. We'll regroup, work hard, and come again with confidence.'

Asked whether he was still enjoying his own role, Lloyd said (without any intentional humour): 'One of the joys of coaching is that there are always plenty of things to work on.' You can say that again.

Meantime, the crowd stayed on to celebrate and a great cheer greeted the announcement that the Zimbabwe team had received a personal message of congratulation from President Robert Mugabe.

Ask most Zimbabweans if they know who was residing at No 10 when England last received a 'well done' message from the Prime Minister, and they would probably hazard a guess at Harold Macmillan. ★ 04/01/97

CAPRIATI'S BROKEN DREAMS
OFFER SALUTARY WARNING TO EARLY RISERS

by ROBERT PHILIP

Back in the swing. Jennifer Capriati in smashing form during her comeback   Mike Blake, Popperfoto/Reuters

ONCE upon a time, Jennifer Capriati was a normal, happy-go-lucky schoolgirl. Well, as normal and happy-go-lucky as any 1990s teenager growing up in Florida. She was born to be Wimbledon champion, so we were told, bestowed with a future of great fame and untold fortune at birth by the good fairy.

Just as destiny had pre-ordained, so it came to pass that on March 6, 1990, the 13-year-old Capriati defeated fellow-American Mary Lou Daniels in her first match as a professional in the Virginia Slims of Florida. She went on to become the youngest player ever to reach the final of a women's tournament, which she lost 6-4, 7-5 to Gabriela Sabatini, then ranked No 3 in the world.

And that is when the terror began . . .

'That wasn't a debut,' said the late Ted Tinling, 'it was a premiere.' Everyone rushed to agree. 'It's really fun for me to see somebody her age and how well she handles things,' enthused Billie Jean King, Capriati's 46-year-old doubles partner for the week of the premiere.

'She can definitely be the leading lady of the 1990s,' concurred Pam Shriver, 'the time is right for a new star,' while television analyst Mary Carillo enthused: 'She was born to do this kind of work. She's happy - that's her secret weapon.'

Initially coached by Chris Evert's father, Jimmy, managed by Chris Evert's

what you will, they are the same in every language and scores of them flared up all over Capriati's face, despite Oil of Ulay's best efforts.

An even uglier blot was to emerge in the shape of Stefano Capriati, father and coach and, in the words of one of Capriati's management team, 'a right, royal pain in the ass'.

By the time Jennifer Capriati was 15, the all-American girl-next-door was wearing black nail varnish, skull and crossbones earrings, a ring on every finger like knuckledusters and a garish assortment of chains and heavy metal paraphernalia. *The National Enquirer*, in one of its more subdued articles, claimed that she was receiving psychiatric help, the latest victim of teenage burn-out which had claimed the tennis careers of Andrea Jaeger, Tracy Austin and a score of lesser-knowns before.

WHEREAS at 13, Capriati had been saying: 'I'm excited . . . it's fun . . . I love all this attention . . . it's kinda groovy', now a careworn 15, the language was that of dark despair and resentment. 'Who's business is it? I mean, why is everyone so wrapped up in everyone else's life? I understand it up to a point but enough is enough. People say, 'I know how you feel.' I'm like, 'Hey, man, what the hell do you know? You're in a totally different thing.' I don't try to tell

SEX, DRUGS AND ROCK'N'ROLL

(PLUS THE ODD BOUT OF SHOPLIFTING)

ON THE MOST SELF-DESTRUCTIVE SCALE

brother, John, and adopted as a younger sister by the great lady herself, Capriati's dearest possession was a gold bracelet engraved: 'To Sparky - Love Chris'; that bangle, plus a weighty portfolio of endorsements, of course, including a $3 million contract to wear Diadora tennis clothes, $1 million to use Prince rackets and a further $2 million in other associated deals.

AT a time when women's tennis was dominated by two foreigners - Martina Navratilova (who was never fully accepted as a US citizen) and Steffi Graf - Capriati was hailed as the new golden girl of American sport. 'I think everyone [everyone in America, that is] hopes so much that Jennifer is going to be the one,' trilled Evert sweetly. 'Everyone wants her to follow Billie Jean and myself by becoming No 1 in the world because Europe has been doing so well. She is the fairy-tale princess of tennis.'

The first blemish appeared on the princess's chin. No sooner had Capriati signed another outrageously lucrative agreement to promote Oil of Ulay skin care products, than she came out in the kind of mischievous rash of spots known to every teenager throughout the generations. Spots, plooks, zits, call them

anyone what they're feeling. Get out of my life, why doncha . . ?'

The rest, as they say, is tragic history: sex, drugs and rock'n'roll (plus the odd bout of shoplifting) on the most self-destructive scale. The youngest player ever to be seeded at Wimbledon, Capriati is 20 now. Olympic champion at Barcelona in 1992, the great championships she was born to dominate will never be hers.

Her latest comeback ended in tears in Melbourne this week when she was beaten in the first round of the Australian Open. How one wishes she would go home, throw her rackets in the trash can, meet someone nice, fall in love, have babies and use her vast wealth to spread happiness. Once upon a future time, perhaps.

Meanwhile in Melbourne, 16-year-old Martina Hingis, the Swiss maid popularly known as Heidi, signed a $10 million clothing sponsorship with Italian company Sergio Tacchini.

Like Capriati, Hingis, ranked world No 4 and rising, was born to be a champion (her Czech mother even named her after Martina Navratilova); like Capriati, her early years have been a fairy tale; and like Capriati, pray for her...

★ 17/01/97

END COLUMN

SPORT AROUND THE WORLD: The snowboarding world championships in Italy this month will feature a new event in which competitors can use virtually any means to outpace their rivals in a high-speed downhill race - including knocking them down. In 'bordercross', four athletes race simultaneously down a run resembling an obstacle course with jumps, bumps and gates. Only the fastest move through to the next round. "It's great to watch, it's exciting...but I don't know if I'll participate," said Marian Posch, the world snowboarding champion. "It's a bit dangerous."

FOOTBALL DIARY: Fining players for shooting from distance, even if they score, is only part of John Gregory's tariff for indiscipline. Wycombe Wanderers players are also fined £5 for turning up late for training or for the team coach, and for wandering around the dressing-room in bare feet. Gregory's foot fetish goes back to his playing days with Aston Villa and a pre-season tour of Yugoslavia, when goalkeeper Jimmy Rimmer wrecked five weeks' preparations by walking on the remains of a lemonade bottle that had smashed on the dressing-room floor. Wycombe's indiscretions have raised £200. That was matched by a local toy shop and £400 worth of presents were distributed to the children's ward at a nearby hospital.

SPORT AROUND THE WORLD: Andre Dawson, a big name in baseball until he retired last year, is paying child support to one air hostess and has been named in a paternity suit by another. Well-known chat-show host Jay Leno cracked: "How can somebody get two flight attendants pregnant? I can't even get an extra bag of peanuts."

FOOTBALL DIARY: Ruud Gullit has eased comfortably into English football and management, though not so easily on the mean streets of west London. He was found at the Chelsea Creek Car Pound - £135 to unclamp your car, guv - the temporary home of all illegally parked cars in that part of town. He had obviously been there before, though, because he was greeted like a regular offender. "Oh no, not you again, Ruud."

FOOTBALL DIARY: The influence of Fabrizio Ravanelli has been minimised in a corner of Derbyshire. Ilkeston Ladies under-14 team have been told by their chairman Wayne Kennedy that they will be substituted if they celebrate goals by pulling their shirts over their heads like the Italian. It did not stop them putting 10 past local rivals Belper, though.

DAY BY DAY REVIEW

1: England thrash Scotland 41-13 to win the Calcutta Cup at Twickenham, while Ireland record a one-point victory over Wales in the other Five Nations match

2: England suffer an humiliating defeat by New Zealand A in the build-up to the second Test

4: Manchester United and Arsenal are both knocked out of the FA Cup, by Wimbledon and Leeds respectively

8: Naseem Hamed adds the IBF featherweight title to the WBO he already holds by stopping America's Tom Johnson; Lennox Lewis claims the vacant WBC heavyweight title against Oliver McCall, who barely throws a punch and says he was awaiting divine intervention

10: England secure their first overseas Test win for two years, a run of 10 matches, when they beat New Zealand by an innings in Wellington; Steve Davis rolls back the years to win the Benson and Hedges Masters by beating Ronnie O'Sullivan in the final

11: John Hall and Bath part company after a 16-year association during which Hall rose from player to director of rugby and team manager; Scotland are held 0-0 by Estonia in the World Cup qualifier replayed in Monte Carlo after the original match was abandoned when Estonia failed to appear

12: Gianfranco Zola's goal at Wembley sends England to their first World Cup defeat and gives Italy the initiative in group two

15: Chesterfield reach the quarter-finals of the FA Cup by defeating Nottingham Forest; England's 40-point victory over Ireland is the biggest winning margin in Five Nations history; France beat Wales in the other match

16: Mike Atherton's unbeaten 94 in the third Test against New Zealand is only the eighth occasion an England opener has carried his bat throughout an innings; Greg Rusedski is forced to pull out injured of the final of the San Jose Open when a set up on Pete Sampras

18: Mike Atherton hits a century as England wrap up the third Test and their first overseas series win for five years

19: Ian Wright and Peter Schmeichel clash during and after the Arsenal v Manchester United game at Highbury; Va'aiga Tuigamala joins Newcastle in rugby union's first £1 million deal

20: England end a run of 12 overseas one-day international defeats by beating New Zealand in Christchurch

22: England take a 2-0 lead in the one-day series in a rain-reduced match against New Zealand; Adrian Maguire rides five winners, worth a combine 355-1, at Kempton Park

23: Tim Henman is beaten in another final, this time by Marc Rosset in Antwerp's European Community Championship

26: England fail to score the two they need off the last ball of the third one-day international and end up tieing with New Zealand; A controversial extra-time penalty decision knocks Leicester out of the FA Cup at Chelsea

AUSTRALIANS UNMOVED BY ENGLAND CELEBRATION

by **PETER FITZSIMONS**

SO ENGLAND have won two Tests in a row. So big deal. This at least seems to be the prevailing mood among Australian cricket followers and media, not to mention the Australian team themselves. There has been wry amusement on this end of the planet at the hoopla that has emerged from ye olde England, about how you've 'turned the corner', 'regained confidence', 'and are ready to take on the Aussies for the Ashes!' And so on, blah, blah, blah.

Frankly, my dears, we've heard it all before.

It's not that there is a lack of interest in the coming battle for the Ashes, starting in May of this year, it's just that we'll need to see far more than two wins on the trot against the New Zealanders before we come to believe that things have really changed. For while we Australians are admittedly deeply impressed at anyone beating those in the land of the Long White Cloud at rugby union, beating them at cricket is not quite so highly regarded. See, the last time we lost to them in cricket was . . . was . . . was . . . so long ago we can't remember, that's how long.

And in terms of the cyclical success, ebb and flow, that most serious teams go through, few would argue that the New Zealand side are at the lowest end of their cycle at this moment.

Look, are you finding me insufferably superior in all this? Me too, but the point is, it's not just me. Most of us Australians feel the same. Few of us have finished chortling over England's woes in Zimbabwe, and that debacle will be some time in the forgetting.

I offer, m'Lud, as evidence of the current disillusionment with English cricket Down Under, a Special Report that has been included in the latest edition of the foremost Australian cricket magazine, *Inside Edge*. Subject: 'What's wrong with English cricket?' (Somehow they've managed to encapsulate that subject in only 2,000 words or so, if you can believe it.)

A few paragraphs, though, should suffice to set the tone.

Mike Atherton's cricketers left Zimbabwe in disarray. Anything less like an Ashes-threatening unit has rarely been seen. The problem is not talent, but attitude, commitment and adaptability . . . . . . the old-age problems of an English system that is out-dated, self-interested, and plainly not working.

Chasing 250 for victory, England were bowled out for 118, courtesy of a chicken farmer.

The problem is that none of England's six batsmen bowl. There's no Waugh, Bevan, Law or Blewett. What are England doing about it? Nothing! Where is the strategy? Nowhere!

DO you kind of get the drift? Of course, this particular edition was put to bed before England's relative success in New Zealand, but fear not. Those two Test victories over there have changed little the Australian attitude.

The reporting of the first Test win in Sydney Town was sprayed all over the back page of the Sydney Morning Herald beneath the following headline: 'Hold the back page: England win a Test match at last.'

WELLINGTON: England have won a Test match. At 1.40 pm the great event occurred as Nick Knight stooped from second slip to take a low catch. Great were the celebrations . . .

Again, you surely get the drift. No one was getting carried away with the fact that England had now registered their third win in 18 starts, just as no one here got carried away when they shortly afterwards made it four wins from 19 starts. It was commendable, but hardly stacked up against what the Australians had just achieved, which was to beat the West Indies in a five-Test series.

Not that our own blokes are without their own troubles, and no mistake. They are currently embarked on what has been unofficially dubbed the Never-Ending Tour, which has seen them go from the subcontinent in August, to the West Indies domestic tour all over our summer, to being in South Africa, to England for the Ashes in May for three months, to God knows where after that.

The mood emanating from our team of late seems to have been a kind of 'If this is February, this must be South Africa' type of thing, and there is a growing sense of the survivors being quite jaded.

For not all *have* survived. This southern summer has seen the final retirement of that great fast-bowling warhorse Craig McDermott, 271 Test wickets after he made his debut in 1984.

NO problem - retiring injured after that length of service is fine. More worrying has been the constant slew of other injuries to close on the entire Test team as bits and pieces break down under the pressure of continuous service without rest.

Shane Warne's finger, Paul Reiffel's hamstring, Steve Waugh's left shoulder, Matthew Elliot's right shoulder, the list goes on.

They all struggle on, though - held together by Band-Aids, fencing wire and good old-fashioned grit - while back in Australia, two players who have been in the recent past considered among our best and brightest sit at home for an entirely different reason. They were, ahem, *dropped*.

Opening batsman Michael Slater, and top-order batsman Ricky Ponting began the summer as solid choices for the Test side, only to lose their way and be unceremoniously omitted. Their absence has been all the more controversial because captain Mark Taylor has desperately and uncharacteristically struggled for runs all season, but has still kept his spot. At the moment, there is some suggestion that he is something of a Mike Brearley selection - put in because of his outstanding captaincy.

The calls for his dropping have been basically muted for the last two months, but grew in volume with his last Test against the Windies, where he once again failed to reach double figures. Should he not get runs in South Africa, it is not out of the question that he will not tour England.

ON the positive side, Glenn McGrath has grown into a genuinely world-class fast bowler after a slow start. Warne goes on, albeit in slightly subdued form, and has oddly enough been taken over in spin-bowling form by an oddly reluctant Michael Bevan - the all-rounder who in the recent past has done quite a long stint at Yorkshire.

I say 'oddly reluctant' because he has been widely quoted in recent days as saying he's sick and tired of being considered as a bowler just because he's got a lot of wickets lately, and he doesn't give a damn if he has got more scalps than Warne lately, he's a *batsman*, OK?

OK. Of course you are, Michael, of course you are - but just roll your arm over a few more times anyway.

Look, it's not as if Australia are actually travelling at the very height of their own cyclical progression at the moment, and it remains to be seen just how much more damage a hefty three-month tour through South Africa will do to them.

But England? In all humility, few doubt that they will be put paid to. ★ **24/02/97**

TAKE THAT! NASEEM HAMED THROWS A MIGHTY RIGHT AGAINST TOM JOHNSON IN THEIR WORLD FEATHERWEIGHT TITLE FIGHT RUSSELL CHEYNE

Telegraph

DIMINUTIVE ROYAL
INSPIRED BY HER VAULTING
AMBITION

by **SARAH EDWORTHY**

YOU know the button on Porsches that convert from manual to automatic? I sometimes think that's what he needs.' We are admiring Tiptronic, a handsome eight-year-old chestnut gelding Princess Haya of Jordan fondly describes as being usefully slow of thought in the ring: 'If he has fear it doesn't register until about 10 minutes after he's over the fence.'

The reference to fast cars is the only verbal clue that indicates this horse-loving young woman knows a life beyond the daily round of mucking out and exercising. The first child of King Hussein and his third wife, the late Queen Alia - and the sixth of the King's 11 children - Princess Haya has swapped life at the Royal Palace in Amman to base herself and her nine horses at showjumper Paul Darragh's Waterside stud in eastern Ireland. Having spent the last 18 months on the farm, she intends to stay until 2000, aiming to compete at the Sydney Olympics.

So here she is, doing some consolidation training before hitting the equestrian-show road again, a four-hour flight away from everything she misses. 'I am homesick for the people, the food, the language, my family, my dad, the cars, the weather, everything.' And she is here, rather than anywhere else in the world, for the simple reason that Darragh, her coach, is one of the few talented showjumpers in the world who understands the problem of being small while in control of a large horse.

'I'm 5ft 2in, and he's shorter than me. It's not only being small that's a disadvantage, but having very short legs. I would never compete with Cindy Crawford or Claudia Schiffer in terms of legs,' explains the Princess, who is anyway so glamorous she can afford to be self-deprecating. It's more difficult getting horses that you fit. All the big horses we have are narrow, so I can get my legs round them. The image of a Thelwell pony and a kid with short legs kicking out can easily be created if you put me on a horse that is too big.'

HER previous trainer, a 6ft 2in German with a 6ft 3in daughter, asked things of her that were physically impossible. 'They used to tell me to shorten my reins but it wasn't my reins that were long, it was just that their arms were so much longer that the positioning looked different.'

Paul Darragh had been on the doorstep for six months before she officially became associated with him. 'I'd been here because of Alain Storme, Paul's partner, but I primarily came here to ride racehorses. I had my jumpers in Germany but when I started spending so much time here - at college I used to fly over from Oxford in the morning and back in the evening - I thought it better to have my showjumpers here as well.

'I went to the Asian Games in Hiroshima in 1995 and saw Paul working with the Kuwaiti team. I was on the lookout for someone whose system I could work with and I ended up seeing the person who was in the stables here all the time.'

Eighteen months down the road, their association has created something which Princess Haya cites as her greatest success, above such individual milestones as winning nine international style prizes, beating her trainer by a place in a World Cup event in Zagreb and taking individual bronze in the Pan Arab Games.

'In a way I would say my survival is the biggest success,' she says wryly, 'but the thing I am really proud of is the team has now been so solidly set up. We have a wonderful team of horses and everyone here is professional about the way the operation works.'

'I WOULD NEVER COMPETE WITH CINDY CRAWFORD OR CLAUDIA SCHIFFER IN TERMS OF LEGS'

The two horses she hopes to ride in Sydney - the big-muscled grey Cera and the feline Scandal - are the talk of the equestrian world. Darragh rides them while training them and Princess Haya for the Olympics. Their progress was marked when Darragh won a World Cup qualifier in Seville before Christmas with Cera and won another class at Olympia on Scandal.

ONE gets the feeling her father demands such an independent attitude. 'When my father gave me my first horse at the age of six, a full-bred Arabian, I don't think he thought I would do it this seriously. But he's started to like the idea a lot. When I finished college and said, 'This is what I'd like to do', he was the only one who said, 'Fine. If that's what you want to do, that's great, but you should do it seriously'.'

After graduating from St Hilda's College, Oxford, with a degree in Politics, Philosophy and Economics, everyone else, she says, 'raised their eyebrows and thought I was crazy'. However she has introduced a rigorous academic approach to showjumping.

'We're dealing now with ideas about nutrition and training programmes that we've observed in sports like athletics, tennis and swimming and we're writing a computer program that will simulate my position and the horse's position over fences.

'It's all at an infantile stage of development, but, if nothing else, it helps me focus 24 hours a day on the fact that I'm trying to be a world-class athlete.'

Equestrianism is a good sport for a modern princess in that, by its very time-consuming, hands-dirtied, weather-chafing nature, it contradicts the image of a spoiled, pampered young royal. Princess Haya admits to being troubled by the notion that people might have a preconception about her because of her background. 'I find this all the time, but what exactly the preconception is I have no idea. If I knew, it would be something I could either combat or live up to. All of that was something I was very concerned about when I started riding.

'The thing I liked here was no one pulled any smooth talk with me or said I am extremely talented. They've always said I've been brought up in the wrong way to go into high-level sport.'

IF Darragh's fortunes revived when he began riding horses owned by Princess Haya, it remains a mutually beneficial association. 'The main influence Paul has had on me is something that has made me happier: it's not so much not to care, but to do your talking in deeds.'

Invited to compete in Atlanta after a mere six months on the international circuit, Princess Haya is glad now she was advised not to. 'I felt while we could find a horse that would take me round, I would just be a passenger.

'While the sporting goal is still there, my eyes have opened to a lot of things in the world. Not that I would be sheltered as a young royal; I've learned the pros and cons of being a young woman around the world, trying to do what she wants to do. I know now that if anything ever happened to me I could look after myself. If I quit tomorrow I know that.' ★ 03/02/97

Princess Haya of Jordan in Ireland Phil Shephard-Lewis

GLOVES ARE OFF FOR NEXT ROUND OF CHAUVINISM

by **BYRON BUTLER**

HISTORY may be a pile of bunk and dust but it does suggest, most earnestly, that tonight's game at Wembley may not be a simple and ethical affair. England and Italy are too much in love with themselves just to let the best team win.

They have been playing international football together for more than 60 years, and the saga has regularly embraced one or two things which have little to do with the higher ideals of the game. Bloodshed and politics will do for a start.

Honours are even in one respect, but out of step in another. They have each won six of the 17 games they have played; but England did not lose to Italy for 40 years and Italy have not lost to England in the last 20.

A relevant fact or damned statistic?

One certain thing, in these wonderfully civilised times, is that this Ash Wednesday meeting will differ in important aspects from the first two confrontations. Mussolini, for example, will not be there.

Il Duce watched the initial game between the two countries on a sweltering day in Rome in 1933; and, by way of tribute, he was struck in the stomach by a wild clearance from Arsenal's Eddie Hapgood. Result: 1-1.

Italy's first visit to England a year later is fondly remembered as 'the Battle of Highbury'. Italy had just won the World Cup but England, who had ignored the tournament, regarded themselves as the best in the universe.

This was Showdown time and Mussolini, for perfectly sound Fascist reasons, offered his players huge bonuses - an Alfa Romeo car each and exemption from military service if they settled the argument once and for all.

England, including seven Arsenal players, took a 3-0 lead at which point Italy went to war.

A nose or two were broken, half the England side finished swathed in bandages and Hapgood, captaining England for the first time, observed later: 'It is hard to play like a gentleman when somebody resembling an enthusiastic member of the Mafia is wiping his studs down your leg.'

Italy, though, lost a player through injury, England won 3-2 and the whole future of international football was debated. Tonight's game? Just a tea-party.

No trouble in Turin, though, in 1948. Italy were still world champions, but England won 4-0 in such dazzling fashion that some Turin shops immediately displayed team pictures of them captioned simply: 'Made in Britain.' England's forward line that day was Matthews, Mortensen, Lawton, Mannion and Finney.

It wasn't until 1973 in Turin, their ninth meeting, that Italy managed to beat England (2-0), but that same year the Azzurri also won by a late goal to nil at Wembley - Bobby Moore's 108th and last cap.

Since when England have never managed a victory over Italy when it mattered.

They beat Italy 3-2 in the Yankee Stadium in New York in 1976, a bizarre and lightweight friendly, and by 2-0 in a World Cup qualifier at Wembley in 1977, although by then England had blown it and Italy were assured of their place in the finals in Argentina.

England were unhinged by an exquisite goal from Tardelli in the European finals in 1980 and edged out of third place by a late penalty in the World Cup finals 10 years later. Both games were skilful and pretty honourable - and both tournaments, remember, were in Italy.

I have seen the last nine meetings between England and Italy and, even more than games against Brazil and Germany they inspire dizzy expectations, muscular chauvinism, doctrinal theories and, just below the surface, doubts which won't go away.

Any old pro will confirm, in so many words, that the only thing we learn from history is that we do not learn from history. What the heck! England to win. ★ **12/02/97.**

McLAREN'S
FLASHY NEW CAR
IS TUNED UP BY **THE SPICE GIRLS** by MARTIN JOHNSON

THE latest trend in subliminal advertising is to waft product-associated smells through air-conditioning vents (freshly baked bread in supermarkets, that sort of thing) but in the surreal world of Formula One, the only aroma that permeates the nostrils is freshly minted fivers.

If those associated with McLaren's new racing car briefly pondered the possibility of unveiling it inside a garage, with the scent of carbon monoxide and old sump oil drifting along the ventilation shaft, the option was rejected in favour of something a trifle more ostentatious, at the rough cost of a small country's gross national product.

If you thought there was tension in the air just before the green lights go out on a grand prix starting grid, you should have been inside London's Alexandra Palace on Thursday night. Five thousand invited guests were assembled to gaze for three hours at a lumpy object hidden underneath a tarpaulin, before congregating in front of a stage to find out what it might possibly be. Slightly surprisingly, judging from the astonished gasp that greeted the unveiling, not a single person had twigged that it might have been a racing car.

The gasp swiftly gave way to roars of delight, which might conceivably have been genuine admiration for the machine's sleek contours and aerodynamic wizardry, but was more likely an involuntary outpouring of joy from the makers of West cigarettes, at the sight of what appeared to be a fag packet on four wheels. There were West stickers everywhere bar the exhaust pipe, but, while it was not easy to see clearly through the dry ice, not a single one identifying it as a McLaren.

It is now only three weeks before the Formula One circus gets under way in Melbourne, and the various teams have been fighting nosecone to nosecone to see who can spend more money on getting their motor car - and, more especially, their sponsors' logos - splashed all over the world's newspapers and TV screens.

McLaren's idea of leaving their rivals stuck in a gravel trap was to hire a teeny-bopper pop group known as the Spice Girls, whose performance made you wonder why the one item of a racing driver's gear that has not yet been covered in a sponsor's logo is their car plugs.

McLaren also engaged (for presumably slightly less money) the services of the BBC sports presenter Steve Rider, who will get no closer to this season's Formula One merry-go-round unless he transfers to ITV. Rider also fronted Jordan's launch at the London Hilton, and however much you suspected him of fighting off an expression not dissimilar to Frank Williams staring at a monitor of one of his cars embedded in a tyre wall, Steve remained irrepressibly excited.

To assist him in this mood, he had the indispensable collaboration of someone by the name of Devina from

something called MTV, who bounced on to the stage to the backcloth of two large video screens advertising Mobil, Loctite and GS Batteries. 'We've got stars, and we've got cars,' cooed Devina, and your heart began to sink.

'This,' she shrilled, 'is the biggest event of its type ever held,' and just in case anyone doubted it, Devina went on to announce that it was being 'broadcast all across the UK on Virgin Radio'.

Your mind tried to take in this picture of millions of people huddled around a transistor awaiting the unveiling of a car, but it wasn't easy. 'Cor, just listen to that bodywork,' you could hear the punters crooning.

Devina then introduced a pop group who sang a song entitled Virtual Insanity, and looking around, it did not seem an inappropriate choice. Next up was Steve, who, lest anyone had forgotten the real purpose of the evening, reminded them. 'West,' he said. 'The fastest growing tobacco company in the world.'

West, a German brand which is not growing all that fast in the UK because they do not sell them here, proclaims itself with the slogan 'The Power Is Now,' which makes the chassis of a racing car an attractive advertising site. However, if Formula One was contested by Trabants, Ladas and Reliant Robins it would still be a seductive medium, as there is practically nowhere else tobacco firms are allowed to peddle their message.

And so to the 'monumental occasion' (Devina's words) of our first glimpse of the MP4/12, an image so powerful that it prompted lots of people wearing ski suits and carrying torches to whizz around the stage on roller skates. Just when you were wondering what a Swiss mountain rescue team had to do with it, Steve came to the rescue by announcing that the suits were replicas of what the McLaren pit crew will be wearing this season. 'This ensures they can't be ignored,' said Steve, somewhat mysteriously.

The two drivers, David Coulthard and Mika Hakkinen were then brought on for a searching interview with Devina, who posed what she described as 'the big question'. Indeed it was. 'David, tell me. Is it Coult-ard, or Coulth-ard?' David, cornered, gave the big answer, 'Coulth-ard.'

Devina then grilled Mika. 'Did you have anything to do with the design?' Mika replied: 'That's a bit technical.' And then we had the Spice Girls. They didn't sing a note out of place, which was not surprising, as this turned out to be a no-expense spared miming exhibition.

The girls, however, were clearly saving their voices to conduct searching driver interviews of their own. 'Tell me,' chirped the girl known as Emma. 'Why aren't there any girl drivers?' Mika's eyes glazed over. Was there no end to these technical questions? How he longed to be alone in his cockpit. Whatever vast amounts of money these boys are getting, it isn't enough. ★ **15/02/97**

> "COR, JUST LISTEN TO THAT BODYWORK," YOU COULD HEAR THE PUNTERS CROONING

DAY BY DAY REVIEW

1: New Zealand hit back in the one-day series with a nine-run win over England; France, 14 points down with 18 minutes to play, beat England at Twickenham, while Scotland crush Ireland in the other Five Nations match

2: Nick Faldo wins the Nissan Open, his first tournament victory since the US Masters, nearly 11 months earlier

4: New Zealand share the one-day series with England 2-2 after winning the fifth match, in Wellington; Newcastle lose 1-0 at home to Monaco in the quarter-final of the UEFA Cup

5: Manchester United run up a four-goal advantage from the home leg of their European Cup quarter-final against Porto

9: David Coulthard wins the first Grand Prix of the season, in Melbourne, as world champion Damon Hill fails to start; Jamie Baulch (400m), high-hurdler Colin Jackson and triple-jumper Ashia Hansen win silver medals at the World Indoor Athletics Championships

11: Martin Pipe's Make A Stand, ridden by Tony McCoy, wins the Champion Hurdle on the first day of Cheltenham

13: Tony McCoy rides his second big winner of the week, the 20-1 shot Mr Mulligan, in the Cheltenham Gold Cup; David Graveney takes over as chairman of England's cricket selectors

15: England complete rugby's triple crown by beating Wales in Cardiff, but France take the Grand Slam by beating Scotland in Paris

18: Monaco end Newcastle's interest in the UEFA Cup with a 4-0 aggregate win

19: Manchester United ease into the European Cup semi-finals after a 0-0 draw in Porto, 4-0 on aggregate

20: Two goals by Robbie Fowler take Liverpool past Brann Bergen and into the last four in the European Cup-Winners' Cup

22: Kaula Lipis wins the first Classic of the season, the Lincoln Handicap at Doncaster; Fiji take the World Cup Sevens rugby title in Hong Kong, beating South Africa in the final, while England are beaten in the quarter-finals

23: Laura Davies wins the Standard Register Ping title for the fourth year

24: Robbie Fowler plays the honesty card by suggesting David Seaman did not foul him for the penalty that helps Liverpool to victory at Arsenal

26: Lola pull out of Formula One racing as a proposed sponsorship collapses

27: Joe Royle and Everton part company 'by mutual consent'; Steve Lomas's £1.6 million move from Manchester City to West Ham is the biggest deal on a record-breaking transfer deadline day

29: England beat Mexico 2-0 in a friendly at Wembley; In World Cup qualifying matches Scotland beat Estonia, Northern Ireland draw with Portugal and Wales are beaten at home by Belgium; Cambridge win the University Boat Race for the fifth successive year

30: Jacques Villeneuve survives a mistake at the first corner to win the Brazilian Grand Prix

31: India fall 39 runs short of their 120 target and lose the third Test against the West Indies

CHANGES TO MENU FAIL TO DETRACT FROM FESTIVE FARE OF BOAT RACE

by **ROBERT PHILIP**

THE secret of the University Boat Race's enduring and utterly mystifying appeal, as it was explained to me, is all to do with the Rip van Winkle theory: if a man, or a woman, was to wake up after being asleep for 100 years and take a stroll down to the Thames on Oxford-Cambridge Saturday, they would instantly recognise the scene.

Nothing changes, insist the romantics; well, nothing, that is, apart from the humungous Beefeater Gin banner which now adorns the middle arch of Putney Bridge for the benefit of the television cameras. Ah, but nothing else has changed save the advent of sponsorship since the two crews first rowed over the present Putney-Mortlake course in 1856. Nothing else? Surely the contour-hugging lycra one-piece cozzies both sets of galley slaves were forced into wearing for the 143rd contest were another innovation? Yes, but that is positively as far as it goes. Old Rip would find everything else exactly as it was a century or so ago when he snuggled down for the big sleep.

To be honest, the traditionalists are still not being strictly honest. For right by the start line, they have built a second 'Putney Bridge', a ritzy, glitzy £3 million glass and steel restaurant which has been open only a fortnight but has been nominated for an architectural award.

As lunch was firmly on my mind, it seemed only fitting to find Chris Kelly, presenter of BBC2's *Food And Drink* programme, milling about in the vast crowds on the towpath some hours before the 'off'. 'I don't mind him,' muttered an Oxford type in a Billy Bunter cap (and waist line) and garish college blazer which appeared to have been stitched together out of unwanted deck-chairs, 'the one that infuriates me is that infernal woman who insists on describing a perfectly reasonable Cabernet Sauvignon as smelling 'like a Turkish wrestler's jockstrap.' Whilst the man from the Beeb departed for a floating lunch aboard a Thames cruiser, I repaired to an upstairs table at 'Putney Bridge' to watch the milling scene below through a leisurely glass of Kir Royale.

'This,' whispered Natalie the waitress, 'is as close as you will ever get to rowing in the race without breaking sweat.' She was not exaggerating; the restaurant 'wall' was solid glass, and the thin copper strip embedded in the wooden floor underneath our table was aligned precisely with the University Stone on Putney Embankment that marks the start line.

A MERE seven tables away, Larry Mayburn was more concerned with the flow of champagne. 'I've been to the Super Bowl, the World Series and the Stanley Cup final, but this is something else. It's like having lunch in the best restaurant in New York with the Fourth of July Parade going past outside.' As a student, Mayburn was a keen rower at Stanford University, California, in the 1960s and retains less than fond memories of one particularly uncompromising assistant coach. 'Franck Jansson. Still gives me a chill just saying the name. He was like Darth Vader without the sense of humour. Actually, that's not wholly fair. When Flower Power arrived I became a real hippy. I let my hair grow long and started a beard. I was dropped from the rowing squad and went to see Jansson to complain. 'Jesus Christ had long hair and a beard' I told him. 'Listen son,' he said, pointing across to the rowing course. 'See that water? Well the day you can walk across it is the day you can wear your goddam hair any goddam way you want'. Aw, hell, I guess if I'd really wanted to get back on his team I shouldn't have been smoking a joint at the time.'

Times - if not tastes - change. As our pampered middle-aged assemblage in 'Putney Bridge' settled down for lunch and the arrival before us of the Isis and Goldie 'reserve' boats, the only substance for which we would almost certainly have tested positive was Bollinger.

Isis and Goldie rowed off into the distance as Larry, champagne glass in hand, hove back into view. 'All your guys are genuine students, right?' Well, up to a point. 'In the States I've known rowers with an IQ less than room temperature get scholarships because of the size of their muscles. My greatest achievement? I never rowed drunk. Hung over, yes, but never drunk.'

As Natalie delivered the Rolls Royce of fish and chips - fillet of salmon deep fried in a blue corn and seaweed batter accompanied by potato wedges to make you purr - talk centred on the differing approaches of Dan Topolski, Oxford's director of coaching, and Rene Mijnders, the Dark Blues' chief coach. Topolski is a graduate of the Franck Jansson school - if it don't hurt then you ain't doin' it right - whilst the Dutchman prescribes to the Jock Stein doctrine: 'Managing a football team is like holding a wounded bird in your hand. Squeeze too tight and you throttle it, not tight enough and it flies away.'

THIS IS AS CLOSE AS YOU WILL EVER GET TO ROWING IN THE RACE WITHOUT BREAKING SWEAT

MIJNDERS, no doubt mindful that fit young men often have other things on their minds apart from rowing, even took his flock to Amsterdam to practise. Thoughts of Amsterdam after dark remind me of another football manager's words: 'It isn't sex that's troublesome . . . it's staying up all night looking for it.' In the pause before pudding - hazelnut ice cream with chocolate samosas - I trawled the downstairs bar of 'Putney Bridge' where bright college things, old buffers and a motley collection of thrill-seekers (no doubt encouraged by the previous day's sinkings during veteran's race) enjoined in a noisome throng. 'There's no such thing as second place today,' pronounced Light Blue voice which made Prince Charles sound like Bernard Manning. 'You're either first or you're last.' 'Ah,' countered soothingly female Dark Blue tones, 'but without losers where would winners be?'

Meanwhile, Natalie had arrived with the pudding trolley, the plate glass windows had been slid open and the sounds of the Thames on Boat Race day drifted across to our little corner of paradise. Larry from Vermont was still intrigued by the academic prowess of the two crews as they came under starter's orders. 'I've been reading their qualifications in the programme and those are real intelligent guys out there. It's totally different back home. A lot of kids on college basketball scholarships, for example, are exposed as witches because they can read and write.'

Off splashed the boats in an angry clash of blades to the intensely satisfying accompaniment of popping corks. Only Steven Fotheringham was ever so slightly miffed. 'The food was fantastic, but at £75 a head I thought there would have been more celebrities here. Patsy Kensit, Liz Hurley, babes like that. I think I saw Hugh Laurie [Boat Race competitor turned comic-actor] and my grandfather insisted he'd spotted the Spice Girls. Turned out it was the Beverley Sisters or something like that.'

Or the Old Spice girls, as someone put it. ★ 31/03/97

CARSON FEARS SILENCE

OF RETIREMENT YEARS AHEAD

by **SUE MOTT**

THE sun threw itself down on a little corner of the Cotswolds and reminded Willie Carson what he has been missing all these years. 'To lie out here in a deckchair when the summer's on, talking on the phone, heat blazing down, nice and comfortable, enjoying meself, with a nice cold can o' Coke beside me.' A thought struck him. 'Now I can upgrade to a can of Budweiser, can't I?' Carson, jockey, retired, now the epitome of a contented man . . . Is he hell.

He is the opposite. At 54 he has retired, almost literally over his own dead body. He strenuously denies that the kicking he received from Meshhed last September at Newbury, and the subsequent hours in intensive care with severe liver damage, hastened his decision to hang up his boots, but sometimes reminders of mortality are just too big to ignore.

'Secretly, I might have given up last year, if I'd had a good one, ending on a high. But my accident put paid to that. When I was first stretchered off, I thought, 'That's it. My riding career's over.' But your immediate reaction when you get hurt is to get up, dust yourself down and get out there fighting again. So I was in the gym. I got myself in pretty good shape. I've only just stopped going in the last five days. Of course, a bit of me wishes I was still riding.' Another thought struck him, as the Flat racing season begins without him for the first time in 40 years. 'I wish I was 21.'

No, contentment is not the word. He sat at the desk in his office surrounded by photos and trophies of the past - images of Nashwan (2,000 Guineas winner with Carson on his back, 1989), Salsabil (1,000 Guineas and the Oaks, 1990), the home-bred Minster Son (St Leger, 1988), Dayjur (beaten in the 1990 Breeders' Cup after fly-jumping the shadow of the winning post) - with his restless feet shoved into red woolly socks and his dejected eyes peering through spectacles at a tottering pile of 'Good Luck, Willie' cards.

'I wish I hadn't done this,' he said quietly. 'What, look through your mail?' I asked. 'No,' he replied. 'Retire.'

Even reference to all those cans of Bud-in-waiting failed to lighten his gloom. Or the fact that he had 12 mares on his Minster Stud in Cirencester, so if he cannot ride a Classic winner any more at least he can breed one. He breeds ducks as well but they're never going to give him the pleasure of coming home first in the 3.35 at Ascot.

'That's the plus side,' he said. 'And the other side is when it's all quiet, will it be too quiet? It's never a happy medium in life, is it? Either you're getting too much or you're not getting enough. Hee, hee, hee.'

He laughs like a court jester, which in some ways he is, having played to the royal courts of the Queen and, latterly, Sheikh Hamdan Al Maktoum. Merriment and mischief are united in his soul, but you know that the son of a Fyffes banana packer from Stirling, barely five feet in his socks, was going to need more in his sporting life than a wicked sense of humour. So he developed a crusading sense of purpose as well. 'It started with me being so small. People would say, 'Oh Billy, aren't you wee. You ought to be a jockey'. So I was brainwashed into it. Then I saw the movie *The Rainbow Jacket* in the cinema and from that day on I was always going to become a jockey. It was about a boy going into racing and riding a Derby winner, I think. Robert Morley and some of those people were in it.'

With an extraordinary sense of destiny he climbed aboard his first saddle (the one on his pushbike) and began the paper round that would pay for his weekly riding lessons with Mrs McFarlane, of Dunblane. He wasn't exactly Sir Gordon Richards in miniature. 'I went to her from the age of

12. In retrospect, I don't think it helped a great deal. But she knew people in the racing fraternity a little bit and wrote away to three trainers for me. I decided in the end on George Armstrong in Middleham.' And why the trainer decided, with rare omniscience, on Carson is not in doubt. 'Cheap labour,' said the former apprentice.

'Oh, I got homesick. Terribly,' said Carson, who appeared to have very little aptitude for his chosen career at the outset. No more, certainly, than his fellow apprentice, Tony Prince, who went on to become a DJ on Radio Luxembourg instead. 'The Royal Ruler,' said Carson, in obvious admiration and adopting the same fake mid-Atlantic accent that afflicted Prince in his prime.

However homesick, Carson was determined. He clung on

to his dream and got his first ride at Redcar, 1959, on Marijar. He was 17. 'It was the horse I used to look after. She was a bit of a lady. The owners and trainer thought she might go for the little boy that looked after her. Because she didn't go for the jockeys.' And did she? 'No. She got left 20 lengths.'

A baptism like that could leave you dejected or ecstatic, but Carson remembered a different reaction. 'I was absolutely ******** myself to be out in public. It's a big, traumatic thing, your first ride. Are you going to make a fool of yerself? Everybody's watching you. It's a big day.'

Not as big as the ones that eventually followed. His first winner on Pinker's Pond, July 17, 1962. His first Classic, the 2,000 Guineas, on High Top in 1972. Winning six on the card at Newcastle in June 1990. Riding his 3,500th winner at Goodwood in July 1993. And a front-page appearance in the *News of the World* (recurring).

For, while his ferocious will was driving him to five champion jockey titles, four Derbys, three St Legers, two 1,000 Guineas, and a fortune, he was also a two-times husband and the father of an illegitimate daughter, sired when he was just a teenager.

'That story coming out wasn't nice. Not nice for the family. But I never denied it. I did my duty. I was taken to court when it was born and I paid right through until it was 16.' *It.* His use of the word strikes you like a sledgehammer. 'Well, I never . . . you see . . . I just blocked it out. It's a girl,

"I WAS NEVER REGARDED AS A GREAT. IT DID WORRY ME AT ONE TIME. BUT I GOT OVER IT."

actually. I feel sorry for her, in a sense, but it's a decision I made years and years ago, rightly or wrongly, that I'd block it out. I mean, I didn't know I was going to be famous, when I was bloody 16. I was 16, for Chrissake. Wait a minute, that's a lie. She was born in '62, same year as my first winner. So I was 18.'

Complications of family life were the inevitable fall-out of his devotion to racing. He was divorced from his first wife, remains estranged from one of his three sons and admits that familial unity came second to his career. 'I really dedicated myself to riding and it came before the family. Oh yes. Unfortunately. I lost out on a lot.'

His second wife, Elaine, bustled in and out of the office and answered, somewhat surprisingly, to the respectful

Allsport

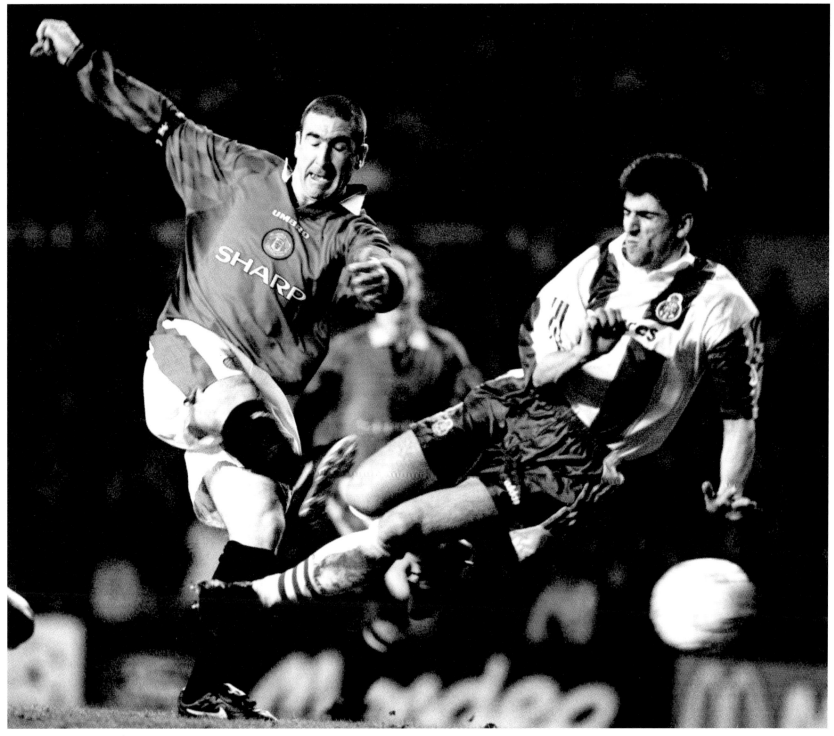

MONSIEUR LE GOALSCORER! ERIC CANTONA SCORES IN MANCHESTER UNITED'S 4-0 VICTORY OVER PORTO IN THE EUROPEAN CUP. RUSSELL CHEYNE

soubriquet 'Madame'. As in: 'We're getting ready for Cheltenham and madame's getting uptight.'

'Twitchy,' she corrected firmly. In that case, she and Carson share a similar nature. For all his bonhomie and cheeky chat that the BBC will now put to good use, Carson has a sensitive side. 'Chips? Oh aye, I've got a bit of a chip. Oh yeah. Oh, I haven't forgotten. There's a few that have said things that were unnecessary. People criticised me. Terrible. They say things . . . said I'd called my son 'stupid'. Well, I had. That's the way I speak. 'You stupid bugger.' They took it serious. They said I'm not loyal to my family. *Not loyal to my family.* It was hurtful. They played on the fact I was hard, or whatever. No heart. But I'm not what they portray. Put it that way.'

He has never been acknowledged as one of the naturally-gifted all-time greats, either. Probably because he wasn't. He grafted, the Calvinist work ethic, planted in his

character by the father, who stayed from apprenticeship to gold watch in the banana factory. 'No, I've never been regarded as a - what's the word? People like the jockeys who are natural. They don't like the people that work for it, grind for it. I got the public's affection but not the professionals in the game. I was never regarded as a great, put it that way. It did worry me at one time. But I got over it, years ago.'

THE cards must help. 'Warmest congratulations, I'll miss you very much,' writes a caring punter. The Maktoums, on the other hand, have been more circumspect. 'They've been very quiet,' he said neutrally. 'Ah, to feel wanted. But they don't say anything, do they? That's the Arab way.'

It has certainly never been the Carson way. Little Billy, mercilessly bullied at school, soon discovered the best route to safety. 'Through the mouth,' he said. 'Talk, talk, talk. I

suppose that's where all the chirpiness comes from. Everyone wants to pick on you when your stature's non-existent. So the only thing you've got is the mouth. It gets you out of trouble.' He thought about this for a minute. 'It gets you into trouble an' all.'

But whether in or out of mischief, he was consistently heroic on a horse. A brilliant tactician and a fearless little grafter. His favourite memory is still winning the Oaks in Jubilee Year on the Queen's horse, Dunfermline.

'That was a fairytale,' he said. 'Her Majesty wasn't there. She was busy. But the Queen Mother wasn't going to miss it. That was a bit special. Even the champagne tasted different somehow.' He can probably still hear the cheers of 20 years ago ringing in his ears, and now it all threatens to go quiet. 'Jesus,' he said. 'The silence is going to be frightening.' ★
15/03/97

WINNING IS NOT EVERYTHING

AS **LOSERS** DISCOVER WAY TO **TAKE ON** THE WORLD

by **STUART BARNES**

TWICKENHAM resonated to the sound of *La Marseillaise* rather than *Swing Low* as an afternoon of enough passion to satiate Sacha Distel reached its glorious and gripping conclusion. That reason alone is enough to make every neutral on the planet raise a glass of Moet et Chandon to a French victory that lifted the spirits of anyone who loves the sport of rugby union.

Of course, there is a price to pay. The four-wheel drives left the West Car Park with deflated tread, the Barbours were tear-stained, but what the hell. To coin the most cliched of phrases from the good old days of amateurism, rugby was the winner.

Paradoxically, so were England. Jack Rowell's team may have lost this particular battle, but the style of the performance emphatically illustrated that they have not lost the war.

England dropped their catapults, picked up some sophisticated weaponry and moved into the territory that was the exclusive domain of our southern hemisphere superiors. Only a blinkered xenophobe would have walked away from Twickenham anything other than uplifted.

Defeat hurts. The stooped frame of Rowell and the glazed eyes of Phil de Glanville at the post-match press conference told the tale of a couple of winners having lost.

But England gained more from this loss than they will ever glean from a facile victory against Scotland. That was a victory spelled with a capital 'P' for pyrrhic. The policy of grind and attrition is a battle strategy that predates the bow and arrow. Alas, physical superiority has enabled England to prevail in the Five Nations despite, not because of, this style.

THOSE who carry no more ambition than to batter second division nations into oblivion will doubtless find such comments heretic, but for all of us who realise that the world stretches beyond the White Cliffs of Dover this was, in so many ways, an inspirational afternoon for England.

A month ago I had the temerity to suggest that England's absence of ambition in the first hour of the match with Scotland was a major impediment to any progress on a global scale. The England captain explained that we critics were unrealistic, that such ambitions were the stuff of fantasy, that Test match rugby was so tight and intense that the very thought of it was ridiculous. Reread the papers, it is all in print. And so, muttering the words 'New Zealand and the semi-final of the World Cup', we humbly bowed before such wisdom.

The script in Dublin was better, but the plot was alarmingly similar. England battened down the hatches before emerging in all their pyrotechnic glory. It was difficult to criticise what was a record-breaking performance, but this was still rugby from another era. Good enough for the Five Nations, inadequate for the world. But the real significance of the day was Rowell's statement of intent, England had 'aspired' to play at pace from the kick-off. Phil had been fooling us all. England really did want to explode from the blocks. And how. England's deeds matched Rowell's pledges as they tore into the heart of France from the kick-off. Such was the intensity of their opening salvo that I thought myself in Auckland for a split-second.

This was the modern world of rugby. A whole universe of untapped potential opened up. Mark Regan, again immensely impressive, found himself in the wide spaces of the wing a la Sean Fitzpatrick; Simon Shaw was constantly carrying the ball . . . and, best of all, Jason Leonard sold a dummy.

THIS was a team with the confidence to explore territory where no white men had previously ventured. As Rowell promised, the comfort zone was left in the dressing room. In search of themselves and the necessary quality to win where it really matters, above and beyond the claustrophobic comfort of the cozy old Five Nations, England asked themselves, as well as the French, questions. If Tony Underwood had outstripped Phillipe Carbonneau, if de Glanville had passed to men outside instead of breaking from his own 22, England could have been out of French sight 20 minutes from the end.

'If' is a small word and the margin between England winning with panache and losing all hopes of a Grand Slam was equally small. The England captain thought his side 'mentally switched off a little bit . . . for 50 minutes we were in their face but, at 20-6, instead of going for the kill we eased back.'

True enough, but mental exhaustion also played a part. England were in pursuit of excellence, not just another win. The result was short-term loss, long-term gain. ★ 15/03/97

END COLUMN

HOLD ON TIGHT! ENGLAND'S TIM STIMPSON JUGGLES AGAINST WALES RUSSELL CHEYNE

SPORT AROUND THE WORLD: Nadezhda Ilyina, first past the post in the Los Angeles Marathon, took a detour to spend a penny during the race, and it cost her £9,000. The Russian said she had a bladder infection, was suffering from cramp, and had to answer a call of nature at a petrol station after 22 miles. However, marathon officials claimed she used the garage as a short-cut and stripped her of first prize. "I had been looking for a bathroom since mile three," she said. "I came back out at the same point that I had left the course."

FOOTBALL DIARY: Jack Charlton, regretfully, has had to turn down Northampton Town's invitation to be the special guest at their centenary dinner. The club have scoured high and low for a replacement. Now, it is reported, they have found "a towering figure whose breath-taking charisma, huge sense of footballing history and demi-god standing in the game worldwide is wholly appropriate for this auspicious occasion". Who else but Nookie Bear.

SPORT AROUND THE WORLD: O J Simpson takes refuge from his problems by golfing on public courses, where he always finds a foursome, even though some of the players don't want him around. Simpson says he gets "some pretty funny reactions" when golfers find he is part of their foursome. "But nobody's walked away yet," he says. Without golf, he says, he'd be lost. "For five hours a day, golf takes all my concentration and nobody bugs me. People are good about it. It's like a golf course is kind of sacred. If I didn't have golf, I'd be in Belle Vue [a psychiatric hospital]."

SPORT AROUND THE WORLD: The ABC of Golf has been published in St Petersburg, the first book about golf written in Russian. There is a print run of only 1,000, not surprising as there are apparently only three golf clubs in Russia, one in St Petersburg, opened last year, and two in Moscow.

LETTERS TO THE SPORTS EDITOR: SIR - Before the campaign to beatify Robbie Fowler develops an unstoppable head of steam, I would like to make a few points. It would appear that Fowler was attempting a high-tariff dive before pulling out when he realised David Seaman wasn't going to touch him. Then, if he genuinely believed that it wasn't a penalty, why did he not just roll the ball to Seaman instead of trying to score. Now that would have been sportsmanship. The referee should have booked Fowler for unsporting behaviour. It is no good players bleating about poor referees when they themselves often set out to con them. - D T DREWERY, Brigg, N Lincs

SPORT AROUND THE WORLD: Just when the Green Bay Packers' fans thought they had every imaginable trinket to honour their Super Bowl heroes, along comes a new product: condoms in the team's green and gold colours.

DAY BY DAY REVIEW

2: The Republic of Ireland and Northern Ireland suffer World Cup qualifying defeats, losing to Macedonia and the Ukraine respectively, though Scotland beat Austria and, in England's group, Italy are held in Poland

5: The Grand National is abandoned after Aintree is evacuated following an IRA bomb warning; Bolton Wanderers win promotion back to the Premier League with a month of the season to go

6: Emile Heskey's late equaliser gives Leicester City a draw in the Coca-Cola Cup final against Middlesbrough; Zimbabwe beat Great Britain 4-1 in their Davis Cup group match at Crystal Palace

7: Tony Dobbin guides Lord Gyllene to win by 25 lengths the postponed Grand National, run at five o'clock on Monday afternoon

9: Borussia Dortmund take the initiative in their European Cup semi-final against Manchester United with a 1-0 win in the first leg

10: Liverpool suffer a 3-0 defeat in the away leg of their European Cup-Winners' Cup semi-final against Paris St. Germain

11: Nick Faldo, the defending champion, misses the cut at the US Masters following a second-round 81 compounded by a nine at the 13th

13: Tiger Woods becomes the youngest US Masters champion, winning by 12 shots; Chelsea reach the FA Cup final after beating Wimbledon, while Middlesbrough are held 3-3 by Second Division Chesterfield in the other game; Liz McColgan finishes two seconds behind Kenya's Joyce Chepchumba in the London Marathon, while Antonio Pinto, of Portugal, takes the men's race

14: Mike Atherton is appointed England captain for the summer's Ashes and one-day series against Australia

16: Steve Claridge's injury-time winner settles the Coca-Cola Cup final in Leicester's favour, against Middlesbrough; Robbie Fowler is sent off in the Merseyside derby for swapping puches with David Unsworth

19: James Hickman wins Britain's only gold at the World Short-Course Swimming Championship, in the 200 metres butterfly

22: Bill Archer announces that he will stand down as chairman of troubled Brighton and hand over to Dick Knight and his consortium; Middlesbrough end Chesterfield's interest in the FA Cup in their semi-final replay

23: Denis Compton, the colourful England opening batsman and Arsenal footballer, dies aged 78; Borussia Dortmund complete their European Cup knock-out of Manchester United with a 1-0 win to the European Cup; Barnsley end their 110-year wait by confirming promotion to the Premier League

27: Heinz-Harald Frentzen makes it a German first and second by beating Michael Schumacher in the San Marino Grand Prix

29: Ireland finish off their first win over county opposition by beating Middlesex by 46 runs in the Benson and Hedges Cup

30: Teddy Sheringham and Alan Shearer score the goals that beat Georgia in a World Cup qualifier at Wembley; elsewhere, Scotland and the Republic of Ireland lose to Sweden and Romania respectively, while Northern Ireland draw in Armenia

THE PARTY MAY BE OVER, BUT OH WHAT A NIGHT...

by **MARCUS ARMYTAGE**

AMONG the small crowd awaiting news, that had gathered outside the gate to Aintree's owners and trainers car park at noon yesterday were trainers, officials, stable lads and a large number of Grand National jockeys, some in their breeches, boots and silks for the 24th consecutive hour.

'Do you want to know the rest of my Sunday?' asked Go Ballistic's jockey Mick Fitzgerald on hearing that the great race would definitely go ahead today. 'Bath, bath, sauna, bath, sauna, bath, bath.'

On Saturday he had been, like so many of his colleagues, trying to pare his 11-stone frame down to less than 10 stone by a process otherwise known as desiccation. In the belief that the race was unlikely to be rescheduled, he had spent most of Saturday night bingeing. 'Two pieces of chicken was all I had for supper last night,' he said glumly. 'And four bags of chips,' added his light-hearted and light-weight colleague John Kavanagh, who partners Turning Trix.

'I daren't get on the scales,' said another of his colleagues. 'I'm not going to until tomorrow morning,' agreed another.

'As far as I know,' rejoined Fitzgerald, 'my saddle is still on the horse.' The whereabouts of 37 other saddles, one of which was left on Scribbler, who proceeded to roll with it, is another of the logistical problems that will have to be sorted out by 5pm today.

The stories of this extraordinary Saturday night in Liverpool were already filtering into the annals of the world's greatest race's history. How jockeys, in their full kit, had to wend their way on foot into town with the crowds and find accommodation. No money, no credit cards, no clothes but if you were in Liverpool on Saturday April 5 1997 dressed to ride a racehorse, then the world was your low-calorie oyster.

In the weighing room, the Melling Road is no longer a gravel-covered lane which you cross four times in the Grand National, it's now a bye-word for Liverpudlian hospitality. Carl Llewellyn stood with us in a pair of loose-fitting jeans and shirt. He'd been passing a local house in Camelot Knight's green and white silks. A man had rushed out. 'Do you want to stay here for the night?' he asked. Llewellyn declined. 'Well the least I can do is lend you some clothes,' he added. The loose-fitting jeans were his, and the shirt. It's one way of losing your shirt on the horses.

Lester Manners, son of Killeshin's trainer, had spent the night on a couch in a front room in the same street. 'We were only allowed to stay there on one condition,' he enthused.

> *NO MONEY, NO CREDIT CARDS, NO CLOTHES, BUT IF YOU WERE IN LIVERPOOL ON APRIL 5 DRESSED TO RIDE A RACEHORESE, THE WORLD WAS YOUR LOW-CALORIE OYSTER*

Lord Gyllene moves clear of Master Oats and Suny Bay when the Grand National was finally run 48 hours late Ed Byrne

DELAY WILL POSE NO PROBLEM FOR LORD GYLLENE

'That we didn't pay a penny. It was far better than the hotel we had the night before and they knocked up a grand meal.'

Adie Smith had been paraded round town like a trophy. 'Do you want to come out with us?' Over The Stream's jockey was asked by a rough-looking bunch in the foyer of the Adelphi Hotel. He looked doubtful. 'We're not robbers,' they reassured him. 'But I haven't a dime on me,' contended Smith. 'We'll pay for you,' they insisted.

'The night of my life,' recollected Smith to his colleagues. At the first nightclub the bouncer had taken one look at him. 'You've had a bad day mate, you can come in for free,' he said. Smith never had to pay for a single beer.

Llewellyn was one of 12 jockeys who slept in David Walsh's room in the Adelphi. 'Who was in there?' he was asked, and he began reeling off names: Carberry, Murphy, Hogan, Brennan, Whitely... before adding with a mischievous grin, 'Jane, Suzy, Amanda, Janet and two Traceys!'

WAS it comfortable? 'Ask Timmy Murphy,' he said. 'He kipped in the bath.' Russ Garrity, Valiant Warrior's jockey, had slept with 300 others in Everton Sports Centre. What was that like? 'En-suite,' he said before adding: 'The only good thing that happened to me on Saturday was that Tiffany from *EastEnders* signed my t-shirt.'

Francis Woods was last seen getting on a plane back to Ireland at Speke Airport - an ordinary everyday sight in his silks. Tony Dobbin, his car locked in the car park, persuaded a colleague from Cumbria to pick him up at a junction on the M57. He had to walk two miles to get there and called in at a McDonalds on the way. 'Got some pretty strange looks,' he laughed.

'Did you get lucky?' asked one jockey to another in the knowledge that breeches, boots and silks were likely to shorten the odds of such an occurrence. 'No,' replied the other. 'But I didn't stop trying until 7am.'

Other jockeys went to the Post House in Runcorn which the Jockeys' Association secretary Michael Caulfield had had the foresight to block book on hearing of the abandonment. They, including Richard Dunwoody, Paul Holley and Andrew Thornton, had all got there via the only form of transport allowed to leave the course on Saturday, a horsebox. In another, Josh Gifford had taken Spuffington to be re-stabled at Haydock Park racecourse - along, of course, with 20 friends. The extra cost to owners, trainers and jockeys for the National's two-day delay is negligible. The cost of a good night out in Liverpool, which is nothing compared to the cost to Aintree Racecourse. 'An extra £19 a night for each lad, and a small transport surcharge,' suggested trainer Tony Balding. 'That's the least of it though.' There will be some small loss in earnings for northern jockeys who were engaged to ride at Kelso today. 'I had four good rides there,' said Tony Dobbin. 'But I'm definitely coming back here. Unfortunately for us, Kelso is the only meeting in the north until Saturday.'

Some of today's runners, like Suny Bay, Master Oats, Smith's Band and Nahthen Lad, were re-stabled at Haydock where they were exercised. Dextra Dove also joined them yesterday. The Irish runners all remained at Aintree where hay from the nearest mounted police stables was shipped in when supplies ran out. Others, like Lord Gyllene, Go Ballistic, River Mandate, General Wolfe, Celtic Abbey and Don't Light Up were all tucked up in their own West Midlands beds.

BACK at the gates to the car park was trainer Charlie Brooks. He has asked the assistant clerk of the course, Ian Renton, if he was thinking of watering the course yesterday. How any official at Aintree had any humour left is beyond me, but Renton found the funny side of it.

After a couple more hours of standing around, Carl Llewellyn's feet were beginning to hurt. Spending most of the night in a pair of thin-soled tight-fitting racing boots is about as practical as a pair of ballet shoes for mountaineering. 'Could I have a quote about your evening last night?' I asked him. 'Tell them,' he said, 'we spent it in the gym.' I was left to ponder on whether or not that was Liverpool's hottest night-spot.

After all the pre-race hype and tension of Saturday's events, the jockeys unwound in time-honoured fashion. Today, however, it will be back to deadly serious work. ★
08/04/97

LORD GYLLENE, who has spent most of the 'lost' two days since the original starting time for the 1997 Martell Grand National in the comfortable surroundings of his Shropshire stable, remains my idea of the likeliest winner of the rearranged race.

Whilst most of his 35 opponents today - the field being depleted by the withdrawal of Belmont King and the likely absence of Over the Stream - have been temporarily lodged a few miles away at Haydock Park, Lord Gyllene was one of a handful able to travel home on Saturday night.

The New Zealand-bred gelding has done plenty of travelling since his formative years in the Southern hemisphere, but six of his last seven races have been at his home track, Uttoxeter, whose chairman Stan Clarke is Lord Gyllene's owner.

Once the police lifted the cordon around Aintree's stable block on Saturday night, Lord Gyllene was one of the first to leave and by 8.30 pm he had made the 65-mile trip home. 'He had to get back,' said trainer Steve Brookshaw yesterday. 'We had no food with us. It's only a short run - and it might be a small advantage that his routine has not been much disturbed. 'I understand some of the other horses were away much longer but even 12 hours, as it was in Lord Gyllene's case, is plenty long enough without food and I'm delighted to say he ate up last night.'

HE SPENT MOST OF THE 'LOST' TWO DAYS IN THE COMFORTABLE SURROUNDINGS OF HIS SHROPSHIRE STABLES

Lord Gyllene was given a canter yesterday morning and his trainer is hopeful that the two-day delay will not prove a problem for this consistent character, who will also not mind any firming of the going following the extra period without either rain or watering. Brookshaw said: 'When I walked the track on Saturday, I thought there was plenty of grass cover, so I do not think there will be a problem of bare patches drying out.'

Lord Gyllene therefore presents the same solid case for selection as he did on Saturday. Winner of three and then a good second in his last four races compares favourably with anything his rivals can boast. My main danger in assessing the original line-up was Tim Forster's General Wolfe, who like Lord Gyllene returned home on Saturday. 'He didn't get back until around midnight,' said assistant trainer Henry Daly, 'but he seemed fine and definitely runs'. Lo Stregone also went home to Tom Tate's stable in Yorkshire, but the drying ground might make the going a little too lively for him.

---

by **TONY STAFFORD**

That is also the fear of trainer Charlie Brooks for Suny Bay and the bookmakers have lengthened his price. When I spoke to Brooks on the Melling Road soon after the abandonment, the trainer looked anxiously skyward. Momentarily, a few spots of rain from the leaden skies offered a promising portent but by yesterday Brooks was declaring Suny Bay '99% certain to run.

Top-weight Master Oats and his stable-companion Glemot were also given the all-clear by their trainer Kim Bailey. 'They spent the night at Haydock and there are no problems,' he said. Glemot's owner will donate a proportion of any prize-money won to charity.

Naturally, the Irish horses were unable to go home and they were all shipped to Haydock. Their most fancied contender is Wylde Hide, whose owner John McManus stands to win a reported £1 million in bets, should he be successful. McManus believes the present ground conditions will favour Wylde Hide, but I prefer the prospects of another Irish runner. Antonin, trained by Sue Bramall, was a high-class handicapper during the 1993-94 season when he won a string of good races, including the Racing Post Chase at Kempton and the Ritz Club Chase at Cheltenham. He lost his form the following season and has struggled to retrieve it since his trainer's move from Yorkshire to a new base in Ireland. Last time out, though, Antonin showed a glimpse of his old excellence when he had today's top-weight Master Oats among his victims at Punchestown. I think he can earn a place.

Despite the Brooks stables' apparent pessimism with regard to Suny Bay, I have to give this grey gelding a serious chance and he can vie with Antonin for third. Jenny Pitman's despair at the events on Saturday was there for all to see. She will be relieved at having a second crack this afternoon and over the past few days, confidence has grown for her Smith's Band, the mount of Richard Dunwoody. He looks to have better prospects than Nahthen Lad, who was pulled up last time in the Gold Cup at Cheltenham. It was that race 13 months ago which clearly illustrated the indelible prospects of Rough Quest, the 1996 National winner. The temptation to regard Go Ballistic, this year's Gold Cup fourth, as having a similar chance, is understandable. Go Ballistic has not only a similar style of racing, but several of his performances have been almost replicas of those previously achieved by Rough Quest.

The snag with Go Ballistic is his tendency to make errors which, as we saw again on Thursday and Friday, are often unforgiven at Aintree. Bookmakers, perhaps fearing an avalanche of bets on a horse with a topical name, have made him their 8-1 favourite. ★ **07/04/97**

WOODS BREAKS THE MOULD TO THREATEN WORLD DOMINATION

MICHAEL WILLIAMS senses fear among top players that they are about to be left behind

IT may only be coincidence but the day after Nick Faldo and Colin Montgomerie played with Tiger Woods, who won the Masters by a record 12 strokes at Augusta National on Sunday, each of them took 81; Faldo in the second round to miss the cut, Montgomerie in the last to tie for 30th place.

Put whatever interpretation you like on that but it was as if both these best of the British, Faldo, three times Masters champion, three times Open champion, and Montgomerie, four times in the last four years the leading money winner in Europe, realised that the game was about to be taken to a level they could never attain.

Even par then and Woods would have smashed the record by five strokes, not one, and while it would be ludicrous to suggest that he is going to win everything in which he plays, there is no doubt that if he sets his mind to it, the rest are going to have one hell of a job stopping him.

Woods himself cited Nicklaus, who had the gift and strength of mind to peak at the right time in winning 18 major championships as a professional and two US Amateurs, as a major influence. Woods, 20 when he turned professional last August, had three US Amateurs under his belt. Since then he has won four US Tour events, two last year and now two this and has exceeded $1 million in prize-money quicker than anyone.

He broke all manner of records in the Masters. He was the youngest winner, by nearly two years when compared with Severiano Ballesteros, who was 23 when he won for the first time in 1980, while his winning margin of 12 strokes from Tom Kite had never been done in any of the four major championships this century.

Most significant of all, however, is that Woods is black and triumphed at a golf club which elected its first non-white member only six years ago. Now there are three, the third being Woods, who as champion becomes an honorary member with the privilege that, when within the grounds of Augusta National though not elsewhere, he can wear the club's distinctive green jacket.

Lee Elder was the first black golfer to play in the Masters, in 1975, and it is only in the last 20 years that players have been allowed to bring their own caddies, regardless of colour. Before that it was the tradition for the club to allocate its own caddies, all of them then black.

'I'm so proud,' said Elder, who had driven up especially from Fort Lauderdale in Florida and picked up a speeding ticket on the way. 'We have a black champion and that's going to be of major significance. It will open doors for more blacks to become members of clubs and it will inspire more minority kids to get involved in golf.'

As Woods walked triumphantly up the 18th fairway, he admitted that one of his thoughts had been of Elder and also Charlie Sifford, another of the first blacks to have played in the tournament. The importance of what he has achieved compares with that of Arthur Ashe when he won Wimbledon. Today is also the 50th anniversary of Jackie Robinson becoming America's first black baseball player.

Quickly on the line with a congratulatory telephone call was President Clinton, who told Woods that 'the best shot I saw all week was the shot of you hugging your dad'.

Throughout Woods's life it has been his father, Earl, who recently underwent heart

WHILE IT WOULD BE LUDICROUS TO SUGGEST THAT HE IS GOING TO WIN EVERYTHING IN WHICH HE PLAYS, THERE IS NO DOUBT THE REST ARE GOING TO HAVE ONE HELL OF A JOB STOPPING HIM

surgery, who has been the force behind him, though his mother, Kultida, a Thai, is also close. The young man they have raised between them is not only an exceptional golfer - one Tom Watson says 'can emerge only once in a millennium' - but also one who promises to be an excellent ambassador.

He is well educated, studied at Stanford, speaks with modesty and good sense and has the looks and athleticism that will make him a role model for the young.

Phil Knight, chairman of Nike, the sportswear company who gave Woods a $40 million contract when he turned professional, said: 'You run out of superlatives. He's off the charts. We expected great things but he's gone way beyond.'

No golf tournament in the world will now be complete unless Woods is in the field. The demand for him will be unprecedented which leaves Hughes Norton, of Mark McCormack's International Management Group, with a mammoth portfolio. So far a balance has been kept. This was, after all, only Woods's ninth tournament of the year, one of which was in Asia and he won that by 10 strokes.

Such is the length that Woods hits the ball he hardly needs 14 clubs in his bag, though he refuted one suggestion that he could have won the Masters with only four. In four rounds he did just about go through the bag but it was the driver, the wedges and the putter that did most of the work.

It is this which is so frightening to every other tournament player. In four historic days they have been left feeling weak and inadequate, asking themselves, as the great Walter Hagen once put it many years ago, 'Who's going to be second?' ★ 15/04/97

This was the last article Michael Williams wrote for The Daily Telegraph. He suffered a fatal heart attack playing golf with his son Roddy at Chelmsford two days later.

Tiger Woods celebrates on the eighteenth green after winning the US Masters at Augusta Timothy A Clary

BATTLING BARNSLEY RISE FROM PITS
TO ATTAIN THEIR PLACE IN THE SUN

by **MICHAEL PARKINSON**

I DON'T know how we survived it, me and Dickie Bird. There was a point in the second half, with Bradford getting on top, when I seriously thought he might invade the pitch and bring them off for bad light. Before the game someone reminded us that the last time Barnsley had an occasion like this was when they won the FA Cup and that was so long ago they had a collection for the Titanic disaster at half-time.

To a natural born witterer like Dickie Bird this was even more reason to become agitated. He spent most of the game worrying in case Oakwell was hit by an iceberg. When the second goal went in and we knew we were there we didn't say much because had we done so I think we might have shed a tear. Silly, isn't it, how the love of a team makes grown men foolish. Why do we feel that way? My father said I was five when I was first taken to Oakwell. At half-time he asked my opinion of what I had seen. Apparently I said: 'It's all right but I think we'll go home now.' We didn't and in that moment I was committed to a lifetime's addiction, not so much to a game as to a club.

At first I stood in the front row, chin on the concrete wall into which my beloved Skinner delivered his bruised opponents. Later, as I grew taller, it became more of a problem to persuade people to let me through. My father devised a brilliant scheme whereby I put on a terrible limp and he would appeal to the spectators' better nature by crying: 'Make way, can't you see the poor little lad's got a bad leg.'

The day I stood alongside the men was a big moment in my life. The day I stood behind them because I had outgrown them was an important rite of passage. In those days my ambition was to buy a house opposite the players' entrance. It was my intention to live there with either Rita Hayworth or Vera Hruba Ralston to give me something to do when Barnsley were playing away. Fifty years on and I'm still thinking of making an offer on the house, although Rita and Vera are both sadly unavailable.

There is no known cure. I tried leaving. All that happened was during a trip to America after reading Barnsley had been beaten by Stockport County 21-1, I spent a small fortune ringing home before discovering the real score was a one-all draw.

Another time, during the Six-Day War in the Middle East, when I was pretending to be a war correspondent, I was also writing a weekly column about sport. At the height of the conflict, I found myself handing the Israeli censor an article about Skinner Normanton and the Barnsley team of my youth. There were a certain number of 'Ayups' and 'Tha' whats' in the article which the censor, a professor of English at Tel Aviv university, was certain were coded messages about Israeli troop movements. Moreover he refused to accept my explanation that Skinner Normanton was a real name and made me delete all references to my hero. He was convinced I was working for British intelligence.

I told Skinner this story some time later when we were brought together in a television studio. When I had finished he thought for a moment and then said: 'There weren't many Barnsley supporters in Israel, then?' Because of my passion for the club and the players of my youth, Sidney Albert Normanton gained a fame beyond the parish boundaries. There was a Skinner Normanton Appreciation Society in Kuala Lumpur. Making a speech in Australia I was introduced as 'the man who made Clogger Normanton famous'.

This information made little impact on the audience who didn't have a clue what the man was talking about. But I did and although Skinner would have objected to being called 'Clogger' - he always thought of himself as competitive rather than crude - I wondered, not for the first time, what it was about the name that captured the imagination of strangers.

I came to the conclusion it was because they thought Skinner was an adjective as well as a nickname. It summed up for them the kind of man who came up the shaft in his pitmuck, pulled on a Barnsley shirt and went out to give people a taste of what it was like to play against a Yorkshire collier. After all, the team were, and still are, called 'Battling Barnsley'.

While it is true a fair number of hard men have spilled blood at Oakwell it must always be remembered Normanton's midfield partner for a while was Danny Blanchflower, and that the Barnsley teams of the Forties and Fifties played their football on the carpet. Danny Wilson's present team play the same way. The other Danny would have approved. He was a purist and a hard man to please.

D ANNY Blanchflower was an important influence in my life. He was the first player who made me want to write about the game. He had a style and intelligence which isolated him from the hoi polloi. Sometimes we would stand outside the ground and get the players' autographs after training and then, like lovelorn swains, follow them to the snooker hall where they spent the afternoons. I don't know why we followed them. We knew where they were going.

One day Danny walked past the snooker hall and continued up the hill to the technical college. He was studying economic theory. The Barnsley team of that time were as pleasant and skilful a combination as I have seen. Pat Kelly was an acrobat of a goalkeeper who would walk on his hands in the penalty area when he was bored and once caught a shot between his knees while upside down (does distance lend enchantment, I wonder?).

Gordon Pallister was a languid and stylish full-back who owned a temperance bar where you could buy pints of sarsaparilla. We used to go to buy a pint between three of us just to sit and gawp. Johnny Kelly was the man who changed the face of English football by giving Alf Ramsey such a towsing when Southampton played Barnsley that Alf vowed vengeance on wingers and banished them from his '66 World Cup team. They have had a hard time ever since.

Blanchflower was the creative soul of the team and for a couple of seasons turned in performances of such imagination and quality they last forever in the minds of those lucky enough to see them. He was happy at Oakwell, except he couldn't understand why, when the players were called back for extra training in the afternoons, they were not allowed the ball.

He was told that if they saw too much of the ball during the week they wouldn't want it on Saturday. Blanchflower pointed out if they didn't see the ball during the week they wouldn't know what it looked like on Saturday. He didn't know his place. He never did. Joe Richards, the Barnsley chairman, sold him to Aston Villa for a few quid. Danny sat in the kitchen with the chairman's chauffeur while he was traded over port and cigars in the dining room. In those days players didn't argue with chairmen, particularly if they owned the only Rolls Royce for miles around and smoked Havana cigars in a Woodbine society. Sir John Hall and Alan Sugar are philanthropic democrats compared to the likes of Richards.

Before the game I drove through the pit villages surrounding Barnsley. This was where I grew up so it was partly a trip down memory lane but also, and more usefully, a reminder of the community served by Barnsley Football Club.

When I was a young man the link between pit and club was obvious. The only difference between player and spectator was one worked down the pit and watched Barnsley and the other worked down the pit and played for Barnsley. Nowadays the pits have gone. The slag heaps are being landscaped, the winding gear is dismantled. The generation singing Barnsley's anthem *It's Just Like Watching Brasil* on Saturday know what a pit looks like but their children won't.

The ground has changed, too, with new stands, although I can't wait to hear what the Manchester United fans think of our visitors' accommodation, which hasn't got a roof. What is more I would love to see Gianfranco Zola's face when he has to stand in line for a bath. We've never been big on pampering in Barnsley. I don't know what it all means because it hasn't yet sunk in. What I am sure of is something special has occurred and it couldn't have happened to nicer or more deserving people. ★ 28/04/97

Going up! Barnsley supporters celebrate the Holy Grail, promotion to the Premiership Chris Laurens

HIGH-FLIER! CHELSEA'S GIANFRANCO ZOLA, THE FOOTBALLER OF THE YEAR, CELEBRATES A GOAL AGAINST WIMBLEDON IN THE FA CUP RUSSELL CHEYNE

SELECTORS IN NEED OF INSPIRATION

by **DONALD TRELFORD**

THERE is a category of sportsmen who have found favour more readily with the fans than with national selectors. The prime current example is Jeremy Guscott at rugby. Before that it was David Gower at cricket.

One thinks of footballers like Matt Le Tissier, Glenn Hoddle and, way back in my childhood, Stanley Matthews. Dean Richards, too, has been inexplicably excluded from some of England's key matches, notably the 1991 Rugby World Cup final.

These players won a sideboard-full of international caps, of course, but it is the times they were sidelined that rankled, and rankle still. The selectors, in their wisdom, may have been privy to fluctuations in form and fitness invisible to the naked eye, but to those of us on the terraces their stubborn stupidity was truly maddening.

What most of these players had in common was an individual artistry that selectors, naturally concerned with choosing a team where talents will blend, seemed to find offensive or even threatening.

INDIVIDUAL GENIUS IS THE QUALITY THAT SPECTATORS PRIZE MOST HIGHLY

Deano hardly falls into this group. What selectors found unforgivable in him was that shambling, socks-down, apparently unathletic divergence from the tidy norm they expected. That image was an illusion, as rugby fans could recognise.

Individual genius is the quality that spectators prize most highly and selectors are constitutionally wary of. To the official mind, especially in this country (foreigners are more tolerant of self-expression), it smacks of showing off and selfishness; it is somehow un-English.

Yet, increasingly, in all international team sports, the capacity to unlock tight defences, to seize an initiative, to do the unexpected, to produce a lethal flash of inspiration, are what mark out the winners from the also-rans. All the players named above, Richards included, have won matches on their own.

Matthews had that quality in spades. Bobby Charlton, who also had it, has told of the joy of watching the winger as a little boy: 'I couldn't take my eyes off him, the feeling that I was actually breathing the same air as he was. Just the sight of Matthews coming out on the pitch gave you a feeling of the magic of the man. People would travel, in the days when it was really difficult, hundreds of miles to see him.'

The magic of Matthews was at its most effective in that greatest of all FA Cup finals, in 1953, when Blackpool came back to beat Bolton 4-3 in injury time. I have a picture on my office wall of the moment Matthews crossed to Bill Perry for the winning goal. I watched the game on a friend's nine-inch black-and-white television set.

The point of this is to remind people that Matthews was the greatest player of his time, greater even than Tom Finney. This may come as a surprise to younger readers, for the Preston plumber's reputation has grown in recent years while that of the so-called wizard of dribble has declined.

This is not to denigrate Finney in any way, either as a player or a man. I had the memorable privilege of sitting next to him at the dinner to mark Matthews' 80th birthday two years ago. He would be included in any team of all-time England greats.

MATTHEWS had that sublime gift of all great sportsmen, shared with the likes of Muhammad Ali, Pele, George Best and Gary Sobers, of seeming to be a mortal touched with divinity. This is captured in a poem by Alan Ross:

The Greatest of all time, meraviglioso Matthews,
Stoke City, Blackpool and England.
Expressionless enchanter, weaving as on strings
Conceptual patterns to a private music, heard
Only by him, to whose slowly emerging theme
He rehearses steps, soloist in compulsions of a dream.

I doubt if anyone would be moved to write a poem about Finney. Why, then, has his reputation soared? The reason came to me as I watched Hugh McIlvanney's brilliant series for the BBC on the great football managers. Bill Shankly, who played behind Finney for Preston North End, has praised him so volubly and colourfully to generations of sports writers that the myth has taken root.

In comparison, Matthews is seen as somewhat effete and flashy, which is far from the truth. He just lacked a Bill Shankly to promote his immortal genius.

SEDBERGH school can claim a clean sweep of England rugby captains with the appointment of James Lofthouse to lead the 18 Group XV. He follows the two Wills, Carling and Greenwood, also from Sedbergh, who captained England and England A respectively.

R M Spencer, from Woodbridge, Suffolk, asks: 'Has any other school achieved this distinction?' ★ **21/04/97**

END COLUMN

SPORT AROUND THE WORLD: A woman went on hunger strike outside the offices of the Argentinian Football Association after being prevented from refereeing first division football matches. Florencia Romano, 25, passed her referee's course with honours and, having controlled 450 non-league games, she was upset when the Argentinian FA refused to accept her. She blamed their 'macho' attitude, appealed to Congress, and the government forced the FA to drop their discrimination. The men at the FA dragged their feet, though, and only after Romano went on hunger strike did they intervene and put her on the official list.

SPORT AROUND THE WORLD: Never mind Manchester United's fixture pile-up, the really hard life for a footballer is in China. To play in the new season of the professional league players had to endure a six-week training camp without a single day off. They had to complete a 10,000-metre run every day - that's 262 miles in their 42-day stay - and the punishment for failure to do so was ineligibility for the whole season. To make sure there was no repeat of last year's carousing, the Chinese FA employed armed police with dogs to patrol the camp at night and make sure no one got out for a drink or a night with the local women. As if they would have had the energy.

ABOUT RUGBY: Walsall have set a national Courage League record but do not know whether to laugh or cry. By losing 44-42 to Reading, they scored the highest number of points yet by a defeated side. Somehow the League Three club allowed a 42-25 advantage to disappear in the final 12 minutes. Even then they had time for a matchwinning dropped goal attempt by Richard Mills, but it was deflected away from the posts.

SPORT AROUND THE WORLD: When Orde Ballantyne, coach of the St Vincent athletics team, refused to stand for the US anthem at the Atlanta Olympics, the chief of the delegation, who happened to be his mother, reported him. Gloria Ballantyne said no son of hers was going to act that way. Now the National Olympic Committee of St Vincent and the Grenadines have suspended Orde Ballantyne for four years. The coach, who will not be eligible to take part in the 2000 Olympics, said he does not stand for any national anthem except St Vincent's.

CRICKET DIARY: Surrey have gone in for a spot of record-breaking, though not the sort which will fill coach Dave Gilbert with pride. The 86 extras they conceded against Somerset beat the Championship 'best' of 81 set no less than four times in 1994, including once by Surrey. Perhaps Surrey should match Malcolm Marshall's initiative at Hampshire last season and introduce a fining system for no balls. Their first half-dozen Championship games yielded only one no ball and that by off-spinner Shaun Udal. If it had applied at the Oval, Chris Lewis's 12 no balls (worth 24 runs) would have left him £60 out of pocket.

ABOUT RUGBY: The Welsh Rugby Union have bowed to sentiment and withdrawn the Cardiff Arms Park goalposts from their auction. But everything else will go, including seats, turf and the scoreboard. "The goalposts are among the most evocative things in the ground," says WRU spokesman Peter Owens. "They will become the centrepiece of a museum in the new national stadium."

DAY BY DAY REVIEW

SURPRISE, LUCK AND CROFT ARE ENGLAND'S BEST BETS

by E.W.SWANTON

THE sun never sets on cricket, as Plum Warner first remarked many years ago, an aphorism even more literally true today than ever. The top players are caught up in a continuous circus which surely calls for some regulation by the International Cricket Council.

Yet the high hopes in an English spring are perennial, and this year there is that special expectation which heralds the coming of Australia and the prospect of yet another fight for the Ashes.

It is 10 years since Mike Gatting, in Australia, retained the Ashes won here two years before by David Gower, and results since have been too depressing to mention. On the evidence of the respective bowling resources it would be foolish to deny that once again the odds over a six-Test series strongly favour Australia.

It might be different but for Shane Warne, and if any England bowler other than the admirable Robert Croft could aspire to the steadfast quality of an Angus Fraser, let alone a Botham or a Bedser. Yet surprise is the essence of cricket, and luck a permanent element. The better side, thank heaven, do not always win.

The crowds who will fill every Test seat and the untold mass of followers everywhere would surely be satisfied if England played with courage to the utmost of their capacity and if they showed a cheerful and generous spirit.

One of the hopes for the new season with the Australians in our midst must be for a general condemnation and action against sledging. The Australians were not the originators of this foul habit of verbal abuse but it has been for many years endemic in their cricket. I hope too that England show a more acceptable demeanour than was apparent at times during the winter, especially in the matter of appealing.

Cricketers, especially young ones, take their cue from what they see on the box. The eyes of the cricket world will be on this Ashes series, which will be genuinely acceptable only if the captains, the umpires and the referees all play their parts in making it so.

TALKING of behaviour, it is 20 years this week since news broke of what turned out to be the most serious assault on the game's accepted values in its history. My recollection of the events of May 1977 is specially clear because after a Thursday's play at Canterbury, Len Maddocks, the Australia manager, with two of his side, came to dine with us at Sandwich.

It was the last happy evening poor Maddocks spent on the tour, for two days later at Hove he learnt that all but four of his team had signed secret contracts binding allegiance to the brash, over-bearing media tycoon, Kerry Packer. There followed the sorry chapter of fractured loyalties, friendships broken, Test cricket played by skeleton sides while the rebels competed in so-called 'Super Tests' against one another.

After two years, a commercial compromise between the Australian board and Packer allowed him television rights on condition that his World Series Cricket ceased to compete with the established game. There is an inclination now in some quarters to say that Packerism was perhaps not such a bad thing as players became better paid. In fact, in England and Australia, improved salary scales were in train anyway.

I have been looking up contemporary comments on WSC in 1977-79. Tony Lewis told *Sunday Telegraph* readers that more bouncers than he had ever seen were destroying the best batsmen. Henry Blofeld wrote of 'despicable' fast bowling. Tony Greig, of the Packer camp, with implicit approval said bowlers were dishing out an unprecedented amount of bouncers at the 'rabbits'.

When the Packer circus ventured to the West Indies, riots occurred in three of the countries visited. At Georgetown, the pavilion was looted and records destroyed. The modern evil of intimidation had its roots in the brutalising of cricket under Packer. I once, by the way, won a £10 cricket wager from his father, Sir Frank, owner of several newspapers in Sydney, who was a genial fellow in comparison.

WHAT memories spring to mind at the news of Denis Compton's passing. For all his 17 Test hundreds, my clearest picture is of his 76 not out in the Lord's Test of 1938 when, on a pitch made difficult by rain and sun, and with Hutton, Barnett, Edrich, Hammond and Verity out, and only 76 runs on the board, he stood, a cool, debonair youth of 20, between Australia and victory, confronting with consummate artistry the spin and lift of O'Reilly and the high speed of McCormick. He used to say it was his best innings - when he remembered.

As a relief from much pain and general ill-health in his last years he could still relish the company of such great friends as Colin Ingleby-Mackenzie and John Warr; but he who had given so much to so many could no longer find pleasure in life. To those old enough to recall the late 1940s there was never such a sporting hero. Wilfred Wooller was another glamorous figure in the world of games for whom I had much admiration. By an ill-fated chance a letter he dictated to his wife congratulating me on my birthday a few days before he died did not reach me until afterwards.

He recalled a friendship going back 60-odd years to his freshman days at Cambridge when he and Cliff Jones led the university in a glorious era on the rugby field. Wooller and Tony O'Reilly were the greatest three-quarters I ever saw, and the break by Wilf which in 1935-36 brought about that most thrilling victory over the All Blacks at Cardiff was the most exciting memory of all of us who were there on that famous day.

As a cricketer he must be accounted one of the two makers of Glamorgan, building on, after the war, the foundation made before it by Maurice Turnbull. He was a belligerent captain — a shade too much so at times — and in particular a pioneer in the aggressive use of catchers round the bat. His winning of the championship in 1948 was a nine-day wonder. ★ 07/05/97

GREAT DIVIDE IS KEY TO REVERSAL OF FORTUNES

by ROBERT HARDMAN

I T IS bizarre to think that we may be only two years away from Wolves v Leek Town or Northwich Victoria v Nottingham Forest on a Football League fixture list. But that is the extent of the League's bold but sensible new consultation document on their future.

Some of those huge League egos will certainly need persuading. But if something is to be done about the declining fortunes at the lower end of professional football then regionalised third divisions with extra part-time clubs seems a good move.

What is striking about all three League divisions - and the Conference - is that they are very well-balanced geographically. Draw a line across England from the Wash, through Walsall and out over Wales and one finds every division has near-equal numbers on either side.

And just as important is the equal divide in both halves of each division, though the Conference do have a stronger southern presence in their bottom half.

The next problem will be titles. The consultants dislike the term 'Third Division North' or 'South', fearing connotations of the old days and a drop in standards. Their solution is either different labels - how about the Mercia and Wessex Divisions? - or else sponsored titles.

In this brave new era, we will simply have to suffer a Hovis Third Division in the north and a Perrier Third Division in the south.

W HAT should we make of Tony Banks's appointment as Sports Minister? I suspect that it signals good news for football fans, bad news for administrators, particularly of the 'posher' sports, and a migraine for British Sky Broadcasting.

No one can question his passion for football nor his capacity to turn a gripe into a parliamentary debate. As one of Westminster's sharpest hecklers, Banks has made a fool of numerous ministers at the Despatch Box, but now it is his turn to be on the receiving end. And there is likely to be plenty of opposition to the Banks manifesto as laid down in recent years. It includes:

Government action to 'persuade' clubs to reduce ticket prices and make Premiership football more accessible to the working man. 'Football is Thatcherism,' Mr Banks told a Labour conference meeting last October. 'If any area of leisure is calling out for some sort of regulation, it's got to be football.'

A ban on national anthems at football internationals. Banks believes that anthems cause aggro and are an aristocratic conspiracy. 'Let the mob have their moment of enjoyment but don't let them ever forget their place,' he said of anthems three months ago, somehow overlooking the fact that communist countries are pretty keen on anthems, too.

An end to point-to-pointing. Banks is a fierce advocate of a ban on hunting which would, inevitably, destroy one of the most popular and cheapest forms of racing since point-to-pointing is inextricably linked to hunting.

A ban on the Grand National and other races which do not meet safety standards laid down by animal welfare groups, a regular Banks demand come Aintree time.

A demand that MCC accept women. In 1991 he called on John Major to resign from MCC after they turned down female members.

Tough action against 'old farts'. In 1995 Banks drew up an Early Day Motion attacking the Rugby Football Union for removing Will Carling as England captain.

Rewriting the rules concerning television coverage of major sporting events to keep the Murdoch sports empire at bay. Telling England to drop the bid for the 2006 World Cup in order to give South Africa's 'rainbow nation' bid a better chance.

Changing his mind about South Africa when he discovered that most voters wanted the World Cup here thanks very much.

Sports fans of all political persuasions may agree with much of the above but the Banks philosophy remains one ill-suited to sport in general: it is the belief that sport's problems should be solved by Whitehall if sport will not solve them itself.

In person, I have always found Banks amiable and accessible (though that may change with the new Blair edict that all ministers must seek Downing Street's permission before speaking or going to the lavatory).

In choosing Banks, Tony Blair has made it clear he wants sport to have a noisy, dynamic profile. And much credit should go to Tom Pendry, Labour's long-serving sport spokesman in Opposition, who devoted many years to the party's sporting manifesto only to be dumped at the hour of victory. Of one thing we can be certain. The new regime will not be dull.

S O Bolton nearly won 100 points in a season (they finished with 99). Big deal. Surely the applause should go to Yeovil Town. They won the ICIS Premier League and promotion to the Conference with 101 points - and they played four games fewer than Bolton. ★ **07/05/97**

GETTING DOWN TO IT. JOHN SOLOMAN OF SUSSEX LINES UP A SHOT AT THE INTER-COUNTY CROQUET CHAMPIONSHIPS PHIL SHEPHARD-LEWIS

GULLIT GOVERNS IN FOREIGN AND DOMESTIC POLICY

by **HENRY WINTER** at the FA Cup final

TO LOSE one final may be considered a misfortune. For Middlesbrough to lose two finals, a place on the Premiership payroll and, in all probability, their leading foreigners hints at something far deeper than being stood up by Lady Luck.

It would take a hard heart and weak-memoried mind to criticise Bryan Robson, Boro's manager, too extensively. Throughout this remarkable period in a likeable club's history, Robson has been the epitome of dignity, dealing with questions honestly and without recourse to rancour, despite lines of inquiry that might have ignited many a man's fuse.

Yet failings persist, not ones that cast clouds on Robson's long-term managerial potential but blips from which the former England captain, as resilient an individual as he was a midfielder, will doubtlessly learn. And they are mistakes highlighted to headline proportion by the contrasting success of Ruud Gullit, a manager of even shorter acquaintance with touchline life, yet one who masterminded the 2-0 defeat of Robson's Boro on Saturday.

Chelsea's preparations, from the early seeds of team assembly to the broad tactical thrust and right down to the match's very minutiae, were impressively thought out. Gullit has bought and built well, bringing in people he values as positive characters as well as formidable footballers. Just look at what his signings have become: Gianfranco Zola is

Footballer of the Year, Roberto Di Matteo is a figure of growing international stature while Frank Leboeuf stands out from the Premiership's admittedly small pool of creative defenders.

All have been committed to the Chelsea cause. The one high-profile foreigner with reason to air grievances, the bench-bound Gianluca Vialli, has never voiced the kind of nonsense occasionally emanating from Emerson and Fabrizio Ravanelli, first-teamers at the Riverside.

Gullit has the advantage over Robson in that foreigners put down roots quicker in a major metropolis. If Robson was handicapped from this perspective, he was also unbelievably let down by Emerson, a shuffling disgrace at Wembley.

At the season's start, Emerson was compared to his manager as a midfielder capable of dominating proceedings from box to box. How short-sighted that verdict proved to be. When the going got tough, a situation Robson relished, Emerson disappeared. There will be a hollow ring whenever the Brazilian claims he once played at the home of football. Robson deserved so much better from a player he invested money, time and faith in. So did Boro's magnificent supporters, who paid Emerson's wages.

Yet if Emerson (and Branco) proved mistakes, Robson deserves praise, thanks even, for inviting Juninho to run across our fields and imaginations. The little man's character and courage have never been in question.

The foreign policy of the Premiership is proving a mixed blessing. It has given us virtuosos such as Juninho, Zola and Di Matteo. Yet these are players who, for all Tony Banks's

cogitations, will never win the World Cup for England. Here again, Gullit has impressed more than Robson by buying and nurturing domestic talent.

Danny Granville, acquired from Cambridge United, and Jody Morris, inherited but given greater projection, are future England internationals. Paul Hughes is so highly regarded that his better-known namesake, the mighty Mark, requires an 'M' before the Hughes on his shirt. Eddie Newton and Michael Duberry are already established in the Premiership consciousness.

AND Boro? Phil Stamp has featured in the England Under-21s, Ben Roberts will learn from his experience and Chris Freestone hints at promise, but the production line needs oiling. As a former pupil of Alex Ferguson, Robson will appreciate the importance of developing from within as well as without.

If Boro have some of their priorities blurred, balance exemplifies Gullit's approach. Take any one player out of Chelsea's team and they would survive; Zola disappointed at Wembley but Di Matteo and Newton assumed responsibility. Remove Juninho and Boro stutter.

Already impressive in his team-building practice, Gullit's preparations intensified with his strategy for the great occasion. Composure and calm professionalism characterised Chelsea's Cup final week. Away from the hype, Gullit and Graham Rix fine-tuned their tactics. In a back-line switching as required from a three to a four, Scott Minto started at left-

We've won the cup! Chelsea supporters salute their side's FA Cup triumph against Middlesbrough at Wembley Russell Cheyne

back but with licence to push forward, complementing the quasi wing-back role of Dan Petrescu on the right.

Newton and Di Matteo largely frustrated Juninho by fair means and foul, the Italian cautioned for the most cynical of trips. Dennis Wise, who looks to have another England squad call in him, proved quietly influential from the left.

Up front, Mark Hughes's task was to provide his usual nuisance factor, creating holes like a cerebral linebacker for colleagues to exploit. No-one quite expected such a plan to produce three cherries on the first pull of the lever. After 43 seconds, Hughes dragged defenders away from Di Matteo, who dipped an exquisite shot over Roberts. The fastest goal in Wembley Cup final history confirmed Boro's position as patients lying awake through an operation.

Di Matteo's wonderful strike should have created an open game. But Emerson, so lax in letting Chelsea's scorer build up steam, failed to become involved. So Boro staggered on, managing only one effort on target when Steve

Vickers was thwarted by Frode Grodas.

Amid all these laboured moves, in a poor final, came 16 offsides for Boro, many the personal responsibility of Mikkel Beck, a naive runner here.

The heart did go out to Robson. He had gambled legitimately on Ravanelli, who departed lame again, so bringing in the far less effective Beck. When victory was assured for Chelsea, following Newton's thoroughly deserved close-range finish, Gullit was able to introduce Vialli, who had lifted the European Cup in his last final .

Vialli had stressed all week the team's importance over the individual. This stretched throughout Club Chelsea, most notably to Rix, who continually dispensed water bottles and advice, and other members of the back-room staff who exhorted the crowd to greater support. The 1997 FA Cup will be remembered as a triumph for Gullit's well-prepared team over Robson's collection of individuals. ★ **19/05/97**

AFTER YEARS OF WAITING ALL WE WANTED WAS TO HEAR THE FINAL WHISTLE by GILES SMITH

JUST as predicted in the song, when Wise went up to lift the FA Cup, we were there. Or thereabouts. From where I was, the trophy was the merest flash of light above a sea of heads and flags, but I don't suppose I'll ever forget the sight, or the collective exhalation of relief from the thousands of people around me. Finally, after a quarter of a century in which the only important silverware we've seen has been Ken Bates's beard, here was the real thing.

Eddie Newton laid to rest some ghosts from 1994 on Saturday (scoring where, three years ago, he gave away a penalty) and he wasn't the only one. For many of us the abiding memory of that Manchester United final is a long trudge home through Wembley's streets in the pouring rain. This time we stayed in the stadium and bopped to *Walking on Sunshine*.

Forgive me if I say that, on a personal level, I thought I played a blinder. As Ruud Gullit himself would doubtless tell you, preparation is the key and experience forms an indispensable guide. No one can say I didn't learn from the mistakes of 1994. The new Continental influence in the game has taught us much about the importance of diet and accordingly I eschewed the disastrous late, greasy-spoon breakfast which cost me so much in terms of stamina last time around, opting instead for a more sustaining chicken sandwich.

And this time I didn't bawl myself hoarse during the warm-up period, an error of judgment which severely limited my contribution late on against Manchester United and which may well have led to their third and fourth goals on that gruesome day.

Travelling light, I went to Wembley armed only with a 12-inch inflatable Ruud Gullit, in case of emergencies, but in the event had no cause to use it. Fright wigs and face paint were the norm. Near me, someone staggered to his seat with a giant tin-foil sculpture on his head. It was meant to look like the FA Cup but it was the size of a flower urn at a stately home. Still, he was much like the rest of us: the Cup had gone to his head in a big way.

Weird scenes. But the strangeness continued. The exclamation I heard again and again was 'I can't believe it'. People were saying it as they took their seats: they were still saying it as Dennis Wise danced past with the Cup in his hands. It was hardly surprising: there was so much not to believe - beginning with Roberto Di Matteo's opening goal. Forty-three seconds, indeed. How could we have been ready for that? By the time Boro kicked off again, we had been jumping around longer than the ball had been in play.

For fans of a neurotic disposition, an early goal is a mixed blessing. Had Chelsea seized the initiative in that first half, and put a couple more away, maybe those of us in the stand could have started to relax and open up. As it was, between that first-minute strike and Newton's clincher 10 minutes from time, I was probably more pre-occupied by the clock than by anything on the pitch. Bizarre, really. You pass whole years longing to see your team play in a Wembley final. Then when it happens, you spend almost the entire 90 minutes willing it to be over.

When it was, a giant weight lifted from some 30,000 pairs of shoulders - and also, perhaps, off the shoulders of their friends. For years we've droned on about Hudson and Cooke and Osgood. At last we have something new to talk about. ★ **19/05/97**

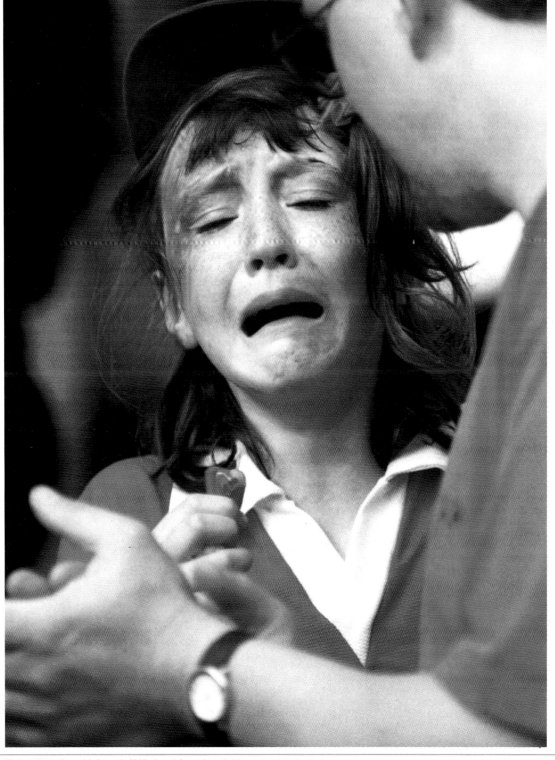

We haven't won the cup! A distraught Middlesbrough fan at the end of the game   Phil Shephard-Lewis

Telegraph

WHACK! ROB TODD OF READING HAS ANDREW BILLSON OF TEDDINGTON ON THE HOP DURING THE HOCKEY ASSOCIATION CUP FINAL   PHILIP BROWN.

NEW LABOUR, NEW RESULT
AGAINST AUSTRALIA

by RORY
BREMNER

NEW Labour, New England. I wonder if next week's new improved, less confrontational Prime Minister's Questions will see John Major rise to his feet to congratulate Tony Blair's Government on adding to a remarkable victory in the Eurovision Song Contest, a memorable one-day triumph over Australia; one which will be celebrated all the more by our cricket-loving former premier for the fact that it was his beloved Surrey wot won it, in the shape of Graham Thorpe and Adam Hollioake.

Ironic, though, that just as the Government threatens to take action against tobacco sponsorship in sport, the first major sporting event of the summer will be... the Ashes.

I remember muttering this time last year in this very column about the disappearance of the Texaco one-day internationals to Sky. This year - another irony - I find myself grateful that, thanks to the satellite channel, I can watch the cricket and write this article as the full moon rises over Glandore Harbour deep in the West of Ireland.

The Irish had only just been celebrating their own Benson and Hedges Cup triumph over Middlesex thanks to that legendary man of Erin, Hans O'Cronje. England's star, too, seems once more in the ascendant, with a team performance fizzing with energy and commitment: whippy bowling, stunning fielding and courageous batting. Let us hope that this one-day wonder at least doesn't live up to its name.

The new season, with its new hopes, means the perennial struggle for fitness. I know this because I've seen Graham Cowdrey in a muck sweat after yet another jog. Even when he isn't trying to get fit, he is one of the funniest men I have ever been lucky enough to meet.

This was apparent during our first game of lawn cricket when he disappeared into the house with a tennis ball, climbed two flights of stairs, appeared at a first-floor window and announced: 'Change of bowling. Curtly Ambrose is coming on. Might just get a bit of lift off a length...'

Having inquired of David Coulthard's manager how much weight grand prix drivers lose in a race, Cowdrey pondered for a while before venturing: 'So, if I drove to Edinburgh and back in my Vectra, with the heater on, do you think I'd make the cut at Canterbury?'

His wife Maxine - herself a champion jockey and a shining personality - despairs that their downstairs bathroom, now full of signed prints, bats, golf umbrellas, benefit ties and other paraphernalia, has been turned into the Graham Cowdrey Benefit Office. 'That's right hon,' he says without a pause. 'I'm auctioning off the shower at the Porter Tun next week.'

AFTER a round of golf, he takes me once again to meet Sir Colin. 'Dad, I've brought Tom Kite to see you...' Sir Colin reminisces. A gentle genius, without a hint of bitterness. This is great, feet-of-the-master stuff. He rates this season's Kent side very highly. 'I think they'd have given our lot a game...'

A highlight of Graham's benefit year so far has been the Rosemary Hawthorne Knicker Talk, where the quite marvellous Miss Hawthorne displayed the contents of two large suitcases of knickers of varying history and design to much amusement at a ladies' lunch at Canterbury. Cardigan Connor's Dodgy Dinner at Hampshire seems a tame gig by comparison.

It is the characters as much as anything that make cricket such a wonderful game. And they don't come much better than Jack Russell, whose book was launched this week. It's one of God's little jokes that most adjectives applied to Jack Russell have canine overtones: dogged, loyal, tenacious and, perhaps above all, barking.

I shared a room with him on a West Indies tour one night and awoke with a fearful hangover. Not, it must be said, from drink, but from the heady fumes of white spirit and turpentine wafting from his collection of rags, brushes and canvasses. I always knew he was a superb artist - on and off the field.

While we were in St Vincent he was distraught because an attempt to starch the sunhat he has worn for 16 years with those years etched into every stitch, rip and ragged line of thread - ended with smoke coming from the oven and Jack desperately trying to repair the scorch marks with yet more white material.

BUT I only knew the half of it. This is a man who, on Christmas Day, had his wife play him the Queen's Message down the phone while he stood proudly to attention in a Harare hotel room.

So concerned is he for his privacy that if he ever invites team-mates round to his house he'll have them blindfolded and drive them there in a van himself. He carries a tumble-drier around in his car throughout the cricket season.

All this and more is in his book, which he launched at the Imperial War Museum ('because I like it here') with a dog (for the cameras) and at a lunch where the main course was jaffa cakes and homewheat digestives (his favourite food).

He is utterly mad and utterly brilliant, I love him. Such has been his misfortune at the hands of selectors that he could well have called the book 'Retired Hurt'. I only hope that in the grim age of total professionalism (new labour, indeed) the next generation does not lose such characters.

Jack's book is ghosted by Pat Murphy, who at last has found a subject rich in character, anecdote and opinion. It was not ever thus. Commissioned in 1979 to write a book with Graham Gooch, Murphy looked forward to his first interview with the future Essex and England captain. What light might the young man shed?

Gooch reflected, then delivered his wisdom: 'If it's in my half of the wicket, I hit it to ****. Oh, and you've got to have confidence in your own ability. (Pause). D'you think you can get 60,000 words out of that?'

The great Viv Richards was similarly enlightening. 'If I see de cherry, I keep my eye on de cherry, an' it disappears.' It says much for Murphy's abilities that he managed the other 59,985 words. But then, Russell and Richards don't work with words. They entertain with skill, hand-eye co-ordination and talent. And Jack paints great pictures.

Today, for England, that picture looks like another new dawn. ★ **24/05/97**

END COLUMN

DAY BY DAY REVIEW

1: Donovan Bailey wins the two-man Challenge of Champions sprint over 150 metres in Toronto when Michael Johnson pulls up injured at halfway

4: England gain revenge for February's World Cup defeat at Wembley by beating Italy 2-0 in Le Tournoi tournament in Nantes with goals by Ian Wright and Paul Scholes

5: England start the Ashes series in sensational style, bowling Australia all out for 118 - they were 54 for eight at one stage - and leading on the first day at Edgbaston by 82 runs

6: Nasser Hussain hits his highest score for England (207) as England pile on the runs in the first Test against Australia

7: Benny The Dip (11-1), ridden by Willie Ryan, trained by John Gosden, wins The Derby by a short-head; Hosts France are beaten by Alan Shearer's goal in England's second game in Le Tournoi in Montpellier; Iva Majoli, of Croatia, upsets Martina Hingis to win the women's French Open title

8: England complete a nine-wicket victory over Australia in the first Test after being set 118 to win; Scotland top their World Cup qualifying group by winning in Belarus; Brazil's Gustavo Kuerten wins his first Grand Slam trophy by beating Sergi Bruguera, the two-time former champion

10: Romario scores for Brazil to end England's unbeaten record in Le Tournoi, though England win the tournament

12: Dean Jones, the Australian, resigns as captain of Derbyshire amid accusations against senior players

15: Jacques Villeneuve crashes on the second lap of his home Grand Prix in Canada, and Michael Schumacher takes maximum points after the race is stopped when Olivier Panis is injured in another smash; Ernie Els ends Colin Montgomerie's hopes of a first major golf title by winning the US Open by one shot; Mark Philippoussis beats Goran Ivanisevic in the final of the Stella Artois tournament at Queen's

19: Celeric and Pat Eddery win the Gold Cup at Royal Ascot; The first day of the Lord's Test between England and Australia is a complete wash-out

21: Glenn McGrath's eight for 38 reduces England to 77 all out in the second Test at Lord's; The British Lions score an unexpected win in the first Test against South Africa, set up by a memorable try by Matt Dawson; Linford Christie wins his eighth successive, and final, European Cup 100 metres, in Munich

22: Great Britain's male athletes win the European Cup by 13 points from Germany, while the women finish third; Jana Novotna and Arantxa Sanchez Vicario share the Direct Line trophy after rain hits their Eastbourne final

23: England bat through the final day to force a draw in the second Test of the Ashes series at Lord's; Wimbledon's Court No 1 is opened on the first, rain-hit day of The Championships

26: Persistent rain means Wimbledon suffers only its fifth blank day in the last 25 years; Rain also leads to the abandonment of Surrey's experiment with floodlit cricket at the Oval

28: British Lions win the second Test, and the series, against South Africa, in Durban, the game settled by Jeremy Guscott's late dropped goal; Mike Tyson is disqualified for twice biting Evander Holyfield's ears during their world heavyweight title fight in Las Vegas

29: Wimbledon stages a proletarian Super Sunday to catch up with the backlog of matches, and Tim Henman entertains a partisan home crowd by beating Paul Haarhuis; Michael Schumacher opens a 14-point lead in the drivers' championship by winning the French Grand Prix

AMERICANS
LOSING THEIR GRIP ON THE COURTS

by JOHN PARSONS

WHILE there has been natural rejoicing over the encouraging number of British players reaching the second round of the men's singles at Wimbledon this year, the truncated events have already served to emphasise the extraordinary decline in American men's tennis.

Back in 1985, when Germany's Boris Becker swept through, unseeded, to become Wimbledon's youngest champion, aged 17, interrupting a run of four consecutive winners from the United States, no less than 54 Americans were either ranked high enough or qualified to be in the 128-man draw. And 32 of them progressed to the second round.

This year the number of American men taking part had dropped to 14, of whom only six (or seven, depending on the outcome of the unfinished contest between Jeff Salzenstein and Patrick Baur of Germany) won their first-round matches - compared with their previous lowest number of first-round winners, which was nine last year.

Although the American problem has been masked to some extent by Andre Agassi winning once (1992) and Pete Sampras three times (1993-95) in the last five years, the worrying signs have been apparent for some time.

In December, when for the first time the Americans could no longer boast of having the greatest number of players in the top 100 of the end-of-year world rankings, being overtaken by Spain, the growing crisis was underlined. A special committee, under the chairmanship of former USTA president Bob Cookson, are now investigating all aspects of player development in America, co-ordinated from the Florida offices in Key Biscayne, and are due to produce a report, which many believe could lead to fundamental changes, by the time of the US Open.

There is added concern because so few outstanding young Americans appear to be on the horizon to take over when players such as Agassi, 27, whose enthusiasm for tennis already seems to have waned severely, Jim Courier, 27, who has slipped to his lowest world ranking (28) for a decade, Michael Chang and Sampras decide they have had enough.

ADMITTEDLY the American impact at Wimbledon this year was likely to be diminished anyway because of injuries to Agassi, Todd Martin and last year's unseeded runner-up MaliVai Washington, but another factor which cannot be ignored is that not one of their players currently in the top 100 is aged under 24, in a time when the lifespan for players at the top seems to have changed from 18-30 or more, to 16-28 at the most.

Few are likely to be so enduring as Jimmy Connors or John McEnroe, whose exploits have figured so prominently as BBC Television have been forced to fill time with great matches from the past.

Justin Gimelstob, the 6ft 5in, 20-year-old from New Jersey, their brightest newcomer who helped them win the Hopman Cup in Perth in January and beat the new French Open champion Gustavo Kuerten here on Tuesday, is still ranked only 117.

Looking beyond him the picture is not much brighter than the one confronting desolate spectators at Wimbledon over the past two days.

Roldolf Rake, ranked 19, is their highest placed representative and one of only three in the top 50 of the International Tennis Federation's world junior rankings.

There are players from 14 other countries above him, with Britain's 6ft 4in, 17-year-old David Sherwood from Sheffield, ranked 36.

In the junior boys' doubles, there is not one American among the top 50. Britain, on the other hand, has five - Sherwood (7), James Trotman (10), Iain Bates (15), Simon Dickson (22) and Daniel Kiernan (35).

BRIAN Teacher, the 1980 Australian Open champion now coaching Greg Rusedski, and Sandy Mayer, who won 11 main tour singles titles, were both part of that dominant contingent of American players in the late 70s and early 80s.

'Of course it's disappointing to see how few Americans there are in events like this now, so you must presume that the wrong people are making the wrong decisions,' said Teacher, who feels the whole attitude to coaching in the United States needs to be looked at afresh.

'Jose Higueras [who used to be with Courier] and Stan Smith have both quit and Tom Gullikson only wants to be involved with the Davis Cup,' added the Californian. He not only finds it strange that he and other former world-class players have not been invited to help but that 'in a country as big as ours there's only one [USTA] training camp and nothing to cater for youngsters on the West Coast.'

Teacher and Mayer both criticise the USTA for not creating a good working relationship with Robert Lansdorp, who coached Tracy Austin and Sampras among others.

'He has produced probably more kids than anyone after [Nick] Bollettieri but he says he always had problems trying to work for the USTA because once he started with promising youngsters, they wanted to own them.'

Mayer nominated Lansdorp as 'the only one great coach in America', and added, 'the level of coaching at the moment is extremely low. People say you don't have to be a great player to be a great coach but if you've been a great player you have a much better chance of being a great coach.'

'We have people who can't play, can't hit the ball where they want their people to hit the ball and then don't want to be evaluated on how their players do.' ★ 27/06/97

> THERE IS CONCERN BECAUSE SO FEW OUTSTANDING YOUNG PLAYERS APPEAR TO BE ON THE HORIZON TO TAKE OVER FROM PLAYERS LIKE AGASSI, COURIER, CHANG AND SAMPRAS

IMAGES OF WIMBLEDON 1997: (CLOCKWISE FROM TOP LEFT) MARCELO RIOS IN AGGRESSIVE MOOD, MARTINA HINGIS IN PETULENT MOOD, AND THE SUPER BRITS, GREG RUSEDSKI AND TIM HENMAN, IN EXUBERANT MOOD. RUSSELL CHEYNE AND FRANK COPPI

GOUGH SETS THE BALL ROLLING AS ENGLAND'S BOWLERS SEIZE DAY

by CHRISTOPHER MARTIN-JENKINS

NOT SINCE EDWARD VII'S REIGN HAS EDGBASTON SEEN ANYTHING LIKE THIS

NOT since the dawn of Edward VII's reign has an Edgbaston Test crowd seen anything quite like the Australian total yesterday morning, when the first Test was only 19 overs old. Their score was 54 for eight and, although there was a recovery of sorts, England were on the way to victory.

It is one thing to be offered a chance, quite another to take it. On a pitch which started a little damp but which will get harder to bat on if, as is likely, its fissures become splits, England took their opportunity superbly and finished a sensational, almost melodramatic opening day of the six-match series with a lead of 82 and seven wickets in hand.

Obeying the command from their captain and coach to pitch the ball up - the key to their success yesterday as it has been to their failure in the past - Darren Gough, Andrew Caddick and Devon Malcolm cut through Australia's predictably vulnerable batting like scythes through thistles.

Despite a spirited counter-attack by Shane Warne, Australia were bowled out for 118 in the sixth over after lunch. This was heady excitement for a crowd of 19,000 and a nasty shock to those who had not read the portents. Offered at 3-1 against to win the game when the morning began, England were 1-4 by lunchtime.

Although they in turn got into early difficulties, Graham Thorpe and Nasser Hussain, with strokeplay as bold as it was handsome, seized the moment still more admirably than the bowlers to take control of what looks suspiciously like another low-scoring Birmingham Test match. When Ken Barrington and Ted Dexter put on 161 for the fourth wicket in 1961, 11 more than Thorpe and Hussain have so far, pitches here were reliable. The way a ball from Michael Kasprowicz exploded from a length past Hussain's gloves 20 minutes from the close yesterday suggested that this one will be predictable only in its unpredictability.

ENGLAND have some good batsmen still in hand but they will have to excel themselves today if the 12,000 who have bought tickets for Sunday are not to be examining the small print for details of how to get their money back.

It was swing rather than uneven bounce which mainly explained Australia's extraordinarily rapid demise, as Warwickshire, whose future as a Test ground is officially under threat, will be quick to argue. This, however, certainly does not look like one of the Edgbaston pitches which get slower and easier.

Jason Gillespie limped off before the close with a strained left hamstring and may not bowl again in the game. Already, with Andrew Bichel still struggling to recover from a bad back, there is talk of a replacement fast bowler, possibly Adam Dale. Such problems are often the lot of England sides when they are on tour. The worm may be turning.

By the time the third wicket fell yesterday, indeed, the beleaguered Mark Taylor was top scorer with seven and only three Australians subsequently did better. He had chosen boldly, but logically enough, to bat first, but a greenish tinge to the pitch and the heaviness of the air on a hot morning made it a good toss for Mike Atherton to lose.

He would also have batted but we shall never know whether Australia's bowlers would have used the thermals in the warm air so effectively as Gough in his incisive spell from the City End. His first ball having fizzed past Taylor's outside edge, he tried a few too many variations at first, whilst Malcolm betrayed slight but understandable signs of nerves as he raced in at the all left-handed opening pair.

Gough's inswinger, bursting through Matthew Elliott's gate in the fifth over, was the first sign of the havoc to come. An over later Taylor drove handsomely past mid-off for four but Malcolm's next ball was pitched up too, a little wider, and Taylor's fast-footed drive succeeded only in slicing the ball to second slip, where Mark Butcher clung on safely to launch his Test career on the right note.

He had been given his cap shortly after the toss by Atherton, but Adam Hollioake had to wait for his. England were not to know that Mark Ealham would not be needed to bowl. Perhaps he might have if Gough had not produced the most important ball of the day, full of length again, to swing in and bowl Mark Waugh between bat and pad.

Gough rested after an eight-over spell of three for 18 and it was Caddick's turn, from the Pavilion End. He took time to shift his line to the off stump rather than outside it, perhaps because there were only two fielders on the legside, but once he did he reminded everyone of his ability to swing the ball away and bounce it above waist-height at a stinging pace. Steve Waugh got the thinnest of outside edges to a ball of just the right length and, next ball, Ian Healy was drawn to play with equally fatal consequence.

MALCOLM produced the ideal ball for Michael Bevan, across his bows and lifting to chest height, producing a simple catch to gully and leaving only the tail. It wagged bravely as Kasprowicz, riding his luck, helped Warne to double the score either side of lunch. Warne's keen eye, and the attacking field, enabled him to hit eight fours before he sliced to third man.

England had 56 overs to ram home their advantage. Atherton got a ball which lifted and left him a fraction in the third over and Butcher, after an encouragingly composed start, received an equally good ball to give Kasprowicz his first Test wicket. Alec Stewart struck the first blows in response before top-edging a pull at a ball too far up for the stroke.

There was no further success for Australia. Thorpe had been dropped a place from the No 4 position which suits him best but he played beautifully from the outset and Hussain's calm defence had already blossomed into elegant control by the time Taylor called on Warne for the first time at 108 for three. This time there was no venom in his magic. Hitting him with impeccable timing off the back foot whenever he dropped short, Thorpe and Hussain left no possible doubt who was in charge. ★ 07/06/97

Nasser Hussain reaches 200 in the first Test at Edgbaston Russell Cheyne

BENNY MAY FOIL MY BOLD EFFORT

FRANKIE DETTORI previews The Derby

IF you had told me two months ago that I would be riding Bold Demand in the Derby I would have laughed at you. He had shown nothing in Dubai all winter, was very lazy and Stowaway seemed our Derby horse. Bold Demand finished second to Single Empire, who went on to win the Italian Derby, in a Newmarket maiden, which was encouraging.

I then rode Stowaway in a gallop with him and he went much better than us so we then ran him in the same maiden that we won with Shantou last year (Shantou was subsequently third in the Derby) which he also won. The improvement he has shown since is remarkable. I am reasonably happy being drawn two. With 13 runners there should not be any hard-luck stories and if things go as smoothly as they did yesterday on Singspiel in the Coronation Cup then we should go close to winning.

Today I hope to have the speed to get an early position but the race really unfolds from Tattenham Corner to the two-furlong marker. The good horses will come through, the bad ones won't pick up, along with the ones which have had problems in training, so we'll all have to be alert.

The Derby is different from any other race because we all put our cards on the table. All the runners are dark horses to a certain extent - even Entrepreneur - because we don't really know that they will stay or just how good they are.

For a jockey, life gets easier after the Derby because the horses sort themselves out. The milers go back to mile races, the stayers go for mile and a half races and the slow ones go to jumping yards.

Although I am hopeful about Bold Demand, Benny The Dip is my selection. I can't understand why he is longer in the betting than Silver Patriarch who he has already beaten at Sandown. He was giving weight away and came home ill that day. That is not to say Silver Patriarch has no chance. I thought he was a big gangly horse who wouldn't handle Epsom until I saw him win at Lingfield, a similar track. He will act well and stay the trip.

You can't disregard Cloudings either, a Group One winner. Though Olivier Peslier also had the choice of Benny The Dip I wouldn't read too much into it. He rides in France, he rode the French Derby winner for Cloudings' trainer Andre Fabre last weekend and, though they obviously have a form line between the two horses, I think his choice was more political than anything else. ★ **07/06/97**

RYAN'S EXPRESS CHARGES THROUGH TO WIN ON THE DIP

by **HOTSPUR** (J. A. McGrath)

RACING'S Classic rematch is on. As the post-mortem examinations continued yesterday into the lack-lustre performance of Entrepreneur, the 4-6 favourite in Saturday's Vodafone Derby at Epsom, connections of the winner, Benny The Dip, and the game runner-up, Silver Patriarch, pinpointed the Budweiser Irish Derby at the Curragh on June 29 as the next target for their colts.

John Gosden announced the Irish Classic as Benny The Dip's immediate objective, though there must have been a temptation to revert to 10 furlongs for the Coral-Eclipse. John Dunlop earmarked Ireland as the next port of call for Silver Patriarch, who failed by the shortest of short heads to overhaul the winner after coming from last on the descent to Tattenham Corner.

It is little wonder that Epsom remains the supreme testing ground of thoroughbred and rider. Nowhere else in the world is the temperament, ability, agility and courage of both tested with such ruthlessness. Entrepreneur, so brilliant in the 2,000 Guineas at Newmarket, floundered when faced with the daunting Epsom roller-coaster.

Hopes that this impeccably bred three-year-old would be wearing the 'champion' tag were dashed after less than three furlongs when the colt appeared uncomfortable after the jostle for early positions. He went from being a handy fifth to toiling in the second half of the field when Cloudings bumped him before the seven-furlong marker.

Mick Kinane tried hard to improve Entrepreneur's position but he was facing a near-impossible task. The fact that the colt battled on for fourth - beaten just over eight lengths - was remarkable in itself, especially considering the way he had been travelling earlier. Sadly, he entered the ever-expanding catalogue of beaten Derby favourites, saving bookmakers a massive payout, estimated at £5 million.

'He finished a very tired horse and he walked back tired,' recalled Kinane, who also reported that the colt was hanging during the race.

If there was a valid veterinary excuse for Entrepreneur's failure - he was routine tested - it would be welcomed by his most ardent followers. But on the face of it, he failed to cope.

Unfailingly, the Derby produces a hero. This year there were almost certainly three. Benny The Dip and Willie Ryan

seized their opportunity at Tattenham Corner after sitting in behind leader Crystal Hearted to that point.

Ryan, understudy to a series of so-called bigger names at Henry Cecil's Warren Place yard at Newmarket, knew the golden chance with which he had been presented and was clearly in no mood to chuck it away. He kicked for home, opened up a gap of five lengths on his opposition and kept riding for all he was worth. Cannily, though, he kept a little up his sleeve for the unexpected.

Nobody could ever have argued that Silver Patriarch, undoubtedly the third hero to emerge from the Derby, was unexpected. But he was trailing the leader by 15 lengths sweeping into the straight and it was not unreasonable to have written him off at that stage.

With Benny The Dip stopping in the last 100 yards and Silver Patriarch relentlessly gathering him in, the crowd of 72,000 roared as the two colts flashed past the post together with Benny The Dip, owned by 72-year-old American Landon Knight, prevailing to give Gosden a major win that he richly deserved after saddling a second and two thirds in the Classic.

'This is a great triumph for my family,' said Gosden, whose father 'Towser' missed saddling Charlottown to win the 1966 Derby when his health failed. Gosden senior had trained Charlottown as a juvenile. 'I'd like to say to my old man, somewhere up there, that we finally got it right,' the trainer added.

Pat Eddery, blamed in most quarters for giving his mount too much to do, was confident Silver Patriarch would reverse the placings in the Irish Derby. In mitigation, Eddery said: 'My horse wouldn't go early and he had trouble handling the track.'

Robert Sangster's Romanov finished third, five lengths behind the second, and will now be aimed at the Coral-Eclipse at Sandown Park. The Fly, backed from 20-1 to 12-1, finished fifth, with Fahris, after being positioned close throughout, in sixth.

The last word belongs to Gosden, who has now won two Classics in the last nine months: 'The funny thing is that Benny The Dip wins by a short head and you're a great trainer, you've won the Derby. If he gets beaten a short head, then you can't train.'

Isn't that racing for you? ★ **09/06/97**

Heading for home. Benny The Dip overtakes Crystal Hearted as the Derby field round Tattenham Corner *Ed Byrne*

LIONS RELISH THOUGHT OF CLEAN SWEEP

by **BRENDAN GALLAGHER** in Durban

NO, YOU were not dreaming. The British Lions did beat South Africa 18-15 at King's Park on Saturday - a remarkable, nigh on miraculous victory that clinched the series and put a spring in the step of every rugby follower in Britain and Ireland. Hopefully your party was as good as ours.

Even now it almost defies belief that the Lions absorbed the unrelenting pressure of the Springboks to win at the death. Rarely can a side have won a major international while so remorselessly under the cosh. Analytically there was absolutely no way the Lions should have won but this squad have rejoiced in making the impossible possible.

As the final whistle blew the Lions' joy was unconfined. Tim Rodber hugged replacement Eric Miller, his great rival for the No 8 shirt, and an exhausted Keith Wood gave a clenched fist of triumph before being helped off by Jason Leonard. Jeremy Guscott, whose 76th-minute dropped goal clinched the issue, stole away from the lap of honour to shake hands with Ian McGeechan, his coach on three strenuous but rewarding Lions tours. A poignant moment indeed.

Captain Martin Johnson, who enjoyed his best game on tour when it was most needed, called all the non-playing reserves on to the field to share the moment while John Bentley wheeled away to a corner of the massive East Stand to applaud the noisiest section of the Barmy Army. The Springboks, meanwhile, sloped off in a state of shock - bemused and beaten.

For the first time in history South Africa, who in truth played immeasurably better than in the first Test, have lost two consecutive home series, having been defeated by the All Blacks last summer. They could also face their first whitewash at home if the Lions can win at Ellis Park on Saturday.

So how did the Lions win? In simple terms they defended with such ferocity and courage that a rampant Springbok side were restricted to three tries. It really did look all over in the 54th minute when Andre Joubert rounded Bentley to score a fine try but the Lions refused to concede any further ground. Scott Gibbs was again an inspiration defensively, making a clutch of crucial tackles.

A storming run midway through the second half also fired the Lions at an important stage, the sight of 20-stone prop Os du Randt rebounding off the Swansea tank lifting their morale.

Goal-kicking was the crux. While the hapless Honiball (two), Montgomery (three), and Joubert (one) missed all six South African attempts at goal, Neil Jenkins, quiet, unobtrusive and astonishingly reliable, kicked five out of five.

The Lions hung on desperately until there was just a sniff of victory, and having got the scent, went for the kill ruthlessly. As the battle raged none did better than Jeremy Davidson, who again commanded the middle of the line-out despite finding himself up against Mark Andrews. It was a great contest and one which included a comical bout of violent finger-wagging, with Andrews uttering a few Afrikaans oaths and Davidson replying in his broad Belfast accent. The message was clear though. Davidson would not tolerate any nonsense.

'That was international sport at its best,' enthused Rob Andrew. 'I am lost in admiration for the team. Test-match rugby is played on a knife edge, you cannot always reproduce the rugby you play against provinces. The Lions clung on by their fingertips and then played it just right when their time came. Jerry's dropped goal was great.'

Inevitably there will be comparisons with Willie John McBride's victorious squad of 1974 - indeed the class of '97 could go one better by winning on Saturday. 'No disrespect to the 1974 team but we have scarcely talked about them,' insisted Bentley afterwards. 'They probably had greater individual players but we have other qualities.' You can say that again. ★ 07/06/97

SATELLITE DISH SERVES UP A FEAST OF FUN

by **GILES SMITH**

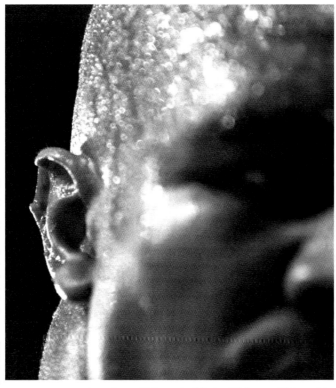

WE wanted to see Tyson as a hungry fighter again,' said Sky Sport's Ian Darke, speaking to us from Las Vegas in the early hours of Sunday morning, 'but not like that.'

Perhaps not. Tyson had just brought the evening to a premature close by snacking on the ears of Evander Holyfield. The rules of boxing are quite clear on this: fighters are not allowed to eat each other. Not even featherweights, who often look like a decent meal wouldn't go amiss.

Naturally, when a boxer ignores this rule, amazing scenes are apt to break out - though only for people with satellite or cable and £14.95 in pay-per-view fees to spare. They are, of course, the kinds of scenes which appal one to the marrow. Which, for £14.95, strikes me as a total bargain.

On Sunday, the ring immediately filled with uniformed security guards, throwing themselves recklessly in the way of a flailing Tyson, who was at this point trying to get over to Holyfield's corner in order, presumably, to finish what he started.

The quantity of people who had suddenly materialised in the ring, and the fact that everyone seemed to be jostling at least one other person, made developments over the next few minutes a little hard to follow. But it was pretty clear that the prospects for finding that missing piece of the defending champion's right ear were now fairly remote.

We next saw Holyfield leave the ring and enjoy an unencumbered retreat through the arena and into the wings. For someone who had recently been cannibalised, he retained a remarkable air of dignity. Unlike Tyson, who seemed to be having to crawl out under the combined weight of half the Las Vegas police force, his own posse and perhaps up to 25 other people involved in fights of their own.

We then cut back to the throng in the ring where Mills Lane, the referee, was telling an interviewer that one bite was probably, in all honesty, enough, but that absolutely he drew the line at a second. If he ever decides to turn his back on the fight game, Mills could walk straight into a job advertising Fun-Size Milky Ways.

Then it was out to the corridor where Holyfield - still preternaturally calm and gracious - confirmed that his plastic surgeon was keen to operate that night, said that he would enjoy a small period of reflection before considering a re-match, and added that he simply wanted to praise the Lord that his injury wasn't any worse than it was. What a guy.

Then back into the ring we went, for further developments in the Security Guards v Aggrieved Members of the Public Free-For-All (rules on biting and head-butting yet to be set in stone); and then out into the corridor we came again, but this time to meet Tyson's manager, who was as mad as hell. He claimed that a Holyfield head-butt had opened up 'a three-inch cut' above his client's eye and he seemed to be saying that, in those circumstances, it stood to reason that you would want to try to bite someone's ear off, twice.

That was pretty much Don King's verdict, too, when he stepped up to the microphone - although Don could see how one might feel differently. In fact, in a classic of

equivocation, which any budding politician would do well to study and get by rote, Don made it clear that he felt there was no excuse for that kind of behaviour while at the same time smoothly excusing it. You would never have known that millions of dollars with Don's name on them might rest on a re-match.

When Tyson himself came out of the dressing room, perhaps as a result of some particularly ingenious cosmetic surgery, the cut above the eye seemed to have shrunk by about two-thirds. But that didn't mean he was any less angry and confused. 'I'm ready to fight him right now,' said Iron Mike, bristling terrifyingly and clearly not committed as yet to a PR make-over. (The unattractive image of street-fighter may well attach to him after all this. But doubtless Don will think of something to do about that.)

Sky, whose capacity for both having and eating cake is unrivalled in sports broadcasting, had called the event *Judgement Night 2*, which seemed to be stretching the Biblical analogy. Whatever next: *Four Further Horsemen of the Apocalypse*?

Everyone in the studio agreed that the original *Judgement Night - Tyson v Holyfield*, back in November - had been a classic. Barry McGuigan called it 'the biggest fight I have ever remembered in my entire life'. This kept open the possibility that there were some pretty enormous ones which he had forgotten, but it was hardly faint praise, even so.

It was generally agreed, though, both in Las Vegas and in the studio back in London, that the second fight had, as an example of sporting brilliance, fallen short of the calibre of the first. Nevertheless, rallying slightly, Darke managed to conclude that it was 'a fight that will go down in history - in its own way.'

Don's own title, for the American market, was *The Sound and the Fury*. Snappy, but with a familiar ring to it. Rumours that he wishes to call the re-match *Tyson v Holyfield: the Second Course*, or even *Tyson v Holyfield: This Time They're Staying for Coffee*, could not be confirmed. ★ 30/06/97

END COLUMN

SPORT AROUND THE WORLD: Elena Dementieva, a Russian tennis player, was told she could not continue her juniors match at the French Open because her shirt bore too many sponsors' names - six instead of the permitted one. Unfortunately she had no spare, so had to leave the court, buy an £18 T-shirt from a vendor and wear that. She lost 6-0, 6-2.

CRICKET DIARY: 'The game must go on' was the response of sides who were confronted by an immovable object while playing in the Torbay Midweek League. The weekend pitch was being prepared at Barton Cricket Club when the heavy roller broke down. Refusing to accept defeat, the company teams playing on an adjacent strip simply slung a tarpaulin over the roller and got on with their match.

SPORT AROUND THE WORLD: A golfer in Elyria, Ohio, who could not wait for the slower-moving foursome ahead of him will serve two years in prison for his impatience. Peter McNamara, 28, broke the nose of John Russo, who was playing with his pregnant wife and two others when McNamara struck a tee shot into the middle of their group.

LETTERS TO THE SPORTS EDITOR: SIR - I feel I must complain in the strongest terms to those who participate in, and those who arrange our countries' international sporting fixtures. For much of June I have been studying for my A Levels, and the members of our national teams have treated my efforts with disdain. The cricket team insisted on beating the Aussies, our footballers selfishly decided to beat Italy, Poland and France in a matter of days, while the Lions romped through South Africa playing exciting and free-flowing rugby. I was forced to watch the action when my nose should have been firmly glued to the inside of a book; if I fail my exams I will only have these teams to blame. - PETER ARNOLD, East Grinstead, West Sussex.

WIMBLEDON DIARY: There was the feeling that Lionel Roux, of France, has not heard the last of what he did at the end of his match with Brett Steven. Having lost in straight sets, the angry Frenchman used his racket to swipe a golf-sized divot from the court. Early the following morning, a groundsman was gathering evidence in the shape of a close-up photograph.

SPORT AROUND THE WORLD: A minor league baseball team in South Carolina planned a match-day raffle to mark Father's Day with an unusual prize: a vasectomy. Among those who didn't like the idea was the local bishop, a season-ticket holder. His complaints led to a change of heart and the raffle was cancelled.

SPORT AROUND THE WORLD: A priest whose favourite local football team had lost four games in succession, the last 15-0, called the players into church for prayer. The divine intervention paid off with a 7-0 victory. Bo Stolpstedt says the special service for the Rumskulla GolF side, from south-east Sweden, was about co-operation and playing as a team. "They took communion and then I passed the football from the altar down the aisle to the entrance of the church where the coach stood. It was symbolic. You have to pass to each other in life," he says. "It was lucky they won. Both my reputation and God's were on the line."

DAY BY DAY REVIEW

2: Tim Henman needs just 36 minutes to complete a 3-1 win over Richard Krajicek, the defending champion, and reach Wimbledon's last eight

3: Tim Henman follows Greg Rusedski out of Wimbledon, losing in straight sets to Michael Stich in the quarter-finals, after Rusedski had lost in four sets to Cedric Pioline. Boris Becker, meanwhile, plays his 79th and final singles match at The Championships, losing to Pete Sampras

5: South Africa prevent a whitewash with a convincing victory in the final Test against the British Lions; Martina Hingis recovers from one set down to become Wimbledon's youngest singles champion this century by beating Jana Novotna

6: Pete Sampras makes light work of Cedric Pioline to take his fourth Wimbledon men's singles title

7: Australia level the Ashes series with a 268-run win over England at Old Trafford, Steve Waugh hitting centuries in both innings

9: Mike Tyson's licence to box is revoked and he is fined $3 million by the Nevada State Athletic Commission for biting Evander Holyfield's ears in their world title fight

11: Cliff Brittle wins the long-running RFU in-fighting when he is re-elected chairman of the Rugby Football Union's management board

12: Australia beat England in the rugby union Test in Sydney, while Wales beat the United States; Ben Hollioake's 98 helps Surrey beat Kent by eight wickets in the Benson and Hedges Cup final at Lord's; Lennox Lewis retains his WBC heavyweight title in Lake Tahoe, Nevada, when Henry Akinwande is disqualified for refusing to fight and holding

13: Jacques Villeneuve wins the British Grand Prix at Silverstone, and Damon Hill claims his first point of the season for sixth place; Greg Rusedski's win in the last singles rubber takes Great Britain to victory in the Davis Cup, Euro-African zone, tie in the Ukraine; Alison Nicholas returns a record 10-under-par card in winning the women's US Open at North Plains, Oregon

16: Group 4, skippered by Mike Golding, are first into Southampton to win the BT Global Challenge round-the-world yacht race

19: Tiger Woods records a course-equalling 64 in the third round of The Open at Royal Troon, but is 10 shots off the lead; Naseem Hamed makes a successful defence of his world featherweight titles by stopping Juan Cabrera in the second round at Wembley Arena

20: Justin Leonard lands The Open at Royal Troon, the first player since 1925 to win the title from five shots behind on the final day; Graham Gooch, the former England captain, announces his retirement from first-class cricket at the age of 44

25: Matthew Elliott and Ricky Ponting stage an unbeaten fourth-wicket stand of 208 to swing the initiative Australia's way in the fourth Test against England at Headingley

26: John Reid rides 16-1 outsider Swain to victory in the King George VI and Queen Elizabeth Diamond Stakes at Ascot; Alan Shearer damages ankle ligaments in Newcastle's pre-season match against Chelsea at Goodison Park, and could be out "for months rather than weeks"

27: Jan Ullrich, who led for 11 days of the three-week race, is the first German winner of the Tour de France; Gerhard Berger makes a triumphant return to Formula One, after missing three races with sinus trouble during which time his father died, by winning the German Grand Prix; Australia's Matthew Elliott finally falls for 199 in the fourth Test at Headingley, and England are kept alive by Nasser Hussain's unbeaten century

28: Australia take a 2-1 lead in the Ashes series with an innings victory over England at Headingley

WILLIAMS
BACK ON TRACK
WHILE FERRARIS FAIL

by TIMOTHY COLLINGS

JACQUES Villeneuve may have delivered only half the result that Frank Williams really wanted by winning yesterday's incident-filled British Grand Prix, but at least it was the important half.

On a day of fluctuating fortunes, pit-lane problems, statistical landmarks and the retirement of both Ferraris, Heinz-Harald Frentzen's failure to complete a lap, let alone score any points, cost Williams a potential one-two finish and, with it, the leadership of the constructors' world championship.

That, inevitably, will matter more to the man at the top of Formula One's most competitive outfit than their 100th victory, or the revival of Villeneuve's challenge to Michael Schumacher for the drivers' crown, by the end of this closely contested season.

Frentzen, who pressed the wrong button and upset his car's sophisticated electronic gearbox, stalled on the grid and then crashed out of the 59-lap contest after colliding with Jos Verstappen's Tyrrell Hart on the first lap, having restarted at the back of the grid. It was his fourth non-finish of the year and a potentially costly one.

'We were lucky today,' said Williams after the race. 'Very, very lucky.' He can say that again. Another of the Williams team's almost-customary wheel-nut problems cost Villeneuve 33 seconds at his first pit stop, after leading for 22 laps, and jeopardised his hopes before Lady Luck intervened to remove Schumacher, who led, his Ferrari team-mate Eddie Irvine, who threatened to, and then Mika Hakkinen, in his McLaren Mercedes-Benz, who was within five laps of his maiden victory.

HILL'S SIXTH PLACE PROMPTED
WILD FLAG-WAVING
ALL AROUND THE TRACK,
TO WHICH HE RESPONDED
WITH A RAISED FIST

Schumacher went out with a failed wheel bearing, Irvine with a broken half-shaft and Hakkinen with an engine failure.

Without these unscheduled excursions, Villeneuve would not have won and Damon Hill could not have exploited the abrupt departure of Shinji Nakano, when his Prost Mugen-Honda expired, to hand him sixth place and a point on the penultimate lap.

That result, for Hill, prompted wild flag-waving all around the track, to which he responded with a raised fist from his cockpit. It signalled also a dream ending to what had started as a nightmare weekend for the world champion and his Arrows Yamaha team.

'It's great for me and the team,' said Hill. 'Everyone has been under so much pressure and now we're going to celebrate. This point is as good as a victory to me. I didn't think we could get it until Nakano's engine blew up - and then I got excited and started waving.'

Hill's happiness was matched by the satisfaction of his team leader Tom Walkinshaw, who had warned Hill last Thursday that he needed to refocus on his job, and by the Benetton Renault team as Jean Alesi and Alexander Wurz finished second and third, thus completing an all-Renault-powered podium. It was also the seventh year in succession that a Renault-engined car had won this race, on the 20th anniversary of the French company's Formula One entry in 1977, the year James Hunt came home as world champion and won.

David Coulthard, who suffered from brake problems which caused him to flat-spot a tyre, finished fourth for McLaren and Ralf Schumacher, the 21-year-old younger brother of Michael, fifth for Jordan Peugeot. Both were disappointed not to claim a podium finish, but could hardly claim as much dejection at their misfortune as Schumacher senior, who has never won at Silverstone. Like Ferrari, who have registered just one victory in Britain in the last 20 years, the twice world champion seems to suffer his worst luck here in July.

WILLIAMS, by contrast, have won six of the last seven and 10 out of 20. That may be remarkable enough, but this victory, which also hoisted them alongside Ferrari (111) and McLaren (105) as the only teams to have reached a century, came from only their 308th start. Their ratio of one win in three also outstrips their rivals.

'Obviously, I am delighted,' said Williams. 'It really is a great achievement, but in reality, today's win represents another 10 points towards the championship.'

Villeneuve led from pole to the end of lap 22 when Schumacher, whose Ferrari had looked capable of winning, took command. Villeneuve's left front wheel became loose (Hill spun out of the race after 27 laps in the lead last year) and Villeneuve said: 'It was so loose it was difficult to drive the car because you had to turn the wheel a lot from one side to the other. It became heavy and the grip wasn't good. The wheel was stuck and that's why we lost so much time.'

The German had already made one fast, early pit stop and he stayed in front, building up a cushion of more than 40 seconds before pitting a second time on lap 38. When he rejoined, it was not as a serious competitor and he retired almost immediately.

It was Ferrari's first reliability problem this season. 'A shame,' said Schumacher. 'But I'm not too disappointed because I was comfortably in the lead when it occurred.'

Schumacher's loss was, briefly, Wurz's gain, but the Austrian pitted after leading for less than a lap and Villeneuve took over again - until his second pit stop after 44 laps.

The Canadian returned to the track, this time behind Hakkinen's McLaren. Despite closing him down to less than a second, he fought in vain for a way by until the Finn's race ended in a cloud of smoke.

Villeneuve said the result was vital for him. 'This was an important race and we needed the points. It was good for me to see Michael retire because it has happened to us a few times and it balances up the championship. I needed to win and see him have a DNF this time.' ★ **14/07/97**

In the wet. Damon Hill warms up in the rain at Silverstone before the British Grand Prix, in which he scored his first point of the season Frank Coppi

BECKER AT END OF GOLDEN ROAD

by **SUE MOTT**

MARS, red and fiery, was in the news this week for having its space invaded by robots. Boris Becker would know how it feels. For 14 years the great champion has inhabited Planet Wimbledon, creating a swashbuckling bridgehead between the star wars of John McEnroe, Bjorn Borg and Jimmy Connors in the early 1980s to the more anonymous, characterless stormtroopers of the modern era. Even Steven Spielberg would have trouble with this lot.

That partially explains the sense of bereftness now, in the wake of his theatrical announcement on Thursday that this Wimbledon is to be his last. Becker may have been arrogant, rule-bending and ambitious to the point of cruelty (especially where poor Ivan Lendl was concerned), but he illuminated the Centre Court with a charismatic passion that could not go unremarked, even by a duchess.

When the 18-year-old Becker won his second successive Wimbledon in 1986, demonstrating a maturity and durability way beyond our ken (and Jeremy), the Duchess of Kent was moved to ask the young German whether he was planning to win five straight titles like Bjorn Borg. 'See you in three years then,' said the precocious boy.

How it all began. Boris Becker, aged 17, at his first Wimbledon in 1986, when he became the youngest winner of the men's singles title Paul Armiger

But we should have known a strawberry blond and Wimbledon would have an affinity. And so it proved. His record on the hallowed turf since he was carted off injured in a wheelchair as a 16-year-old - a premonition of the emperor's litter that awaited him - is little short of astonishing. Three times the champion, four times runner-up, twice a semi-finalist and double quarter-finalist; no wonder he claimed 10 years ago: 'It seems like my court.'

He brought the power game to tennis with displays of uninhibited aggression that exploded like mortar fire around his rivals, leaving them in a state of shellshocked surrender. 'I felt a little bit that I was playing uphill today,' said Stefan Edberg, plucking from the smorgasbord of classic understatement to describe the first set of their 1989 final. The Swede had won precisely 10 points in the first set, which he lost equally precisely 6-0.

But above all, the young Mars, god of war, had the head for it. Possibly no other man has played the so-called big points with more radiant intensity. His will to win was almost visible. It was ignited behind those famous blue eyes like a pilot light. Full beam, it was virtually irresistible.

As a youngster, even younger than the child he was when he won his first Wimbledon, he would weep and rant and tear his shirt and hurl his rackets round the locker-room, so deep was his hatred of losing. After defeat in the Orange Bowl, the world junior champion-ship, his former coach, Gunther Bosch, remembered him 'not only pounding his racket on the court but he also hit himself. It was horrible.'

He was always going to rage at the dying of the light. It accounts for his willingness to walk away from Wimbledon, nothing less than his spiritual home, at the relatively young age of 29. No way would he have tolerated a long, slow decline into tennis dotage.

'I feel like I've come to the end of the road with my head held up high. It's not like I'm going out there and losing to people I shouldn't lose to. I always wanted to go out on top. I feel right now I'm on top, on top of the mountain, and I can only go down.'

THE timing was typical of the drama king. He chose to tell Pete Sampras, the world No 1, as they shook hands at the net following the American's 6-1, 6-7, 6-1, 6-4 quarter-final victory. Sampras looked as though he had been hit by a stun gun. 'He had sort of a shock in his eyes, yes,' said Becker, satisfied. 'I said to him that it was my last match. And I was glad it would be against him because I respect him so much and because he's such a great champion.'

Then he turned to face the Centre Court crowd, bowing extravagantly to the cheering throng and his mind's eye wandering back perhaps down a vista of years: all those ovations, all those aces, all those glares, all those goalkeeper dives, until it reached the moment in 1985 when he defeated - unseeded, unheralded, unheard of - the South African, Kevin Curren, to secure his place on the roll-call of champions.

'He could become the best player in the world,' said Curren then. Becker, just a kid, could not absorb such profundity'. £130,000?' he said of his winnings. 'That's a lot. Maybe tonight I'll have a good dinner and a glass of champagne.'

He could have been a freak, a one-tournament wonder. His fresh, freckle-face could have come and gone like a rare outbreak of sunshine this Wimbledon.

Germany had no great tradition here, not since Baron Gottfried von Cramm was taking phone calls from Hitler and Wilhelm Bungert lost to John Newcombe in the 1967 final. But Becker changed all that.

'The whole tennis world questioned whether 1985 was a fluke. That's why 1986 was my biggest achievement. That tournament I felt the most pressure ever and yet I played my best ever.'

AS usual, at the expense of Lendl. The Czech was well into his grass dearth by then, desperate to win the only Grand Slam tournament that had eluded him but almost comi-tragically unable to find his footing and confidence on the alien surface. Becker did for him every time. First, he was one of the greatest serve-volleyers the world had ever seen. Then, he would joke with a line judge. Lendl, of delicate robotic wiring at the best of times, would become madly distracted and simply self-destruct in face of Becker's arrant gamesmanship.

Becker won the 1986 final in straight sets ('that makes me the second-youngest champion after myself') then lost to a little-known Australian, even in Australia, Peter Doohan, in the second round in 1987. That secured his fame. When a 19-year-old has the perspective to say: 'I lost a tennis match. It was not a war. Nobody died,' the seeds of sporting heroism have come to fruition. Plus, one of the stewards from the London Fire Brigade that year had named his pet tarantula Boris. There are few finer accolades.

And so he strong-armed his way into Wimbledon lore. He invented the power game and leaves with dignity before he finds himself overpowered.

'I never saw myself as a tennis machine,' he said. 'I see myself mainly as a human being with a heart and soul. Then, at No 2, a tennis player.' His sense of another life beyond the tramlines is perhaps what makes it possible for him to speak of the 'relief' of retiring from Wimbledon. His marriage four years ago to singer/model/actress Barbara Feltus and the birth of his son, Noah Gabriel, have turned him into a man with different priorities. 'It's very important for me to win and I really hate to lose but it's not at all a question of life or death.'

YOU wonder what he will remember most from the 'Boom-Boom' years. The 'Bonking Boris' story, when the tabloids gleefully latched on to the fact that his manager, Ion Tiriac, requested that the distracting police chief's daughter from Monaco should stay away from The Championships? The 'Witt Bit' when the tabloids joyfully reported the fact that the German ice-skating star, Katarina Witt, was his guest in the VIP box? The 'Great Gateman' scandal (recurring), when some jobsworth refused to let him into the arena he virtually owns?

But those are the trite momentos. More likely, as he sat in the deserted Royal Box last Thursday waiting for the rain to abate mid-match, he was absorbing the sights and sounds of his greatest triumphs as though they were still locked in the special ether there.

'I felt very much at home here obviously,' he said. 'You know, we can almost talk of a relationship we had because I've been here so many times. . . I always felt they knew how to treat me and I was always trying to give them the best that I've got. I feel half English, you know.' God, now he tells us. ★ 22/05/97

How it all ended. Boris Becker walks off Centre Court for the last time. *Frank Coppi.*

CARTER LANDING BLOWS AS FREEDOM FIGHTER

by
STEVE
BUNCE

THIS is the story of The Hurricane. In 1967, Rubin Hurricane Carter was wrongfully convicted of triple murder in New Jersey and sentenced to three life terms in prison. At the time he was the leading contender for the world middleweight title.

Carter is now 60 and lives in Toronto. A small, bald, gentle man who has devoted what is left of his life to fighting for the rights of the wrongfully convicted and the justice he never received.

In 1966, Carter was the man. He was the most ferocious boxer in the world. A fighter nobody wanted to meet. In Paterson, New Jersey, he was a familiar sight in his white Dodge with The Hurricane written on the doors. When he went out he parked where he liked. On the night of June 16, 1966, he parked outside the Nite Spot in Paterson.

After 2am, Carter and two others returned to his apartment to get some money. The police stopped them but let them continue to the Nite Spot. It was late, and Carter and the two others left. Carter dropped off the first man and then, two blocks from the home of John Artis, the other passenger who was a young athlete, the same police officer stopped them again. He was about to let them go when more cars arrived. It was nearly 3am and Carter's life would never be the same again.

At the Lafayette Bar and Grill, 12 blocks from the Nite Spot, two customers and the barman had been shot and murdered at about the time Carter was driving home for money. Carter had never been in the Lafayette. The police were looking for two black men in a white car.

Carter recalled: 'I thought it was just harassment. They told us to follow them, we did. There were several cars and the police were leaning out through the windows with shotguns pointing at us. We drove to a bar I'd never even heard of. They told us to get out. There were a lot of people crying and standing around and I started to get a bad feeling. It was like a lynching. They put us in one of their cars and drove us to the hospital, to the operating room, where we were placed in front of a man. The police asked him if we shot him. He said 'No'. It was after 4am.

Nevertheless, Carter and Artis were taken to the police station and asked to take a lie detector test. They agreed. The results showed that neither was involved in the shooting. It was just the start of Carter's nightmare that would last 30 years, nearly 20 spent in prison before he was again a free man.

SEVENTEEN hours after Carter and Artis were taken to the police station they were released. Carter's car had been torn apart but no evidence of guns had been found. Neither Carter nor Artis had been given a paraffin test to determine if they had fired a gun. They left behind a group of determined men in the police station who would stop at nothing to get a conviction. The police wanted Carter for the murders and they would get him.

He was, as Bob Dylan wrote in the song The Hurricane, *'just a crazy nigger, no one doubted that he pulled the trigger'*. Nobody proved it. There was no evidence, just the testimony of two petty criminals who indicated Carter as the killer.

Alfred Bello and Arthur Bradley were suspects in the Lafayette slayings. They admitted being in the bar and taking money from the till but claimed it was after the killings. They saw, they later said, two black men leaving the Lafayette bar. They said they were chased by Carter and Artis but escaped. Bello, who is now in a witness protection programme in New Mexico, claimed that, though he was fat and wearing trendy high-heel shoes, he managed to sprint away from Carter and Artis. Bradley is dead.

There was a trial and after six weeks the white jury needed just 90 minutes to sentence the pair to three life terms for the murders. There was no motive and the only evidence was the testimony of Bello and Bradley. Carter's planned fight for the middleweight title of the world against Dick Tiger was postponed. His career was at an end. It was May 1967.

Carter, a friend of Martin Luther King in the Sixties, said: 'That night I was out driving with friends meeting with people and trying to set up my next training camp.

'I was isolated long before the murders. In 1964 I spoke out after the Harlem fruit riots, when New York police killed a little black child, and I spoke out and said black people ought to have died in the street protecting their children. Instead they were forced to watch by police holding guns on them as the children were shot. On June 17, 1966, they put the handles on me.

'When I was convicted they wanted the electric chair. The amazing thing is that the white jury came back with guilty with a recommendation for mercy. If they just for one second believed that I killed those people they would have burnt me to death.'

In New Jersey's prisons Carter was a celebrity. He never wore prison clothes, worked prison jobs or ate prison food. He was known as Lord. He spent most of his sentence in solitary confinement. The hole, as he called it. In 1974 his autobiography, *The 16th Round*, was published. It led to a revival of his case. Dylan wrote the song, gave benefit concerts and Muhammad Ali was involved. In March 1976, Carter and Artis were released on bail.

Ali picked up Carter from Trenton State Prison, drove the fighter to New York and gave him several thousand dollars. On Dec 22, he and Artis were reconvicted at a second trial and their initial life sentences were reimposed. This time, the New Jersey prosecutors came up with a motive: the murders were racial, they claimed.

Carter and Artis were taken back to prison. On Dec 23, Carter's second child, Rahim, was born. Carter was refused permission to see the baby. His first child had been three when he was sentenced. She was 13 in 1977.

Carter watched his daughter, Theodora, grow up through bullet-proof glass. One day each month, for 30 minutes, he was a father again. He often missed visits because he was in solitary. Carter still has contact with his two children and his wife but after his second conviction he filed for divorce. 'I was not angry with her. They were starting to use her because they knew it was the only way to break me. I set her free because I loved her.'

Carter continued to think like a free man. In prison his status remained high. He was still the man, The Hurricane. His road to freedom started in 1980 when a group of Canadians took an interest in his case after a boy from New York who they had decided to take care of, discovered Carter's book. New York lawyer Myron Beldock devoted 15 years in pursuit of justice.

IN November 1985, Carter was released, four years after Artis. There was no bail, the game was over for the New Jersey officials. In August 1987, the original conviction was thrown out by the United States Supreme Court of Appeals. However, it was not until February 1988 that a judge in Passaic county, which covers Paterson, formally dismissed the indictments. Carter has never received a cent in compensation or an apology. To this day he will not even fly over New Jersey. He left for Canada in March 1988, a free man living a quiet life, and that is where I spoke to him.

'The 16th round was my final release. I had to win that round to get clear of the iron bars and the stone walls and to thank everybody who campaigned for me and believed in me. I won,' said Carter as the twilight closed the last light in his living room and left his shaven skull flickering in the wayward beams of a street light. For several minutes he sat in silence and then he was gone. I never saw him again. I let myself out. ★ 25/07/97

The way he was. Rubin Carter attacks during his victory over Bootle's Harry Scott at the Royal Albert Hall in 1965

LEONARD CLAWS BACK FIVE SHOTS TO STUN PARNEVIK

by LEWINE MAIR

JUSTIN Leonard holed three grand putts down the closing stretch at Royal Troon yesterday to become the first player since 1925 to win the Open from five shots behind.

None was finer by the American than the 15-footer he made for his two at the short 17th. That paved the way for his inward 34 and a last-round 65 which had him winning by three shots from Jesper Parnevik and Darren Clarke.

The roar which greeted Leonard's all-important putt at the 17th had disturbed Parnevik, who was at the time preparing to tackle a four-footer at the 16th. He backed away from the ball, walked about a bit, and then missed. Before leaving the green, he did what he had failed to do at Turnberry in 1994 and checked the leaderboard. It told him the worst.

Leonard was now 12 under to his 11 under. 'The air went out of my sails,' said Parnevik, who made no attempt to pretend that he was anything other than shattered at the end. If ever there was a time when he would like to have pulled down the peak of his cap, it must have been then.

Freddie Couples, who played alongside Leonard, 25, was the first to pay tribute to the new champion, who went into the last round five behind leader Parnevik. 'Justin's front nine was phenomenal, his back nine terrific. When you putt like he putted, it's not luck. He made some putts which were huge.'

Couples agreed that it was no bad thing from Leonard's point of view that he was playing with someone as laid-back as himself. They chatted all the while and always looked to be having rather more fun than the leaders behind them.

Clarke came to grief on the tee of the second where, armed with a three-iron, he hit his first shank in seven years as a professional. It finished on the beach and it cost him a double-bogey six. Parnevik felt then that the Irishman had ruined his title chance.

PARNEVIK thought that the fatal hole as far as he was concerned was the long sixth. He had hit a second as good as he could hit, but it had leapt into a fairway bunker and under the lip. He blasted it out as well but then made what many felt to be a mistake. Where, on Saturday, he had used his putter with telling effect from far down the fairway, this time his attempt at such a shot left him woefully short.

As Clarke said, the two of them would have scored better had they been able to feed off each other but that never happened. Clarke showed plenty of steel as he finished with two birdies in the last three holes to sign off alongside the Swede in a share of second place but, to his credit, he was far from satisfied. Like Parnevik, he thought he should have won.

Parnevik's performance came as a bitter blow to the Swedish federation, who have long thought that their men should start matching their women in the matter of winning majors. Of all their players, they felt that Parnevik was the most likely to win in such a situation, for they like the way in which he has done his own thing and played in the States.

The federation suspect that they may be at fault in that the Swedes have cars and sponsors' badges all over their person. They are not the hungry fighters they could be.

The general consensus of opinion yesterday was that much depended on what Tiger Woods did at the start of his round. If he could pin down some early birdies, there was the chance that the leaders would feel doubly tight as they teed up at the first.

At 9pm on Saturday, Woods had strolled back to the course and put in a thoroughly peaceful practice session. Yesterday morning, with the help of neighbours who, noticing that the curtains were still drawn, desisted from cutting their lawns, he slept until 11.15. Off the tee at 2pm, he opened with a mammoth drive which finished in the edge of the right rough but, from a lie which seemingly troubled him not at all, he hauled his next into sand.

HE had said after his 64 that the secret of shooting a really low round is to start with a birdie but, before too long, he had three debilitating pars on his card. They were neither going to set him alight nor were they going to cause the rest to take fright.

On the walk from the tee of the 557-yard fourth, his caddie, Fluff, confided: 'We need something to happen.' With the Woods drive having travelled all of 395 yards, Fluff was clearly thinking in terms of an eagle but, in the event, they collected a birdie. There was another birdie at the short fifth, where Woods holed from 15 feet to go to five under for the tournament but the seventh and eighth proved his undoing. He missed from three feet at the seventh and failed to escape the far right-hand bunker at the eighth at his first attempt. The magic had gone.

Intriguingly, word has it that the moment he sets a second major alongside his Masters victory, his Nike contract for $40 million over five years is automatically scrapped. Nike, it seems, would be happy to pay double to keep him.

The prize-giving ceremony was full of emotion, and not least as far as the winner was concerned because Tom Kite had come back from Prestwick airport to congratulate his friend. 'Welcome to the Ryder Cup team,' he said.

Leonard, whose aim over his 40-footer at the last was simply to get the first one close enough so he did not have to think about the second, tailed off in mid-speech as the tears flowed. He was thinking of his parents, his grandmother and his sister and his coach, Randy Smith, none of whom was with him in his finest hour. It was just him and his caddie.

Earlier in the week the club captain, Ian Valentine, who presented the trophy and cheque for £250,000, had given Michael Bonallack and the rest of the Royal & Ancient something of a shock in connection with the 1997 Open's closing moments. After a discussion as to what the caddies might be getting paid for wearing Sky TV visors on the course, Valentine had taken them all in for a moment when he said, lightly: 'I don't know what they're getting, but I'm getting £50,000 for wearing one at the prize-giving.' ★

21/07/97

> 'JUSTIN'S FRONT NINE WAS PHENOMENAL, HIS BACK NINE TERRIFIC. WHEN YOU PUTT LIKE HE PUTTED, IT'S NOT LUCK. HE MADE SOME PUTTS WHICH WERE HUGE'

END COLUMN

Telegraph

DAY BY DAY REVIEW

2: Kelly Holmes pulls up injured at the World Championships in the heats of the 1,500 metres, for which she was a gold-medal contender

3: Manchester United win the Charity Shield on penalties after a 1-1 draw with Chelsea at Wembley; Maurice Greene, of the United States, lands the world 100 metres title in Athens, ahead of Donavan Bailey

4: Denise Lewis claims Britain's first medal at the World Championships, a silver in the heptathlon; Tony Hallett, secretary of the RFU, resigns following Cliff Brittle's success at the AGM last month

5: Lord MacLaurin, chairman of the England and Wales Cricket Board, unveils his blueprint, Raising the Standard, which proposes a three- conference county championship, end-of-season play-offs and a two division 50-over league; Sanarth Jayasuriya and Roshan Mahanama compile an unbroken second-wicket partnership of 548, a record for all wickets in Test cricket, for Sri Lanka against India; Steve Backley takes silver in the javelin at the World Championships

6: Sri Lanka's 952 for six against India is a Test record total, as is their second-wicket partnership of 576, while Sanarth Jayasuriya's 340 is the fourth highest individual Test score. The match is drawn

7: Britain's third silver at the World Championships goes to Colin Jackson in the hurdles, while Sally Gunnell announces her retirement

8: Jonathan Edwards relinquishes his world triple-jump title to Cuba's Yoelvis Quesada, and settles for Britain's fourth silver

10: Australia wrap up the Ashes with one Test to go, thanks to a 264-run victory over England at Trent Bridge; Damon Hill's car fails on the last lap in Hungary, handing victory to Jacques Villeneuve; Great Britain end the World Championships with just six medals, bolstered by silver in the 4x400 metres and bronze in the sprint relay; United States golfers inflict a 18-6 defeat on Britain in the Walker Cup.

12: Essex's NatWest Trophy tie against Glamorgan is marred by a push-and-shove between Mark Ilott and Robert Croft in the gloom

13: Newcastle beat Croatia Zagreb 2-1 in the first leg of their European Cup qualifying round match

14: Essex and Glamorgan fine Mark Ilott and Robert Croft £1,000 each for their argy-bargy in the NatWest Trophy; Denmark's Wilson Kipketer finally erases Seb Coe's name from the 800 metres world record in Zurich, and improves the record he equalled last month

17: Davis Love III lands his first major golf title with three rounds of 66 in a five-shot victory in the US PGA Championship; Karrie Webb wins the women's British Open by eight shots; Michael Doohan's victory at the British Grand Prix seals the world motorcycling title

19: Paul Palmer wins gold for Britain over 200 metres at the European Swimming Championships in Seville

20: Jack Rowell resigns as England's rugby union coach to concentrate on his business interests; Britain's 4x200 metres men take the gold at the European Swimming Championships, where Michelle de Bruin wins her second gold; Wales are on the wrong end of a 10-goal thriller in a World Cup qualifier, losing 6-4 to Turkey, while Germany beat Northern Ireland and the Republic are held by Lithuania

21: Glenn McGrath takes seven for 76 as England are dismissed for 180 in the sixth Test against Australia at the Oval

22: Phil Tufnell, in his first Test of the summer, takes seven Australian wickets for 64 as England fight back in the sixth Test

23: England win the sixth Test by 19 runs, though losing the series 3-2, after setting Australia just 124

24: Michael Schumacher's mastery of wet conditions helps him win the Belgian Grand Prix and extend his lead over Jacques Villeneuve

27: Newcastle equalise in the last minute of extra time to move past Croatia Zagreb into the European Champions' League

29: Despite England's defeat in the Ashes series, Michael Atherton announces he will remain captain for the tour to the West Indies

CHASM APPEARS AT TRENT BRIDGE AS INFERIOR ENGLAND COLLAPSE

by **CHRISTOPHER MARTIN-JENKINS**

C'EST *magnifique, mais ce n'est pas la guerre*,' said a certain Marechal Bosquet of the charge of the Light Brigade. England went magnificently enough to their death on the fourth afternoon at Nottingham yesterday, invited to do so by the attacking fields and constantly challenging bowling of the Australians, and the approach, personified by Graham Thorpe's brilliant 82 not out, was splendidly entertaining for the fourth successive capacity crowd.

Alas, the way that England played in being bowled out in the second to last over of the extra half hour to lose the match, the series and the Ashes in one vainglorious and lemming-like dash to destruction, was wholly out of keeping with the gritty traditions of Anglo-Australian cricket.

'I want them to die for their country,' said Lord MacLaurin, chairman of the ECB, of the attitude he hoped to see from the national team. But sane men do not go frivolously to their death.

THIS WAS A RECKLESS DISPLAY WHICH ALLOWED AUSTRALIA TO TAKE THEIR HITHERTO HARD-EARNED PRIZE FAR TOO EASILY

This was a reckless display which allowed Australia to take their hitherto hard-earned prize far too easily.

England might have helped them by their lack of backbone yesterday and last Thursday's toss was certainly an unlucky one for Mike Atherton to have lost, but it was the sheer quality of Australia's cricket all-round which swamped them in the end.

Edgbaston, and the national euphoria which followed, was a cruel delusion, although it was brought about by genuine enough cricket from England. For Australians it was merely, as they would say, 'a hurry-up'. Mark Taylor said that he had never seen his side bowl so badly as they did then.

Since then this strong character, decent man and wholly admirable cricketer has led them to one triumph after another, prolonging his own reign as a Test captain but bringing Atherton's to an end.

Having been appointed by the

SOME RELIEF AT LAST! MICHAEL ATHERTON AND ALEC STEWART CELEBRATE ENGLAND'S VICTORY OVER AUSTRALIA IN THE FINAL TEST AT THE OVAL PHILIP BROWN

selectors for the full series, Atherton reiterated his intention to captain England for the 46th time at the Oval next week but had nothing to add to the weekend statement which followed the meeting last Thursday night with Lord MacLaurin and other members of England's 'management and organisation'.

'Australia were simply just too good for us,' he said. 'In the last two games the gulf has been pretty big. When they get into a big lead and start bowling in the fourth innings they are are almost unstoppable. But it's not much consolation in defeat that they are such a good side.

'I hope there won't be a whole lot of changes at the end of the series. I think we've got some good cricketers in the players we've had this summer who can compete on even terms with most teams in the world. I will back us to win in the West Indies. But Australia are the best side in the world.'

From the first over of the second Test at Lord's the Australians have been unstoppable and the conclusion has to be that they would have won there too had the rain not given England considerable assistance. In the three matches which have followed they have swept irresistibly to victory, by 268 runs, an innings and 61 and now, to go 3-1 up, by 264 runs.

In the last over before tea, with 25 on the board, Atherton was caught behind off his glove from a ball which lifted so quickly that only a genius could have avoided it. He was thus out to Glenn McGrath for the sixth time in his nine dismissals in the series, a remarkable confirmation of the champion fast bowler's ability to get the wicket which matters most. He did the same to Brian Lara against the West Indies last winter.

Atherton's dismissal was followed in the first full over after tea by that of Alec Stewart, caught in the gully from a leading edge, and the skid had started.

Stewart had earlier made some brilliant takes standing up but had also missed another tricky stumping off Robert Croft and a run-out as England's fielding, so good for most of the game, disintegrated in the latter stages of the Australian innings, Atherton himself making mistakes which betrayed his pre-occupation with all that was to come.

He alone could have provided the steel and unyielding concentration required to save the game when England finally bowled out Australia a second time shortly before 3pm and set out to bat for a minimum of 132 overs.

They had taken a wicket with only the second ball of the morning, when Andrew Caddick prodded a McGrath-like lifter to take the gloves of Steve Waugh, but hopelessly inconsistent bowling in the hour that followed and the dashing style and unbreakable confidence of Ian Healy ended any possibility that England's steadier bowling performance on Saturday afternoon could be exploited to the point where they might have faced a more realistic victory target.

Healy, cutting with devastating elan, made fifty off only 49 balls and Ricky Ponting was compact and utterly secure in sensible support as Australia added an extraordinary 75 in 12 overs in the first hour of a hazy morning.

Adam Hollioake and Robert Croft, flighting it well and at last getting just a little turn, proved the right combination to staunch the flow after Caddick and Dean Headley, who had bowled so well on Saturday, had retired to lick their wounds.

The 451 England needed to win, though victory alone would have kept the issue of the Ashes alive, was out of the serious question. A long rearguard on a pitch which was still so beautifully even in bounce that Atherton went out to bat without an arm-guard, should not have been impossible. England's spirit has been broken, however, whether they realise it or not, on the wheel of Australia's complete superiority in all departments.

The fight which was so evident in the earlier stages of the match was altogether absent in this display, except in Thorpe's severe dismissal of the short ball on his way to 50 out of 62 in the first 10 overs of his two-hour innings, a 68-minute innings by John Crawley which ended unluckily with another leg-side catch, and some stout defence by Headley in the extra half hour as England almost avoided the ignominy of being bowled out inside 50 overs.

A quite brilliant diving catch to the right of first slip by Healy, worthily the man of the match, ended that possibility and McGrath administered the coup de grace when Devon Malcolm edged his second ball to second slip where Mark Waugh, of course, caught it, though it reached him like a bullet from a high-velocity rifle.

The Australians immediately embraced in a tight knot of triumph in the middle of the square. Their victory in the end has been an unalloyed triumph. ★ 24/08/97

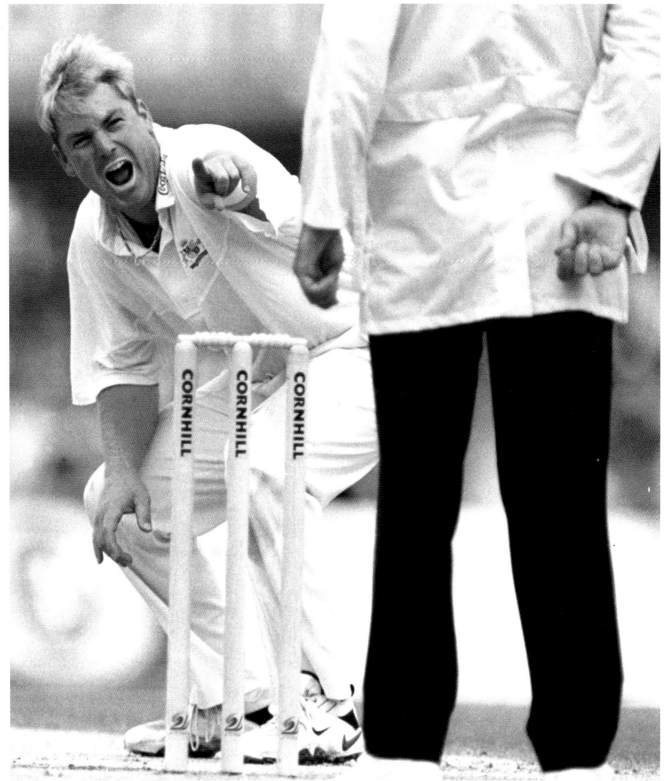

A familiar scene from the Ashes series. Australia's Shane Warne appeals for a wicket *Philip Brown*

UP AND OVER. COLIN JACKSON, SECOND FROM RIGHT, HEADS FOR VICTORY IN THE 110M HURDLES SEMI-FINAL AT THE WORLD CHAMPIONSHIPS

AFRICANS
RUNNING OUT OF SIGHT
by IAIN MACLEOD

WORLD RECORDS		
800M	1-41.24	W KIPKETER (AUG 13)
5,000M	12-41.86	H GEBRSELASSIE (AUG 13)
3,000S	7-59.08	W B KIPKETER (AUG 13)
5,000M	12-39.74	D KOMEN (AUG 22)
10,000M	26-27.85	P TERGAT (AUG 22)
800M	1-41.11	W KIPKETER (AUG 24)
3,000M	7-55.72	B BARMASAI (AUG 24)

OUT of Africa, into Europe and an offensive on history unparalleled in the modern era. African athletes have this summer set 11 world records, seven of them in a 12-day spell in Zurich, Brussels and Cologne; events which have demonstrated the widening gulf between Africa and the rest of the world.

This has, indeed, been a summer of eternal achievements: three records in the 800 metres, two at two miles, two each in the 3,000m steeplechase, the 5,000m and 10,000m, will not last for ever, but the timeless quality of so many accomplishments in this unique season will live in the memory long after another generation of Africans have enhanced their lore.

With respect to men's middle and long-distance running, the Africans, largely Kenyan and Ethiopian, but also including Algerians and Moroccans, are putting that aspect of the sport beyond any non-African. 'I was not born to be a champion, and it's only because of the training I'm doing that I am,' Moses Kiptanui said yesterday.

Kiptanui, the greatest exponent of the 3,000m steeplechase in history and the first athlete to run the distance in under eight minutes, was making an important point: hard work as much as talent is a requisite for those who aspire to greatness; a work ethic - at least by Kenyan standards - it seems is not shared by the majority of European athletes. Kiptanui said that their average training load consisted of running 200km a week.

'Why are the Africans running so good?' Kiptanui said, 'It can take five years to become a champion. We are brought up differently to the Europeans, who have a more comfortable life. They don't like being away from home. I believe that when athletes train together there are many advantages.'

Kiptanui, who has a wife and children on his farm in Kenya, is at home for only two months of the year. The assessment of European athletes was more an observation designed to assist rather than simple criticism, for his primary argument was the advantage gained by the Africans from training in groups.

Daniel Komen, the 21-year-old who, in July, became the first athlete to run two miles in under eight minutes - back-to-back sub-four-minute miles - and, in Brussels last Friday, broke Haile Gebrselassie's world 5,000m record, is the latest Kenyan to join the ranks of African greats.

Kiptanui, who takes a paternal interest in his protege, believes Komen is 'the most talented athlete I've trained with'. Kiptanui added: 'He listens because he wants to know more, because he wants to be the best. Any time he can break a record.'

KOMEN is a part of the training group Kiptanui promotes, his versatility such that he is the closest since Said Aouita - who once said he could break every world record between 800m and 10,000m - to have that ability over so many distances. 'Moses is important to me because we train together; I follow in his footsteps - that's why I've succeeded.'

'Very few of the Europeans are training in groups,' Kiptanui explained. Those who are, such as the Spanish and the Germans, have benefited recently. The Spanish took gold and silver in the World Championships marathon in Athens earlier this month, Fermin Cacho was second in the 1500m final, while the German, Dieter Baumann, who visited Kenya last winter, recently broke the European 5,000m record.

Kiptanui does not believe this is coincidental. 'I believe there are many advantages,' he said. 'Some athletes, especially if they are up-and-coming, can't afford a coach, but a coach can train 20 athletes, or more, and they can understand from athlete to athlete how his body works.

'In Kenya, people who are training as a group tend to give others advice - and not just on running, but on other aspects of life as well. I believe anyone can run fast so long as they are exposed to good training. I don't know how much the Europeans train, but it seems they are not doing enough distance running. Compared with what I'm doing, they are not doing enough.'

He cited the difference between Baumann, who clearly found the Kenyan experience highly beneficial, and the Briton, Andrew Pearson, who also went to Kenya, but did not like what he saw. 'Pearson didn't want to train in Kenya,' said Kiptanui. 'So how can he expect to run well when he doesn't want to train with us.'

Steve Cram, the former 1500m and mile world record holder, was not, he admitted - at least in his day - the greatest advocate of group training, but he did have training partners such as the talented David Sharpe, who provided valuable benefits. Cram did not subscribe to the view that all Europeans were 'soft' but acknowledged that the Africans had a 'different attitude towards running and training'.

Cram added: 'I think the groups probably help a lot, for too many of our athletes train on their own. I think they [the Africans] have a different attitude; a few of our lot could learn from it.' There is, in effect, no answer to talent, and little doubt that, for years to come, the African hegemony of distance running is set to astound the world even more. ★
29/08/97

McGEECHAN TURNS BACK ON THE GRANDEST STAGE OF ALL
by MICK CLEARY

TO LOOK forward to a new season it is imperative to look back: back to wonderful days across a challenging South African landscape when British and Irish rugby came of age once again. Then was the time for pure indulgence, a time to revel in the heroic defiance of a squad whose deep commitment to each other and to the cause won the Test series. Now is the proper occasion to reflect on the means which produced that triumph.

If the Lions are only recalled in beery, nostalgic moments for their denting of Springbok manhood then the tour itself will be but a swiftly passing glory. If, however, club coaches pore over the video tapes of every game played then the tour will prove to be a turning point for the sport in these parts. So many people have talked the expansive game in recent years; only Ian McGeechan has managed to deliver it successfully at the highest level. Small wonder that England wanted him on board.

That we did not see that much overt evidence of the style in the two winning Tests was due entirely to the pressure exerted on the day. This was pressure induced by the opposition, not by the occasion. The Lions were not cautious and conservative in the way England had been in the early Nineties, stalked by a fear of failure. England had a priceless commodity during that era of dominance - the ball. The Lions, in contrast, had to lay their skin bare to get a sighting of it. But when they did they were prepared to use it. Crucially they knew how to use it. And the credit for that is all McGeechan's.

McGeechan's way is the only way the game can now be played. This has nothing to do with a cliched notion of providing entertainment and everything to do with playing rugby in the most effective way. The All Blacks, unbeaten and a country mile ahead, have proved that beyond all doubt. Such a dynamic, intelligent style just happens to be easier on the eye also.

In laying to waste all but one of South Africa's top provincial sides the Lions debunked two deep-rooted myths: that the British are a stilted, unimaginative rugby breed by nature and, secondly, that it takes months of dreary squad sessions to make it all happen. It is the quality of time available, and the calibre of people directing that time, which is crucial. Hence the attempts of Fran Cotton, Lions manager and the new RFU vice-chairman (playing), to bring McGeechan into the fold.

Yesterday McGeechan turned down the opportunity to become England coach. 'It was the worst decision of my life to make,' he said. There were various stumbling blocks, notably the £500,000 compensation placed on McGeechan's head by his club, Northampton, the offer of only a two-year contract and his sense of loyalty to his players at Northampton.

That McGeechan is a Scot (he both played for and coached Scotland) was not a factor at all in his decision. He called the England post 'one of the top jobs in sport'. There is a counter approach from Scotland but, though too decent a man to say so, McGeechan knows that England had far more potential. With Scotland there is little chance of winning a World Cup: with England there is every chance. In the end

RUNNING MAN. BATH'S VICTOR UBOGU PICKS UP THE BALL AND HEADS SINGLE-MINDEDLY FOR THE HARLEQUINS' LINE PHILIP BROWN

there were too many tangled strands for McGeechan to make a definite commitment to England. It is a decision which deep down you feel he may regret for the rest of his days. With him overseeing English rugby and his Lions assistant, Jim Telfer, performing a similar role in Scotland, rugby in these two territories would have been in very good hands.

Whatever now happens it seems untenable for Cotton and Jack Rowell to strike any sort of working relationship. Cotton remarked over the weekend that aspects of Rowell's man management and selection left something to be desired. It is one thing for it to be correct but quite another for it to be said as a public statement.

The RFU want the position of England coach to be a full-time one. At the rate they are filling the calendar with Tests even that may not afford enough time. The gravest problem for the game as it enters a new season is that of overkill. Every year the season is stretched at either end. The Allied Dunbar Premiership begins this Saturday, less than six weeks after the English Lions returned from their labours in South Africa and then Australia. The Heineken European Cup is now to be played on a home-and-away basis.

England will play 13 Tests in the next 10 months, four in the autumn against New Zealand (twice), Australia and South Africa followed by the Five Nations before heading off

to play New Zealand, Australia and South Africa again. They have also tacked on a game at the start, against the US in Los Angeles. Let's hope the pilot doesn't refuel in Morocco on the way back from South Africa or there will be an administrator hustling for a ball, a set of posts and a game.

'IT WAS THE WORST DECISION OF MY LIFE TO MAKE'

It is not just England who are guilty of chasing the fast buck. Wales play Romania on Saturday week. This glut of international rugby serves no benefit. It treats the players as slabs of meat and the spectators as mugs. The rugby world is

very small and the opposition will only go around so many times before the boredom threshold is reached. It is the scarcity of a product which increases its value not its availability.

Maybe now that the RFU seem to have spent all their fury and spilled all their blood in their internal battles proper focus can be restored. There is a horrible nagging feeling, though, that too many people high up are still uncomfortable with the concept of professionalism. Cliff Brittle, the hero of the masses and the new chairman of the RFU management board, insists he is progressive. He must prove it quickly. There is nothing to fear in professionalism. There was not one dissenting voice among the celebrating British thousands in Cape Town and Durban. Not one of them was quibbling about the Johnsons and the Guscotts earning £150,000 a year. It is the clubs who nurture these top players. Without their support and sustenance the shop window would be threadbare.

The season has so much to offer. Shame about McGeechan, though. The big stage suits him.

Mick Cleary took over this month as The Daily Telegraph rugby union correspondent from John Mason, who retired after 20 years service with the newspaper. ★
19/08/97

COUNTY EGOS CONTINUE
TO GET IN WAY OF PROGRESS

by MARK NICHOLAS

LORD MacLaurin and Tim Lamb have done a pretty good job considering the extraordinary resistance to change that confronts any imaginative administration of English cricket. Here we are, with a substandard county system feeding a Test team who could not beat Zimbabwe let alone Australia, and still the restructuring of our game hints at loose ends and compromise. MacLaurin is not a man for either but even he, with his remarkable CV in business planning, is shackled by the indifference and self-interest of the counties. He has gone half-hog because the counties would have lobbed the whole hog out of the window.

The fact is that English cricket will continue to massage its own over-inflated ego while it is run by the county clubs and therefore by their members. It should be run by the newly constituted 38 regional boards who should be at the top of a pyramid which begins with cricket in the schools and moves right the way through the amateur game, financing a strong premier league in each county or region, to the county team itself. Only then, when the county clubs are answerable to their boards and the county boards answerable to the management committee of the ECB and their chairman, will English cricket have a structure that the amazing and continued enthusiasm for the game in this country deserves.

Still, at least we have something brave in its departure from the past and fresh in its possibilities for the future to be excited about. I spoke to a handful of first-class cricketers yesterday and could sense the energy in their support for three competitions with new purpose and potential drama. It was as if a layer of dust had been lifted off the game and the furniture which had been dulled by time and routine now had the chance to stand proudly again.

Three conferences and play-offs, which sound more complicated than they are, will increase the intensity of championship cricket and provide a focus not only for the players but also for the supporters who have been short-changed by teams who are out of the hunt in late July. We should have had two divisions with promotion and relegation but because the counties are not prepared to face and understand their true responsibilities to the English game in general, rather than of their own patch, we do not.

The shock of relegation should have been a challenge to get the house back in order; the opportunity for promotion should have been the catalyst for freer, more incisive play. There was nothing to be scared of, only more testing competition from which players, marketing men and money men would have benefited. As it is, the conferences will create spice and the play-offs a climax for all teams, rather than the lucky few, to enjoy at the season's end.

Craftily, MacLaurin and Lamb have given us the chance to evaluate promotion and relegation by including it in the one-day rethink. There may be more matches but now they have an obvious pattern and will therefore be easier to follow. Clearly, they are there to make money and the flexibility of the scheduling will allow for experiments with evening play, night matches under lights and further exploiting the midweek corporate audience. The television companies are delighted with the potential of this National League and will therefore retain their confidence in the value of covering the domestic game.

Phasing out second - XI cricket and reducing county staffs is a good way to go, not least because a professional sportsman's lifestyle must be the privilege of the elite, not of the hangers-on. However, this will only work if money, and a lot of it, initiative and support are given to the amateur game. Premier leagues are a must as are two-day matches between all cricketers outside the county teams. We have plenty of gifted 15- and 16-year-olds in England but very few who realise their talent at first-class level. The under-17 age group must assume greater importance - probably in place of the under-19 age group - and the club cricket circuit which follows must have the facilities and the standards to act as the provider for the first-class game.

The board must provide money more specifically. The county clubs should be able to sustain their own first-class team, wages and overheads, through their own revenue. The handout from the ECB should be to the county boards and should provide exclusively for the development of the game.

A last thought in the wake of yesterday's gale-force wind of change. The quality of pitches and the standard of coaching and management in English cricket leave a deal to be desired. County pitches must not conform to a rule of thumb, they must retain their indigenous characteristics and most importantly must have enough life to encourage bowlers.

English coaches must be prepared to branch out, to explore and embrace the modern thinking that is evident in much of the rest of the world, otherwise overseas coaches will become the norm in county cricket and our own ability to influence the game will diminish.

The job of management is dependent on the counties who must decide whether or not they are prepared to appoint the sort of forward-thinking people whose methods can take the game into the 21st century. ★ **06/08/97**

The counties subsequently voted against the report and in favour of the status quo.

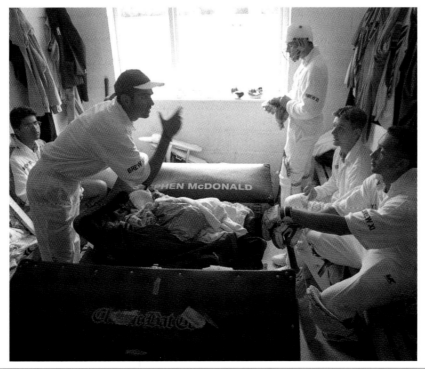

SPORT AROUND THE WORLD: Diego Maradona and Claudio Caniggia renewed their partnership at Argentinian side Boca Juniors, but their goals will no longer be sealed with a kiss. Last year they caused raised eyebrows by celebrating a goal for Boca with a long kiss on the lips. Now Caniggia's wife, former model Mariana Nannis, has laid down the rules: they can hug, but they can't kiss on the lips. "It's immoral," she said.

CRICKET DIARY: An unemployed Sri Lankan cricketer, Wasantha Kumara, committed suicide after being scolded repeatedly by his mother for devoting too much time to the game, and not enough to getting a job. Kumara, 20, drank insecticide after leaving a request to be buried with his cricket bat and ball, hoping that he would be a better player in the next life.

FOOTBALL DIARY: Robbie Savage soon became the butt of dressing-room banter at Leicester following his move from Crewe. His new Porsche, flowing blond locks and dodgy dress sense explains why he was nicknamed, 'Lily'. As in drag queen Lily Savage.

LETTERS TO THE SPORTS EDITOR: SIR - Last week The Daily Telegraph published the top 20 first-class averages for batting and bowling. It was not surprising to note that in the England side at Trent Bridge - a game we had to win - not one of the 11 players featured in these top 20s. - D E MEEKINS, Tonbridge, Kent.

SPORT AROUND THE WORLD: Adelino Barros, one of Portugal's top goalkeepers, broke his jaw in a bizarre training accident when his teeth got caught up in the netting. Barros, of first division Vitoria Guimaraes, ran from the pitch with blood streaming from his mouth and needed hospital surgery. Barros said: "I leapt to punch the ball and, as I fell, my teeth got stuck in the net. My whole body weight was being supported by my teeth and my upper jaw bone was yanked out of place."

FOOTBALL DIARY: The Sixties and Seventies fad for naming offspring after the line-up of your favourite team has finally come home to roost in the guise of Charlie Oatway. His father was a Queens Park Rangers fan, and Oatway jnr was duly named after the team, circa 1973: Anthony Phillip David Terry Frank Donald Stanley Gerry Gordon Stephen James Oatway. "You can see why people call me Charlie," he says. Unfortunately, he has just signed for nearby Brentford, where QPR are despised.

CRICKET DIARY: Jack Russell for England is the cry, not from the predictable quarter of Gloucestershire, but from the Isle of Wight. The Jack Russell in question is a dog called Bodie, who is confirming his reputation for having a safe set of paws in Shanklin, passing his career total of 500 balls retrieved, and homing in on his season's best of 135. Owner Harold Renouf, 86, said: "He's on 131 found balls for this season, but with a month still to go I'm sure he'll pass the record." Bodie's annual contribution to the club has been rewarded with four tins of dog food.

DAY BY DAY REVIEW

1: Greg Rusedski beats Daniel Vacek to become the first Briton to reach the quarter-finals of the US Open since 1984

2: Glenn Hoddle drops West Ham's Rio Ferdinand, 18, from England's squad for the Moldova game after he is convicted of drink-driving

3: Greg Rusedski beats Richard Krajicek in straight sets in the quarter-finals of the US Open

5: Athens is named as host for the 2004 Olympic Games

6: Sport is cancelled in Britain as a mark of respect for the funeral of Diana, Princess of Wales; Greg Rusedski reaches the US Open final by beating Jonas Bjorkman; Steve Redgrave and Matthew Pinsent are in Britain's coxless four who win gold at the World Rowing Championships; The Republic of Ireland beat Iceland in a World Cup qualifier

7: Greg Rusedski, the first Briton in 61 years to reach a US Open final, goes down to Pat Rafter; Martina Hingis drops just four games in her victory over Venus Williams in the women's final; David Coulthard records his second grand prix win of the season, in Italy; Essex need less than half their 60 overs to overhaul Warwickshire and win the NatWest Trophy; Scotland beat Belarus in a World Cup qualifier

10: Ian Wright scores twice as England beat Moldova 4-0 at Wembley, and go top of their World Cup group as Italy are held by Georgia; Republic of Ireland beat Lithuania in another World Cup match

13: Silver Patriarch, first in the St Leger at Doncaster, gives Pat Eddery the 4,000th winner of his career

14: Tim Henman emerges from the shadows of Greg Rusedski to win the ATP Tour tournament in Tashkent, beating Marc Rosset in the final; Warwickshire's victory over Gloucestershire, aided and abetted by Kent's defeat at Yorkshire, seals the Axa Life Sunday League title

15: Cricket's counties reject Lord MacLaurin's plans to restructure the Championship in favour of the status quo; Sir John Hall ends his 5½-year reign as chairman of Newcastle United

16: Steve McManaman's solo goal earns Liverpool a draw at Celtic in the UEFA Cup, while Aston Villa hold Bordeaux and Arsenal, Leicester and Rangers all lose their away legs; Clive Woodward is appointed Jack Rowell's successor as England rugby coach

17: Faustino Asprilla's hat-trick helps Newcastle to a 3-2 win over Barcelona in the European Champions' League, in which Manchester United are also successful in Kosice, Slovakia

18: Chelsea build a two-goal advantage in the first leg of their European Cup-Winners' Cup tie against Slovan Bratislava; Justin Rose and Rebecca Hudson win The Daily Telegraph Junior Golf titles

20: Kent's victory over Surrey is not enough to prevent Glamorgan, winners over Somerset, claiming the County Championship for the first time since 1969

21: Jacques Villeneuve cuts Michael Schumacher's lead in the drivers' championship to one point with victory in the Austrian GP

24: Fulham announce that Kevin Keegan is to return to football as their chief operating officer

26: Europe and the United States are level after the storm-hit first day's fourballs and foursomes in the Ryder Cup at Valderrama

27: Europe build a 9-4 lead over the United States after the second day of the Ryder Cup; Frankie Dettori, who won all seven races at Ascot a year ago, manages just one this time, on Jaseur in the last race

28: Europe hold on to win the Ryder Cup 14½ - 13½, after which Severiano Ballestero announces he will stand down as captain for 1999; Michael Schumacher's collision with brother Ralf hands Jacques Villeneuve victory in the Luxembourg GP and opens a nine-point gap

30: Liverpool are held at home by Celtic in the second leg of their UEFA Cup encounter, though win on away goals, while Aston Villa are the only other British club to go through, beating Bordeaux in extra-time; Arsenal, Leicester and Rangers are all beaten on aggregate

by **MIHIR BOSE**

SPORTS COUNCIL
BACK CENTRAL BID TO RUN
ACADEMY

THE British Academy of Sport will be run by the Central Consortium. The Midlands-based group have successfully defeated bids by the city of Sheffield and the British Olympic Association.

The decision was made when the UK Sports Council met under the chairmanship of Sir Rodney Walker on Monday. However, in keeping with the British traditions of compromise, the two unsuccessful bidders will get a consolation prize.

The Central Consortium will also be told that they cannot use Lilleshall as one of the three sites - Loughborough and Holme Pierrepont are the others - at which they were hoping to base the academy.

Lilleshall is considered too far away and the English Sports Council Trust, who own the site, are reluctant to let it be used solely for the academy. Instead it will become one of the regional centres underpinning the main academy site.

Central will also be told that they will have to give the British Olympic Association a role in the running of the academy. There is some sympathy among sports administrators that because of the nature of British sports, the British Olympic Association do not play as crucial a role as associations in other countries. The academy will concentrate on a core of some eight sports, all of them Olympic, and a role for the BOA is considered crucial.

The sop for Sheffield, whose bid has been impressive, is that it will become a strong regional centre. There will also be other regional centres in England, Scotland, Northern Ireland and Wales. England could have as many as 10 regional centres and other failed bidders who were eliminated in earlier rounds, such as Bath, Birmingham and Manchester, could get a regional centre. A notional figure of £100 million from lottery funds is allocated for the academy but it is still to be decided how this will be divided between the central site and the regions. From Nov 1 sport, along with the existing five good causes that benefit from lottery funds, will start getting less money. That is when education and health become the sixth good cause and sport could lose something like £60 million a year.

The UK Sports Council's decision has to be ratified by Tony Banks, the Minister for Sport, who has the ultimate power to decide. It would be a major surprise, however, if he were to throw out the recommendation, which is expected to be announced next month.

BRITISH television viewers will be able to choose whether to follow Manchester United or Newcastle in their Champions' League matches this season - provided they have access to the Carlton Select cable channel.

While ITV have the British rights, they cannot screen both teams live as their games kick off at the same time. So they have sold on three of the matches to Carlton Select, who will start by showing Manchester United in Kosice on Wednesday while ITV screen Newcastle v Barcelona. Carlton do not yet know what games they have bought, as ITV will decide round by round which of the two teams to show live.

Aware of the problems for TV companies this season, when countries like England, Italy, Spain and Germany have more than one team in the Champions' League, UEFA have already indicated a willingness to change their strict schedules.

For the round of matches on Nov 26 - Manchester United are at home to Kosice and Newcastle away to Barcelona - UEFA will allow the rescheduling of certain games on the Thursday. They are considering a similar plan for the fifth round of fixtures on Dec 10, when Manchester United are away to Juventus and Newcastle at home to Dinamo Kiev. If the English games are affected, ITV could show live football on Wednesday and Thursday.

This is a radical change from UEFA's previous rules, under which UEFA Cup ties are played on a Tuesday, Champions' League games on a Wednesday and Cup-Winners' Cup matches on a Thursday. On the two dates in question the UEFA Cup, with a far bigger entry, has a round of knockout ties while the Cup Winners' Cup does not, thus leaving two Thursdays clear.

Frits Ahlstrom, a UEFA spokesman, made it clear that concern about television coverage was the reason for the changes. By moving games a whole day, they give non-subscription channels the chance to show two live games.

'We are very keen that as many matches as possible should be on terrestrial television,' he said. 'And terrestrial television as opposed to satellite does not have many channels.'

ITV will have more than five hours of Champions' League coverage on Wednesday night/Thursday morning, and anyone without Carlton Select will be able to watch a delayed transmission of the Manchester United match at 2.15am. That will be after the Newcastle game (7.30-10pm) and a separate highlights programme at 11.40pm.

THE Football Association, euphoric after Wednesday's results, are already making plans about where England might be based if they reach the World Cup finals in France next year. One suggestion was that they might stay in England, at a hotel in the south-east, and fly to France for matches, returning immediately afterwards.

There is nothing in FIFA's regulations compelling a team to stay inside the borders of the host country, and that plan might make sense, especially as England would not be based in the same city for their group games. They would, like all the other teams except hosts France and holders Brazil, be moved around the country and play in at least three different cities in the group stage.

A FIFA spokesman said: 'It would be an unusual request but the regulations don't say anything about where they should be based.'

Steve Double, a spokesman for the FA, laughed away such ideas and said England were likely to follow the system they had for Le Tournoi this summer, when they were based in Nantes. But do not be surprised if, given a favourable draw with no long flights, they think again about staying in England. ★ **13/9/97**

Telegraph

WRIGHT
PUBLICITY STUNT
BACKED A LOST CAUSE

by **MICHAEL PARKINSON**

WE said at the time it would all end in tears and trust Ian Wright not to let us down, or keep us waiting. Only a couple of weeks after the FA dressed him in Thirties gear and mutton chop whiskers and plastered him all over the press promoting the so-called beautiful game, he finds himself in front of his bosses charged with misconduct because of an ugly confrontation on the field of play.

It is difficult to decide who was the more stupid, Wright for getting involved - not on the spur of the moment, but after having made a special journey from the subs bench - or the dunderheads at the FA who thought him worthy of being their ambassador.

Football needs to improve its manners. Recent events both here and abroad have done nothing but reinforce the notion that players, managers, directors, the men who run the FA and the Premier League, not forgetting lickspittles in the media and crackpots on the terraces, need to be made aware that all is not well. And that is putting it mildly. Ian Wright is not the sickness but the symptom and the FA's decision to employ him a mere indication of how football lacks sensible leadership.

What we get instead of firm action to improve the game's countenance is David Mellor's task force. Chosen carefully so as to offend no one, Mellor and his team are examples of what happens when the concern is more about image than action. They are rocking-horse soldiers. What we want is the cavalry.

In any event, in the final analysis, football must sort itself out. It would greatly help if referees were given the sort of protection they enjoy in other games. For instance, if the referee at Leicester the other night had been in charge at either code of rugby the players who surrounded him would have spent the rest of the season watching their team on television. It would also help if the responsibility for time-keeping was taken away from referees, as it is in other sports. They have enough on their plates nowadays without having to fiddle with stop watches.

It would also much improve the general situation if managers started behaving like bosses and not players'

poodles. Arsene Wenger's reaction to Wright's stupidity was to suggest the player is being picked on. How he can say it with a straight face beats me. Wright is a serial offender. His record proves it. If he gets a suspension for his latest misdemeanour then great harm will be done to Arsenal's chances of winning the championship.

If that happens, will Wenger feed his player's paranoia by patting him on the head or will he get tough and point out that for all Wright's fine talk about being 'one of the lads' in the Arsenal squad he is not a team player at all but a selfish and wilful man whose behaviour discredits the club and threatens his team's ambitions?

Wright claims he is picked on. 'Why me?' he asks. Because he sits up and begs for it is the answer. He should study his rap sheet and if he still believes he is being

discriminated against ought to apply to be registered as an oppressed minority.

Isn't it curious that in a game which oozes machismo and likes to think it looks the world in the eye there are many so-called heroes who are wimps when it comes to the ultimate manly virtue of accepting responsibility for what they do?

When David Batty was rightly dismissed for trying to separate an opponent's legs from the rest of his body, having already been shown one yellow card, his manager, Kenny Dalglish, complained he was hard done by because he should not have been booked for the first offence. But what about a player who, knowing he is under threat, reoffends with a tackle so crude it left the referee no room for discretion? Shouldn't that be the manager's main area of concern?

DALGLISH, along with Wenger and their fellow managers, would do well to consider the opinion of those shareholders at last week's Arsenal annual meeting who made it clear they are fed up with Wright and wish he would take his angst elsewhere. Wenger's reply that it would cost the club £15-20 million to replace the player only indicated he hadn't understood the wider issue involved.

It also defined what is at the root of most of the problems in the modern game. The truth is football knows how to count its riches but not how to be accountable for them.

Already ahead of his appearance before the FA there are clear indications of a campaign within the game to win sympathy for Wright.

Glenn Hoddle, the England manager, says authority has 'an obsession' about the player. The fact is he demands attention like a naughty child. At Leicester he demonstrated his ability to create a problem for himself where none existed. In other words it was a controversy entirely of his own making.

This makes nonsense of Hoddle's theory which, of course, has nothing to do with him not wanting to lose a key player with the World Cup qualifiers coming up.

First with Paul Gascoigne and now with Wright, the England manager has established himself as the Patron Saint of Lost Causes. We shouldn't be surprised. A belief in miracles is a prerequisite of anyone managing the England team.

Justifying his selection, Hoddle said he thought a ban would be 'very unfair on the lad'. He is entitled to his opinion but the fact is Wright is long past being a lad. He is a man in his thirties only a few years younger than Hoddle, who would no doubt get shirty if anyone referred to him as a youth.

Like Eric Cantona, Wright needs time to contemplate the error of his ways, to take stock, as Cantona did, and hopefully reach the same conclusions. It is said he is visiting a therapist to help him control his temper. The FA should afford him the opportunity of a lengthy course of treatment free from the terrible temptation of playing football.

To be cynical (football makes you that way) it doesn't really matter if the FA back off getting tough with Wright. They are only postponing the inevitable. It is a racing certainty he will continue his foolish ways. There was evidence of this on Saturday in the game against Spurs when he was booked for an illegal tackle when his opponent was off the field of play. Perhaps, in the final analysis, Wright is neither a victim nor a villain. Simply a twerp. ★ **01/09/97**

Avoiding action. Ian Wright leaps above Leicester's Robbie Savage and Matt Elliott Raymonds

O'NEILL MAKES A LIVELY IMPACT NURTURING SPARSE RESOURCES

by DAVID MILLER

TO adapt Groucho Marx, clubs he had hardly even heard of rejected management applications from Martin O'Neill. It is strange how, over the years, there should have been a profusion of successful Scottish managers in the English game, yet only a handful of Irishmen. O'Neill, with rising Leicester - and Sammy McIlroy at small-time Macclesfield - may be about to correct the balance.

'The number of clubs, including Fourth Division ones, who didn't even give me an interview shows how soon you're forgotten,' O'Neill recalls without rancour. He has the least envious task of any manager in European competition this week. Leicester go to Madrid tomorrow to face Atletico in the club's biggest match since the articulate side of Matt Gillies vainly attempted to prevent Spurs' Double in the 1961 FA Cup final.

O'Neill regards Atletico as one of the best teams in the Continent, let alone Spain. He is well placed to judge. As a player during the four years of Nottingham Forest's prime, 1977-80, he won more medals than any current Premiership manager other than Kenny Dalglish, Bryan Robson and Ruud Gullit. His 18 months at Leicester have, thus far, been beyond expectation: promotion, and a League Cup title.

O'Neill coaches, manages and talks like he played - staccato, instinctive, perpetual motion, occasionally risk-taking for the thrill of the adrenalin it pumps into his players. And him. He conveys an infectious quality, of living for this moment, for now, so don't waste a moment of opportunity.

I remember him coming off the field 15 years ago, on that humid night in Valencia, when Northern Ireland, under his leadership, had for the second time in their history just reached the quarter-finals of the World Cup by defeating Spain, the hosts. His vitality remained electric. It was as though he were ready immediately to play another match.

HIS words rattle out at a greater rate than Clive Anderson's, but without that smug vanity. The charm of the Irish is the self-mockery of their humour. Maybe that is why most club chairmen feel less than comfortable with an Irish manager. Themselves predominantly being without a sense of humour, and wanting daily to receive assurance on prospects as cast iron as wedding vows, they never know whether an Irish manager is being serious.

There are more asides, footnotes and oblique cross-references in an O'Neill conversation than in a legal reference book; perhaps unsurprisingly, since he studied law. Journalists, and no doubt club directors, are left trailing in the wake of his post-match analyses, with their uncommon strands of truth, doubt, and refusal to be held in awe by the imponderables of his and the team's future.

More than most, the Irish have a way of keeping sport in perspective. Perhaps it is the long proximity to national hardship or misfortune. Listen to O'Neill, and you hear the echoes of north and south; of managers such as Johnny Carey, Danny Blanchflower, Noel Cantwell, Charlie Hurley, Billy Bingham, Terry O'Neill. A boardroom conference between John Cobbold, late of Ipswich, and Martin O'Neill would have been riotous. If Tom Smeaton at Leicester has confidence in O'Neill, as indeed he should, then Smeaton must be a good man.

When your manager is making fun of his own half-time talk to the players, it needs a steady nerve in the boardroom. After Saturday's three-goal flourish against woeful

'WE'RE SHORT OF GENUINE QUALITY ALL ROUND, BUT WE'VE DONE OUR BEST TO HIDE OUR DEFICIENCIES'

Tottenham, when Leicester might have been two up at half-time but were still goal-less, O'Neill said: 'I told them 'keep playing the same way, a goal will come'. Whether I believed it is another matter!'

The vein of self-mockery, that protective don't-get-too-confident streak, is ever-present. 'We can play a little bit now and again. It's a decent team - I haven't a clue for how long.'

You can detect there something of the banter of Brian Clough or Tommy Docherty, but without Clough's Yorkshire sarcasm or Docherty's quips that were usually at an individual player's expense. O'Neill's reference to his players is unwaveringly affectionate.

'I'd have to be thick not to learn from him [Clough],' O'Neill says. 'He was brilliant. I didn't get on with him, but I tried to put his ideas to use. It wouldn't work in total. You've got to be you, and I haven't changed in character since I was 15. If I treat players as fairly as I can, and they return it, that's all I can expect.'

There are many schools of management: the technical (Greenwood, Nicholson, Allison), the pragmatic (Shankly, Catterick, Revie, Mee), the tactical (Graham, Dalglish), the simplistic (Cullis, Gould, Bassett, Kinnear), the cosmopolitan (Busby, Paisley, Ferguson). And there are those who, by a combination of their own and their players' personalities, manage to achieve results that are beyond the perceived talents at their disposal: Ramsey with Ipswich, Stein with Celtic, Ashman with West Bromwich, Stock with QPR and

Fulham, Clough with Derby and Nottingham Forest.

You sense that O'Neill may belong in this category. Certainly it is true of his performance with Leicester so far. The ceiling on his/their achievement may prove to be the absurd wages, as opposed merely to transfer fees, now being paid by the big city clubs.

ASK him what is Leicester's strength, and the answer is immediate. The camaraderie. The willingness to work for each other. 'Some might have thought that [work] would not last more than a season, but there's no sign of this in the last few games,' O'Neill said, before the victory over Tottenham. 'We're short of genuine quality all round, but we've done our best to hide our deficiencies.' And some.

The ethic of fairness runs deep. 'What players want, even sometimes if it hurts, is an honest assessment of their ability,' he says. So much of coaching is no more than advice. Clough never coached, he reflects. 'He just used to drive home, repeatedly, basic points. Such as the responsibility of a full-back in closing down a winger, being not to force him to cross the ball - thereby shifting the responsibility elsewhere - but to prevent the cross.'

And, of course, learning to play without the ball. 'It's a cliche,' O'Neill says, 'and we'll experience it, not having the ball, in Madrid. I believe we've drawn the short straw [against Atletico] but the experience of last season, when good opposition would pass the ball through us, may be helpful. Sure, Tuesday is worrying, I saw Atletico thrash Valladolid and they were brilliant. But the performance against Tottenham gives us confidence.'

Managers are chided for endlessly talking about 'getting a result'. Never underestimate the importance, insists O'Neill. 'The first-team result - as opposed to performance - is the only factor that gives you time to do anything else.' he says. 'Some managers may go on about getting a youth squad underway, but that's running away from the issue. That's what I learnt in my five years at Wycombe and brief spell with Norwich.'

Yet his anxiety now lies less in results than in whether a club flotation can raise the money to buy an occasional established international player rather than those such as Matt Elliott, from Oxford, and Mustafa Izzet from Chelsea, still striving to make their mark at the top.

'The most difficult task is turning Leicester from a medium into a big city club,' he admits. 'From a yo-yo side, into one that's competing on a level financial playing field.'

Leicester's outlay for the current season has been £600,000 net, with the sale of Grayson, for Graham Fenton, Tony Cottee and Robbie Savage. 'That's not big thinking,' O'Neill admits.

On the other hand, he concedes, impishly, that he finds perverse enjoyment from out-manoeuvring the likes of Liverpool, Arsenal and Spurs on the third-smallest wages bill in the top division. Even if flotation should generate the fee for, say, the unsettled Steve Stone at Forest, the wages would destroy Leicester's financial structure.

'I'm reluctant to put anyone on ferociously more money than those who've done such a lot already,' he says. Come rain or shine, O'Neill will live by loyalty. It might just be enough, remembering what Clough contrived with an average workforce including the likes of Hinton, O'Hare, Robertson, McGovern, Burns, Clark, Birtles… and O'Neill. ★
15/09/97

BALLESTEROS
THE DRIVING FORCE

ROBERT PHILIP
at Valderrama

SOMEWHERE over the rainbow lay his destiny; as he stood alone on the terrace of the Valderrama clubhouse on Saturday morning, gazing out across the still-deserted velvet fairways to a far-off spot on the horizon where the departing raindrops shimmered brilliantly in the sun's rays, Severiano Ballesteros felt the fall of a strong hand on his shoulder. 'Whatever happens this day,' smiled Bernhard Langer, 'always remember that nobody in the world could have done more for this team. Nobody.'

The tribute had come full circle; for it was at Kiawah Island, South Carolina, six years ago that Ballesteros, already a Ryder Cup captain-in-waiting though still a supposedly humble foot-soldier serving under Bernard Gallacher, comforted the distraught German whose missed six-foot putt on the 18th green against Hale Irwin had just deprived Europe of victory by a single point. 'Nobody in the world could have made that putt,' whispered Ballesteros as Langer stood alone amid a veritable mardi gras of whooping and hollering Americans, 'nobody.' Langer never forgot that kindness.

When the events of another nerve-frayingly traumatic Ryder Cup final day had been recorded in prosaic red-and-blue numbers on the great scoreboard by the 18th green here on the Costa del Monsoon, it was the European XII's turn to unloose the tear ducts and enjoin in riotous celebration; and nobody had done more to secure a fifth success in seven contests than the 13th man, Seve Ballesteros. And I mean nobody.

When Thomas Bjorn's shoulders slumped after he fell four behind on the fourth green despite producing highly respectable golf against Open champion Justin Leonard, there was Ballesteros to extend a punched fist of defiance. When Darren Clarke disappeared into the trees on the 10th, there was Ballesteros plunging noisily through the undergrowth like an angry rhino to help sniff out the errant ball. When Ian Woosnam hung his head in defeated anguish after 11 holes of misery against Fred Couples, there was Ballesteros waiting with a smiling shrug of sympathy. When Costantino Rocca conjured up his latest miracle against Tiger Woods on the 16th, there was Ballesteros with a celebratory kiss and a cuddle. And when Mark O'Meara sank a three-mile putt on the 14th to crush Jesper Parnevik, there was Ballesteros scowling that special Spanish scowl he reserves for Yanks who have had the audacity to challenge his authority.

In short, he prowled here, there and everywhere, encouraging, consoling, cajoling, careering around Valderrama at the wheel of his blue-and-white buggy as though it bore the livery of a Williams-Renault Formula One car. 'Seve's very relaxed,' noted Colin Montgomerie in a wonderfully accurate 10-word thumbsketch of the Great One, 'in his own intense sort of way.'

Did Montgomerie say 'relaxed'? As Europe's points tally briefly stalled on the tortuous struggle towards the all-important total of 14½ during the climactic series of singles, Ballesteros was as relaxed as a soon-to-be new dad pacing the hospital waiting-room floor.

Each victorious European was welcomed home like a long-lost son, each American was treated to a perfunctory handshake and the kind of demonic smile Dracula usually bestowed upon potential victims. Perhaps he achieved the illusion of being in attendance on 12 holes at the same time with the aid of mirrors or maybe he employed a huge army of *doppelgangers* as stand-ins, but wherever and whenever something of import occurred on the course, there hovered Ballesteros - his handsome features a constantly changing kaleidoscope of emotions - at the very epicentre of the drama. Whereas some players - notably his fellow Latins Ignacio Garrido, Jose Maria Olazabal and Rocca - welcomed this 'track-suit manager' approach, others were less certain about allowing Seve room to meddle in their affairs.

> 'IN HIS HEART I THINK HE HIT EVERY BALL IN EVERY MATCH. EVERY TIME I LOOKED OVER HE WAS THERE'

'We were doing all right,' said Monty in a tone of mock-exasperation following his tense last-hole foursomes victory in the company of Langer on Saturday night, 'until he showed up.'

But if *he* intimidated Monty, then *he* terrified the life out of the Americans. 'You can feel this incredible life-force blasting out of Seve,' said Couples after his eight and seven annihilation of Woosnam. 'I met Muhammad Ali at an awards dinner one time and he gave off the same powerful aura. With Seve, you kinda get the feeling if you ran a Geiger counter over him the reading would go off the scale.'

THOUGH he was criticised by some in the final countdown to this contest - particularly for his clumsy cameo role in the highly embarrassing Miguel Angel Martin shenanigans - the passion Ballesteros brought inspired everyone around him.

At Kiawah Island, Nick Faldo studiously ignored Dave Gilford, then a trembling rookie, during every step of their seven and six mauling by Paul Azinger and O'Meara. Here at Valderrama, Faldo, Ballesteros's on-course aide-de-camp, coaxed Lee Westwood through his remarkably composed debut like a protective big brother. The one-time doggedly insular Faldo also made sure he had a quiet word with every team-mate before going out to confront Jim Furyk in the penultimate singles.

'It's like Oak Hill two years ago,' beamed Rocca, a crucial three and two victor over Woods and another man who feels comfortable wearing his heart on his sleeve. 'I win Ryder Cup but I win something more important - I win 12 friends for life. Everyone have same importance except Seve; he is the most important man on team. Maybe you do not see him hit a ball but in here [he points to his heart] I

think he hit every ball in every match. Every time I looked over he was there and if you ask rest of players I think they all tell you the same.'

Like Ballesteros, Rocca was born into relative poverty, taught himself to play while serving as a caddie, and views golf in romantic rather than epic images. 'In between holes,' he says softly, 'I talk to the angels.'

Normally the most charming, amusing and carefree of men, Rocca shares his captain's burning dislike of what he regards as American arrogance. (As one leading US writer put it on the 17th green yesterday after Langer, appropriately, had ensured Europe's continued possession of the trophy by beating Brad Faxon two and one: 'This will in no way affect our inherent superiority complex. These guys could lose the Ryder Cup 28-0 and they'd still think they were the 12 best players on the planet'.)

At The Belfry four years ago, the Americans dubbed the Italian 'Rocca the Choker' when they wrongly blamed Europe's defeat on his inability to beat Davis Love III despite leading by one hole with two to play. Yesterday they were calling him 'Il Rocca Gibraltar'.

From the moment he teed off with Olazabal in the opening fourball match on Friday morning until he sank the final putt against Woods in his singles, Rocca played without fear of failure. 'What I have to fear? Just as I no win the Ryder Cup by myself today, I no lose the Ryder Cup at The Belfry in '93. I love this. It is like nothing else in golf. For people like me and Seve to play in the Ryder Cup is a miracle.' A miracle indeed; the son of a quartz mine worker in Bergamo, the teenage Rocca used to climb over the wall of the local golf club late at night to hone his talents armed with a three-iron, a pocketful of balls and a torch.

Olazabal, too, seemed to thrive against Lee Janzen whenever Seve came into view to lend a word of encouragement; at times, Ballesteros, driving like Batman, appeared to overtake Olazabal's shots in mid-flight so determined was he to cheer the landing of his Spanish compatriot's ball on the green.

Sadly, the inspiration which had accompanied Olazabal throughout his duties with Rocca in the previous two days' fourballs and foursomes mysteriously deserted him when left to his own devices and he lost on the 18th green after being two ahead with three to play.

'No one can understand what it means to have Seve at your shoulder,' confirmed Janzen. 'Even when the European guys hit a bad shot, he seems able to *will* the ball down the middle of the fairway, around the bunker or into the hole. We've always thought Seve's a bit unnatural.'

And so, after being a Spanish captain on Spanish turf, Seve now wants only to play when Europe defend the trophy in Brookline, Massachusetts, in 1999. That depends on his being able to shake off the chronic back injury which has wreaked havoc on his career in recent seasons.

'Please do not ask me about sore back,' he pleaded with one interviewer at Valderrama. 'I wasn't going to mention your bad back,' came the retort. 'Good,' sayeth Seve, 'I don't know why, but every time someone ask me to talk about sore back it give me sore head.'

To Per-Ulrik Johansson, Rocca, Langer, Bjorn and Montgomerie - who scored the ultimately triumphal half-point against Scott Hoch - went the glory on the last afternoon; but nobody contributed more than Seve. Nobody... ★ **29/09/97**

THE CLASP OF TRIUMPH. LEE WESTWOOD AND NICK FALDO JOIN HANDS TO SALUTE EUROPE'S
VICTORY IN THE RYDER CUP AFP

END COLUMN

SPORT AROUND THE WORLD: For 20 years Earl Woods had been hoping to hear from his great friend Col Tiger Phong, the South Vietnamese soldier after whom he named his son, the golfer Tiger Woods. It was only after undercover work in Vietnam by an American journalist that it was discovered Phong, whom Woods Snr met while on two tours of duty with the Green Berets and named Tiger for his bravery in battle, had starved to death in 1976 in a communist "re-education" camp. "Earl cried for a couple of days after he learnt that Phong had died," said Tom Callaghan, the journalist. "He said it was like losing a relative, and that Tiger was his shoulder to cry on."

CRICKET DIARY: Steve Waugh, a keen collector of cricketana, found himself outbid in a Melbourne auction room. Waugh had hoped that his wife's telephoned bid of £4,000 would secure the cap worn by Victor Trumper on the 1902 tour of England. But interest was so keen that the cap fetched a staggering £15,000. The same amount was paid for Trumper's diary of the same tour by British collector and bookseller John McKenzie.

FOOTBALL DIARY: Ever wondered what really happens on those end-of-season tours when players let down their hair and provide copious copy for the tabloids during their silly season? Well, Leeds United obviously have complete faith in their players because they have come up with an innovative prize for the winner of a fantasy football competition in the club programme: a trip for two with the team. "You do what the players do," says the blurb, "you go where the players go." Second prize? You have to go back next year.

LETTERS TO THE SPORTS EDITOR: SIR - Something urgently needs to be done about the ridiculous annual ritual of playing the final of the NatWest Trophy in one day in September. The likelihood of this important match being decided on the toss of a coin is grossly unfair to the players. Furthermore, I, for one, will never again pay £47 to see a "showpiece" match decided in this unsatisfactory manner. - A N WILSON, Hadley Wood, Herts.

SPORT AROUND THE WORLD: An artist claims to have been tortured and has gone on a hunger strike in Cairo, because of a mascot for the under-17 football World Cup. Mohammed Abdel-Aziz Taeeb, 28, says he drew a cartoon of Tutankhamen kicking a ball as a mascot for the tournament. He claims the image was stolen and sold on to an advertising company who made £170,000, while offering him £4,000 in compensation. Taeeb says: "I will either die or get my rights." After his first complaint he was picked up by police, stripped to his underwear, beaten and forced to sign a document transferring his rights to the advertising firm's owner.

FOOTBALL DIARY: Jessica Rizzo, Italy's most popular film star, is to sponsor Montecatini's women's football team to promote her pay-per-view adult channel. Clea Giannecchini, one of Montecatini's strikers, says: "We've had a laugh about it, it's nothing vulgar. Maybe it will offend opponents and the public, but we're not scared of gossip." However, Natalina Levati, the president of women's football in Italy, is not so broad-minded. "We don't want to go back 30 years to when spectators came just to watch the girls' legs," she said. "Over the years, we've achieved some dignity by offering sport for sport's sake. This type of sponsorship goes against what we've been working for."

DAY BY DAY REVIEW

1: Manchester United recover from going a goal down after 24 seconds to beat Juventus 3-2 in their Champions' League match, while Newcastle fight back from 2-0 behind to draw at Dynamo Kiev

2: Chelsea complete their comprehensive aggregate win over Slovan Bratislava in the first round of the European Cup-Winners' Cup; Steve Collins announces his retirement from boxing after the WBO refuse to recognise him as their super-middleweight champion; The first female amateur boxing bout to be held in Britain, between 13-year-olds Emma Brammer and Andrea Prime in Stoke, is cancelled when Brammer's parents bow to 'media pressure'

4: Lennox Lewis needs just 95 seconds to stop Andrzej Golota and retain his WBC heavyweight time in Atlantic City

5: Peintre Celebre, partnered by Olivier Peslier, wins the Prix de l'Arc de Triomphe by five lengths in a record time; Greg Rusedski beats Mark Philippoussis in straight sets to win the Swiss indoor title in Basle

8: Lord Archer, the former deputy chairman of the Conservative party, is elected president of the World Professional Billiards and Snooker Association; Ashar Mahmood and Mushtaq Ahmed equal the world record for a last-wicket stand in Test cricket by putting on 151 for Pakistan against South Africa in Rawalpindi, Mahmood's unbeaten 128 making him only the second Pakistani to score a century on his debut

9: John Merricks, who with Ian Walker won an Olympic silver yachting medal in 1996, dies in a road accident aged 26

11: England qualify for the 1998 World Cup finals by holding Italy to a 0-0 draw in Rome, and gaining the point required in a match marred by fighting involving Italian police and England supporters; Scotland also qualify automatically as the best second-placed country, while the Republic of Ireland must play off; Greg Rusedski beats Tim Henman 6-4, 6-4 in the semi-final of the Austrian indoor championships; Chris Eubank's is beaten for the vacant WBO super-middleweight title by Joe Calzaghe at the Sheffield Arena, where Nassem Hamed stops Jose Badillo to retain his WBO featherweight crown, and undercard boxer Carl Wright requires neurosurgery after his fight

12: Some good, balking teamwork by Eddie Irvine holds up Jacques Villeneuve and smoothes Michael Schumacher's path to victory in the Japanese Grand Prix at Suzuka, though Villeneuve may have damaged his own hopes by ignoring a yellow flag in practice, being suspended and only driving in the race pending an appeal; Vijay Singh wins the World Matchplay Golf Championship at Wentworth, beating Ernie Els by one hole in the final; Greg Rusedski loses to Goran Ivanisevic in the final of the Austrian indoor championships

14: The British Athletic Federation announce that they have called in a Birmingham insolvency firm after identifying a deficit of £530,000 coupled with monthly running costs of £130,000; Ipswich knock weakened Manchester United out of the Coca-Cola Cup,.

19: South Africa beat Sweden to win golf's Dunhill Cup at St Andrews

21: Liverpool suffer a disastrous night in France where they are beaten 3-0 in the UEFA Cup by Strasbourg, while Aston Villa do better by holding Athletic Bilbao in Spain; Paul Cayard, on his debut in the Whitbread Round the World yacht race, steers EF Language into Cape Town to win the first stage.

22: Manchester United maintain their 100 per cent record in the Champions' League by beating Feyenoord 2-1 at Old Trafford, while Newcastle go down 1-0 at PSV Eindhoven; The United States name Ben Crenshaw as successor to Tom Kite as Ryder Cup captain

23: Chelsea are beaten 3-2 by Tromso in a European Cup-Winners' Cup tie reduced to farce by a blinding snowstorm which hit the Norwegian town 350 miles inside the Arctic Circle

24: Phil Tufnell is fined £1,250 by the England and Wales Cricket Board for failing to take a random drugs test, though an 18-month ban from the game was suspended providing he undertakes further testing

26: Jacques Villeneuve lands the world drivers' title, his third place in the European GP in Jerez enough when Michael Schumacher spins off after a controversial collision with Villeneuve, Mikka Hakkinen winning the race

28: Walter Smith confirms he is to stand down as Rangers manager at the end of the season; Michael Schumacher fails to convince when he claims he made a mistake at the European Grand Prix, denying he attempted to ram Jacques Villeneuve

29: Lawrence Dallaglio is announced as the England rugby union captain; The Republic of Ireland are held 1-1 in Dublin by Belgium in the first leg of their World Cup play-off

EUBANK TACKLES AGENT PROVOCATEUR ON THE FLOOR AT CAMBRIDGE UNION'S CHAMBER OF HORRORS

by GILES SMITH

TO the debating chamber of the Cambridge Union - for some, a training ground for the nation's future political big shots, a white-hot workshop in which the country's very future is forged; for others, a place where students go to take themselves too seriously and pretend to be 50 before their time. For most, a subtle blend of the two.

Tonight the motion is: 'This house believes that in modern sport it's the money, not the taking part, that counts.' And here, among the guest speakers in the leather seats, are some people who should know. Like Eric Hall, shy, retiring East End boy, forced reluctantly into multi-media self-promotion and the wearing of deafening clothes by a small problem with his licence, which has recently prevented him from trading as a football agent. Eric will be speaking on behalf of the motion and, by implication, on behalf of money.

So, too, will Gareth Rees, a Canadian rugby union player who plays for Wasps, and can thus speak from a position of some authority within a sport which has taken to professionalism like a duck to a motorway. Rees will provide the evening's most measured speech - an admission of the reality of the motion from a position of reluctance - though, to be frank, the truth and clarity of his words will be significantly overshadowed by the less formal contributions of his fellow speakers.

And denying this gross slur upon the Olympian purity of sporting motivation, who else but John Fashanu, aka Fash the Bash, aka Fash the Cash, who, as was demonstrated to everyone's total satisfaction recently in a court of law, has never in his life been paid to influence the outcome of a football match. (Even by his own manager, some rueful Aston Villa fans might add.)

Fashanu's partner in opposition? Chris Eubank: boxer, philosopher, actor, monocle-wearer, truck driver, person who lives in Brighton - his talents expand to surround us. Chris is, as someone observes, 'fresh from his latest bout' - a punch-up with Naseem Hamed in the lounge at Heathrow Airport during which Eubank may or may not have sent one of Hamed's trophy belts skidding across the polished floor.

What a dramatic and unconventional encounter that must have been, and yet one which somehow brought the words 'stunt' and 'publicity' to mind. (What was Hamed doing wearing one of those bulky championship belts at Heathrow? Does he really find them comfortable enough to slip into for flights? And if so, is he obliged to leave them in that plastic dish in order to pass through the metal scanner? Questions, questions.)

The guests enter in a flurry of pricey clothes through the main door and head up the carpet, Hall at some speed, Eubank very slowly, draped in caramel-coloured linen, swishing his cane and looking up at the balconies with mild curiosity. It's as well for the level playing field of the debate - and particularly for the integrity of those in opposition - that none of them are on a fee tonight. Just expenses, dinner, and a hotel if they need one.

The debate is led off by Tom Dixon, a graduate student with some form in this area - billed, indeed, as a 'World Championship Debater'. 'Have you got an agent?' Eric Hall is moved to ask him at one point, and understandably. (Dixon replies: 'An agent? I haven't even got any friends.')

A hand is raised on the opposite bench. 'Can I ask a question?' says Chris Eubank. 'Am I against the motion?' This, it is pointed out, is roughly the idea. But Eubank - even though it isn't officially his turn to speak - thinks we should be clear from the beginning what his approach is and he stands to say: 'I will be neither for nor against. I will understand.' Then, to great applause, he calls for a double espresso with cream and four sugars and sits down.

Now Eric Hall is at the dispatch box. He is wearing a mustard-yellow jacket and the pink of his tie so very nearly matches the pink of his shirt. His eight-inch cigar is unlit. 'I tried to get Fash to fix me a match,' Hall says, by way of an opening, 'but he couldn't manage it.'

It's not immediately clear how hard Hall has been preparing for this debate on the train up from London. He goes for a largely free-form approach, but he is in a good position to do so, having a big bag of old chestnuts to dip into when silence threatens. 'My clients take 80 per cent of my earnings,' he points out for roughly the 400th time in living memory. Then he boldly contradicts The Beatles - invariably a risky tactic. 'Money can buy you love,' he says. 'The only thing money can't buy you is poverty.'

> *'MONEY CAN BUY YOU LOVE. THE ONLY THING MONEY CAN'T BUY YOU IS POVERTY'*

THESE gems do at least relate to the subject under scrutiny. Others don't. 'I nearly married a girl once,' Eric says, apropos of nothing at all. 'She had everything a man could want. A hairy chest, a low voice and a beard.'

But Eric is warming to his theme and he begins to walk about a bit. He says he's glad to see footballers earning big money. In the past it was only the chairmen who banked the cash - and you don't go to football to watch the chairman. Except, possibly, at Chelsea. 'I'm a Tory and I love the Tory party,' Eric says, finishing with a flourish. 'I propose, don't knock money. Don't be a communist. Applaud the people who make money, because they're winners and I love a winner.'

Now Fashanu stands up, in a brown and cream striped jacket and a black roll-neck. He is confident and passionate and a big user of his arms - as those who played against him may have cause to recall. No way was he ever motivated by anything as base as money, says the presenter of *Gladiators*, a programme in which body builders knock each other about with rubber truncheons. Monaco, Newcastle United, Manchester United - they had all come in for Fash, but he had stayed at Wimbledon. 'I loved the supporters - and I knew every one of them personally. I loved the buzz as we were going into the showers and fighting and messing about. I would have played for Wimbledon for nothing,' Fashanu says, slamming his finger repeatedly on the dispatch box.

But, of course, he never had to. In his last season at the club - before his contract ran out and he was sold to Aston Villa - he was on £80 per week basic. Which doesn't sound like much, until you learn that he got £10,000 every time he played. And another £2,000 if he scored. And £5,000 if he scored twice. (Someone will point out later that it should really have been the other way around: £2,000 for playing, £10,000 for scoring. But, hey, that's football.)

Now Gareth Rees stands up. Rees has a little niggle at Fashanu. He reckons Fash would have gone to Monaco, or Newcastle or Manchester if the money had been right. Then he moves on to lament the entry of the word 'product' into sport. People nod. They see the sense. ★ **25/10/97**

BATTY THRIVES ON CENTRE-STAGE AS ENGLAND HARNESS BRAIN AND BRAWN

by **HENRY WINTER** in Rome

WHEN a frustrated Gianfranco Zola is observed fouling David Batty then life's normal order must be re-assessed. When England are seen time-wasting and counter-attacking cannily against Italy then football's world really has been turned upside down. England, with Batty a picture of composure, did to Italy what Zola and his forefathers have been doing to others for years.

England's Roman stalemate, a result that sends Batty and Co to France and Italy into the play-offs, does not quite herald a complete reversal in fortunes. Serie A remains a more cerebral league than the Premiership. Italy, with a more distinguished history than England's, will doubtless qualify for the World Cup finals and be installed among the favourites. What Saturday showed was that England are maturing rapidly as an international force.

The Three Lions have changed. Their elevated thought patterns, and their willingness to accept tactical alterations, have lifted them to their present prominence while never compromising the age-old English virtue of commitment. Brain and brawn now combine well.

Such have been England's recent strides, that it was no surprise that the night's most significant performers, Batty and Tony Adams, used to be known as archetypal English bulldog professionals, adherents to the philosophy of muscle over mind. But Batty was calm throughout, ignoring the rough challenges, which began early from Demetrio Albertini, who is really too good a player to stoop to leaving his foot in. If Italy's midfield were looking for mental vulnerabilities, for signs of short-fuses, they picked the wrong opponents. Batty would have taken longer to wind up than Big Ben. 'Batty has been magnificent for 12 months,' Hoddle reflected. 'He's not put a foot wrong. He's not flamboyant. He wins possession and very rarely gives the ball away. We've worked on him, telling him that when he has won the ball to play forward first. He's doing that much better now and he's getting balls into Teddy [Sheringham] and the midfield players.'

It stands as a particular tribute to the Newcastle player that England's midfield was not over-run on the two occasions Ince disappeared for stitches in his cut head. Batty's assuredness under pressure, his refusal to waste possession, was shared by England's well-balanced central-midfield triangle, also including the excellent Pauls, Ince and Gascoigne. 'England are a very good team, especially in the middle,' said Italy's Cesare Maldini, his face as drawn as the match. 'They have players in there with strong characters.'

Even the terrace disturbances, with riot police engaging visiting fans in skirmishing throughout the first half, failed to divert England's completely focused attention. Batty was pushed as man of the match by Adams. The Arsenal centre-half, who does not need an armband to lead, organised his defence impressively, despite the (admittedly lop-sided) deployment of a three-man attack against England. Despite the concentration of activity around him, Adams kept reading the game with near-perfect vision.

TWO first-half challenges on the disappointing Filippo Inzaghi and the more dangerous Christian Vieri provided ample testament to Adams's influence. After the break, he proved important in the air, particularly against Vieri.

Adams's more thoughtful mood was encapsulated by events after the final whistle. He stood on the pitch, chatting with the coach Glenn Roeder. All around Adams, his team-mates were jumping into each others' arms and punching the air in front of the crowd. Eventually, Adams jogged over to where the England Travel Club were corralled and gave a simple thumbs-up. Gone was the excess of yesteryear. But the intensity of commitment remains.

Composure, allied to well-channelled commitment, had been the key for England, who kept their shape and discipline. Italy did not - as six cautions and Angelo di Livio's dismissal indicated. 'We were very professional, very intelligent and very controlled,' said Glenn Hoddle, England's coach. 'We needed 1), a strong referee which we got and 2), to keep 11 players on the pitch. It was always going to be that sort of game.'

Chances were few and far between. England enjoyed the better ones. Ince fired powerfully at Angelo Peruzzi. David Beckham, after a good one-two with Sheringham, shot over. Yet England remained indebted to David Seaman, who negated a brief flurry of danger from Enrico Chiesa. The match climaxed in heart-stoppage time. Beckham missed the target. Then Ian Wright hit the post and Sheringham failed from the follow-up.

It was surely over... but there was more. Vieri rose to head at Seaman, and for a split second a stadium stood transfixed, aware of the fine line between success and failure. When the ball flashed wide, both sides knew that the last throw of the dice had been made.

For Hoddle, described in the programme as 'a young technician with a great personality', the final whistle provided a moment of supreme satisfaction. When he followed Terry Venables after Euro 96, he had to live with increased expectations but with no time to prepare for a World Cup qualification programme. He has learnt well on the hoof.

'As a coach, you get a massive pat on the back or a massive knife in the back.' The back-patting may have begun but Hoddle is too determined an individual to rest on his laurels. ★13/10/97

England's Braveheart. The bandaged Paul Ince slides in to dispossess Italy's Angelo Di Livio. Russell Cheyne.

MONTGOMERIE & CO
TEMPTED TO GIVE UP
ROUGH FOR THE SMOOTH

by **MARTIN JOHNSON**

AS Greg Turner strolled down the 18th fairway, the sun was glinting off the orange trees, the mediaeval clubhouse was silhouetted against the backcloth of the 10th century town of Jerez, and the air of tranquillity was disturbed only by a gaggle of geese flapping across the lake. 'So how do you like Montecastillo, then Greg?' His native New Zealand is not short of aesthetically pleasing vistas such as this, and Turner cast an expert eye around him - in much the same way as Arthur Negus used to examine a piece of antique pottery - before delivering his verdict. 'No question about it,' he said. 'It's a tip.'

Turner none the less conceded that Montecastillo was an appropriate venue for the European Tour's showcase event - 'we play on tips most weeks, so the place is at least representative' - before adding that the only reason the golfers' end-of-term beano was being held here was the Formula One race track next door.

'The Volvo clients can get to race around the circuit, and then come and watch us play golf. But I've got a better idea for next year. They can drive their Volvos around the golf course, and we'll go and play on the race track.'

As ever with a professional golfer (and Turner is certainly not one of the tour's prima donnas), everything boils down to the course. Too much sand in the bunkers, not enough sand in the bunkers. Greens too fast, greens too slow. Too much rough, not enough rough. When it comes to moaning, bitching and griping, these boys are off a minimum handicap of plus four.

However, all too often on the European Tour they have a point. When they staged the British Masters at Collingtree last year, the greens were green all right, not so much because they had been treated with Fison's, as in fertiliser, but Dulux, as in paint. The fertiliser is mostly reserved for hitting the fan, as it did at the Swiss Open in Crans sur Sierre, where the greens were rougher than the spectators' parking lot.

That is not so much the case here, for the simple reason that there are hardly any spectators. Neil Armstrong had more of a gallery when he played his seven iron, or whatever it was, on the moon, and even Sky TV, not normally shy of tub-thumping their own broadcasts, cannot be finding it that easy when their cameras are honing in on big-name golfers being accompanied by a scorer, a bunker raker, and a goat.

On Thursday morning, free admission notwithstanding, half a dozen spectators were gathered around the first tee, where a man in a blazer was introducing the players. 'En el tee del uno, de Escocia, Sam Torrance!' Sam sunk his peg into the turf, and in acknowledgment of the deafening silence, doffed his visor and said (taking an irony off the tee, so to speak): 'Thank you very much.' Turner said yesterday: 'I've just played a round in southern Spain, in lovely sunshine, with Seve Ballesteros. A national hero. And we had more marshals with us than spectators.'

Meantime, across the Atlantic in Houston, the American equivalent of this tournament is being played on the usual lagoon-dotted billiard table, with a million dollars between 30 players, and attended by crowds of 60,000 per day. Which is why, next season, many Europeans will be trading in the polite ripple they occasionally get for a crushed two-iron to six inches from the hole, to the ghastly prospect of a whoop, holler, and a 'you're the man' for a routine wedge shot into a contoured dartboard.

Nothing gets up Colin Montgomerie's nose quite as much as being introduced to American audiences as 'Coalin Mantgameree', but once this tournament is over Monty will announce that this is the price he is prepared to pay in search of better playing conditions.

It is also rumoured that most of the Swedes will be heading for the US Tour as well, and while this will hardly make much of a dent in the European Tour's charisma quotient, protracted absences from the likes of Montgomerie (along with Nick Faldo and Jesper Parnevik) are hardly calculated to have the sponsors falling over each other to get their name attached to the Moroccan Open or the German Masters.

IT was a little unfair of one of the players' managers to compare Montecastillo to a 'football pitch', but the analogy is appropriate in terms of the European Tour scoring a series of own goals with many of its venues. Several boffins from the tour's expanding agronomy department were dispatched here, but it was a bit too late to pluck a manicured masterpiece from a course currently in receivership, a greenkeeping staff of six (if you include those whose duties do not extend beyond tending the flower beds) and equipment not too far advanced from garden shears.

Turner, for one, is not surprised that so many European Tour players are about to defect. 'If a young guy has aspirations to become a world-class golfer, then this tour as it stands at the moment is no more than a stepping-stone. To an extent it's the players' fault, because they've been only too happy to go along with the tour's short-term solution for keeping us sweet - throw more money at us.

'We play for big money now, and the tour has done an excellent job in that area, but a continuing problem is the standard of courses we play. With a few exceptions, it's pretty desperate. I realise we often sound like whingeing prima donnas, and let's face it, there are a lot of worse ways to earn a good living, but when you're in your early 20s, it's as much to do with romance as money.

'You dream of being the best in the world, and playing in front of large, enthusiastic galleries. Then you end up playing in terrible conditions in front of a man and two dogs. It's depressing. I don't really understand it, because most of our tournaments are sponsored by blue-chip companies, like Volvo and BMW, whose whole marketing strategy is built on excellence and quality. But they then hold their events on rubbish tips. This place, for instance, is in disrepair. There's a tour rule allowing us to move stones out of bunkers, but I had to get clarification about whether that included boulders as well.'

MANY European courses are not a stern enough test for players of this quality, and Montgomerie's attempt to win this event has been handicapped by the fact that, unless you've had a hard night on the sangria, it is pretty hard to miss a fairway. As one of the straightest hitters in the world, Monty's ideal fairway is not quite as wide as Ian Woosnam's, but at Montecastillo you can get away with driving like Michael Schumacher did just across the road here last weekend.

Monty's defection (although he will probably still play as many European events as, say, Woosnam does) will hit the tour hard, not least the golfing media. His eyes misted over the other day when one of the writers told him how much he would be missed, which is certainly true, if as much for his quotability as his golf. Whether he is hitting a golf ball or inside a press tent, Monty performs almost exclusively by instinct. He does not practise much because he does not really understand the mechanics of an entirely natural swing. Likewise, he rarely visits the practice ground when it involves saying what is on his mind. And his mind, currently, is on America. It will surprise many that there is so much discontent in the ranks over such an agreeable way of life, but it is difficult to understate the insular, hermetically sealed world of the professional golfer.

When half the Middle East was on fire during the Gulf War, the burning question among this lot was not 'is this the start of World War III?' but 'will they have to cancel the Dubai Desert Classic?'

They have people to drive them around, people to carry their bags, people to smooth out their bunkers, and people to replace their divots. Pro golfers react to a delayed courtesy car like babies being parted from a mother's breast. They even lose the ability to make unilateral decisions about the weather.

Hence, when Padraig Harrington was playing with Montgomerie in the first round, he threw up a bit of grass and discovered that the wind was coming slightly from the left. 'Slightly from the left?' he asked his caddie, and his caddie solemnly reassured him that it was.

When a golfer makes a decision on his own, be it whether to take a fiveiron, go to America, or what to have for dinner, it is an even bigger event than the Volvo Masters. ★
01/11/97

Bernhard Langer splashes out of a bunker during the Volvo Masters at Montecastillo Popperfoto Reuters

A QUEST FOR EQUESTRIAN
GOLD IS GUNNELL'S NEXT
OLYMPIC HURDLE

by LUCINDA GREEN

UNTIL a dismal injury-stricken Atlanta put an end to Sally Gunnell's hopes of a second gold medal in the lung-busting 400 metres hurdles, the nearest she had ever been to a horse was sharing a stubborn old family pony on her father's 300-acre Essex farm.

Now, following her retirement, she intends to replace some of the buzz with learning to ride. She even has long-term ambitions to own a horse which competes in the 2004 Olympic Games.

My inspiration to event was the mutual love and trust my horse and I shared, along with the thrill of flying through the air over those impossible fences. For Gunnell, 31, the only woman in track history to have held all four titles at once - European, world, Commonwealth and Olympic - the inspiration to run was different.

'It was something I was good at. I was never particularly good academically and I found that I could win races both at school and at home when my friends and I raced across the hay bales. By the time I got to about 11 I realised I was better than average and it was becoming embarrassing and I tried not to win by too much.' It was a further 10 years, however, before she believed she could 'go all the way'.

At 14 she was talent-spotted at her local athletics club by Bruce Longden, who trained her for the rest of her 16-year career. 'Sally's father Les used to bring her up to training sessions at Crystal Palace,' remembers Longden. 'The others used to call her stick insect or grasshopper.' Gunnell could always hurdle. Despite her forte being jumping and physical strength rather than speed, she did not enjoy the high jump nor the throwing aspect of the heptathlon.

At 18 she took a job for two years as a nanny. 'And blew up. I suppose I just ate the children's left-overs and I got to 10 stone when my race weight was eight stone 12 pounds.' (She is 5ft 5 1/2 in and size 8-10.) Nevertheless, at 19 she went on an under-23 tour of Australia and there her future husband, Jonathan Bigg, fell out of a cupboard.

The sleeping arrangements on the trip were organised with the strictest discriminatory rules. Bigg, however, had been the only one to leave his window open during the day and his room was filled with mosquitoes. He thought he would find more peace sleeping on Gunnell's floor. A knock on her door in the morning resulted in Bigg leaping for cover into the cupboard. 'It was all completely innocent,' insisted Gunnell, 'and if you knew Jon, you'd know it was the most unlikely thing for him to do anyway.'

That was the beginning of Sally Gunnell finding the other part of herself. Jon Bigg has been her inner strength, her guide for 12 years and it seems abundantly clear that his wife would not be Britain's most celebrated female athlete if it were not for him.

An 800m athlete himself till a spike tear to his Achilles tendon finished his career, Bigg understood what it took. He trained every year with Gunnell six days a week starting in mid-October following a six-week break. They pursued a punishing nine months' build-up to her peak summer fitness, an annual routine which makes racehorses' look fairly tame. It began with a month of daily 20-minute runs and gym work and continued through a two-month slog of 'reps' (repetition).

A further two months of indoor racing continued until March to ease the boredom. Then another hard slog bringing in speed work and hurdles. 'In May I started racing and for me my eighth race was my peak. The last two weeks before that I would just do speed work, and suddenly I would turn and find I had another gear.'

Apart from a weekly session in Crystal Palace with Longden, training took place in the park and on the track near her home in Brighton. The 1992 Barcelona gold bought an investment in a black-timbered house set in open country half a mile from the foot of the sharply rising, beautiful South Downs.

In 1995, the year before Atlanta, Gunnell suffered her first significant injury. No athlete that she could recall had ever survived so many years at top level without injury.

In Atlanta the other Achilles went. As so often happens with horses as well as people, the good leg, the recipient of increased strain, then succumbs too. On the way back from America Gunnell vowed to learn to ride - 'I wanted to do something dangerous and I wanted to support Jon.'

HE HAD ridden for four years and started competing recently, finding it replaced the adrenalin fix of athletics. 'But I found the muscles used in riding were so different that I started getting stiff running and it is only now that I have retired that I can start to concentrate on it. It's not a million miles from running, you know, except that something else is in charge underneath you. I went out for my first ride alone last week - what a buzz.'

Both of them learn at Chris Ellis's stable near Worthing, and so intrigued have they become by the horse world, and how maybe their own experiences in training can in some way help, that they have bought into some impressive young show jumpers with Ellis. They hope to build a string of six, sharing their costs with Ellis, thus enabling him to keep and ride his most talented horses himself. Two he has sold on have already made the Olympic team. This adventure will be a consuming hobby and surprisingly is something Bigg might need more than Gunnell. He is going to miss the nurturing of his wife and her fitness almost more than Gunnell is her career. ★ **20/10/97**

End of the line. Michael Schumacher watches disconsolately as Jaques Villenueve races away to win the Formula One drivers' title in the last grand prix of the season at Jerez EMPICS.

UNLIKELY STAGE FOR VILLENEUVE TRIUMPH

by **SIMON HUGHES**

THE paddock has been awash throughout this final race weekend with fanciful conspiracy theories and collusion rumours surrounding the destination of the championship. Some were so far-fetched Steven Spielberg couldn't have dreamt them up. The Ferrari *tifosi's* script, on a banner unfurled over a wall, told a more likely tale: *'Il secno di un domino rosso'* - 'This race is under red control'. Wrong. With the two McLaren drivers and Jacques Villeneuve finishing on the podium, the appropriate title would have been 'Three Colours Blue'.

The fantasists were, however, right to predict an afternoon of high drama, periodically stirring various German and French commentators in the press room to hysterical yelling and brandishing of fists. It is not often that an over-hyped event actually delivers more twists and turns than anticipated. This one did, careering between sport and theatre for 90 enthralling minutes, and continuing in the same vein afterwards when the stewards declared that Michael Schumacher's attempt to barge Villeneuve off the track was 'a racing incident'. 'Fairground incident' would have been more accurate. Amid all this, Gerhard Berger's Formula One farewell after a 13-year, 210-race career was utterly eclipsed.

Surrounded on the grid at the start by hordes of cameramen and Prada-clad Italian dignitaries, Schumacher gave his car a final optimistic glance before climbing into the cockpit. The Ferrari racing director, Jean Todt, nodded sagely to his master driver while a technician stuck what looked like Sellotape over the bonnet hinges and tightened a couple of screws. What he should also have done was to attach a six-inch spike to the right wing, a weapon to puncture Villeneuve's hopes in the collision they would inevitably have.

Schumacher's dastardly manoeuvre back-fired, and humiliatingly he was transported back to the pits riding pillion on the back of a moped. His car was winched out of the gravel, but having battled for two years to come to terms with outgoing designer John Barnard's chassis, Schumacher would have happily left it where it was. The scrap metal merchants will be popping in today.

So the hoarse *tifosi* trudged away to drown their sorrows goodness knows where (Jerez is hardly a throbbing entertainment zone), and the big moment for their last world champion, Jody Scheckter - presenting the title to Schumacher - was put on hold for another year. Standing forlornly beside the Ferrari motorhome, having attended his first grand prix for 10 years, he reflected on how the sport had changed since his triumphant day in 1979. 'Less girls, more technology,' he said dejectedly.

Much of it British technology, too. Making off with the spoils at the start and finish of the championship, McLaren gave the season a neat symmetry, and look a genuine force for next year, especially now that Mika Hakkinen has at last broken his duck. Realistically though, it has always been a two-horse race. Well, four-horse to be strictly accurate. Villeneuve could not have won 10 pole positions and his first championship without Frank Williams' shrewd racing brain and the peerless facilities he has assimilated. Meanwhile the nobbly, teacake-faced Frenchman Todt aligned the disorderly Ferrari forces behind Schumacher's expertise and total discipline - until yesterday. In motor racing, you get what you pay for, and the two richest teams - both with budgets around £70 million - were hardest to beat.

But how different the two leading drivers are. On a nightclub dance floor after his first win of the year in Brazil, Villeneuve looked, with his round glasses and his shirt hanging out and his woosy smile, like a geography student who had just passed his finals. He was in his element, talking animatedly to anyone who approached, male or female. Reacting against the austerity of Williams, he dyed his hair blond, went roller-blading and late in the season, returned to Canada to patch up an ailing relationship rather than spend more time testing at Silverstone. He need not have worried: everyone loves a flawed hero.

You would be as likely to find Schumacher at a nightclub as Paul Gascoigne in a public library. Instead, he takes his extended family everywhere, including his three dogs on this occasion (one hotel guest apparently complained about the barking) and often actually shares a room with his brother, Ralf. Occasionally he interrupts his routine to visit the Sultan of Brunei, owner of Asprey, one of his sponsors, but is rarely deflected from a rigorous training programme. His body is built for speed, even down to his sharp, aerodynamic jaw. Rarely betraying any emotion, never perspiring (a unique feature of both Schumachers, despite serious heat in the cockpit) he is man metamorphosing into machine.

WHAT a travesty, then, that two such expensively assembled, finely honed teams should have been contesting the title on such a sandy, dust-strewn track in such a ramshackle town. Jerez is inaccessible, the monasterial hotels and sherry houses of which make it more suitable to host the world bridge championships than a fiesta for petrol-heads. With its tuppeny-ha'penny airport, its unkempt harbour and scraggy hinterland, it represents the equivalent of France staging the World Cup final at Le Touquet.

There is another irony, too, in this lavish technological world. The competition between multi-million pound cars has been settled by the correct choice of a few £300 lumps of rubber. On a wet Monaco day in May, Williams opted for the wrong tyres and Ferrari stole the championship lead. Teams closely guard their tyre preferences, with decoy sets often piled outside individual garages to deceive unwary snoopers. Ferrari played cat and mouse in this way on Saturday, appearing to struggle with hard tyres during practice, then suddenly sneaking up on the grid during qualifying on softer ones (for the race, teams must stick with the same type of tyres they ran in qualifying).

Yesterday, Villeneuve blamed his poor start to the race on beginning with used tyres, then attributed regaining the lead in the 47th lap to a poor third set of tyres on Schumacher's Ferrari. It is a baffling subject, complicated by stringent regulations and Goodyear, the vastly superior supplier, manufacturing 83 different compounds during the year.

Confused and confounded? Not, surely, as much as the Ferrari faithful, who arrive perennially in their thousands to hail a world champion, idolise a phenomenal driver and his mercurial team-mate but still cannot overtake the old Renault. Embarrassingly, 150,000 caps, one worn after the race by Eddie Irvine, and 200,000 shirts emblazoned with 'Michael Schumacher World Champion 1997' will have to be binned. Not only do the French build the most refined engines, they can show everyone else how to actually savour champagne, rather than just throw it around. ★ **27/10/97**

'BARKING' RUSSELL LAUGHS OFF WORRIES OF A MAD, MAD WORLD

The **MICHAEL PARKINSON** Interview with Jack Russell

I AM wise to the ways of wicketkeepers. I played with one who wore a balaclava and an overcoat on cold days and looked like a bank robber behind the stumps. There was another who strapped his box - a huge corrugated metal affair - outside of his trousers and another who used to fit hair clips into the toes of his boots with which to tap the stumps and dislodge the bail. I have known for a while they are not like the rest of us, but nothing prepared me for Jack Russell. There are two Jack Russells. One is arguably the best wicketkeeper in Britain and a fine and sensitive artist to boot. The other has subtitled his biography *Barking*, as in mad, and asks me, having read it, whether or not I think he is crackers.

I had breakfast with Jack, which is to say I had scrambled eggs, bacon, tomatoes and toast and he had Weetabix of such sogginess his plate looked like a farmyard puddle. It achieves this texture by being soaked in milk for precisely 12 minutes. This is how long he likes his cereals soaked and who is to argue? He will have the same for lunch and during the day eats a pack of Jaffa Cakes and one of wholemeal biscuits. If he feels like a meal in the evening it will be mashed potato mixed with plain rice with baked beans and brown sauce. During a tour of India he ate steak (cremated) and chips for 28 consecutive days and wonders if this is a record.

At his side while we ate was a holdall containing his wicketkeeping gloves and his famous white hat. They are never out of his sight. He has worn the hat in every first-class game since 1981. It looks its age. It is whiteish on the outside but if you look under the rim you can see it was once set on fire. This happened after it was placed in an oven when it was 13 years old. Don't ask why.

During the 1996 World Cup the authorities ordered Russell to wear the official hat. He refused and threatened to walk out of the tournament. The officials relented.

He lives in fear of losing his hat. The rest of us ought to be terrified of finding it. It is the sort of object to be approached by men wearing protective clothing and carrying flame-throwers .

When he opened the boot of his car he apologised for the absence of the tumble-drier which he normally carries around with him because he washes his own kit. By now the sight of a cricketer carrying cricket gear in one hand and a box of paints in the other seemed perfectly normal. We were at the Oval - Gloucestershire playing Surrey. I met up with my old friend Dickie Bird, who was umpiring. I told him I was writing an article about Jack Russell. 'Oh, he's not playing, is he?' asked Mr Bird, becoming agitated. 'He'll start jumping up and down and getting me going like he always does. He's a beauty that Jack Russell, a beauty. Much worse than me.' It takes one to know one.

Like Dickie Bird, Jack Russell has the sublime ability to be able to laugh at himself. He doesn't take himself seriously but he is very serious about the job he does. For all he makes fun of himself and his eccentric ways he also thinks deeply about the game of cricket. It is typical that the England and Wales Cricket Board wasted time searching for reasons to censor his book when a copy should have been sent to every committee member in every county so they might begin to understand what they have to do to produce better cricketers.

What Russell makes clear is the grinding monotony of the county season, the way the system blunts the competitive edge, numbs ambition, turns players into robots. As someone who on recent tours spent most of his time watching other people play, he was ideally placed to observe and comment upon the way touring parties are organised. He is not too impressed. His account of Raymond Illingworth's handling of the South Africa tour is a sad portrait of the generation gap at work. None the less it is a picnic compared with his description of what happened in Zimbabwe. He says: 'Some of the team decided they didn't like the place from the start. They didn't care for the country, underestimated the opposition. I couldn't understand them. I thought it was a fascinating adventure. When they complained about the hotels I told them they should have been on a tour of Pakistan when we slept in a biscuit factory and were eaten alive by mosquitoes.'

After the defeat by Mashonaland, Russell stood up at a team meeting and said he felt we weren't bowling with enough discipline and when we batted were being careless when there was a need for graft. His observations were ignored. As the tour progressed so the siege mentality increased to the point where players and management refused to go to the Christmas party thrown by the media. Jack Russell told them it was not the right decision. 'You can't blame the press if you're playing badly,' he said. Again he found himself in a minority.

He feels not enough attention is paid to preparing our cricketers psychologically for what is required on a tour. 'We have to get inside their heads much more than we do,' he said. Man-management skills are either lacking or non-existent.

HE has evidence of both, including the farcical approach to touring. When he was sent for as a replacement on our last tour to Australia he didn't have a visa. The TCCB told him there wouldn't be a problem. When he arrived in Australia there was no one to meet him to help through the red tape. After considerable delay with immigration officers he eventually reached the hotel, where the tour manager, MJK Smith, told him there was nothing to worry about.

Russell spent the next two days sitting in a visa office waiting to be called, wondering why Mr Smith and his Australian friends didn't do something about his predicament.

As he points out, had England been in urgent need of him at that time he would have been unable to play because he didn't have the necessary permit. No wonder the tour was a shambles and the Aussies treated us as a joke. They still do.

It is doubtful if Jack Russell will play against the Aussies this season. It could be his international career is over because we are unable to find an all-rounder. According to Russell the deeper significance of this is a tendency towards employing batsmen who can keep wicket rather than keepers who bat at seven. He sees the day arriving when the specialist keeper will be a relic.

HE THINKS HE MIGHT END UP A RECLUSE **LIKE GETTY OR HOWARD HUGHES.** SOMEHOW I DON'T THINK SO

Johannesburg, Jack received a message from John Paul Getty. It said: 'Thank you for enriching my life. That was one of the bravest and most dogged innings ever played.'

He thinks he might end up a recluse like Getty or Howard Hughes. Somehow I don't think so. There is so much to do and so little time. Apart from his ambitions in cricket, painting takes up more and more of his life. At present it is a toss-up if he is a cricketer who paints or vice versa. He wants to spend more time researching military history, he has ambition to become a jockey. Again, don't ask.

On the one hand it is possible to look at Russell's career as a cricketer and lament the circumstances which have made him as much a reluctant observer of the international game as a participant. On the other hand he has too much humour and talent in other fields to become a forlorn figure propping up the bar in his retirement.

He has the future taped, including his funeral. He has left instructions his hands are to be amputated, embalmed and on display at his art gallery in Chipping Sodbury. He wants his coffin placed on top of a British tank on the journey from home to church. When the coffin is taken into church it must be to the sound of Lee Marvin singing *Wanderin' Star*. On his tombstone the inscription: 'I used to wander through graveyards like you, hoping that one day I would be famous so that people would wonder who I was. Life is too short for you to be stood here. Thank you for your interest - off you go and do something beneficial before you end up like me'.

I should tell you - if you hadn't already guessed - Jack Russell has a twinkle in his eye. When he ran on to the field at the Oval he went straight to Dickie Bird and for a minute or two they were in animated conversation. I observed them from high in the press box and thought, not for ★ the first time, how cricket makes children of us all. ★ **17/05/97**

For a purist like Russell this is almost too terrible to contemplate. Imagine a game deprived of the skills of Alan Knott or Bob Taylor. Imagine how much would be missing from the joy of watching Warne bowl if behind the stumps stood a fielder with gloves on and not Ian Healy. 'I would love to have kept to Warne. The ultimate challenge,' said Russell.

He reckons he has another five years or more as a top-class player, then he would like to be in charge of Gloucestershire's cricket. He wants to be the director of cricket with complete control. 'I don't want committees. They are the dry rot of English cricket. They take up too much time, are not productive and are a platform for too many egos,' he says.

Hear, hear, but I doubt he will get his way, not unless he can persuade a platoon of his beloved commandos to occupy Lord's on behalf of those of us who believe. Lord MacLaurin notwithstanding, only armed insurrection will save the game.

Jack Russell's obsession with the military started at an early age. When he was 12 his mother returned from work to find her son wearing an army jacket covered in military badges, a camouflaged hat and carrying a kitbag containing a sleeping bag and a tin plate. He told her he was about to embark on a secret mission. Twenty years later he sustained his heroic partnership with Michael Atherton against the South Africans by recalling Rorke's Drift. He is obsessed by

the courage of men under fire and his painting of the Cockleshell Heroes hangs in the Imperial War Museum. He haunts the museum whenever he is in London and often sits in the reconstruction of the trenches from World War One battlefields just to imagine what it must have been like.

You get the feeling he wouldn't mind becoming a macho hunk. Instead he stands 5ft 8¼in high and weighs 9½ stone. There is an endearing account in the book of Jack trying to look mean and hard after being told by Atherton he didn't impose himself enough on the opposition. When Gloucestershire next played Lancashire, Russell decided to show his captain he could hang tough with the best of them. When he went out to bat he ignored their greetings with a stony stare. When Peter Martin tried to be genial, Jack threatened to deck him. It all went wrong when, during a staring match with Graham Lloyd, Jack decided to show his contempt by spitting. Being short of practice the spittle collided with the grill on his helmet and just dangled there. The Lancashire team collapsed in laughter to be joined after a moment by their hitherto aggressive protagonist.

THE fact is Jack Russell is tough without having to look the part. No one who has watched him play cricket can doubt he is made of the real stuff. After he and Atherton defied the South Africans in

ARCHER
IS RELISHING HIS BREAK

The **SUE MOTT**
Interview with **Lord Archer**

'Juan Antonio Samaranch today announced that snooker will be a fully recognised sport when London hosts the Olympic Games in 2012. He said that the opening ceremony would be performed jointly by the Prince of Wales and Jimmy White. White, the former snooker player, who renounced beer, biryanis, fags and gambling in 2005, said he was sensible of the honour and that he owed it all to one man. . .'

THAT man is upstairs. Quite a long way upstairs, as this is where he maintains his two-storey penthouse on the Albert Embankment. Battersea Power Station to port, the Houses of Parliament to starboard: a fine summation of his 57-year life to date, unless the Marshalsea debtors' prison should also hove into view through his panoramic windows.

It took some finding, this place. Partly because I had the address written wrongly and partly because his apartment block rises from a very anti-establishment South Bank jumble of crooked mews and dodgy-hinged garages. 'It must be that one,' said my taxi driver finally. 'I don't reckon Lord Jeffrey would live in a lock-up.'

Arthur Daly in ermine. There's a thought. But Lord Archer of Weston-super-Mare ('Jeffrey will be all right') is in the news for another reason. He has been anointed the new president of the World Professional Billiards and Snooker Association. It is a great move for the sport and an even greater one for him, since he declares himself a

> ## "I LOVE MY SPORT. I LOVE MY RUGBY, MY CRICKET, MY RUNNING, MY SNOOKER. AND I FEEL SORRY FOR PEOPLE WHO ONLY DO POLITICS"

'snooker nut' and once played a frame against Steve Davis in a charity match at the Dorchester. His breaks were 11, 9, 7, 3, 1, 1 and 1.

'I love snooker. I'm a nutter. It's an open-ended appointment and I will stay for as long as I've got something to offer. I think that might be for the rest of my life. I was playing yesterday at the Erith and Crayford Conservative Club and was soundly beaten by the club captain. I think, actually, humiliated would be a better word.'

Lord Archer, Jeffrey rather, talks in short, sharp, emphatic sentences, which could be due to his sore throat from auctioneering, Conservative Party politicking or the books he writes full of short, sharp, emphatic sentences. Anyway, you rarely miss the point.

'Now your greatest break is 32,' I said, proving the value of research. 'Would've been 39 if I hadn't gone in off a black,' he replied. I venture this is not very good. 'That's very cruel,' he declared mock-hotly, trying to impose a frown on that Cheshire Cat grin of his. 'You're obviously a very nasty press person. I think it's terrific. . . No, it isn't very good.' But then anyone can have a bad day. Even Stephen Hendry, first-round loser in the Grand Prix at Bournemouth.

So, at a time of life when many old ermined dears in the Lords are ready for the squelch of slippers and an ear-trumpet, Jeffrey is taking on the revivification of snooker with a three-pronged assault: ambassador, troubleshooter and irresistible sponsor-grabber. 'Lord Chadlington, Peter Gummer, runs one of the biggest advertising agencies in the country. His ankle's already been kicked.'

This will by no means preclude his other activities, which this morning have included a 70-minute cardiovascular weight-training workout in his basement gym, a 30-minute radio interview, heaven knows how many short, sharp sentences for the latest book ('I've never had writer's block') and his continuing campaign to be Mayor of London.

But surely the fulfilment of this last ambition would knock snooker and the rest on the head. He gives me a look of scathing pity. 'Frankly, it would be a pretty second-rate person who couldn't combine love of one's sport and doing a job. In fact, I would be critical of someone who did nothing else. I love my sport. I love my rugby, my cricket, my running, my snooker. And I feel sorry for people who only do politics,' he said, the former Member for Louth, who left the Commons when he faced bankruptcy in 1974.

He is then, I suggested, of the John Major/Tony Banks school that combines Parliament with a plastic seat at Chelsea. 'And the Tony Blair school,' he amended, never one not to walk through a fractionally open door. 'Big football fan of Newcastle isn't he? Anyway, be interesting to see how he reacts when I invite him to the final of the world snooker championship. Why not? I shall invite everyone. All three leaders.'

HERE we go. We may now confidently predict that for the first time in the history of the championship Nelson Mandela and Hilary Clinton will be invited to break up the monopoly of tight-permed white-haired old ladies, who usually make up the hushed Crucible crowd. 'Are you being rude about them?' cried Jeffrey, ever the knight in armour at full tilt. 'Those ladies are in love with Steve Davis. And Jimmy White, poor darling.' But surely he cannot be serious about bringing No 10 to Sheffield? 'Wait and see,' he said.

By now, few people would put anything past Jeffrey, who was described recently as 'a shameless tart' by Julia Langdon, of *The Guardian*, to his own intense delight. 'It was after my speech at the Tory Party Conference this year. 'Jeffrey,' she said, 'you're a shameless tart, but I loved every minute of it.' Coming from an old socialist like her, I took it as a great compliment.'

It sounds like a wonderful running slogan for the office of London's Mayor. 'Jeffrey Archer - your shameless tart candidate', but in fact the former Tory deputy chairman has a slightly more cogent political message.

'The major things are crime, transport, traffic, environment, planning. What people in London want is to get to work and back again quicker. People say to me: 'Jeffrey, get me to work quicker,'' which makes him sound rather like a rickshaw driver. Nevertheless, his

boundless enthusiasm is evident and when the referendum comes (May 7, 1998) sport will be a vital arrow in his quiver (to borrow from one of his book titles).

'Sport is not a minor issue. I think securing the Olympic Games for this city is very important. It would bring great prosperity and employment, and we deserve the Games. It would be one of the first things I'd do were I to be elected,' he electioneered.

'The trouble is, we've got nowhere to put them,' I pointed out.

'That's a defeatist attitude,' he boomed. 'From the moment you walked in the door I knew you were a defeatist.'

'Why?' I said, hurt and outrage warring for expression.

'Oh, she rises easily doesn't she?' he said gleefully. 'You're being wimpish.'

'You're being hectoring.'

'Well, at least I won't have you walking out of here saying 'He's an old smoothie'.' He is, of course. His bantering bravado has been one of the keys to his scarcely believable success since he was £400,000 in debt at the age of 34. He remains close friends with Margaret Thatcher and John Major. William Hague and, perhaps more to the point, Samaranch are just a matter of time. 'I've been to every Olympics, I ran myself, and there's virtually no one on the Olympic committee I don't know.'

I F those Olympics are not on British soil by 2012 (he has identified Northolt and Docklands, by the way, as provisional venues) Jeffrey will want to know the reason why.

'Do you still think you will be involved then?' I asked tactfully, when really meaning 'alive then'.

'What a statement!' he expostulated. 'Put her in the Tower of London. Should I only do things that will reflect well on me? I am fighting for London.'

'You're very competitive, aren't you,' I said, huffily.

'You'd better believe it. I don't like losing.' This was not why his fleeting career as an international sprinter ('carthorse more than butterfly') drew to a halt when he was 26. It was rather because there was no money in it. 'We didn't get £10,000 for going to Oslo in those days.' He remembered the authorities docking sixpence from his 10s expenses to White City because they refused to pay his bus fare.

Bearing in mind that Jeffrey likes to call himself 'a storyteller' I checked his athletic credentials. Sure enough, Sir Arthur Gold, the British team chief in 1966, remembers him running against Sweden. 'He wasn't our No1 sprinter,' said Sir Arthur with slow and steady emphasis. 'But he was an extrovert personality.' All the better to be Mayor of London with.

'You'd be the second most powerful man in Britain,' I said to Jeffrey. He cleared his throat. 'Hard to tell,' he said brusquely. But, in the meantime, snooker has the full-beam benefit of his gall and persuasion. Give him a few years, a disciplined diet and do not dare bet against our opening fantasy coming true.

'Great life,' I said, surveying the wonder and artworks of his Thames-lapping penthouse. 'You have to work for it,' he countered sternly. 'It wasn't given to me. I went out and got it.'

He turned to the innocently snapping photographer. 'Isn't she awful?' he said. ★ **25/10/97**

Phil Shephard-Lewis

BRUCIE PLAYS HIS CARDS RIGHT DESPITE A JOKER IN THE PACK

The **GILES SMITH**
Interview with Bruce Forsyth

ISHOULD say straight away that it wasn't Bruce Forsyth's idea to play golf with me at Wentworth this week. The Jackie Alliss Pro/Celebrity Golf Day, a charity fund-raiser marking the 10th anniversary of the Lady Taverners, was sponsored by Flavell Divett International, a computer consultancy firm from Brighton, and it was FDI who offered me a place in Bruce's four-ball.

They had read in these pages about my efforts to hatch as a golfer (efforts which leave me still surprisingly larval after a year) and reasoned, I suppose, that, along with the Head twins, Samantha and Johanna, I was just the kind of young talent whose performance could give the day the lift it needed.

Anyway, I was delighted at the prospect - the chance to go mano a mano with Brucie, maybe offer him some help with his game, and then have a good old laugh in the clubhouse afterwards over a Cinzano with lemonade. A warning bell sounded, however, a couple of days before the tournament when Peter Alliss phoned me at home, which doesn't often happen. There was a note of consternation in his voice which I do not recall ever having heard on the telly, and he said he hoped I wouldn't mind if he 'shot from the hip' about a matter which 'has set a few nerves jangling at this end'.

He and his wife, Jackie, had been going through the team-lists and couldn't help noticing that the sponsors had me down as a 36-handicap which was a) impossible, given that male handicaps only go up to 24, and b) not entirely compatible with Bruce's 12-handicap. Alliss just wanted to be sure I was comfortable with this – especially with it being Bruce, who really is very good, and with the fact that the course at Wentworth is not exactly famous for going gently on beginners.

Slightly put out, I told Alliss that I could indeed, as he put it, 'get it away' and that, though there was as yet little hard statistical evidence for my gifts as a golfer, I had a subtle inkling that in Wentworth's luscious spaces my game would come alive in a new and exciting way, enabling me to get round in about 100. That would be a first for me anywhere, actually, let alone on the championship West Course, but this was not dishonesty. It was simply an example of what the sports psychologist Dr Bob Rotella - in his valuably obvious book *Golf is Not a Game of Perfect* - calls 'creating your own reality'.

In any case, let's put this in perspective. Bruce Forsyth was for a long time the host of *The Generation Game*. How could my golf, even at its worst, tax the patience of someone who spent all those years watching couples from Oldham trying to plait marzipan and fold napkins into the shape of horses?

How indeed. Didn't I do well? No, I did not.

I suppose the nerves first bit as I drove towards Wentworth's familiar castle-style clubhouse, past the expensively shrubbed and electric-gated mansions which dot the estate, one of which has been, for the last 20 years, Bruce's home. With a nicely judged four-iron from the centre of the fairway on the first, you could probably take out his television aerial.

There at breakfast were Russ Abbot, Virginia Wade and Bob Wilson with his wife, Meg. And there was Bruce, in a golf shirt with golfers embroidered around the neck, in conversation with Peter Alliss. They were denouncing the complication of video recorders. 'Why can't they be simple?' Bruce was saying.

Later, as everyone began to ready themselves for play, I crept along the back of the driving-range bays to sneak a look at Bruce. My idea of a pre-round warm-up is to stretch just after getting out of the car. But Bruce was earnestly doing what everyone knows they should - working his way systematically through the clubs. His swing was fast and effective: the ball flew far and straight. Later he would go to the putting green and play himself in there, too. These were worrying sights.

As 12.30pm neared, John and Rod from FDI, myself and the host of *Play Your Cards Right* climbed to the first tee where the organisers and a few other bystanders were looking on. I wished that they weren't. 'Where did you get these clubs?' said Rachael Heyhoe-Flint. 'The Oxfam shop?' I tried to raise a smile, but somewhere along the line I had lost all feeling in my facial muscles, as if under anaesthetic at the dentist.

To quote Dr Bob Rotella again: 'A sound pre-shot routine is the rod and staff of the golfer under pressure, a comfort in times of affliction and challenge.' So much for that. I had prepared a new 'swing thought' for the occasion - at the start of the club-head's descent, I would concentrate my mind with the single, talismanic word 'Tarby' - but all my good intentions were lost to the wind now as a variety of internal worries competed for the honour of destroying me first. I got my arms up and swung and hoped.

The ball rose to grouse-height, veered sharply right and landed, perhaps some 75 yards away, in a wood. A chilly silence stole across the air. I was left with a second shot which could only be rendered uncomplicated by judicious use of a chainsaw. I thrashed at it twice, noticed Bruce idling nearby in his buggy, was swallowed by self-consciousness, picked up my ball and waved the others ahead.

This set the pattern for pretty much my entire round, one in which I completed just three holes and carried my ball a good deal further than I hit it. At the third, my drive did drop on to the green. Unfortunately, it was the green we had just left. 'I think it's going to be a hole in one,' said Bruce, as the ball rolled mockingly towards the pin. I picked it up and we moved on.

And so the afternoon passed. Bruce, who was using top-of-the-range Callaway clubs with heads the size of footballs, would boom his tee-shot off into the heart of the fairway, casually saying something afterwards like, 'I think that's just about perfect'. Then Rod and John would do much the same. And then I would balloon my ball into the nearest available hedge and, out of embarrassment and anxiety, promptly surrender.

Luckily we were playing as a team, whose best score counted at each hole. Thus, though I could not advance our cause, I could not destroy it, either. I was letting down no one but myself. But that seemed to be enough at the time.

I'm used to courses on which the fairway is at least visible from the tee. Whereas at Wentworth, the fairway and the tee only rarely seem to be in the same county and to reach the one from the other, you have to cross a small forest or a field of bracken.

I WAS LETTING DOWN NO ONE BUT MYSELF. BUT THAT SEEMED TO BE ENOUGH AT THE TIME

For the most part, Bruce was 200 yards ahead of me in his buggy and - who can blame him? - had pretty much tuned me out. These were difficult circumstances in which to bond. But at the ninth, we stopped off at the drinks hut where Bruce asked me what I fancied. I toyed with the idea of asking for chloroform, but in the end joined Bruce in a pot of tea and a packeted slice of dark fruit cake. Bruce told me he first came to Wentworth with the Stage Golfing Society and little imagined that he would ever afford to live there. These days he works 34 weeks of the year and spends the other 18 playing golf. I suppose he ought to be good.

Somewhere along the back nine, Rod holed a 30-foot putt. 'Lovely,' Bruce said. 'Now go and have a lie down.' But this was a rare moment of light-heartedness. I would hazard a guess that a similar atmosphere of clenched concentration prevailed in Russ Abbot's four-ball, too. The golf course is not somewhere entertainers go to relax; it's somewhere they go to be more serious than their professional life ever allows.

Bruce twice stood away from his ball to let a train pass so that he might work in silence. And each of the rest of us received at least one ticking-off for standing in his line as he putted, or for encroaching upon his peripheral vision as he drove. My turn came when I had given up on a hole and had gone on ahead to the next tee. I was some 30 feet uphill of Bruce and 50 yards away when I heard him call. 'What are you doing?' he shouted. 'I'm looking for some water,' I said. 'But you're in my line!' he said, and there was genuine exasperation in his voice.

He's a serious golfer, then, Bruce. But he's also a kind and thoughtful man who does not bear a grudge: when his buggy finally swung alongside me again, he reached out to pass me one of his bottles of water.

At the end we shook hands warmly. Yet somehow I knew that in the future, when that spare place suddenly falls open on a four-ball with Tarby and Russ, mine may not be the number Bruce tries first. Not until some improvements are in place. In 40 years' time, say. ★ **21/06/97**

TRAGIC ACCIDENT
FAILS TO DIMINISH GEORGE'S LIFELONG
LOVE of RUGBY

IT IS intensely gratifying to discover that the pitiless bank manager of whom many of us live in mortal fear is frequently called to account by an even higher authority. As Governor of the Bank of England, Eddie George is the bank manager's bank manager. Seated in front of his accusing gaze in an office of intimidating dimensions above Threadneedle Street, the mightiest financial figures in the land have been known to squirm like errant schoolboys summoned before the Head. A kris, a ceremonial Malay dagger, is displayed within easy reach as a warning to recalcitrant bank managers. If the glass case is closed, then they are likely to be let off with the City's equivalent of 100 lines; if left open, then self-immolation probably offers the least bloody means of escape.

The **ROBERT PHILIP**
Interview with **EDDIE GEORGE**

On the day of my appointment, the dagger was safely locked away, the daffodils on the Governor's roof garden were in riotous bloom, and Eddie George was wrestling with a major problem. Inflation? Interest rates? European Monetary Union? The possibility of having to establish a working relationship with a new Chancellor of the Exchequer after the General Election? The exchange rate mechanism? Alas, 'twas much more complex than that. A previously arranged skiing trip meant he would be unable to attend England's Triple Crown decider at Cardiff Arms Park. 'Very bad organisation,' he admitted. 'I'll have to find a way of phoning home to hear the result.'

The nation's finances apart, Eddie George seldom allows anything to interfere with his abiding passion for rugby union, a passion which survived - though only just - a tragic accident some 40 years ago in which a fellow school pupil at Dulwich College was killed. 'We were training for a sevens tournament and I pushed him away with a simple hand-off,' recalled the Governor, now 58, in a voice of terrible sadness undimmed by the passage of time. 'But it turned out this chap's artery to the brain came over rather than under the bone which is supposed to

protect it. It transpired it was a congenital condition. Anyway, his artery was severed, he went into a coma and later died.

'The College coach, John Gwilliam, who was one of the world's

great rugby players, was fantastic. He kept telling me it wasn't my fault and that I hadn't done anything wrong. Not that I thought it was my fault, but without John I might have been scarred for life. It was a hand-off, just a simple hand-off. After that, although I continued to play rugby, I was never as uninhibited on the pitch again and I suppose it was that incident which prevented me going on to play at any serious level.'

Ironically, the 17-year-old Eddie George had actually given up rugby 12 months earlier in order to devote his time and energies cramming for an Oxbridge place. 'That was a terrible mistake, my exam results were a disaster. But it was a great lesson because it showed me that if you focus entirely on work and ignore all other outside interests, then your work just goes to pot. At least, it did in my case.' And so he returned to the Dulwich College first XV at scrum-half, promptly sailing through the entrance exam for Emmanuel College, Cambridge, where he gained a second in economics before joining the Bank of England in 1962 as a specialist in East European affairs.

Now he sits atop a veritable mountain of gold ('I'm not supposed to tell you how much we have in the vaults beneath us') as one of the most powerful - yet least pretentious - men on the planet. He insists on writing his own speeches, very few of which are played without laughs. At one global conference, Eddie George told delegates there were three categories of economists: 1, those who can add up; and 2, those who cannot. Afterwards, he revealed with devilish glee, a German banker had asked him what the third category was.

Yet when sitting in his favourite seat in the Twickenham grandstand, does he ever wish he had chosen a sporting rather than financial career? 'If I'd been good enough I would probably have

thought. I think it's terrific that so many great players have been attracted to English club rugby. The game is visibly improving and not solely because of the arrival of European players, but also because of those from the Southern Hemisphere.'

Is there not a danger, however, that professionalism will destroy rugby union as we know it, leaving it prey for an American Football-style marketing blitz and the wheeler-dealers (aka agents) of English football? 'I don't think club rugby will ever lose that special spirit - everyone in the bath after the game singing songs. My impression is that even at international level there is still great camaraderie between both sides. It's silly to say there is no danger but professionalism hasn't changed tennis or golf in any fundamental kind of way. My heart tells me you can adopt a professional approach and the challenge is to do that while retaining traditional values. Everything in life is a risk but the opportunities for rugby are terrific. Anyway, I don't think there is any option. The idea that you can ignore the rest of the world is just not right. A global competition in the new millennium involving Bath, say, and Auckland would be no bad thing at all.'

A past-master in the twin arts of negotiation and compromise, Eddie George remains diplomatic on the subject of whom he believes should be running English rugby, Will Carling's '57 old farts', or an amalgam of paid officials, former players, sponsors and the marketing people. 'I honestly don't know the answer. It's very new all of this, and in my experience when you get major change, it takes years for everything to settle down. It's part of the democratic process in a way. The arguments are made from people in entrenched positions. People who have vested interests, of course. It's a terribly sad thing that you suddenly get this

'I HAVE A FEELING WE MIGHT HAVE A SPOT OF DIFFICULTY OVER THE CALCUTTA CUP BUT IT WOULD BE NICE TO HAVE SOMEONE TO TALK RUGBY WITH AT No 11'

become a rugby league player to earn some money. Of course, I would have loved to have been able to earn a living playing rugby union as so many do now. Still, it's probably all been for the best.' But would he swap the trappings of high office to savour a single afternoon spent with the red rose of England above his heart? 'Well, you do exactly that in a vicarious way, don't you? Yes, I can associate with those chaps who are actually playing, but I'm too old, too fat, too puffed to imagine myself in their place.' Oh, I don't know, ventured I to the Governor's guffaws, if Rob Andrew can come back. . .

THOUGH politically neutral in public, for purely sporting reasons Eddie George professes an electoral preference for Shadow Chancellor Gordon Brown, a keen rugger type, over the incumbent Kenneth Clarke, a rabid footy fan. 'I have a feeling we might have a spot of difficulty over the Calcutta Cup but it would be nice to have someone to talk rugby with at No 11. Ken's a great football fan - Nottingham Forest - as are most of the people involved in our discussions. The Deputy Governor is Manchester City, our economics director here is vice-president of Aston Villa, another senior adviser follows Queens Park Rangers and when they all start talking soccer I haven't the foggiest what they're on about.'

Just how we should be expected to put our faith in a Chancellor who supports Nottingham Forest inspires another outbreak of mischievous laughter before we turn attention to this nation's expanding rugby links with our neighbours. 'I think there's more convergence in the 'European Rugby Union' [pause, again, for delighted cackles] than there is in the European monetary systems just at the moment. Is ERU more acceptable than EMU? That's a very interesting

great influx of money and the world begins to spread apart. It's when you don't have enough money you should feel the pressure.

'What's clear is that you have to evolve into a situation in which the interests of the professional superstructure and the club understructure are both brought together under the same management. Now precisely what that means, I don't know. I think it will mean a strong executive. It will all take quite a long time to determine what the relationship is between the professional people and the amateur people. But I don't think there's any need to panic. It's in both sides' interests to work in harmony. The professionals need the updraught of the club game, and the clubs need the encouragement and support of the professional side because they need money. I don't have a blueprint because I'm not close enough to the game but what I see is the early stages in a process of evolution.'

HAVING brought wretched unhappiness into his life at a very young age, rugby has never lost the magic to send the Governor's heart soaring. 'I played tennis - hopelessly - and a lot of hockey, but rugby was always my game, even after the artery incident. I just love to see a centre tear through the middle. What a sight that is. Probably my most memorable experience of rugby was Ellis Park, Johannesburg, on World Cup final day. That was such a fantastic occasion. The sense of national emotion was a dimension beyond anything I've ever experienced. There was no way New Zealand could win - and they deserved to win, as a matter of fact - but South Africa were carried along by this tide of emotion. Wonderful, just wonderful. What a pleasant change it's been to talk about something other than interest rates. . .' ★ **17/3/97**

RAINEY HAS NO REGRETS AS HE SURVEYS LIFE FROM SLOW LANE

The **MARTIN JOHNSON**
Interview with Wayne Rainey

EVEN for someone whose every waking moment was consumed by nothing else but motorcycle racing and winning, it would have been permissible just this once to let his mind stray towards more important matters. Such as whether he had only a couple more seconds left to live.

However, on the day Wayne Rainey found himself flying through the air - minus his bike - at 130 mph, it did not immediately occur to him that he might never see his wife and son again, only that he would not be seeing the chequered flag that afternoon. 'Damn it,' (or something a little stronger) he groaned, 'I've just handed the world championship to Schwantz.'

His next thought was that he could have done without hitting the kerb, a collision which turned what might otherwise have been a controlled slide along the gravel trap into a series of high-speed somersaults. From then on, Rainey went from around 120 mph down to zero employing the same, albeit involuntary, method as Barnes Wallis's bouncing bomb, used by the RAF to breach Germany's Ruhr dams in the Second World War.

It was only during the final flip, when he heard the 'pop' which turned out to be his spinal column breaking, that Rainey began to suspect that the consequences of turning himself into a human missile might be a touch graver than conceding his world title to his arch-rival from Texas.

'When I finally stopped flipping over, I realised something was badly wrong. Everything started going black in one eye, and I was in so much pain. Then when the pain went away, and everything felt relaxed, I realised I was going. Slipping away. Dying. It felt so easy to die, and that was scary. My whole focus in life had been racing, but now I just wanted to see my wife and son again. Getting to the next breath was the only thing that mattered.'

Not surprisingly in the circumstances, Rainey found God in those moments of hovering between life and death. 'Until I fell off,' he said (as though it was the equivalent of a small boy coming a cropper on his tricycle), 'I didn't have a strong faith - but that was enough to convince me. I spoke out loud, 'God, I'm sorry for all the bad things I've done, but I'm not ready to leave yet'.'

Rainey's prayer to carry on living was answered, but the consequences of his accident on the Italian racetrack at Misano in 1993 condemned him to an altogether different type of life on two wheels. Now they're propelled by his own forearms rather than a 500 cc, 200-horsepower Yamaha engine.

The accident also pushed him rather earlier than he had planned into team owner-managership, and tomorrow afternoon will see him at Donington Park, charting his team's progress in the British Grand Prix from the pit lane. His Yamahas won't win, because, he says, his two riders are inexperienced. 'The press keep saying that the bike is bad, but if I had my legs back, I'd dig out my old leathers and helmet and show them otherwise.'

It was the British Grand Prix in 1993 which indirectly led to Rainey's final, career-terminating accident in Misano. A crash in practice at Donington had left him concussed, and while he knew he should not have raced, not competing would have effectively handed the championship to the man leading it, Kevin Schwantz.

WE disliked each other at the time,' said Rainey. 'We were both good, and he was from Texas while I was from California. In the States, that's real rivalry.' How intense, exactly? 'Well, we deliberately drove into each other a couple of times during races,' said Rainey, almost matter of factly. At what sort of speed? 'About 140.'

'Anyway, the concussion left me with no depth perception, and I knew I couldn't possibly attempt any overtaking, so my only chance in the race was to open the throttle and get into the first corner ahead. I managed it, and almost at once the pit sign went up 'Schwantz off.' So

'I SPOKE OUT LOUD, GOD, I'M SORRY FOR ALL THE BAD THINGS I'VE DONE, BUT I'M NOT READY TO LEAVE YET'

he coasted round for second place, and instead of being out of the title race, he found himself three points behind Schwantz before the next round at Misano.

If Rainey had not raced at Donington, he would probably not have been in a position to win his fourth championship, and would not have been, in his own words, 'pushing too hard'. As it was, he opened up a narrow lead over Schwantz at Misano, and came into the fateful corner 'a bit too fast'.

'In racing terms, it was only a fraction too quick, but I was already right on the edge, and when I opened the throttle to come out of the corner, the bike just slid away. Ninety per cent of the time you just walk away after an accident like that,' said Rainey, but after this one, walking away from anything was no longer an option for him.

He does not, however, look back on anything - including the accident - with regrets. 'I dreamt of racing motorbikes as a small boy, and I started riding at the age of nine. It was my whole life, and unbelievably thrilling. It gave me nothing but pleasure.

'Sure, I didn't want to break my back, but before the accident, I didn't realise how much my family meant to me. All I thought about was racing, testing and lap times. Now, believe it or not, I'm happier in my everyday life than I've ever been.'

It wasn't always like that, and Rainey experienced many dark moments of despair in the months after the accident. However, his eventual rehabilitation was helped by a hospital visit from Frank Williams, the even more badly crippled Formula One team owner, and now he views being in a wheelchair as simply something to 'deal with' while getting on with the rest of his life.

LOOK at Christopher Reeve, he's got a far worse problem than I have. Plus, all those people in poor countries who can't afford the equipment that helps someone more privileged like me. A lot of them end up being pushed around in wheelbarrows, which is why all the proceeds from my book are going to wheelchair charities.

'Life can never be as easy as it was before, whatever help you get. It's the little things you miss most. Such as, when my kid fell down, I'd just run over and pick him up. Now I can't do that. There's always an up-side to everything, though, and he's gonna grow up to be a pretty tough kid.'

Given what's happened to him, would he encourage his son to take up the sport? Rainey ponders for a moment, and says: 'Frankly, no. But if he asks me, then it'll be OK. You have to enjoy life, and if you do something that puts you in risk of losing it, then that's all part of it.'

At the age of 36, Rainey clearly remains a speed freak. There is talk of attempting a world land speed record - 'I'd love to see what it's like travelling at 500 mph' - and the boat he has at home is his pride and joy. 'It's got a 415-horsepower Chevvy engine,' he purrs. 'She'll do 70 mph across Lake Tahoe, and that's with 15 people.'

Further proof, if any were needed, came shortly after the conclusion of our interview. Crossing the waxed floor of the hotel lobby, a wheelchair came blurring past, hugging the corner of the coffee shop and almost cleaning up a indoor plant as the driver hurled it round on the racing line. Jamming on the brakes, Rainey glanced over his shoulder in the same way he once used to check that Schwantz was still behind him. 'Sorry,' he chuckled. 'I'm heading for the swimming pool.' A remarkable man, Wayne Rainey. ★ **16/08/97**

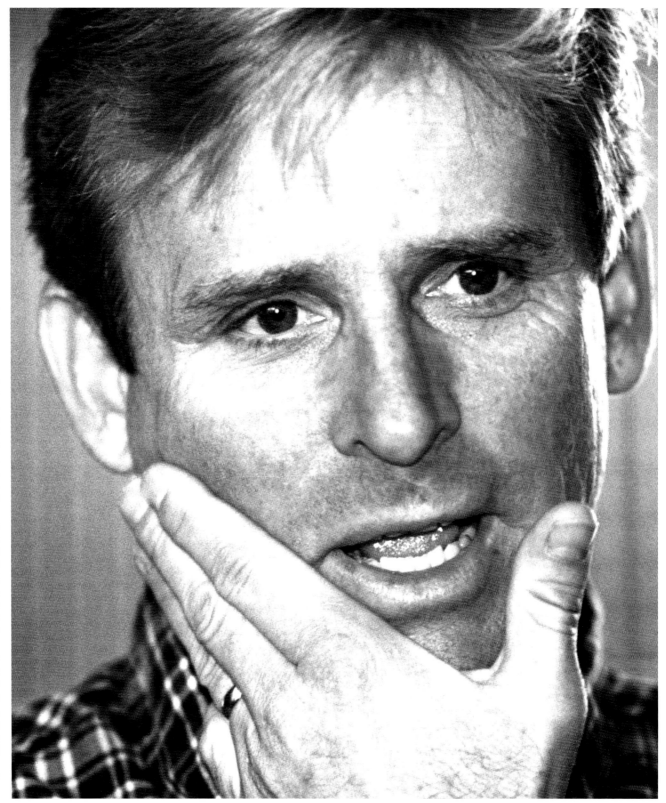

Phil Shephard-Lewis

REMEMBER WOMEN?

WELL, THIS WILL BE THE YEAR OF JANE COUCH AND LAURA DAVIES

SUE MOTT PREDICTS THE NAMES TO WATCH OUT FOR IN 1998

YOU MIGHT think that having interviewed Sean Bean at 1.33 pm on Jan 3, 1996, in the snug bar of the Orange Tree Pub, Totteridge (weather overcast, alcohol consumption modest, times lipstick reapplied - about 47), there was no other pleasure left in life. Actually, I think so too.

Nevertheless, though 1997 was not a vintage sporting year, one from which you would blow the dust and lovingly inhale its intoxicating bouquet, it had moments that I, personally, will never forget. I met Willie Carson's ducks, our new Sports Minister, Tony Banks, whose position is more tenuous than Kenny Dalglish's grasp of the English language, and the rocket/jockey Frankie Dettori eating a breadstick that his calorie-deprived figure so closely resembles.

I also saw an impressive British male tennis player on the massage table in Bournemouth. I've no idea who he was. On the other hand, we all, by the end of Wimbledon, knew all about Greg Rusedski and Tim Henman. They were quarter-finalists, patriotic heroes and inexplicable.

Why suddenly should these twin towers of rival-murdering manhood burst to prominence after 60 years of relative failure? Our cruel disappointment had been coming up for its bus pass when these great, white (and, in one case, Canadian) hopes of British tennis thwarted a lifetime of carping. Rusedski went on to reach the US Open final and have his parentage more discussed than the Prince of Wales. But already he and

"I WAS AN ANIMAL. LIVING ON A DIET OF BEER, FISH'N'CHIPS AND ROCK"

Henman had achieved beyond our wildest dreams. They had taken a humble and much-maligned sport, more famous for its cucumber sandwiches than Colossi, and made it respectable again.

As far left as you can go from respectable, sat Banks at the Ministry of Fun. '**** me!' he said when the Prime Minister asked him to open the red box marked 'Sport'. 'I thought when the call came from No 10 Downing Street that perhaps the lavatories were blocked. Could I possibly come round with me plunger,' he admitted in the first flush of office.

After multiple gaffes and superficial wounds to his party, it is more likely that Peter Mandleson will be coming round with his plunger. But for sheer, unbridled character ('I wish I had the courage to wear an ear-ring'), the Minister of Sport and Member for West Ham did much... well, to make us laugh anyway.

As for the laughing matters of 1998, they remain to be seen. We can assume Gazza has binned the plastic breasts or at least sent them on to Christie's for an auction in the year 2010 when bits of his cruciate ligaments may also be up for sale. He has, perhaps, taken a turn for the serious. He is certainly not a 'new star' anymore, more a recurring nuisance like one of those clapped-out old satellites that worries us all because you never know where it will drop.

But there will be emergent stars in the constellation of '98 and at the World Cup in France, the two most romantic choices would be Michael Owen, 17, of Liverpool and Tony Adams of Arsenal, born with typical patriotic timing in 1966. Is it just me or can everyone imagine that Adams prowls the England locker-room before a match, declaiming: 'The game's afoot: follow your spirit and upon this [FA disciplinary] charge cry 'God for Gary [Lineker], England and St Glenn!'?

The Arsenal captain was as born to lead as any son of Henry IV, has endured more grief from the 'donkey'-mocking populace and had drunk Falstaffian lakes before his hugely brave admission of alcoholism. If he could coax his old limbs into one summer's swansong for England, there is no doubt he would deserve to be hailed the talismanic hero of the French campaign.

Owen, the nerveless wonder of Merseyside, who smashed Ian Rush's 20-year record for scoring in the Deeside Primary Schools Under-11s, is likely to be included in the World Cup squad, and will certainly be only 18. Pele once proved that youth was no bar to genius, scoring a hat-trick in the semi-final and twice in the World Cup final. If Owen, who already possesses a Blue Peter badge, can perform a fifth as well, it will be the start of a glittering international career (Baby Spice optional).

Which reminds me. Remember women? You must have seen them. Those creatures: legs, nagging, over-emotional, no heading ability, who must not on any account be allowed to box or beat you on the golf course. It gives me, therefore, great pleasure to assign 1998 as the Year of Jane Couch and Laura Davies.

Couch, the 'Fleetwood Assassin' is a boxer who laid out a London policewoman on her professional debut during a Thai kick-boxing show in Wigan. This was no more

than she had been doing for years in Blackpool although the policewomen (and men) were on duty at the time. 'I was an animal. Living on a diet of beer, fish'n'chips and rock,' she said of her former life.

She became the welterweight champion of the world, and now, thanks to the reluctant embrace of female emancipation on the part of the Amateur Boxing Association, she may become the icon of a generation of British women boxers. Men may balk at the thought of the little woman presenting a smile like Peter Beardsley, spitting her gumshield and a few teeth in the ringside bucket, but there is clearly no stopping them now.

As for Davies, if she does not become Britain's best loved high-performance sporting ambassador for the dizzying combination of a hugely skilled golf game, an unremitting sense of humour, Ivana Trump-style shopping sprees, that red Ferrari and the instincts of a predator up front for the women golfers' football team, then there is absolutely no justice in this world. She is also, thanks to the odd bet, second to Sheikh Mohammed al Maktoum in keeping the horse-racing industry alive.

Lester Piggott had this privilege once. Now the electric Dettori. Who will head the next cavalcade is a question that only time and rides will answer. But Laura could do worse than stick her Merit Money on Royston Ffrench, the leading apprentice from the stables of Luca Cumani whose driving, fluid style belies the stuttering effs of his name.

He is black, 22, and a former factory hand hammering wooden pallets together. Then his Uncle Errol introduced him to riding. He had lesson one on a runaway. Lesson two, he fell off. But there have been enough smug punters from Sandown to Ayr this season to justify faith in his future.

More futures: Dwaine Chambers cannot really be the world's fastest teenager, given the speed at which young offenders can shift at the sound of a police car siren, but he will be fast enough (10.06 for the 100 metres) to frighten his elders. Lee Westwood cannot really be the world's slowest golfer, he merely had the misfortune to be paired with Nick Faldo in the 1997 Ryder Cup. Unfettered, watch him go in 1998.

David Sale will be cricket's rising sensation, a batsman of belligerent ferocity and the sort of build you would call beefy until either Ian Botham or Mad Cow Disease brought the whole concept into disrepute. And how can we not predict a glorious future for Cracknell/Foster, the rowing pair who are making up the foursome in Steve Redgrave's boat? James Cracknell (a trained geography teacher with the tattoo of a skull on his ankle) and Tim Foster (blond, two ear-rings and plays in a dubious band with no name) are coping brilliantly well with their supporting roles. 'Put it this way,' said Cracknell, 'if I stop rowing he'll lose.'

Will Greenwood will become the England rugby union team's unconditional centre, making his reawakening from unconsciousness in a tunnel in Orange Free State all the more worthwhile. At the time the British Lions' doctor had a scalpel in his hand ready to perform an emergency tracheotomy on Greenwood's prone and unresponsive form. But from ER to Ooh Ah. As no less a man than Fran Cotton has said: 'There are no chinks to his make-up.'

Not like me with Sean Bean then. ★

THE ENGLAND
CRICKET TEAM FACE A
RELENTLESS
INTERNATIONAL
PROGRAMME IN '98

CHRISTOPHER MARTIN-JENKINS REALISTICALLY ASSESSES THEIR CHANCES

NO-ONE would guess England's current standing in world cricket - sixth out of nine - from the international programme planned for them this year. Only world champions, surely, would take on this sort of schedule. After five Tests and five one-day internationals in the West Indies from January to April, the players will go straight into a home season studded with three one-day internationals and five Tests against South Africa, a triangular one-day tournament with South Africa and Sri Lanka, and a Test against Sri Lanka, all squashed into the summer between June and August. The climax of the county season will follow in September, then it will be off to Australia in October for the toughest tour of the lot.

By the time the third match has been played in the first few days of 1999, England will have played 14 Tests in 11 months and will probably have gone most of the way towards a sixth successive defeat in an Ashes series. As a recipe for exhaustion for all concerned the programme is as good as could be imagined. It is out of the question that a fast bowler - let us say Darren Gough - could play in all 14 Tests; certainly unless our administrators change their intention to continue with the weak voluntary code by which England players may be released from county cricket duties by mutual consent between the chairman of selectors and the chairman of the county club concerned.

This is an absolutely black-and-white issue. If England want to get the best from Gough - and from Andrew Caddick and Dean Headley - they have to cut the red tape and employ them centrally. All the top cricketers, indeed, need to be managed, trained, coached and honed specifically for England matches.

It will be expensive. County clubs will have to be properly compensated if they are to release players, whom they have nurtured, for a full season. About £20,000 per player would be a reasonable investment, given the undeniable premise that the great majority of the income is generated by England matches.

There were a sufficient number of impressive performances against Australia last summer to suggest that England's present band of players could compete on level terms if they were allowed to concentrate solely on their international responsibilities. As things stand, however, it is long odds on another year of unequal struggle in 1998.

All England supporters hope not, of course, but they should never have been confronted with this sort of itinerary for the year. Tim Lamb, the England and Wales Cricket Board's chief executive, has now publicly pledged that there will never again be a West Indies and Australian tour in the same year. His predecessor expressed the same intention, but it has happened. It is no good our administrators reiterating how difficult it is to fit into a world schedule without upsetting people. This is the sort of issue on which a stand has to be made on principle.

Not that there are easy series against anyone these days. There may be nothing for it in 1998 but to forget patriotism and to enjoy the skills of our opponents. The West Indies will be attractive to watch when they bat, as they always are. Brian Lara has had a relatively lean time since he batted so dazzlingly in the second half of the West Indies tour of England in 1995, and was even placed outside the world's top 20 players in one of the various lists of international ratings last October, but, like many, he seems to reserve his best performances for English opposition. The key to England's chances may lie in shackling Lara and somehow finding a way of negating the less spectacular, but no less effective left-hander, Shivnarine Chanderpaul. He is a batsman of the highest class and if these two have a good series, England's bowlers will not.

The West Indies fast attack is fashionably described as being less good than it was. Yet they found two useful new recruits last year in Franklyn Rose and Mervyn Dillon and they have not given up hope in a mountainous young fellow called Nixon McClean, who did well in the Hong Kong Sixes last September.

They will work around the vastly experienced pair of Curtly Ambrose and Courtney Walsh, about whom there is nothing new to say. If Gough, Caddick, Headley and young Ashley Cowan want to learn, they only have to watch how Ambrose so consistently fires the ball at the off stump on the length he wants. Only Angus Fraser has achieved that regularly among the England fast bowlers picked for the tour and it will be a delight for all concerned if he can prove the selectors right to recall him.

THERE WAS A SUFFICIENT NUMBER OF IMPRESSIVE PERFORMANCES AGAINST AUSTRALIA LAST SUMMER TO SUGGEST THAT ENGLAND'S PRESENT BAND OF PLAYERS COULD COMPETE ON LEVEL TERMS IF THEY WERE ALLOWED TO CONCENTRATE SOLELY ON THEIR INTERNATIONAL RESPONSIBILITIES

South Africa, of course, have their own Ambrose in the lean thoroughbred Allan Donald and their team in England for the summer will be all the more formidable for the experience in county cricket of Donald, Shaun Pollock and Jacques Kallis. They are going to be an excellent team for sure; good to watch, tough to play against. Curiously, however,

there will be equally high expectations for the second touring side, Sri Lanka. There was widespread indignation at the old TCCB's failure to accelerate their return to England after their brilliant triumph in the World Cup in 1995-96, but the sometimes myopic administrators at Lord's need have no fears about the attraction to the public of these superb cricketers.

On ability alone Aravinda de Silva has been in my world XI for the last 10 years. The World Cup revealed another world-class player in Sanath Jayasuriya as he proved himself so much more than a one-day dasher with his marathon innings against India in August, 1996: 340, the fourth highest Test score in history. Arjuna Ranatunga, Muttiah Muralitheran, Hashas Tillekeratne, the multi-initialled W.P.U.J.C. Vaas, the bustling Dennis Lillee protege, Kuruppuarachchige Pushpakumara (what fun they are to commentate upon!) and the rising talent, Marvon Atapattu, are all players capable of taking Sri Lanka towards their stated goal of becoming the best *Test* team in the world by 2000. Beating England at Lord's would be an ideal achievement in pursuit of that dream.

Meanwhile, the oldest domestic cricket competition in the world, the County Championship, will continue, happily unmolested. The title will be passionately defended by last year's worthy winners, Glamorgan, and keenly contested as usual by those involved. The quality will be varied and so will the crowds, but the same goes for the Sheffield Shield and all the other major domestic competitions. It doesn't stop outstanding overseas players from wanting to come to county cricket to round off their education.

There was a tremendous controversy last year about whether the format should be changed. It was only in 1993, however, that it became an all four-day competition for the first time, so it has hardly been staid or static. The fashionable view, especially among those journalists who practically never watch the Championship, was that the rejection of the idea of splitting the tournament into two divisions, was unforgivably reactionary on the part of the 11 counties who voted emphatically against it. They appeared to believe that England would become more competitive by concentrating the best players into nine clubs, who would, inevitably, given a few seasons of sorting themselves out, be the wealthier ones.

However, given the probability that, centrally employed squad or not, England players will be available to their counties increasingly less in an increasingly demanding international programme, an awful lot would have been lost by making nine other counties second-class, even with three promotions and relegations a year, and too many flowers would have blossomed unseen. At least the reforms of the recreational game will begin in earnest in 1998 and it is only by investing time, effort and money in the base of the amateur game that the professional level at the top will improve in the long term. ★

Philip Brown

BBC BOUNCE BACK
WITH A RICH BILL OF FARE

GILES SMITH LOOKS AHEAD TO WHAT THE COUCH POTATOES WILL BE WATCHING IN AN ACTION-PACKED **YEAR OF TELEVISED SPORT**

TOWARDS the end of 1997, ITV began to run an advertising campaign for their sports coverage, attached to which was the mellifluous slogan: 'Sport is free on ITV, as it should be.' Strictly speaking, this is not true: attempt to watch ITV, or any other television channel, for free in this country and someone from the television licensing department comes round in a detector van and insists on removing half the furniture in your sitting-room in lieu of the fine.

But one got the point, and the point was that, on ITV, there would be no additional charges levied for sports events, no pay-per-view - the dark practice, from time to time, of a certain satellite organisation called Sky.

Here's an issue for sports broadcasting which will burn and niggle through 1998: whether we should pay, how much we should pay, and when. Should sport be free on television? (It would be interesting to hear ITV make the moral case that their slogan seems to imply.) Whatever, the fact is, to a significant extent it still is.

It is the BBC who are regularly said to have been knocked hardest in the scrap for sports franchises - though there is a decent argument which says they have merely been stirred from their complacency. In any case, even setting aside their recent franchise

losses (two of the most substantial of which - Formula One motor racing and the FA Cup final - have been to ITV and therefore are not lost to terrestrial viewers), we are still some way from a world in which the BBC are forced to fill *Grandstand* with bowling from an American-style fun-rink near you. Let alone a world in which a quiz game *A Question of Sport* becomes the channel's flagship sports programme.

I have before me a list of the BBC's scheduled sports events for next year, and it includes: the Winter Olympics in February, the Grand National in April, the Rugby League Challenge Cup, football and Wimbledon tennis in June, British Open golf in July, the

European Athletics Championships in August and the Commonwealth Games in September. Far from convincing one that the BBC are slumped against the ropes, the list rather suggests that someone in Sky Sports franchise-purchasing department isn't working hard enough.

Channel 5 have also expanded the options for many people who can't afford a cable or satellite link. C5 was meant to be terrestrial television's comedy routine. How we laughed at the thought of their video re-tuning men going from door-to-door nationwide. How we hooted when they

proposed to show us snowboarding at two o'clock in the morning. And then how we started watching when they began bringing us Arsenal's, Aston Villa's and Chelsea's football matches in Europe. Late last year the channel snatched Evander Holyfield's title fight with Michael Moorer - not a massive box-office draw, perhaps, but the first time Holyfield had stepped out since Tyson had tucked into his ear, and thus an event of some resonance. What's more, a major sports event, free, on a low-budget terrestrial.

What threatens to affect sports broadcasting in 1998 far more than the defection of some major events to a place where the majority will not see them, is the simple passage of time. An entire generation of commentators who have become, in our minds, the voices of their sports is coming to the end of its professional life. The Voice of Horse Racing, Peter O'Sullevan, has retired. The Voice of Athletics, David Coleman, has begun to scale down his workload. For how many more seasons can we reasonably rely on the energy and commitment of the Voice of Football, Brian Moore, and The Voice of Motor Racing, Murray Walker? There is only so much shouting one can expect a man to do in his lifetime.

What connects these valuable people is that in many ways they share very little with the spirit of television as it has become. What, to them, is the Super Sunday, the Mega Monday, the Throbbing Thursday, the four-hour, cafe-format build-up with its bogus enthusiasm for the views of a Celebrity to hand? How the wearying hype and sheer financial panic of televised sport in the late 1990s must grate on the nerves of those who learnt their art in another age - those who grew to understand the weight of silence and who realised that sometimes sport must be left to speak for itself. Sport on television will give us everything now, except a minute's peace.

Nevertheless, the fact is, in 1998 there will be more sport than ever before on terrestrial television. And yet we will still hear the complaint that it has all been sold off. So maybe we have to conclude that the appetite for sport has grown so exponentially that we have moved to the stage where there could never be enough sport on television. Which would explain the modern pursuit of sports-related programming: documentaries, comedy quiz games, chat-shows, phone-ins, previews, reviews. *They Think It's All Over*, *Under the Moon*, *Turnstyle*, *Motormouth*... even when terrestrial television isn't showing sport, they're talking about it.

Indeed, between the European Cup final and the cricket and the motor racing this year, you may care to look out for the

following programmes, which are by no means guaranteed to reach your screen, but all of which were rumoured to be enjoying successful pilots and try-outs at the time of writing.

They Think They've Got Sports News For You: Comedy quiz game in which contestants take it in turns to pretend to be a television sports news correspondent, charged with enthusiastically delivering a story which the other contestants already know because they watched it live earlier in the evening. Hilarious. Points awarded for sincerity and the ability to maintain a straight face. Compere: David Baddiel. Team captains: Jo Brand and Rory McGrath. Guest appearances from Ally McCoist, Nick Hancock and Nicholas Witchell.

Whose Linesman Is It Anyway? Another comedy quiz game, in which contestants sit in judgment on the week's most controversial refereeing or umpiring decisions. Compere: John Motson. Team captains: Nick Hancock and David Baddiel. Guest appearances from Rory McGrath, Ally McCoist, Rory McCoist, Ally McGrath and Jo Brand.

Have I Got Lines All Over? Yet another comedy quiz game, in which teams must put on brightly coloured clothing and then decide whether what they are wearing is a genuine piece of *haute couture*, an item from a pantomime costume rental company, or the change-strip of a league-affiliated football club. Compered by Rory McGrath. Team captains: Rory McGrath and Rory McGrath.

THE LIST RATHER SUGGESTS THAT SOMEONE IN SKY SPORTS FRANCHISE-PURCHASING DEPARTMENT ISN'T WORKING HARD ENOUGH

With guests: Rory McGrath, Rory McGrath, Rory McGrath and Rory McGrath.

PavilionEnders: Television's first cricket-based soap opera. Watch, enthralled, as the regulars come and go in the square. Episodes spread over five days, with a special abridged one-day version to be screened on Sundays. Starring Geoffrey Boycott, Jonathan Agnew and Barbara Windsor.

Putt It Away, For Goodness Sake! Saucy fun with Peter Alliss and friends, who exhaust an unimaginably large slice of the BBC's budget by travelling to the world's most exotic golf courses for a round of golf and a drink afterwards. Special guests: Bruce Forsyth, Jimmy Tarbuck, Ronnie Corbett and Rory McGrath.

Burning Rubber: The big one for the summer - the definitive history of the plimsoll, in 14 weekly, hour-long parts, narrated by Donald Sinden, and accompanied by a lavishly illustrated book with an introduction by Richard Attenborough. The theme music, by Barrington Pheloung of *Inspector Morse* fame, will be made available on CD in early autumn. ★

ENGLAND'S FOOTBALLERS

COULD WELL BE WORLD CUP FINALISTS IN PARIS IN JULY

HENRY WINTER LOOKS FORWARD TO AN ENTHRALLING COMPETITION AND A YEAR OF **REVOLUTION** IN THE DOMESTIC GAME

JULY IN France is not a bad time for revolutions. On this occasion, though, the threat to the established orders comes from England, whose footballers have the look of possible finalists when the World Cup reaches its climax in Paris on July 12.

Lining up against such perennial powerhouses as Brazil, Germany and Argentina, not forgetting the dangerous-looking Dutch and French, it will be a magnificent achievement for Glenn Hoddle's men to work their passage to the ultimate test but one that can be realised. If England then prevail, it will be the greatest moment in the Three Lions' history, superior even to the

summer of 66 when success was secured on home soil. The feeling that '98 will be sent spinning by revolutions runs deep. Throughout the year, young English players, such as Rio Ferdinand, Michael Owen and John Curtis, will come to the fore, pushing aside better-known names. Yet the real headline stars, those expected to feature on French fields, will become even more untouchable by a revolution in the transfer system commencing on July 1. Some will earn a million simply for signing their name. It could be them.

The financial gains are gargantuan, intoxicating, alarming even. Yet there are many footballers, already rich beyond their

boyhood dreams, who are driven by simple glory, of pure sporting excellence, of silver on the sideboard not in the bank. Such a player is Alan Shearer, cut down by injury in 1997, but expected to be fit and hungry for France 98. Indeed, the timing may be right for Shearer, a centre-forward capable of dominating the World Cup. Remember Marco Van Basten? The great Dutch striker recovered from injury to direct Holland to European Championship triumph a decade ago. Shearer can emulate that achievement.

Footballers like Shearer, David Seaman, Tony Adams and Paul Ince form the backbone to England's French crusade. And youngsters like David Beckham and Paul Scholes will simply confirm the qualities they showed last summer in winning the Tournoi de France.

The year's French flavour is pertinent. Hoddle's grounding as a knowledgeable coach commenced while a player at Monaco under Arsene Wenger, now Arsenal's guiding light. Eric Cantona's legacy to Manchester United and England comes in the form of the hard-working, hard-training posse of young players like Beckham and Scholes, who learnt so much from their French tutor.

Jamie Redknapp deserves to be. Hoddle has searched high and low for the pivotal central defender capable of delivering the first-time howitzer pass. Redknapp, earmarked for this role at the Tournoi before injury intervened, may find '98 an uplifting year.

His club-mate, Jamie Carragher, full of vim and versatility, may gradually make his mark in midfield or defence. Still young and perhaps impressionable, Carragher currently has a tendency to pass the ball short, usually to Ince, but he may soon spread play as confidence and experience takes hold. Owen, pacey and predatory, already looks squad material for France '98.

Liverpool's plans for the future Carraghers and Owens will continue to take concrete shape at their new academy on the outskirts of town. Along with the positive philosophy in operation at Old Trafford, it will provide the benchmark for all clubs. Those who have the money that is.

Hoddle has plentiful options, reflecting the improvement in standards English football's return to European competition, following the Heysel ban which has made players tactically sharper. The emergence of enlightened coaches and managers, many with experience of Continental ways, has also helped. Furthermore, a new wave of

THROUGHOUT THE YEAR, YOUNG ENGLISH PLAYERS SUCH AS RIO FERDINAND, MICHAEL OWEN AND JOHN CURTIS, WILL COME TO THE FORE, PUSHING ASIDE BETTER-KNOWN NAMES

France 98 provides the ideal opportunity for the Football Association to accelerate their bid to host the finals of 2006. As the programme unfolds, the FA's blazered persuaders will be out lobbying anyone with influence within FIFA, the game's global governors.

The FA and all those who hold England dear will hope that the team are not followed by unruly camp followers. Outbreaks of hooliganism will tarnish further England's image and perhaps temper enthusiasm for the FA's 2006 campaign. The World Cup's proximity to England, and the organisers' desire for supporters to move around so making train stations international melting-pots, may lead to bouts of ugliness.

England's feelgood factor, domestically and internationally, is partly rooted in the growing promise of young players spread across the land, players who could blossom as the Millennium draws ever closer. At West Ham United, Rio Ferdinand looks to possess the control and composure needed in modern defences. Manchester United continue to polish footballing gems. Scholes could force his way into the starting line-up in France. The central playmaking platform will surely belong to Beckham when Paul Gascoigne tires. Even younger than these two is the talented, mobile Curtis, maturing nicely on the fringes of United's first team.

United's old rivals, Liverpool, will also provide booted catalysts for the rebirth of English football. Robbie Fowler and Steve McManaman are established in the squad.

independently wealthy managers has arrived, past players who made their money from the game and thus do not have to worry so unduly about the P45's impact. They can build teams rather than seek short-term gain to appease clamorous chairmen.

A revolution will also occur in the deal-making world. July heralds a transformation in the transfer system, which has been in a state of flux since the Bosman ruling triggered freedom of movement. Out-of-contract players over the age of 24 can now join another English club without a fee being demanded by the club being left. Players moving within contract will still command fees as will those under 24 years.

An even bigger star system will be created. The power is now with the player, who when his contract expires will be able to command huge salaries and signing-on fees. His new club will simply see this as preferable to the old form of a transfer fee. Players will become millionaires overnight. The top professionals enjoy a win-win situation here. If they sign short-term deals, as will be the temptation, they increase their number of out-of-contract bonanzas. If such luminaries agree to long-term contracts, which clubs will desire to safeguard their investment, the players and their agents can insist on even bigger contracts, knowing the club will get a fee if there is movement mid-contract. Lengthy contracts can also be a burden for clubs if a player gets injured or loses form. From the lush lawns of France, to the negotiating chambers of Premiership clubs, 1998 is the year for the elite footballer. ★

Old head on young shoulders. Teddy Sheringham will provide the experience for England and Manchester United. Steve Yarnell

BEING THERE

MARTIN JOHNSON LOOKS ON IN WONDER AT THE **EXTRAORDINARY DEDICATION** OF THE GROWING ARMY OF THE UK'S TRAVELLING FANS

The Ryder Cup was in the bag, and the majority of Europe's supporters could scarcely have cared less when Severiano Ballesteros strode on to Valderrama's 18th green to concede Scott Hoch's 15ft putt for a half. On the other hand, a by no means insignificant number leapt from their armchairs in frothing indignation - not so much because the American had earlier asked Monty to hole a putt that a 24-handicapper could have knocked in with his umbrella, but because, for those who were following the event with their wallets as well as their heartstrings, putting one over on the Yanks would not have been half as satisfying as putting one over on the bookies.

Not that long ago, serious betting in sport extended not very much further than the equine variety, inside dingy shops where people in flat caps waded their way across a floor littered with Park Drive packets to find out what Hotspur was recommending in the 3.15 at Uttoxeter. The only non-regulars to make a meaningful contribution to the Ladbroke coffers were the small army of housewives who had a once-a-year 50p each-way on the Derby. They'd have backed a Skegness donkey, just so long as Lester Piggott was piloting it.

Nowadays, however, the bookmakers have expanded their horizons to embrace almost anything, and you can doubtless already get a quote on how many boxes of Kleenex Gazza will get through should England win the World Cup, or whether England's cricketers will regain the Ashes before or after the first McDonalds opens on Mars.

Hence the small outpouring of grief for Ballesteros's act of chivalry from all those punters clutching tickets for a 15-13 European victory in the Ryder Cup. More and more wagers on sporting events are now centred around margins rather than the actual result - largely through the growth of the spread-betting industry.

This even embraces such things as how many minutes will have elapsed before the first throw-in in a football match, or how many runs a batsman might make in a Test series. On England's last tour to the West Indies, Sporting Index quoted Brian Lara at 375, which was precisely the number he had scored before his final innings. Potentially, there wasn't much profit either way, until Lara made another 375 in one outing.

This kind of made-to-measure sporting wager is set to grow even further in 1998, although the one thing you can bet on with total certainty in the year ahead is that the number of runs scored by the entire England team in this winter's Caribbean Test series will scarcely match (not on current form anyway) the number of visiting supporters there to see them do it. The bookmakers might take a tidy sum from the vast public interest in England's cricketers in the West Indies, and England and Scotland at football's World Cup, but not half as much as the likes of Thomas Cook and Gullivers' Travels.

There was a time when British sportsmen could travel abroad and feel as though they were a long way from home. Not any more they can't. What do you think England's cricketers will hear when they take on the West Indies in Port of Spain and Bridgetown. Calypso music through the loudspeakers? Steel drums during Curtly Ambrose's run-up? Do me a favour. 'Ingerlund, Ingerlund' is what they'll be hearing, intermingled with: 'Here we go, here we go' and 'We are the cacophony of whistling and abuse from the MCG's notorious Bay 13 is more likely to be drowned out by thousands of cheering Brits perched up in the Northern Stand - coating the railings with Union Jacks with Worksop CC written across them, and the messages for the lads in the snug bar at the Fuzzock and Firkin. And as a batsman, when you get out, there is the cheery prospect of being intercepted by Sky TV for a quick interview on the pavilion steps for the benefit of the small percentage of folks still back at home.

Similarly, in this year's World Cup, there will be a huge influx of British supporters, the interest in England's cricket tour to Sharjah in December, for a handful of relatively unimportant one-day internationals in an uncomfortably hot environment, where the relief of a light breeze is counterbalanced by the involuntary swallowing of the clouds of red dust blown up as a result, not to mention licensing laws precluding even half a shandy with which to clear the throat.

The really dedicated cricket fan will find it extremely hard to make ends meet this year in that England's tour of the West Indies ends in April, and they're off again in October to Australia. What with Sharjah as well, it will be

THERE IS NEVER MORE WORK FOR THE MISSING PERSONS BUREAU THAN AFTER A SCOTLAND FOOTBALL MATCH ABROAD

Army, the Barmy, Barmy Army'. Whoever it was who penned the old proverb about travel broadening the mind has never been on an overseas cricket tour with the Barmies.

Once upon a time, England (or MCC as it was then) cricket tours were followed largely by slipping a crystal set under the pillow, out of which poured more hiss, crackle and static than the average taxi driver's walkie-talkie. 'Welcome to the Melbourne Cricket Ground, where you join us with England two hundred and ssssss, kkkrrr, ssssss for kkkrrr.'

These days, however, an England cricket tour to Australia means that Melbourne High Street will be wall-to-wall with pink-faced, flaky-nosed punters, mostly wearing the traditional uniform of blue England cricket shirt, baggy shorts, black ankle socks, sandals, and Gullivers' travel-bag slung over the shoulder.

Devon Malcolm runs into bowl, and the combination of affluence and relatively cheap air travel making this kind of pilgrimage a more popular holiday than the erstwhile 10 days in Torremolinos. With Scotland in attendance, it also seems unlikely that the Falklands War scenario - 'I counted them all out, and I counted them all back' - has much chance of applying. There is never more work for the Missing Persons Bureau than after a Scotland football match abroad.

With the vast majority of the 30,000 (per day) spectators at the Ryder Cup being made up of Brits, it does seem to be a peculiarly British phenomenon, even though the travel specialists receive relatively little business for Davis Cup relegation battles in Zagreb and Nairobi, or the world surfing championships in Newcastle - New South Wales, as opposed to on Tyne.

There was even a remarkable degree of far from easy to fit all three in, but some will certainly manage it.

It is also a triumph of hope over expectation, in that it is comparatively rare for their team to reward them for their loyal support. The last English spectator to see his side win the Ashes in Australia is now 12 years older, and England have failed to win an overseas series anywhere, other than New Zealand, since 1986.

The phenomenon is all the more remarkable given that you can watch everything at home now for the price of a satellite dish. And even, as was the case with England's World Cup football qualifier against Italy in Rome, get the benefit of incisive comments ('they're both great footballing nations / Gazza is a great footballer') from studio guests like Michael Caine. On the other hand, perhaps that's why so many people are keen to get away. ★

The Barmy Army prepare for their winter holiday in the West Indies sunshine. Dave Burges

1997 QUOTES OF THE YEAR

"I'm delighted they don't start as they finish"

Brian Ashton, the Ireland coach, after England scored four tries in the last nine minutes to win 41-6

"When I'm playing tennis I'm not this nice guy everyone imagines me to be. I'm cold and ruthless. As far as I'm concerned, it's kill or be killed"

Jekyll and Hyde by Tim Henman

"We could pick three different sides and they would all beat England"

Stuart Law, Essex's Australian batsman, left out of the tour party for the Ashes

"Everyone wants more money and it's better in my bank account than theirs"

Eddie Irvine after Ferrari extend his contract for another season

"If you ever hear me complain about signing autographs, just hit me. Please"

Justin Leonard on the price of fame after winning The Open

"He was not a captain, he was like a father for us. We put our hands on the clubs but he was the one who played the shots"

Ignacio Garrido on the debt Europe owed Severiano Ballesteros for winning the Ryder Cup

"You must understand that time is just a linear measurement of successive increments of now"

Earl Woods's advice to son Tiger

"Dance sport has the potential to become one of the jewels in the crown in the sporting world"

Mark McCormack after his company IMG signed an agreement aimed at raising the profile of the International DanceSport Federation

"The sun is going to rise tomorrow, and I'll be on a plane following it"

Jim Courier after his first-round defeat at the French Open

"Waiting for God is boring so I thought I would be better off back behind the wheel"

The Countess of Arran, on her decision to return to powerboat racing at the age of 79

SPORT DIARY

1998

1997

JANUARY
```
M  .  6  13  20  27
T  .  7  12  21  28
W  1  8  15  22  29
T  2  9  16  23  30
F  3  10  17  24  31
S  4  11  18  25  .
S  5  12  19  26  .
```

FEBRUARY
```
M  .  3  10  17  24
T  .  4  11  18  25
W  .  5  12  19  26
T  .  6  13  20  27
F  .  7  14  21  28
S  1  8  15  22  .
S  2  9  16  23  .
```

MARCH
```
M  .  3  10  17  24  31
T  .  4  11  18  25  .
W  .  5  12  19  26  .
T  .  6  13  20  27  .
F  .  7  14  21  28  .
S  1  8  15  22  29  .
S  2  9  16  23  30  .
```

APRIL
```
M  .  7  14  21  28
T  1  8  15  22  29
W  2  9  16  23  30
T  3  10  17  24  .
F  4  11  18  25  .
S  5  12  19  26  .
S  6  13  20  27  .
```

MAY
```
M  .  5  12  19  26
T  .  6  13  20  27
W  .  7  14  21  28
T  1  8  15  22  29
F  2  9  16  23  30
S  3  10  17  24  31
S  4  11  18  25  .
```

JUNE
```
M  .  2  9  16  23  30
T  .  3  10  17  24  .
W  .  4  11  18  25  .
T  .  5  12  19  26  .
F  .  6  13  20  27  .
S  .  7  14  21  28  .
S  1  8  15  22  29  .
```

1998

JANUARY
```
M  .  5  12  19  26
T  .  6  13  20  27
W  .  7  14  21  28
T  1  8  15  22  29
F  2  9  16  23  30
S  3  10  17  24  31
S  4  11  18  25  .
```

FEBRUARY
```
M  .  2  9  16  23
T  .  3  10  17  24
W  .  4  11  18  25
T  .  5  12  19  26
F  .  6  13  20  27
S  .  7  14  21  28
S  1  8  15  22  .
```

MARCH
```
M  .  2  9  16  23  30
T  .  3  10  17  24  31
W  .  4  11  18  25  .
T  .  5  12  19  26  .
F  .  6  13  20  27  .
S  .  7  14  21  28  .
S  1  8  15  22  29  .
```

APRIL
```
M  .  6  13  20  27
T  .  7  14  21  28
W  1  8  15  22  29
T  2  9  16  23  30
F  3  10  17  24  .
S  4  11  18  25  .
S  5  12  19  26  .
```

MAY
```
M  .  4  11  18  25
T  .  5  12  19  26
W  .  6  13  20  27
T  .  7  14  21  28
F  1  8  15  22  29
S  2  9  16  23  30
S  3  10  17  24  31
```

JUNE
```
M  1  8  15  22  29
T  2  9  16  23  30
W  3  10  17  24  .
T  4  11  18  25  .
F  5  12  19  26  .
S  6  13  20  27  .
S  7  14  21  28  .
```

1999

JANUARY
```
M  .  4  11  18  25
T  .  5  12  19  26
W  .  6  13  20  27
T  .  7  14  21  28
F  1  8  15  22  29
S  2  9  16  23  30
S  3  10  17  24  31
```

FEBRUARY
```
M  1  8  15  22
T  2  9  16  23
W  3  10  17  24
T  4  11  18  25
F  5  12  19  26
S  6  13  20  27
S  7  14  21  28
```

MARCH
```
M  1  8  15  22  29
T  2  9  16  23  30
W  3  10  17  24  31
T  4  11  18  25  .
F  5  12  19  26  .
S  6  13  20  27  .
S  7  14  21  28  .
```

APRIL
```
M  .  5  12  19  26
T  .  6  13  20  27
W  .  7  14  21  28
T  1  8  15  22  29
F  2  9  16  23  30
S  3  10  17  24  .
S  4  11  18  25  .
```

MAY
```
M  .  3  10  17  24  31
T  .  4  11  18  25  .
W  .  5  12  19  26  .
T  .  6  13  20  27  .
F  .  7  14  21  28  .
S  1  8  15  22  29  .
S  2  9  16  23  30  .
```

JUNE
```
M  .  7  14  21  28
T  1  8  15  22  29
W  2  9  16  23  30
T  3  10  17  24  .
F  4  11  18  25  .
S  5  12  19  26  .
S  6  13  20  27  .
```

1997

JULY
```
M  .  7 14 21 28
T  1  8 15 22 29
W  2  9 16 23 30
T  3 10 17 24 31
F  4 11 18 25  .
S  5 12 19 26  .
S  6 13 20 27  .
```

SEPTEMBER
```
M  1  8 15 22 29
T  2  9 16 23 30
W  3 10 17 24  .
T  4 11 18 25  .
F  5 12 19 26  .
S  6 13 20 27  .
S  7 14 21 28  .
```

NOVEMBER
```
M  .  3 10 17 24
T  .  4 11 18 25
W  .  5 12 19 26
T  .  6 13 20 27
F  .  7 14 21 28
S  1  8 15 22 29
S  2  9 16 23 30
```

AUGUST
```
M  .  4 11 18 25
T  .  5 12 19 26
W  .  6 13 20 27
T  .  7 14 21 28
F  1  8 15 22 29
S  2  9 16 23 30
S  3 10 17 24 31
```

OCTOBER
```
M  .  6 13 20 27
T  .  7 14 21 28
W  1  8 15 22 29
T  2  9 16 23 30
F  3 10 17 24 31
S  4 11 18 25  .
S  5 12 19 26  .
```

DECEMBER
```
M  1  8 15 22 29
T  2  9 16 23 30
W  3 10 17 24 31
T  4 11 18 25  .
F  5 12 19 26  .
S  6 13 20 27  .
S  7 14 21 28  .
```

1998

JULY
```
M  .  6 13 20 27
T  .  7 14 21 28
W  1  8 15 22 29
T  2  9 16 23 30
F  3 10 17 24 31
S  4 11 18 25  .
S  5 12 19 26  .
```

SEPTEMBER
```
M  .  7 14 21 28
T  1  8 15 22 29
W  2  9 16 23 30
T  3 10 17 24  .
F  4 11 18 25  .
S  5 12 19 26  .
S  6 13 20 27  .
```

NOVEMBER
```
M  .  2  9 16 23 30
T  .  3 10 17 24  .
W  .  4 11 18 25  .
T  .  5 12 19 26  .
F  .  6 13 20 27  .
S  .  7 14 21 28  .
S  1  8 15 22 29  .
```

AUGUST
```
M  .  3 10 17 24 31
T  .  4 11 18 25  .
W  .  5 12 19 26  .
T  .  6 13 20 27  .
F  .  7 14 21 28  .
S  1  8 15 22 29  .
S  2  9 16 23 30  .
```

OCTOBER
```
M  .  5 12 19 26
T  .  6 13 20 27
W  .  7 14 21 28
T  1  8 15 22 29
F  2  9 16 23 30
S  3 10 17 24 31
S  4 11 18 25  .
```

DECEMBER
```
M  .  7 14 21 28
T  1  8 15 22 29
W  2  9 16 23 30
T  3 10 17 24 31
F  4 11 18 25  .
S  5 12 19 26  .
S  6 13 20 27  .
```

1999

JULY
```
M  .  5 12 19 26
T  .  6 13 20 27
W  .  7 14 21 28
T  1  8 15 22 29
F  2  9 16 23 30
S  3 10 17 24 31
S  4 11 18 25  .
```

SEPTEMBER
```
M  .  6 13 20 27
T  .  7 14 21 28
W  1  8 15 22 29
T  2  9 16 23 30
F  3 10 17 24  .
S  4 11 18 25  .
S  5 12 19 26  .
```

NOVEMBER
```
M  1  8 15 22 29
T  2  9 16 23 30
W  3 10 17 24  .
T  4 11 18 25  .
F  5 12 19 26  .
S  6 13 20 27  .
S  7 14 21 28  .
```

AUGUST
```
M  .  2  9 16 23 30
T  .  3 10 17 24 31
W  .  4 11 18 25  .
T  .  5 12 19 26  .
F  .  6 13 20 27  .
S  .  7 14 21 28  .
S  1  8 15 22 29  .
```

OCTOBER
```
M  .  4 11 18 25
T  .  5 12 19 26
W  .  6 13 20 27
T  .  7 14 21 28
F  1  8 15 22 29
S  2  9 16 23 30
S  3 10 17 24 31
```

DECEMBER
```
M  .  6 13 20 27
T  .  7 14 21 28
W  1  8 15 22 29
T  2  9 16 23 30
F  3 10 17 24 31
S  4 11 18 25  .
S  5 12 19 26  .
```

JANUARY	FEBRUARY	MARCH	APRIL	MAY	JUNE
1 T	1 S	1 S	1 W	1 F	1 M
2 F	2 M	2 M	2 T	2 S	2 T
3 S	3 T	3 T	3 F	3 S	3 W
4 S	4 W	4 W	4 S	4 M	4 T
5 M	5 T	5 T	5 S	5 T	5 F
6 T	6 F	6 F	6 M	6 W	6 S
7 W	7 S	7 S	7 T	7 T	7 S
8 T	8 S	8 S	8 W	8 F	8 M
9 F	9 M	9 M	9 T	9 S	9 T
10 S	10 T	10 T	10 F	10 S	10 W
11 S	11 W	11 W	11 S	11 M	11 T
12 M	12 T	12 T	12 S	12 T	12 F
13 T	13 F	13 F	13 M	13 W	13 S
14 W	14 S	14 S	14 T	14 T	14 S
15 T	15 S	15 S	15 W	15 F	15 M
16 F	16 M	16 M	16 T	16 S	16 T
17 S	17 T	17 T	17 F	17 S	17 W
18 S	18 W	18 W	18 S	18 M	18 T
19 M	19 T	19 T	19 S	19 T	19 F
20 T	20 F	20 F	20 M	20 W	20 S
21 W	21 S	21 S	21 T	21 T	21 S
22 T	22 S	22 S	22 W	22 F	22 M
23 F	23 M	23 M	23 T	23 S	23 T
24 S	24 T	24 T	24 F	24 S	24 W
25 S	25 W	25 W	25 S	25 M	25 T
26 M	26 T	26 T	26 S	26 T	26 F
27 T	27 F	27 F	27 M	27 W	27 S
28 W	28 S	28 S	28 T	28 T	28 S
29 T		29 S	29 W	29 F	29 M
30 F		30 M	30 T	30 S	30 T
31 S		31 T		31 S	

JULY	AUGUST	SEPTEMBER	OCTOBER	NOVEMBER	DECEMBER
1 W	1 S	1 T	1 T	1 S	1 T
2 T	2 S	2 W	2 F	2 M	2 W
3 F	3 M	3 T	3 S	3 T	3 T
4 S	4 T	4 F	4 S	4 W	4 F
5 S	5 W	5 S	5 M	5 T	5 S
6 M	6 T	6 S	6 T	6 F	6 S
7 T	7 F	7 M	7 W	7 S	7 M
8 W	8 S	8 I	8 T	8 S	8 T
9 T	9 S	9 W	9 F	9 M	9 W
10 F	10 M	10 T	10 S	10 T	10 T
11 S	11 T	11 F	11 S	11 W	11 F
12 S	12 W	12 S	12 M	12 T	12 S
13 M	13 T	13 S	13 T	13 F	13 S
14 T	14 F	14 M	14 W	14 S	14 M
15 W	15 S	15 T	15 T	15 S	15 T
16 T	16 S	16 W	16 F	16 M	16 W
17 F	17 M	17 T	17 S	17 T	17 T
18 S	18 T	18 F	18 S	18 W	18 F
19 S	19 W	19 S	19 M	19 T	19 S
20 M	20 T	20 S	20 T	20 F	20 S
21 T	21 F	21 M	21 W	21 S	21 M
22 W	22 S	22 T	22 T	22 S	22 T
23 T	23 S	23 W	23 F	23 M	23 W
24 F	24 M	24 T	24 S	24 T	24 T
25 S	25 T	25 F	25 S	25 W	25 F
26 S	26 W	26 S	26 M	26 T	26 S
27 M	27 T	27 S	27 T	27 F	27 S
28 T	28 F	28 M	28 W	28 S	28 M
29 W	29 S	29 T	29 T	29 S	29 T
30 T	30 S	30 W	30 F	30 M	30 W
31 F	31 M		31 S		31 T

15 monday

first-half

second-half

extra-time

SPORTING FIXTURES

CRICKET: Sharjah Champions Trophy, Pakistan v England, *Sharjah, UAE*

FOOTBALL: FIFA Confederation Cup - King Fahd Trophy, Czech Republic v Uruguay, *Riyadh, Saudi Arabia*
FIFA Confederation Cup - King Fahd Trophy, UAE v South Africa, *Riyadh, Saudi Arabia*

SKIING: World Cup Skiing, *Sestriere, Italy*

YACHTING: Mistral World Championships Finish, *Fremantle, Australia*

16 tuesday

SPORTING FIXTURES

CRICKET: Sharjah Champions Trophy, India v West Indies, *Sharjah, UAE*

FOOTBALL: FIFA Confederation Cup - King Fahd Trophy, Brazil v Mexico, *Riyadh, Saudi Arabia*
FIFA Confederation Cup - King Fahd Trophy, Saudi Arabia v Australia, *Riyadh, Saudi Arabia*

YACHTING: 1997 Windsurfer World Championships Start (Finish 23rd Dec), *Fremantle, Australia*

17 wednesday

SPORTING FIXTURES

CRICKET: Carlton & United Breweries World Series, New Zealand v Australia, *Melbourne, Australia*

FOOTBALL: FIFA Confederation Cup - King Fahd Trophy, Uruguay v South Africa, *Riyadh, Saudi Arabia*
FIFA Confederation Cup - King Fahd Trophy, UAE v Czech Republic, *Riyadh, Saudi Arabia*

20 saturday

first-half

second-half

extra-time

SPORTING FIXTURES

RUGBY UNION: Italy v Ireland, *Bologna, Italy*
Heineken European Rugby Cup, Bath v Pau, *Bath,*

SKIING: World Cup Skiing, *Val Gardena, Italy*

18 thursday

first-half

second-half

extra-time

SPORTING FIXTURES

BIATHLON: World Cup 3 Starts (Finishes 21st Dec), *Kontiolahti, Finland*

EQUESTRIAN: Olympia International Championships Start (Finish 22nd Dec), *London*

TABLE TENNIS: ITTF Pro-Tour Grand Finals Start (Finish 21st Dec), *Hong Kong*

19 friday

BOXING: Prince Naseem Hamed (GBR) v Kevin Kelley(USA), *Madison Square Garden, USA*

CRICKET: Sharjah Champions Trophy Final, *Sharjah, UAE*

FOOTBALL: FIFA Confederation Cup - King Fahd Trophy, Semi-Finals, *Riyadh, Saudi Arabia*

SKIING: World Cup Skiing Starts (Finishes 21st Dec), *Veysonnaz, Switzerland*

notes

21 sunday

Michaelmas Law Sittings end   *4th in Advent*   ☾ Last Quarter   Winter Solstice

first-half

second-half

extra-time

SPORTING FIXTURES

ATHLETICS: IAAF World Cross Challenge - ASLK/CGER Crosscup, *Brussels, Belgium*

BIATHLON: World Cup 3 Finishes, *Kontiolahti, Finland*

FOOTBALL: FIFA Confederation Cup - King Fahd Trophy, Final, *Riyadh, Saudi Arabia*

RUGBY UNION: Heineken European Rugby Cup, Toulouse v Brive, *Toulouse, France*

SKIING: World Cup Skiing Finishes, *Veysonnaz, Switzerland*

TABLE TENNIS: ITTF Pro-Tour Grand Finals Finish, *Hong Kong*

22 monday

first-half

second-half

extra-time

SPORTING FIXTURES

CRICKET: 1st One Day International, India v Sri Lanka,
Guwahati, India

EQUESTRIAN: Olympia International Championships Finish,
London

SKIING: World Cup Skiing,
Madonna di Campiglio, Italy

YACHTING: Whitbread Round The World Race
- Finish Leg Three, *Sydney, Australia*

23 tuesday

BOARDSAILING: ISAF World Championships Finish,
Perth, Australia

YACHTING: 1997 Windsurfer World Championships Finish,
Fremantle, Australia

24 wednesday

27 saturday

first-half

second-half

extra-time

SPORTING FIXTURES

AMERICAN FOOTBALL: Wild-Card Play-Off Games,
tbc, USA

BASKETBALL: Women's International - England v New Zealand,
tbc

CANOEING: Murray Marathon Starts (Finishes 31st Dec),
Yarrawonga, Australia

CRICKET: 1st Test, Australia v South Africa - Day 2,
Melbourne, Australia

HORSE RACING: The Coral Welsh National,
Chepstow
The Bonusprint Christmas Hurdle,
Kempton Park

SKIING: World Cup Skiing Starts (Finishes 28th Dec),
Lienz, Austria

25 thursday

Christmas Day (Quarter Day)

first-half

second-half

extra-time

SPORTING FIXTURES

CRICKET: 2nd One Day International, India v Sri Lanka, *Gwalior, India*

26 friday

Boxing Day, Bank Holiday UK & Republic of Ireland

CRICKET: 1st Test, Australia v South Africa - Day 1, *Melbourne, Australia*

HORSE RACING: The Rowland Meyrick Handicap Steeple Chase, *Wetherby*
The King George VI Steeple Chase, *Kempton Park*

YACHTING: World Fireball Championships Start (Finish 11th Jan), *Melbourne, Australia*

notes

28 sunday

Christmas 1

first-half

second-half

extra-time

SPORTING FIXTURES

AMERICAN FOOTBALL: Wild-Card Play-Offs, *tbc, USA*

BASKETBALL: Women's International - England v New Zealand, *tbc*

CRICKET: 3rd One Day International, India v Sri Lanka, *Goa, India*
Women's World Cup Final, *Calcutta, India*
1st Test, Australia v South Africa - Day 3, *Melbourne, Australia*

SKIING: World Cup Skiing Finishes, *Lienz, Austria*

RUSSELL CHEYNE

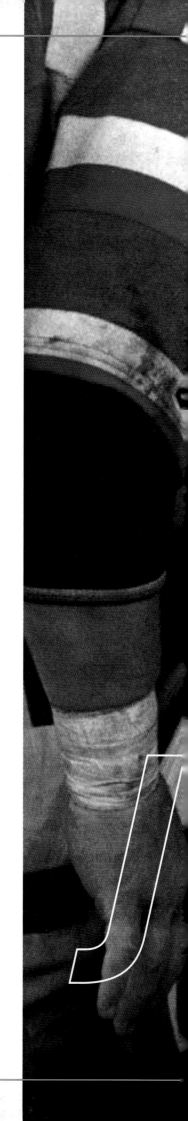

```
M  .   5  12  19  26
T  .   6  13  20  27
W  .   7  14  21  28
T  1   8  15  22  29
F  2   9  16  23  30
S  3  10  17  24  31
S  4  11  18  25   .
```

1998
JANUARY

★ **BUPA DURHAM INTERNATIONAL CROSS COUNTRY** ATHLETICS **3 JAN** Maiden Castle
★ **EMBASSY WORLD PROFESSIONAL CHAMPIONSHIPS** DARTS **3 - 11 JAN** Frimley Green
★ **WORLD CHAMPIONSHIPS** SWIMMING **7 - 18 JAN** Perth, Australia
★ **MONTE CARLO RALLY** MOTOR RALLYING **17 - 21 JAN** Monte Carlo, Monaco
★ **AUSTRALIAN OPEN CHAMPIONSHIPS** TENNIS **19 JAN - 1 FEB** Melbourne, Australia
★ **COCA-COLA INTERNATIONAL** CROSS COUNTRY ATHLETICS **24 JAN** Belfast
★ **FA CUP 4TH ROUND** FOOTBALL **24 JAN** Various venues
★ **SUPERBOWL XXXII** AMERICAN FOOTBALL **25 JAN** San Diego, USA
★ **COCA-COLA CUP SEMI-FINALS 1ST LEG** FOOTBALL **28 JAN** To be confirmed
★ **CABLE & WIRELESS 1ST TEST MATCH- WEST INDIES V ENGLAND** CRICKET **29 JAN - 2 FEB** Kingston, Jamaica
★ **HEINEKEN EUROPEAN RUGBY CUP FINAL** RUGBY UNION **31 JAN** Twickenham

anuary

29 monday

● New Moon

first-half

second-half

extra-time

SPORTING FIXTURES

CRICKET: 1st Test, Australia v South Africa - Day 4,
Melbourne, Australia

SKIING: World Cup Skiing,
Bormio, Italy

30 tuesday

BASKETBALL: Eurostars 1997- East v West,
Tel Aviv, Israel

CRICKET: 1st Test, Australia v South Africa - Day 5,
Melbourne, Australia

31 wednesday

First Day of Ramadan

CANOEING: Murray Marathon Finishes,
Yarrawonga, Australia

YACHTING: International Contender World Championship
Starts (Finish 11th Jan),
Sydney, Australia

3 saturday

first-half

second-half

extra-time

SPORTING FIXTURES

AMERICAN FOOTBALL: Divisional Play-Offs,
USA (BSkyB)

ATHLETICS: Durham International Cross Country,
Durham (BBC)

CRICKET: 2nd Test, Australia v South Africa - Day 2,
Sydney, Australia (BSkyB)
South Africa U19 v England U19,
Benoni, South Africa
Kenya v England A,
Nairobi, Kenya

DARTS: Embassy World Professional Championships Start
(Finish 11th Jan),
Frimley Green (BBC)

GOLF: Andersen Consulting WCOG Finals - Day 1,
Scottsdale, USA (BSkyB)

SKIING: Men's World Cup Skiing - Day 1,
Kranjska Gora, Slovenia (Eurosport)

YACHTING: International OK Dinghy World Championships
Start (Finish 10th Jan),
Glenelg, Australia

SLEDDOG: BSHRA Championship Series
(Finish 4th Jan),
Kent

1 thursday

New Year's Day, Bank Holiday UK & Republic of Ireland

first-half

second-half

extra-time

SPORTING FIXTURES

CHESS: World Championships Starts (Finish 9th Jan),
Lausanne, Switzerland

MOTOR RALLYING: Paris-Dakar Starts (Finishes 17th Jan),
Paris, France (Eurosport)

YACHTING: 49ER World Championships Starts
(Finishes 4th Jan), *Perth, Australia*

2 friday

CRICKET: 2nd Test, Australia v South Africa - Day 1,
Sydney, Australia (BSkyB)

SNOOKER: Qualifying For Embassy World Championships Starts
(Finishes 14th Jan), *Blackpool*

notes

4 sunday

Christmas 2

first-half

second-half

extra-time

SPORTING FIXTURES

AMERICAN FOOTBALL: Divisional Play-Offs,
tbc, USA (BSkyB)

CRICKET: Kenya v England A,
Nairobi, Kenya
South Africa U19 v England U19,
Fochville, South Africa
2nd Test, Australia v South Africa - Day 3,
Sydney, Australia (BSkyB)

GOLF: Andersen Consulting WCOG Finals - Day 2, *Scottsdale,
USA (BSkyB)*

SKIING: Men's World Cup Skiing - Day 2,
Kranjska Gora, Slovenia (Eurosport)

YACHTING: Whitbread Round The World Race
- Start Leg Four,
Sydney, Australia (BBC)
49ER World Championships Finishes,
Perth, Australia

5 monday

☽ First Quarter

first-half

second-half

extra-time

SPORTING FIXTURES

CRICKET: 2nd Test, Australia v South Africa - Day 4,
Sydney, Australia (BSkyB)

LAWN TENNIS: ATP Tour - Australian Hardcourt Championships Starts,
Adelaide, Australia

SKIING: Women's World Cup Skiing - Day 1,
Ofterschwang, Germany (Eurosport)

YACHTING: International Contender World Championship Starts (Finishes 9th Jan),
Sydney, Australia

6 tuesday

Epiphany

SPORTING FIXTURES

BADMINTON: Korean World Grand Prix Starts (Finish 11th Jan),
Seoul, Korea

CRICKET: 2nd Test, Australia v South Africa - Day 5,
Sydney, Australia (BSkyB)
Kenya v England A - Day 1,
Nairobi, Kenya

SKIING: Women's World Cup Skiing - Day 2,
Ofterschwang, Germany (Eurosport)

7 wednesday

SPORTING FIXTURES

CRICKET: Kenya v England A - Day 2,
Nairobi, Kenya

SQUASH: European Champion Of Champions Start (Finishes 10th Jan),
Stavanger, Norway

SWIMMING: VIII Fina World Championships - Day 1,
Perth, Australia (BBC)

10 saturday

first-half

second-half

extra-time

SPORTING FIXTURES

CRICKET: Silver Jubilee Independence Cup, India v Bangladesh,
Dhaka, Bangladesh
Kenya v England A,
Nairobi, Kenya

RUGBY UNION: Richmond v Bath,
Richmond (BSkyB)

SKIING: Women's World Cup Skiing - Day 1,
Maribor, Slovenia (Eurosport)

SQUASH: European Champion Of Champions Finishes,
Stavanger, Norway

SWIMMING: VIII Fina World Championships - Day 4,
Perth, Australia (BBC)

YACHTING: International OK Dinghy World Championships Finish,
Glenelg, Australia

8 thursday

first-half

second-half

extra-time

SPORTING FIXTURES

CRICKET: Kenya v England A - Day 3,
Nairobi, Kenya

FOOTBALL: European Super Cup Final 1st Leg
- FC Barcelona v Borussia Dortmund,
Barcelona, Spain

SKIING: British Land Senior Championships
Start (Finish 14th Jan),
Tignes, France

SWIMMING: VIII Fina World Championships - Day 2,
Perth, Australia (BBC)

9 friday

CHESS: World Championships Finish,
Lausanne, Switzerland

CRICKET: Carlton & United Breweries World Series,
New Zealand v South Africa,
Brisbane, Australia (BSkyB)

SWIMMING: VIII Fina World Championships - Day 3,
Perth, Australia (BBC)

YACHTING: International Contender World Championship
Finish,
Sydney, Australia
Whitbread Round The World Race - Finish Leg Four,
Auckland, New Zealand (BBC)

notes

11 sunday

Hilary Law Sittings begin   *Epiphany 1*

first-half

second-half

extra-time

SPORTING FIXTURES

AMERICAN FOOTBALL: AFC & NFC Championships,
tbc, USA (BSkyB)

ATHLETICS: 38th Cross International Zornotza,
Amorebieta, Spain (Eurosport)

CRICKET: Silver Jubilee Independence Cup, India v Pakistan,
Dhaka, Bangladesh
Carlton & United Breweries World Series, Australia v South Africa,
Brisbane, Australia (BSkyB)

DARTS: Embassy World Professional Championships Finish,
Frimley Green (BBC)

LAWN TENNIS: ATP Tour - Australian Hardcourt
Championships Finish,
Adelaide, Australia

RUGBY UNION: Saracens v Harlequins,
Watford (BSkyB)

SKATING: European Figure Skating Championships Start
(Finish 18th Jan),
Milan, Italy (Eurosport)

SKIING: Women's World Cup Skiing - Day 2,
Maribor, Slovenia (Eurosport)

SWIMMING: VIII Fina World Championships - Day 5,
Perth, Australia (BBC)

12 monday

○ Full Moon

first-half

second-half

extra-time

SPORTING FIXTURES

CRICKET: Silver Jubilee Independence Cup,
Bangladesh v Pakistan,
Dhaka, Bangladesh

LAWN TENNIS: ATP & WTA Tour- Sydney International Starts
(Finishes 18th Jan),
Sydney, Australia

SWIMMING: VIII Fina World Championships - Day 6,
Perth, Australia (BBC)

13 tuesday

BADMINTON: Yonex Open Japan Starts (Finishes 18th Jan),
Tokyo, Japan

BOBSLEIGH: World Cup 5 / European Championships Start
(Finish 18th Jan),
Igls, Austria (Eurosport)

SKIING: Men's World Cup Skiing,
Adelboden, Switzerland (Eurosport)

SWIMMING: VIII Fina World Championships - Day 7,
Perth, Australia (BBC)

14 wednesday

CRICKET: Carlton & United Breweries World Series,
New Zealand v Australia,
Sydney, Australia (BSkyB)
Silver Jubilee Independence Cup 1st Final,
Dhaka, Bangladesh

SKIING: British Land Senior Championships Finish,
Tignes, France

SNOOKER: Qualifying For Embassy World Championships
Finishes, **Blackpool**

SWIMMING: VIII Fina World Championships - Day 8,
Perth, Australia (BBC)

17 saturday

first-half

second-half

extra-time

SPORTING FIXTURES

BASKETBALL: Men's National Trophy Final,
Sheffield (BBC)

MOTOR RALLYING: Paris-Dakar Finishes,
Dakar, Senegal (Eurosport)
Rallye Automobile de Monte Carlo Starts (Finishes 21st Jan),
Monte Carlo, Monaco (Eurosport)

RUGBY UNION: Leicester v Wasps,
Leicester (BSkyB)

SKIING: Freestyle World Cup Finishes,
Lake Placid, USA
Women's World Cup Skiing - Day 1,
Kitzbuhel, Austria (Eurosport)

SWIMMING: VIII Fina World Championships - Day 11,
Perth, Australia (BBC)

SLEDDOG: BSHRA Championship Series (Finish 18th Jan),
Kent

15 thursday

first-half

second-half

extra-time

SPORTING FIXTURES

SKIING: Freestyle World Cup Starts (Finishes 17th Jan),
Lake Placid, USA

SWIMMING: VIII Fina World Championships - Day 9,
Perth, Australia (BBC)

16 friday

CRICKET: Carlton & United Breweries World Series,
New Zealand v South Africa,
Perth, Australia (BSkyB)
Silver Jubilee Independence Cup 2nd Final,
Dhaka, Bangladesh

SNOOKER: Regal Welsh Open Starts (Finishes 25th Jan),
Newport (BSKYB)

SWIMMING: VIII Fina World Championships - Day 10,
Perth, Australia (BBC)

TABLE TENNIS: European Nations Cup Starts
(Finishes 18th Jan), *Bayreuth, Germany*

notes

18 sunday

Epiphany 2

first-half

second-half

extra-time

SPORTING FIXTURES

BADMINTON: Yonex Open Japan Finish,
Tokyo, Japan

BOBSLEIGH: World Cup 5 / European Championships Finish,
Igls, Austria (Eurosport)

CRICKET: Carlton & United Breweries World Series,
Australia v South Africa,
Perth, Australia (BSkyB)
Silver Jubilee Independence Cup 3rd Final,
Dhaka, Bangladesh

LAWN TENNIS: ATP & WTA Tour- Sydney International
Finishes,
Sydney, Australia

RUGBY UNION: Newcastle v Bath,
Newcastle (BSkyB)

SKATING: European Figure Skating Championships Finish,
Milan, Italy (Eurosport)

SKIING: Women's World Cup Skiing - Day 2,
Kitzbuhel, Austria (Eurosport)

SWIMMING: VIII Fina World Championships - Day 12,
Perth, Australia (BBC)

TABLE TENNIS: European Nations Cup Finishes,
Bayreuth, Germany

19 monday

first-half

second-half

extra-time

SPORTING FIXTURES

BOWLS: World Indoor Championships for Men Starts (Finish 1st Feb), *Preston (BBC)*

CRICKET: Under-19 World Cup Starts (Finishes 1st Feb), *Various, South Africa*

LAWN TENNIS: Australian Open Championships - Day 1, *Melbourne, Australia*

20 tuesday

☾ Last Quarter

LAWN TENNIS: Australian Open Championships - Day 2, *Melbourne, Australia*

21 wednesday

CRICKET: Carlton & United Breweries World Series, New Zealand v Australia, *Melbourne, Australia (BSkyB)*

LAWN TENNIS: Australian Open Championships - Day 3, *Melbourne, Australia*

MOTOR RALLYING: Rallye Automobile de Monte Carlo Finishes, *Monte Carlo, Monaco (Eurosport)*

24 saturday

first-half

second-half

extra-time

SPORTING FIXTURES

ATHLETICS: Coca-Cola International Cross Country, *Belfast (BBC)*

FENCING: Corble Cup - Men's Sabre F.I.E., *Guildford*

GOLF: Johnnie Walker Classic - Round 3, *Phuket, Thailand*

LAWN TENNIS: Australian Open Championships - Day 6, *Melbourne, Australia*

RUGBY UNION: Italy v Scotland, *tbc, Italy*

22 thursday

first-half

second-half

extra-time

SPORTING FIXTURES

GOLF: Johnnie Walker Classic - Round 1,
Phuket, Thailand

LAWN TENNIS: Australian Open Championships - Day 4,
Melbourne, Australia

23 friday

CRICKET: Carlton & United Breweries World Series 1st Final,
Melbourne, Australia (BSkyB)

GOLF: Johnnie Walker Classic - Round 2,
Phuket, Thailand

HOCKEY: Womens Indoor European Nations Cup Starts
(Finishes 25th Jan), *Orense, Spain*

LAWN TENNIS: Australian Open Championships - Day 5,
Melbourne, Australia

SKATING: European Short Track Speed Skating Championships
Start, *Budapest, Hungary*

notes

25 sunday

Epiphany 3

first-half

second-half

extra-time

SPORTING FIXTURES

AMERICAN FOOTBALL: Superbowl XXXII,
San Diego, USA (BSkyB)

CRICKET: Carlton & United Breweries World Series 2nd Final,
Sydney, Australia (BSkyB)

GOLF: Johnnie Walker Classic - Round 4,
Phuket, Thailand

HOCKEY: Womens Indoor European Nations Cup Finishes,
Orense, Spain

ICE HOCKEY: European Hockey League - Final Four
- Final And 3rd/4th Place Playoff, *tbc*

LAWN TENNIS: Australian Open Championships - Day 7,
Melbourne, Australia

SKATING: European Short Track Speed Skating Championships
Finish, *Budapest, Hungary*

SNOOKER: Regal Welsh Open Finishes,
Newport (BSkyB)

Februar

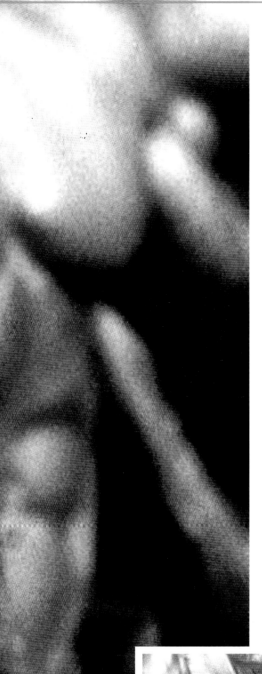

M	.	2	9	16	23
T	.	3	10	17	24
W	.	4	11	18	25
T	.	5	12	19	26
F	.	6	13	20	27
S	.	7	14	21	28
S	1	8	15	22	.

1998

FEBRUARY

★ **FRANCE V ENGLAND** RUGBY UNION **7 FEB** Paris, France

★ **IRELAND V SCOTLAND** RUGBY UNION **7 FEB** Lansdowne Rd, Ireland

★ **18TH WINTER OLYMPIC GAMES** OLYMPICS **7 - 22 FEB** Nagano, Japan

★ **CABLE & WIRELESS 2ND TEST MATCH WEST INDIES V ENGLAND**
CRICKET **13 - 17 FEB** Port-Of-Spain, Trinidad & Tobago

★ **FA CUP 5TH ROUND** FOOTBALL **14 FEB** Various Venues

★ **BUPA INDOOR GRAND PRIX - RICOH TOUR** ATHLETICS **15 FEB** Birmingham

★ **DAYTONA 500** NASCAR **15 FEB** Daytona Beach, USA

★ **COCA-COLA CUP SEMI FINALS 2ND LEG** FOOTBALL **18 FEB** To be confirmed

★ **ENGLAND V WALES** RUGBY UNION **21 FEB** Twickenham

★ **SCOTLAND V FRANCE** RUGBY UNION **21 FEB** Murrayfield

★ **LONDON INDOORS** TENNIS **23 FEB - 1 MAR** London

★ **CABLE & WIRELESS 3RD TEST MATCH- WEST INDIES V ENGLAND**
CRICKET **27 FEB - 3 MAR** Georgetown, Guyana

★ **ENGLAND V ISRAEL** BASKETBALL **28 FEB** Manchester

RUSSELL CHEYNE

26 monday

first-half

second-half

extra-time

SPORTING FIXTURES

BOBSLEIGH: Europa Cup 4 Starts (Finishes 1st Feb),
St Moritz, Switzerland

LAWN TENNIS: Australian Open Championships - Day 8,
Melbourne, Australia

27 tuesday

CRICKET: Carlton & United Breweries World Series 3rd Final,
Sydney, Australia (BSkyB)

LAWN TENNIS: Australian Open Championships - Day 9,
Melbourne, Australia

SQUASH: British National Championships Start (Finish 2nd Feb),
Manchester

28 wednesday

Chinese New Year ● New Moon

LAWN TENNIS: Australian Open Championships - Day 10,
Melbourne, Australia

SKIING: Men's World Cup Skiing - Day 1,
Garmisch Partenkirchen, Germany (Eurosport)

31 saturday

first-half

second-half

extra-time

SPORTING FIXTURES

ATHLETICS: Cross Auchan Lille Metropole,
Tourcoing, France

CRICKET: Cable & Wireless 1st Test,
West Indies v England - Day 3,
Kingston, Jamaica (BSkyB)
3rd Test, Australia v South Africa - Day 2,
Adelaide, Australia (BSkyB)

LAWN TENNIS: Australian Open Championships - Women's
Final, *Melbourne, Australia*

RUGBY UNION: Heineken European Rugby Cup Final,
Twickenham (BSkyB)

SKIING: Men's World Cup Skiing - Day 4,
Garmisch Partenkirchen, Germany (Eurosport)

YACHTING: Whitbread Round The World Race - Start Leg Five,
Auckland, New Zealand (BBC)

29 thursday

first-half

second-half

extra-time

SPORTING FIXTURES

CRICKET: Cable & Wireless 1st Test,
West Indies v England - Day 1,
Kingston, Jamaica (BSkyB)

LAWN TENNIS: Australian Open Championships
- Women's Semi-Finals,
Melbourne, Australia

SKIING: Men's World Cup Skiing - Day 2,
Garmisch Partenkirchen, Germany (Eurosport)

30 friday

BADMINTON: Liverpool Victoria Nationals Start (Finish 1st Feb),
Haywards Heath

CRICKET: 3rd Test Australia v South Africa - Day 1,
Adelaide, Australia (BSkyB)
Cable & Wireless 1st Test, West Indies v England - Day 2,
Kingston, Jamaica (BSkyB)

LAWN TENNIS: Australian Open Championships
- Men's Semi-Finals, *Melbourne, Australia*

SKIING: Men's World Cup Skiing - Day 3,
Garmisch Partenkirchen, Germany (Eurosport)

notes

1 sunday

Epiphany 4

first-half

second-half

extra-time

SPORTING FIXTURES

AMERICAN FOOTBALL: AFC/NFC Pro-Bowl,
Honolulu, USA (BSkyB)

ATHLETICS: Tokyo International Marathon,
Tokyo, Japan

BADMINTON: Liverpool Victoria Nationals Finish,
Haywards Heath

BOBSLEIGH: Europa Cup 4 Finishes,
St Moritz, Switzerland

BOWLS: World Indoor Championships for Men Finish,
Preston (BBC)

CRICKET: Under-19 World Cup Finishes,
Various, South Africa
Cable & Wireless 1st Test, West Indies v England - Day 4,
Kingston, Jamaica (BSkyB)
3rd Test Australia v South Africa - Day 3,
Adelaide, Australia (BSkyB)

LAWN TENNIS: Australian Open Championships - Men's Final,
Melbourne, Australia

SNOOKER: Benson & Hedges Masters Start (Finish 8th Feb),
Wembley (BBC)

2 monday

Candlemas (Scottish Term Day)

first-half

second-half

extra-time

SPORTING FIXTURES

CRICKET: Cable & Wireless 1st Test,
West Indies v England - Day 5,
Kingston, Jamaica (BSkyB)
3rd Test, Australia v South Africa - Day 4,
Adelaide, Australia (BSkyB)

SQUASH: British National Championships Finish,
Manchester

3 tuesday

☽ First Quarter

SPORTING FIXTURES

ATHLETICS: Memorial Jose Ma Cagival,
Madrid, Spain

CRICKET: 3rd Test, Australia v South Africa - Day 5,
Adelaide, Australia (BSkyB)

LIFE SAVING: World Championships Start
(Finish 15th Feb),
Auckland, New Zealand

4 wednesday

SPORTING FIXTURES

BOBSLEIGH: World Cup Starts (Finishes 7th Feb),
Calgary, Canada

CRICKET: 1st One Day International,
New Zealand v Zimbabwe,
Hamilton, New Zealand

7 saturday

first-half

second-half

extra-time

SPORTING FIXTURES

BOBSLEIGH: World Cup Finishes,
Calgary, Canada

FOOTBALL: African Nations Cup Starts (Finishes 28th Feb),
Ouagadougou, Burkina Faso

ICE HOCKEY: 18th Winter Olympic Games - Germany v Japan,
Nagano, Japan (BBC)

RUGBY UNION: Ireland v Scotland,
Lansdowne Road, Ireland (BBC)
France v England,
Paris, France (BSkyB)
Wales v Italy, **tbc** (BBC)

5 thursday

first-half

second-half

extra-time

SPORTING FIXTURES

BASKETBALL: NBA All Star Weekend Starts (Finish 8th Feb),
New York, USA (BSkyB)

MOTOR RALLYING: International Swedish Rally Starts
(Finishes 8th Feb),
Karlstad, Sweden (Eurosport)

6 friday

Accession of Queen Elizabeth II

BADMINTON: Friends Provident Grand Slam Starts
(Finishes 8th Feb),
Kirkham

CRICKET: 2nd One Day International,
New Zealand v Zimbabwe,
Wellington, New Zealand

notes

8 sunday

Septuagesima, 9th before Easter

first-half

second-half

extra-time

SPORTING FIXTURES

ATHLETICS: Almond Blossom Cross Country,
Vilamoura, Portugal
Flanders Indoors,
Ghent, Belgium

BADMINTON: Friends Provident Grand Slam Finishes,
Kirkham

BASKETBALL: NBA All Star Game,
New York, USA (BSkyB)

CRICKET: 1st One Day International New Zealand v Australia,
Christchurch, New Zealand (BSkyB)

MOTOR RALLYING: International Swedish Rally Finishes,
Karlstad, Sweden

NETBALL: Wales v England, *Cardiff*

SKATING: 18th Winter Olympic Games - Pair Short Program,
Nagano, Japan (BBC)

SKIING: Winter Olympic Games - Men's Downhill,
Hakuba, Japan (BBC)

SNOOKER: Benson & Hedges Masters Finish,
Wembley (BBC)

9 monday

10 tuesday

11 wednesday

○ Full Moon

first-half

second-half

extra-time

SPORTING FIXTURES

LAWN TENNIS: Dubai Tennis Open Starts (Finishes 15th Feb),
Dubai, UAE (Eurosport)
Open Gaz De France Starts (Finishes 15th Feb),
Paris, France

SKIING: Winter Olympic Games - Men's Combined Downhill,
Hakuba, Japan (BBC)

CRICKET: 2nd One Day International, New Zealand v Australia,
Wellington, New Zealand (BSkyB)

SKATING: Winter Olympic Games - Pair Free Program,
Nagano, Japan (BBC)

SKIING: Winter Olympic Games - Women's Super G,
Hakuba, Japan (BBC)

SNOOKER: Scottish Open Starts (Finish 22nd Feb),
Aberdeen (BSkyB)

BIATHLON: Winter Olympic Games - Men's 20km,
Nozawa, Japan (BBC)

SKIING: Winter Olympic Games - Men's Combined Slalom,
Shiga Kogen, Japan (BBC)

14 saturday

St Valentine's Day

first-half

second-half

extra-time

SPORTING FIXTURES

BOBSLEIGH: Winter Olympic Games - Two Man
- 1st & 2nd Runs,
Nagano, Japan (BBC)

CRICKET: 4th One Day International, New Zealand v Australia,
Auckland, New Zealand (BSkyB)
1st Test, South Africa v Pakistan - Day 2,
Johannesburg, South Africa
Cable & Wireless 2nd Test, West Indies v England - Day 2,
Port-Of-Spain, Trinidad & Tobago (BSkyB)

GOLF: Alfred Dunhill South African PGA Championship
- Round 3,
Johannesburg, South Africa

SKIING: Winter Olympic Games - Women's Downhill,
Hakuba, Japan (BBC)

12 thursday

first-half

second-half

extra-time

SPORTING FIXTURES

CRICKET: 3rd One Day International, New Zealand v Australia, **Napier, New Zealand** (BSkyB)

GOLF: Alfred Dunhill South African PGA Championship - Round 1, **Johannesburg, South Africa**

SKATING: 18th Winter Olympic Games - Men's Short Program, **Nagano, Japan** (BBC)

SNOWBOARDING: 18th Winter Olympic Games - Halfpipe Final, **Shiga Kogen, Japan** (BBC)

13 friday

SPORTING FIXTURES

CRICKET: 1st Test South Africa v Pakistan - Day 1, **Johannesburg, South Africa**
Cable & Wireless 2nd Test, West Indies v England - Day 1, **Port-Of-Spain, Trinidad & Tobago** (BSkyB)

GOLF: Alfred Dunhill South African PGA Championship - Round 2, **Johannesburg, South Africa**

SKATING: 18th Winter Olympic Games - Ice Dancing, **Nagano, Japan** (BBC)

SKIING: 18th Winter Olympic Games - Men's Super G, **Hakuba, Japan** (BBC)

notes

15 sunday

Sexagesima, 8th before Easter

first-half

second-half

extra-time

SPORTING FIXTURES

ATHLETICS: BUPA Indoor Grand Prix Ricoh Tour, **Birmingham**

BOBSLEIGH: 18th Winter Olympic Games - Two Man - 3rd and 4th Run, **Nagano, Japan** (BBC)

CRICKET: Cable & Wireless 2nd Test, West Indies v England - Day 3, **Port-Of-Spain, Trinidad & Tobago** (BSkyB)
1st Test, South Africa v Pakistan - Day 3, **Johannesburg, South Africa**

GOLF: Alfred Dunhill South African PGA Championship - Round 4, **Johannesburg, South Africa**

LAWN TENNIS: Open Gaz De France Finishes, **Paris, France**
Dubai Tennis Open Finishes, **Dubai, UAE** (Eurosport)

LIFE SAVING: World Championships Finish, **Auckland, New Zealand**

MOTOR RACING: Daytona 500, **Daytona Beach, USA** (Eurosport)

SKIING: 18th Winter Olympic Games - Women's Combined Downhill, **Hakuba, Japan** (BBC)

16 monday

first-half

second-half

extra-time

SPORTING FIXTURES

CRICKET: Cable & Wireless 2nd Test,
West Indies v England - Day 4,
Port-Of-Spain, Trinidad & Tobago (BSkyB)
1st Test, South Africa v Pakistan - Day 4,
Johannesburg, South Africa

LAWN TENNIS: European Community Championships Starts
(Finishes 22nd Feb),
Antwerp, Belgium (Eurosport)
Kroger St. Jude International Starts (Finishes 22nd Feb),
Memphis, USA (Eurosport)

SKATING: 18th Winter Olympic Games - Ice Dancing, *Nagano,
Japan (BBC)*

17 tuesday

SPORTING FIXTURES

CRICKET: Cable & Wireless 2nd Test,
West Indies v England - Day 5,
Port-Of-Spain, Trinidad & Tobago (BSkyB)
1st Test, South Africa v Pakistan - Day 5,
Johannesburg, South Africa

DRAGON BOAT RACING: IDBF World Club Crew
Championships Start (Finish 22nd Feb),
Wellington, New Zealand

SKIING: 18th Winter Olympic Games
- Women's Combined Slalom,
Shiga Kogen, Japan (BBC)

18 wednesday

SPORTING FIXTURES

SKATING: 18th Winter Olympic Games
- Women's Short Program,
Nagano, Japan (BBC)

SKIING: 18th Winter Olympic Games - Men's Giant Slalom,
Shiga Kogen, Japan (BBC)

21 saturday

first-half

second-half

extra-time

SPORTING FIXTURES

BOBSLEIGH: 18th Winter Olympic Games
- Four Man 3rd and 4th Runs,
Nagano, Japan (BBC)

CRICKET: 1st Test, New Zealand v Zimbabwe - Day 3,
Wellington, New Zealand

MOTOR RALLYING: RAC British Rally Championship -
Rallysprint, *Silverstone*

RUGBY UNION: Scotland v France,
Murrayfield (BBC)
England v Wales,
Twickenham (BSkyB)

SKATING: 18th Winter Olympic Games - Exhibition,
Nagano, Japan (BBC)

SLEDDOG: BSHRA Championship Series - Day 1,
Thetford

19 thursday

☾ Last Quarter

first-half

second-half

extra-time

SPORTING FIXTURES

ATHLETICS: DN Games,
Stockholm, Sweden

CRICKET: 1st Test, New Zealand v Zimbabwe - Day 1,
Wellington, New Zealand

SKIING: 18th Winter Olympic Games - Women's Slalom,
Shiga Kogen, Japan (BBC)

20 friday

BOBSLEIGH: 18th Winter Olympic Games - Four Man
- 1st and 2nd Runs,
Nagano, Japan (BBC)

CRICKET: 1st Test, New Zealand v Zimbabwe - Day 2,
Wellington, New Zealand

HOCKEY: Mens Indoor European Club Championship Start
(Finishes 22nd Feb),
Hamburg, Germany

SKIING: 18th Winter Olympic Games - Women's Giant Slalom,
Shiga Kogen, Japan (BBC)

notes

22 sunday

Quinquagesima, 7th before Easter

first-half

second-half

extra-time

SPORTING FIXTURES

ATHLETICS: Meeting Vittel Du Pas De Calais,
Lievin, France

CRICKET: 1st Test, New Zealand v Zimbabwe - Day 4,
Wellington, New Zealand

DRAGON BOAT RACING: IDBF World Club Crew
Championships Finish,
Wellington, New Zealand

HOCKEY: Mens Indoor European Club Championship Finishes,
Hamburg, Germany

ICE HOCKEY: 18th Winter Olympic Games - Final,
Nagano, Japan (BBC)

LAWN TENNIS: European Community Championships Finish,
Antwerp, Belgium (Eurosport)
Kroger St. Jude International Finishes,
Memphis, USA (Eurosport)

SKIING: 18th Winter Olympic Games - Men's Slalom,
Shiga Kogen, Japan (BBC)

SLEDDOG: BSHRA Championship Series - Day 2,
Thetford

SNOOKER: Scottish Open Finishes,
Aberdeen (BSkyB)

M	.	2	9	16	23	30
T	.	3	10	17	24	31
W	.	4	11	18	25	.
T	.	5	12	19	26	.
F	.	6	13	20	27	.
S	.	7	14	21	28	.
S	1	8	15	22	29	.

1998
MARCH

RUSSELL CHEYNE

★ **FRANCE V IRELAND** RUGBY UNION **7 MAR** Paris, France

★ **WALES V SCOTLAND** RUGBY UNION **7 MAR** Wembley

★ **QANTAS AUSTRALIAN GRAND PRIX** FORMULA 1 **8 MAR** Melbourne, Australia

★ **THE YONEX ALL ENGLAND BADMINTON CHAMPIONSHIPS** BADMINTON **9 - 16 MAR** Birmingham

★ **CABLE & WIRELESS 4TH TEST MATCH - WEST INDIES V ENGLAND**
CRICKET **12 - 16 MAR** Barbados

★ **CHELTENHAM FESTIVAL** HORSE RACING **17 - 19 MAR** Cheltenham

★ **CABLE & WIRELESS 5TH TEST MATCH- WEST INDIES V ENGLAND**
CRICKET **20 - 24 MAR** Antigua

★ **IRELAND V WALES** RUGBY UNION **21 MAR** Lansdowne Rd, Ireland

★ **SCOTLAND V ENGLAND** RUGBY UNION **22 MAR** Edinburgh

★ **26TH WORLD CROSS COUNTRY CHAMPIONSHIPS** ATHLETICS **22 - 23 MAR** Marakesch, Morocco

★ **OXFORD V CAMBRIDGE UNIVERSITY BOAT RACE** ROWING **28 MAR** London

★ **CABLE & WIRELESS 1ST ONE DAY INTERNATIONAL- WEST INDIES V ENGLAND**
CRICKET **29 MAR** Barbados

★ **COCA-COLA CUP FINAL** FOOTBALL **29 MAR** Wembley

★ **HONG KONG RUGBY SEVENS** RUGBY UNION **29 - 31 MAR** Hong Kong

★ **WORLD FIGURE SKATING CHAMPIONSHIPS** SKATING **29 MAR - 5 APR** Minneapolis, USA

23 monday

first-half

second-half

extra-time

SPORTING FIXTURES

CRICKET: 1st Test, New Zealand v Zimbabwe - Day 5,
Wellington, New Zealand

LAWN TENNIS: IGA Tennis Classic Starts (Finishes 1st March),
Oklahoma City, USA
London Indoors Day 1, **London**

YACHTING: Whitbread Round The World Race - Finish Leg Five,
Sao Sebastiao, Brazil (BBC)

24 tuesday

Shrove Tuesday

LAWN TENNIS: London Indoors Day 2,
London

SKIING: FIS Freestyle World Cup,
Muju, Korea

25 wednesday

Ash Wednesday

BASKETBALL: Euro Championships Semi-Finals Round
- Belarus v England, **Belarus**

LAWN TENNIS: London Indoors Day 3, **London**

28 saturday

first-half

second-half

extra-time

SPORTING FIXTURES

ATHLETICS: European Indoor Championships Day 2,
Valencia, Spain (Eurosport)
Mombasa International Cross, **Mombasa, Kenya**

BASKETBALL: Euro Championships Semi-Finals Round -
England v Israel, **Manchester**

CRICKET: Cable & Wireless 3rd Test,
West Indies v England - Day 2,
Georgetown, Guyana (BSkyB)
2nd Test South Africa v Pakistan - Day 3,
Durban, South Africa

FOOTBALL: African Nations Cup Final,
Ouagadougou, Burkina Faso

GOLF: Dubai Desert Classic - Round 3,
Dubai, UAE

LAWN TENNIS: London Indoors Day 6, **London**

26 thursday

● New Moon

first-half

second-half

extra-time

SPORTING FIXTURES

CRICKET: 2nd Test, South Africa v Pakistan - Day 1,
Durban, South Africa

GOLF: Dubai Desert Classic - Round 1,
Dubai, UAE

LAWN TENNIS: London Indoors Day 4, *London*

SNOOKER: Liverpool Victoria Charity Challenge Starts
(Finishes 1st March), *Derby (ITV)*

27 friday

SPORTING FIXTURES

ATHLETICS: European Indoor Championships - Day 1,
Valencia, Spain (Eurosport)

CRICKET: 2nd Test, South Africa v Pakistan - Day 2,
Durban, South Africa
Cable & Wireless 3rd Test, West Indies v England - Day 1,
Georgetown, Guyana (BSkyB)

GOLF: Dubai Desert Classic - Round 2,
Dubai, UAE

LAWN TENNIS: London Indoors Day 5, *London*

notes

1 sunday

St David's Day, Wales *Quadragesima, 1st in Lent*

first-half

second-half

extra-time

SPORTING FIXTURES

ATHLETICS: European Indoor Championships - Day 3,
Valencia, Spain (Eurosport)
BAF Cross Country Championships & World Trials,
Belfast

CRICKET: Cable & Wireless 3rd Test, West Indies v England
- Day 3, *Georgetown, Guyana (BSkyB)*
2nd Test, South Africa v Pakistan - Day 4,
Durban, South Africa

GOLF: Dubai Desert Classic - Round 4,
Dubai, UAE

HORSE RACING: Hong Kong Derby,
Shae Tin, Hong Kong

LAWN TENNIS: IGA Tennis Classic Finishes,
Oklahoma City, USA
London Indoors Final, *London*

SNOOKER: Liverpool Victoria Charity Challenge Finishes,
Derby (ITV)

YACHTING: ISAF World Sailing Championship Starts
(Finishes 14th March),
Dubai, UAE

2 monday

first-half

second-half

extra-time

SPORTING FIXTURES

CRICKET: 2nd Test, South Africa v Pakistan - Day 5,
Durban, South Africa
Cable & Wireless 3rd Test, West Indies v England - Day 4,
***Georgetown, Guyana** (BSkyB)*

LAWN TENNIS: WTA Tour - State Farm Evert Cup Starts
(Finishes 15th March),
Indian Wells, USA
ATP Tour ABN/AMRO World Tennis Tournament Starts
(Finishes 8th March),
***Rotterdam, Holland** (Eurosport)*

3 tuesday

CRICKET: Cable & Wireless 3rd Test, West Indies v England -
Day 5,
***Georgetown, Guyana** (BSkyB)*

FOOTBALL: UEFA Cup - Quarter Final 1st Leg, ***tbc***

4 wednesday

BOXING: ABA Championships,
Birmingham

CRICKET: 3rd One Day International,
New Zealand v Zimbabwe,
Christchurch, New Zealand

FOOTBALL: UEFA Champions League - Quarter Final 1st Leg,
***tbc** (ITV)*

7 saturday

first-half

second-half

extra-time

SPORTING FIXTURES

CRICKET: 3rd Test, South Africa v Pakistan Day 2,
Port Elizabeth, South Africa

GOLF: Qatar Masters - Round 3,
Doha, Qatar

RUGBY UNION: France v Ireland,
***Paris, France** (BSkyB)*
Wales v Scotland,
***Wembley** (BBC)*

SKIING: Women's World Cup Skiing - Day 1,
***Morzine, France** (Eurosport)*

SNOOKER: Thailand Open Starts (Finishes 15th March),
Bangkok, Thailand

SWIMMING: National Synchronised Swimming Championships
Start (Finish 8th March),
Halifax

5 thursday

First Quarter

first-half

second-half

extra-time

SPORTING FIXTURES

DISABLED: Winter Paralympic Games Start (Finish 14th March), *Nagano, Japan*

GOLF: Qatar Masters - Round 1, *Doha, Qatar*

6 friday

CRICKET: 3rd Test, South Africa v Pakistan - Day 1, *Port Elizabeth, South Africa*
4th One Day International, New Zealand v Zimbabwe, *Napier, New Zealand*

GOLF: Qatar Masters - Round 2, *Doha, Qatar*

TABLE TENNIS: English National Championships Start (Finish 8th March), *tbc*

notes

8 sunday

2nd in Lent

first-half

second-half

extra-time

SPORTING FIXTURES

BASKETBALL: 7UP League Trophy Final, *Birmingham*

CRICKET: 5th One Day International, New Zealand v Zimbabwe, *Auckland, New Zealand*
3rd Test, South Africa v Pakistan - Day 3, *Port Elizabeth, South Africa*

GOLF: Qatar Masters - Round 4, *Doha, Qatar*

LAWN TENNIS: ABN/AMRO World Tennis Tournament Finishes, *Rotterdam, Holland (Eurosport)*

MOTOR RACING: Australian Grand Prix, *Melbourne, Australia (ITV)*

SKIING: Women's World Cup Skiing - Day 2, *Morzine, France (Eurosport)*

SWIMMING: National Synchronised Swimming Championships Finish, *Halifax*

TABLE TENNIS: English National Championships Finish, *tbc*

9 monday

Commonwealth Day

first-half

second-half

extra-time

SPORTING FIXTURES

BADMINTON: Yonex All England Championships - Day 1,
Birmingham (BSkyB)

BOWLS: British International Indoor Series for Men Starts
(Finishes 13th Mar), *Swansea*

CRICKET: 3rd Test, South Africa v Pakistan - Day 4,
Port Elizabeth, South Africa

LAWN TENNIS: ATP Tour - Newsweek Champions Cup Starts
(Finishes 15th March),
Indian Wells, USA (Eurosport)

10 tuesday

SPORTING FIXTURES

BADMINTON: Yonex All England Championships - Day 2,
Birmingham (BSkyB)

CRICKET: 3rd Test, South Africa v Pakistan - Day 5,
Port Elizabeth, South Africa

11 wednesday

SPORTING FIXTURES

BADMINTON: Yonex All England Championships - Day 3,
Birmingham (BSkyB)

BASKETBALL: Budweiser League All Star Game,
tbc (BSkyB)

FOOTBALL: European Super Cup Final 2nd Leg
- Borussia Dortmund v FC Barcelona,
Dortmund, Germany

SKIING: FIS World Cup Finals - Day 1,
Crans Montana, Switzerland (Eurosport)

14 saturday

first-half

second-half

extra-time

SPORTING FIXTURES

ATHLETICS: English National Cross Country Championships,
Leeds

BADMINTON: Yonex All England Championships - Finals,
Birmingham (BSkyB)

CRICKET: 1st Test, Zimbabwe v Pakistan - Day 1,
Bulawayo, Zimbabwe
Cable & Wireless 4th Test, West Indies v England - Day 3,
St Michael, Barbados (BSkyB)

DISABLED: Winter Paralympic Games Finish,
Nagano, Japan

GOLF: Moroccan Open - Round 3,
Rabat, Morocco

GYMNASTICS: British Team Championships for Men,
Guildford

SKIING: FIS World Cup Finals - Day 4,
Crans Montana, Switzerland (Eurosport)

YACHTING: Whitbread Round The World Race - Start Leg Six,
Sao Sebastiao, Brazil (BBC)
ISAF World Sailing Championship Finishes,
Dubai, UAE

12 thursday

first-half

second-half

extra-time

SPORTING FIXTURES

BADMINTON: Yonex All England Championships - Day 4, *Birmingham (BSkyB)*

CRICKET: Cable & Wireless 4th Test, West Indies v England - Day 1, *St Michael, Barbados (BSkyB)*

GOLF: Moroccan Open - Round 1, *Rabat, Morocco*

SKIING: FIS World Cup Finals - Day 2, *Crans Montana, Switzerland (Eurosport)*

13 friday

○ Full Moon

SPORTING FIXTURES

BADMINTON: Yonex All England Championships - Day 5, *Birmingham (BSkyB)*

BOWLS: British International Indoor Series for Men Finish, *Swansea*

CRICKET: Cable & Wireless 4th Test, West Indies v England - Day 2, *St Michael, Barbados (BSkyB)*

GOLF: Moroccan Open - Round 2, *Rabat, Morocco*

SKIING: FIS World Cup Finals - Day 3, *Crans Montana, Switzerland (Eurosport)*

notes

15 sunday

3rd in Lent

first-half

second-half

extra-time

SPORTING FIXTURES

CRICKET: 1st Test, Zimbabwe v Pakistan - Day 2, *Bulawayo, Zimbabwe*
Cable & Wireless 4th Test, West Indies v England - Day 4, *St Michael, Barbados (BSkyB)*

GOLF: Moroccan Open - Round 4, *Rabat, Morocco*

LAWN TENNIS: ATP Tour - Newsweek Champions Cup Finishes, *Indian Wells, USA (Eurosport)*
WTA Tour - State Farm Evert Cup Finishes, *Indian Wells, USA*

MOTOR CYCLING: SBK Superbike World Championship, *Sentul, Indonesia (BSkyB)*

MOTOR RACING: CART - Marlboro Grand Prix Of Miami, *Homestead, USA (Eurosport)*

SKIING: FIS World Cup Finals - Day 5, *Crans Montana, Switzerland (Eurosport)*

SNOOKER: Thailand Open Finishes, *Bangkok, Thailand*

16 monday

first-half

second-half

extra-time

SPORTING FIXTURES

BOWLS: British International Indoor Series for Women Starts, *Durlington*

CRICKET: 1st Test, Zimbabwe v Pakistan - Day 3, *Bulawayo, Zimbabwe*
Cable & Wireless 4th Test, West Indies v England - Day 5, *St Michael, Barbados (BSkyB)*

SKATING: British Precision Team Championships Starts (Finishes 17th March), *Bracknell*

LAWN TENNIS: ATP & WTA Tour - The Lipton Championships Starts (Finishes 29th March), *Key Biscayne, USA (Eurosport)*

17 tuesday

St Patrick's Day, Holiday Ireland

CRICKET: 1st Test, Zimbabwe v Pakistan - Day 4, *Bulawayo, Zimbabwe*

HORSE RACING: Cheltenham Festival - Day 1, *Cheltenham (C4)*

SKATING: British Precision Team Championships Finishes, *Bracknell*

18 wednesday

CRICKET: 1st Test, Zimbabwe v Pakistan - Day 5, *Bulawayo, Zimbabwe*

FOOTBALL: UEFA Champions League - Quarter Final 2nd Leg, *tbc (ITV)*

HORSE RACING: Cheltenham Festival - Day 2, *Cheltenham (C4)*

21 saturday

☾ Last Quarter

first-half

second-half

extra-time

SPORTING FIXTURES

CRICKET: 1st Test, South Africa v Sri Lanka - Day 3, *Cape Town, South Africa*
Cable & Wireless 5th Test, West Indies v England - Day 2, *St Johns, Antigua (BSkyB)*
2nd Test, Zimbabwe v Pakistan - Day 1, *Harare, Zimbabwe*

CYCLING: World Cup Milano-San Remo, *Milan, Italy (Eurosport)*

FENCING: British 100th Sabre Championships, *London*

GOLF: Portuguese Open - Round 3, *Lisbon, Portugal*

MOTOR RALLYING: RAC British Rally Championship - Vauxhall Rally Of Wales Finish, *Chester*

ROWING: Head Of The River, *London*

RUGBY UNION: Ireland v Wales, *Lansdowne Road, Ireland (BBC)*

19 thursday

first-half

second-half

extra-time

SPORTING FIXTURES

CRICKET: 1st Test, South Africa v Sri Lanka - Day 1,
Cape Town, South Africa

GOLF: Portuguese Open - Round 1,
Lisbon, Portugal

HORSE RACING: Cheltenham Festival - Day 3,
Cheltenham (C4)

20 friday

Vernal Equinox

BOWLS: British International Indoor Series for Women Finishes,
Durlington

CRICKET. 1st Test, South Africa v Sri Lanka - Day 2,
Cape Town, South Africa
Cable & Wireless 5th Test, West Indies v England - Day 1,
St Johns, Antigua (BSkyB)

GOLF: Portuguese Open - Round 2, *Lisbon, Portugal*

MOTOR RALLYING: RAC British Rally Championship - Vauxhall
Rally Of Wales Start, *Chester*

notes

22 sunday

Mothering Sunday   *4th in Lent*

first-half

second-half

extra-time

SPORTING FIXTURES

ATHLETICS: IAAF World Cross Country Championships Start,
Marrakech, Morocco (Eurosport)

CRICKET: 1st Test, South Africa v Sri Lanka - Day 4,
Cape Town, South Africa
Cable & Wireless 5th Test, West Indies v England - Day 3,
St Johns, Antigua (BSkyB)
2nd Test, Zimbabwe v Pakistan - Day 2,
Harare, Zimbabwe

GOLF: Portuguese Open - Round 4,
Lisbon, Portugal

MOTOR CYCLING: SBK Superbike World Championship,
Phillip Island, Australia (BSkyB)

MOTOR RACING: Autosport British Formula 3 Championship,
Donington Park

MOTOR RALLYING: TAP Rallye Du Portugal Starts
(Finishes 25th March), *Figuera Da Foz, Portugal*

RUGBY UNION: Scotland v England,
Murrayfield (BBC)

23 monday

first-half

second-half

extra-time

SPORTING FIXTURES

CRICKET: 1st Test, South Africa v Sri Lanka - Day 5,
Cape Town, South Africa
Cable & Wireless 5th Test, West Indies v England - Day 4,
St Johns, Antigua (BSkyB)
2nd Test, Zimbabwe v Pakistan - Day 3,
Harare, Zimbabwe

24 tuesday

SPORTING FIXTURES

CRICKET: Cable & Wireless 5th Test, West Indies v England - Day 5,
St Johns, Antigua (BSkyB)
2nd Test, Zimbabwe v Pakistan - Day 4,
Harare, Zimbabwe

SNOOKER: Benson & Hedges Irish Masters Start
(Finish 29th March), *County Kildare, Ireland*

25 wednesday

Lady Day (Quarter Day)

first-half

SPORTING FIXTURES

BASKETBALL: Final of the Korac Cup - 1st leg,
tbc

CRICKET: 2nd Test, Zimbabwe v Pakistan - Day 5,
Harare, Zimbabwe

MOTOR RALLYING: TAP Rallye Du Portugal Finishes,
Figuera Da Foz, Portugal

28 saturday

● New Moon

first-half

second-half

extra-time

SPORTING FIXTURES

BOWLS: English National Indoor Championships for Men Start
(Finish 5th April),
Melton Mowbray

CRICKET: 2nd Test, South Africa v Sri Lanka - Day 2,
Verwoerdburg, South Africa
1st One Day International, Zimbabwe v Pakistan,
Harare, Zimbabwe

GOLF: The Players Championship - Round 3,
Ponte Vedra Beach, USA (BSkyB)

HORSE RACING: The Lincoln,
Doncaster

MOTOR RACING: CART - Budweiser 500,
Motegi, Japan (Eurosport)

RHYTHMIC GYMNASTICS: British Championships for Women
Start (Finish 29th March),
Bletchley

ROWING: Oxford v Cambridge Boat Race,
River Thames (BBC)

26 thursday

first-half

second-half

extra-time

SPORTING FIXTURES

GOLF: The Players Championship - Round 1,
Ponte Vedra Beach, USA (BSkyB)

SQUASH: British Open Starts (Finishes 6th April),
Grantham

27 friday

CRICKET: 2nd Test, South Africa v Sri Lanka - Day 1,
Verwoerdburg, South Africa

GOLF: The Players Championship - Round 2,
Ponte Vedra Beach, USA (BSkyB)

GYMNASTICS: British Championships for Women Start
(Finish 29th March), *Guildford*

MOTOR CYCLING: British Superbike Championship Starts,
Brands Hatch (BBC)

notes

29 sunday

British Summer Time begins   *5th in Lent*

first-half

second-half

extra-time

SPORTING FIXTURES

CRICKET: Cable & Wireless 1st One Day International,
West Indies v England,
St Michael, Barbados (BSkyB)

FOOTBALL: Coca-Cola Cup Final,
Wembley (ITV/BSkyB)

GOLF: The Players Championship - Round 4,
Ponte Vedra Beach, USA (BSkyB)

MOTOR CYCLING: Malaysian GP,
Shah Alam, Malaysia (Eurosport)
British Superbike Championship Finishes,
Brands Hatch (BBC)

MOTOR RACING: Brazilian Grand Prix,
Interlagos, Brazil (ITV)

LAWN TENNIS: ATP & WTA Tour - The Lipton Championships
Finishes, *Key Biscayne, USA (Eurosport)*

RUGBY UNION: Hong Kong Rugby Sevens Start
(Finish 31st March), *Hong Kong (BSkyB)*

SKATING: World Figure Skating Championships Start
(Finish 5th April),
Minneapolis, USA (Eurosport)

SNOOKER: Benson & Hedges Irish Masters Finish,
County Kildare, Ireland

M	.	6	13	20	27
T	.	7	14	21	28
W	1	8	15	22	29
T	2	9	16	23	30
F	3	10	17	24	.
S	4	11	18	25	.
S	5	12	19	26	.

1998
APRIL

RUSSELL CHEYNE

★ CABLE & WIRELESS 2ND ONE DAY INTERNATIONAL- WEST INDIES V ENGLAND
CRICKET **1 APRIL** Barbados

★ UEFA CHAMPIONS CUP - SEMI FINAL 1ST LEG
FOOTBALL **1 APRIL** Various venues

★ DAVIS CUP - GREAT BRITAIN V UKRAINE/DENMARK
TENNIS **3 - 5 APRIL** To be confirmed

★ CABLE & WIRELESS 3RD ONE DAY INTERNATIONAL- WEST INDIES V ENGLAND
CRICKET **4 APRIL** St. Vincent

★THE MARTELL GRAND NATIONAL HORSE RACING **4 APRIL** Aintree

★ ENGLAND V IRELAND RUGBY UNION **4 APRIL** Twickenham

★ CABLE & WIRELESS 4TH ONE DAY INTERNATIONAL - WEST INDIES V ENGLAND
CRICKET **5 APRIL** St. Vincent

★ WALES V FRANCE RUGBY UNION **5 APRIL** Wembley

★ CABLE & WIRELESS 5TH ONE DAY INTERNATIONAL- WEST INDIES V ENGLAND
CRICKET **8 APRIL** Port-Of-Spain Trinidad & Tobago

★ THE US MASTERS GOLF **9 - 12 APRIL** Augusta, USA

★ SBK SUPERBIKE WORLD CHAMPIONSHIP MOTOR CYCLING **13 APRIL** Donington Park

★ EMBASSY WORLD CHAMPIONSHIPS SNOOKER **18 APRIL - 4 MAY** Sheffield

★ FLORA LONDON MARATHON ATHLETICS **26 APRIL** London

30 monday

first-half

second-half

extra-time

SPORTING FIXTURES

CRICKET: 2nd Test, South Africa v Sri Lanka - Day 4,
Verwoerdburg, South Africa

LAWN TENNIS: WTA Tour - Family Circle Magazine Cup Starts
(Finishes 5th April),
Hilton Head Island, USA

31 tuesday

(cont. sporting fixtures)

CRICKET: 2nd Test, South Africa v Sri Lanka - Day 5,
Verwoerdburg, South Africa

FOOTBALL: UEFA Cup - Semi-Final 1st Leg,
Various, tbc

RUGBY UNION: Hong Kong Rugby Sevens Finish,
Hong Kong (BSkyB)

SNOOKER: British Open Starts (Finishes 12th April),
Plymouth (BSkyB)

1 wednesday

All Fools' Day

BASKETBALL: Final of the Korac Cup - 2nd leg,
tbc

CRICKET: Cable & Wireless 2nd One Day International,
West Indies v England, *St Michael, Barbados (BSkyB)*

FOOTBALL: UEFA Champions League- Semi-Final 1st Leg,
Various, tbc (ITV)

SKIING: British Universities Ski Championships Start
(Finish 5th April), *Les Arcs, France*

4 saturday

first-half

second-half

extra-time

SPORTING FIXTURES

ATHLETICS: FISU Cross Country Championships, *Luton*

CRICKET: Cable & Wireless 3rd One Day International,
West Indies v England,
Arnos Vale, St Vincent (BSkyB)

HORSE RACING: The Martell Grand National Steeple Chase,
Aintree (BBC)

LAWN TENNIS: Davis Cup - Great Britain v Ukraine/Denmark
Doubles Match,
tbc (BSkyB)

RUGBY UNION: England v Ireland,
Twickenham (BSkyB)

SKATING: British Short Track Speed Relay Championships,
Basingstoke

2 thursday

first-half

second-half

extra-time

SPORTING FIXTURES

FOOTBALL: European Cup Winners Cup - Semi-Final 1st Leg,
Various, tbc

YACHTING: Whitbread Round The World Race - Finish Leg Six,
Fort Lauderdale, USA (BBC)

3 friday

☽ First Quarter

SPORTING FIXTURES

CRICKET: Triangular Series, South Africa v Pakistan,
Durban, South Africa

LAWN TENNIS: Davis Cup - Great Britain v Ukraine/Denmark
1st Singles Matches,
tbc (BSkyB)

notes

---

5 sunday

Tax Year ends   *Palm Sunday*

first-half

second-half

extra-time

SPORTING FIXTURES

AMERICAN FOOTBALL: England v Frankfurt,
Crystal Palace (BSkyB)

BOWLS: English National Indoor Championships for Men Finish,
Melton Mowbray

CRICKET: Cable & Wireless 4th One Day International,
West Indies v England,
Arnos Vale, St Vincent (BSkyB)

LAWN TENNIS: Davis Cup - Great Britain v Ukraine/Denmark
2nd Singles Matches, *tbc (BSkyB)*
WTA Tour - Family Circle Magazine Cup Finishes,
Hilton Head Island, USA

MOTOR CYCLING: Japanese GP,
Suzuka, Japan (Eurosport)

RUGBY UNION: Wales v France,
Wembley (BBC)

SKATING: World Figure Skating Championships Finish,
Minneapolis, USA (Eurosport)

SKIING: British Universities Ski Championships Finish,
Les Arcs, France
English Ski Council Alpine Race Championships Start
(Finish 10th April),
Les Arcs, France

6 monday

first-half

second-half

extra-time

SPORTING FIXTURES

SQUASH: British Open Finishes, *Grantham*

LAWN TENNIS: WTA Tour - Bausch & Lomb Championships Start (Finish 12th April),
Amelia Island, USA
ATP Tour - Estoril Open Starts (Finishes 12th April),
Estoril, Portugal (Eurosport)

7 tuesday

BASKETBALL: Women's Euroleague - Final Four Starts (Finishes 9th April),
Bourges, France

CRICKET: Triangular Series, Pakistan v Sri Lanka,
Kimberley, South Africa

8 wednesday

Hilary Law Sittings end

CRICKET: Cable & Wireless 5th One Day International, West Indies v England,
Port-Of-Spain, Trinidad & Tobago (BSkyB)

SKATING: ISU World Precision Team Skating Challenge Cup Start (Finish 12th Apr),
Bordeaux, France

11 saturday

First Day of Passover (Pesach) ◯ Full Moon

first-half

second-half

extra-time

SPORTING FIXTURES

AMERICAN FOOTBALL: England v Rhein,
Bristol (BSkyB)

CRICKET: Triangular Series, Pakistan v South Africa,
East London, South Africa

GOLF: The Masters - Round 3,
Augusta, USA (BBC)

HORSE RACING: Easter Cup,
Melbourne, Australia

JUDO: British Open Championships Start (Finish 12th April),
Birmingham

ROWING: International Spring Regatta Starts
(Finishes 12th April),
Ghent, Belgium

9 thursday

first-half

second-half

extra-time

SPORTING FIXTURES

BASKETBALL: Women's Euroleague - Final Four Finishes, *Bourges, France*

CRICKET: Triangular Series, Pakistan v Sri Lanka, *Paarl, South Africa*

GOLF: The Masters - Round 1, *Augusta, USA (BBC)*

10 friday

Good Friday, Holiday UK & Republic of Ireland

FIELD HOCKEY: Mens European Club Championship - A Division Starts (Finish 13th Apr), *Terassa, Spain*

GOLF: The Masters - Round 2, *Augusta, USA (BBC)*

SKIING: English Ski Council Alpine Race Championships Finish, *Les Arcs, France*

notes

12 sunday

Easter Day

first-half

second-half

extra-time

SPORTING FIXTURES

AMERICAN FOOTBALL: Amsterdam v Scotland, *Amsterdam, Holland (BSkyB)*

CYCLING: World Cup Paris-Roubaix, *Paris, France (Eurosport)*

GOLF: The Masters - Round 4, *Augusta, USA (BBC)*

JUDO: British Open Championships Finish, *Birmingham*

LAWN TENNIS: WTA Tour - Bausch & Lomb Championships Finish, *Amelia Island, USA*
ATP Tour - Estoril Open Finishes, *Estoril, Portugal (Eurosport)*

MOTOR RACING: Argentine Grand Prix, *Buenos Aires, Argentina (ITV)*

ROWING: International Spring Regatta Finishes, *Ghent, Belgium*

SKATING: ISU World Precision Team Skating Challenge Cup Finish, *Bordeaux, France*

SNOOKER: British Open Finishes, *Plymouth (BSkyB)*

13 monday

Bank Holiday UK & Republic of Ireland

first-half

second-half

extra-time

SPORTING FIXTURES

CRICKET: Triangular Series, Sri Lanka v South Africa, *Port Elizabeth, South Africa*

LAWN TENNIS: ATP & WTA Tour - Japan Open Starts (19th April), *Tokyo, Japan (Eurosport)*

MOTOR CYCLING: SBK Superbike World Championship, *Donington Park (BSkyB)*

MOTOR RACING: RAC Touring Car Championship, *Thruxton (BBC)*

14 tuesday

SPORTING FIXTURES

BASKETBALL: Final of the Eurocup, *Belgrade, Yugoslavia*

FOOTBALL: UEFA Cup - Semi-Final 2nd Leg, *Various, tbc*

15 wednesday

SPORTING FIXTURES

CRICKET: Triangular Series, Sri Lanka v Pakistan, *Benoni, South Africa*

EQUESTRIAN: Volvo World Cup Show Jumping Final Starts (Finishes 19th April), *Helsinki, Finland*

FOOTBALL: UEFA Champions League- Semi-Final 2nd Leg, *Various, tbc (ITV)*

ICE HOCKEY: World Championship Pool B Starts (Finishes 24th April), *Ljubljana & Jesenice, Slovenia*

18 saturday

first-half

second-half

extra-time

SPORTING FIXTURES

AMERICAN FOOTBALL: Frankfurt v England, *Frankfurt, Germany (BSkyB)*

ATHLETICS: IAAF World Road Relay Championships Start (Finish 19th April), *Manaus, Brazil*

BADMINTON: European Championships Start (Finish 25th April), *Sofia, Bulgaria*

DRAGON BOAT RACING: Euro-Cup Races (Finish 19th April), *Rome, Italy*

GOLF: Air France Cannes Open - Round 3, *Cannes, France*

GYMNASTICS: World Cup for Men & Women - Sagit Cup Finishes, *Vancouver, Canada*

LAWN TENNIS: KB Fed Cup - Round 1 - Day 1, *Various (BSkyB)*

SNOOKER: Embassy World Championships Start (Finish 4th May), *Sheffield (BBC)*

16 thursday

first-half

second-half

extra-time

SPORTING FIXTURES

FOOTBALL: European Cup Winners Cup - Semi-Final 2nd Leg,
Various, tbc

GOLF: Air France Cannes Open - Round 1,
Cannes, France

17 friday

CRICKET: Triangular Series, South Africa v Pakistan,
Verwoerdburg, South Africa

GOLF: Air France Cannes Open - Round 2,
Cannes, France

GYMNASTICS: World Cup for Men & Women - Sagit Cup Starts
(Finishes 18th April),
Vancouver, Canada

notes

19 sunday

Low Sunday, Easter 1 ☾ Last Quarter

first-half

second-half

extra-time

SPORTING FIXTURES

ATHLETICS: IAAF World Road Relay Championships Finish,
Manaus, Brazil

CRICKET: Triangular Series, South Africa v Sri Lanka,
Bloemfontein, South Africa

CYCLING: World Cup Liege-Bastogne-Liege,
Belgium (Eurosport)

EQUESTRIAN: Volvo World Cup Show Jumping Final Finishes,
Helsinki, Finland

GOLF: Air France Cannes Open - Round 4,
Cannes, France

LAWN TENNIS: ATP & WTA Tour - Japan Open Finishes,
Tokyo, Japan (Eurosport)
KB Fed Cup - Round 1 - Day 2,
Various (BSkyB)

MOTOR CYCLING: Indonesian GP,
Sentul, Indonesia (Eurosport)

MOTOR RALLYING: 32 Rallye De Catalunya Costa Brava
- Rallye Of Spain Starts,
Lloret De Mar, Spain

YACHTING: Whitbread Round The World Race
- Start Leg Seven,
Fort Lauderdale, USA (BBC)

20 monday

first-half

second-half

extra-time

SPORTING FIXTURES

ATHLETICS: Boston Marathon,
Hopkinton To Boston, USA

LAWN TENNIS: ATP Tour - Monte Carlo Open Starts
(Finishes 26th April),
Monte Carlo, Monaco (Eurosport)
WTA Tour - Budapest Lotto Ladies Open Starts
(Finishes 26th April),
Budapest, Hungary

21 tuesday

Easter Law Sittings begin   Birthday, HM Queen Elizabeth II, b. 1926

BASKETBALL: Final Four Euroleague For Men Starts
(Finishes 23rd April),
Barcelona, Spain

22 wednesday

CRICKET: Triangular Series Final,
Cape Town, South Africa

MOTOR RALLYING: 32 Rallye De Catalunya Costa Brava
- Rallye Of Spain Finishes,
Lloret De Mar, Spain

YACHTING: Whitbread Round The World Race
- Finish Leg Seven,
Baltimore, USA (BBC)

25 saturday

first-half

second-half

extra-time

SPORTING FIXTURES

ATHLETICS: European Cup - Race Walking,
Dudince, Slovakia

BADMINTON: European Championships Finish,
Sofia, Bulgaria

BOWLS: English Bowls Players Association Singles
Championship Finals,
Wellingborough

CYCLING: World Cup Amstel Gold Race,
Heerlen - Maastrich, Holland (Eurosport)

GOLF: Turespana Masters - Round 3,
Maspalomas, Spain

JUDO: BSJA National Individual Championships,
Cannock

MOTOR RALLYING: RAC British Rally Championship
- Pirelli International Rally, *Carlisle*

23 thursday

St George's Day, England

first-half

second-half

extra-time

SPORTING FIXTURES

BASKETBALL: Final Four Euroleague For Men Finishes,
Barcelona, Spain
NBA Play-Offs Begin, *tbc, USA (BSkyB/C4)*

GOLF: Turespana Masters - Round 1, *Maspalomas, Spain*

SQUASH: European Team Championships Start
(Finish 26th April), *Lahti, Finland*

TABLE TENNIS: European Championships Start
(Finish 3rd May), *Eindhoven, Holland*

24 friday

GOLF: Turespana Masters - Round 2,
Maspalomas, Spain

ICE HOCKEY: World Championship Pool B Finishes,
Ljubljana & Jesenice, Slovenia

MOTOR CYCLING: British Superbike Championship Start
(Finish 26th April)
Oulton Park (BBC)

notes

26 sunday

Easter 2 ● New Moon

first-half

second-half

extra-time

SPORTING FIXTURES

AMERICAN FOOTBALL: England v Scotland,
Birmingham (BSkyB)

ATHLETICS: Flora London Marathon,
London (BBC)

BOWLS: English Bowls Players Association Singles Championship
Finals, *Wellingborough*

GOLF: Turespana Masters - Round 4, *Maspalomas, Spain*

LAWN TENNIS: WTA Tour - Budapest Lotto Ladies Open
Finishes,
Budapest, Hungary
ATP Tour - Monte Carlo Open Finishes,
Monte Carlo, Monaco (Eurosport)

MOTOR CYCLING: British Superbike Championship Finish,
Oulton Park (BBC)

MOTOR RACING: RAC Touring Car Championship,
Silverstone (BBC)
San Marino Grand Prix,
Imola, Italy (ITV)

SQUASH: European Team Championships Finish,
Lahti, Finland

RUSSELL CHEYNE

M	.	4	11	18	25
T	.	5	12	19	26
W	.	6	13	20	27
T	.	7	14	21	28
F	1	8	15	22	29
S	2	9	16	23	30
S	3	10	17	24	31

1998 MAY

★ **THE SAGITTA 2000 GUINEAS** HORSE RACING **2 MAY** Newmarket

★ **THE SAGITTA 1000 GUINEAS** HORSE RACING **3 MAY** Newmarket

★ **UEFA CUP - FINAL** FOOTBALL **6 MAY** To be confirmed

★ **MITSUBISHI MOTORS BADMINTON HORSE TRIALS** EQUESTRIAN **7 - 10 MAY** Badminton

★ **THE WELSH INTERNATIONAL OPEN** TENNIS **10 - 17 MAY** Cardiff

★ **EUROPEAN CUP WINNERS' CUP - FINAL** FOOTBALL **13 MAY** To be confirmed

★ **MIDDLESEX SEVENS** RUGBY UNION **16 MAY** Twickenham

★ **FA CUP FINAL** FOOTBALL **16 MAY** Wembley

★ **UEFA CHAMPIONS CUP- FINAL** FOOTBALL **20 MAY** To be confirmed

★ **1ST TEXACO TROPHY ONE-DAY INTERNATIONAL - ENGLAND V SOUTH AFRICA**
CRICKET **21 MAY** The Oval

★ **VOLVO PGA CHAMPIONSHIP** GOLF **22 - 25 MAY** Wentworth

★ **2ND TEXACO TROPHY ONE-DAY INTERNATIONAL - ENGLAND V SOUTH AFRICA**
CRICKET **23 MAY** Old Trafford

★ **3RD TEXACO TROPHY ONE-DAY INTERNATIONAL - ENGLAND V SOUTH AFRICA**
CRICKET **24 MAY** Headingley

★ **MONACO GRAND PRIX** FORMULA 1 **24 MAY** Monte Carlo, Monaco

★ **WHITBREAD ROUND THE WORLD RACE FOR THE VOLVO TROPHY - FINISH**
YACHTING **24 MAY** Southampton

★ **FRENCH OPEN CHAMPIONSHIPS** TENNIS **25 MAY - 7 JUN** Paris, France

★ **BRITISH NATIONS CUP AND GRAND PRIX** EQUESTRIAN **28 - 31 MAY** To be confirmed

27 monday

first-half

second-half

extra-time

SPORTING FIXTURES

LAWN TENNIS: ATP Tour - BMW Open - Day 1,
Munich, Germany *(Eurosport)*
WTA Tour - Rexona Cup - Day 1,
Hamburg, Germany

28 tuesday

Islamic New Year 1419

SPORTING FIXTURES

LAWN TENNIS: ATP Tour - BMW Open - Day 2,
Munich, Germany *(Eurosport)*
WTA Tour - Rexona Cup - Day 2,
Hamburg, Germany

29 wednesday

SPORTING FIXTURES

LAWN TENNIS: ATP Tour - BMW Open - Day 3,
Munich, Germany *(Eurosport)*
WTA Tour - Rexona Cup - Day 3,
Hamburg, Germany

2 saturday

first-half

second-half

extra-time

SPORTING FIXTURES

AMERICAN FOOTBALL: Amsterdam v England,
Amsterdam, Holland *(BSkyB)*

BASKETBALL: Budweiser Championship Finals,
tbc *(BSkyB)*
NBA Conference Semi-Finals Begin,
tbc, USA *(BSkyB/C4)*

GOLF: Conte Of Florence Italian Open - Round 3,
Brescia, Italy

HORSE RACING: Visa Triple Crown Championship Series -
Kentucky Derby,
Churchill Downs, USA
The Sagitta 2000 Guineas Stakes,
Newmarket *(C4)*

LAWN TENNIS: ATP Tour - BMW Open - Day 6,
Munich, Germany *(Eurosport)*
WTA Tour - Rexona Cup - Day 6,
Hamburg, Germany

RUGBY LEAGUE: Silk Cut Challenge Cup Final,
Wembley *(BBC)*

RUGBY UNION: Womens Rugby World Cup Starts
(Finishes 16th May),
Amsterdam, Holland

30 thursday

first-half

second-half

extra-time

SPORTING FIXTURES

GOLF: Conte Of Florence Italian Open - Round 1,
Brescia, Italy

GYMNASTICS: European Championships For Women Start
(Finish 3rd May),
St Petersburg, Russia

LAWN TENNIS: ATP Tour - BMW Open - Day 4,
Munich, Germany (Eurosport)
WTA Tour - Rexona Cup - Day 4,
Hamburg, Germany

1 friday

Holiday Republic of Ireland

SPORTING FIXTURES

GOLF: Conte Of Florence Italian Open - Round 2, *Brescia, Italy*

ICE HOCKEY: World Championship Pool A Starts (Finishes 17th
May), *Basel & Zurich, Switzerland (Eurosport)*

LAWN TENNIS: WTA Tour - Rexona Cup - Day 5, *Hamburg,
Germany*
ATP Tour - BMW Open - Day 5, *Munich, Germany (Eurosport)*

SPEEDWAY: Individual World Championship Qualifier, *Mureck,
Austria*

notes

3 sunday

Easter 3 ◗ First Quarter

first-half

second-half

extra-time

SPORTING FIXTURES

BASKETBALL: Budweiser Championship Finals,
tbc (BSkyB)

GOLF: Conte Of Florence Italian Open - Round 4,
Brescia, Italy

GYMNASTICS: European Championships For Men Finish,
St Petersburg, Russia

HORSE RACING: The Sagitta 1000 Guineas Stakes,
Newmarket (C4)

LAWN TENNIS: WTA Tour - Rexona Cup- Final,
Hamburg, Germany
ATP Tour - BMW Open - Final,
Munich, Germany (Eurosport)

MOTOR CYCLING: Spanish Grand Prix,
Jerez De La Frontera, Spain (Eurosport)
British Superbike Championship Starts,
Thruxton (BBC)

TABLE TENNIS: European Championships Finish, *Eindhoven,
Holland*

YACHTING: Whitbread Round The World Race
- Start Leg Eight,
Baltimore, USA (BBC)

4 monday

Bank Holiday UK

first-half

second-half

extra-time

SPORTING FIXTURES

LAWN TENNIS: WTA Tour - Italian Open - Day 1, *Rome, Italy*
ATP Tour - German Open - Day 1, *Hamburg, Germany*
(Eurosport)

MOTOR CYCLING: British Superbike Championship Finishes,
Thruxton (BBC)

MOTOR RACING: RAC Touring Car Championship,
Donington Park, (BBC)

SNOOKER: Embassy World Championships Finish,
Sheffield (BBC)

5 tuesday

LAWN TENNIS: ATP Tour - German Open - Day 2,
Hamburg, Germany (Eurosport)
WTA Tour - Italian Open - Day 2,
Rome, Italy

6 wednesday

FOOTBALL: UEFA Cup - Final, *tbc*

LAWN TENNIS: WTA Tour - Italian Open - Day 3,
Rome, Italy
ATP Tour - German Open - Day 3,
Hamburg, Germany (Eurosport)

9 saturday

first-half

second-half

extra-time

SPORTING FIXTURES

AMERICAN FOOTBALL: Rhein v Scotland,
Rhein, Germany (BSkyB)

ATHLETICS: IAAF Grand Prix In Osaka,
Osaka, Japan

FENCING: British Foil Championships,
Reading

GOLF: Peugeot Open De Espana - Round 3,
Madrid, Spain

LAWN TENNIS: WTA Tour - Italian Open - Day 6,
Rome, Italy
ATP Tour - German Open - Day 6,
Hamburg, Germany (Eurosport)

RUGBY UNION: Tetley Bitter Cup Final,
Twickenham (BBC)

SPEEDWAY: Individual World Championship Qualifying,
Krsko, Slovenia

7 thursday

first-half

second-half

extra-time

SPORTING FIXTURES

EQUESTRIAN: Badminton Horse Trials Start
(Finish 10th May),
Badminton (BBC)

GOLF: Peugeot Open De Espana - Round 1,
Madrid, Spain

LAWN TENNIS: ATP Tour - German Open - Day 4,
Hamburg, Germany (Eurosport)
WTA Tour - Italian Open - Day 4,
Rome, Italy

8 friday

GOLF: Peugeot Open De Espana - Round 2,
Madrid, Spain

LAWN TENNIS: WTA Tour - Italian Open - Day 5,
Rome, Italy
ATP Tour - German Open - Day 5,
Hamburg, Germany (Eurosport)

MOTOR CYCLING: British Superbike Championship Start,
Snetterton (BBC)

notes

10 sunday

Easter 4

first-half

second-half

extra-time

SPORTING FIXTURES

AMERICAN FOOTBALL: England v Amsterdam,
Crystal Palace (BSkyB)

EQUESTRIAN: Badminton Horse Trials Finish,
Badminton (BBC)

GOLF: Peugeot Open De Espana - Round 4,
Madrid, Spain

HOCKEY: AEWHA Cup Finals, *Milton Keynes*

LAWN TENNIS: ATP Tour - German Open - Final,
Hamburg, Germany (Eurosport)
WTA Tour - Italian Open - Final,
Rome, Italy

MOTOR CYCLING: British Superbike Championship Finish,
Snetterton (BBC)
SBK Superbike World Championship,
Monza, Italy (BSkyB)

MOTOR RACING: Spanish Grand Prix,
Barcelona, Spain (ITV)
CART - Rio 400,
Rio De Janeiro, Brazil (Eurosport)

11 monday

○ Full Moon

first-half

second-half

extra-time

SPORTING FIXTURES

AMERICAN FOOTBALL: Barcelona v Frankfurt,
***Barcelona, Spain** (BSkyB)*

LAWN TENNIS: ATP Tour - Campionati Internazionali D'Italia
- TIM Cup - Day 1,
***Rome, Italy** (Eurosport)*

12 tuesday

LAWN TENNIS: ATP Tour - Campionati Internazionali D'Italia
- TIM Cup - Day 2,
***Rome, Italy** (Eurosport)*

POLO: Prince Of Wales Trophy Starts (Finishes 24th May),
Royal County of Berkshire Polo Club

13 wednesday

FOOTBALL: European Cup Winners Cup - Final,
tbc

LAWN TENNIS: ATP Tour - Campionati Internazionali D'Italia
- TIM Cup - Day 3,
***Rome, Italy** (Eurosport)*

16 saturday

first-half

second-half

extra-time

SPORTING FIXTURES

BASKETBALL: NBA Conference Finals Begin,
***USA** (BSkyB/C4)*

BOXING: European Championships Start (Finish 26th May),
Minsk, Belarus

CYCLING: Giro D'Italia Starts (Finishes 7th June),
***Various, Italy** (Eurosport)*

FOOTBALL: FA Cup Final,
***Wembley** (ITV)*

GOLF: Benson & Hedges International Open - Round 3,
***Oxford** (BBC)*

LAWN TENNIS: ATP Tour - Campionati Internazionali D'Italia
- TIM Cup - Day 6,
***Rome, Italy** (Eurosport)*

MOTOR RACING: Formula 3000 International Championship
Round 1, ***Silverstone***

RUGBY UNION: Middlesex Sevens, ***Twickenham** (BBC)*
3rd Womens Rugby World Cup Finishes,
Amsterdam, Holland

YACHTING: Whitbread Round The World Race
- Finish Leg Eight,
***La Rochelle, France** (BBC)*

14 thursday

first-half

second-half

extra-time

SPORTING FIXTURES

GOLF: Benson & Hedges International Open - Round 1,
Oxford (BBC)

JUDO: European Championships Start (Finish 17th May),
Oviedo, Spain

LAWN TENNIS: ATP Tour - Campionati Internazionali D'Italia
- TIM Cup - Day 4,
Rome, Italy (Eurosport)

15 friday

Whitsunday (Scottish Term Day)

SPORTING FIXTURES

GOLF: Brabazon Trophy Starts (Finishes 17th May),
Liverpool
Benson & Hedges International Open - Round 2,
Oxford (BBC)

GYMNASTICS: World Aerobic Championships Start
(Finish 17th May),
Catania, Italy

LAWN TENNIS: ATP Tour - Campionati Internazionali D'Italia
- TIM Cup - Day 5,
Rome, Italy (Eurosport)

notes

17 sunday

Rogation Sunday

first-half

second-half

extra-time

SPORTING FIXTURES

AMERICAN FOOTBALL: Scotland v England,
Murrayfield (BSkyB)

GOLF: Benson & Hedges International Open - Round 4,
Oxford (BBC)
Brabazon Trophy Finishes, *Liverpool*

GYMNASTICS: World Aerobic Championships Finish,
Catania, Italy

ICE HOCKEY: World Championship Pool A Finishes,
Basel & Zurich, Switzerland (Eurosport)

JUDO: European Championships Finish,
Oviedo, Spain

LAWN TENNIS: ATP Tour - Campionati Internazionali D'Italia
- TIM Cup - Final,
Rome, Italy (Eurosport)

MOTOR CYCLING: Italian GP,
Mugello, Italy (Eurosport)

MOTOR RACING: RAC Touring Car Championship,
Brands Hatch (BBC)

18 monday

first-half

second-half

extra-time

SPORTING FIXTURES

CANOEING: Wildwater Racing World Championships Start
(Finish 24th May),
Garmisch-Partenkirchen, Germany

LAWN TENNIS: Peugeot ATP Tour World Team Championship
Start (Finish 24th May),
Dusseldorf, Germany (Eurosport)
WTA Tour - Internationaux De Strasbourg Starts
(Finishes 24th May),
Strasbourg, France

19 tuesday

☾ Last Quarter

BADMINTON: Thomas & Uber Cup Finals Start
(Finish 24th May),
Hong Kong

POLO: Gerald Balding Cup Starts (Finishes 31st May),
Cirencester

20 wednesday

FOOTBALL: UEFA Champions League Final,
tbc (ITV)

HOCKEY: World Cup Hockey Starts (Finishes 1st June),
Utrecht, Holland

MOTOR RALLYING: Rally Argentina Starts (Finishes 23rd May),
Cordoba, Argentina (Eurosport)

23 saturday

first-half

second-half

extra-time

SPORTING FIXTURES

AMERICAN FOOTBALL: Rhein v England,
Rhein, Germany (BSkyB)

CRICKET: 2nd Texaco Trophy One-Day International,
England v South Africa,
Old Trafford (BSkyB)

CYCLING: The Prudential Tour of Britain Starts (Finish 31st May),
Various

GOLF: Volvo PGA Championship - Round 2,
Wentworth (BBC)

MOTOR RACING: CART - Motorola 300,
Madison, USA (Eurosport)

MOTOR RALLYING: Rally Argentina Finishes,
Cordoba, Argentina (Eurosport)

RUGBY UNION: The Sanyo Cup,
Twickenham

21 thursday

Ascension Day (Holy Thursday)

first-half

second-half

extra-time

SPORTING FIXTURES

CRICKET: 1st Texaco Trophy One-Day International,
England v South Africa,
The Oval (BSkvB)

EQUESTRIAN: The Chubb Insurance Windsor International
Horse Trials Start, *Windsor*

22 friday

Easter Law Sittings end

notes

GOLF: Volvo PGA Championship - Round I,
Wentworth (BBC)

YACHTING: Whitbread Round The World Race - Start Leg Nine,
La Rochelle, France (BBC)

24 sunday

Sunday after Ascension

first-half

second-half

extra-time

SPORTING FIXTURES

BADMINTON: Thomas & Uber Cup Finals Finish,
Hong Kong

CRICKET: 3rd Texaco Trophy One-Day International,
England v South Africa,
Headingley (BSkyB)

EQUESTRIAN: The Chubb Insurance Windsor International
Horse Trials Finish, *Windsor*

GOLF: Volvo PGA Championship - Round 3,
Wentworth (BBC)

LAWN TENNIS: WTA Tour - Internationaux De Strasbourg
Finish, *Strasbourg, France*
Peugeot ATP Tour World Team Championship Finish,
Dusseldorf, Germany (Eurosport)

MOTOR CYCLING: SBK Superbike World Championship,
Albacete, Spain (BSkyB)

MOTOR RACING: Monaco Grand Prix,
Monte Carlo, Monaco (ITV)

YACHTING: Whitbread Round The World Race
- Finish Leg Nine, *Southampton (BBC)*

25 monday

Bank Holiday UK ● New Moon

first-half

second-half

extra-time

SPORTING FIXTURES

GOLF: Volvo PGA Championship - Round 4, *Wentworth (BBC)*

LAWN TENNIS: French Open Championships - Day 1, *Paris, France (Eurosport/BBC)*

MOTOR RACING: RAC Touring Car Championship, *Oulton Park (BBC)*

26 tuesday

SPORTING FIXTURES

BASKETBALL: World Championship For Women Start (Finish 7th June), *Germany*

BOXING: European Championships Finish, *Minsk, Belarus*

LAWN TENNIS: French Open Championships - Day 2, *Paris, France (Eurosport/BBC)*

POLO: Queens Cup Starts (Finishes 14th June), *Guards*

27 wednesday

SPORTING FIXTURES

LAWN TENNIS: French Open Championships - Day 3, *Paris, France (Eurosport/BBC)*

SWIMMING: National Age Group Diving Competitions Start (Finish 31st May), *Crystal Palace*

30 saturday

first-half

second-half

extra-time

SPORTING FIXTURES

CANOEING: Wildwater World Cup Starts (Finishes 31st May), *Valsesia, Italy*

GOLF: Deutsche Bank/Sap Open TPC Of Europe - Round 3, *Hamburg, Germany*

GYMNASTICS: World Cup Final for Men & Women Starts (Finishes 31st May), *Sadae, Japan*

LAWN TENNIS: French Open Championships - Day 6, *Paris, France (Eurosport/BBC)*

POLO: Arthur Lucas Cup Starts (Finishes 7th June), *Beaufort*

ROWING: FISA Regatta Series Starts (Finishes 31st May), *Munich, Germany*

28 thursday

first-half

second-half

extra-time

SPORTING FIXTURES

GOLF: Deutsche Bank/Sap Open TPC Of Europe - Round 1,
Hamburg, Germany

HANDBALL: 3rd Mens European Championships Starts
(Finishes 7th June), *Bolzano & Merana, Italy*

LAWN TENNIS: French Open Championships - Day 4,
Paris, France (Eurosport/BBC)

RHYTHMIC GYMNASTICS: European Championships Start
(Finish 31st May), *Porto, Portugal*

29 friday

GOLF: Deutsche Bank/Sap Open TPC Of Europe - Round 2,
Hamburg, Germany

LAWN TENNIS: French Open Championships - Day 5,
Paris, France (Eurosport/BBC)

SWIMMING: Speedo British Swimming Grand Prix Super Final
Start (Finish 31st May), *Sheffield*

notes

31 sunday

Feast of Weeks (Shavuot)   *Whit Sunday (Pentecost)*

first-half

second-half

extra-time

SPORTING FIXTURES

AMERICAN FOOTBALL: England v Barcelona,
Crystal Palace (BSkyB)

ATHLETICS: Prefontaine Classic,
Eugene, USA

BASKETBALL: NBA Finals Begin,
tbc, USA (BSkyB/C4)

CYCLING: The Prudential Tour of Britain Finishes,
Various

GOLF: Deutsche Bank/Sap Open TPC Of Europe - Round 4,
Hamburg, Germany

LAWN TENNIS: French Open Championships - Day 7,
Paris, France (Eurosport/BBC)

MOTOR CYCLING: French GP,
Paul Ricard, France (ITV)

POLO: Gerald Balding Cup Finishes,
Cirencester

RHYTHMIC GYMNASTICS: European Championships Finish,
Porto, Portugal

SWIMMING: Speedo British Swimming Grand Prix Super Final
Finishes, *Sheffield*

M	1	8	15	22	29
T	2	9	16	23	30
W	3	10	17	24	.
T	4	11	18	25	.
F	5	12	19	26	.
S	6	13	20	27	.
S	7	14	21	28	.

JULIAN HERBERT/ALLSPORT

JUNE 1998

★ **1ST CORNHILL TEST MATCH - ENGLAND V SOUTH AFRICA** CRICKET **4 - 8 JUNE** Edgbaston

★ **THE VODAFONE OAKS** HORSE RACING **5 JUNE** Epsom

★ **THE VODAFONE DERBY** HORSE RACING **6 JUNE** Epsom

★ **DFS CLASSIC** TENNIS **8 - 14 JUNE** Birmingham

★ **THE STELLA ARTOIS GRASS COURT CHAMPIONSHIPS** TENNIS **8 - 14 JUNE** Queen's Club

★ **WORLD CUP** FOOTBALL **10 JUNE - 12 JULY** Various venues France

★ **THE NOTTINGHAM OPEN** TENNIS **15 - 20 JUNE** Nottingham

★ **DIRECT LINE INSURANCE CHAMPIONSHIPS** TENNIS **15 - 21 JUNE** Eastbourne

★ **ROYAL ASCOT** HORSE RACING **16 - 19 JUNE** Ascot

★ **US OPEN** GOLF **18 - 21 JUNE** San Francisco, USA

★ **2ND CORNHILL TEST MATCH - ENGLAND V SOUTH AFRICA** CRICKET **18 - 22 JUNE** Lord's

★ **NEW ZEALAND V ENGLAND** RUGBY UNION **20 JUNE** Dunedin, New Zealand

★ **THE WIMBLEDON LAWN TENNIS CHAMPIONSHIPS** TENNIS **22 JUNE - 5 JULY** Wimbledon

★ **NEW ZEALAND V ENGLAND** RUGBY UNION **27 JUNE** Auckland, New Zealand

★ **EUROPEAN SUPER LEAGUE CUP FINAL** ATHLETICS **27 - 28 JUNE** St. Petersburg, Russia

★ **FRENCH GRAND PRIX** FORMULA 1 **28 JUNE** Magny Cours, France

1 monday

Holiday Republic of Ireland

first-half

second-half

extra-time

SPORTING FIXTURES

GOLF: British Amateur Championships Start (Finish 6th June),
East Lothian

HOCKEY: World Cup Hockey Finishes,
Utrecht, Holland

LAWN TENNIS: French Open Championships - Day 8,
Paris, France (Eurosport/BBC)

MOTOR RACING: Formula 3000 International Championship
Round 2, *Pau, France*

2 tuesday

Trinity Law Sittings begin   Coronation Day   ☽ First Quarter

LAWN TENNIS: French Open Championships - Day 9,
Paris, France (Eurosport/BBC)

3 wednesday

EQUESTRIAN: World Cup Show Jumping Starts
(Finishes 7th June),
Spruce Meadows, Canada

LAWN TENNIS: French Open Championships - Day 10,
Paris, France (Eurosport/BBC)

6 saturday

first-half

second-half

extra-time

SPORTING FIXTURES

AMERICAN FOOTBALL: Barcelona v England,
Barcelona, Spain (BSkyB)

CRICKET: 1st Cornhill Test, England v South Africa - Day 3,
Edgbaston (BBC)

GOLF: British Amateur Championships Finish,
East Lothian
Alamo English Open - Round 3,
tbc (BSkyB)

HORSE RACING: Visa 3 Year-Old Championship Series -
Preakness Stakes,
Pimlico, USA
The Vodafone Derby,
Epsom (C4)

LAWN TENNIS. French Open Championships - Women's Final,
Paris, France (Eurosport/BBC)

MOTOR RACING: Le Mans 24 Hours Starts (Finishes 7th June),
France (Eurosport)

4 thursday

first-half

second-half

extra-time

SPORTING FIXTURES

CRICKET: 1st Cornhill Test, England v South Africa - Day 1,
Edgbaston (BBC)

GOLF: Alamo English Open - Round 1,
tbc (BSkyB)

LAWN TENNIS: French Open Championships - Women's
Semi-Finals, *Paris, France (Eurosport/BBC)*

5 friday

ATHLETICS: Golden Gala, *Rome, Italy*

CRICKET: 1st Cornhill Test, England v South Africa - Day 2,
Edgbaston (BBC)

GOLF: Alamo English Open - Round 2, *tbc (BSkyB)*

HORSE RACING: The Vodafone Oaks, *Epsom (C4)*

LAWN TENNIS: French Open Championships - Men's
Semi-Finals, *Paris, France (Eurosport/BBC)*

notes

7 sunday

Trinity Sunday, Pentecost 1

first-half

second-half

extra-time

SPORTING FIXTURES

AMERICAN FOOTBALL: Scotland v Amsterdam,
Murrayfield (BSkyB)

ATHLETICS: Znamensky Memorial,
Moscow, Russia

BASKETBALL: World Championship For Women Finish,
Germany

CRICKET: 1st Cornhill Test, England v South Africa - Day 4,
Edgbaston (BBC)

CYCLING: Giro D'Italia Finishes,
Various, Italy (Eurosport)

GOLF: Alamo English Open - Round 4,
tbc (BSkyB)

LAWN TENNIS: French Open Championships - Men's Final,
Paris, France (Eurosport/BBC)

MOTOR CYCLING: SBK Superbike World Championship,
tbc, Germany (BSkyB)

MOTOR RACING: Canadian Grand Prix,
Montreal, Canada (ITV)
Le Mans 24 Hours Finishes,
France (Eurosport)

POLO: Arthur Lucas Cup Finishes,
Beaufort

8 monday

first-half

second-half

extra-time

SPORTING FIXTURES

CRICKET: 1st Cornhill Test, England v South Africa - Day 5, *Edgbaston (BBC)*

CROQUET: Mens and Womens National Championships Start (Finish 14th June), *Cheltenham*

LAWN TENNIS: The Stella Artois Grass Court Championships - Day 1, *Queen's, London (BBC)*
DFS Classic Starts (Finishes 14th June), *Birmingham*

9 tuesday

LAWN TENNIS: The Stella Artois Grass Court Championships - Day 2, *Queen's, London (BBC)*

10 wednesday

Birthday, HRH Prince Philip, Duke of Edinburgh, b. 1921   ○ Full Moon

FOOTBALL: World Cup Opening Ceremony & Brazil v A2, *Paris, France (BBC/ITV)*
World Cup Match - A3 v A4, *Montpellier, France (BBC/ITV)*

LAWN TENNIS: The Stella Artois Grass Court Championships - Day 3, *Queen's, London (BBC)*

POLO: Royal Windsor Cup Starts (Finishes 21st June), *Guards*

13 saturday

first-half

second-half

extra-time

SPORTING FIXTURES

BOXING: World Cup Starts (Finishes 21st June), *Chongqing, People's Republic Of China (BBC/ITV)*

FENCING: British Men's Epee Open, *London*

FOOTBALL: World Cup Match - E3 v E4, *Lyon, France (BBC/ITV)*

FOOTBALL: World Cup Match - D1 v D2, *Nantes, France (BBC/ITV)*
World Cup Match - E1 v E2, *Paris, France (BBC/ITV)*

LAWN TENNIS: The Stella Artois Grass Court Championships - Day 6, *Queen's, London (BBC)*

RUGBY UNION: New Zealand A v England, *Hamilton, New Zealand*

11 thursday

Corpus Christi

first-half

second-half

extra-time

SPORTING FIXTURES

EQUESTRIAN: Bramham International Horse Trials Start (Finish 14th June), *Bramham*

FOOTBALL: World Cup Match - B1 v B2, *Bordeaux, France (BBC/ITV)* World Cup Match - B3 v B4, *Toulouse, France (BBC/ITV)*

LAWN TENNIS: The Stella Artois Grass Court Championships - Day 4, *Queen's, London (BBC)*

12 friday

SPORTING FIXTURES

FOOTBALL: World Cup - C1 v C2, *Marseilles, France (BBC/ITV)* World Cup Match - C3 v C4, *Lens, France (BBC/ITV)* World Cup Match - D3 v D4, *Montpellier, France (BBC/ITV)*

LAWN TENNIS: The Stella Artois Grass Court Championships - Day 5, *Queen's, London (BBC)*

notes

14 sunday

Pentecost 2

first-half

second-half

extra-time

SPORTING FIXTURES

AMERICAN FOOTBALL: World League Of American Football - World Bowl, *Frankfurt, Germany (BSkyB)*

CROQUET: Mens and Womens National Championships Finish, *Cheltenham*

EQUESTRIAN: Bramham International Horse Trials Finish, *Bramham*

FOOTBALL: World Cup Match - H1 v H2, *Toulouse, France (BBC/ITV)*

FOOTBALL: World Cup Match - F3 v F4, *Saint-Etienne, France (BBC/ITV)* World Cup Match - H3 v H4, *Lens, France (BBC/ITV)*

LAWN TENNIS: The Stella Artois Grass Court Championships Final, *Queen's, London, (BBC)* DFS Classic Final, *Birmingham*

MOTOR CYCLING: Portuguese GP, *Estoril, Portugal (Eurosport)*

MOTOR RACING: RAC Touring Car Championship, *Donington Park (BBC)*

15 monday

first-half

second-half

extra-time

SPORTING FIXTURES

FOOTBALL: World Cup Match - F1 v F2,
Paris, France (BBC/ITV)
World Cup Match - G1 v G2,
Lyon, France (BBC/ITV)
World Cup Match - G3 v G4,
Marseilles, France (BBC/ITV)

LAWN TENNIS: Direct Line Insurance Championships Starts
(Finishes 21st June),
Eastbourne (BBC)
The Nottingham Open Starts (Finishes 20th June),
Nottingham (BSkyB)

16 tuesday

SPORTING FIXTURES

FOOTBALL: World Cup Match - Brazil v A3,
Nantes, France (BBC/ITV)
World Cup Match - A2 v A4,
Bordeaux, France (BBC/ITV)

HORSE RACING: Royal Ascot - Day 1, *Ascot (BBC)*

POLO: Eduardo Moore Tournament Starts (Finishes 5th July),
Royal County of Berkshire Polo Club

RUGBY UNION: New Zealand Academy v England,
Invercargill, New Zealand

17 wednesday

☾ Last Quarter

SPORTING FIXTURES

FOOTBALL: World Cup Match - B1 v B3,
Montpellier, France (BBC/ITV)
World Cup Match - B2 v B4,
Saint-Etienne, France (BBC/ITV)

HORSE RACING: Royal Ascot - Day 2,
Ascot (BBC)

20 saturday

first-half

second-half

extra-time

SPORTING FIXTURES

CRICKET: 2nd Cornhill Test, England v South Africa - Day 3,
Lord's (BBC)

FOOTBALL: World Cup Match - E2 v E4,
Bordeaux, France (BBC/ITV)
World Cup Match - H2 v H4,
Nantes, France (BBC/ITV)
World Cup Match - E1 v E3,
Marseilles, France (BBC/ITV)

GOLF: US Open Round 3,
San Francisco, USA (BSkyB)

LAWN TENNIS: The Nottingham Open Final,
Nottingham (BSkyB)

RUGBY UNION: New Zealand v England,
Dunedin, New Zealand

YACHTING: Round The Islands Race,
Various

18 thursday

first-half

second-half

extra-time

SPORTING FIXTURES

CRICKET: 2nd Cornhill Test, England v South Africa - Day 1,
Lord's (BBC)

FOOTBALL: World Cup Match - C1 v C3,
Paris, France (BBC/ITV)
World Cup Match - C2 v C4,
Toulouse, France (BBC/ITV)

GOLF: US Open - Round 1,
San Francisco, USA (BSkyB)

HORSE RACING: Royal Ascot - Day 3,
Ascot (BBC)

19 friday

SPORTING FIXTURES

CRICKET: 2nd Cornhill Test, England v South Africa - Day 2,
Lord's (BBC)

FOOTBALL: World Cup Matches - D1 v D3,
Saint-Etienne, France (BBC/ITV)
World Cup Matches - D2 v D4,
Paris, France (BBC/ITV)

GOLF: US Open - Round 2,
San Francisco, USA (BSkyB)

HORSE RACING: Royal Ascot - Day 4, *Ascot (BBC)*

notes

21 sunday

Birthday, HRH Prince William, b. 1982   *Pentecost 3*   Summer Solstice

first-half

second-half

extra-time

SPORTING FIXTURES

BOXING: World Cup Finishes,
Chongqing, People's Republic Of China

CRICKET: 2nd Cornhill Test, England v South Africa - Day 4,
Lord's (BBC)

FOOTBALL: World Cup Matches - F1 v F3,
Lens, France (BBC/ITV)
World Cup Matches - F2 v F4,
Lyon, France (BBC/ITV)

FOOTBALL: World Cup Matches - H1 v H3,
Paris, France (BBC/ITV)

GOLF: US Open - Round 4,
San Francisco, USA (BSkyB)

LAWN TENNIS: Direct Line Insurance Championships Finishes,
Eastbourne (BBC)

MOTOR CYCLING: SBK Superbike World Championship,
San Marino (BSkyB) `

POLO: Royal Windsor Cup Finishes, *Guards*

22 monday

first-half

second-half

extra-time

SPORTING FIXTURES

CRICKET: 2nd Cornhill Test, England v South Africa - Day 5, *Lord's (BBC)*

FOOTBALL: World Cup Matches - G1 v G3, *Toulouse, France (BBC/ITV)*
World Cup Matches - G2 v G4, *Montpellier, France (BBC/ITV)*

LAWN TENNIS: The Wimbledon Championships - Day 1, *Wimbledon (BBC)*

23 tuesday

FOOTBALL: World Cup Match - B1 v B4, *Paris, France (BBC/ITV)*
World Cup Match - B2 v B3, *Nantes, France (BBC/ITV)*
World Cup Match - Brazil v A4, *Marseilles, France (BBC/ITV)*
World Cup Match - A2 v A3, *Saint-Etienne, France (BBC/ITV)*

LAWN TENNIS: The Wimbledon Championships - Day 2, *Wimbledon (BBC)*

24 wednesday

● New Moon Midsummer's Day (Quarter Day)

FOOTBALL: World Cup Match - D1 v D4, *Lens, France (BBC/ITV)*
World Cup Match - D2 v D3, *Toulouse, France (BBC/ITV)*
World Cup Match - C1 v C4, *Lyon, France (BBC/ITV)*
World Cup Match - C2 v C3, *Bordeaux, France (BBC/ITV)*

LAWN TENNIS: The Wimbledon Championships - Day 3, *Wimbledon (BBC)*

27 saturday

first-half

second-half

extra-time

SPORTING FIXTURES

ATHLETICS: European Super League Cup Final - Day 1, *St Petersburg, Russia (BBC)*

FOOTBALL: World Cup Match - 1A v 2B, *Paris, France (BBC/ITV)*
World Cup Match - 1B v 2A, *Marseilles, France (BBC/ITV)*

LAWN TENNIS: The Wimbledon Championships - Day 6, *Wimbledon (BBC)*

MOTOR CYCLING: Dutch GP, *Assen, Holland (Eurosport)*

RUGBY UNION: New Zealand v England, *Auckland, New Zealand*

25 thursday

first-half

second-half

extra-time

SPORTING FIXTURES

FOOTBALL: World Cup Match - F2 v F3,
Nantes, France (BBC/ITV)
World Cup Match - F1 v F4,
Montpellier, France (BBC/ITV)
World Cup Match - E2 v E3,
Paris, France (BBC/ITV)
World Cup Match - E1 v E4,
Saint-Etienne, France (BBC/ITV)

LAWN TENNIS: The Wimbledon Championships
- Day 4, *Wimbledon (BBC)*

26 friday

SPORTING FIXTURES

FOOTBALL: World Cup Match - G2 v G3,
Lens, France (BBC/ITV)
World Cup Match - H1 v H4,
Bordeaux, France (BBC/ITV)
World Cup Match - H2 v H3,
Lyon, France (BBC/ITV)
World Cup Match - G1 v G4,
Paris, France (BBC/ITV)

TENNIS: The Wimbledon Championships
- Day 5, *Wimbledon (BBC)*

notes

28 sunday

Pentecost 4

first-half

second-half

extra-time

SPORTING FIXTURES

ATHLETICS: European Super League Cup Final - Day 2,
St Petersburg, Russia (BBC)

CANOEING: Slalom World Cup 3,
Augsburg, Germany

FOOTBALL: World Cup Match - 1D v 2C,
Paris, France (BBC/ITV)
World Cup Match - 1C v 2D,
Lens, France (BBC/ITV)

LAWN TENNIS: The Wimbledon Championships
- Day 7, *Wimbledon (BBC)*

MOTOR RACING: FIA GT Championship Round 5,
Nurburgring, Germany
RAC Touring Car Championship,
Croft On Tees (BBC)

SPEEDWAY: Team World Championship Group A,
Togliatti, Russia

RUSSELL CHEYNE

M	.	6	13	20	27
T	.	7	14	21	28
W	1	8	15	22	29
T	2	9	16	23	30
F	3	10	17	24	31
S	4	11	18	25	.
S	5	12	19	26	.

JULY
1998

★ **HENLEY ROYAL REGATTA** ROWING **1 - 5 JULY** Henley
★ **3RD CORNHILL TEST MATCH - ENGLAND V SOUTH AFRICA** CRICKET **2 - 6 JULY** Old Trafford
★ **BRITISH GRAND PRIX** MOTOR CYCLING **5 JULY** Donington Park
★ **ROYAL INTERNATIONAL HORSE SHOW** EQUESTRIAN **7 - 12 JULY** Hickstead
★ **TOUR DE FRANCE** CYCLING **11 JULY - 2 AUG**
★ **RAC BRITISH GRAND PRIX** FORMULA 1 **12 JULY** Silverstone
★ **THE OPEN** GOLF **16 - 19 JULY** Royal Birkdale
★ **GOODWILL GAMES** GAMES **19 JULY - 2 AUG** New York, USA
★ **4TH CORNHILL TEST MATCH - ENGLAND V SOUTH AFRICA** CRICKET **23 - 27 JULY** Trent Bridge
★ **THE KING GEORGE VI AND THE QUEEN ELIZABETH DIAMOND STAKES** HORSE RACING **25 JULY** Ascot
★ **GLORIOUS GOODWOOD** HORSE RACING **28 JULY - 1 AUG** Goodwood
★ **13TH AMWAY WORLD CHAMPIONSHIP FOR MEN** BASKETBALL **29 JULY - 9 AUG** Greece

29 monday

Feast of SS Peter & Paul

first-half

second-half

extra-time

SPORTING FIXTURES

BOWLS: British Isles International Outdoor Series for Men Starts,
Ayr, Scotland

FOOTBALL: World Cup Match - 1F v 2E,
Montpellier, France (BBC/ITV)
World Cup Match - 1E v 2F,
Toulouse, France (BBC/ITV)

LAWN TENNIS: The Wimbledon Championships
- Day 8, *Wimbledon (BBC)*

30 tuesday

SPORTING FIXTURES

FOOTBALL: World Cup Match - 1H v 2G,
Saint-Etienne, France (BBC/ITV)
World Cup Match - 1G v 2H,
Bordeaux, France (BBC/ITV)

LAWN TENNIS: The Wimbledon Championships
- Day 9, *Wimbledon (BBC)*

POLO: Veuve Clicquot Gold Cup Starts (Finishes 19th July),
Cowdray

1 wednesday

☽ First Quarter

SPORTING FIXTURES

ATHLETICS: Meeting Gaz De France,
Paris, France

LAWN TENNIS: The Wimbledon Championships
- Day 10, *Wimbledon (BBC)*

ROWING: Henley Royal Regatta Starts (Finishes 5th July),
River Thames

4 saturday

first-half

second-half

extra-time

SPORTING FIXTURES

CRICKET: 3rd Cornhill Test, England v South Africa - Day 3,
Old Trafford (BBC)

FOOTBALL: World Cup Quarter Final Match,
Marseilles, France (BBC/ITV)
World Cup Quarter Final Match,
Lyon, France (BBC/ITV)

GOLF: US Womens Open - Round 3,
Kohler, USA

HORSE RACING: The Coral-Eclipse Stakes,
Sandown Park

LAWN TENNIS: The Wimbledon Championships
- Women's Final,
Wimbledon (BBC)

2 thursday

first-half

second-half

extra-time

SPORTING FIXTURES

CRICKET: 3rd Cornhill Test, England v South Africa - Day 1,
Old Trafford *(BBC)*

GOLF: US Womens Open - Round 1,
Kohler, USA

LAWN TENNIS: The Wimbledon Championships
- Women's Semi-Finals,
Wimbledon *(BBC)*

3 friday

SPORTING FIXTURES

CRICKET: 3rd Cornhill Test, England v South Africa - Day 2,
Old Trafford *(BBC)*

FOOTBALL: World Cup Quarter Final Match,
Nantes, France *(BBC/ITV)*
World Cup Quarter Final Match,
Paris, France *(BBC/ITV)*

GOLF: US Womens Open - Round 2, ***Kohler, USA***

LAWN TENNIS: The Wimbledon Championships
- Men's Semi-Finals, ***Wimbledon*** *(BBC)*

notes

5 sunday

Pentecost 5

first-half

second-half

extra-time

SPORTING FIXTURES

CRICKET: 3rd Cornhill Test, England v South Africa - Day 4,
Old Trafford *(BBC)*

GOLF: US Womens Open - Round 4,
Kohler, USA

LAWN TENNIS: The Wimbledon Championships
- Men's Final, ***Wimbledon*** *(BBC)*

MOTOR CYCLING: British GP,
Donington Park *(BBC)*

POLO: Eduardo Moore Tournament Finishes,
Royal County of Berkshire Polo Club

ROWING: Henley Royal Regatta Finishes,
River Thames

6 monday

first-half

second-half

extra-time

SPORTING FIXTURES

CRICKET: 3rd Cornhill Test, England v South Africa - Day 5,
Old Trafford (BBC)

LAWN TENNIS: WTA Tour - Skoda Czech Open Starts
(Finishes 12th July),
Karlovy Vary, Czech Republic
ATP Tour - Rado Swiss Open Starts (Finishes 12th July),
Gstaad, Switzerland (Eurosport)

7 tuesday

BASEBALL: All-Star Game,
Denver, USA (Ch5)

FOOTBALL: World Cup Semi-Final 1,
Marseilles, France (BBC/ITV)

POLO: Duke Of Beaufort's Cup Starts (Finishes 12th July),
Beaufort

8 wednesday

CRICKET: Natwest Trophy 2nd Round,
Various (BBC)

EQUESTRIAN: Royal International Horse Show Starts
(Finishes 12th July),
Hickstead (BBC)

FOOTBALL: World Cup - Semi- Final 2,
Paris, France (BBC/ITV)

GOLF: Gulf Stream World Invitational - Round 1,
Glasgow (BBC)

11 saturday

first-half

second-half

extra-time

SPORTING FIXTURES

BMX BIKE: European Championships Finish,
Schwedt, Germany

CRICKET: Benson & Hedges Cup Final, *Lord's*

CYCLING: Tour de France Prologue,
Dublin, Ireland (Eurosport/C4)

FOOTBALL: World Cup Match - 3rd Place Play-Off,
Paris, France (BBC/ITV)

GOLF: Gulf Stream World Invitational - Round 4,
Glasgow (BBC)

MOTOR RACING: Autosport British Formula 3 Championship,
Silverstone

ROWING: Lucerne Regatta Starts (Finishes 12th July),
Lucerne, Switzerland

9 thursday

○ Full Moon

first-half

second-half

extra-time

SPORTING FIXTURES

GOLF: Gulf Stream World Invitational - Round 2,
Glasgow *(BBC)*

SWIMMING: ASA British Commonwealth Trials Start
(Finish 12th July), ***Sheffield*** *(BBC)*

10 friday

SPORTING FIXTURES

BMX BIKE: European Championships Start
(Finish 11th July),
Schwedt, Germany

GOLF: Gulf Stream World Invitational - Round 3,
Glasgow *(BBC)*

notes

12 sunday

Pentecost 6

first-half

second-half

extra-time

SPORTING FIXTURES

CYCLING: Tour de France - 1st Stage,
Dublin, Ireland *(Eurosport/C4)*

EQUESTRIAN: Royal International Horse Show Finishes,
Hickstead *(BBC)*

FOOTBALL: World Cup Final,
Paris, France *(BBC/ITV)*

LAWN TENNIS: WTA Tour - Skoda Czech Open Finishes,
Karlovy Vary, Czech Republic
ATP Tour - Rado Swiss Open Finishes,
Gstaad, Switzerland *(Eurosport)*

MOTOR CYCLING: SBK Superbike World Championship,
Laguna Seca, USA *(BSkyB)*

MOTOR RACING: RAC British Grand Prix,
Silverstone *(ITV)*

POLO: Duke Of Beaufort's Cup Finishes,
Beaufort

ROWING: Lucerne Regatta Finishes,
Lucerne, Switzerland

SWIMMING: ASA British Commonwealth Trials Finish,
Sheffield *(BBC)*

13 monday

Holiday Northern Ireland

first-half

second-half

extra-time

SPORTING FIXTURES

CYCLING: Tour de France - Stage 2,
***Enniscorthy-Cork, Ireland** (Eurosport/C4)*

LAWN TENNIS: Torneo Internazionale - Day 1,
Palermo, Italy

POLO: RCBPC 8 Goal Tournament Starts (Finishes 18th July),
Royal County of Berkshire Polo Club

14 tuesday

SPORTING FIXTURES

CYCLING: Tour de France - Stage 3,
***Roscoff-Lorient, France** (Eurosport/C4)*

LAWN TENNIS: Torneo Internazionale - Day 2,
Palermo, Italy

15 wednesday

St Swithin's Day

SPORTING FIXTURES

ATHLETICS: Nikaia Meeting,
Nice, France

CYCLING: Tour de France - Stage 4,
***Plouay-Cholet, France** (Eurosport/C4)*

LAWN TENNIS: Torneo Internazionale - Day 3,
Palermo, Italy

18 saturday

first-half

second-half

extra-time

SPORTING FIXTURES

CYCLING: Tour de France - Stage 7,
***Meyrignac L'Eglise-Correze, France** (Eurosport/C4)*

GLIDING: European Gliding Championships Start
(Finish 2nd August),
Leszno, Poland

GOLF: British Open - Round 3,
***Southport** (BBC)*

LAWN TENNIS: Torneo Internazionale - Day 6,
Palermo, Italy

POLO: RCBPC 8 Goal Tournament Finishes,
Royal County of Berkshire Polo Club

SWIMMING: European Long Distance Swimming Cup,
Holme Pierrepont

16 thursday

☾ Last Quarter

first-half

second-half

extra-time

SPORTING FIXTURES

CYCLING: Tour de France - Stage 5,
Cholet-Chateau, France (Eurosport/C4)

GOLF: British Open - Round 1, *Southport (BBC)*

LAWN TENNIS: Torneo Internazionale - Day 4,
Palermo, Italy

17 friday

SPORTING FIXTURES

ATHLETICS: Mobil Bislett Games, *Oslo, Norway*

CYCLING: Tour de France - Stage 6,
La Chatre-Brive La Gaillarde, France (Eurosport/C4)

GOLF: British Open - Round 2, *Southport (BBC)*

LAWN TENNIS: Torneo Internazionale - Day 5, *Palermo, Italy*

MOTOR CYCLING: British Superbike Championship Start,
Oulton Park (BBC)

notes

19 sunday

Pentecost 7

first-half

second-half

extra-time

SPORTING FIXTURES

ATHLETICS: IAAF Grand Prix II,
Gateshead

CYCLING: Tour de France - Stage 8,
Brive La Gaillarde-Montauban, France (Eurosport/C4)

GOLF: British Open - Round 4,
Southport (BBC)

LAWN TENNIS: Torneo Internazionale - Final,
Palermo, Italy

MOTOR CYCLING: British Superbike Championship Finish,
Oulton Park (BBC)
German Grand Prix,
Nurburg-Eifel, Germany (Eurosport)

MOTOR RACING: CART - Molson Indy,
Toronto, Canada (Eurosport)

MULTI-EVENT GAMES: Goodwill Games - Day 1,
New York, USA

POLO: Veuve Clicquot Gold Cup Finishes, *Cowdray*

SWIMMING: ASA 25km National Championships,
Holme Pierrepont

20 monday

first-half

second-half

extra-time

SPORTING FIXTURES

CYCLING: Tour de France - Stage 9,
Montauban-Pau, France (Eurosport/C4)

LAWN TENNIS: Legg Mason Tennis Classic Starts
(Finishes 26th July),
Washington, USA (Eurosport)
Mercedes Cup - Stuttgart - Day 1,
Stuttgart, Germany (Eurosport)

MULTI-EVENT GAMES: Goodwill Games - Day 2,
New York, USA

21 tuesday

SPORTING FIXTURES

CYCLING: Tour de France - Stage 10,
Pau-Luchon, France (Eurosport/C4)

LAWN TENNIS: Mercedes Cup - Stuttgart - Day 2,
Stuttgart, Germany (Eurosport)

MULTI-EVENT GAMES: Goodwill Games - Day 3,
New York, USA

22 wednesday

SPORTING FIXTURES

CYCLING: Tour de France - Stage 11,
Luchon-Plateau De Beille, France (Eurosport/C4)

FOOTBALL: UEFA Champions League First Qualifying Round
1st Leg, *Various, tbc*
UEFA Cup First Qualifying Round 1st Leg, *Various, tbc*

LAWN TENNIS: Mercedes Cup - Stuttgart - Day 3,
Stuttgart, Germany (Eurosport)

MULTI-EVENT GAMES: Goodwill Games - Day 4,
New York, USA

25 saturday

first-half

second-half

extra-time

SPORTING FIXTURES

ATHLETICS: AAA Championships - European And
Commonwealth Trials - Day 2, *Birmingham*

CRICKET: 4th Cornhill Test, England v South Africa - Day 3,
Trent Bridge (BBC)

CYCLING: Tour de France - Stage 13,
Frontigan La Peyrade-Carpentras, France (Eurosport/C4)

HORSE RACING: The King George VI And
The Queen Elizabeth Diamond Stakes,
Ascot (BBC)

LAWN TENNIS: Mercedes Cup - Stuttgart - Day 6,
Stuttgart, Germany (Eurosport)

MULTI-EVENT GAMES: Goodwill Games - Day 7,
New York, USA

23 thursday

● New Moon

first-half

second-half

extra-time

SPORTING FIXTURES

CRICKET: 4th Cornhill Test, England v South Africa - Day 1, *Trent Bridge (BBC)*

GOLF: Sun Microsystems Dutch Open Starts (Finishes 26th July), *Hilversum, Holland*

LAWN TENNIS: Mercedes Cup - Stuttgart - Day 4, *Stuttgart, Germany (Eurosport)*

MULTI-EVENT GAMES: Goodwill Games - Day 5, *New York, USA*

24 friday

ATHLETICS: AAA Championships - European And Commonwealth Trials - Day 1, *Birmingham*

CRICKET: 4th Cornhill Test, England v South Africa - Day 2, *Trent Bridge (BBC)*

CYCLING: Tour de France - Stage 12, *Tarascon Sur Ariege-Cap D'Agde, France (Eurosport/C4)*

LAWN TENNIS: Mercedes Cup - Stuttgart - Day 5, *Stuttgart, Germany (Eurosport)*

MULTI-EVENT GAMES: Goodwill Games - Day 6, *New York, USA*

notes

26 sunday

Pentecost 8

first-half

second-half

extra-time

SPORTING FIXTURES

ATHLETICS: AAA Championships - European And Commonwealth Trials - Day 3, *Birmingham*

CRICKET: 4th Cornhill Test, England v South Africa - Day 4, *Trent Bridge (BBC)*

CYCLING: Tour de France - Stage 14, *Valreas-Grenoble, France (Eurosport/C4)*

GOLF: Sun Microsystems Dutch Open Finishes, *Hilversum, Holland*

LAWN TENNIS: Mercedes Cup - Stuttgart - Final, *Stuttgart, Germany (Eurosport)*
Legg Mason Tennis Classic Finishes, *Washington, USA* *(Eurosport)*

MOTOR RACING: RAC Touring Car Championship, *Snetterton (BBC)*
Austrian Grand Prix, *A1 Ring, Austria (ITV)*

MULTI-EVENT GAMES: Goodwill Games - Day 8, *New York, USA*

RUSSELL CHEYNE

AUGUST
1998

M	.	3	10	17	24	31
T	.	4	11	18	25	.
W	.	5	12	19	26	.
T	.	6	13	20	27	.
F	.	7	14	21	28	.
S	1	8	15	22	29	.
S	2	9	16	23	30	.

★ **SKANDIA LIFE COWES WEEK** YACHTING **1 - 8 AUG** Cowes
★ **SBK SUPERBIKE WORLD CHAMPIONSHIPS** MOTORCYCLING **2 AUG** Brands Hatch
★ **5TH CORNHILL TEST MATCH - ENGLAND V SOUTH AFRICA** CRICKET **6 - 10 AUG** Headingley
★ **CHARITY SHIELD** FOOTBALL **9 AUG** Wembley
★ **HICKSTEAD DERBY** EQUESTRIAN **12 - 16 AUG** Hickstead
★ **80TH PGA CHAMPIONSHIP** GOLF **13 - 16 AUG** Seattle, USA
★ **PREMIERSHIP SEASON BEGINS** FOOTBALL **15 AUG** Various venues
★ **TRIANGULAR TOURNAMENT - ENGLAND V SRI LANKA** CRICKET **16 AUG** Lord's
★ **WORLD CUP- LEEDS INTERNATIONAL CLASSIC** CYCLING **16 AUG** Leeds
★ **17TH EUROPEAN ATHLETICS CHAMPIONSHIPS** ATHLETICS **17 - 23 AUG** Budapest, Hungary
★ **TRIANGULAR TOURNAMENT - ENGLAND V SOUTH AFRICA** CRICKET **18 AUG** Edgbaston
★ **TRIANGULAR TOURNAMENT FINAL** CRICKET **20 AUG** Lord's
★ **WORLD TRACK CHAMPIONSHIPS** CYCLING **24 - 30 AUG** Bordeaux, France
★ **1ST CORNHILL TEST MATCH - ENGLAND V SRI LANKA** CRICKET **27 - 31 AUG** The Oval
★ **US OPEN CHAMPIONSHIPS** TENNIS **31 AUG - 13 SEP** Flushing Meadows, USA

27 monday

first-half

second-half

extra-time

SPORTING FIXTURES

CRICKET: 4th Cornhill Test, England v South Africa - Day 5, **Trent Bridge** (BBC)

CYCLING: Tour de France - Stage 15, **Grenoble-Les Deux Alpes, France** (Eurosport/C4)

GOLF: English Amateur Championships Start (Finish 1st August), **Woodhall Spa**

LAWN TENNIS: EA Generali Open Starts (Finishes 2nd August), **Kitzbuhel, Austria** (Eurosport)

MULTI-EVENT GAMES: Goodwill Games - Day 9, **New York**

28 tuesday

SPORTING FIXTURES

CYCLING: Tour de France - Stage 16, **Vizille-Albertville, France** (Eurosport/C4)

HORSE RACING: Glorious Goodwood - Day 1, **Goodwood** (BBC)

MULTI-EVENT GAMES: Goodwill Games - Day 10, **New York, USA**

29 wednesday

SPORTING FIXTURES

CYCLING: Tour de France - Stage 17, **Albertville-Aix Les Bains, France** (Eurosport/C4)

FOOTBALL: UEFA Champions League First Qualifying Round 2nd Leg, **Various, tbc**
UEFA Cup First Qualifying Round 2nd Leg, **Various, tbc**

HORSE RACING: Glorious Goodwood - Day 2, **Goodwood** (BBC)

MULTI-EVENT GAMES: Goodwill Games - Day 11, **New York, USA**

1 saturday

Lammas (Scottish Term Day)

first-half

second-half

extra-time

SPORTING FIXTURES

CYCLING: Tour de France - Stage 20, **Montceau Les Mines-Le Creusot, France** (Eurosport/C4)

GOLF: Volvo Scandinavian Masters - Round 3, **Malmo, Sweden**
Curtis Cup - Day 1, **Minnesota, USA**
English Amateur Championships Finish, **Woodhall Spa**

HORSE RACING: Glorious Goodwood - Day 5, **Goodwood** (BBC)

MOTOR RALLYING: Mobil 1 RAC British Rally Championship - Stena Line Ulster Rally, **Belfast**

MULTI-EVENT GAMES: Goodwill Games - Day 14, **New York, USA**

YACHTING: Skandia Life Cowes Week Starts (Finishes 8th August), **The Solent**

30 thursday

first-half

second-half

extra-time

SPORTING FIXTURES

CYCLING: Tour de France - Stage 18,
Aix Les Bains-Neuchatel, France (Eurosport/C4)

GOLF: Volvo Scandinavian Masters - Round 1,
Malmo, Sweden

HORSE RACING: Glorious Goodwood - Day 3,
Goodwood (BBC)

MULTI-EVENT GAMES: Goodwill Games - Day 12,
New York, USA

31 friday

Trinity Law Sittings end   ☽ First Quarter

SPORTING FIXTURES

CYCLING: Tour de France - Stage 19,
Le Chau De Fonds-Autun, France (Eurosport/C4)

GOLF: Volvo Scandinavian Masters - Round 2, *Malmo, Sweden*

HORSE RACING: Glorious Goodwood - Day 4, *Goodwood (BBC)*

MOTOR RALLYING: Mobil 1 RAC British Rally Championship - Stena Line Ulster Rally, *Belfast*

MULTI-EVENT GAMES: Goodwill Games - Day 13,
New York, USA

notes

2 sunday

Pentecost 9

first-half

second-half

extra-time

SPORTING FIXTURES

ATHLETICS: IAAF Grand Prix I, *Sheffield*

CYCLING: Tour de France - Final Stage,
Melun-Paris, France (Eurosport/C4)

GLIDING: European Gliding Championships Finish,
Leszno, Poland

GOLF: Curtis Cup - Day 2, *Minnesota, USA*
Volvo Scandinavian Masters - Round 4,
Malmo, Sweden

LAWN TENNIS: EA Generali Open Finishes,
Kitzbuhel, Austria (Eurosport)

MOTOR CYCLING: SBK Superbike World Championship,
Brands Hatch (BSkyB)

MOTOR RACING: RAC Touring Car Championship,
Thruxton (BBC)

MULTI-EVENT GAMES: Goodwill Games - Day 15,
New York, USA

3 monday

Holiday Republic of Ireland

first-half

second-half

extra-time

SPORTING FIXTURES

ARCHERY: World Field Championships Start
(Finish 9th August), *Tyrol, Austria*

BOWLS: English National Championships for Women Start
(Finish 15th Aug), *Royal Leamington Spa*

LAWN TENNIS: ATP Tour - Du Maurier Open - Day 1,
Toronto, Canada (Eurosport)
Enka Ladies Open Starts (Finishes 9th August),
Istanbul, Turkey

4 tuesday

Birthday, HM Queen Elizabeth the Queen Mother, b. 1900

SPORTING FIXTURES

LAWN TENNIS: ATP Tour - Du Maurier Open - Day 2,
Toronto, Canada (Eurosport)

POLO: National 15 Goal Championships Start
(Finish 16th August),
Cirencester

5 wednesday

SPORTING FIXTURES

LAWN TENNIS: ATP Tour - Du Maurier Open - Day 3,
Toronto, Canada (Eurosport)

ROWING: World Junior Championships Start (Finish 9th August),
Ottensheim, Austria

8 saturday

○ Full Moon

first-half

second-half

extra-time

SPORTING FIXTURES

ATHLETICS: Herculis Zepter 98, *Monte Carlo, Monaco*

CRICKET: 5th Cornhill Test, England v South Africa - Day 3,
Headingley (BBC)

CYCLING: World Cup San Sebastian,
Spain (Eurosport)

GLIDING: Open Class National Championships Start
(Finish 16th August), *Lasham*

GOLF: Chemapol Trophy Czech Open - Round 3,
Prague, Czech Republic

LAWN TENNIS: ATP Tour - Du Maurier Open - Day 6,
Toronto, Canada (Eurosport)

MULTI-EVENT GAMES: Central America and Caribbean Games
Start (Finish 22nd August), *Maracaibo, Venezuela*

YACHTING: Skandia Life Cowes Week Finishes,
The Solent

6 thursday

first-half

second-half

extra-time

SPORTING FIXTURES

CRICKET: 5th Cornhill Test, England v South Africa - Day 1, *Headingley (BBC)*

GOLF: Chemapol Trophy Czech Open - Round 1, *Prague, Czech Republic*

LAWN TENNIS: ATP Tour - Du Maurier Open - Day 4, *Toronto, Canada (Eurosport)*

7 friday

SPORTING FIXTURES

CRICKET: 5th Cornhill Test, England v South Africa - Day 2, *Headingley (BBC)*

GOLF: Chemapol Trophy Czech Open - Round 2, *Prague, Czech Republic*

LAWN TENNIS: ATP Tour - Du Maurier Open - Day 5, *Toronto, Canada (Eurosport)*

MOTOR CYCLING: British Superbike Championship Starts, *Knockhill (BBC)*

SPEEDWAY: Individual World Championship GP, *Bradford*

notes

9 sunday

Pentecost 10

first-half

second-half

extra-time

SPORTING FIXTURES

ARCHERY: World Field Championships Finish, *Tyrol, Austria*

CRICKET: 5th Cornhill Test, England v South Africa - Day 4, *Headingley (BBC)*

GOLF: Chemapol Trophy Czech Open - Round 4, *Prague, Czech Republic*

LAWN TENNIS: Enka Ladies Open Finishes, *Istanbul, Turkey*
ATP Tour - Du Maurier Open - Final, *Toronto, Canada (Eurosport)*

MOTOR CYCLING: British Superbike Championship Finishes, *Knockhill (BBC)*

MOTOR RACING: CART - Miller Lite 200, *Lexington, USA (Eurosport)*

ROWING: World Junior Championships Finish, *Ottensheim, Austria*

YACHTING: Falmouth Week Starts (Finishes 15th August), *Falmouth*

10 monday

first-half

second-half

extra-time

SPORTING FIXTURES

CRICKET: 5th Cornhill Test, England v South Africa - Day 5,
Headingley (BBC)

LAWN TENNIS: ATP Tour - Great American Insurance ATP
Championship - Day 1,
Cincinnati, USA (Eurosport)

POLO: National 8 Goal Championship Starts (Finish 16th August),
Little Budworth

11 tuesday

SPORTING FIXTURES

FOOTBALL: UEFA Cup Second Qualifying Round 1st Leg,
Various, tbc

LAWN TENNIS: ATP Tour - Great American Insurance ATP
Championship - Day 2,
Cincinnati, USA (Eurosport)

12 wednesday

FOOTBALL: UEFA Champions League Second Qualifying Round
1st Leg,
Various, tbc

LAWN TENNIS: ATP Tour - Great American Insurance ATP
Championship - Day 3,
Cincinnati, USA (Eurosport)

15 saturday

Feast of the Assumption

first-half

second-half

extra-time

SPORTING FIXTURES

BOWLS: English National Championships for Women Finish,
Royal Leamington Spa

EQUESTRIAN: Pedigree Chum Scottish Championship Horse
Trials Thirlestane Castle,
Thirlestane Castle

GOLF: PGA Championship - Round 3,
Seattle, USA (BSkyB)
Weetabix Women's British Open - Round 3,
Lytham St Annes

LAWN TENNIS: ATP Tour - Great American Insurance ATP
Championship - Day 6,
Cincinnati, USA (Eurosport)

YACHTING: Falmouth Week Finishes,
Falmouth

13 thursday

first-half

second-half

extra-time

SPORTING FIXTURES

EQUESTRIAN: Hickstead Derby Starts (Finishes 16th August), *Hickstead (BBC)*

FOOTBALL: European Cup Winners Cup Qualifying Round 1st Leg, *Various, tbc*

GOLF: PGA Championship - Round 1, *Seattle, USA (BSkyB)* Weetabix Women's British Open - Round 1, *Lytham St Annes,*

LAWN TENNIS: ATP Tour - Great American Insurance ATP Championship - Day 4, *Cincinnati, USA (Eurosport)*

14 friday

☾ Last Quarter

CRICKET: Triangular Tournament, South Africa v Sri Lanka, *Trent Bridge (BSkyB)*

GOLF: PGA Championship - Round 2, *Seattle, USA (BSkyB)* Weetabix Women's British Open - Round 2, *Lytham St Annes*

LAWN TENNIS: ATP Tour - Great American Insurance ATP Championship - Day 5, *Cincinnati, USA (Eurosport)*

MOTOR CYCLING: British Superbike Championship Starts, *Kirkby (BBC)*

notes

16 sunday

Pentecost 11

first-half

second-half

extra-time

SPORTING FIXTURES

BOWLS: English National Championships for Men Start (Finish 29th August), *Worthing*

CRICKET: Triangular Tournament, England v Sri Lanka, *Lord's (BSkyB)*

CYCLING: World Cup Leeds International Classic, *Leeds (Eurosport)*

EQUESTRIAN: Hickstead Derby Finishes, *Hickstead (BBC)*

GOLF: Weetabix Women's British Open - Round 4, *Lytham St Annes* PGA Championship - Round 4, *Seattle, USA (BSkyB)*

LAWN TENNIS: ATP Tour - Great American Insurance ATP Championship - Final, *Cincinnati, USA (Eurosport)*

MOTOR CYCLING: British Superbike Championship Finishes, *Kirkby (BBC)*

MOTOR RACING: Hungarian Grand Prix, *Budapest, Hungary (ITV)* RAC Touring Car Championship, *Dunfermline (BBC)*

17 monday

first-half

second-half

extra-time

SPORTING FIXTURES

LAWN TENNIS: RCA Championships - Day 1,
Indianapolis, USA (Eurosport)
Du Maurier Open Starts (Finishes 23rd August),
Montreal, Canada

18 tuesday

ATHLETICS: European Athletics Championships - Day 1,
Budapest, Hungary (BBC/Eurosport)

CRICKET: Triangular Tournament, England v South Africa,
Edgbaston (BSkyB)

LAWN TENNIS: RCA Championships - Day 2,
Indianapolis, USA (Eurosport)

POLO: World Championships Start (Finish 30th August),
Santa Barbara, USA

19 wednesday

ATHLETICS: European Athletics Championships - Day 2,
Budapest, Hungary (BBC/Eurosport)

LAWN TENNIS: RCA Championships - Day 3,
Indianapolis, USA (Eurosport)

22 saturday

● New Moon

first-half

second-half

extra-time

SPORTING FIXTURES

ANGLING: National Championships Division 4,
Keadby

ATHLETICS: European Athletics Championships - Day 5,
Budapest, Hungary (BBC/Eurosport)

EQUESTRIAN: British Open Championship Gatcombe Park Starts
(Finish 23rd Aug), **Gatcombe Park**

GOLF: Smurfit European Open - Round 3,
Dublin, Ireland (BSkyB)

LAWN TENNIS: RCA Championships - Day 6,
Indianapolis, USA (Eurosport)

MULTI-EVENT GAMES: Central America and Caribbean
Games Finish, **Maracaibo, Venezuela**

20 thursday

first-half

second-half

extra-time

SPORTING FIXTURES

ATHLETICS: European Athletics Championships - Day 3,
Budapest, Hungary *(BBC/Eurosport)*

CRICKET: Triangular Tournament Final,
Lord's *(BSkyB)*

GOLF: Smurfit European Open - Round 1,
Dublin, Ireland *(BSkyB)*

LAWN TENNIS: RCA Championships - Day 4,
Indianapolis, USA *(Eurosport)*

21 friday

SPORTING FIXTURES

ATHLETICS: European Athletics Championships - Day 4,
Budapest, Hungary *(BBC/Eurosport)*

GOLF: Smurfit European Open - Round 2,
Dublin, Ireland *(BSkyB)*

LAWN TENNIS: RCA Championships - Day 5, ***Indianapolis,
USA*** *(Eurosport)*

SPEEDWAY: Individual World Championship Intercontinental
Final, ***Vojens, Denmark***

YACHTING: Largs Regatta Week Starts (Finishes 30th August),

notes

23 sunday

Pentecost 12

first-half

second-half

extra-time

SPORTING FIXTURES

ATHLETICS: European Athletics Championships - Final Day,
Budapest, Hungary *(BBC/Eurosport)*

CYCLING: World Cup Grand Prix Of Switzerland,
Various, Switzerland *(Eurosport)*

EQUESTRIAN: British Open Championship Gatcombe Park
Finishes, ***Gatcombe Park***

GOLF: Smurfit European Open - Round 4,
Dublin, Ireland *(BSkyB)*

LAWN TENNIS: RCA Championships - Final,
Indianapolis, USA *(Eurosport)*
Du Maurier Open Finishes,
Montreal, Canada

MOTOR CYCLING: Czech Republic GP,
Brno, Czech Republic *(Eurosport)*

MOTOR RACING: FIA GT Championship Round 7,
Suzuka, Japan

24 monday

first-half

second-half

extra-time

SPORTING FIXTURES

CYCLING: World Track Championships Start
(Finish 30th August),
Bordeaux, France (Eurosport)

LAWN TENNIS: MFS Pro Tennis Championships - Day 1,
Boston, USA (Eurosport)
US Womens Hardcourt Championships Start (Finish 30th August),
Atlanta, USA

MOTOR RACING: Autosport British Formula 3 Championship,
Pembrey

25 tuesday

SPORTING FIXTURES

ATHLETICS: Athletissima 98,
Lausanne, Switzerland

FOOTBALL: UEFA Cup Second Qualifying Round 2nd Leg,
Various, tbc

LAWN TENNIS: MFS Pro-Tennis Championships - Day 2,
Boston, USA (Eurosport)

26 wednesday

SPORTING FIXTURES

BADMINTON: Russia World Grand Prix Starts
(Finishes 30th August),
Moscow, Russia

LAWN TENNIS: MFS Pro-Tennis Championships - Day 3,
Boston, USA (Eurosport)

29 saturday

first-half

second-half

extra-time

SPORTING FIXTURES

BOWLS: English National Championships for Men Finish,
Worthing

CRICKET: 1st Cornhill Test, England v Sri Lanka - Day 3,
The Oval (BBC)

GOLF: BMW International Open - Round 3,
Munich, Germany

LAWN TENNIS: MFS Pro-Tennis Championships - Day 6,
Boston, USA (Eurosport)

MOTOR CYCLING: British Superbike Championship Starts,
Cadwell Park (BBC)

MOTOR RACING: Formula 3000 International Championship
Round 5,
Spa-Francorchamps, Belgium

27 thursday

first-half

second-half

extra-time

SPORTING FIXTURES

CRICKET: 1st Cornhill Test, England v Sri Lanka - Day 1,
The Oval (BBC)

EQUESTRIAN: Blair Castle International Horse Trials Start
(Finish 30th August), *Blair Castle*

FOOTBALL: European Cup Winners Cup Qualifying Round 2nd
Leg, *Various, tbc*

GOLF: BMW International Open - Round 1, *Munich, Germany*

LAWN TENNIS: MFS Pro-Tennis Championships - Day 4, *Boston,
USA (Eurosport)*

28 friday

SPORTING FIXTURES

CRICKET: 1st Cornhill Test, England v Sri Lanka - Day 2,
The Oval (BBC)

GOLF: BMW International Open - Round 2,
Munich, Germany

LAWN TENNIS: MFS Pro-Tennis Championships - Day 5,
Boston, USA (Eurosport)

SPEEDWAY: Individual World Championship Grand Prix,
Linkoping, Sweden

notes

30 sunday

Pentecost 13   ☽ First Quarter

first-half

second-half

extra-time

SPORTING FIXTURES

CRICKET: 1st Cornhill Test, England v Sri Lanka - Day 4,
The Oval (BBC)

CYCLING: World Track Championships Finish,
Bordeaux, France (Eurosport)

EQUESTRIAN: Blair Castle International Horse Trials Finish,
Blair Castle

GOLF: BMW International Open - Round 4, *Munich, Germany*

LAWN TENNIS: US Womens Hardcourt Championships Finish,
Atlanta, USA
MFS Pro-Tennis Championships - Final,
Boston, USA (Eurosport)

MOTOR CYCLING: SBK Superbike World Championship,
A1 Ring, Austria (BSkyB)

MOTOR RACING: Belgian Grand Prix,
Spa-Francorchamps, Belgium (ITV)

POLO: World Championships Finish,
Santa Barbara, USA

YACHTING: Largs Regatta Week Finishes,
Largs

September

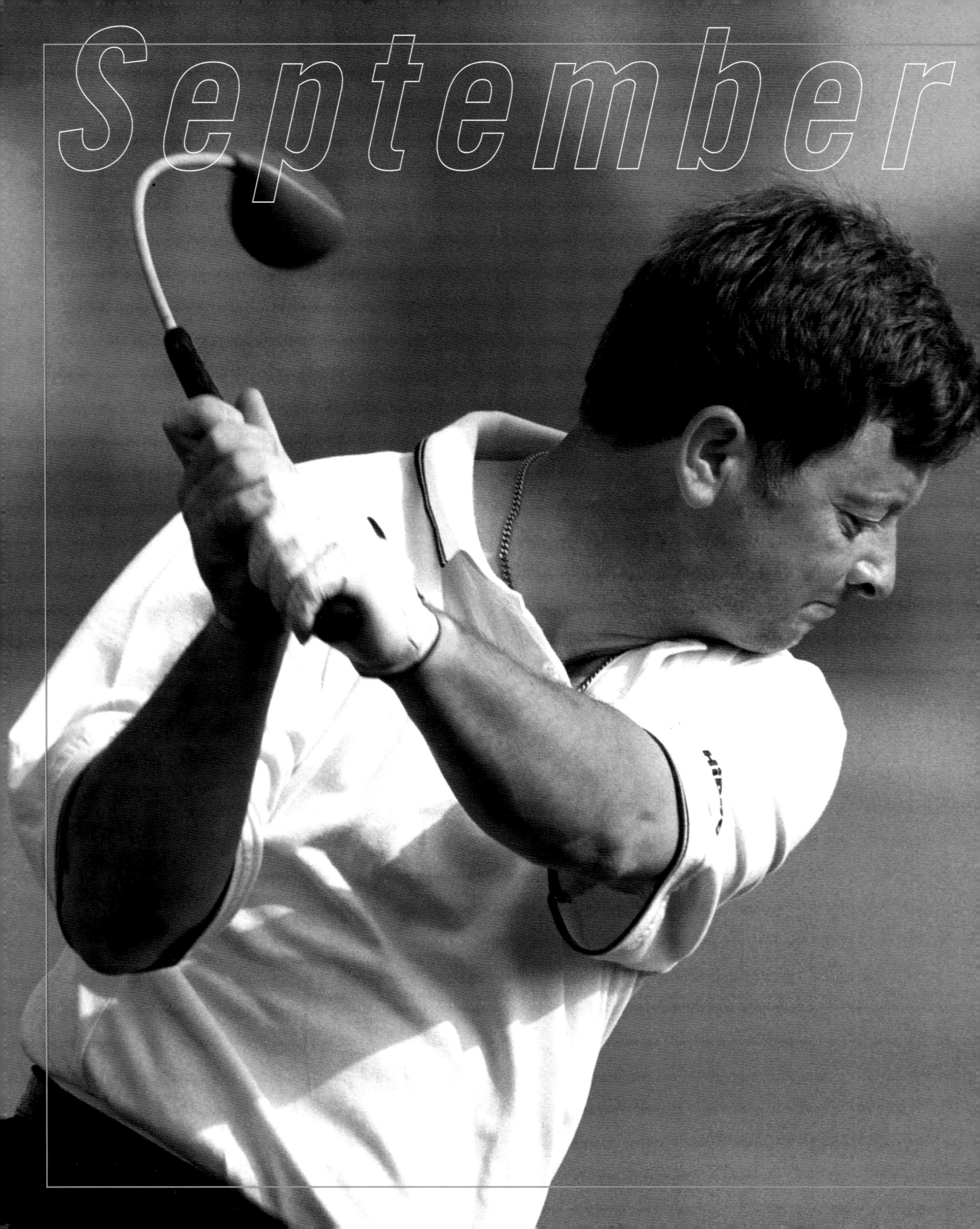

PHILIP BROWN

SEPTEMBER 1998

M	.	7	14	21	28
T	1	8	15	22	29
W	2	9	16	23	30
T	3	10	17	24	.
F	4	11	18	25	.
S	5	12	19	26	.
S	6	13	20	27	.

★ **BURGHLEY PEDIGREE CHUM HORSE TRIALS** EQUESTRIAN **3 - 6 SEPT** Burghley

★ **IAAF 14TH GRAND PRIX FINAL** ATHLETICS **5 SEPT** Moscow, Russia

★ **VUELTA A ESPAÒA** CYCLING **5 - 27 SEPT** Various venues, Spain

★ **WORLD CHAMPIONSHIPS** ROWING **6 - 13 SEPT** Cologne, Germany

★ **ONE 2 ONE BRITISH MASTERS** GOLF **10 - 13 SEPT** To be confirmed

★ **16TH COMMONWEALTH GAMES** GAMES **10 - 20 SEPT** Kuala Lumpur, Malaysia

★ **IAAF 8TH WORLD CUP OF ATHLETICS** ATHLETICS **11 - 13 SEPT** Johannesberg, S. Africa

★ **ITALIAN GRAND PRIX** FORMULA 1 **13 SEPT** Monza, Italy

★ **THE SAMSUNG OPEN** TENNIS **14 - 20 SEPT** Bournemouth

★ **SOLHEIM CUP** GOLF **18 - 20 SEPT** Dublin, Ohio USA

★ **KB FED CUP FINAL** TENNIS **19 - 20 SEPT** To be confirmed

★ **THE QUEEN ELIZABETH II STAKES** HORSE RACING **26 SEPT** Ascot

★ **HORSE OF THE YEAR SHOW** EQUESTRIAN **30 SEPT - 4 OCT** Wembley

★ **ST. LEGER** FLAT RACING **12 SEPT** Doncaster

31 monday

Bank Holiday UK

first-half

second-half

extra-time

SPORTING FIXTURES

CRICKET: 1st Cornhill Test, England v Sri Lanka - Day 5,
The Oval (BBC)

LAWN TENNIS: US Open Championships - Day 1,
New York, USA (BSkyB)

MOTOR CYCLING: British Superbike Championship Finishes,
Cadwell Park (BBC)

MOTOR RACING: RAC Touring Car Championship,
Brands Hatch (BBC)

1 tuesday

SPORTING FIXTURES

LAWN TENNIS: US Open Championships - Day 2,
New York, USA (BSkyB)

YACHTING: International Hobie 16 World Championship Starts
(Finish 30th Sep),
Airlie Beach, Australia

2 wednesday

ATHLETICS: ISTAF '98,
Berlin, Germany

LAWN TENNIS: US Open Championships - Day 3,
New York, USA (BSkyB)

5 saturday

first-half

second-half

extra-time

SPORTING FIXTURES

ATHLETICS: IAAF Grand Prix Final,
Moscow, Russia

CYCLING: Vuelta a Espana - Stage 1,
Cordoba-Cordoba, Spain (Eurosport)

GOLF: Canon European Masters - Round 3,
Crans-Sur-Sierre, Switzerland

LAWN TENNIS: US Open Championships - Day 6,
New York, USA (BSkyB)

MOTOR RACING: Formula 3000 International Championship
Round 6,
Donington Park

MOUNTAIN BIKE: Grundig/UCI Mountain Bike Cross Country
World Cup Final Starts,
Bromont, Canada

3 thursday

first-half

second-half

extra-time

SPORTING FIXTURES

CANOEING: Flatwater Racing World Championships Start
(Finish 6th Sep),
Szeged, Hungary

EQUESTRIAN: Burghley Pedigree Chum Horse Trials Start
(Finish 6th Sep), *Burghley*

GOLF: Canon European Masters - Round 1,
Crans-Sur-Sierre, Switzerland

LAWN TENNIS: US Open Championships - Day 4,
New York, USA (BSkyB)

4 friday

first-half

second-half

extra-time

GOLF: Canon European Masters - Round 2,
Crans-Sur-Sierre, Switzerland

LAWN TENNIS: US Open Championships - Day 5,
New York, USA (BSkyB)

MOTOR CYCLING: British Superbike Championship Start,
Silverstone (BBC)

notes

---

6 sunday

Pentecost 14 ○ Full Moon

first-half

second-half

extra-time

SPORTING FIXTURES

AMERICAN FOOTBALL: NFL Season Begins,
Various, USA (BSkyB/C4)

CYCLING: Vuelta a Espana - Stage 2,
Cordoba-Cadiz, Spain (Eurosport)

EQUESTRIAN: Burghley Pedigree Chum Horse Trials Finish,
Burghley

GOLF: Canon European Masters - Round 4,
Crans-Sur-Sierre, Switzerland

LAWN TENNIS: US Open Championships - Day 7,
New York, USA (BSkyB)

MOTOR CYCLING: Imola GP,
Imola, San Marino (Eurosport)
SBK Superbike World Championship,
Assen, Holland (BSkyB)

MOTOR RACING: FIA GT Championship Round 8,
Donington Park

MOUNTAIN BIKE: Grundig/UCI Mountain Bike Cross Country
World Cup Final Finishes, *Bromont, Canada*

ROWING: World Championships Start (Finish 13th Sep),
Cologne, Germany

7 monday

first-half

second-half

extra-time

SPORTING FIXTURES

CYCLING: Vuelta a Espana - Stage 3,
Cadiz-Estepona, Spain (Eurosport)

LAWN TENNIS: US Open Championships - Day 8,
New York, USA (BSkyB)

8 tuesday

SPORTING FIXTURES

CYCLING: Vuelta a Espana - Stage 4,
Marbella-Granada, Spain (Eurosport)

LAWN TENNIS: US Open Championships - Day 9,
New York, USA (BSkyB)

WRESTLING: World Mens Freestyle Championships Start (Finish 11th Sep),
Tehran, Iran

9 wednesday

SPORTING FIXTURES

CYCLING: Vuelta a Espana - Stage 5,
Oula Del Rio-Murcia, Spain (Eurosport)

LAWN TENNIS: US Open Championships - Day 10,
New York, USA (BSkyB)

12 saturday

first-half

second-half

extra-time

SPORTING FIXTURES

ANGLING: National Championships Division 1,
The River Thames

CYCLING: Vuelta a Espana - Stage 8,
Palma De Mallorca-Palma De Mallorca, Spain (Eurosport)

GOLF: One 2 One British Masters - Round 3,
tbc (BSkyB)

HORSE RACING: St Leger, **Doncaster**

LAWN TENNIS: US Open Championships - Women's Final,
New York, USA (BSkyB)

MOTOR RALLYING: RAC British Rally Championship
- Manx International Rally,
Douglas

MOUNTAIN BIKE: UCI Mountain Bike World Championships Start (Finish 20th Sep),
Mont Sainte Anne, Canada

MULTI-EVENT GAMES: 16th Commonwealth Games - Day 2,
Kuala Lumpur, Malaysia (BBC)

10 thursday | 11 friday | notes

first-half

second-half

extra-time

CYCLING: Vuelta a Espana - Stage 6, *Murcia-Alicante, Spain* *(Eurosport)*

EQUESTRIAN: Blenheim International Horse Trials Starts (Finish 13th Sep), *Blenheim*

GOLF: One 2 One British Masters - Round 1, *tbc (BSkyB)*

LAWN TENNIS: US Open Championships - Women's Semi-Finals, *New York, USA (BSkyB)*

MOTOR RALLYING: RAC British Rally Championship - Manx International Rally, *Douglas*

ATHLETICS: IAAF 8th World Cup Of Athletics Starts (Finishes 13th Sep), *Johannesberg, South Africa*

CYCLING: Vuelta a Espana - Stage 7, *Alicante-Valencia, Spain* *(Eurosport)*

GOLF: One 2 One British Masters - Round 2, *tbc (BSkyB)*

LAWN TENNIS: US Open Championships - Men's Semi-Finals, *New York, USA (BSkyB)*

MULTI-EVENT GAMES: 16th Commonwealth Games Opening Ceremony, *Kuala Lumpur, Malaysia (BBC)*

13 sunday

Pentecost 15 ☾ Last Quarter

first-half | second-half | extra-time

ATHLETICS: IAAF 8th World Cup Of Athletics Finishes, *Johannesberg, South Africa*

CYCLING: Vuelta a Espana - Stage 9, *Alcudia-Alcudia, Spain (Eurosport)*

EQUESTRIAN: Blenheim International Horse Trials Finish, *Blenheim*

GOLF: One 2 One British Masters - Round 4, *tbc (BSkyB)*

HURLING: Guinness All Ireland Hurling Championships Final, *Dublin, Ireland*

LAWN TENNIS: US Open Championships - Men's Final, *New York, USA (BSkyB)*

MOTOR RACING: Italian Grand Prix, *Monza, Italy (ITV)* Auto Trader RAC Touring Car Championship, *Oulton Park (BBC)*

MULTI-EVENT GAMES: 16th Commonwealth Games - Day 3, *Kuala Lumpur, Malaysia (BBC)*

ROWING: World Championships Finish, *Cologne, Germany*

14 monday

Battle of Britain

first-half

second-half

extra-time

SPORTING FIXTURES

LAWN TENNIS: Samsung Open - Day 1,
Bournemouth (BBC)

MULTI-EVENT GAMES: 16th Commonwealth Games - Day 4,
Kuala Lumpur, Malaysia (BBC)

15 tuesday

Birthday, HRH Prince Harry, b. 1984

CYCLING: Vuelta a Espana - Stage 10,
Vic-Andorra, Spain (Eurosport)

FOOTBALL: UEFA Cup First Round 1st Leg,
Various, tbc

LAWN TENNIS: Samsung Open - Day 2,
Bournemouth (BBC)

MULTI-EVENT GAMES: 16th Commonwealth Games - Day 5,
Kuala Lumpur, Malaysia (BBC)

16 wednesday

CYCLING: Vuelta a Espana - Stage 11,
Andorra-Ampriu, Spain (Eurosport)

FOOTBALL: UEFA Champions League Group Match 1,
Various, tbc

LAWN TENNIS: Samsung Open - Day 3,
Bournemouth (BBC)

MULTI-EVENT GAMES: 16th Commonwealth Games - Day 6,
Kuala Lumpur, Malaysia (BBC)

19 saturday

first-half

second-half

extra-time

SPORTING FIXTURES

CROQUET: All England Final Starts (Finishes 20th Sep),
Wrest Park

CYCLING: Vuelta a Espana - Stage 14,
Biesca-Zaragoza, Spain (Eurosport)

MULTI-EVENT GAMES: 16th Commonwealth Games - Day 9,
Kuala Lumpur, Malaysia (BBC)

GOLF: Solheim Cup - Day 2,
Dublin, Ohio, USA (BSkyB)

LAWN TENNIS: Samsung Open - Day 6,
Bournemouth (BBC)
KB Fed Cup - World Group 1 - Final Starts (Finishes 20th Sep),
tbc (BSkyB)

17 thursday

first-half

second-half

extra-time

SPORTING FIXTURES

CYCLING: Vuelta a Espana - Stage 12,
Benasque-Jaca, Spain (Eurosport)

FOOTBALL: European Cup Winners Cup First Round 1st Leg,
Various, tbc

LAWN TENNIS: Samsung Open - Day 4,
Bournemouth (BBC)

MULTI-EVENT GAMES: 16th Commonwealth Games - Day 7,
Kuala Lumpur, Malaysia (BBC)

18 friday

SPORTING FIXTURES

CYCLING: Vuelta a Espana - Stage 13,
Sabinanigo-Sabinanigo, Spain (Eurosport)

GOLF: Solheim Cup - Day 1,
Dublin, Ohio, USA (BSkyB)

LAWN TENNIS: Samsung Open - Day 5,
Bournemouth (BBC)

MULTI-EVENT GAMES: 16th Commonwealth Games - Day 8,
Kuala Lumpur, Malaysia (BBC)

SPEEDWAY: Individual World Championship Grand Prix,
Bydgoszcz, Poland

notes

20 sunday

Pentecost 16 ● New Moon

first-half

second-half

extra-time

SPORTING FIXTURES

CROQUET: All England Final Finishes,
Wrest Park

CYCLING: Vuelta a Espana - Stage 15,
Zaragoza-Soria, Spain (Eurosport)

GOLF: Solheim Cup - Day 3,
Dublin, Ohio, USA (BSkyB)

LAWN TENNIS: Samsung Open - Final,
Bournemouth (BBC)
KB Fed Cup - World Group 1 - Final Finishes,
tbc (BSkyB)

MOTOR CYCLING: Catalonian GP,
Barcelona, Spain (Eurosport)

MOTOR RACING: RAC Touring Car Championship,
Silverstone (BBC)

MOUNTAIN BIKE: UCI Mountain Bike World Championships
Finish,
Mont Sainte Anne, Canada

MULTI-EVENT GAMES: 16th Commonwealth Games - Day 10,
Kuala Lumpur, Malaysia (BBC)

21 monday

Jewish New Year (Rosh Hashanah) 5759

first-half

second-half

extra-time

SPORTING FIXTURES

CYCLING: Vuelta a Espana - Stage 16,
Soria-Laguna Negra De Neila, Spain *(Eurosport)*

LAWN TENNIS: Toyota Princess Cup - Day 1,
Tokyo, Japan

MULTI-EVENT GAMES: 16th Commonwealth Games - Day 11,
Kuala Lumpur, Malaysia *(BBC)*

22 tuesday

SPORTING FIXTURES

CYCLING: Vuelta a Espana - Stage 17,
Burgos-Leon, Spain *(Eurosport)*

LAWN TENNIS: Toyota Princess Cup - Day 2,
Tokyo, Japan

23 wednesday

Autumnal Equinox

SPORTING FIXTURES

CYCLING: Vuelta a Espana - Stage 18,
Leon-Salamanca, Spain *(Eurosport)*

LAWN TENNIS: Toyota Princess Cup - Day 3,
Tokyo, Japan

26 saturday

first-half

second-half

extra-time

SPORTING FIXTURES

ANGLING: National Championships Division 5,
Bridgewater

CYCLING: Vuelta a Espana - Stage 21,
Fuenlabrada-Fuenlabrada, Spain *(Eurosport)*

GOLF: Linde German Masters - Round 3,
Berlin, Germany

HORSE RACING: The Queen Elizabeth II Stakes,
Ascot *(BBC)*

LAWN TENNIS: Toyota Princess Cup - Day 6,
Tokyo, Japan

24 thursday

first-half

second-half

extra-time

SPORTING FIXTURES

BADMINTON: World Junior Championships Start
(Finish 27th Sep),
Jakarta, Indonesia

CYCLING: Vuelta a Espana - Stage 19,
Salamanca-Segovia, Spain (Eurosport)

GOLF: Linde German Masters - Round 1,
Berlin, Germany

LAWN TENNIS: Toyota Princess Cup - Day 4,
Tokyo, Japan

25 friday

first-half

second-half

extra-time

SPORTING FIXTURES

CHESS: 23rd Olympiad Starts (Finishes 10th Oct),
Kalmykia, Russia

CYCLING: Vuelta a Espana - Stage 20,
Segovia-Alto De Navacerrada, Spain (Eurosport)

GOLF: Linde German Masters - Round 2, *Berlin, Germany*

LAWN TENNIS: Toyota Princess Cup - Day 5, *Tokyo, Japan*

MOTOR CYCLING: British Superbike Championship Starts,
Donington Park (BBC)

notes

27 sunday

Pentecost 17

first-half

second-half

extra-time

SPORTING FIXTURES

ATHLETICS: IAAF World Half Marathon Championships,
Zurich, Switzerland

BADMINTON: World Junior Championships Finish,
Jakarta, Indonesia

CYCLING: Vuelta a Espana - Stage 22,
Madrid, Spain (Eurosport)

GAELIC FOOTBALL: Bank Of Ireland, All Ireland Football Final,
Dublin, Ireland

GOLF: Linde German Masters - Round 4,
Berlin, Germany

HORSE RACING: The Mail On Sunday Final,
Ascot

LAWN TENNIS: Toyota Princess Cup - Final,
Tokyo, Japan

MOTOR CYCLING: Motor Cycle News British Superbike
Championship Finishes,
Donington Park (BBC)

MOTOR RACING: Autosport British Formula 3 Championship,
Spa, Belgium
Luxembourg Grand Prix,
Nurburgring, Germany (ITV)

FRANK COPPI

M	.	5	12	19	26
T	.	6	13	20	27
W	.	7	14	21	28
T	1	8	15	22	29
F	2	9	16	23	30
S	3	10	17	24	31
S	4	11	18	25	.

1998

OCTOBER

★ **WORLD EQUESTRIAN GAMES** EQUESTRIAN **2 - 11 OCT** Rome & Pratoni Del Vivaro, Italy
★ **FORTE MERIDIEN PRIX DE L'ARC DE TRIOMPHE** HORSE RACING **4 OCT** Longchamp, France
★ **WORLD ROAD CHAMPIONSHIPS** CYCLING **7 - 11 OCT** Valkenburg/Maastricht, Holland
★ **ALFRED DUNHILL CUP** GOLF **8 - 11 OCT** St. Andrews
★ **SAN REMO RALLY** MOTOR RALLYING **10 - 14 OCT** San Remo, Italy
★ **PORTUGUESE GRAND PRIX** FORMULA 1 **11 OCT** Estoril, Portugal
★ **TOYOTA WORLD MATCHPLAY CHAMPIONSHIP** GOLF **15 - 18 OCT** To be confirmed
★ **THE TOTE CESAREWITCH** HORSE RACING **17 OCT** Newmarket
★ **CHAMPIONS TROPHY** FIELD HOCKEY **31 OCT - 8 NOV** Lahore, Pakistan

28 monday

First Quarter

first-half

second-half

extra-time

SPORTING FIXTURES

LAWN TENNIS: ATP Tour - Grand Prix De Tennis De Toulouse - Day 1, *Toulouse, France (Eurosport)*
WTA Tour - Sparkasen Cup International Grand Prix - Day 1, *Leipzig, Germany*

29 tuesday

Michaelmas (Quarter Day)

FOOTBALL: UEFA Cup First Round 2nd Leg, *Various, tbc*

LAWN TENNIS: ATP Tour - Grand Prix De Tennis De Toulouse - Day 2, *Toulouse, France (Eurosport)*
WTA Tour - Sparkasen Cup International Grand Prix - Day 2, *Leipzig, Germany*

30 wednesday

Day of Atonement (Yom Kippur)

EQUESTRIAN: Horse Of The Year Show Starts (Finishes 4th Oct), *Wembley, London (BSkyB)*

FOOTBALL: UEFA Champions League Group Match 2, *Various, tbc*

LAWN TENNIS: WTA Tour - Sparkasen Cup International Grand Prix - Day 3, *Leipzig, Germany*
ATP Tour - Grand Prix De Tennis De Toulouse - Day 3, *Toulouse, France (Eurosport)*

YACHTING: International Hobie 16 World Championship Finish, *Airlie Beach, Australia*

3 saturday

first-half

second-half

extra-time

SPORTING FIXTURES

CHESS: Monarch Assurance 7th International Open Starts (Finishes 11th Oct), *Port Erin*

DRAGON BOAT RACING: BDA National Cup Grand Finals Start (Finish 4th Oct), *Nottingham*

HORSE RACING: The TOTE Cambridgeshire Handicap Stakes, *Newmarket (C4)*

LAWN TENNIS: ATP Tour - Grand Prix De Tennis De Toulouse - Day 6, *Toulouse, France (Eurosport)*
WTA Tour - Sparkasen Cup International Grand Prix - Day 6, *Leipzig, Germany*

SPEEDWAY: Individual World Championship Grand Prix, *Pardubice, Czech Republic*

1 thursday

Michaelmas Law Sittings begin

first-half

second-half

extra-time

SPORTING FIXTURES

EQUESTRIAN: Tweseldown Novice Horse Trials Start
(Finish 4th Oct), *Tweseldown*

FOOTBALL: European Cup Winners Cup First Round 2nd Leg,
Various, tbc

LAWN TENNIS: ATP Tour - Grand Prix De Tennis De Toulouse -
Day 4, *Toulouse, France (Eurosport)*
WTA Tour - Sparkasen Cup International Grand Prix - Day 4,
Leipzig, Germany

2 friday

SPORTING FIXTURES

JUDO: Welsh Senior Open Championships,
Cardiff

LAWN TENNIS: ATP Tour - Grand Prix De Tennis De Toulouse -
Day 5, *Toulouse, France (Eurosport)*
WTA Tour - Sparkasen Cup International Grand Prix - Day 5,
Leipzig, Germany

notes

4 sunday

Pentecost 18

first-half

second-half

extra-time

SPORTING FIXTURES

CYCLING: World Cup Paris Tours,
Paris, France (Eurosport)

DRAGON BOAT RACING: BDA National Cup Grand Finals
Finish, *Nottingham*

EQUESTRIAN: Horse Of The Year Show Finishes,
Wembley (BSkyB)

EQUESTRIAN: Tweseldown Novice Horse Trials Finish,
Tweseldown

HORSE RACING: Forte Meridien Prix De L'Arc De Triomphe,
Longchamp, France (BBC)

LAWN TENNIS: WTA Tour - Sparkasen Cup International
Grand Prix - Final,
Leipzig, Germany
ATP Tour - Grand Prix De Tennis De
Toulouse - Final, *Toulouse, France (Eurosport)*

MOTOR CYCLING: Australian GP,
Phillip Island, Australia (Eurosport)
SBK Superbike World Championship,
Miyagi-Ken, Japan (BSkyB)

MOTOR RACING: Autosport British Formula 3 Championship,
Silverstone

5 monday

First Day of Tabernacles (Succoth)   ○ Full Moon

first-half

second-half

extra-time

SPORTING FIXTURES

FENCING: World Championships Start (Finish 11th Oct),
La Chaux De Fonds, Switzerland

LAWN TENNIS: WTA Tour - Porsche Tennis Grand Prix Starts
(Finishes 11th Oct),
Filderstadt, Germany
ATP Tour - Davidoff Swiss Indoors Basle - Day 1,
Basle, Switzerland (Eurosport)

6 tuesday

SPORTING FIXTURES

CYCLING: World Road Championships Start (Finish 11th Oct),
Valkenburg / Maastricht, Holland (Eurosport)

EQUESTRIAN: World Equestrian Games - Day 1,
Rome & Pratoni Del Vivaro, Italy

LAWN TENNIS: ATP Tour - Davidoff Swiss Indoors Basle
- Day 2,
Basle, Switzerland (Eurosport)

7 wednesday

SPORTING FIXTURES

EQUESTRIAN: World Equestrian Games - Day 2,
Rome & Pratoni Del Vivaro, Italy

LAWN TENNIS: ATP Tour - Davidoff Swiss Indoors Basle
- Day 3,
Basle, Switzerland (Eurosport)

10 saturday

first-half

second-half

extra-time

SPORTING FIXTURES

CHESS: 23rd Olympiad Finishes,
Kalmykia, Russia

EQUESTRIAN: World Equestrian Games - Day 5,
Rome & Pratoni Del Vivaro, Italy

GOLF: Alfred Dunhill Cup - Day 3, *St. Andrews, Fife*

HORSE RACING: The Princess Royal Stakes,
Ascot

LAWN TENNIS: ATP Tour - Davidoff Swiss Indoors Basle
- Day 6,
Basle, Switzerland (Eurosport)

MOTOR RALLYING: Rallye San Remo - Rallye D'Italia Starts
(Finishes 14th Oct),
San Remo, Italy (Eurosport)

8 thursday

first-half

second-half

extra-time

SPORTING FIXTURES

EQUESTRIAN: World Equestrian Games - Day 3,
Rome & Pratoni Del Vivaro, Italy

GOLF: Alfred Dunhill Cup - Day 1,
St. Andrews, Fife

LAWN TENNIS: ATP Tour - Davidoff Swiss Indoors Basle - Day 4,
Basle, Switzerland (Eurosport)

9 friday

SPORTING FIXTURES

EQUESTRIAN: World Equestrian Games - Day 4,
Rome & Pratoni Del Vivaro, Italy

GOLF: Alfred Dunhill Cup - Day 2,
St. Andrews, Fife

GYMNASTICS: British Championships for Women Start
(Finish 11th Oct), *Guildford*

HORSE RACING: The Bonusprint October Stakes, *Ascot*

LAWN TENNIS: ATP Tour - Davidoff Swiss Indoors Basle -
Day 5, *Basle, Switzerland (Eurosport)*

notes

11 sunday

Pentecost 19

first-half

second-half

extra-time

SPORTING FIXTURES

ATHLETICS: Lasalle Banks Chicago Marathon,
Chicago, USA

CYCLING: World Road Championships Finish,
Valkenburg, Holland (Eurosport)

EQUESTRIAN: World Equestrian Games - Final Day,
Rome & Pratoni Del Vivaro, Italy

FENCING: World Championships Finish,
La Chaux De Fonds, Switzerland

GOLF: Alfred Dunhill Cup - Day 4,
St. Andrews, Fife

LAWN TENNIS: ATP Tour - Davidoff Swiss Indoors Basle - Final,
Basle, Switzerland (Eurosport)
WTA Tour - Porsche Tennis Grand Prix Finishes,
Filderstadt, Germany

MOTOR CYCLING: SBK Superbike World Championship,
Shah Alam, Malaysia (BSkyB)

MOTOR RACING: Portuguese Grand Prix,
Estoril, Portugal (ITV)

SNOOKER: Grand Prix Starts (Finishes 24th Oct),
Preston (BBC)

12 monday

☽ Last Quarter

first-half

second-half

extra-time

SPORTING FIXTURES

LAWN TENNIS: ATP Tour - CA Tennis Trophy - Day 1, *Vienna, Austria (Eurosport)*
WTA Tour - European Indoor Championships - Day 1, *Zurich, Switzerland*

13 tuesday

SPORTING FIXTURES

LAWN TENNIS: ATP Tour - CA Tennis Trophy - Day 2, *Vienna, Austria (Eurosport)*
WTA Tour - European Indoor Championships - Day 2, *Zurich, Switzerland*

14 wednesday

SPORTING FIXTURES

BADMINTON: Denmark World Grand Prix Starts (Finishes 18th Oct),
Denmark

LAWN TENNIS: ATP Tour - CA Tennis Trophy - Day 3, *Vienna, Austria (Eurosport)*

MOTOR RALLYING: Rallye San Remo - Rallye D'Italia Finishes, *San Remo, Italy (Eurosport)*
WTA Tour - European Indoor Championships - Day 3, *Zurich, Switzerland*

17 saturday

first-half

second-half

extra-time

SPORTING FIXTURES

CYCLING: World Cup Giro Di Lombardia, *Italy (Eurosport)*

GOLF: Toyota World Matchplay Championship - Day 3, *tbc (BBC)*

JUDO: European Team Championships Start (Finish 18th Oct), *Villach, Austria*

LAWN TENNIS: ATP Tour - CA Tennis Trophy - Day 6, *Vienna, Austria (Eurosport)*
WTA Tour - European Indoor Championships - Day 6, *Zurich, Switzerland*

SWIMMING: Inter-County Swimming Competition, *Sheffield*

15 thursday

first-half

second-half

extra-time

SPORTING FIXTURES

GOLF: Toyota World Matchplay Championship - Day 1,
tbc (BBC)

LAWN TENNIS: ATP Tour - CA Tennis Trophy - Day 4,
Vienna, Austria (Eurosport)
WTA Tour - European Indoor Championships - Day 4,
Zurich, Switzerland

16 friday

SPORTING FIXTURES

GOLF: Toyota World Matchplay Championship - Day 2,
tbc (BBC)

LAWN TENNIS: ATP Tour - CA Tennis Trophy - Day 5,
Vienna, Austria (Eurosport)
WTA Tour - European Indoor Championships - Day 5,
Zurich, Switzerland

notes

18 sunday

Pentecost 20

first-half

second-half

extra-time

SPORTING FIXTURES

BADMINTON: Denmark World Grand Prix Finishes,
Denmark

GOLF: Toyota World Matchplay Championship - Day 4,
tbc (BBC)

JUDO: European Team Championships Finish, *Villach, Austria*

LAWN TENNIS: ATP Tour - CA Tennis Trophy - Final,
Vienna, Austria (Eurosport)
WTA Tour - European Indoor Championships - Final, *Zurich, Switzerland*

MOTOR CYCLING: Rio GP,
Autodromo Nelson Piquet, Brazil (Eurosport)

MOTOR RACING: Indy Carnival Australia,
Gold Coast, Australia

ROWING: Head Of The Charles, *Boston, USA*

19 monday

first-half

second-half

extra-time

SPORTING FIXTURES

LAWN TENNIS: ATP Tour - IPB Czech Indoor - Day 1,
Ostrava, Czech Republic (Eurosport)
Ladies Kremlin Cup Starts (Finishes 25th Oct),
Moscow, Russia

20 tuesday

● New Moon

FOOTBALL: UEFA Cup Second Round 1st Leg,
Various, tbc

LAWN TENNIS: ATP Tour - IPB Czech Indoor - Day 2,
Ostrava, Czech Republic (Eurosport)

21 wednesday

FOOTBALL: UEFA Champions League Group Match 3,
Various, tbc

LAWN TENNIS: ATP Tour - IPB Czech Indoor - Day 3, *Ostrava,
Czech Republic (Eurosport)*

24 saturday

United Nations Day

first-half

second-half

extra-time

SPORTING FIXTURES

DANCE SPORT: IDSF European Ten Dance Championship,
Bratislava, Slovakia

EQUESTRIAN: International Jumping Event Starts
(Finishes 26th Oct), *Clonshire, Ireland*

GOLF: OKI Pro-Am - Round 3,
Madrid, Spain

HORSE RACING: The Racing Post Trophy,
Doncaster (C4)

LAWN TENNIS: ATP Tour - IPB Czech Indoor - Day 6, *Ostrava,
Czech Republic (Eurosport)*

SNOOKER: Grand Prix Finishes, *Preston (BBC)*

22 thursday

first-half

second-half

extra-time

SPORTING FIXTURES

FOOTBALL: European Cup Winners Cup, Second Round 1st Leg, *Various, tbc*

GOLF: OKI Pro-Am - Round 1, *Madrid, Spain*

LAWN TENNIS: ATP Tour - IPB Czech Indoor - Day 4, *Ostrava, Czech Republic (Eurosport)*

23 friday

SPORTING FIXTURES

GOLF: OKI Pro-Am - Round 2, *Madrid, Spain*

LAWN TENNIS: ATP Tour - IPB Czech Indoor - Day 5, *Ostrava, Czech Republic (Eurosport)*

notes

25 sunday

British Summer Time ends   *9th before Christmas*

first-half

second-half

extra-time

SPORTING FIXTURES

GOLF: OKI Pro-Am - Round 4, *Madrid, Spain*

LAWN TENNIS: Ladies Kremlin Cup Finishes, *Moscow, Russia*
ATP Tour - IPB Czech Indoor - Final, *Ostrava, Czech Republic (Eurosport)*

MOTOR CYCLING: Argentine GP, *Buenos Aires, Argentina (Eurosport)*

M	.	2	9	16	23	30
T	.	3	10	17	24	.
W	.	4	11	18	25	.
T	.	5	12	19	26	.
F	.	6	13	20	27	.
S	.	7	14	21	28	.
S	1	8	15	22	29	.

FRANK COPPI

1998
NOVEMBER

- ★ **JAPANESE GRAND PRIX** FORMULA 1 **1 NOV** Suzuka, Japan
- ★ **MELBOURNE CUP** HORSE RACING **3 NOV** Flemington, Australia
- ★ **API RALLY AUSTRALIA** MOTOR RALLYING **5 - 8 NOV** Perth, Australia
- ★ **BREEDERS CUP** HORSE RACING **7 NOV** Inglewood, USA
- ★ **CHASE CHAMPIONSHIPS OF THE COREL WTA TOUR** TENNIS **16 - 22 NOV** New York, USA
- ★ **WORLD CUP OF GOLF** GOLF **19 - 22 NOV** Kiawah Island USA
- ★ **NETWORK Q RAC RALLY** MOTOR RALLYING **21 - 23 NOV** Various venues
- ★ **JAPAN CUP** HORSE RACING **22 NOV** Tokyo, Japan
- ★ **ATP TOUR WORLD CHAMPIONSHIPS** TENNIS **23 - 29 NOV** Hanover, Germany
- ★ **THE HENNESSY COGNAC GOLD CUP HANDICAP STEEPLECHASE**
  HORSE RACING **28 NOV** Newbury

26 monday

first-half

second-half

extra-time

SPORTING FIXTURES

EQUESTRIAN: International Jumping Event Finishes, *Clonshire, Ireland*

LAWN TENNIS: ATP Tour - Eurocard Open - Day 1, *Stuttgart, Germany* (Eurosport)
WTA Tour - Seat Luxembourg Open - Day 1, *Kockelscheuer, Luxembourg*

27 tuesday

SPORTING FIXTURES

LAWN TENNIS: ATP Tour - Eurocard Open - Day 2, *Stuttgart, Germany* (Eurosport)
WTA Tour - Seat Luxembourg Open - Day 2, *Kockelscheuer, Luxembourg*

28 wednesday

☽ First Quarter

LAWN TENNIS: WTA Tour - Seat Luxembourg Open - Day 3, *Kockelscheuer, Luxembourg*
ATP Tour - Eurocard Open - Day 3, *Stuttgart, Germany* (Eurosport)

31 saturday

Halloween

first-half

second-half

extra-time

SPORTING FIXTURES

ANGLING: Shore Angling World Championships Start (Finish 7th Nov), *Langeland, Germany*

DISABLED: National Swimming Championships Start (Finish 1st Nov), *Darlington*

GOLF: Volvo Masters - Round 3, *Spain*

HOCKEY: Champions Trophy Starts (Finishes 8th Nov), *Lahore, Pakistan*

LAWN TENNIS: WTA Tour - Seat Luxembourg Open - Day 6, *Kockelscheuer, Luxembourg*
ATP Tour - Eurocard Open - Day 6, *Stuttgart, Germany* (Eurosport)

29 thursday

first-half

second-half

extra-time

SPORTING FIXTURES

GOLF: Volvo Masters - Round 1,
Spain

LAWN TENNIS: ATP Tour - Eurocard Open - Day 4, *Stuttgart,*
Germany (Eurosport)
WTA Tour - Seat Luxembourg Open - Day 4,
Kockelscheuer, Luxembourg

30 friday

SPORTING FIXTURES

GOLF: Volvo Masters - Round 2,
Spain

LAWN TENNIS: ATP Tour - Eurocard Open - Day 5,
Stuttgart, Germany (Eurosport)
WTA Tour - Seat Luxembourg Open - Day 5,
Kockelscheuer, Luxembourg

notes

1 sunday

All Saints' Day   *8th before Christmas*

first-half

second-half

extra-time

SPORTING FIXTURES

ATHLETICS: New York City Marathon,
New York, USA

DISABLED: National Swimming Championships Finish,
Darlington

GOLF: Volvo Masters - Round 4,
Spain

LAWN TENNIS: ATP Tour - Eurocard Open - Final,
Stuttgart, Germany (Eurosport)
WTA Tour - Seat Luxembourg Open - Final,
Kockelscheuer, Luxembourg

MOTOR RACING: Japanese Grand Prix,
Suzuka, Japan (ITV)
CART - Marlboro 500, *Fontana, USA* (Eurosport)

SQUASH: Women's World Open Starts (Finishes 8th Nov),
Stuttgart, Germany

2 monday

first-half

second-half

extra-time

SPORTING FIXTURES

LAWN TENNIS: ATP Tour - Open De La Ville De Paris - Day 1, *Paris, France (Eurosport)*
WTA Tour - Ameritech Cup Starts (Finishes 8th Nov), *Chicago, USA*

3 tuesday

FOOTBALL: UEFA Cup Second Round 2nd Leg, *Various, tbc*

HORSE RACING: Melbourne Cup, *Flemington, Australia*

LAWN TENNIS: ATP Tour - Open De La Ville De Paris - Day 2, *Paris, France (Eurosport)*

VOLLEYBALL: Womens World Championships Start (Finish 12th Nov), *Various, Japan*

4 wednesday

○ Full Moon

FOOTBALL: UEFA Champions League Group Match 4, *Various, tbc*

LAWN TENNIS: ATP Tour - Open De La Ville De Paris - Day 3, *Paris, France (Eurosport)*

7 saturday

first-half

second-half

extra-time

SPORTING FIXTURES

ANGLING: Shore Angling World Championships Finish, *Langeland, Germany*

GOLF: Subaru Sarazen World Open Championship - Round 3, *Braselton, USA*

HORSE RACING: Visa 3-Year-Old Championship Series - Breeders' Cup, *Hollywood Park, USA (C4)*

LAWN TENNIS: ATP Tour - Open De La Ville De Paris - Day 6, *Paris, France (Eurosport)*

NETBALL: International Netball, *Wembley*

5 thursday

first-half

second-half

extra-time

SPORTING FIXTURES

FOOTBALL: European Cup Winners Cup Second Round 2nd Leg,
Various, tbc

GOLF: Subaru Sarazen World Open Championship - Round 1,
Braselton, USA

LAWN TENNIS: ATP Tour - Open De La Ville De Paris
- Day 4, *Paris, France (Eurosport)*

MOTOR RALLYING: API Rally Australia Starts
(Finishes 8th Nov),
Perth, Australia

6 friday

SPORTING FIXTURES

BOXING: World Championships - Under 19 Start
(Finishes 16th Nov),
Buenos Aires, Argentina

GOLF: Subaru Sarazen World Open Championship - Round 2,
Braselton, USA

LAWN TENNIS: ATP Tour - Open De La Ville De Paris - Day 5,
Paris, France (Eurosport)

notes

8 sunday

Remembrance Sunday   *7th before Christmas*

first-half

second-half

extra-time

SPORTING FIXTURES

GOLF: Subaru Sarazen World Open Championship - Round 4,
Braselton, USA

HOCKEY: Champions Trophy Finishes,
Lahore, Pakistan

LAWN TENNIS: WTA Tour - Ameritech Cup Finishes, *Chicago, USA*
ATP Tour - Open De La Ville De Paris - Final, *Paris, France (Eurosport)*

MOTOR RALLYING: API Rally Australia Finishes,
Perth, Australia

SQUASH: Women's World Open Finishes,
Stuttgart, Germany

9 monday

first-half

second-half

extra-time

SPORTING FIXTURES

LAWN TENNIS: ATP Tour - Kremlin Cup - Day 1,
Moscow, Russia *(Eurosport)*
WTA Tour - Advanta Championships - Day 1,
Philadelphia, USA

SQUASH: Women's World Team Championship Starts
(Finishes 15th Nov), *Stuttgart, Germany*

10 tuesday

SPORTING FIXTURES

LAWN TENNIS: ATP Tour - Kremlin Cup - Day 2,
Moscow, Russia *(Eurosport)*
WTA Tour - Advanta Championships - Day 2,
Philadelphia, USA

11 wednesday

Martinmas (Scottish Term Day)   Armistice Day   ☾ Last Quarter

first-half

SPORTING FIXTURES

LAWN TENNIS: WTA Tour - Advanta Championships
- Day 3, *Philadelphia, USA*
ATP Tour - Kremlin Cup - Day 3,
Moscow, Russia *(Eurosport)*

14 saturday

Birthday, HRH The Prince of Wales, b. 1948

first-half

second-half

extra-time

SPORTING FIXTURES

DANCE SPORT: IDSF World Latin Competition,
Frankfurt, Germany

GYMNASTICS: British Championships for Men Start
(Finish 15th Nov), *tbc*

HORSE RACING: The Murphys Gold Cup Handicap
Steeple Chase, *Cheltenham*

LAWN TENNIS: WTA Tour - Advanta Championships
- Day 6, *Philadelphia, USA*
ATP Tour - Kremlin Cup - Day 6,
Moscow, Russia *(Eurosport)*

12 thursday

first-half

second-half

extra-time

SPORTING FIXTURES

LAWN TENNIS: WTA Tour - Advanta Championships - Day 4,
Philadelphia, USA
ATP Tour - Kremlin Cup - Day 4,
Moscow, Russia (Eurosport)

VOLLEYBALL: Womens World Championships Final,
Osaka, Japan

13 friday

LAWN TENNIS: ATP Tour - Kremlin Cup - Day 5,
Moscow, Russia (Eurosport)
WTA Tour - Advanta Championships - Day 5,
Philadelphia, USA

SNOOKER: Liverpool Victoria UK Championships Start
(Finish 29th Nov), *Bournemouth (BBC)*

VOLLEYBALL: Mens World Championships Start
(Finish 29th Nov), *Various, Japan*

notes

15 sunday

6th before Christmas

first-half

second-half

extra-time

SPORTING FIXTURES

GYMNASTICS: British Championships for Men Finish,
tbc

LAWN TENNIS: ATP Tour - Kremlin Cup - Final,
Moscow, Russia (Eurosport)
WTA Tour - Advanta Championships - Final,
Philadelphia, USA

SQUASH: Women's World Team Championship Finishes,
Stuttgart, Germany

16 monday

first-half

second-half

extra-time

SPORTING FIXTURES

BOXING: World Championships - Under 19 Finish,
Buenos Aires, Argentina

LAWN TENNIS: Chase Championships Of The Corel WTA Tour
- Day 1, *New York, USA*
Phoenix / ATP Tour World Doubles Championship - Day 1,
Hartford, USA (Eurosport)

17 tuesday

LAWN TENNIS: Chase Championships Of The Corel
WTA Tour - Day 2, *New York, USA*
Phoenix / ATP Tour World Doubles Championship - Day 2,
Hartford, USA (Eurosport)

18 wednesday

LAWN TENNIS: Chase Championships Of The Corel
WTA Tour - Day 3, *New York, USA*
Phoenix / ATP Tour World Doubles Championship - Day 3,
Hartford, USA (Eurosport)

21 saturday

first-half

second-half

extra-time

SPORTING FIXTURES

GOLF: World Cup Of Golf - Round 3,
Kiawah Island, USA (BSkyB)

HORSE RACING: The First National Bank Gold Cup Chase,
Ascot

LAWN TENNIS: Phoenix / ATP Tour World Doubles
Championship - Day 6, *Hartford, USA (Eurosport)*
Chase Championships Of The Corel WTA Tour - Day 6,
New York, USA

MOTOR RALLYING: Network Q RAC Rally Day 1,
Cheltenham (BBC)

19 thursday

● New Moon

first-half

second-half

extra-time

SPORTING FIXTURES

GOLF: World Cup Of Golf - Round 1,
Kiawah Island, USA (BSkyB)

JUDO: European Junior Championships Start (Finish 22nd Nov),
Rome, Italy

LAWN TENNIS: Chase Championships Of The Corel
WTA Tour - Day 4, *New York, USA*
Phoenix / ATP Tour World Doubles Championship - Day 4,
Hartford, USA (Eurosport)

20 friday

SPORTING FIXTURES

GOLF: World Cup Of Golf - Round 2, *Kiawah Island, USA*
(BSkyB)

HORSE RACING: The Coopers & Lybrand Ascot Hurdle, *Ascot*

LAWN TENNIS: Phoenix / ATP Tour World Doubles
Championship - Day 5, *Hartford, USA (Eurosport)*
Chase Championships Of The Corel WTA Tour - Day 5,
New York, USA

YACHTING: Tornado World Championship Starts
(Finishes 27th Nov), *Buzios, Brazil*

notes

22 sunday

5th before Christmas

first-half

second-half

extra-time

SPORTING FIXTURES

GOLF: World Cup Of Golf - Round 4,
Kiawah Island, USA (BSkyB)

HORSE RACING: Japan Cup,
Tokyo, Japan

JUDO: European Junior Championships Finish,
Rome, Italy

LAWN TENNIS: Chase Championships Of The Corel
WTA Tour - Final, *New York, USA*
Phoenix / ATP Tour World Doubles Championship - Final,
Hartford, USA (Eurosport)

MOTOR RACING: F3 Intercontinental Cup,
TBC, Macao

MOTOR RALLYING: Network Q RAC Rally Day 2,
Cheltenham (BBC)

SKATING: World Junior Figure Skating Championships Start
(Finish 29th Nov),
Zagreb, Croatia

23 monday

first-half

second-half

extra-time

SPORTING FIXTURES

LAWN TENNIS: IBM/ATP Tour World Championship - Day 1, **Hanover, Germany** (Eurosport)

MOTOR RALLYING: Network Q RAC Rally Day 3, **Cheltenham** (BBC)

24 tuesday

FOOTBALL: UEFA Cup Third Round 1st Leg, **Various, tbc**

LAWN TENNIS: IBM/ATP Tour World Championship - Day 2, **Hanover, Germany** (Eurosport)

25 wednesday

BASKETBALL: Euro Championships Semi-Final Round (Men) England v Denmark, **Sheffield**

FOOTBALL: UEFA Champions League Group Match 5, **Various, tbc**

LAWN TENNIS: IBM/ATP Tour World Championship - Day 3, **Hanover, Germany** (Eurosport)

28 saturday

first-half

second-half

extra-time

SPORTING FIXTURES

BASKETBALL: Euro Championships Semi-Final Round (Men) Spain v England, **Spain**

DISABLED: National Basketball Championships Start (Finish 29th Nov), **Aylesbury**

HORSE RACING: The Hennessy Cognac Gold Cup Handicap Steeple Chase, **Newbury** (BBC)

LAWN TENNIS: IBM/ATP Tour World Championship - Day 6, **Hanover, Germany** (Eurosport)

26 thursday

first-half

second-half

extra-time

SPORTING FIXTURES

BODY-BUILDING: Commonwealth Body-Building
Championships Start (Finish 30th Nov),
Malacca, Malaysia

LAWN TENNIS: IBM/ATP Tour World Championship - Day 4,
Hanover, Germany (Eurosport)

TABLE TENNIS: Swedish Open Starts (Finishes 29th Nov),
Sweden

27 friday

☽ First Quarter

LAWN TENNIS: IBM/ATP Tour World Championship - Day 5,
Hanover, Germany (Eurosport)

RUGBY UNION: Dubai International Sevens Start
(Finish 29th Nov),
Dubai, UAE

YACHTING: Tornado World Championship Finishes,
Buzios, Brazil

notes

29 sunday

1st in Advent

first-half

second-half

extra-time

SPORTING FIXTURES

DISABLED: National Basketball Championships Finish,
Aylesbury

LAWN TENNIS: IBM/ATP Tour World Championship
- Final, *Hanover, Germany (Eurosport)*

RUGBY UNION: Dubai International Sevens Finish,
Dubai, UAE

SKATING: World Junior Figure Skating Championships Finish,
Zagreb, Croatia

SNOOKER: Liverpool Victoria UK Championships Finish,
Bournemouth (BBC)

TABLE TENNIS: Swedish Open Finishes, *tbc, Sweden*

VOLLEYBALL: Mens World Championships Final,
Tokyo, Japan

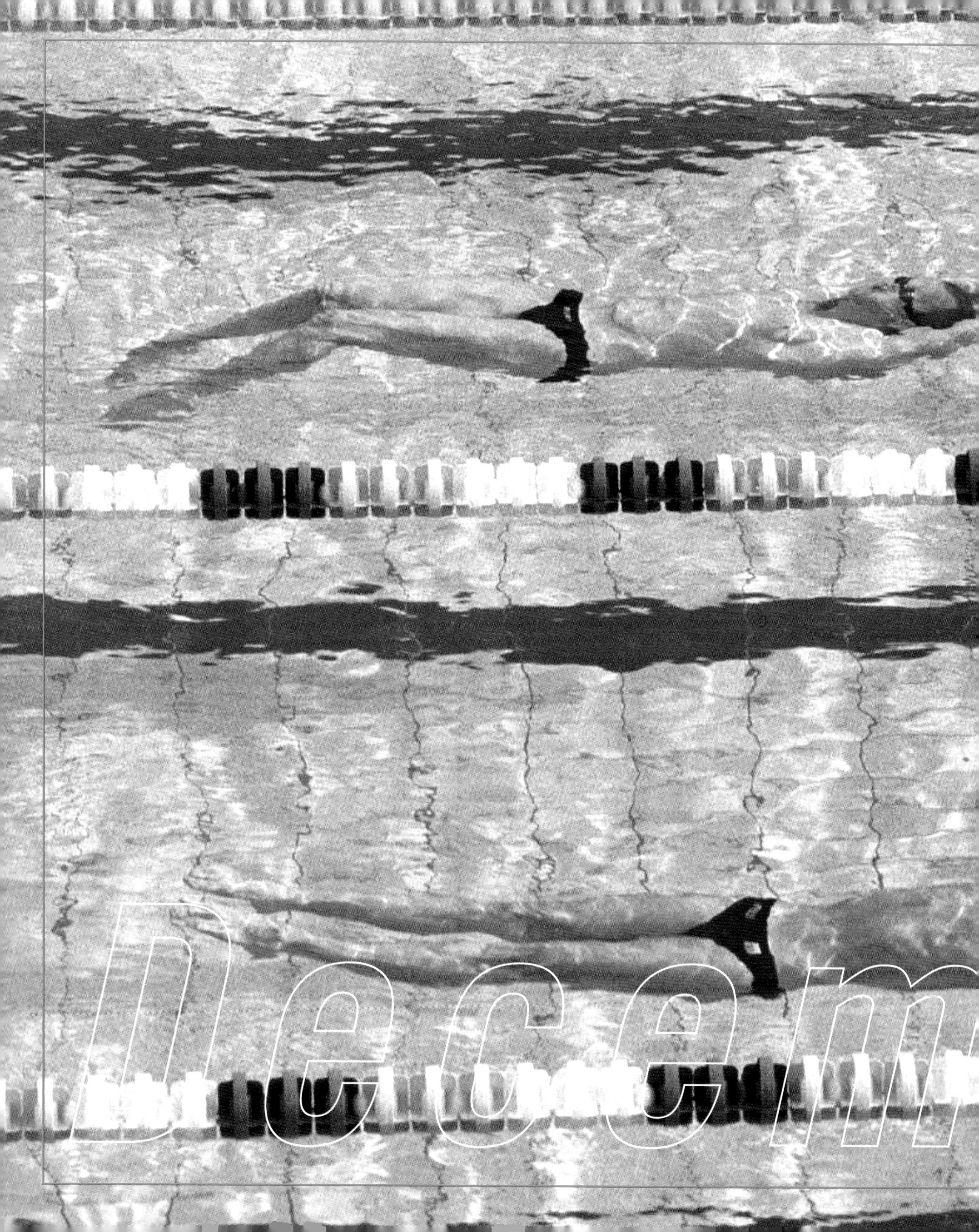
Decem

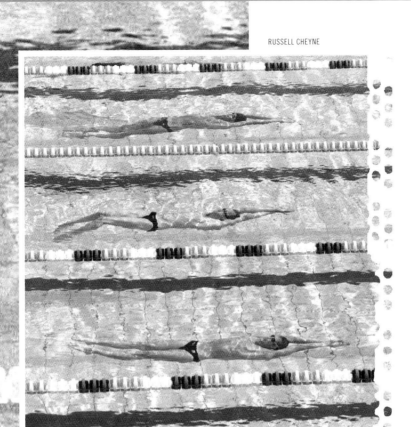

RUSSELL CHEYNE

M	.	7	14	21	28
T	1	8	15	22	29
W	2	9	16	23	30
T	3	10	17	24	31
F	4	11	18	25	.
S	5	12	19	26	.
S	6	13	20	27	.

1998
DECEMBER

★ **ENGLAND TOUR OF AUSTRALIA** CRICKET **DEC** Various venues, Australia

★ **MEN'S WORLD OPEN** SQUASH **1 - 6 DEC** Bombay, India

★ **ENGLAND V UKRAINE- EUROPEAN CHAMPIONSHIPS QUALIFYING**
BASKETBALL **2 DEC** Sheffield

★ **NEDBANK 19 SUN CITY MILLION DOLLAR CHALLENGE**
GOLF **3 - 6 DEC** Sun City, South Africa

★ **DAVIS CUP FINAL** TENNIS **4 - 6 DEC** To be confirmed

★ **13TH ASIAN GAMES** GAMES **6 - 20 DEC** Bangkok, Thailand

★ **BRITISH ICE FIGURE AND DANCE CHAMPIONSHIPS**
SKATING **9 - 13 DEC** Hull

★ **EUROPEAN SPRINTS** SWIMMING **10 - 13 DEC** Sheffield

★ **OLYMPIA INTERNATIONAL CHAMPIONSHIPS**
EQUESTRIAN **17 - 21 DEC** Olympia

★ **CAFE DE COLOMBIA ALPINE WORLD CUP**
SKIING-ALPINE **19 DEC** Val Gardena, Italy

★ **KING GEORGE VI CHASE** **26 DEC** Kempton

30 monday

St Andrew's Day, Scotland

first-half

second-half

extra-time

SPORTING FIXTURES

BOBSLEIGH: European Cup Starts (Finishes 7th Dec),
Igls, Austria

BODY-BUILDING: Commonwealth Body-Building
Championships Finish,
Malacca, Malaysia

1 tuesday

SQUASH: Men's World Open Starts (Finishes 6th Dec),
Bombay, India

TRAMPOLINE: European Youth Championships Start (Finish
5th Dec),
Portugal

2 wednesday

BASKETBALL: Euro Championships Semi-Final Round (Men)
Ukraine v England, *Sheffield*

5 saturday

first-half

second-half

extra-time

SPORTING FIXTURES

CURLING: European Curling Championships Start
(Finish 12th Dec),
Flims, Switzerland

HORSE RACING: The Henry VIII Novices' Steeple Chase,
Sandown Park

LAWN TENNIS: Davis Cup Final - Day 2, *tbc (BSkyB)*

SWIMMING: Women's Inter-District Water Polo Championships
Start (Finish 6th Dec),
Walsall

TRAMPOLINE: European Youth Championships Finish,
Portugal

3 thursday

○ Full Moon

first-half

second-half

extra-time

SPORTING FIXTURES

GOLF: JC Penny Classic Starts (Finishes 6th Dec),
Palm Harbour, USA (BSkyB)

VOLLEYBALL: Men's Beach Volleyball World Tour Starts
(Finishes 6th Dec),
Fortaleza, Brazil

4 friday

EQUESTRIAN: International Show Jumping Event Starts
(Finishes 6th Dec),
Munich, Germany

LAWN TENNIS: Davis Cup Final - Day 1,
tbc (BSkyB)

notes

6 sunday

2nd in Advent

first-half

second-half

extra-time

SPORTING FIXTURES

EQUESTRIAN: International Show Jumping Event Finishes,
Munich, Germany

GOLF: JC Penny Classic Finishes,
Palm Harbour, USA (BSkyB)

LAWN TENNIS: Davis Cup Final - Day 3,
tbc (BSkyB)

MULTI-EVENT GAMES: Asian Games Start (Finish 20th Dec),
Bangkok, Thailand

SQUASH: Men's World Open Finishes,
Bombay, India

SWIMMING: Womens Inter District Water Polo
Championships Finish, *Walsall*

VOLLEYBALL: Mens Beach Volleyball World Tour Finishes,
Fortaleza, Brazil

7 monday

first-half

second-half

extra-time

SPORTING FIXTURES

BOBSLEIGH: European Cup Finishes,
Igls, Austria

8 tuesday

SPORTING FIXTURES

BOBSLEIGH: World Cup Starts (Finishes 13th Dec),
Germany (Eurosport)

FOOTBALL: UEFA Cup Third Round 2nd Leg,
Various, tbc

9 wednesday

SPORTING FIXTURES

FOOTBALL: UEFA Champions League Group Match 6,
Various, tbc

12 saturday

first-half

second-half

extra-time

SPORTING FIXTURES

CURLING: European Curling Championships Finish,
Flims, Switzerland

DANCE SPORT: IDSF World Formation Standard Competition,
Braunschweig, Germany

HORSE RACING: The Tripleprint Gold Cup, *Cheltenham*
The Bonusprint Bula Hurdle, *Cheltenham*

LUGE: World Cup Starts (Finishes 13th Dec), *Altenberg,
Germany*

10 thursday | 11 friday | notes

☾ Last Quarter

first-half

first-half

second-half

extra-time

SPORTING FIXTURES

EQUESTRIAN: International Show Jumping Event Starts
(Finishes 13th Dec),
Geneva, Switzerland

SWIMMING: European Sprints Start (Finish 13th Dec),
Sheffield *(BBC)*

EQUESTRIAN: Frankfurt Equestrian Festival Starts
(Finishes 13th Dec),
Frankfurt, Germany

HANDBALL: 3rd Womens European Championships Start
(Finish 20th Dec),
Rotterdam, Netherlands

13 sunday

3rd in Advent

first-half | second-half | extra-time

SPORTING FIXTURES

ATHLETICS: SPAR European Cross Country Championships,
Ferrara, Italy *(Eurosport)*

BOBSLEIGH: World Cup Finishes,
Germany *(Eurosport)*

EQUESTRIAN: Frankfurt Equestrian Festival Finishes,
Frankfurt, Germany
International Show Jumping Event Finishes,
Geneva, Switzerland

JUDO: British Senior Closed Men & Women's Championships
Cardiff

LUGE: World Cup Finishes,
Altenberg, Germany

SWIMMING: European Sprints Finish,
Sheffield *(BBC)*

14 monday

first-half

second-half

extra-time

SPORTING FIXTURES

BOBSLEIGH: European Cup Starts (Finishes 20th Dec),
Cortina d'Ampezzo, Italy

EQUESTRIAN: Three Day Event Starts (Finishes 18th Dec),
Punchestown, Ireland

15 tuesday

16 wednesday

first-half

second-half

extra-time

JUDO: World Student Championships Start (Finish 20th Dec),
Prague, Czech Republic

19 saturday

first-half

second-half

extra-time

SPORTING FIXTURES

GOLF: Wendys Three Tour Challenge Starts (Finishes 20th Dec),
Henderson, USA

HORSE RACING: The Betterware Cup,
Ascot

LUGE: World Cup Starts (Finishes 20th Dec),
Igls, Austria

SKIING: World Cup Skiing,
Val Gardena, Italy (Eurosport)

17 thursday

first-half

second-half

extra-time

SPORTING FIXTURES

EQUESTRIAN: Olympia International Championships Start
(Finish 21st Dec), *Olympia*

SWIMMING: British Swimming Championships Start
(Finish 20th Dec),
Glasgow (BBC)

18 friday

● New Moon

EQUESTRIAN: Three Day Event Finishes,
Punchestown, Ireland

notes

20 sunday

First Day of Ramadan   *4th in Advent*

first-half

second-half

extra-time

SPORTING FIXTURES

BOBSLEIGH: European Cup Finishes,
Cortina d'Ampezzo, Italy

GOLF: Wendys Three Tour Challenge Finishes,
Henderson, USA

HANDBALL: Womens European Championships Finish,
Rotterdam, Holland

JUDO: World Student Championships Finish,
Prague, Czech Republic

LUGE: World Cup Finishes,
Igls, Austria

MULTI-EVENT GAMES: Asian Games Finish,
Bangkok, Thailand

SNOWBOARDING: Grundig Snowboard World Cup Starts
(Finishes 21st Dec),
Mont. Ste. Anne, Canada

SWIMMING: British Swimming Championships Finish,
Glasgow

21 monday

Michaelmas Law Sittings end

first-half

second-half

extra-time

SPORTING FIXTURES

EQUESTRIAN: Olympia International Championships Finish, *Olympia*

SNOWBOARDING: Grundig Snowboard World Cup Finishes, *Mont. Ste. Anne, Canada*

22 tuesday

Winter Solstice

23 wednesday

26 saturday

☽ First Quarter

first-half

second-half

extra-time

SPORTING FIXTURES

HORSE RACING: King George V Chase, *Kempton Park*
The Rowland Meyrick Handicap Steeple Chase, *Wetherby*

YACHTING: Christmas Race Starts (Finishes 31st Dec), *Palamos, Spain*

24 thursday

first-half

second-half

extra-time

SPORTING FIXTURES

25 friday

Christmas Day (Quarter Day)

notes

27 sunday

Christmas 1

first-half

second-half

extra-time

SPORTING FIXTURES

CANOEING: Murray Marathon Starts (Finishes 31st Dec),
Yarrawonga, Australia

GYMNASTICS: Grand Prix DTB Pokal Starts (Finishes 29th Dec),
Stuttgart, Germany

SPEED SKATING: Christmas Cup Starts (Finishes 28th Dec),
Baselga di Pine, Italy

RUSSELL CHEYNE

M	.	4	11	18	25
T	.	5	12	19	26
W	.	6	13	20	27
T	.	7	14	21	28
F	1	8	15	22	29
S	2	9	16	23	30
S	3	10	17	24	31

1999
JANUARY

★ **EUROPEAN CHAMPIONSHIPS** BOBSLEIGH **11 - 17 JAN** Winterberg, Germany
★ **AUSTRALIAN OPEN CHAMPIONSHIPS** TENNIS **18 - 31 JAN** Melbourne, Australia
★ **WORLD CUP** BOBSLEIGH **19 - 24 JAN** St. Moritz, Switzerland
★ **SHORT TRACK SPEED SKATING- EUROPEAN CHAMPIONSHIPS** SPEED SKATING **22 - 24 JAN** Oberstdorf, Germany
★ **EUROPEAN FIGURE SKATING CHAMPIONSHIPS** SKATING **24 - 31 JAN** Prague, Czech Republic
★ **CAFE DE COLOMBIA ALPINE WORLD CUP** SKIING-ALPINE **28 - 31 JAN** Garmisch Partenkirchen, Germany
★ **SUPERBOWL XXXIII** AMERICAN FOOTBALL **31 JAN** Miami, USA

January

28 monday

Bank Holiday UK & Republic of Ireland

first-half

second-half

extra-time

SPORTING FIXTURES

HORSE RACING: The Coral Welsh National,
Chepstow

SPEED SKATING: Christmas Cup Finishes,
Baselga di Pine, Italy

29 tuesday

SPORTING FIXTURES

BASKETBALL: Eurostars 1998 East v West, *tbc*

GYMNASTICS: Grand Prix DTB Pokal Finishes,
Stuttgart, Germany

30 wednesday

SPORTING FIXTURES

HANDBALL: Men's University Championships Start
(Finish 7th Jan),
Novi Sad, Yugoslavia

2 saturday

○ Full Moon

first-half

second-half

extra-time

SPORTING FIXTURES

AMERICAN FOOTBALL: Wild-Card Play-Off Games Start
(Finish 3rd Jan),
tbc, USA (BSkyB)

31 thursday

first-half

second-half

extra-time

SPORTING FIXTURES

CANOEING: Murray Marathon Finishes, *Yarrawonga, Australia*

GOLF: Diners' Club Matches Start (Finishes 3rd Jan),
La Quinta, USA

YACHTING: Christmas Race Finishes, *Palamos, Spain*

1 friday

New Year's Day, Bank Holiday UK & Republic of Ireland

notes

3 sunday

Christmas 2

first-half

second-half

extra-time

SPORTING FIXTURES

AMERICAN FOOTBALL: Wild-Card Play-Off Games Finish, *tbc,*
USA (BSkyB)

GOLF: Diners' Club Matches Finish, *La Quinta, USA*

4 monday

first-half

second-half

extra-time

SPORTING FIXTURES

5 tuesday

6 wednesday

Epiphany

BADMINTON: Korean World Grand Prix Starts
(Finishes 10th Jan), **Korea**

TABLE TENNIS: English Open Starts (Finishes 11th Jan), **tbc**

9 saturday

☾ Last Quarter

first-half

second-half

extra-time

SPORTING FIXTURES

AMERICAN FOOTBALL: Divisional Play-Offs Start
(Finish 10th Jan),
tbc, USA (BSkyB)

FOOTBALL: First African Women's Championships Final,
tbc

7 thursday

first-half

second-half

extra-time

SPORTING FIXTURES

HANDBALL: Men's University Championships Finish,
Novi Sad, Yugoslavia

TABLE TENNIS: ITTF Pro Tour Finals Start (Finish 10th Jan),
tbc

YACHTING: Sail Melbourne '99 Starts (Finishes 14th Jan),
Melbourne, Australia

8 friday

first-half

second-half

SPEED SKATING: European Championships Start
(Finish 11th Jan), *Heerenveen, Holland* (Eurosport)

notes

10 sunday

Epiphany 1

first-half

second-half

extra-time

SPORTING FIXTURES

AMERICAN FOOTBALL: Divisional Play-Offs Finish,
tbc, USA (BSkyB)

BADMINTON: Korean World Grand Prix Finishes,
Korea

TABLE TENNIS: ITTF Pro Tour Finals Finish,
tbc

11 monday

Hilary Law Sittings begin

first-half

second-half

extra-time

SPORTING FIXTURES

BOBSLEIGH: European Championships Start (Finish 17th Jan),
Winterberg, Germany (Eurosport)

SPEED SKATING: European Championships Finish,
Heerenveen, Holland (Eurosport)

TABLE TENNIS: English Open Finishes,
tbc

12 tuesday

SPORTING FIXTURES

BADMINTON: Japanese World Grand Prix Starts
(Finishes 17th Jan),
Japan

13 wednesday

16 saturday

first-half

second-half

extra-time

SPORTING FIXTURES

FENCING: Grand Prix Martini Starts (Finishes 17th Jan),
Budapest, Hungary

14 thursday

first-half

second-half

extra-time

SPORTING FIXTURES

YACHTING: Sail Melbourne Finishes,
Melbourne, Australia

15 friday

notes

HOCKEY: Mens European Indoor Nations Cup Starts
(Finishes 17th Jan), *tbc*

SPEED SKATING: World Junior Short Track Championships
Start (Finish 17th Jan),
Montreal, Canada

17 sunday

Epiphany 2 ● New Moon

first-half

second-half

extra-time

SPORTING FIXTURES

AMERICAN FOOTBALL: AFC & NFC Championships,
tbc, USA (BSkyB)

BADMINTON: Japanese World Grand Prix Finishes,
Japan

BOBSLEIGH: European Championships Finish,
Winterberg, Germany (Eurosport)

FENCING: Grand Prix Martini Finishes,
Budapest, Hungary

HOCKEY: Mens European Indoor Nations Cup Finishes,
tbc

SPEED SKATING: World Junior Short Track
Championships Finish,
Montreal, Canada

18 monday

first-half

second-half

extra-time

SPORTING FIXTURES

LAWN TENNIS: Australian Open Championships - Day 1,
Melbourne, Australia

19 tuesday

(center column fixtures)

BOBSLEIGH: World Cup Starts (Finishes 24th Jan),
St. Moritz, Switzerland

LAWN TENNIS: Australian Open Championships - Day 2,
Melbourne, Australia

20 wednesday

LAWN TENNIS: Australian Open Championships - Day 3,
Melbourne, Australia

23 saturday

first-half

second-half

extra-time

SPORTING FIXTURES

FENCING: Grand Prix Paris Starts (Finishes 24th Jan), *Paris,
France*

LAWN TENNIS: Australian Open Championships - Day 6,
Melbourne, Australia

SKI-ORIENTEERING: World Cup Round 1 Starts
(Finishes 26th Jan), *tbc, Switzerland*

21 thursday

first-half

second-half

extra-time

SPORTING FIXTURES

LAWN TENNIS: Australian Open Championships
- Day 4, *Melbourne, Australia*

22 friday

HOCKEY: European Nations Cup Starts (Finishes 24th Jan),
Belgium

LAWN TENNIS: Australian Open Championships
- Day 5, *Melbourne, Australia*

SPEED SKATING: Short Track European Championships Start
(Finish 24th Jan), *Oberstdorf, Germany*

notes

24 sunday

Epiphany 3   First Quarter

first-half

second-half

extra-time

SPORTING FIXTURES

BOBSLEIGH: World Cup Finishes,
St. Moritz, Switzerland

FENCING: Grand Prix Paris Finishes,
Paris, France

FIELD HOCKEY: European Nations Cup Finishes,
Belgium

LAWN TENNIS: Australian Open Championships
- Day 7, *Melbourne, Australia*

SKATING: European Figure Skating Championships Start
(Finish 31st Jan),
Prague, Czech Republic (Eurosport)

SPEED SKATING: Short Track European Championships Finish,
Oberstdorf, Germany

25 monday

first-half

second-half

extra-time

SPORTING FIXTURES

LAWN TENNIS: Australian Open Championships - Day 8, *Melbourne, Australia*

26 tuesday

LAWN TENNIS: Australian Open Championships - Day 9, *Melbourne, Australia*

SKI-ORIENTEERING: World Cup Round 1 Finishes, *Switzerland*

27 wednesday

LAWN TENNIS: Australian Open Championships - Day 10, *Melbourne, Australia*

30 saturday

first-half

second-half

extra-time

SPORTING FIXTURES

CYCLO-CROSS: World Championships Start (Finish 31st Jan), *Poprak, Slovakia*

MULTI-EVENT GAMES: Winter Asian Games Start (Finish 6th Feb), *Kangwon, Korea*

LAWN TENNIS: Australian Open Championships - Women's Final, *Melbourne, Australia*

LUGE: World Championships Finish, *Koenigsee, Germany*

28 thursday

first-half

second-half

extra-time

SPORTING FIXTURES

LAWN TENNIS: Australian Open Championships
- Women's Semi-Finals, *Melbourne, Australia*

SKIING: World Cup Skiing Starts (Finishes 31st Jan),
Garmisch Partenkirchen, Germany

29 friday

LUGE: World Championships Start (Finish 30th Jan),
Koenigsee, Germany

LAWN TENNIS: Australian Open Championships
- Men's Semi-Finals, *Melbourne, Australia*

notes

31 sunday

Septuagesima, 9th before Easter ○ Full Moon

first-half

second-half

extra-time

SPORTING FIXTURES

AMERICAN FOOTBALL: Superbowl XXXIII,
Miami, USA

CYCLO-CROSS: World Championships Finish,
Poprak, Slovakia

LAWN TENNIS: Australian Open Championships
- Men's Final,
Melbourne, Australia

SKATING: European Figure Skating Championships Finish,
Prague, Czech Republic (Eurosport)

SKIING: World Cup Skiing Finishes,
Garmisch Partenkirchen, Germany

FIXTURES 1998

AMERICAN FOOTBALL

NFL

3-4 Jan	Divisional Play-Offs, tbc, USA
11 Jan	AFC & NFC Championships, tbc, USA
25 Jan	Superbowl XXXII, San Diego, USA
1 Feb	AFC/NFC Pro Bowl, Honolulu, USA
6 Sep	NFL Season Begins, Various, USA

WORLD LEAGUE

4 Apr	Barcelona v Scotland, Barcelona, Spain
4 Apr	Rhein v Amsterdam, Rhein, Germany
5 Apr	England v Frankfurt, Crystal Palace
11 Apr	England v Rhein, Bristol
11 Apr	Frankfurt v Barcelona, Frankfurt, Germany
12 Apr	Amsterdam v Scotland, Amsterdam, Holland
18 Apr	Barcelona v Amsterdam, Barcelona, Spain
18 Apr	Frankfurt v England, Frankfurt, Germany
19 Apr	Scotland v Rhein, Murrayfield
25 Apr	Amsterdam v Frankfurt, Amsterdam, Holland
25 Apr	Rhein v Barcelona, Rhein, Germany
26 Apr	England v Scotland, Birmingham
2 May	Frankfurt v Rhein, Frankfurt, Germany
2 May	Amsterdam v England, Amsterdam, Holland
3 May	Scotland v Barcelona, Murrayfield
9 May	Rhein v Scotland, Rhein, Germany
10 May	England v Amsterdam, Crystal Palace
11 May	Barcelona v Frankfurt, Barcelona, Spain
16 May	Barcelona v Rhein, Barcelona, Spain
16 May	Frankfurt v Amsterdam, Frankfurt, Germany
17 May	Scotland v England, Murrayfield
23 May	Amsterdam v Barcelona, Amsterdam, Holland
23 May	Rhein v England, Rhein, Germany
24 May	Scotland v Frankfurt, Glasgow
30 May	Amsterdam v Rhein, Amsterdam, Holland
31 May	England v Barcelona, Crystal Palace
31 May	Frankfurt v Scotland, Frankfurt, Germany
6 June	Barcelona v England, Barcelona, Spain
6 June	Rhein v Frankfurt, Rhein, Germany
7 June	Scotland v Amsterdam, Murrayfield
14 June	World League Of American Football - World Bowl, Frankfurt, Germany

ANGLING

4 Jul	National Championships Division 3, Milton Keynes
11 Jul	Junior National Championships, Tring
18 Jul	National Championships Division 2, Middle Trent
1 Aug	National Womens Championships, Mersey Canal
22 Aug	National Championships Division 4, Keadby
12 Sep	National Championships Division 1, The River Thames
20 Sep-20 Oct	Boat Angling World Championships, tbc, Slovenia
26 Sep	National Championships Division 5, Bridgewater
31 Oct-7 Nov	Shore Angling World Championships, Langeland, Germany

ARCHERY

30 Jan-1 Feb	World Ski-Archery Championships, Cogne, Italy
22-26 Jul	Junior World Target Championships, Sunne, Sweden
3-9 Aug	World Field Championships, Tyrol, Austria

ATHLETICS

3 Jan	Durham International Cross Country, Durham
10 Jan	UKCAU Championships, Luton
11 Jan	Cross International Zornotza, Amorebieta, Spain
18 Jan	Cross Internacional De Italica, Seville, Spain
24 Jan	Coca-Cola International Cross Country, Belfast
31 Jan	Cross Auchan Lille Metropole, Tourcoing, France
1 Feb	Tokyo International Marathon, Tokyo, Japan
3 Feb	Memorial Jose Ma Cagival, Madrid, Spain
8 Feb	Almond Blossom Cross Country, Vilamoura, Portugal
8 Feb	Flanders Indoors, Ghent, Belgium
8 Feb	Reebok British Challenge 5, Birmingham
15 Feb	Eurocross, Dierkirch, Luxembourg
15 Feb	Chiba International Cross, Chiba, Japan
15 Feb	Bupa Indoor Grand Prix Ricoh Tour, Birmingham
19 Feb	DN Games, Stockholm, Sweden
22 Feb	Meeting Vittel Du Pas De Calais, Lievin, France
27 Feb-1 Mar	European Indoor Championships, Valencia, Spain
28 Feb	Mombasa International Cross, Mombasa, Kenya
1 Mar	BAF Champs & World Trials, Belfast
8 Mar	Cinque Mulini, San Vittore, Italy
8 Mar	Volksbanken Raiffeisenbanken Leichtathletik Grand Prix, Sindelfingen, Germany
14 Mar	English National Cross Country Championships, Leeds
22-23 Mar	IAAF World Cross Country Championships, Marrakech, Morocco
4 Apr	FISU Cross Country Championships, Luton
18 Apr	AAA 12 Stage Road Relay, Sutton Park, Birmingham
18-19 Apr	IAAF World Road Relay Championships, Manaus, Brazil
19 Apr	Generale Bank Rotterdam Marathon, Rotterdam, Holland
20 Apr	Boston Marathon, Hopkinton To Boston, USA
25 Apr	European Cup- Race Walking, Dudince, Slovakia
26 Apr	Flora London Marathon, London
3 May	Grand Prix Brasil de Atletismo, Rio De Janeiro, Brazil
9 May	IAAF Grand Prix In Osaka, Japan
28 May-3 June	South American Games, Cuenca, Ecuador
31 May	Prefontaine Classic, Eugene, USA
5 June	Golden Gala, Rome, Italy
7 June	Znamensky Memorial, Moscow, Russia
16 June	Comrades Marathon, Durban, South Africa
27-28 June	European Super League Cup Final, St Petersburg, Russia
1 Jul	Meeting Gaz De France, Paris, France
15 Jul	Nikaia Meeting, Nice, France
17 Jul	Mobil Bislett Games, Oslo, Norway
19 Jul	IAAF Grand Prix II, Gateshead
19 Jul-2 Aug	Goodwill Games, New York, USA
24 Jul	US Open Meet, Durham, USA
24-26 Jul	AAA Championships - European And Commonwealth Trials, Birmingham
2 Aug	IAAF Grand Prix I, Sheffield
tbc Aug	DN Galan, Stockholm, Sweden
8 Aug	Herculis Zepter, Monte Carlo, Monaco
tbc Aug	Weltklasse in Zurich, Switzerland
18-23 Aug	European Athletics Championships, Budapest, Hungary
25 Aug	Athletissima 98, Lausanne, Switzerland
tbc Aug	Memorial Van Damme, Brussels, Belgium
tbc Aug	Weltklasse in Cologne, Germany
2 Sep	ISTAF, Berlin, Germany
5 Sep	IAAF Grand Prix Final, Moscow, Russia
11-13 Sep	IAAF World Cup Of Athletics, Johannesberg, South Africa
11-21 Sep	16th Commonwealth Games, Kuala Lumpur, Malaysia
27 Sep	IAAF World Half Marathon Championships, Zurich, Switzerland
11 Oct	Lasalle Banks Chicago Marathon, Chicago, USA
1 Nov	New York City Marathon, New York, USA
13 Dec	SPAR European Cross Country Championships, Ferrara, Italy

BADMINTON

6-11 Jan	Korean World Grand Prix, Seoul, Korea
13-18 Jan	Yonex Open Japan, Tokyo, Japan
30 Jan-1 Feb	Liverpool Victoria Nationals, Haywards Heath
6-8 Feb	Friends Provident Grand Slam, Kirkham
14-21 Feb	Thomas & Uber Cup Preliminary Rounds, Sandefjord, Norway
15-22 Feb	Thomas & Uber Cup Preliminary Rounds, Manila, Phillipines
20-22 Feb	English National Under 19 Championships, Milton Keynes
4-8 Mar	Ericsson Swedish World Grand Prix, Borlange, Sweden
7-8 Mar	All England Veterans Championships, Wimbledon
9-14 Mar	Yonex All England Championships, Birmingham
17-22 Mar	Swiss World Grand Prix, Basel, Switzerland
27-29 Mar	Friends Provident Grand Slam, Cardiff
1-5 Apr	Heros Polish World Grand Prix, Spala, Poland
8-12 Apr	Brunei World Grand Prix, Brunei
13-19 Apr	Vietnam World Grand Prix, Vietnam
18-25 Apr	European Championships, Sofia, Bulgaria
1-3 May	Friends Provident Grand Slam
19-24 May	Thomas & Uber Cup Finals, Hong Kong
tbc June	USA World Grand Prix, California, USA
1-5 Jul	Malaysia World Grand Prix, Malaysia
8-12 Jul	Thailand World Grand Prix, Bangkok, Thailand
5-9 Aug	Indonesia World Grand Prix, North Sulawesi, Indonesia
11-16 Aug	Singapore World Grand Prix, Singapore, Singapore
26-30 Aug	Russia World Grand Prix, Moscow, Russia
3-6 Sep	World University Badminton Championships, Istanbul, Turkey
11-21 Sep	Commonwealth Games, Kuala Lumpur, Malaysia
24-27 Sep	World Junior Championships, Jakarta, Indonesia
1-4 Oct	Netherland World Grand Prix, Holland
7-11 Oct	Germany World Grand Prix, Saarbrucken, Germany
14-18 Oct	Denmark World Grand Prix, Denmark
1-5 Nov	India World Grand Prix, Delhi, India
5-8 Nov	Chinese Taipei World Grand Prix, Chinese Taipei
19-22 Nov	China World Grand Prix, PR China
25-29 Nov	Hong Kong World Grand Prix, Hong Kong

BASEBALL

7 Jul	All-Star Game, Denver, USA
tbc Oct	World Series, tbc, USA

BASKETBALL

17 Jan	Men's National Trophy Final, Sheffield
5-8 Feb	NBA All Star Game, New York, USA
25 Feb	Belarus v England Euro Championships Semi-Finals Round, Belarus
28 Feb	England v Israel, Manchester
25 Mar	Final of the Korac Cup - 1st leg, tbc
1 Apr	Final of the Korac Cup - 2nd leg, tbc
14 Apr	Final of the Eurocup, Belgrade, Yugoslavia
21-23 Apr	Final Four Euroleague For Men, Barcelona, Spain
23 Apr	NBA Play-Offs Begin, tbc, USA
2 May	NBA Conference Semi-Finals Begin, tbc, USA
2-3 May	Budweiser Championship Finals
16 May	NBA Conference Finals Begin, tbc, USA
26 May-7 June	World Championship For Women, Germany
31 May	NBA Finals Begin, tbc, USA
19 Jul-2 Aug	Goodwill Games, New York, USA
29 Jul-9 Aug	Amway World Championship For Men, Athens, Greece
25 Nov	Euro Championships Semi-Final Round (Men) England v Denmark, tbc
28 Nov	Euro Championships Semi-Final Round (Men) Spain v England, Spain
2 Dec	Euro Championships Semi-Final Round (Men) Ukraine v England, Ukraine
29 Dec	Eurostars East v West, tbc

BOBSLEIGH

4-9 Jan	BBA Selection Camp, Germany
12-18 Jan	Europa Cup 3, Winterberg, Germany
13-18 Jan	World Cup 5 / Europeans, Igls, Austria
19-25 Jan	World Junior Championships, Cortina D'Ampezza, Switzerland
20-25 Jan	World Cup 6, St Moritz, Switzerland
26 Jan-1 Feb	Europa Cup 4, St Moritz, Switzerland
7-22 Feb	Winter Olympic Games, Nagano, Japan

BOWLS

19 Jan-1 Feb	World Indoor Championships for Men, Preston
9-13 Mar	British Isles International Indoor Series for Men, Swansea
16-20 Mar	British Isles International Indoor Series for Women, Durlington
28 Mar-5 Apr	English National Indoor Championships for Men, Melton Mowbray
25-26 Apr	English Bowls Players Association Singles Championship Finals, Wellingborough
17-22 June	British Isles International Outdoor Series for Women, tbc
29-3 June	British Isles International Outdoor Series for Men, Ayr, Scotland
3-15 Aug	English National Championships for Women, Royal Leamington Spa
16-29 Aug	English National Championships for Men, Worthing
11-21 Sep	16th Commonwealth Games, Kuala Lumpur, Malaysia

BOXING

4 Mar	ABA Championships, Birmingham
16-26 May	European Championships, Minsk, Belarus
13-21 June	World Cup, Chongqing, People's Republic Of China
22-28 June	Boxing Festival, Liverpool
19 Jul-2 Aug	Goodwill Games, New York, USA
11-21 Sep	16th Commonwealth Games, Kuala Lumpur, Malaysia
6-16 Nov	World Championships- Under 19, Buenos Aires, Argentina

CANOEING

10-12 Apr	International Regatta Flatwater World Cup 1, Curitiba, Brazil
15-17 May	International Regatta Flatwater World Cup 2, Poznan, Poland
18-24 May	Wildwater Racing World Championships for Seniors, Garmisch- Partenkirchen, Germany
30-31 May	Wildwater World Cup, Valsesia, Italy

5-7 June	Copenhagen Olympic Open - Flatwater World Cup 3, Denmark
14 June	Slalom World Cup 1, Liptovsky Mikulas, Slovakia
21 June	Slalom World Cup 2, Tacen, Slovenia
26-28 June	XVII International Regatta Flatwater World Cup 4, Duisburg, Germany
28 June	Slalom World Cup 3, Augsburg, Germany
4-5 Jul	Wildwater World Cup, Muothal, Switzerland
11-12 Jul	Wildwater World Cup Final, Lofer, Austria
24-26 Jul	European Flatwater Championships for Juniors, Nykoping, Sweden
30 Jul-2 Aug	World University Canoe-Kayak Championships(FISU), Zagreb, Croatia
2 Aug	Slalom World Cup 4, Waussau, USA
16-23 Aug	Interceltic Watersports Festival, Bude
tbc Sep	Canoe Polo World Championships, Portugal
3-6 Sep	Flatwater Racing World Championships, Szeged, Hungary
13 Sep	Slalom World Cup Finals, La Seu D'urgell, Spain
25-26 Sep	Marathon Racing World Championships, Pietermaritzburg, South Africa

CRICKET

2-6 Jan	2nd Test Australia v South Africa, Sydney, Australia
3 Jan	South Africa U19 v England U19, Benoni, South Africa
3 Jan	Kenya v England A, Nairobi, Kenya
4 Jan	Kenya v England A, Nairobi, Kenya
4 Jan	South Africa U19 v England U19, Fochville, South Africa
6 Jan	South Africa U19 v England U19, Centurion, South Africa
6-8 Jan	Kenya v England A, Nairobi, Kenya
9 Jan	Carlton & United Breweries World Series, New Zealand v South Africa, Brisbane, Australia
10 Jan	Silver Jubilee Independence Cup, India v Bangladesh, Dhaka, Bangladesh
10 Jan	Kenya v England A, Nairobi, Kenya
11 Jan	Carlton & United Breweries World Series, Australia v South Africa, Brisbane, Australia
11 Jan	Silver Jubilee Independence Cup, India v Pakistan, Dhaka, Bangladesh
12 Jan	Silver Jubilee Independence Cup, Bangladesh v Pakistan, Dhaka, Bangladesh
14 Jan	Carlton & United Breweries World Series, New Zealand v Australia, Sydney, Australia
14 Jan	Silver Jubilee Independence Cup 1st Final, Dhaka, Bangladesh
16 Jan	Carlton & United Breweries World Series, New Zealand v South Africa, Perth, Australia
16 Jan	Silver Jubilee Independence Cup 2nd Final, Dhaka, Bangladesh
18 Jan	Carlton & United Breweries World Series, Australia v South Africa, Perth, Australia
18 Jan	Silver Jubilee Independence Cup 3rd Final, Dhaka, Bangladesh
19 Jan-1 Feb	Under-19 World Cup, Various, South Africa
21 Jan	Carlton & United Breweries World Series, New Zealand v Australia, Melbourne, Australia
23 Jan	Carlton & United Breweries World Series 1st Final, Melbourne, Australia
25 Jan	Carlton & United Breweries World Series 2nd Final, Sydney, Australia
27 Jan	Carlton & United Breweries World Series 3rd Final, Sydney, Australia
29 Jan-2 Feb	Cable & Wireless 1st Test, West Indies v England, Kingston, Jamaica
30 Jan-3 Feb	3rd Test Australia v South Africa, Adelaide, Australia
4 Feb	1st One Day International, New Zealand v Zimbabwe, Hamilton, New Zealand
6 Feb	2nd One Day International, New Zealand v Zimbabwe, Wellington, New Zealand
8 Feb	1st One Day International, New Zealand v Australia, Christchurch, New Zealand
10 Feb	2nd One Day International, New Zealand v Australia, Wellington, New Zealand
12 Feb	3rd One Day International, New Zealand v Australia, Napier, New Zealand
13-17 Feb	1st Test, South Africa v Pakistan, Johannesburg, South Africa
13-17 Feb	Cable & Wireless 2nd Test, West Indies v England, Port-Of-Spain, Trinidad & Tobago
14 Feb	4th One Day International, New Zealand v Australia, Auckland, New Zealand
19-23 Feb	1st Test, New Zealand v Zimbabwe, Wellington, New Zealand
26 Feb-2 Mar	2nd Test, New Zealand v Zimbabwe, Auckland, New Zealand
26 Feb-2 Mar	2nd Test, South Africa v Pakistan, Durban, South Africa
27 Feb-3 Mar	Cable & Wireless 3rd Test, West Indies v England, Georgetown, Guyana

4 Mar	3rd One Day International, New Zealand v Zimbabwe, Christchurch, New Zealand
6 Mar	4th One Day International, New Zealand v Zimbabwe, Napier, New Zealand
6-10 Mar	3rd Test, South Africa v Pakistan, Port Elizabeth, South Africa
8 Mar	5th One Day International, New Zealand v Zimbabwe, Auckland, New Zealand
12-16 Mar	Cable & Wireless 4th Test, West Indies v England, Barbados
14-18 Mar	1st Test, Zimbabwe v Pakistan, Bulawayo, Zimbabwe
19-23 Mar	1st Test, South Africa v Sri Lanka, Cape Town, South Africa
20-24 Mar	Cable & Wireless 5th Test, West Indies v England, St Johns, Antigua
21-25 Mar	2nd Test, Zimbabwe v Pakistan, Harare, Zimbabwe
27-31 Mar	2nd Test, South Africa v Sri Lanka, Verwoerdburg, South Africa
28 Mar	1st One Day International, Zimbabwe v Pakistan, Harare, Zimbabwe
29 Mar	Cable & Wireless 1st One Day International, West Indies v England, Barbados
29 Mar	2nd One Day International, Zimbabwe v Pakistan, Harare, Zimbabwe
1 Apr	Cable & Wireless 2nd One Day International, West Indies v England, St Michael, Barbados
3 Apr	Triangular Series, South Africa v Pakistan, Durban, South Africa
4 Apr	Cable & Wireless 3rd One Day International, West Indies v England, St Vincent
5 Apr	Cable & Wireless 4th One Day International, West Indies v England, St Vincent
5 Apr	Triangular Series, South Africa v Sri Lanka, Johannesburg, South Africa
7 Apr	Triangular Series, Pakistan v Sri Lanka, Kimberley, South Africa
8 Apr	Cable & Wireless 5th One Day International, West Indies v England, Port-Of-Spain, Trinidad & Tobago
9 Apr	Triangular Series, Pakistan v Sri Lanka, Paarl, South Africa
11 Apr	Triangular Series, Pakistan v South Africa, East London, South Africa
13 Apr	Triangular Series, Sri Lanka v South Africa, Port Elizabeth, South Africa
13 Apr	Triangular Series, Sri Lanka v Pakistan, Benoni, South Africa
17 Apr	Triangular Series, South Africa v Pakistan, Verwoerdburg, South Africa
19 Apr	Triangular Series, South Africa v Sri Lanka, Bloemfontein, South Africa
22 Apr	Triangular Series Final, Cape Town, South Africa
21 May	1st Texaco Trophy One-Day International, England v South Africa, The Oval
23 May	2nd Texaco Trophy One-Day International, England v South Africa, Old Trafford
24 May	3rd Texaco Trophy One-Day International, England v South Africa, Headingley
4-8 June	1st Cornhill Test, England v South Africa, Edgbaston
18-22 June	2nd Cornhill Test, England v South Africa, Lord's
23 June	Natwest Trophy 1st Round
2-6 Jul	3rd Cornhill Test, England v South Africa, Old Trafford
8 Jul	Natwest Trophy 2nd Round
11 Jul	Benson & Hedges Cup Final, Lord's
23-27 Jul	4th Cornhill Test, England v South Africa, Trent Bridge
6-10 Aug	5th Cornhill Test, Enghland v South Africa, Headingley
14 Aug	Triangular Tournament, South Africa v Sri Lanka, Trent Bridge
16 Aug	Triangular Tournament, England v Sri Lanka, Lord's
18 Aug	Triangular Tournament, England v South Africa, Edgbaston
20 Aug	Triangular Tournament Final, Lord's
27-31 Aug	1st Cornhill Test, England v Sri Lanka, The Oval
29 Aug/5 Sept tbc	Natwest Trophy Final, Lord's

CROQUET

6-7 June	Home Internationals, Southport
8-14 June	Mens and Womens Championships, Cheltenham
2-5 Jul	Senior Championships, Southwick
12-19 Jul	Open Championships, Hurlingham
10-13 Sep	Presidents Cup, Parkstone
19-20 Sep	All England Final, Wrest Park
26-27 Sep	CA Finals Weekend, Cheltenham

CYCLING

21 Mar	World Cup Milano-San Remo, Milan, Italy
5 Apr	World Cup Tour Des Flandres, Flanders, Belgium
12 Apr	World Cup Paris-Roubaix, Paris, France
19 Apr	World Cup Liege-Bastogne-Liege, Belgium
25 Apr	World Cup Amstel Gold Race, Heerlen - Mastrich, Holland
16 May-7 June	Giro D'italia, Various, Italy
23-31 May	The Prudential Tour of Britain, Various
11 Jul-2 Aug	Tour De France, Various
19 Jul-2 Aug	Goodwill Games, New York, USA
8 Aug	World Cup, San Sebastian, Spain
16 Aug	Hew-Cyclassics Cup, Hamburg, Germany
16 Aug	World Cup, Leeds International Classic, Leeds
23 Aug	World Cup, Grand Prix Of Switzerland, Various, Switzerland
24-30 Aug	World Track Championships, Bordeaux, France
5-27 Sep	Vuelta A Espana, Various, Spain
11-21 Sep	16th Commonwealth Games, Kuala Lumpur, Malaysia
4 Oct	World Cup, Paris Tours, Paris, France
8-11 Oct	World Road Championships, Valkenburg, Holland
17 Oct	World Cup Giro Di Lombardia, Italy

DARTS

3-11 Jan	Embassy World Professional Championships, Frimley Green

DISABLED SPORTS

8 Feb	IPC World Cup Athletics (Cross Country), Villa Moura, Portugal
5-14 Mar	Winter Paralympic Games, Nagano, Japan
23 May	Sempach Marathon, Sempach
12-20 June	CP-ISRA World Boccia Championships, New York, USA
15-24 June	Mediterranean Games, Bari, Italy
15-30 June	World Shooting Championships, Santander, Spain
18-26 Jul	World Judo Championships, Madrid, Spain
21 Jul-1 Aug	World Archery Championships, Stoke Mandeville
tbc Aug	World Championships, Berlin, Germany
1-11 Aug	World Athletics Championships tbc
1-11 Aug	World Powerlifting Championships, Bruges, Belgium
1-11 Aug	World Team Cup Tennis, Poland
8-15 Aug	World Cycling Championships, Colorado Springs, USA
2-21 Sep	World Bowls Championships, Johannesburg, South Africa
15-27 Sep	World Cup Soccer Championships, Rio De Janeiro, Brazil
19 Oct-1 Nov	Gold Cup Wheelchair Basketball, Sydney, Australia
1-8 Nov	World Table Tennis Championships, Paris, France

EQUESTRIAN

13-15 Mar	Internationales Reitturnier Westfalenhallen, Dortmund, Germany
19-22 Mar	International Jumping Event, Hertogensbosch, Holland
2-5 Apr	Volvo World Cup Dressage Final, Gothenburg, Sweden
15-19 Apr	Volvo World Cup Show Jumping Final, Helsinki, Finland
30 Apr-2 May	International Jumping Event, Monte Carlo, Monaco
7-10 May	Mitsubishi Motors Badminton Horse Trials, Badminton
7-10 May	International Jumping Event, La Baule, France
21-24 May	International Jumping Event, Rome, Italy
21-24 May	Pferd International, Munich, Germany
21-24 May	The Chubb Insurance Windsor International Horse Trials, Windsor
28-31 May	Albert E Sharp Sansaw Park Horse Trials, Sansaw Park
4-7 June	International Jumping Event, Lucerne, Switzerland
11-14 June	Bramham International Horse Trials, Bramham
11-14 June	International Jumping Event, Modena, Italy
12-14 June	International Dressage Event, Rennes, France
12-14 June	International Jumping Event, Helsinki, Finland
18-21 June	Macallan Burgie Horse Trials, Elgin
8-12 Jul	Royal International Horse Show, Hickstead
9-12 Jul	International Jumping Event, Falsterbo, Sweden
23-26 Jul	European Show Jumping Championships, Lisbon, Portugal
23-26 Jul	International Vaulting Event, Stoneliegh
6-9 Aug	International Jumping Event, Bratislava, Slovakia
11-16 Aug	International Jumping Event, Aachen, Germany
13-16 Aug	Hickstead Derby, Hickstead
15-16 Aug	Pedigree Chum Scottish Championship Horse Trials, Thirlestane Castle
20-23 Aug	International Jumping and Dressage Event, Rotterdam, Holland
22-23 Aug	British Open Championship, Gatcombe Park
27-30 Aug	Blair Castle International Horse Trials, Blair Castle

Date	Event
3-6 Sep	Burghley Pedigree Chum Horse Trials, Burghley
4-6 Sep	International Jumping Event, Plovdiv, Bulgaria
9-13 Sep	International Jumping Event, Spruce Meadows, Canada
10-13 Sep	Blenheim International Horse Trials, Blenheim
17-20 Sep	International Jumping Event, Linz-Ebelsberg, Austria
17-20 Sep	International Jumping Event, Donaueschingen, Germany
17-20 Sep	International Jumping Event, Linz-Ebelsberg, Austria
17-20 Sep	International Jumping Event, Prague, Czech Republic
24-27 Sep	International Jumping Event, Zagreb, Croatia
30 Sep-4 Oct	Horse Of The Year Show, Wembley, London
1-4 Oct	International Jumping Event, Athens, Greece
1-4 Oct	Tweseldown Novice Horse Trials, Tweseldown
2-4 Oct	German Classics, Bremen, Germany
6-11 Oct	World Equestrian Games, Rome & Pratoni Del Vivaro, Italy
8-11 Oct	Weston Park Horse Trials, Weston Park
4-15 Nov	International Jumping Event, Toronto, Canada
12-15 Nov	Internationales Reitturnier Berlin, Berlin, Germany
11-13 Dec	Frankfurt Equestrian Festival, Frankfurt, Germany
17-21 Dec	Olympia International Championships, London

FENCING

10 Jan	British Under 20 Women's Foil Championships, Oldham
24 Jan	Corble Cup - Men's Sabre F.I.E. 'A' Grade, Guildford
7 Mar	City of Glasgow Men's Epee F.I.E. 'A' Grade, Glasgow
21 Mar	British Sabre Championships, London
28 Mar	Scottish International Sabre, Glasgow
11 Apr	Birmingham International, Birmingham
25 Apr	Ipswich Cup - Women's Epee, Ipswich
2 May	Edinburgh Open, Edinburgh
9 May	British Foil Championships, Reading
16 May	British Epee Championships, London
13 June	British Men's Epee Open, London
17-22 Aug	Commonwealth Fencing Tournament, Kuala Lumpar, Malaysia
5-11 Oct	World Championships, La Chaux De Fonds, Switzerland

FOOTBALL

8 Jan	European Super Cup Final 1st Leg - FC Barcelona v Borussia Dortmund
1-15 Feb	Concacaf Gold Cup, Oakland/Miami & Los Angeles, USA
7-28 Feb	African Nations Cup, Ouagadougou, Burkina Faso
4 Mar	UEFA Champions League - Quarter-Final 1st Leg, Various, tbc
11 Mar	European Super Cup Final 2nd Leg - Borussia Dortmund v FC Barcelona
18 Mar	UEFA Champions League - Quarter-Final 2nd Leg, Various, tbc
29 Mar	Coca-Cola Cup Final, Wembley
31 Mar	UEFA Cup - Semi-Final 1st Leg, Various, tbc
1 Apr	UEFA Champions League - Semi-Final 1st Leg, Various, tbc
2 Apr	European Cup Winners Cup - Semi-Final 1st Leg, Various, tbc
14 Apr	UEFA Cup - Semi-Final 2nd Leg, Various, tbc
15 Apr	UEFA Champions League - Semi-Final 2nd Leg, Various, tbc
16 Apr	European Cup Winners Cup -Semi-Final 2nd Leg, Various, tbc
19 Apr	Auto Windscreens Shield Final, Wembley
6 May	UEFA Cup - Final, tbc
10 May	Nationwide League Playoffs Semi-Finals 1st Leg, Various
13 May	European Cup Winners Cup - Final, tbc
13 May	Nationwide League Playoffs Semi-Finals 2nd Leg, Various
16 May	FA Cup Final, Wembley
20 May	UEFA Champions League Final, tbc
23 May	Nationwide League 3rd Division Playoff Final, Wembley
24 May	Nationwide League 2nd Division Playoff Final, Wembley
25 May	Division 1 Premiership Play-Off, Wembley
10 Jun-12 Jul	World Cup 1998, France

HOCKEY

tbc Jan	Four Nations Tournament, tbc, India
23-25 Jan	Womens Indoor European Nations Cup A Division, Orense, Spain
20-22 Feb	Men's Indoor European Club Championship - B Division, Dundee
20-22 Feb	Men's Indoor European Club Championship - C Division, Belgrade, Yugoslavia
20-22 Feb	Mens Indoor European Club Championship - A Division, Hamburg, Germany

Date	Event
27 Feb-1 Mar	Women's Indoor European Club Championship - A Division, tbc
27 Feb-1 Mar	Women's Indoor European Club Championship - B Division, Vienna, Austria
1 Mar	British Aerospace Women's Under 18 School Championship, Milton Keynes
2 Mar	British Areospace Women's Under 16 School Championships, Milton Keynes
3-5 Apr	Men's Inter League Tournament, Milton Keynes
4 Apr	Men's Vets & Vintage Cup Finals, Milton Keynes
5 Apr	Men's Trophy & Cup Finals, Milton Keynes
9 Apr	U16/U18 European Six Nations Tournament, Milton Keynes
10-13 Apr	Mens European Club Championship - A Division, Terassa, Spain
10-13 Apr	Womens European Club Championship - A Division, tbc
18-19 Apr	Women's Inter League Tournament, Milton Keynes
tbc 2/3 May	County Championships, tbc
9 May	U19 Club Championships, Milton Keynes
9-17 May	Five Nations Tournament, Kuala Lumpar, Malaysia
10 May	AEWHA Cup Finals, Milton Keynes
17 May	Women's Vets Finals, Milton Keynes
20 May-1 June	World Cup Hockey, Utrecht, Holland
29 May-1 June	Men's European Club Championship - B Division, Swansea
29 May-1 June	Men's European Club Championship - C Division, Glasgow
4-11 Jul	Mens European Nations Cup Qualifiers, Dundee
5-12 Jul	Womens European Nations Cup Qualifiers, Helsinki, Finland
6-12 Jul	Mens European Nations Cup Qualifiers, Prague, Czech Republic
6-12 Jul	Mens European Nations Cup Qualifiers, Alicante, Spain
19-26 Jul	Womens European Nations Cup Qualifiers, Mora, Sweden
11-21 Sep	16th Commonwealth Games, Kuala Lumpar, Malaysia
31 Oct-8 Nov	Champions Trophy, Lahore, Pakistan

GAELIC FOOTBALL

27 Sep	Bank Of Ireland All Ireland Football Final, Dublin

MULTI-EVENT GAMES

7-22 Feb	18th Winter Olympic Games, Nagano, Japan
24 May-4 June	6th South American Games, Cuenca, Ecuador
19 Jul-2 Aug	Goodwill Games, New York, USA
8-22 Aug	18th Central America and Caribbean Games, Maracaibo, Venezuela
11-21 Sep	16th Commonwealth Games, Kuala Lumpar, Malaysia
6-20 Dec	13th Asian Games, Bangkok, Thailand

GLIDING

6-14 June	Standard Class National Championships, London G.C.
4-12 Jul	15 Metre Class National Championships, Cambridge
4-12 Jul	Club Class Championships, Yorkshire G.C.
18 Jul-2 Aug	European Gliding Championships, Leszno, Poland
8-16 Aug	Open Class National Championships, Lasham
22-30 Aug	Junior Championships, Lasham

GOLF

EUROPEAN PGA

12-15 Feb	Alfred Dunhill South African PGA Championship, Johannesburg, South Africa
26 Feb-1 Mar	Dubai Desert Classic, Dubai, UAE
5-8 Mar	Qatar Masters, Doha, Qatar
12-15 Mar	Moroccan Open, Rabat, Morocco
19-22 Mar	Portuguese Open, Lisbon, Portugal
16-19 Apr	Air France Cannes Open, Cannes, France
23-26 Apr	Turespana Masters, Maspalomas, Spain
30 Apr-3 May	Conte Of Florence Italian Open, Brescia, Italy
7-10 May	Peugeot Open De Espana, Madrid, Spain
14-17 May	Benson & Hedges International Open, Oxford
22-25 May	Volvo PGA Championship, Wentworth
28-31 May	Deutsche Bank/Sap Open TPC Of Europe, Hamburg, Germany
4-7 June	Alamo English Open, tbc
11-14 June	Compaq European Grand Prix, tbc
18-21 June	Madeira Island Open, Madeira, Portugal
25-28 June	Peugeot Open De France, Paris, France
2-5 Jul	Murphys Irish Open, Dublin, Ireland
8-11 Jul	Gulf Stream World Invitational, Glasgow
16-19 Jul	The Open, Southport

Date	Event
23-26 Jul	Sun Microsystems Dutch Open, Hilversum, Holland
30 Jul-2 Aug	Volvo Scandinavian Masters, Malmo, Sweden
6-9 Aug	Chemapol Trophy Czech Open, Prague, Czech Republic
20-23 Aug	Smurfit European Open, Dublin, Ireland
27-30 Aug	BMW International Open, Munich, Germany
3-6 Sep	Canon European Masters, Crans-Sur-Sierre, Switzerland
10-13 Sep	One 2 One British Masters, tbc
17-20 Sep	Trophee Lancome, Paris, France
24-27 Sep	Linde German Masters, Berlin, Germany
tbc Oct	Volvo German Open, Stuttgart, Germany
8-11 Oct	Alfred Dunhill Cup, St. Andrews
15-18 Oct	Toyota World Matchplay Championship, tbc
22-25 Oct	OKI Pro-Am, Madrid, Spain
29 Oct-1 Nov	Volvo Masters, tbc, Spain

WPGET

4-7 June	Evian Masters, Evian-Les Bains, France
11-14 June	Danish Open, Vejle, Denmark
6-9 Aug	McDonald's WPGA Championships Of Europe, Gleneagles
13-16 Aug	Weetabix Women's British Open, Lytham St. Annes
20-23 Aug	Compaq Open, tbc, Sweden

US PGA

3-4 Jan	Andersen Consulting WCOG, Scottsdale
8-11 Jan	Mercedes Championships, Carlsbad
14-18 Jan	Bob Hope Chrysler Classic, Indian Wells
22-25 Jan	Phoenix Open, Scottsdale
29 Jan-1 Feb	AT&T Pebble Beach National Pro-Am, Pebble Beach
5-8 Feb	Buick Invitational, Lajolla
12-15 Feb	United Airlines Hawaiian Open, Honolulu
19-22 Feb	Tucson Chrysler Classic, Tucson
26 Feb-1 Mar	Nissan Open, Los Angeles
5-8 Mar	Doral-Ryder Open, Miami
12-15 Mar	Honda Classic, Coral Springs
19-22 Mar	Bay Hill Invitational, Orlando
26-29 Mar	The Players Championship, Ponte Vedra Beach
2-5 Apr	Freeport-McDermott Classic, New Orleans
9-12 Apr	The Masters, Augusta
16-19 Apr	MCI Classic, Hilton Head Island
23-26 Apr	Greater Greensboro Chrysler Classic, Greensboro
30 Apr-3 May	Shell Houston Open, The Woodlands
7-10 May	Bellsouth Classic, Marietta
14-17 May	GTE Byron Nelson Classic, Irving
21-24 May	Mastercard Colonial, Ft. Worth
28-31 May	Memorial Tournament, Dublin
4-7 June	Kemper Open, Potomac
11-14 June	Buick Classic, Rye
18-21 June	US Open, San Francisco
25-28 June	Motorola Western Open, Lemont
2-5 Jul	Canon Greater Hartford Open, Cromwell
9-12 Jul	Quad City Classic, Coal Valley
16-19 Jul	Deposit Guaranty Golf Classic, Madison
23-26 Jul	CVS Charity Classic, Sutton
30 Jul-2 Aug	FedEx St. Jude Classic, Memphis
6-9 Aug	Buick Open, Grand Blanc
13-16 Aug	PGA Championship, Seattle
20-23 Aug	The Sprint International, Castle Rock
27-30 Aug	Greater Vancouver Open, Surrey, Canada
27-30 Aug	NEC World Series Of Golf, Akron
3-6 Sep	Greater Milwaukee Open, Milwaukee
10-13 Sep	Bell Canadian Open, Montreal, Canada
17-20 Sep	BC Open, Endicott
24-27 Sep	La Cantera Texas Open Presented By Lite Beer, San Antonio
1-4 Oct	Buick Challenge, Pine Mountain
8-11 Oct	Michelob Championship At Kingsmill, Williamsburg
14-18 Oct	Las Vegas Invitational, Las Vegas
22-25 Oct	Walt Disney World Oldsmobile Golf Classic, Lake Buena Vista
30 Oct-1 Nov	The Tour Championship, Houston
5-8 Nov	Lincoln-Mercury Kapulua International, Lahina,maui
5-8 Nov	Subaru Sarazen World Open Championship, Braselton
13-15 Nov	Franklin Templeton Shark Shootout, Thousand Oaks
19-22 Nov	World Cup Of Golf, Kiawah Island
28-29 Nov	Skins Game, La Quinta
3-6 Dec	JC Penny Classic, Palm Harbour
19-20 Dec	Wendys Three Tour Challenge, Henderson

US LPGA

2-5 Jul	US Womens Open, Kohler
18-20 Sep	Solheim Cup, Dublin, Ohio

AMATEUR

15-17 May	Brabazon Trophy, Liverpool
23-24 May	St Andrew Links Trophy, St. Andrews
1-6 June	British Amateur Championships, East Lothian
21-23 Jul	Doug Sanders World Boys Final, Aberdeen
27 Jul-1 Aug	English Amateur Championships, Woodhall Spa

| 1-2 Aug | Curtis Cup, Minnesota, USA |
| 5-7 Aug | Boys Home Internationals, St. Andrews |

GYMNASTICS

14 Mar	British Team Championships for Men, Guildford
20-22 Mar	World Stars for Men & Women, Moscow, Russia
27-28 Mar	Reebok International Team Championships for Men & Women, Knoxville, USA
27-29 Mar	Women's International, Great Britain vs. Spain, Guildford
27-29 Mar	World Cup France Telecom International Tournament, Paris, France
4-5 Apr	British Sport Acrobatics National Finals, Kings Lynn
17-18 Apr	FIG World Cup for Men & Women - Sagit Cup, Vancouver, Canada
23-26 Apr	European Championships For Men, St Petersburg, Russia
30 Apr-3 May	European Championships For Women, St Petersburg, Russia
15-17 May	World Aerobic Championships, Catania, Italy
21-24 May	Euroteam - General Gymnastics, Odense, Denmark
30-31 May	FIG World Cup Final for Men & Women, Sadae, Japan
19 Jul-2 Aug	Goodwill Games, New York, USA
11-21 Sep	16th Commonwealth Games, Kuala Lumpur, Malaysia
9-11 Oct	British Championships for Women, Guildford
14-15 Nov	British Championships for Men, tbc

HORSE RACING

FLAT RACING

1 Mar	Hong Kong Derby, Shae Tin, Hong Kong
28 Mar	The Lincoln, Doncaster
2 May	The Haydock Park Spring Trophy Rated Stakes, Haydock Park
2 May	The Sagitta 2000 Guineas Stakes, Newmarket
2 May	Visa Triple Crown Championship Series - Kentucky Derby, Churchill Downs, USA
3 May	The Sagitta 1000 Guineas Stakes, Newmarket
25 May	The Bonusprint Henry II Stakes, Sandown Park
25 May	The Tote Zetland Gold Cup, Redcar
25 May	The Tripleprint Temple Stakes, Sandown Park
5 June	The Vodafone Coronation Cup, Epsom
5 June	The Vodafone Oaks, Epsom
5 June	The Vodata Woodcote Stakes, Epsom
6 June	The Vodac Dash Rated Stakes, Epsom
6 June	The Vodafone Derby, Epsom
6 June	The Vodafone Diomed Stakes, Epsom
6 June	Visa 3-Year-Old Championship Series - Preakness Stakes, Pimlico, USA
16 June	The Prince Of Wales's Stakes, Ascot
16-19 June	Royal Ascot, Ascot
4 Jul	The Coral-Eclipse Stakes, Sandown Park
12 Sep	St. Leger, Doncaster
25 Jul	The King George VI And The Queen Elizabeth Diamond Stakes, Ascot
25 Jul	The Princess Margaret Stakes, Ascot
28 Jul-1 Aug	Glorious Goodwood, Goodwood
26 Sep	The Racal Diadem Stakes, Ascot
26 Sep	The Queen Elizabeth II Stakes, Ascot
26 Sep	The Tote Festival Handicap, Ascot
27 Sep	The Tote Sunday Special Handicap, Ascot
27 Sep	The Mail On Sunday Final, Ascot
27 Sep	The Fillies' Mile, Ascot
27 Sep	The Harvest Stakes, Ascot
4 Oct	Forte Meridien Prix De L'Arc De Triomphe, Longchamp, France
9 Oct	The Bonusprint October Stakes, Ascot
10 Oct	The McGee Autumn Stakes, Ascot
10 Oct	The Princess Royal Stakes, Ascot
10 Oct	The Willmott Dixon Cornwallis Stakes, Ascot
3 Nov	Melbourne Cup, Flemington, Australia
7 Nov	Visa 3-Year-Old Championship Series - Breeders' Cup, Hollywood Park, USA
22 Nov	Japan Cup, Tokyo, Japan

NATIONAL HUNT

28 Feb	The Greenalls Grand National Trial, Haydock Park
17-19 Mar	Cheltenham Festival, Cheltenham
2 Apr	The Martell Cup Steeple Chase, Aintree
2 Apr	The Sandeman Maghull Novices' Steeple Chase, Aintree
2 Apr	The Seagram Top Novices' Hurdle, Aintree
3 Apr	The Belle Epoque Sefton Novices' Hurdle, Aintree
3 Apr	The Martell Mersey Novices' Hurdle, Aintree
3 Apr	The Mumm Melling Steeple Chase, Aintree
3 Apr	The Mumm Mildmay Novices' Steeple Chase, Aintree
4 Apr	The Martell Aintree Hurdle, Aintree
4 Apr	The Martell Champion Standard Bumper, Aintree
4 Apr	The Martell Grand National Steeple Chase, Aintree

4 Apr	The Martell Red Rum Steeple Chase, Aintree
14 Nov	The Murphys Gold Cup Handicap Steeple Chase, Cheltenham
20 Nov	The Coopers & Lybrand Ascot Hurdle, Ascot
21 Nov	The First National Bank Gold Cup Chase, Ascot
28 Nov	The Hennessy Cognac Gold Cup Handicap Steeple Chase, Newbury
5 Dec	The Henry VIII Novices' Steeple Chase, Sandown Park
12 Dec	The Bonusprint Bula Hurdle, Cheltenham
12 Dec	The Tripleprint Gold Cup, Cheltenham
26 Dec	King George V Chase, Kempton Park
26 Dec	The Rowland Meyrick Handicap Steeple Chase, Wetherby

HURLING

| 13 Sep | Guinness All Ireland Hurling Championships Final, Dublin |

ICE HOCKEY

4 Jan	European Hockey League - Quarter-Finals - 1st Leg, Various, tbc
6 Jan	European Hockey League - Quarter-Finals - 2nd Leg, Various, tbc
24 Jan	European Hockey League - Final Four - Semi-Finals, Various, tbc
25 Jan	European Hockey League - Final Four - Final And 3rd/4th Place Playoff, tbc
1-3 Feb	Pre-Olympic Tournament, Tomakomai & Sapporo, Japan
7-22 Feb	Winter Olympic Games, Nagano, Japan
15-24 Apr	World Championship Pool B, Ljubljana & Jesenice, Slovenia
1-17 May	World Championship Pool A, Basel & Zurich, Switzerland

JUDO

15 Feb	BSJA National Trials, Cannock
28 Feb	BSJA National Team Championships, Cradley Heath
21 Mar	Commonwealth Tournament, Edinburgh
11-12 Apr	British Open Championships, Birmingham
25 Apr	BSJA National Individual Championships, Cannock
14-17 May	European Senior Championships, Oviedo, Spain
2 Oct	Welsh Senior Open Championships, Cardiff
8-11 Oct	World Junior Championships, Cali, Colombia
17-18 Oct	European Team Championships, Villach, Austria
19-22 Nov	European Junior Championships, Rome, Italy
13 Dec	British Senior Closed Men & Women's Championships, Cardiff
16-20 Dec	World Student Championships, Prague, Czech Republic

LAWN TENNIS

GRAND SLAM

19 Jan-1 Feb	Australian Open Championships, Melbourne, Australia
25 May-7 June	French Open Championships, Paris, France
22 June-5 Jul	The Wimbledon Championships
31 Aug-13 Sep	US Open Championships, New York, USA

ATP TOUR

5-11 Jan	Australian Men's Hardcourt Championships, Adelaide, Australia
5-11 Jan	Qatar Mobil Open, Doha, Qatar
12-18 Jan	Bellsouth Open, Auckland, New Zealand
12-18 Jan	Sydney International, Australia
2-8 Feb	Croatian Indoors, Zagreb, Croatia
9-15 Feb	Dubai Open, Dubai, UAE
9-15 Feb	St Petersburg Open, St Petersburg, Russia
9-15 Feb	Sybase Open - San Jose, San Jose, USA
16-22 Feb	European Community Championships, Antwerp, Belgium
16-22 Feb	Kroger St. Jude International - Memphis, USA
23 Feb-1 Mar	Advanta Championships, Philadelphia, USA
23 Feb-1 Mar	Guardian Direct, London
2-8 Mar	ABN/AMRO World Tennis Tournament, Rotterdam, Holland
2-8 Mar	Franklin Templeton Tennis Classic, Scottsdale, USA
9-15 Mar	Copenhagen Open, Denmark
9-15 Mar	Newsweek Champions Cup, Indian Wells, USA
16-29 Mar	The Lipton Championships, Key Biscayne, USA
23-29 Mar	Grand Prix Hassan, Casablanca, Morocco
6-12 Apr	Estoril Open, Portugal
6-12 Apr	Gold Flake Open, Chennai, India
6-12 Apr	Salem Open - Hong Kong

13-19 Apr	Japan Open, Tokyo
13-19 Apr	Open - Godo, Barcelona, Spain
20-26 Apr	Monte Carlo Open, Monaco
20-26 Apr	U.S. Clay Court Championships, Orlando, USA
27 Apr-3 May	Paegas Czech Open, Prague, Czech Republic
27 Apr-3 May	AT&T Challenge, Atlanta, USA
27 Apr-3 May	BMW Open, Munich, Germany
4-10 May	German Open, Hamburg
4-10 May	America's Red Clay Tennis Championship, Coral Springs
11-17 May	Campionati Internazionali D'Italia - TIM Cup, Rome, Italy
18-23 May	Internationaler Raiffeisen Grand Prix, St Polten, Austria
18-24 May	Peugeot ATP Tour World Team Championship, Dusseldorf, Germany
8-14 June	Gerry Weber Open, Halle In Westfalen, Germany
8-14 June	Internazionali Di Tennis Carisbo, Bologna, Italy
8-14 June	The Stella Artois Grass Court Championships, Queen's
15-20 June	The Nottingham Open, Nottingham
15-21 June	Heineken Trophy, Hertogenbosch, Holland
6-12 Jul	Rado Swiss Open, Gstaad, Switzerland
6-12 Jul	Swedish Open - Bastad, Sweden
6-12 Jul	Miller Lite Hall Of Fame Tennis Championships, Newport, USA
20-26 Jul	Mercedes Cup - Stuttgart, Germany
20-26 Jul	Legg Mason Tennis Classic, Washington, USA
27 Jul-2 Aug	International Championship Of Croatia - Umag, Croatia
27 Jul-2 Aug	EA Generali Open, Kitzbuhel, Austria
27 Jul-2 Aug	Infiniti Open, Los Angeles, USA
3-9 Aug	Du Maurier Open, Toronto, Canada
3-9 Aug	Grolsch Open, Amsterdam, Holland
10-16 Aug	Great American Insurance ATP Championship, Cincinnati, USA
10-16 Aug	Internazionali Di Tennis Di San Marino, San Marino
17-23 Aug	Pilot Pen International Tennis Tournament, New Haven, USA
17-23 Aug	RCA Championships, Indianapolis, USA
24-30 Aug	MFS Pro-Tennis Championships, Boston, USA
24-30 Aug	Waldbaum's Hamlet Cup, Long Island, USA
14-20 Sep	Presidents Cup, Tashkent, Uzbekistan
14-20 Sep	Samsung Open, Bournemouth
14-20 Sep	Marbella Open, Marbella, Spain
28 Sep-4 Oct	Grand Prix De Tennis De Toulouse, France
28 Sep-4 Oct	Open Romania, Bucharest, Romania
5-11 Oct	Campionati Internazionali Di Sicilia, Palermo, Italy
5-11 Oct	Davidoff Swiss Indoors Basle, Switzerland
5-11 Oct	Shanghai Tennis Open, PR China
12-18 Oct	CA Tennis Trophy, Vienna, Austria
12-18 Oct	Heineken Open - Singapore
19-25 Oct	Beijing Open, PR China
19-25 Oct	Grand Prix De Tennis De Lyon, Lyon, France
19-25 Oct	IPB Czech Indoor, Ostrava, Czech Republic
26 Oct-1 Nov	Abierto Mexicano De Tenis, Mexico City
26 Oct-1 Nov	Eurocard Open, Stuttgart, Germany
2-8 Nov	Cerveza Club Colombia Open, Bogota, Colombia
2-8 Nov	Open De La Ville De Paris, France
9-15 Nov	Kremlin Cup, Moscow, Russia
9-15 Nov	Scania Stockholm Open, Sweden
9-15 Nov	Chevrolet Cup, Santiago, Chile
16-22 Nov	Phoenix / ATP Tour World Doubles Championship, Hartford, USA
23-29 Nov	IBM/ATP Tour World Championship, Hanover, Germany

WTA TOUR

5-11 Jan	A.S.B. Bank Classic, Auckland, New Zealand
5-11 Jan	Australian Womens Hardcourt Championships, Gold Coast, Australia
12-18 Jan	ANZ Tasmania International, Hobart, Australia
12-18 Jan	Sydney International, Sydney, Australia
2-8 Feb	Toray Pan Pacific Open, Tokyo, Japan
9-15 Feb	Open Gaz De France, Paris, France
16-22 Feb	Copa Colsanitas, Bogota, Colombia
16-22 Feb	Faber Grand Prix, Hanover, Germany
23 Feb-1 Mar	EA-Generali Ladies Austrian Open, Linz, Austria
23 Feb-1 Mar	IGA Tennis Classic, Oklahoma City, USA
2-15 Mar	State Farm Evert Cup, Indian Wells, USA
16-29 Mar	The Lipton Championships, Key Biscayne, USA
30 Mar-5 Apr	Family Circle Magazine Cup, Hilton Head Island, USA
6-12 Apr	Bausch & Lomb Championships, Amelia Island, USA
13-19 Apr	Japan Open, Tokyo, Japan
13-19 Apr	Makarska Ladies Open, Croatia
20-26 Apr	Budapest Lotto Ladies Open, Hungary
20-26 Apr	Danamon Open, Jakarta, Indonesia
27 Apr-3 May	Croatian Bol Ladies Open, Bol, Croatia
27 Apr-3 May	Rexona Cup, Hamburg, Germany
4-10 May	Italian Open, Rome, Italy
11-17 May	German Open, Berlin, Germany
18-24 May	Open Paginas Amarillas Villa De Madrid, Madrid, Spain
18-24 May	Internationaux De Strasbourg, France
8-14 June	DFS Classic, Birmingham
15-21 June	Direct Line Insurance Championships, Eastbourne
15-21 June	Heineken Trophy, Rosmalen, Holland

6-12 Jul   Skoda Czech Open, Karlovy Vary, Czech Republic
6-12 Jul   Styria Open Maria Lankowitz, Maria Lankowitz, Austria
13-19 Jul   Torneo Internazionale, Italy
13-19 Jul   Warsaw Cup, Poland
27 Jul-2 Aug   Bank Of The West Classic, Stanford, USA
3-9 Aug   Enka Ladies Open, Istanbul, Turkey
3-9 Aug   Toshiba Tennis Classic, San Diego, USA
10-16 Aug   Acura Classic, Los Angeles, USA
17-23 Aug   Du Maurier Open, Montreal, Canada
24-30 Aug   US Womens Hardcourt Championships, Atlanta, USA
14-20 Sep   Samsung Womens Open, Seoul, Korea
21-27 Sep   Toyota Princess Cup, Tokyo, Japan
28 Sep-4 Oct   Sparkasen Cup International Grand Prix, Leipzig, Germany
28 Sep-4 Oct   Wismilak International, Surabaya, Indonesia
5-11 Oct   Porsche Tennis Grand Prix, Filderstadt, Germany
12-18 Oct   European Indoor Championships, Zurich, Switzerland
19-25 Oct   Ladies Kremlin Cup, Moscow, Russia
26-31 Oct   Seat Luxembourg Open, Kockelscheuer, Luxembourg
26 Oct-1 Nov   Bell Challenge, Quebec City, Canada
2-8 Nov   Ameritech Cup, Chicago, USA
9-15 Nov   Advanta Championships, Philadelphia, USA
16-22 Nov   Chase Championships Of The Corel WTA Tour, New York, USA
16-22 Nov   Volvo Womens Open, Pattaya City, Thailand

DAVIS & FED CUP

3-5 Apr   Davis Cup Round 1 - Italy v India, Italy
3-5 Apr   Davis Cup Round 1 - Switzerland v Czech Republic, Switzerland
3-5 Apr   Davis Cup Round 1 - USA v Russia, USA
3-5 Apr   Davis Cup Round 1 - Slovakia v Sweden, Slovakia
3-5 Apr   Davis Cup Round 1 - Germany v South Africa, Germany
3-5 Apr   Davis Cup Round 1 - Brazil v Spain, Brazil
3-5 Apr   Davis Cup Round 1 - Belgium v Holland, Belgium
3-5 Apr   Davis Cup - Great Britain v Ukraine/Denmark
3-5 Apr   Davis Cup Round 1 - Australia v Zimbabwe, Australia
18-19 Apr   KB Fed Cup - Australia v Russia, Australia
18-19 Apr   KB Fed Cup - Italy v Austria, Italy
18-19 Apr   KB Fed Cup - USA v Holland, USA
18-19 Apr   KB Fed Cup - Germany v Spain, Germany
18-19 Apr   KB Fed Cup - Belgium v Holland, Belgium
18-19 Apr   KB Fed Cup - Argentina v Slovakia, Argentina
18-19 Apr   KB Fed Cup - Croatia v Japan, Croatia
18-19 Apr   KB Fed Cup - Czech Republic v Switzerland, Czech Republic
17-19 Jul   Davis Cup Round 2, Various, tbc
25-26 Jul   KB Fed Cup - World Group 1 - Semi-Finals, tbc
19-20 Sep   KB Fed Cup - World Group 1 - Final, tbc
25-27 Sep   Davis Cup Round 3, Various
4-6 Dec   Davis Cup Final, tbc

MOTOR CYCLING

WORLD MOTOR CYCLING CHAMPIONSHIPS

29 Mar   Malaysian GP, Shah Alam, Malaysia
5 Apr   Japanese GP, Suzuka, Japan
19 Apr   Indonesian GP, Sentul, Indonesia
3 May   Spanish GP, Jerez De La Frontera, Spain
17 May   Italian GP, Mugello, Italy
31 May   French GP, Paul Ricard, France
14 June   Portuguese GP, Estoril, Portugal
27 June   Dutch GP, Assen, Holland
5 Jul   British GP, Donington Park
19 Jul   German GP, Nurburg-Eifel, Germany
23 Aug   Czech Republic GP, Brno, Czech Republic
6 Sep   Imola GP, Imola, San Marino
20 Sep   Catalonian GP, Barcelona, Spain
4 Oct   Australian GP, Phillip Island, Australia
18 Oct   Rio GP, Autodromo Nelson Piquet, Brazil
25 Oct   Argentine GP, Buenos Aires, Argentina

SBK SUPERBIKE WORLD CHAMPIONSHIP

15 Mar   Sentul, Indonesia
22 Mar   Phillip Island, Australia
13 Apr   Donington Park
10 May   Monza, Italy
24 May   Albacete, Spain
7 June   tbc, Germany
21 June   tbc, San Marino
5 Jul   tbc
12 Jul   Laguna Seca, USA
2 Aug   Brands Hatch
30 Aug   A1 Ring, Austria
6 Sep   Assen, Holland
20 Sep   tbc
4 Oct   Miyagi-Ken, Japan
11 Oct   Shah Alam, Malaysia

BRITISH SUPERBIKE CHAMPIONSHIP

27-29 Mar   Brands Hatch
24-26 Apr   Oulton Park
3-4 May   Thruxton
8-10 May   Snetterton
19-21 June   Donington Park
17-19 Jul   Oulton Park
7-9 Aug   Knockhill
14-16 Aug   Kirkby
29-31 Aug   Cadwell Park
4-6 Sep   Silverstone
18-20 Sep   Brands Hatch
25-27 Sep   Donington Park

MOTOR RACING

FORMULA ONE

8 Mar   Australian Grand Prix, Melbourne, Australia
29 Mar   Brazilian Grand Prix, Interlagos, Brazil
12 Apr   Argentine Grand Prix, Buenos Aires, Argentina
26 Apr   San Marino Grand Prix, Imola, Italy
10 May   Spanish Grand Prix, Barcelona, Spain
24 May   Monaco Grand Prix, Monte Carlo, Monaco
7 June   Canadian Grand Prix, Montreal, Canada
12 Jul   British Grand Prix, Silverstone
26 Jul   Austrian Grand Prix, Zeltweg, Austria
16 Aug   Hungarian Grand Prix, Budapest, Hungary
30 Aug   Belgian Grand Prix, Spa-Francorchamps, Belgium
13 Sep   Italian Grand Prix, Monza, Italy
27 Sep   Luxembourg Grand Prix, Nurburgring, Germany
11 Oct   Portuguese Grand Prix, Estoril, Portugal
1 Nov   Japanese Grand Prix, Suzuka, Japan

INDY CART

15 Mar   Marlboro Grand Prix Of Miami, Homestead, USA
28 Mar   Budweiser 500, Motegi, Japan
5 Apr   Toyota Grand Prix Of Long Beach, Long Beach, USA
26 Apr   Bosch Spark Plug Grand Prix, Nazareth, USA
10 May   Rio 400, Rio De Janeiro, Brazil
23 May   Motorola 300, Madison, USA
31 May   Miller 200, West Allis, USA
7 June   ITT Automotive Detroit Grand Prix, Detroit, USA
21 June   Budweiser/GI Joes 200, Portland, USA
12 Jul   Medic Drug Grand Prix Of Cleveland, Cleveland, USA
19 Jul   Molson Indy, Toronto, Canada
26 Jul   US 500, Brooklyn, USA
9 Aug   Miller Lite 200, Lexington, USA
16 Aug   Texaco/Havoline 200, Elkhart Lake, USA
6 Sep   Molson Indy Vancouver, Vancouver, Canada
13 Sep   Grand Prix Of Monterey, Laguna Seca, USA
4 Oct   Texaco Grand Prix Of Houston, Houston, USA
18 Oct   IndyCarnival Austrlia, Gold Coast, Australia
1 Nov   Marlboro 500, Fontana, USA

FIA GT CHAMPIONSHIP

22 Mar   Round 1, tbc, France
5 Apr   Round 2, Estoril, Portugal
19 Apr   Round 3, tbc, Germany
17 May   Round 4, Silverstone
28 June   Round 5, Nurburgring, Germany
19 Jul   Round 6, Spa-Francorchamps, Belgium
23 Aug   Round 7, Suzuka, Japan
6 Sep   Round 8, Donington Park
20 Sep   Round 9, Zeltweg, Austria
4 Oct   Round 10, Mugello, Italy

FORMULA 3000 CHAMPIONSHIP

16 May   Round 1, Silverstone
1 June   Round 2, Pau, France
14 June   Round 3, Helsinki, Finland
19 Jul   Round 4, Enna-Pergusa, Italy
29 Aug   Round 5, Spa-Francorchamps, Belgium
5 Sep   Round 6, Donington Park
27 Sep   Round 7, Mugello, Italy
11 Oct   Round 8, Magny Cours, France

OTHER MAJOR EVENTS

15 Feb   Daytona 500, Daytona Beach, USA
6-7 June   Le Mans 24 Hours, France

BRITISH TOURING CARS

13 Apr   RAC Touring Car Championship, Thruxton
26 Apr   RAC Touring Car Championship, Silverstone
4 May   RAC Touring Car Championship, Donington Park
17 May   RAC Touring Car Championship, Brands Hatch
25 May   RAC Touring Car Championship, Oulton Park
14 June   RAC Touring Car Championship, Donington Park
28 June   RAC Touring Car Championship, Croft On Tees
26 Jul   RAC Touring Car Championship, Snetterton
2 Aug   RAC Touring Car Championship, Thruxton
16 Aug   RAC Touring Car Championship, Dunfermline
31 Aug   RAC Touring Car Championship, Brands Hatch
13 Sep   RAC Touring Car Championship, Oulton Park
20 Sep   RAC Touring Car Championship, Silverstone

BRITISH FORMULA THREE

22 Mar   Donington Park
29 Mar   Thruxton
5 Apr   Silverstone
26 Apr   Brands Hatch
4 May   Oulton Park
17 May   Silverstone
24 May   Croft On Tees
14 June   Snetterton
11 Jul   Silverstone
24 Aug   Pembrey
30 Aug   Donington Park
13 Sep   Thruxton
27 Sep   Spa, Belgium
4 Oct   Silverstone
22 Nov   F3 Intercontinental Cup, tbc, Macao

MOTOR RALLYING

1-17 Jan   20th Paris-Dakar
17-21 Jan   Rallye Automobile de Monte Carlo, Monte Carlo, Monaco
5-8 Feb   International Swedish Rally, Karlstad
21 Feb   Mobil 1 RAC British Rally Championship - Rallysprint, Silverstone
27 Feb-2 Mar   Safari Rally, Nairobi, Kenya
20-21 Mar   Mobil 1 RAC British Rally Championship - Vauxhall Rally Of Wales, Chester
22-25 Mar   TAP Rallye Du Portugal, Figuera Da Foz, Portugal
19-22 Apr   32 Rallye De Catalunya Costa Brava - Rallye Of Spain, Lloret De Mar, Spain
25-26 Apr   Mobil 1 RAC British Rally Championship - Pirelli International Rally, Carlisle
3-6 May   Rallye De France - Tour de Corse, Ajaccio, France
20-23 May   Rally Argentina, Cordoba, Argentina
5-6 June   Mobil 1 RAC British Rally Championship - Scottish International Rally, Dumfries
5-9 June   Acropolis Rally Athens, Athens, Greece
25-28 Jul   Rally Of New Zealand, Manukau, New Zealand
31 Jul-1 Aug   Mobil 1 RAC British Rally Championship - Stena Line Ulster Rally, Belfast
21-23 Aug   Neste Rally Finland, Jyvaskyla, Finland
10-12 Sep   Mobil 1 RAC British Rally Championship - Manx International Rally, Douglas
18-20 Sep   Rally Of Indonesia, Medan, Indonesia
10-14 Oct   Rallye San Remo - Rallye D'Italia, San Remo, Italy
5-8 Nov   API Rally Australia, Perth, Australia
21-23 Nov   Network Q RAC Rally, various

NETBALL

17 Jan   English Counties League, various
7 Feb   English Counties League, various
8 Feb   Wales v England, Cardiff
7 Mar   English Counties League, various
17-19 Apr   European Netball Championships, tbc
5 Jul   National Junior Championships Finals, tbc
11-21 Sep   16th Commonwealth Games, Kuala Lumpur, Malaysia
7 Nov   International Netball, Wembley

POINT-TO-POINT

BANK HOLIDAY WEEKEND EVENTS

11 Apr   Vale of Lune at Whittington
11 Apr   Ashford Valley Foxhounds at Charing
11 Apr   Woodland Fytchley at Dingley
11 Apr   Vale of Aylesbury at Kimble
11 Apr   Tescott Foxhounds at Lifton
11 Apr   Royal Artillery at Larkhill
11 Apr   Puckeridge at Horseheath
11 Apr   North Staffordshire at Sandon
11 Apr   Middleton at Whitwell on the Hill
11 Apr   Ladlow at Bitterley
11 Apr   Glamorgan at St. Hilary
11 Apr   Blackmore & Sparkford Vale at Charlton Horethorne
11 Apr   Cotswold Vale Farmer's at Maismore Park
11 Apr   Percy at Alnwick

13 Apr	Eggesford Foxhounds at Bishopsleigh
13 Apr	South Notts at Thorpe
13 Apr	Old Berkshire at Lockinge
13 Apr	North Shropshire at Eyton on Severn
13 Apr	North Cotswold at Paxford
13 Apr	Braes Of Derwent at Corbridge
13 Apr	Essex Farmers & Union at Marks Tey
13 Apr	East Kent at Aldington
13 Apr	Southdown & Eridge at Heathfield
13 Apr	Staintondale at Charm Park
13 Apr	Four Burrow at Wadebridge
13 Apr	Taunton Vale Foxhounds at Kingston St Mary
13 Apr	Vine and Craven at Hackwood Park
13 Apr	South Pembrokeshire at Lydstep
2 May	Surrey Union at Peper Harrow, Godalming
2 May	Albrighton at Weston Park
2 May	Devon & Somerset Staghounds at Holnicote
2 May	Gelligaer Farmer's at Bonvilston
2 May	Modbury Harriers at Flete Park
2 May	Pendle Forest & Craven at Gisburn
3 May	Radnor & West Herefordshire at Cursneh Hill
3 May	Fernie at Dingley
3 May	Lauderdale at Mosshouses
4 May	Cotley at Cotley
4 May	Zetland at Witton Castle, Zetland
4 May	West Street Tickham at Aldington
4 May	Warwickshire at Ashorne
4 May	Stevenstone Foxhounds at High Bickington
4 May	Enfield Chase Foxhounds at Northaw
4 May	Banwen Miners at Pantyderi
4 May	South Shropshire at Eyton on Severn
23 May	Dulverton East Foxhounds at Mounsey Hill Gate
23 May	Melton Club at Garthorpe
23 May	Tredegar Farmers at Bassaleg
24 May	Berks & Bucks Draghounds at Kingston Blount
25 May	South Tercott Foxhounds at Lifton
25 May	Albrighton Woodland at Chaddesley Corbett

POLO

12-24 May	Prince Of Wales Trophy, Royal County of Berkshire Polo Club
19-24 May	Dollar Cup, Cowdray
19-31 May	Gerald Balding Cup, Cirencester
26 May-14 June	Queens Cup, Guards
30 May-7 June	Arthur Lucas Cup, Beaufort
10-21 June	Royal Windsor Cup, Guards
15-28 June	Archie David Cup, Guards
16-28 June	Warwickshire Cup, Cirencester
16 June-5 Jul	Eduardo Moore Tournament, Royal County of Berkshire Polo Club
20 June-27 Jul	Prince Of Wales Cup, Beaufort
30 June-19 Jul	Veuve Clicquot Gold Cup, Cowdray
7-12 Jul	Duke Of Beaufort's Cup, Beaufort
13-18 Jul	RCBPC 8 Goal Tournament, Royal County of Berkshire Polo Club
26 Jul	International Day Sponsored By Cartier, Guards
4-16 Aug	National 15 Goal Championships, Cirencester
10-16 Aug	National 8 Goal Championships, Little Budworth
18-29 Aug	Duke Of Wellington Trophy, Guards
18-30 Aug	World Championships, Santa Barbara, USA

RHYTHMIC GYMNASTICS

28-29 Mar	British Championships for Women, Bletchley
8-10 May	World Rhythmic Championships for Groups, Seville, Spain
28-31 May	European Championships, Porto, Portugal

ROWING

1 Mar	FISA Team Cup, Seville, Spain
21 Mar	Head Of The River, London
28 Mar	Oxford v Cambridge Boat Race, River Thames
18-19 Apr	Strathclyde International, Strathclyde
30-31 May	FISA Regatta Series, Munich, Germany
13-14 June	International Regatta, Bled, Slovenia
20-21 June	Henley Womens Regatta, River Thames
20-21 June	FISA Regatta Series, Hazewinkel, Belgium
1-5 Jul	Henley Royal Regatta, River Thames
11-12 Jul	FISA Regatta Series, Lucerne, Switzerland
25-26 Jul	The Nations Cup, Ioannina, Greece
5-9 Aug	World Junior Championships, Ottensheim, Austria
3-6 Sep	FISA Masters Regatta, Munich, Germany
6-13 Sep	World Championships, Cologne, Germany
18 Oct	Head Of The Charles, Boston, USA

RUGBY LEAGUE

tbc Apr	Start Of Super League, Various
2 May	Silk Cut Challenge Cup Final, Wembley
tbc Sep	Super League Playoffs, Various
tbc Oct	World Cup, Various, Australia

RUGBY UNION

FIVE NATIONS

7 Feb	France v England, Paris, France
7 Feb	Ireland v Scotland, Lansdowne Road, Ireland
21 Feb	England v Wales, Twickenham
21 Feb	Scotland v France, Murrayfield
7 Mar	France v Ireland, Paris, France
7 Mar	Wales v Scotland, Wembley
21 Mar	Ireland v Wales, Lansdowne Road, Ireland
22 Mar	Scotland v England, Murrayfield
4 Apr	England v Ireland, Twickenham
5 Apr	Wales v France, Wembley

OTHER MAJOR EVENTS

24 Jan	Italy v Scotland, tbc
31 Jan	Heineken European Rugby Cup Final, Twickenham
7 Feb	Wales v Italy, tbc
tbc May	Scotland Tour Of Australia, Various, Australia
2-16 May	Womens Rugby World Cup, Amsterdam, Holland
9 May	Tetley Bitter Cup Final, Twickenham
23 May	The Sanyo Cup, Twickenham
13 June	New Zealand A v England, Hamilton, New Zealand
16 June	New Zealand Academy v England, Invercargill, New Zealand
20 June	New Zealand v England, Dunedin, New Zealand
23 June	New Zealand Maoris v England, Rotorua, New Zealand
27 June	New Zealand v England, Auckland, New Zealand
11-21 Sep	16th Commonwealth Games, Kuala Lumpur, Malaysia

RUGBY SEVENS

11 Jan	Tournoi Punta Del Este, Punta Del Este, Uruguay
29-31 Mar	Hong Kong Rugby Sevens, Hong Kong
15-17 May	The Air France Paris Sevens, Paris, France
16 May	Middlesex Sevens, Twickenham
27-29 Nov	Dubai International Sevens, Dubai, UAE

SHOOTING

21-30 Mar	UIT World Cup In Clay Target, Cairo, Egypt
1-7 May	UIT World Cup In Clay Target, Darussalam, Brunei
11-18 May	UIT World Cup In Rifle, Pistol, Clay Target and RT, Atlanta, USA
19-25 May	UIT World Cup In Rifle, Pistol & RT, Munich, Germany
25 May-1 June	UIT World Cup In Rifle, Pistol & RT, Milan, Italy
25 May-1 June	UIT World Cup in RT, Guatemala City, Guatemala
10-16 Jul	UIT World Cup In Clay Target, Lonato, Italy
16-30 Jul	World Championships, Barcelona, Spain
11-21 Sep	16th Commonwealth Games, Kuala Lumpur, Malaysia
16-21 Sep	UIT World Cup Final In Clay Target, Montecatini, Italy
16-21 Sep	UIT World Cup In Rifle & Pistol, Buenos Aires, Argentina

SKATING

9-11 Jan	European Speed Skating Championships, Helsinki, Finland
11-18 Jan	European Figure Skating Championships, Milan, Italy
23-25 Jan	European Short Track Speed Skating Championships, Budapest, Hungary
24-25 Jan	World Sprint Speed Skating Championships, Berlin, Germany
7-22 Feb	Winter Olympic Games, Nagano, Japan
13-15 Mar	World Speed Skating Championships, Heerenveen, Holland
16-17 Mar	British Precision Team Championships, Bracknell
20-22 Mar	World Short Track Speed Skating Championships, Vienna, Austria
29 Mar-5 Apr	World Figure Skating Championships, Minneapolis, USA
4 Apr	British Short Track Speed Relay Championships, Basingstoke
8-12 Apr	ISU World Precision Team Skating Challenge Cup, Bordeaux, France

19 Jul-2 Aug	Goodwill Games, New York, USA
22-29 Nov	World Junior Figure Skating Championships, Zagreb, Croatia

SKIING

3-4 Jan	Pokal Vitranc, Kranjska Gora, Slovenia
5-6 Jan	WC-Rennen Damen, Ofterschwang, Germany
6 Jan	Cafe De Colombia Alpine World Cup, Hinterstoder, Austria
8-10 Jan	Cafe De Colombia Alpine World Cup, Schladming, Austria
8-14 Jan	British Land Senior Championships, Tignes, France
10-11 Jan	Zlata Lisica - Pohorski pokal, Maribor, Slovenia
13 Jan	Herren-Weltcup-Riesenslalom, Adelboden, Switzerland
17-18 Jan	Internationale Lauberhornrennen, Wengen, Switzerland
17-18 Jan	Int. Hahnenkammrennen, Kitzbuhel, Austria
23-25 Jan	Int. Hahnenkammrennen, Kitzbuhel, Austria
23-25 Jan	Cortina Super Ski Trophy, Cortina D'Ampezzo, Italy
28 Jan-1 Feb	WC-Rennen-Herren, Garmisch Partenkirchen, Germany
29 Jan-1 Feb	Cafe De Colombia Alpine World Cup, Are, Sweden
28 Feb-1 Mar	Cafe De Colombia Alpine World Cup, Saalbach, Austria
28 Feb-1 Mar	Yongpyong Cup Alpine Ski Games, Yong Pyong, Korea
7-8 Mar	Coupe Du Monde, Morzine, France
7-8 Mar	Cafe De Colombia Alpine World Cup, Kvitfjell, Norway
10-14 Mar	European Cup Final, Aviemore
11-15 Mar	FIS World Cup Final, Crans Montana, Switzerland
11-15 Mar	FIS World Cup Final, Crans Montana, Switzerland
28 Mar-3 Apr	British Land Junior & Childrens Championships, Tignes, France
1-5 Apr	British Universities Ski Championships, Les Arcs, France
5-10 Apr	English Ski Council Alpine Race Championships, Les Arcs, France

SNOOKER

2-14 Jan	Qualifying For Embassy World Championships, Blackpool
16-25 Jan	Regal Welsh, Newport
1-8 Feb	Benson & Hedges Masters, Wembley Conference Centre
10-22 Feb	Scottish Open, Aberdeen
26 Feb-1 Mar	Liverpool Victoria Charity Challenge, Derby
7-15 Mar	Thailand Open, Bangkok, Thailand
24-29 Mar	Benson & Hedges Irish Masters, County Kildare, Ireland
31 Mar-12 Apr	British Open, Plymouth
18 Apr-4 May	Embassy World Championships, Sheffield
11-24 Oct	Grand Prix, Preston
17-18 Oct	National Championships, Stirling
13-29 Nov	Liverpool Victoria UK Championships, Bournemouth

SPEEDWAY

1 May	Individual World Championship Qualifier, Mureck, Austria
9 May	Individual World Championship Qualifying, Krsko, Slovenia
10 May	Individual World Championship Qualifier, Gniezno, Poland
10 May	Individual World Championship Qualifier, Moorwinkelsdamm, Germany
15 May	Individual World Championship Grand Prix, Prague, Czech Republic
5 June	Individual World Championship Grand Prix, Pocking, Germany
7 June	Team World Championship Group B, Daugavpils, Latvia
13 June	Individual World Championship Continental Semi-Finals, Lonigo, Italy
14 June	Individual World Championship Continental Semi-Finals, Prelog, Croatia
14 June	Individual World Championship Overseas Final, Poole
19 June	Individual World Championship Grand Prix, Vojens, Denmark
28 June	Team World Championship Group A, Togliatti, Russia
4 Jul	Individual World Championship Scandinavian Final, Norrkoping, Sweden
25 Jul	Individual World Championship Continental Final, Debrecen, Hungary
7 Aug	Individual World Championship Grand Prix, Bradford
21 Aug	Individual World Championship Intercontinental Final, Vojens, Denmark
28 Aug	Individual World Championship Grand Prix, Linkoping, Sweden
11 Sep	Team World Championship Final, Vojens, Denmark

18 Sep	Individual World Championship Grand Prix, Bydgoszcz, Poland
3 Oct	Individual World Championship Grand Prix, Pardubice, Czech Republic

SQUASH

7-10 Jan	European Champion Of Champions, Stavanger, Norway
27 Jan-2 Feb	British National Championships, Manchester
26 Mar-6 Apr	British Open, Grantham
23-26 Apr	European Team Championships, Helsinki, Finland
11-21 Sep	16th Commonwealth Games, Kuala Lumpur, Malaysia
1-8 Nov	Women's World Open, Stuttgart, Germany
9-15 Nov	Women's World Team Championship, Stuttgart, Germany
1-6 Dec	Men's World Open, Bombay, India

SWIMMING

7-18 Jan	VIII Fina World Championships, Perth, Australia
21-22 Jan	World Cup Series, Sydney, Australia
30 Jan-2 Feb	Speedo British Swimming Grand Prix, Swansea
20-22 Feb	Winter Age Group Diving Championships, Plymouth
20-23 Feb	Speedo British Swimming Grand Prix, Leeds
21-22 Feb	World Cup Series, Hong Kong
25-26 Feb	World Cup Series, Beijing, PR China
27-28 Feb	GB Club Team Championships, Stockport
6-8 Mar	Fina IV Diving Grand Prix Internationaler Springertag, Rostok, Germany
7-8 Mar	National Synchronised Swimming Championships, Halifax
7-8 Mar	World Cup Series, Rio De Janeiro, Brazil
12-15 Mar	Fina IV Diving Grand Prix, Moscow, Russia
13-14 Mar	World Cup Series, Sheffield
14-15 Mar	Winter Diving Championships, Sheffield
17-18 Mar	World Cup Series, Malmo, Sweden
20-22 Mar	National Masters Diving Competitions, Sheffield
21-22 Mar	World Cup Series, Gelsenkirchen, Germany
25-26 Mar	World Cup Series, Imperia, Italy
28-29 Mar	World Cup Series, Paris, France
2-5 Apr	North Sea Water Polo Tournament, Sheffield
9-11 Apr	Womens International Water Polo Tournament, Millfield
30 Apr-2 May	Fina IV Diving Grand Prix, Winnipeg, Canada
2-4 May	Speedo British Swimming Grand Prix Final, Cardiff
7-10 May	Fina IV Diving Grand Prix, tbc, USA
15-17 May	Fina IV Diving Grand Prix, tbc, Mexico
16 May	Water Polo Championship Finals, Walsall
27-31 May	National Age Group Diving Competitions, Crystal Palace
29-31 May	GB Masters Championships, Glasgow
29-31 May	Speedo British Swimming Grand Prix Super Final, Sheffield
19-21 June	Fina IV Diving Grand Prix, Madrid, Spain
26-28 June	Fina IV Diving Grand Prix - Hungarian Grand Prix, Budapest, Hungary
30 June-2 Jul	Fina IV Diving Grand Prix, Rome, Italy
3-5 Jul	Fina IV Diving Grand Prix Volksbank Diving Grand Prix, Vienna, Austria
8-10 Jul	Fina IV Diving Grand Prix, Jonkoping, Sweden
9-12 Jul	ASA British Commonwealth Trials, Sheffield
9-12 Jul	National Summer Diving Competitions, Sheffield
18 Jul	European Long Distance Swimming Cup, Holme Pierrepont
18-19 Jul	ASA Open Water & Masters Championships, Holme Pierrepont
19 Jul	ASA 25km National Championships, Holme Pierrepont
19 Jul-2 Aug	Goodwill Games, New York, USA
24 Jul-2 Aug	European Junior Womens Water Polo Championship, Millfield
3-8 Aug	National Age Group Championships, Leeds
11-21 Sep	16th Commonwealth Games, Bukit Jalil, Malaysia
19 Sep	Inter District Synchronised Swimming Competition, tbc
17 Oct	Inter County Swimming Competition, Sheffield
23-25 Oct	National Masters Championships, Sheffield
7-8 Nov	National Age Group Synchronised Swimming Competitions, tbc
7-8 Nov	Novices Diving Competitions, Trowbridge
21-22 Nov	Womens Under 20 Inter District Water Polo Championship, Walsall
22 Nov	Mens County Junior Water Polo Final, Walsall
5-6 Dec	Womens Inter District Water Polo Championships, Walsall
10-13 Dec	European Sprints, Sheffield
17-20 Dec	British Swimming Championships, Glasgow

TABLE TENNIS

16-18 Jan	European Nations Cup, Bayreuth, Germany
18 Jan	British League, Various
24-25 Jan	European Womens Team Cup, Bremen, Germany
25 Jan	British League, Various
30 Jan-1 Feb	European Top 12, Halmstad, Sweden
7-8 Feb	Welsh Open, Cardiff
22 Feb	British League, Various
23-27 Feb	Qatar Open, Doha, Qatar
6-8 Mar	English Senior Nationals, Various
12-15 Mar	Croatian Open, Zagreb, Croatia
15 Mar	British League, Various
22 Mar	British League, Various
5 Apr	British League, Various
23 Apr-3 May	European Championships, Eindhoven, Holland
3 May	British League, Various
4-7 June	Malaysian Open, Joho Baru, Malaysia
11-14 June	Japan Open, Wakayama, Japan
17-27 June	World Veterans Championships, Manchester
1-5 Jul	US Open (Pro Challenge Tour), Houston, USA
13-16 Aug	Australian Open, Melbourne, Australia
27-30 Aug	Korea Open, Seoul, Korea
3-6 Sep	China Open, tbc, PR China
11-13 Sep	Womens World Cup, tbc
15-18 Oct	Mens World Cup, tbc
22-25 Oct	Lebanon Open, Beirut, Lebanon
29 Oct-1 Nov	Italian Open, Palermo, Italy
12-15 Nov	Brazil Open, Rio de Janeiro, Brazil
19-22 Nov	Yugoslav Open, tbc, Yugoslavia
26-29 Nov	Swedish Open, tbc, Sweden
3-6 Dec	Finlandia Open, Turkku, Finland

VOLLEYBALL

19 Jul-2 Aug	Goodwill Games, New York, USA
3-12 Nov	Womens World Championships, Various, Japan
13-29 Nov	Mens World Championships, Various, Japan

WRESTLING

23-26 Apr	European Mens Greco-Roman Championships, Minsk, Belarus
7-9 May	European Womens Freestyle Championships, Bratislava, Slovakia
7-10 May	European Mens Freestyle Championships, Bratislava, Slovakia
6-7 June	European Junior Womens Freestyle Championships, Patras, Greece
25-28 June	European Junior Mens Freestyle Championships, Radovis, Macedonia
9-12 Jul	European Junior Mens Greco-Roman Championships, Tirana, Albania
7-9 Aug	World Junior Womens Freestyle Championships, Fredrikstad, Norway
7-10 Aug	World Junior Mens Freestyle Championships, Primm, USA
18-21 Aug	World Junior Mens Greco-Roman Championships, Cairo, Egypt
27-30 Aug	World Mens Greco-Roman Championships, Gavle, Sweden
2-4 Sep	World Womens Freestyle Championships, Poznan, Poland
8-11 Sep	World Mens Freestyle Championships, Tehran, Iran

YACHTING

1-4 Jan	49ER World Championships, Perth, Australia
1-31 Jan	Hobie 16 World Championship, Airlie Beach, Australia
3-10 Jan	International OK Dinghy World Championships, Glenelg, Australia
3-11 Jan	International Fireball World Championship, Frankston, Australia
4 Jan	Whitbread Round The World Race - Start Leg Four, Sydney, Australia
5-9 Jan	International Contender World Championship, Sydney, Australia
9 Jan	Whitbread Round The World Race - Finish Leg Four, Auckland, New Zealand
31 Jan	Whitbread Round The World Race - Start Leg Four, Auckland, New Zealand
23 Feb	Whitbread Round The World Race - Finish Leg Five, Sao Sebastiao, Brazil
1-14 Mar	Dubai ISAF World Sailing Championship, Dubai, UAE
14 Mar	Whitbread Round The World Race - Start Leg Six, Sao Sebastiao, Brazil
2 Apr	Whitbread Round The World Race - Finish Leg Six, Fort Lauderdale, USA
5-11 Apr	International 5.5 World Championship, Nassau, Bahamas
19 Apr	Whitbread Round The World Race - Start Leg Seven, Fort Lauderdale, USA
22 Apr	Whitbread Round The World Race - Finish Leg Seven, Baltimore, USA
3 May	Whitbread Round The World Race - Start Leg Eight, Baltimore, USA
16 May	Whitbread Round The World Race - Finish Leg Eight, La Rochelle, France
22 May	Whitbread Round The World Race - Start Leg Nine, La Rochelle, France
24 May	Whitbread Round The World Race - Finish Leg Nine, Southampton
14-22 June	International 5.5 European Championship, Cowes
20 June	Round The Islands Race, Various
7-14 Jul	International 420 Class World Championship, Palamos, Spain
11-19 Jul	Myrd World Championship, Viry Chatillon, France
12-17 Jul	Yngling World Championship, Wolfgansee, Austria
1-8 Aug	Skandia Life Cowes Week, The Solent
1-30 Aug	Int. 505 World Championship, Hyannis, USA
4-11 Aug	International Flying Dutchman World Championship, Medemblik, Holland
9-15 Aug	Falmouth Week, Falmouth
16-23 Aug	Fowey Royal Regatta, Fowey
16-23 Aug	Interceltic Waterports Festival, Bude
21-30 Aug	Largs Regatta Week, Largs
1-30 Sep	Etchells World Championship, Marblehead, USA
1-30 Sep	International Hobie 16 World Championship, Airlie Beach, Australia
20-27 Nov	Tornado World Championship, Buzios, Brazil

AMERICAN FOOTBALL

SUPER BOWL XXXI
Jan 27 New Orleans
Green Bay Packers 35-21 New England Patriots

ATHLETICS

LONDON MARATHON
Apr 13

Men
1 Antonio Pinto POR 2:07:55

Women
1 Joyce Chepchumba KEN 2:26:51

BOSTON MARATHON
Apr 21

Men
1 Lameck Aguta KEN 2:10:34

Women
1 Fatuma Roba ETH 2:26:24

WORLD CHAMPIONSHIP
Aug 2-10 Athens

Men's 100m
1 Maurice Greene USA 9.86
2 Donovan Bailey CAN 9.91
3 Tim Montgomery USA 9.94

Women's 100m
1 Marion Jones USA 10.83
2 Zhanna Pintussevich UKR 10.85
3 Sevatheda Fynes BAH 11.03

Men's 200m
1 Ato Boldon TRI 20.04
2 Frank Fredericks NAM 20.23
3 Claudinei Da Silva BRA 20.26

Women's 200m
1 Zhanna Pintussevich UKR 22.32
2 Susanthika Jayasinghe SRI 22.39
3 Merlene Ottey JAM 22.40

Men's 400m
1 Michael Johnson USA 44.12
2 Davis Kamoga UGA 44.37
3 Tyree Washington USA 44.39

Women's 400m
1 Cathy Freeman AUS 49.77
2 Sandie Richards JAM 49.79
3 Jearl Miles-Clark USA 49.90

Men's 800m
1 Wilson Kipketer DEN 1:43.38
2 Norberto Tellez CUB 1:44.00
3 Rich Kenah USA 1:44.25

Women's 800m
1 Ana Fidelia Quirot CUB 1:57.14
2 Yelena Afanasyeva RUS 1:57.56
3 Maria Mutola MOZ 1:57.59

Men's 1500m
1 Hicham El Guerrouj MAR 3:35.83
2 Fermin Cacho ESP 3:36.63
3 Reyes Estevez ESP 3:37.26

Women's 1500m
1 Carla Sacramento POR 4:04.24
2 Regina Jacobs USA 4:04.63
3 Anita Weyermann SUI 4:04.70

Men's 5000m
1 Daniel Komen KEN 13:07.38
2 Khalid Boulami MAR 13:09.34
3 Tom Nyariki KEN 13:11.09

Women's 5000m
1 Gabriela Szabo ROM 14:57.68
2 Roberta Brunet ITA 14:58.29
3 Fernanda Ribeiro POR 14:58.85

Men's 10,000m
1 Haile Gebreselassie ETH 27:24.58
2 Paul Tergat KEN 27:25.62
3 Salah Hissou MAR 27:28.67

Women's 10,000m
1 Sally Barsosio KEN 31:32.92
2 Fernanda Ribeiro POR 31:39.15
3 Masako Chiba JPN 31:41.93

Men's Marathon
1 Abel Anton ESP 2:13:16
2 Martin Fiz ESP 2:13:21
3 Steve Moneghetti AUS 2:14:16

Women's Marathon
1 Hiromi Suzuki JPN 2:29:48
2 Manuela Machado POR 2:31:12
3 Lidia Simon ROM 2:31:55

Men's 110m Hurdles
1 Allen Johnson USA 12.93
2 Colin Jackson GBR 13.05
3 Igor Kovac SVK 13.18

Women's 100m Hurdles
1 Ludmila Engquist SWE 12.50
2 Svetla Dimitrova BUL 12.58
3 Michelle Freeman JAM 12.61

Men's 400m Hurdles
1 Stephane Diagana FRA 47.70
2 Llewellyn Herbert RSA 47.86
3 Bryan Bronson USA 47.88

Women's 400m Hurdles
1 Nezha Bidouane MAR 52.97
2 Deon Hemmings JAM 53.09
3 Kim Batten USA 53.52

Men's 3000m Steeplechase
1 Wilson Boit Kipketer KEN 8:05.84
2 Moses Kiptanui KEN 8:06.04
3 Bernard Barmasai KEN 8:06.04

Men's 4x100m Relay
1 Canada 37.86
2 Nigeria 38.07
3 Great Britain 38.14

Women's 4x100m Relay
1 USA 41.47
2 Jamaica 42.10
3 France 42.21

Men's 4x400m Relay
1 USA 2:56.47
2 Great Britain 2:56.65
3 Jamaica 2:56.75

Women's 4x400m Relay
1 Germany 3:20.92
2 USA 3:21.03
3 Jamaica 3:21.30

Men's 20k Walk
1 Daniel Garcia MEX 1:21:43
2 Mikhail Shchennikov RUS 1:21:53
3 Mikhail Khmelnitskiy BLR 1:22:01

Women's 10k Walk
1 Annarita Sidoti ITA 42:55.49
2 Olimpiada Ivanova RUS 43:07.63
3 Olga Kardopoltseva BLS 43:30.20

Men's 50km Walk
1 Robert Korzeniowski POL 3:44:46
2 Jesus Angel Garcia ESP 3:44:59
3 Miguel Angel Rodriguez MEX 3:48:30

Men's Decathlon
1 Tomas Dvorak CZE 8837
2 Eduard Hamalainen FIN 8730
3 Frank Busemann GER 8652

Women's Heptathlon
1 Sabine Braun GER 6739
2 Denise Lewis GBR 6654
3 Remigija Nazaroviene LIT 6566

Men's Discus
1 Lars Riedel GER 68.54
2 Virgilijus Alekna LIT 66.70
3 Jurgen Schult GER 66.14

Women's Discus
1 Beatrice Faumuina NZL 66.82
2 Ellina Zvereva BLR 65.90
3 Natalya Sadova RUS 65.14

Men's High Jump
1 Javier Sotomayor CUB 2.37
2 Artur Partyka POL 2.35
3 Tim Forsyth AUS 2.35

Women's High Jump
1 Hanne Haugland NOR 1.99
2 Olga Kaliturina RUS 1.96
2 Inga Babakova UKR 1.96

Men's Shot Put
1 John Godina USA 21.44
2 Oliver-Sven Buber GER 21.24
3 C.J. Hunter USA 20.33

Women's Shot Put
1 Astrid Kumbernuss GER 20.71
2 Vita Pavlysh UKR 20.66
3 Stephanie Storp GER 19.22

Men's Triple Jump
1 Yoelvis Quesada CUB 17.85
2 Jonathan Edwards GBR 17.69
3 Aliecer Urrutia CUB 17.64

Women's Triple Jump
1 Sarka Kasparkova CZE 15.20
2 Rodica Mateescu ROM 15.16
3 Yelena Govorova UKR 14.67

Men's Long Jump
1 Ivan Pedroso CUB 8.42
2 Erik Waber USA 8.38
3 Kirill Sosunov RUS 8.18

Women's Long Jump
1 Liudmila Galkina RUS 7.05
2 Niki Xanthou GRE 6.94
3 Fiona May ITA 6.91

Men's Javelin
1 Marius Corbett RSA 88.40
2 Steve Backley GBR 86.80
3 Konstantinos Gatzioudis GRE 86.64

Women's Javelin
1 Trine Hattestad NOR 68.78
2 Joanna Stone AUS 68.64
3 Tanja Damaske GER 67.12

Men's Pole Vault
1 Sergey Bubka UKR 6.01
2 Maksim Tarasov RUS 5.96
3 Dean Starkey USA 5.91

Men's Hammer
1 Heinz Weis GER 81.78
2 Andrey Skvaruk UKR 81.46
3 Vasiliy Sidorenko RUS 80.76

NEW YORK MARATHON
Nov 2

Men
1 John Kagwe KEN 2:08:12

Women
1 Fraziska Rochat-Moser SWI 2:28:09

1997 GRAND PRIX STANDINGS

Men			points
1 Wilson Kipketer	800m	DEN	114
2 Lars Riedel	discus	GER	99
3 Mark Crear	110m H	USA	95

Women			points
1 Astrid Kumbernuss	Shot	GER	99
2 Deon Hemmings	400m H	JAM	93
3 Kim Batten	400m H	USA	91

1997 WORLD RECORDS

Men
Feb 2 Stuttgart
1500m (indoor) 3:31.18 Hicham El Guerrouj MAR
Feb 12 Ghent
Mile (indoor) 3:48.45 Hicham El Guerrouj MAR
Feb 20 Stockholm
5000m (indoor) 12:59.04 Haile Gebrselassie ETH
Mar 1 Sindelfin
Triple jump (indoor) 17.83 Aliecer Urrutia CUB
Mar 9 Paris
800m (indoor) 1:42.67 Wilson Kipketer DEN
May 31 Hengels
2 miles 8:01.08 Haile Gebrselassie ETH
Jul 4 Oslo
10000m 26:31.32 Haile Gebrselassie ETH
Jul 19 Hechtel
2 miles 7:58.61 Daniel Komen KEN
Aug 13 Zurich
5000m 12:41.86 Haile Gebrselassie ETH
Aug 13 Zurich
3000m steeplechase 7:59.08 Wilson Boit KEN
Aug 22 Brussels
10000m 26:27.85 Paul Tergat KEN
Aug 22 Brussels
5000m 12:39.74 Daniel Komen KEN
Aug 24 Cologne
800m 1:41.11 Wilson Kipketer DEN
Aug 24 Cologne
3000m steeplechase 7:55.72 Bernard Barmasai KEN
Sep 21 Zaanden
10 miles 44:45 Paul Koech KEN
Oct 5 Adelaide
24 hours 303.5k Yiannis Kouros AUS

Women
Feb 8 Melbourne
Pole vault 4.50 Emma George AUS
Feb 10 Tampere
100m H (indoor) 12.64 Ludmila Engquist SWE
Feb 20 Melbourne
Pole vault 4.55 Emma George AUS
Mar 3 Bucharest
Hammer 69.58 Mihaela Melinte ROM
Mar 9 Paris
Pole vault (indoor) 4.40 Stacy Dragila USA
Jun 16 Smolensk
Hammer 70.78 Olga Kuzenkova RUS
Jun 27 Munich
Hammer 7.22 Olga Kuzenkova RUS
Jun 22 Munich
Hammer 73.10 Olga Kuzenkova RUS
Jul 25 Guadalajara
600m 1:22.63 Ana Quirot CUB
Oct 21 Shanghai
5000m 14:31.27 Dong Yanmei CHN
Oct 23 Shanghai
5000m 14:28.09 Jiang Bo CHN
Some records await ratification.

BADMINTON

WORLD CHAMPIONSHIP
May 25-Jun 1 Glasgow

Men's Singles Final
P Rasmussen DEN beat Sun Jun CHI
16-17; 15-13; 15-10

Men's Doubles Final
B Sigit IND and C Wijaya IND
beat
Yap Kim Hock MAL and Cheah Soon Kit MAL
8-15; 18-17; 15-10

Women's Singles Final
Ye Zhaoying CHI beat Gong Zhichao CHI
12-11;11-8

Women's Doubles Final
Gu Jun CHI and Ge Fei CHI
beat
Tang Yongshu CHI and Qin Yiyuan CHI
15-1; 15-8

Mixed Doubles Final
Liu Yong CHI and Ge Fei CHI
beat
J Eriksen DEN and M Thomsen DEN

BASEBALL

WORLD SERIES

1996-97 Champions: Florida Marlins
Florida Marlins beat Cleveland Indians 4-3 in a best of seven series

Oct 19	Cleveland	4	Florida	7
Oct 20	Cleveland	6	Florida	1
Oct 22	Florida	14	Cleveland	11
Oct 23	Florida	3	Cleveland	10
Oct 24	Florida	8	Cleveland	7
Oct 26	Cleveland	4	Florida	1
Oct 27	Cleveland	2	Florida	3

BASKETBALL

NBA

1996-97 Champions: Chicago Bulls
Chicago Bulls beat Utah Jazz 4-2 in a best of seven series

Jun 1	Chicago	84	Utah	82
Jun 4	Chicago	97	Utah	85
Jun 6	Utah	104	Chicago	93
Jun 8	Utah	78	Chicago	73
Jun 11	Utah	88	Chicago	90
Jun 13	Chicago	90	Utah	86

BUDWEISER LEAGUE

1996-97 Champions: London Towers

Budweiser Championships Final
May 4 Wembley
Leopards 88-89 London Towers

1996-97 League

	P	W	L	Pts
1 Leopards	36	28	8	56
2 London Towers	36	26	10	52
3 Sheffield	36	26	10	52
4 Birmingham	36	25	11	50
5 Chester	36	24	12	48
6 Manchester	36	22	14	44
7 Newcastle	36	21	15	42
8 Leicester	36	15	21	30
9 Derby	36	14	22	28
10 Thames Valley	36	14	22	28
11 Worthing	36	12	24	24
12 Crystal Palace	36	5	31	10
13 Hemel & Watford	36	2	34	4

BOWLS

ALL-ENGLAND CHAMPIONSHIP
Aug17-29 Worthing

Semi-Finals
R Brittan (Eridlington) beat
P Broderick (Wellingborough) 21-12

M Coles (Garston) beat
A Thomson (Blackheath & Greenwich)

Final
R Brittan (Erdlington) beat
M Coles (Garston) 21-17

BOXING

Feb 8 **IBF Featherweight Title** London Arena
Naseem Hamed stopped Tom Johnson Rnd 8

Mar 1 Atlantic City
Hector Camacho stopped Sugar Ray Leonard Rnd 5

Mar 21 **WBC Light Heavyweight Title** Atlantic City
Roy Jones disqualified against Montell Griffin Rnd 9

Apr 12 **WBC Welterweight Title** Las Vegas
O. De La Hoya won decision over P. Whitaker Rnd 12

Jun 28 **WBA Heavyweight Title** Las Vegas
Mike Tyson disqualified against Evander Holyfield Rnd 3

Aug 7 **WBC Light Heavyweight Title** Leddyard, Conn.
Roy Jones knocked out Montell Griffin Rnd 1

Aug 9 **WBC Jr Middleweight Title** Kansas City
Terry Norris knocked out Joaquin Velasquez Rnd 2

Sep 13 **WBC Welterweight Title** Las Vegas
O. de la Hoya won decision over H. Camacho Rnd 12

Oct 4 **WBC Heavyweight Title** Atlantic City
Lennox Lewis stopped Andrew Golota Rnd !

Oct 11 **WBO Super Middleweight Title** Sheffield
Joe Calzaghe won decision over Chris Eubank Rnd 12

CRICKET

ENGLAND TOUR OF NEW ZEALAND

Jan 24-28 **First Test** Auckland
New Zealand 390 & 248-9 dec
England 521
Match drawn

Feb 6-10 **Second Test** Wellington
New Zealand 124 & 191
England 383
England won by an innings and 68 runs

Feb 14-18 **Third Test** Christchurch
New Zealand 346 & 186
England 228 & 307-6
England won by 4 wickets
England won series 2-0

AUSTRALIA TOUR OF ENGLAND

Texaco Trophy

May 22 **First One Day International** Headingley
Australia 170-8 (50 overs)
England 175-4 (40.1 overs)
England won by 6 wickets

May 24 **Second One Day International** The Oval
Australia 249-6 (50 overs)
England 253-4 (48.2 overs)
England won by 6 wickets

May 25 **Third One Day International** Lord's
Australia 269 (49.2 overs)
England 270-4 (49 overs)
England won by 6 wickets
England won series 3-0

CORNHILL INSURANCE TESTS

Jun 5-8 **First Test** Edgbaston
Australia 118 & 477
England 478 & 119-1
England won by 9 wickets

Jun 19-23 **Second Test** Lord's
England 77 (McGrath 8 for 38) & 266-4 dec
Australia 213-7 dec
Match drawn

Jul 3-7 **Third Test** Old Trafford
Australia 235 & 395
England 162 & 200
Australia won by 268 runs

Jul 24-28 **Fourth Test** Headingley
England 172 & 268
Australia 501-9 dec
Australia won by an innings & 61 runs

Aug 7-10 **Fifth Test** Trent Bridge
Australia 427 & 336
England 313 & 186
Australia won by 264 runs

Aug 21-23 **Sixth Test** The Oval
England 180 & 163
Australia 220 & 104
England won by 19 runs
Australia won series 3-2

BENSON & HEDGES CUP

Jul 12 **Final** Lord's
Kent 212-9 (50 overs)
Surrey 215-2 (45 overs)
Surrey won by 8 wickets

NATWEST TROPHY

Sep 6 **Final** Lord's
Warwickshire 170 (60 overs)
Essex 171-1 (26.3 overs)
Essex won by 9 wickets

BRITANNIC ASSURANCE CHAMPIONSHIP

1997 Champions: Glamorgan

1997 Britannic Assurance Championship

		P	W	L	D	Bat	Bwl	Pts
1	Glamorgan	17	8	2	7	50	57	256
2	Kent	17	8	4	5	44	60	252
3	Worcestershire	17	6	3	8	49	54	228
4	Middlesex	17	7	4	6	33	56	219
5	Warwickshire	17	7	2	8	32	51	219
6	Yorkshire	17	6	3	8	41	54	215
7	Gloucestershire	17	6	6	5	35	60	206
8	Surrey	17	5	5	7	39	52	192
9	Essex	17	5	6	6	39	55	192
10	Leicestershire	17	4	1	12	37	54	191
11	Lancashire	17	5	6	6	34	54	186
12	Somerset	17	3	3	11	38	64	183
13	Nottinghamshire	17	4	3	10	26	55	175
14	Hampshire	17	3	5	9	42	41	158
15	Northamptonshire	17	3	5	9	33	48	156
16	Derbyshire	17	2	9	6	32	59	141
17	Durham	17	2	8	7	22	56	131
18	Sussex	17	1	10	6	24	57	115

AXA LIFE SUNDAY LEAGUE

1997 Champions: Warwickshire

1997 AXA Life Sunday League

		P	W	L	T	NR	Pts	RR
1	Warwickshire	17	13	4	0	0	52	14.14
2	Kent	17	12	4	0	1	50	7.70
3	Lancashire	17	10	4	1	2	46	1.89
4	Leicestershire	17	9	5	1	2	42	7.11
5	Surrey	17	9	5	0	3	42	1.06
6	Somerset	17	9	6	0	2	40	4.31
7	Essex	17	9	6	1	1	40	-2.38
8	Worcestershire	17	8	6	1	2	38	6.87
9	Northamptonshire	17	8	6	0	3	38	2.78
10	Yorkshire	17	8	7	1	1	36	5.24
11	Gloucestershire	17	7	6	0	4	36	1.01
12	Nottinghamshire	17	7	7	0	3	34	-0.19
13	Glamorgan	17	5	9	0	3	26	-4.01
14	Derbyshire	17	4	9	0	4	24	-3.04
15	Hampshire	17	5	11	0	1	22	-4.73
16	Middlesex	17	3	10	1	3	20	-8.28
17	Durham	17	3	13	0	1	14	-12.27
18	Sussex	17	2	13	0	2	12	-16.72

LEADING FIRST-CLASS AVERAGES

Batting

		M	I	NO	Runs	HS	Ave
1	G A Hick	18	28	6	1524	303	69.27
2	S P James	18	30	4	1775	162	68.26
3	M P Maynard	18	25	7	1170	161	65.00
4	R T Ponting	8	12	3	571	127	63.44
5	D S Lehmann	17	27	2	1575	182	63.00
6	N C Johnson	12	18	5	819	150	63.00
7	G P Thorpe	14	23	4	1160	222	61.05
8	M T G Elliott	12	19	0	1091	199	57.42
9	S G Law	17	28	2	1482	175	57.00
10	M R Ramprakash	19	30	4	1453	190	55.88

Bowling

		Overs	M	Runs	W	Av	Best
1	A A Donald	387.5	123	938	60	15.63	6-55
2	A M Smith	512.2	125	1464	83	17.63	6-45
3	P R Reiffel	188.4	49	520	28	18.57	5-49
4	K D James	161.1	37	504	27	18.66	8-49
5	D R Brown	521.3	135	1560	81	19.25	8-89
6	Saqlain Mushtaq	254.5	75	617	32	19.28	5-17
7	B J Phillips	282.1	73	877	44	19.93	5-47
8	P M Hutchison	233.1	56	741	37	20.02	7-38
9	S K Warne	433.4	112	1154	57	20.24	7-10
10	J H Kallis	234.3	61	655	32	20.46	5-54

CYCLING

TOUR DE FRANCE
Jul 5-27

Stage winners:

P	C Boardman	GBR	Gan	8:20
1	M Cipollini	ITA	Saeco	4:39:59
2	M Cipollini	ITA	Saeco	6:27:47
3	E Zabel	GER	Telekom	4:54:33
4	N Minali	ITA	Batik	5:46:42
5	C Vasseur	FRA	Gan	6:16:44
6	J Blijlevens	NED	TVM	5:58:09
7	E Zabel	GER	Telekom	4:11:15
8	E Zabel	GER	Telekom	3:22:42
9	L Brochard	FRA	Festina	5:24:57
10	J Ullrich	GER	Telekom	7:46:06
11	L Desbiens	FRA	Cofidis	5:05:05
12	J Ullrich	GER	Telekom	1:16:24
13	M Pantani	ITA	Mercatone	5:02:42
14	R Virenque	FRA	Festina	4:34:16
15	M Pantani	ITA	Mercatone	5:57:16
16	C Mengin	FRA	FDJ	4:30:11
17	N Stephens	AUS	Festina	4:54:38
18	D Rous	FRA	Festina	4:24:48
19	M Traversoni	ITA	Mercatone	4:03:43
20	A Olano	SPA	Banesto	1:15:57
21	N Minali	ITA	Batik	3:54:36

Overall Standings

1	J Ullrich	GER	TEL	100h 30m 35s
2	R Virenque	FRA	FES	+ 9:09
3	M Pantani	ITA	MER	+ 14:03
4	A Olano	SPA	BAN	+ 15:55
5	F Escartin	SPA	KEL	+ 20:32
6	F Casagrande	ITA	SAE	+ 22:47
7	B Riis	DEN	TEL	+ 26:34
8	J-M Jiminez	SPA	BA	+ 31:17
9	L Dufaux	SUI	FES	+ 31:55
10	R Conti	ITA	MER	+ 32:26

Teams:

1	Telekom	301:51:30
2	Mercatone Uno	+ 31:56
3	Festina	+ 47.52

WORLD CHAMPIONSHIPS
Oct 8 - 12 San Sebastian

Time Trials

Men **(42.6km)**
1 L Jalabert FRA 52:01

Women **(28km)**
1 J Longo FRA 39:15

Road Races

Men **(256.5km)**
1 L Brochard FRA 6:16:48

Women **(108km)**
1 A Cappellotto ITA 2:44:37

EQUESTRIANISM

BADMINTON THREE-DAY EVENT
May 8-11

Mitsubishi Trophy
Final leading placings
1 Custom Made 49.25 D O'Connor USA
2 Star Appeal 55.00 M King GBR
3 Cosmopolitan II 55.60 W Fox-Pitt GBR

ROYAL INTERNATIONAL HORSE SHOW
Jul 10-13 Hickstead

Hickstead Chase
1 Carat G Goosen GBR
2 Edgar H Engemann GER
3 Virtual Village Ashley M Whitaker GBR

July Stakes
1 T'Aime P Charles IRE
2 Elco M Hecart FRA
3 Pinon Voice J Fisher GBR

Grand Prix
1 Virtual Village Ashely M Whitaker GBR
2 T'Aime P Charles IRE
3 Virtual Village Tinka's Boy N Skelton GBR

Speed Challenge
1 LBH Fedor P Geerink NED
2 Virtual Village Hunters Level M Whitaker GBR
3 Convent Hill Diamond R Splaine IRE

UPS Speed Classic
1 Convent Hill Diamond R Splaine IRE
2 Blue Bayu P Charles IRE
3 Virtual Village Hunters Level J Whitaker GBR

Sussex Stakes
1 LBH Fedor P Geerink NED
2 Cat Balou H Engemann GER
3 Shurlands Viking D Charles GBR

King George V Gold Cup
1 Virtual Village Welham J Whitaker GBR
2 Carthago J Lanski NED
3 Virtual Village It's Otto G Billington GBR

Queen Elizabeth II Cup
1 Grafton Magna L Bevan GBR
2 Pipakie J Annett GBR
3 Ferdinand H Weinberg GER

Dressage Grand Prix
1 Legal Democrat C Hester GBR
2 Commanche M Barisone USA
3 Flim Flam S Binks USA

EUROPEAN OPEN THREE-DAY EVENT
Sept 12-13 Burghley

Pedigree Chum European Open Championship

Individual
1 Broadcast News M Todd NZL
2 Watermill Stream B Overesch-Boker GER
3 Cosmopolitan II W Fox-Pitt GBR

Teams
1 Great Britain
2 New Zealand
3 Sweden

EUROPEAN CHAMPIONSHIP
(held in conjunction with the Open Three Day Event)

Individual
1 Watermill Stream B Overesch-Boker GER
2 Cosmopolitan II W Fox-Pitt GBR
3 General Jock T Gifford GBR

Teams
1 Great Britain
2 Sweden
3 France

HORSE OF THE YEAR SHOW
Sept 24-28 Wembley

Daewoo Series Championship Final
1 Moneymore C Edwards GBR
2 Eldorado V Whitaker GBR
3 Virtual Village Magic Carpet M Whitaker GBR

Martin Collins Leading Showjumper of the Year
1 Virtual Village Heyman J Whitaker GBR
2 Virtual Village Zalza N Skelton GBR
3 Virtual Village It's Otto G Billington GBR

Porterbrook Venue of Legends
1 Virtual Village Silk M Whitaker GBR
2 Virtual Village Zalza N Skelton GBR
3 Desire E Castellini ITA

FOOTBALL

1996/97 SEASON FINAL LEAGUE TABLES

FA Carling Premier League:

		P	W	D	L	F	A	Pts
1	Man Utd	38	21	12	5	76	44	75
2	Newcastle	38	19	11	8	73	40	68
3	Arsenal	38	19	11	8	62	32	68
4	Liverpool	38	19	11	8	62	37	68
5	Aston Villa	38	17	10	11	47	34	61
6	Chelsea	38	16	11	11	58	55	59
7	Sheff Wed	38	14	15	9	50	51	57
8	Wimbledon	38	15	11	12	49	46	56
9	Leicester	38	12	11	15	46	54	47
10	Tottenham	38	13	7	18	44	51	46
11	Leeds	38	11	13	14	28	38	46
12	Derby	38	11	13	14	45	58	46
13	Blackburn	38	9	15	14	42	43	42
14	West Ham	38	10	12	16	39	48	42
15	Everton	38	10	12	16	44	57	42
16	Southampton	38	10	11	17	50	56	41
17	Coventry	38	9	14	15	38	54	41
18	Sunderland	38	10	10	18	35	53	40
19	Middlesbrough	38	10	12	16	51	60	39
20	Nottm Forest	38	6	16	16	31	59	34

Nationwide League Division One:

		P	W	D	L	F	A	Pts
1	Bolton	46	28	14	4	100	53	98
2	Barnsley	46	22	14	10	76	55	80
3	Wolves	46	22	10	14	68	51	76
4	Ipswich	46	20	14	12	68	50	74
5	Sheff Utd	46	20	13	13	75	52	73
6	Crystal Palace	46	19	14	13	78	48	71
7	Portsmouth	46	20	8	18	59	53	68

		P	W	D	L	F	A	Pts
8	Port Vale	46	17	16	13	58	55	67
9	QPR	46	18	12	16	64	60	66
10	Birmingham	46	17	15	14	52	48	66
11	Tranmere	46	17	14	15	63	56	65
12	Stoke	46	18	10	18	51	57	64
13	Norwich	46	17	12	17	63	68	63
14	Man City	46	17	10	19	59	60	61
15	Charlton	46	16	11	19	52	66	59
16	West Brom	46	14	15	17	68	72	57
17	Oxford	46	16	9	21	64	68	57
18	Reading	46	15	12	19	58	67	57
19	Swindon	46	15	9	22	52	71	54
20	Huddersfield	46	13	15	18	48	61	54
21	Bradford	46	12	12	22	47	72	48
22	Grimsby	46	11	13	22	60	81	46
23	Oldham	46	10	13	23	51	66	43
24	Southend	46	8	15	23	42	86	39

Nationwide League Division Two:

		P	W	D	L	F	A	Pts
1	Bury	46	24	12	10	62	38	84
2	Stockport	46	23	13	10	59	41	82
3	Luton	46	21	15	10	71	45	78
4	Brentford	46	20	14	12	56	43	74
5	Bristol City	46	21	10	15	69	51	73
6	Crewe	46	22	7	17	56	47	73
7	Blackpool	46	18	15	13	59	47	69
8	Wrexham	46	17	18	11	54	50	69
9	Burnley	46	19	11	16	71	55	68
10	Chesterfield	46	18	14	14	42	39	68
11	Gillingham	46	19	10	17	60	59	67
12	Walsall	46	19	10	17	54	53	67
13	Watford	46	16	19	11	45	38	67
14	Millwall	46	16	13	17	50	54	61
15	Preston	46	18	7	21	49	55	61
16	Bournemouth	46	15	15	16	43	45	60
17	Bristol Rovers	46	15	11	20	47	50	56
18	Wycombe	46	15	10	21	51	56	55
19	Plymouth	46	12	18	16	47	58	54
20	York	46	13	13	20	47	68	52
21	Peterborough	46	11	14	21	55	73	47
22	Shrewsbury	46	11	13	22	49	74	46
23	Rotherham	46	7	14	25	39	70	35
24	Notts County	46	7	14	25	33	59	35

Nationwide League Division Three:

		P	W	D	L	F	A	Pts
1	Wigan	46	26	9	11	84	51	87
2	Fulham	46	25	12	9	72	38	87
3	Carlisle	46	24	12	10	67	44	84
4	Northampton	46	20	12	14	67	44	72
5	Swansea	46	21	8	17	62	58	71
6	Chester	46	18	16	12	55	43	70
7	Cardiff	46	20	9	17	56	54	69
8	Colchester	46	17	17	12	62	51	68
9	Lincoln	46	18	12	16	70	69	66
10	Cambridge	46	18	11	17	53	59	65
11	Mansfield	46	16	16	14	47	45	64
12	Scarborough	46	16	15	15	65	68	63
13	Scunthorpe	46	18	9	19	59	62	63
14	Rochdale	46	14	16	16	58	58	58
15	Barnet	46	14	16	16	46	51	58
16	Leyton Orient	46	15	12	19	50	58	57
17	Hull City	46	13	18	15	44	50	57
18	Darlington	46	14	10	22	64	78	52
19	Doncaster	46	14	10	22	52	66	52
20	Hartlepool	46	14	9	23	53	66	51
21	Torquay	46	13	11	22	46	62	50
22	Exeter	46	12	12	22	48	73	48
23	Brighton	46	13	10	23	53	70	47
24	Hereford	46	11	14	21	50	65	47

Bell's Scottish Premier Division:

		P	W	D	L	F	A	Pts
1	Rangers	36	25	5	6	85	33	80
2	Celtic	36	23	6	7	78	32	75
3	Dundee Utd	36	17	9	10	46	33	60
4	Hearts	36	14	10	12	46	43	52
5	Dunfermline	36	12	9	15	52	65	45
6	Aberdeen	36	10	14	12	45	54	44
7	Kilmarnock	36	11	6	19	41	61	39
8	Motherwell	36	9	11	16	44	55	38
9	Hibernian	36	9	11	16	38	55	38
10	Raith	36	6	7	23	29	73	25

Bell's Scottish First Division:

		P	W	D	L	F	A	Pts
1	St Johnstone	36	24	8	4	74	23	80
2	Airdrie	36	15	15	6	56	34	60
3	Dundee	36	15	13	8	47	33	58
4	St Mirren	36	17	7	12	48	41	58
5	Falkirk	36	15	9	12	42	39	54
6	Partick	36	12	12	12	49	48	48
7	Stirling	36	12	10	14	54	61	46
8	G Morton	36	12	9	15	42	41	45
9	Clydebank	36	7	7	22	31	59	28
10	East Fife	36	2	8	26	28	92	14

COCA-COLA CUP FINAL
6 Apr — Wembley
Middlesbrough (0) 1 — Leicester City (0) 1
Heskey 118 — Ravanelli 95
after extra time

COCA-COLA CUP FINAL REPLAY
16 Apr — Hillsborough
Leicester City (0) 1 — Middlebrough (0) 0
Claridge 100

UEFA CUP FINAL FIRST LEG
7 May — Gelsenkirchen
Schalke (0) 1 — Internazionale (0) 0
Wilmots 71

UEFA CUP FINAL SECOND LEG
21 May — San Siro, Milan
Internazionale (0) 1 — Schalke (0) 0
Zamorano 84
Schalke won 4-1 on penalties

EUROPEAN CUP-WINNERS' CUP FINAL
14 May — Rotterdam
Barcelona (1) 1 — Paris St Germain (0) 0
Ronaldo 38 (pen)

FA CUP FINAL
17 May — Wembley
Chelsea (1) 2 — Middlesbrough (0) 0
di Matteo 1
Newton 82

SCOTTISH FA CUP FINAL
24 May — Ibrox
Kilmarnock (1) 1 — Falkirk (0) 0
Wright 20

EUROPEAN CHAMPIONS' CUP FINAL
28 May — Munich
Borussia Dortmund (2) 3 — Juventus (0) 1
Riedle 29, 34 — Del Piero 64
Ricken 71

TOURNOI DE FRANCE
4 Jun — Nantes
Italy (0) 0 — England (2) 2
Wright, I 26
Scholes 43

7 Jun — Montpellier
France (0) 0 — England (0) 1
Shearer 86

10 Jun — Parc des Princes, Paris
England (0) 0 — Brazil (0) 1
Romario 60

FA CHARITY SHIELD
3 Aug — Wembley
Chelsea (0) 1 — Manchester United (0) 1
Hughes, M 52 — Johnsen 58

OTHER INTERNATIONALS
22 Jan — Palermo
Italy (1) 2 — Northern Ireland (0) 0
Zola 8
Del Piero 88
11 Feb — Windsor Park
Northern Ireland (1) 3 — Belgium (0) 0
Quinn 14
Magilton 62 (pen)
Mulryne 88
11 Feb — Cardiff
Wales (0) 0 — Rep of Ireland (0) 0
29 Mar — Wembley
England (1) 2 — Mexico (0) 0
Sheringham 20 (pen)
Fowler 55
24 May — Old Trafford
England (1) 2 — South Africa (1) 1
Lee 21 — Masinga 43
Wright, I 75
27 May — Rugby Park
Scotland (0) 0 — Wales (0) 1
Hartson 46

1 Jun — Valletta
Malta (1) 2 — Scotland (2) 3
Suda 17 — Dailly 4
Sultana 57 — Jackson 44, 81

WORLD CUP QUALIFYING

Groups involving UK and Republic of Ireland

Group Two
Moldova (0) 0 — England (2) 3
Barmby 24, Gascoigne 25
Shearer 61

Moldova (1) 1 — Italy (1) 3
England (2) 2 — Poland (1) 1
Shearer 25, 37 — Citko 6
Italy (1) 1 — Georgia (0) 0
Georgia (0) 0 — England (2) 2
Sheringham 15
Ferdinand 37

Poland (1) 2 — Moldova (0) 1
England (0) 0 — Italy (1) 1
Zola 18

Italy (2) 3 — Moldova (0) 0
Poland (0) 0 — Italy (0) 0
England (1) 2 — Georgia (0) 0
Sheringham 43
Shearer 90
Italy (2) 3 — Poland (0) 0
Poland (0) 0 — England (1) 2
Shearer 5
Sheringham 90

Georgia (1) 2 — Moldova (0) 0
Poland (2) 4 — Georgia (1) 1
England (1) 4 — Moldova (0) 0
Scholes 29
Wright, I 46, 90
Gascoigne 81
Georgia (0) 0 — Italy (0) 0
Moldova (0) 0 — Georgia (1) 1
Moldova (0) 0 — Poland (1) 3
Italy (0) 0 — England (0) 0
Georgia (0) 3 — Poland (0) 0

Group Two final table:

	P	W	D	L	F	A	Pts
England	8	6	1	1	15	2	19
Italy	8	5	3	0	11	1	18
Poland	8	3	1	4	10	12	10
Georgia	8	3	1	4	7	9	10
Moldova	8	0	0	8	2	21	0

Group Four
Sweden (2) 5 — Belarus (0) 1
Austria (0) 0 — Scotland (0) 0
Belarus (0) 1 — Estonia (0) 0
Latvia (0) 1 — Sweden (2) 2
Latvia (0) 0 — Scotland (1) 2
Collins 18
Jackson 78

Estonia (0) 1 — Belarus (0) 0
Sweden (0) 0 — Austria (1) 1
Belarus (0) 1 — Latvia (1) 1
Austria (1) 2 — Latvia (1) 1
Scotland (1) 1 — Sweden (0) 0
McGinlay 8
Estonia (0) 0 — Scotland (0) 0
Scotland (1) 2 — Estonia (0) 0
Boyd 25
Meet 51 (og)
Scotland (1) 2 — Austria (0) 0
Gallacher 24, 78
Sweden (1) 2 — Scotland (0) 1
Andersson, K 43, 69
Gallacher 83

Latvia (1) 2 — Belarus (0) 0
Austria (0) 2 — Estonia (0) 0
Estonia (1) 1 — Latvia (0) 3
Belarus (0) 0 — Scotland (0) 1
McAllister, G 49 (pen)

Latvia (0) 1 — Austria (0) 3
Estonia (0) 2 — Sweden (1) 3
Belarus (1) 1 — Sweden (0) 2
Estonia (0) 0 — Austria (0) 3
Latvia (0) 1 — Estonia (0) 0
Austria (0) 1 — Sweden (0) 0
Scotland (1) 4 — Belarus (0) 1
Gallacher 5, 58
Kachuro 75 (pen)
Hopkin 55, 87
Belarus (0) 0 — Austria (0) 1
Sweden (0) 1 — Latvia (0) 0
Scotland (1) 2 — Latvia (0) 0
Gallacher 43
Durie 79
Austria (4) 4 — Belarus (0) 0
Sweden (1) 1 — Estonia (0) 0

Group Four final table:

	P	W	D	L	F	A	Pts
Austria	10	8	1	1	17	4	25
Scotland	10	7	2	1	15	3	23
Sweden	10	7	0	3	16	9	21
Latvia	10	3	1	6	10	14	10
Estonia	10	1	1	8	4	16	4
Belarus	10	1	1	8	5	21	4

Group 7
San Marino (0) 0 — Wales (3) 5
Melville 20
Hughes 32, 43
Giggs 50
Pembridge 85
Wales (4) 6 — San Marino (0) 0
Saunders 1, 78
Hughes 24, 56
Melville 33
Robinson 44
Belgium (2) 2 — Turkey (0) 1
Wales (1) 1 — Holland (0) 3
Saunders 17 — van Hooijdonk 72, 75
de Boer, R 79

San Marino (0) 0 — Belgium (2) 3
Holland (4) 7 — Wales (1) 1
Bergkamp 22, 72, 78 — Saunders 40
de Boer, R 33
Jonk 34, de Boer, F 45
Cocu 61

Turkey (2) 7 — San Marino (0) 0
Wales (0) 0 — Turkey (0) 0
Belgium (0) 0 — Holland (2) 3
Wales (0) 1 — Belgium (2) 2
Speed 68 — Crassen 24
Staelens 44

Holland (1) 4 — San Marino (0) 0
Turkey (0) 1 — Holland (0) 0
Turkey (1) 1 — Belgium (3) 3
San Marino (0) 0 — Holland (1) 6
Belgium (5) 6 — San Marino (0) 0
Turkey (3) 6 — Wales (3) 4
Hakan 5, 36, 76, 82 — Blake 17
Saffet 8 — Savage 20
Oguz 60 — Saunders 32
Melville 52

Holland (1) 3 — Belgium (0) 1
San Marino (0) 0 — Turkey (2) 5
Belgium (3) 3 — Wales (0) 2
Staelens 4 (pen) — Pembridge 52 (pen)
Claessons 32 — Giggs 60
Wilmots 39
Holland (0) 0 — Turkey (0) 0

Group Seven final table:

	P	W	D	L	F	A	Pts
Holland	8	6	1	1	26	4	19
Belgium	8	6	0	2	20	11	18
Turkey	8	4	2	2	21	9	14
Wales	8	2	1	5	20	21	7
San Marino	8	0	0	8	0	42	0

Group Eight
Macedonia (1) 3 — Liechtenstein (0) 0
Iceland (0) 1 — Macedonia (0) 1
Liechtenstein (0) 0 — Rep of Ireland (4) 5
Townsend 5
O'Neill 9
Quinn 12, 61
Harte 20
Romania (1) 3 — Lithuania (0) 0
Lithuania (1) 2 — Iceland (0) 0
Rep of Ireland (1) 3 — Macedonia (0) 0
McAteer 8
Cascarino 46, 70
Lithuania (1) 2 — Liechtenstein (0) 1
Iceland (0) 0 — Romania (1) 4
Liechtenstein (0) 1 — Macedonia (6) 11
Rep of Ireland (0) 0 — Iceland (0) 0
Macedonia (0) 0 — Romania (2) 3
Romania (4) 8 — Liechtenstein (0) 0
Macedonia (2) 3 — Rep of Ireland (1) 2
Stojkovski 28(pen), — McLoughlin 8
44(pen), Hristov 59 — Kelly, D 78
Lithuania (0) 0 — Romania (0) 1
Romania (1) 1 — Rep of Ireland (0) 0
Ilie A 32
Liechtenstein (0) 0 — Lithuania (0) 2
Rep of Ireland (3) 5 — Liechtenstein (0) 0
Connolly 29, 34, 40
Cascarino 60, 77
Macedonia (0) 1 — Iceland (0) 0
Iceland (0) 0 — Lithuania (0) 0
Rep of Ireland (0) 0 — Lithuania (0) 0
Liechtenstein (0) 0 — Iceland (2) 4
Romania (2) 4 — Macedonia (0) 2
Iceland (1) 2 — Rep of Ireland (1) 4
Gunnarsson 45 — Connelly 13, Keane 54, 64
H Sigurdsson 47 — Finnbogason (og) 79
Liechtenstein (0) 1 — Romania (6) 8
Lithuania (1) 2 — Macedonia (0) 0
Lithuania (0) 1 — Rep of Ireland (1) 2
Zlukas 52 — Cascarino 17, 71
Romania (2) 4 — Iceland (0) 0
Rep of Ireland (0) 1 — Romania (0) 1
Cascarino 84 — Hagi 53
Iceland (0) 4 — Liechtenstein (0) 0
Macedonia (1) 1 — Lithuania (0) 2

Group Eight final table:

	P	W	D	L	F	A	Pts
Romania	10	9	1	0	37	4	28
Rep of Ireland	10	5	3	2	22	8	18
Lithuania	10	5	2	3	11	8	17
FYR Macedonia	10	4	1	5	22	18	13
Iceland	10	2	3	5	11	16	9
Liechtenstein	10	0	0	10	3	52	0

Group Nine
N Ireland (0) 0 — Ukraine (0) 1
Rebrov79
Armenia (0) 0 — Portugal (0) 0
N Ireland (1) 1 — Armenia (1) 1
Lennon 29
Ukraine (1) 2 — Portugal (0) 1
Armenia (0) 0 — Germany (3) 5
Albania (0) 0 — Portugal (1) 3
Germany (1) 1 — N Ireland (1) 1
Moller 41 — Taggart 39
Albania (0) 1 — Armenia (0) 1
Portugal (0) 1 — Ukraine (0) 0
N Ireland (2) 2 — Albania (0) 0
Dowie 12, 21

Portugal (0) 0 Germany (0) 0
N Ireland (0) 0 Portugal (0) 0
Albania (0) 0 Ukraine (1) 1
Ukraine (1) 2 N Ireland 1) 1
Kossovski V 2 Dowie 14 pen
Shevchenko 70
Albania (0) 2 Germany (0) 3
Armenia (0) 0 N Ireland (0) 0
Germany (0) 2 Ukraine (0) 0
Ukraine (1) 1 Armenia (0) 1
Ukraine (0) 0 Germany (0) 0
Portugal (1) 2 Albania (0) 0
N Ireland (0) 1 Germany (0) 3
Hughes 59 Bierhoff 73, 77, 79
Portugal (2) 3 Armenia (0) 1
Ukraine (0) 1 Albania (0) 0
Armenia (0) 3 Albania (0) 0
Germany (0) 1 Portugal (0) 1
Albania (0) 1 N Ireland (0) 0
Haxhi 69
Germany (0) 4 Armenia (0) 0
Portugal (1) 1 N Ireland (0) 0
Conceicao 17
Germany (0) 4 Albania (0) 3
Armenia (0) 0 Ukraine (1) 2

Group Nine final table:

	P	W	D	L	F	A	Pts
Germany	10	6	4	0	23	9	22
Ukraine	10	6	2	2	10	6	20
Portugal	10	5	4	1	12	4	19
Armenia	10	1	5	4	8	17	8
N Ireland	10	1	5	4	6	10	7
Albania	10	1	1	8	7	20	4

GOLF

MAJORS

US MASTERS
Apr 10-13 Auga National, Georgia

Leading final scores:
270 T Woods USA 70 66 65 69
282 T Kite USA 77 69 66 70
283 T Tolles USA 72 72 72 67
284 T Watson USA 75 68 69 72
285 P Stankowski USA 68 74 69 74
C Rocca ITA 71 69 70 74
286 B Langer GER 72 72 74 68
J Leonard USA 76 69 71 70
D Love III USA 72 71 72 71
F Couples USA 72 69 73 72
J Sluman USA 74 67 72 73
287 S Elkington AUS 76 72 72 67
W Wood USA 72 76 71 68
P-U Johansson SWE 72 73 73 69
T Lehman USA 73 76 69 69
J M Olazabal SPA 71 70 74 72
288 M Calcavecchia USA 74 73 72 69
V Singh FIJ 75 74 69 70
F Funk USA 73 74 69 72
E Els RSA 73 70 71 74

US OPEN CHAMPIONSHIP
Jun 12-15 Congressional, Washington

Leading final scores:
276 E Els RSA 71 67 69 69
277 C Montgomerie GBR 65 76 67 69
278 T Lehman USA 67 70 68 73
281 J Maggert USA 73 66 68 74
282 J Furyk USA 74 68 69 71
O Browne USA 71 71 69 71
B Tway USA 71 71 70 70
T Tolles USA 74 67 69 72
J Haas USA 73 69 68 72
283 S McCarron USA 73 71 69 70
S Hoch USA 71 68 72 72
D Ogrin USA 70 69 71 73
284 L Roberts USA 72 69 72 71
S Cink USA 71 67 74 72
B Andrade USA 75 67 69 73
285 D Love III USA 75 70 69 71
J M Olazabal SPA 71 72 71 71
B Hughes AUS 75 70 71 69
286 P Stankowski USA 75 70 68 73
H Sutton USA 66 73 73 74
T Woods USA 74 67 73 72
N Price ZIM 71 74 71 70
L Westwood GBR 71 71 73 71

THE OPEN CHAMPIONSHIP
Jul 17-20 Royal Troon

Leading final scores:
272 J Leonard USA 69 66 72 65
275 D Clarke GBR 67 66 71 71
J Parnevik SWE 70 66 66 73
279 J Furyk USA 67 72 70 70
280 P Harrington IRE 75 69 69 67
S Ames TRI 74 69 66 71
281 P O'Malley AUS 73 70 70 68
E Romero ARG 74 68 67 72
F Couples USA 69 68 70 74
282 D Love III USA 70 71 74 67
R Goosen RSA 75 69 70 68
F Nobilo NZE 74 72 68 68
T Kite USA 72 67 74 69
M Calcavecchia USA 74 67 72 69
S Maruyama JAP 74 69 70 69
E Els RSA 75 69 69 69
T Watson USA 71 70 70 71
R Allenby AUS 76 68 66 72
L Westwood GBR 73 70 67 72
283 J-M Olazabal SPA 75 68 73 67
B Faxon USA 77 67 72 67
M James GBR 76 67 70 70
284 T Lehmann USA 74 72 72 66
D A Russell GBR 75 72 68 69
J Haas USA 71 70 73 70
C Montgomerie GBR 76 69 69 70
P Mickleson USA 76 68 69 71
I Woosnam GBR 71 73 69 71
T Woods USA 72 74 64 74
P Lonard AUS 72 70 69 73

US PGA CHAMPIONSHIP
Aug 14-17 Winged Foot, New York

Leading final scores:
269 D Love III USA 66 71 66 66
274 J Leonard USA 68 70 65 71
276 J Maggert USA 69 69 73 65
279 L Janzen USA 69 67 74 69
280 T Kite USA 68 71 71 70
281 J Furyk USA 69 72 72 68
P Blackmar USA 70 68 74 69
S Hoch USA 71 72 68 70
282 T Byrom USA 69 73 70 70
283 J Sindelar USA 72 71 71 69
T Lehman USA 69 72 72 70
S McCarron USA 74 71 67 71
284 D Duval USA 70 70 71 73
T Tolles USA 75 70 73 66
M O'Meara USA 69 73 75 67
V Singh FIJ 73 66 76 69
N Price ZIM 72 70 72 70
K Triplett USA 73 70 71 70
G Norman AUS 68 71 74 71
T Herron USA 72 73 68 71
C Montgomerie USA 74 71 67 72

RYDER CUP
Sep 26-28 Valderrama
Europe 14 1/2 beat USA 13 1/2

Day One

Fourballs
J M Olazabal & C Rocca beat
D Love III & P Mickleson 1 hole
N Faldo & L Westwood lost to
F Couples & B Faxon 1 hole
J Parvenik & P-U Johansson beat
T Lehman & F Furyk 1 hole
C Montgomerie & B Langer Lost to
T Woods & M O'Meara 3 & 2

Foursomes
J M Olazabal & C Rocca ;ost to
S Hoch & L Janzen 1 hole
B Langer & C Montgomerie beat
T Woods & M O'Meara 5 & 3
N Faldo & L Westwood beat
J Leonard & J Maggert 3 & 2
I Garrido & J Parvenik halved with
P Micklelson & T Lehman
Day One score: Europe 4 1/2 USA 3 1/2

Day Two

Fourballs
C Montgomerie & D Clarke beat
F Couples & D Love III 1 hole
I Woosnam & T Bjorn beat
J Leonard & B Faxon 2 & 1
N Faldo & L Westwood beat
T Woods & M O'Meara 2 & 1
J M Olazabal & I Garrido halved with
P Mickelson & T Lehman

Foursomes
C Montgomerie & B Langer beat
L Janzen & J Furyk 1 hole
N Faldo & L Westwood lost to
S Hoch & J Maggert 2 & 1
J Parvenik & I Garrido halved with
T Woods & J Leonard
J M Olazabal & C Rocca beat
F Couples & D Love III 5 & 4
Day Two score: Europe 6 USA 2

Day Three

Singles
I Woosnam lost to F Couples 8 & 7
P-U Johansson beat D Love III 3 & 2
C Rocca beat T Woods 4 & 2
T Bjorn halved with J Leonard
D Clarke lost to P Mickleson 2 & 1
J Parvenik lost to M O'Meara 5 & 4
J M Olazabal lost to L Janzen 1 hole
B Langer beat B Faxon 2 & 1
L Westwood lost to J Maggert 3 & 2
C Montgomerie halved with S Hoch
N Faldo lost to J Furyk 3 & 2
I Garrido lost to T Lehman 7 & 6
Day Three score: Europe 4 USA 8

Overall result:

EUROPE 14 1/2
USA 13 1/2

Captains:
Europe: S Ballesteros
USA: T Kite

Individual points:

Europe

Name	Matches	Points
C Montgomerie	5	3 1/2
B Langer	4	3
C Rocca	4	3
J-M Olazabal	5	2 1/2
P-U Johansson	2	2
N Faldo	5	2
L Westwood	5	2
J Parvenik	4	2
T Bjorn	2	1 1/2
I Garrido	4	1 1/2
D Clarke	2	1
I Woosnam	2	1

USA

Name	Matches	Points
S Hoch	3	2 1/2
L Janzen	3	2
J Maggert	3	2
F Couples	4	2
T Lehman	4	2
P Mickleson	4	2
M O'Meara	4	2
T Woods	5	1 1/2
J Leonard	4	1
B Faxon	3	1
J Furyk	3	1
D Love III	4	0

EUROPEAN PGA TOUR

Johnnie Walker Classic
Jan 23-26 Queensland
278 E Els RSA ... 70 68 71 69

Heineken Classic
Jan 30-Feb 2 Perth
273 M A Martin SPS ... 70 67 65 71

South African Open
Feb 6-9 Johannesburg
270 Vijay Singh FIJ 69 66 66 69

Dimension Data Pro-Am
Feb 13-16 Sun City
268 N Price ZIM 67 66 66 69

Alfred Dunhill PGA
Feb 20-23 Johannesburg
269 Nick Price ZIM 67 66 70 66
David Frost RSA 69 63 66 71

Dubai Desert Classic
Feb 27-Mar 2 Dubai
272 Richard Green AUS 70 68 66 68
G Norman AUS 71 68 67 66
I Woosnam GBR 69 67 67 69
(Green won play-off at first extra hole)

Moroccan Open
Mar 6-9 Agadir
277 C Whitelaw RSA 68 71 69 69

Portuguese Open
Mar 13-16 Lisbon
269 Michael Jonzon SWE 67 65 68 69

Turespana Masters
Mar 20-23 Las Palomas
272 J-M Olazabal SPA 70 67 68 67

Madeira Island Open
Mar 27-29 Madeira
204 P Mitchell GBR 70 63 71

Cannes Open
Apr 17-20 Cannes
270 S Cage GBR 68 67 69 66

Spanish Open
Apr 24-27 Madrid
277 M James GBR 67 68 73 69
G Norman AUS 69 70 68 70
(James won at third play-off hole)

Italian Open
May 1-4 Brescia
273 B Langer GER 71 69 69 64

Benson and Hedges International Open
May 8-11 Thame
276 B Langer GER 70 66 71 69

Alamo English Open
May 15-18 Hanbury Manor
269 P-U Johansson SWE 70 68 64 67

Volvo PGA Championship
May 23-25 Wentworth
275 I Woosnam GBR 67 68 70 70

Deutsche Bank Open
May 29-Jun 1 Hamburg
282 R McFarlane GBR 70 73 68 71

Compaq European Grand Prix
Jun 5-8 Slaley Hall, Northumberland
270 C Montgomerie GBR 69 68 68 65

German Open
Jun 19-22 Stuttgart
271 I Garrido SPA 65 67 67 72

Peugeot French Open
Jun 26-29 Paris
271 R Goosen RSA 64 67 70 70

Irish Open
Jul 3-6 Druid's Glen
269 C Montgomerie GBR 68 70 69 62

Gulfstream World Invitational
Jul 10-13 Loch Lomond
265 T Lehman USA 65 66 67 67

Holland Open
Jul 24-27 Hilversum
266 S Struver GER 67 64 69 66

Volvo Scandinavian Masters
Jul 31-Aug 3 Malmo
270 J Haeggman SWE 67 69 65 69

Czech Open
Aug 7-10 Prague
264 B Langer GER 70 67 64 63

Smurfit European Open
Aug 21-24 County Kildare
267 P-U Johansson SWE 68 64 66 69

BMW International Open
Aug 28-31 Munich
264 R Karlsson SWE 67 67 64 66
Carl Watts GBR 64 68 67 65
(Karlsson won play-off at third extra hole)

European Open
Sep 4-7 Crans-sur-Sierre
266 C Rocca ITA 72 64 68 62

Lancome Trophy
Sep 11-14 Saint-Nom-la Breteche
271 M O'Meara USA 69 67 66 69

One 2 One British Masters
Sep 18-21 Forest of Ardern
275 G Turner NZL 68 71 66 70

Linde German Masters
Oct 2-5 Berlin
267 B Langer GER 68 69 60 70

Oki Pro-Am
Oct 23-26 Madrid
266 P McGinley GBR 66 67 64 69

Volvo Masters
Oct 30-Nov 2 Jerez, Spain
200 L Westwood GBR 65 67 68

1997 European Order of Merit:

1	C Montgomerie	GBR	£798,947
2	B Langer	GER	£692,398
3	L Westwood	GBR	£588,718
4	D Clarke	GBR	£537,409
5	I Woosnam	GBR	£503,562
6	I Garrido	SPA	£411,479
7	R Goosen	RSA	£394,597
8	P Harrington	IRE	£388,982
9	J M Olazabal	SPA	£385,648
10	R Karlsson	SWE	£364,542
11	P-U Johansson	SWE	£354,580
12	C Rocca	ITA	£315,077
13	E Romero	ARG	£290,469
14	M James	GRB	£271,510

15	T Bjorn	DEN	£264,938
16	R Russell	GBR	£250,633
17	P Sjoland	SWE	£245,274
18	G Turner	NZL	£239,869
19	J Haeggman	SWE	£228,479
20	R Claydon	GBR	£225,005

Facts and figures on the 1997 European Tour:

Lowest round:
60 (-12) B Langer (Linde German Masters)
Lowest total:
264 (-24) R Karlsson (BMW International), C Watts (BMW International)
Biggest win:
8 shots by N Price (Dimension Data Pro-am)
Most wins:
4 B Langer (Italian Open, Benson and Hedges International, Czech Open, German Masters)
Low 1st 18:
61 (-10) G Orr (Canon European Masters)
Low 1st 36:
128 (-14) S Henderson (Canon European Masters)
Low 1st 54:
197 (-19) P McGinley (Oki Pro-Am), B Langer (Linde German Masters), 197 (-16) I Garrido (Chemapol Trophy Czech Open)
Highest winning score:
282 (-6) R McFarlane (Deutsche Bank Open-TPC of Europe)
Lowest start by winner:
64 (-8) R Goosen (Peugeot French Open)
Highest start by winner:
72 (+1) C Rocca (Canon European Masters)
Lowest finish by winner:
62 (-9) C Montgomerie (Murphy's Irish Open), C Rocca (Canon European Masters)
Highest finish by winner:
72 (+1) I Garrido (Volvo German Open)
Most under par:
-177 C Montgomerie (325 birdies, 13 eagles)
Lowest cut:
139 (-5) BMW International, Canon European Masters
Highest cut:
147 (+5) Cannes Open, Open championship, 147 (+3) Moroccan Open, Volvo PGA, 148 (+4) German Masters
Holes-in-one:
21

1997 US PGA Tour Money List:

1	T Woods	USA	$2,066,833
2	D Duval	USA	$1,885,308
3	D Love III	USA	$1,635,953
4	J Fyryk	USA	$1,619,480
5	J Leonard	USA	$1,587,531
6	S Hoch	USA	$1,393,788
7	G Norman	AUS	$1,345,856
8	S Elkington	AUS	$1,320,411
9	E Els	RSA	$1,243,008
10	B Faxon	USA	$1,233,505
11	P Mickleson	USA	$1,225,390
12	J Parnevik	SWE	$1,217,587
13	M O'Meara	USA	$1,124,560
14	M Calcavecchia	USA	$1,117,365
15	L Roberts	USA	$1,089,140
16	V Singh	FIJ	$1,059,236
17	N Price	ZIM	$1,053,845
18	S Appleby	USA	$1,003,356
19	T Lehman	USA	$960,584
20	S Jones	USA	$959,108

HOCKEY

May 12

HA MEN'S CUP FINAL
Reading 1-2 Teddington

AEWHA WOMEN'S CUP FINAL
Hightown 2-2 Clifton
(Hightown won 4-3 on penalties)

MEN'S NATIONAL LEAGUE

1996-97 Premier Champions: Reading

National League Premier Division

		P	W	D	L	F	A	Pts
1	Reading	22	15	2	5	79	53	47
2	Teddington	22	15	1	6	78	56	46
3	Southgate	22	13	2	7	68	55	41
4	Cannock	22	12	3	7	79	52	39
5	Canterbury	22	10	5	7	65	59	35
6	East Grinstead	22	9	7	6	65	52	34
7	Guildford	22	10	3	9	76	64	33
8	Old Loughtonians	22	10	2	10	59	56	32
9	Houndslow	22	5	6	11	43	65	21
10	Barford Tigers	22	6	2	14	36	70	20
11	Surbiton	22	4	7	11	44	73	19
	Havant	22	2	2	18	36	73	8

WOMEN'S NATIONAL LEAGUE

1996-97 Premier Champions: Slough

National League Premier Division

		P	W	D	L	F	A	Pts
1	Slough	14	11	1	2	41	15	34
2	Ipswich	14	9	3	2	36	17	30
3	Clifton	14	7	4	3	33	20	25
4	Sutton Coldfield	14	4	5	5	26	32	17
5	Doncaster	14	3	4	7	21	28	13
6	Hightown	14	4	1	9	19	38	13
7	Trojans	14	3	3	8	18	29	12
8	Balsam Leicester	14	3	3	8	17	32	12

HORSE RACING

The Ladbroke Hurdle Grade 1
Jan 11 Leopardstown
1 Master Tribe 7-10-4 N Williamson
(Jebel Ali Racing Stables) 18-1 hd 23 ran

Hennessy Cognac Gold Cup Grade 1
Feb 2 Leopardstown
1 Danoli 9-12-0 T P Treacy
(D J O'Neill) 6-1 2L 8 ran

The Smurfit Champion Hurdle Challenge Trophy Grade 1
Mar 1 Cheltenham
1 Make A Stand 6-12-0 A P McCoy
(P A Deal) 7-1 5L 17 ran

The Queen Mother Champion Chase Grade 1
Mar 12 Cheltenham
1 Martha's Son 5-12-0 R Farrant
(Mr P J Hartigan) 9-1 21/2L 17 ran

The Tote Cheltenham Gold Cup Grade 1
Mar 13 Cheltenham
1 Mr Mulligan 4-12-0 A P McCoy
(Michael & Jerry Worcester) 20-1 9L 28 ran

The Sporting Life Doncaster Mile Listed
Mar 20 Doncaster
1 Canyon Creek 4-8-12 L Dettori
(Sheihk Mohammed) 7-2 4L 24 ran

The Jameson Irish Grand National Chase Handicap
Mar 31 Fairyhouse
1 Mudahim 11-10-3 J Titley
(In Touch Racing Club) 13-2 shd 20 ran

The Shadwell Stud Nell Gwyn Stakes Group 3
Apr 15 Newmarket
1 Reunion 3-8-9 R Hills
(Highclere T'bred Racing) 8-1 1L 9 ran

Scottish Grand National H'cap Chase Grade 3
Apr 19 Ayr
1 Belmont King 5-11-10 A P McCoy
(Mrs Billie Bond) 16-1 11/2L 18 ran

The Heineken Gold Cup Grade 1
Apr 23 Punchestown
1 Noyan 7-11-1 N Williamson
(C H McGhie) 13-2 15L 18 ran

The Whitbread Gold Cup Handicap Chase Grade 3
Apr 26 Sandown Park
1 Harwell Lad 5-10-0 Mr R Nutall
(Mr H Wellstead) 14-1 4L 10 ran

The Pertemps 2000 Guineas Stakes Group 1
May 3 Newmarket
1 Entrepreneur 3-9-0 M J Kinane
(Mr M Tabor & Mrs J Magnier) 11-2 3/4L 6 ran

The R L Davison Pretty Polly Stakes Listed
May 4 Newmarket
1 Siyadah 3-8-8 L Dettori
(Godolphin) 10-3F 3/4L 6 ran

The Pertemps 1000 Guineas Stakes Group 1
May 4 Newmarket
1 Sleepytime 3-9-0 K Fallon
(Greenbay Stables Ltd) 5-1 4L 6 ran

The Vodafone Oaks Group 1
Jun 6 Epsom
1 Reams of Verse 3-9-0 K Fallon
(Mr K Abdullah) 5-6F 11/2L 8 ran

The Vodafone Coronation Cup Group 1
Jun6 Epsom
1 **Singspiel** 5-9-0 L Dettori
(Sheihk Mohammed) 5/4F 5L 5 ran

The Vodafone Derby Stakes Group 1
Jun 7 Epsom
1 **Benny The Dip** 3-9-0 W Ryan
(Mr L Knight & Claiborne Farm) 11-1 shd 13 ran

The Queen Anne Stakes Group 2
Jun 17 Royal Ascot
1 Allied Forces 3-9-5 L Dettori
(Godolphin) 10-1 nk 11 ran

The Prince Of Wales Stakes Group 2
Jun 17 Royal Ascot
1 Bosra Sham 3-9-5 K Fallon
(Mr Wafic Said) 4-11F 8L 11 ran

The Coronation Stakes Group 1
Jun 18 Royal Ascot
1 Rebecca Sharp 3-9-0 M Hills
(Mr A E Oppenheimer) 25-1 3/4L 20 ran

The Gold Cup Group 1
Jun 19 Royal Ascot
1 Celeric 4-9-2 Pat Eddery
(Mr Christopher Spence) 11-2 3/4L 9 ran

The King Edward VII Stakes Group 2
Jun 20 Royal Ascot
1 Kingfisher Mill 3-8-8 Pat Eddery
(Lord Howard De Walden) 9-4F 8L 14 ran

The Budweiser Irish Derby Group 1
Jun 29 Curragh
1 Desert King 3-9-0 C Roche
(M Tabor) 11-2 1L 10 ran

The Kildangen Stud Irish Oaks Group 1
Jul 13 Curragh
1 Ebadiyla 3-9-0 J P Murtagh
(H H Aga Khan) 9-2 3L 11 ran

The King George VI & Queen Elizabeth Diamond Stakes Group 1
Jul 26 Ascot
1 Swain 3-9-7 J Reid
(Godolphin) 16-1 1L 8 ran

The Sussex Stakes Group 1
Jul 30 Goodwood
1 Ali-Royal 3-9-7 K Fallon
(Greenbay Stables Ltd) 13-2 3/4L 12 Ran

The Crowson Goodwood Cup Group 2
Jul 31 Goodwood
1 Double Trigger 3-9-0 M Roberts
(Mr R W Huggins) 16-1 11/2L 8 ran

The Heinz 57 Phoenix Stakes Group 1
Aug 10 Leopardstown
1 Princely Heir 2-9-0 J Weaver
(Maktoum Al Maktoum) 12-1 hd 9 ran

The Tote Ebor Handicap
Aug 20 York
1 Far Ahead 3-8-0 T Williams
(Sunpak Potatoes) 33-1 nk 16 ran

The Pertemps St Leger Stakes Group 1
Sep 13 Doncaster
1 Silver Patriarch 3-9-0 Pat Eddery
(Mr Peter S Winfield) 5-4F 3L 6 ran

The Queen Elizabeth II Stakes Group 1
Sep 27 Ascot
1 Air Express 3-8-11 O Peslier
(Mr Mohamed Obaidah) 9-1 shd 8 ran

The Shadwell Stud Chevely Park Stakes Stakes Group 1
Sep 30 Newmarket
1 Embassy 2-8-11 K Fallon
(Sheikh Mohammed) 5-2 21/2L 15 ran

The Champion Stakes Group 1
Oct 18 Newmarket
1 Pilsudski 3-9-2 M J Kinane
(Lord Weinstock) EvensF 2L 30 ran

Foster's Melbourne Cup Group 1
Nov 4 Flemington, Aus
1 Might And Power (NZ) 4-8-11 J Cassidy
(Mr N Moraltis) 7/2F shd 22 ran

Breeders' Cup Classic Grade 1
Nov 8 Hollywood Park USA
1 Skip Away (USA) 4-9-0 M E Smith
(Mrs C Hine) 18/10F 6L 9 ran

JUDO

WORLD CHAMPIONSHIP
Oct 8-12 Paris

Men's Over 95kg
D Douillet FRA beat S Shinohara JAP
Bronze: Pong Son CHI and T Tmenov RUS

Men's 95kg
P Nastula POL beat A Miguel BRA
Bronze: C Lemaire FRA and I Radu ROM

Men's 86kg
Jeon Ki-young SKO beat M Spitkka GER
Bronze: B Olsen USA and M Monti ITA

Men's 78g
Cho In-chol SKO beat D Bouras FRA
Bronze: P Reiter AUT and Kwak Ok-Choi SKO

Men's 71g
K Nakamura JAP beat C Gagliano FRA
Bronze: G Bentes POR and V Zelenij LAT

Men's 65kg
Kim Hyuk SKO beat L Benboudaoud FRA
Bronze:
G Vazagashvili GEO and V Bivol MOL

Men's 60kg
T Nomura JAP beat G Revazishvili GEO
Bronze: C Taymans BEL and F Miyata BRA

Men's Open
R Kubacki POL beat Y Makishi JAP
Bronze:
D van der Greest NED and H Van Barneveld BEL

Women's Over 72kg
C Cicot FRA beat M Ninomiya JAP
Bronze:
Sun Fuming CHI and B Maksymow POL

Women's 72kg
N Anno JAP beat D Luna CUB
Bronze:
U Werbrouck BEL and E Silva BRA

Women's 66kg
K Howey GBR beat A von Rekowski GER
Bronze:
E Pierantozzi ITA and Cho Min-Sun SKO

Women's 61kg
S Vandenhende FRA beat G Vandecaveye BEL
Bronze: S Alvarez SPA and Jung-Sungsook SKO

Women's 56kg
I Fernandez SPA beat D Gonzales CUB
Bronze: C Tateno JAP and M Baton FRA

Women's 52kg
M C Restoux FRA beat Kye Sun-hui NKO
Bronze:
N Falgothier BEL and Hyun Sook-hee SKO

Women's Open:
D Beltran CUB beat R Barrientos SPA
Bronze: Yuan Hua CHI and M Ninomiya JAP

MOTOR CYCLING

FIM WORLD CHAMPIONSHIP

1997 Grand Prix Final Point Standings

Individual 500cc

1	M Doohan	AUS	Repsol Honda	340
2	T Okada	JAP	Repsol Honda	197
3	N Aoki	JAP	Rheos ELF	179

Team 500cc

1	Honda	375
2	Yamaha	188
3	Suzuki	90

Individual 250cc

1	M Biaggi	ITA	MTK Honda	250
2	R Waldmann	GER	Marlboro Honda	248
3	T Harada	JAP	Aprilia RT	235

Team 250cc

1	Honda	360
2	Aprilia	268
3	TS Honda	109

Individual 125cc

1	V Rossi	ITA	Nastro Aprilia	321
2	N Ueda	JAP	Team Pileri	238
3	T Manako	JAP	Team UGT3000	235

Team 125cc

1	Aprilia	351
2	Honda	287
3	Yamaha	139

SUPERBIKE WORLD CHAMPIONSHIP

1997 Grand Prix Final Point Standings

1	J Kocinski	USA	Honda	416
2	C Fogarty	GBR	Ducati	358
3	A Slight	NZL	Honda	343

Manufacturers

Honda	486
Ducati	440
Kawasaki	359

MOTOR RACING

FIA FORMULA ONE WORLD CHAMPIONSHIP

Australian Grand Prix

Mar 9 — Melbourne

1	D Coulthard	GBR	McLaren	1:30:28.718
2	M Schumacher	GER	Ferrari	1:30:48.764
3	M Hakkinen	FIN	McLaren	1:30:50.895

Brazilian Grand Prix

Mar 30 — Interlagos

1	J Villeneuve	CAN	Williams	1:36:06.990
2	G Berger	AUT	Benetton	1:36:11.180
3	O Panis	FRA	Prost	1:36:22.860

Argentinian Grand Prix

Apr 13 — Buenos Aires

1	J Villeneuve	CAN	Williams	1:52:01.715
2	E Irvine	GBR	Ferrari	1:52:02.694
3	R Schumacher	GER	Jordan	1:52:13.804

San Marino Grand Prix

Apr 27 — Imola

1	H-H Frentzen	GER	Williams	1:31:00.573
2	M Schumacher	GER	Ferrari	1:31:01.910
3	E Irvine	GBR	Ferrari	1:32:19.016

Monaco Grand Prix

May 11 — Monte Carlo

1	M Schumacher	GER	Ferrari	2:00:05.654
2	R Barrichello	BRA	Stewart	2:00:58.960
3	E Irvine	GBR	Ferrari	2:01:27.762

Spanish Grand Prix

May 25 — Barcelona

1	J Villeneuve	CAN	Williams	1:30:35.896
2	O Panis	FRA	Prost	1:30:41.700
3	J Alesi	FRA	Benetton	1:30:481.430

Canadian Grand Prix

Jun 15 — Montreal

1	M Schumacher	GER	Ferrari	1:17:40:646
2	J Alesi	FRA	Benetton	1:17:43.211
3	G Fisichella	ITA	Jordan	1:17:43.865

French Grand Prix

Jun 29 — Magny-Cours

1	M Schumacher	GER	Ferrari	1:38:50.492
2	H-H Frentzen	GER	Williams	1:39:14.029
3	E Irvine	GBR	Ferrari	1:40:05.293

British Grand Prix

Jul 13 — Silverstone

1	J Villeneuve	CAN	Williams	1:28:01.665
2	J Alesi	FRA	Benetton	1:28:11.870
3	A Wurz	AUT	Benetton	1:28:12.961

German Grand Prix

Jul 27 — Hockenheim

1	G Berger	AUT	Benetton	1:20:59.046
2	M Schumacher	GER	Ferrari	1:21:16.573
3	M Hakkinen	FIN	McLaren	1:21:23.816

Hungarian Grand Prix

Aug 10 — Hungaroring

1	J Villeneuve	CAN	Williams	1:45:47.149
2	D Hill	GBR	Arrows	1:45:56.228
3	J Herbert	GBR	Sauber	1:46:07.594

Belgian Grand Prix

Aug 24 — Spa

1	M Schumacher	GER	Ferrari	1:33:46.717
2	G Fisichella	ITA	Jordan	1:34:13.470
3	M Hakkinen	FIN	McLaren	1:34:17.573

Italian Grand Prix

Sep 7 — Monza

1	D Coulthard	GBR	McLaren	1:17:04.609
2	J Alesi	FRA	Benetton	1:17:06.546
3	H-H Frentzen	GER	Williams	1:17:08.952

Austrian Grand Prix

Sep 21 — A1-Ring

1	J Villeneuve	CAN	Williams	1:27:35.999
2	D Coulthard	GBR	McLaren	1:27:38.908
3	H-H Frentzen	GER	Williams	1:27:39.961

Luxembourg Grand Prix

Sep 28 — Nurburgring

1	J Villeneuve	CAN	Williams	1:31:27.843
2	J Alesi	FRA	Benetton	1:31:39.613
3	H-H Frentzen	GER	Williams	1:31:41.323

Japanese Grand Prix

Oct 12 — Suzuka

1	M Schumacher	GER	Ferrari	1:29:48.446
2	H-H Frentzen	GER	Williams	1:29:49.824
3	E Irvine	GBR	Ferrari	1:30:14830

European Grand Prix

Oct 26 — Jerez

1	M Hakkinen	FIN	McLaren	1:38:57.771
2	D Coulthard	GBR	McLaren	1:38:59.425
3	J Villeneuve	CAN	Williams	1:38:59.574

Drivers' Championship:

1	J Villeneuve	CAN	Williams	81
2	H-H Frentzen	GER	Williams	42
3	D Coulthard	GB	McLaren	36
4	J Alesi	FRA	Benetton	36
5	G Berger	AUT	Benetton	27
6	M Hakkinen	FIN	McLaren	27
7	E Irvine	GBR	Ferrari	24
8	G Fisichella	ITA	Jordan	20
9	O Panis	FRA	Prost	16
10	J Herbert	GB	Sauber	14
11	R Schumacher	GER	Jordan	13
12	D Hill	GB	Arrows	7
13	R Barrichello	BRA	Stewart	6
14	A Wurz	AUT	Benetton	4
15	J Trulli	ITA	Prost	3
16	M Salo	FIN	Tyrrell	2
	P Diniz	BRA	Arrows	2
18	S Nakano	JPN	Prost	2
19	N Larini	ITA	Sauber	1
20	G Morbidelli	ITA	Sauber	0
	N Fontana	ARG	Sauber	0
	T Marques	BRA	Minardi	0
	J Verstappen	HOL	Tyrrell	0
	J Magnussen	DEN	Stewart	0
	U Katayama	JPN	Minardi	0
	M Schumacher	GER	Ferrari	0

Constructors' Championship:

1	Williams Renault	123
2	Ferrari	102
3	Benetton Renault	67
4	McLaren Mercedes	63
5	Jordan Peugeot	33
6	Prost Mugen Honda	21
7	Sauber Petronas	16
8	Arrows Yamaha	9
9	Stewart Ford	6
10	Tyrrell Ford	2
11	Minardi Hart	0

INDIANAPOLIS 500

May 27

1	A Luyendyk	NED	G F-Aurora	3:25:43.388
2	S Goodyear	CAN	G F-Aurora	3:25:43.958
3	J Ward	USA	G F-Aurora	3:25:44.286

LE MANS 24 HOUR

Jun 14-15

			laps	Av kmh
1	Joest	Joest TWR Porsche	361	204.186
2	Gulf Team Davidoff	McLaren BMW	360	202.993
3	Team BMW Motorsport	McLaren BMW	358	201.858

ROWING

BEEFEATER GIN UNIVERSITY BOAT RACE

Mar 29 — River Thames

Cambridge (17mins 38secs) beat
Oxford (17mins 42secs) by two lengths

WORLD CHAMPIONSHIPS

Sep 6 — Lac Aiguebelette, France

Men's Coxless Fours

1 Britain 5:52.40
(J Cracknell, S Redgrave, T Foster, M Pinsent)
2 France 5:56.34
3 Romania 5:57.10

Women's Coxless Fours

1 Britain 6:40.30
(S Walker, A Beever, E Henshilwood, L Eyre)
2 Romania 6:41.13
3 Germany 6:45.70

RUGBY LEAGUE

SILK CUT CHALLENGE CUP FINAL

May 3 — Wembley

Bradford Bulls 22-32 St Helens

Bradford Bulls: Peacock, Loughlin, Tomlinson, Lowes. Goals: McNamara 3

St Helens: Tries: Martyn 2, Hammond , Joynt, Sullivan. Goals: Goulding 6

STONES SUPER LEAGUE

1997 Stones Super League Champions: Bradford Bulls

Stones Super League:

		P	W	D	L	F	A	Pts
1	Bradford Bulls	22	20	0	2	769	397	40
2	London Broncos	22	15	3	4	616	418	33
3	St Helens	22	14	1	7	592	506	29
4	Wigan Warriors	22	14	0	8	683	398	28
5	Leeds Rhinos	22	13	1	8	544	463	27
6	Salford Reds	22	11	0	11	428	495	22
7	Halifax Blue Sox	22	8	2	12	524	549	18
8	Sheffield Eagles	22	9	0	13	415	574	18
9	Warrington Wolves	22	8	0	14	437	647	16
10	Castleford Tigers	22	5	2	15	334	515	12
11	Paris St Germain	22	6	0	16	362	572	12
12	Oldham Bears	22	4	1	17	461	631	9

Stones Premiership Final

Sep 28 — Old Trafford

St Helens 20-33 Wigan Warriors

St Helens: Tries: Anderson, Hammond, McVey, Newlove. Goals: Long 2

Wigan Warriors: Tries: Farrell, Haughton A Johnson, Radlinski, Robinson. Goals: Farrell 6. Drop Goal: Farrell

Super League Visa World Club Champs Final

Oct 17 — Auckland

Brisbane 36-12 Hunter Mariners

RUGBY UNION

INTERNATIONALS

Jan 11 — Cardiff Arms Park

Wales 34-14 United States

Wales: Tries: Evans 2, Gibbs, penalty try. Conversions: A Thomas 4. Penalties: A Thomas 2

United States: Try: Bachelet. Penalties: Alexander 3

Jul 12 — Sydney

Australia 25-6 England

Australia: Tries: Burke, Gregan, Horan, Tune. Conversion: Burke: Penalty: Eales

England: Penalty: Stimson. Drop Goal: Catt

Jul 12 — San Francisco

United States 23-28 Wales

United States: Tries: Anitoni, Walker. Conversions: Alexander 2. Penalties: Alexander 3

Wales: Tries: Proctor 3, A Thomas. Conversion: A Thomas. Penalties: A Thomas 2

HEINEKEN EUROPEAN CUP FINAL

Jan 25 — Cardiff Arms Park

Brive 28-9 Leicester

Brive: Tries: Carrat 2, Viars, Fabre. Conversion: Lamaison. Penalty: Lamaison. Drop Goal: Lamaison

Leicester: Penalties: Liley 3

FIVE NATIONS CHAMPIONSHIP

Five Nations Championship Champions: France

Jan 18 — Murrayfield

Scotland 19-34 Wales

Scotland: Try: Hastings. Conversion: Shepherd. Penalties: Shepherd 3. Drop Goal: Chalmers

Wales: Tries: S Quinnell, Jenkins, A Thomas, Evans. Conversions: Jenkins 4. Penalties: Jenkins 2

Jan 18 — Lansdowne Road

Ireland 15-32 France

Ireland: Penalties: Elwood 5

France: Tries: Venditti 3, Galthie. Conversions: Castaignede 3. Penalties: Castaignede 2

Feb 1 — Twickenham

England 41-13 Scotland

England: Tries: penalty try, Carling, Gomarsall, de Glanville. Conversions: Grayson 3. Penalties: Grayson 5

Scotland: Try: Eriksson. Conversion: Shepherd. Penalties: Shepherd 2

Feb 1 — Cardiff Arms Park

Wales 25-26 Ireland

Wales: Tries: Evans 2, S Quinnell. Conversions: Jenkins 2. Penalties: Jenkins 2

Ireland: Tries: Bell, Miller, Hickie. Conversion: Elwood. Penalties: Elwood 3

Feb 15 — Lansdowne Road

Ireland 6-46 England

Ireland: Penalties: Elwood 2

England: Tries: Sleightholme 2, Underwood 2, Gomarsall, Hill. Conversions: Grayson 2. Penalties: Grayson 4

Feb 15 — Parc des Princes

France 27-22 Wales

France: Tries: Leflamand 2, Merle, Venditti. Conversions: Dourthe, Aucagne. Penalty: Aucagne.

Wales: Tries: G Thomas, Bateman, Howley. Conversions: Jenkins 2. Penalty: Jenkins

Mar 1 — Twickenham

England 20-23 France

England: Try: Dallaglio. Penalties: Grayson 4. Drop Goal: Grayson

France: Tries: Leflamand, Lamaison. Conversions: Lamaison 2. Penalies: Lamaison 2. Drop Goal: Lamaison

Mar 1 — Murrayfield

Scotland 38-10 Ireland

Scotland: Tries: Tait, Townsend, Weir, Walton, Stanger. Conversions: Shepherd 5. Penalty: Shepherd.

Ireland: Try: Hickie. Conversion: Humphreys. Penalty: Humphreys

Mar 15 — Parc des Princes

France 47-20 Scotland

France: Tries: Benazzi, Leflamand, Magne, Tournaire Conversions: Lamaison 3. Penalies: Lamaison 6. Drop Goal: Sadournay

Scotland: Tries: Tait 2. Conversions: Shepherd 2 Penalties: Shepherd 2

Mar 15 — Cardiff Arms Park

Wales 13-34 England

Wales: Try: Howley. Conversion: J Davies. Penalties: J Davies 2

England: Tries: Stimpson, Underwood, Hill, de Glanville. Conversions: Catt 4. Penalties: Catt 2

Five Nations Championship Final Table:

		P	W	D	L	F	A	Pts
1	France	4	4	0	0	129	77	8
2	England	4	3	0	1	141	55	6
3	Wales	4	1	0	3	94	106	2
4	Scotland	4	1	0	3	90	132	2
5	Ireland	4	1	0	3	57	141	2

WORLD CUP SEVENS FINAL

Mar 23 — Hong Kong

Fiji 24-21 South Arica

Fiji: Tries: Koroi 2, Erenavula, Vunibaka. Conversions: Serevi2.

S Africa: Tries: Venter 2, Brink. Conversions: Brink 3

COURAGE LEAGUE

1996-97 National Division One Champions: Wasps

Courage League National Division One:

		P	W	D	L	F	A	Pts
1	Wasps	22	18	1	3	685	406	37
2	Bath	22	15	1	6	863	411	31
3	NEC Harlequins	22	15	0	7	755	416	30
4	Leicester	22	14	1	7	600	395	29
5	Sale	22	13	2	7	603	525	28
6	Saracens	22	12	1	9	568	459	25
7	Gloucester	22	11	1	10	476	589	23
8	Northampton	22	10	0	12	515	477	20
9	Bristol	22	8	1	13	432	625	17
10	London Irish	22	6	0	16	502	747	12
11	W Hartlepool	22	3	0	19	382	795	6
12	Orrell	22	3	0	19	360	886	6

TENNENTS PREMIERSHIP

1996-97 Division One Champions: Melrose

SRU Tennents Premiership Division One:

		P	W	D	L	F	A	Pts
1	Melrose	14	14	0	0	582	215	28
2	Watsonians	14	12	0	2	587	226	24
3	Currie	14	9	0	5	379	259	18
4	Boroughmuir	14	6	1	7	394	325	13
5	Hawick	14	5	0	9	268	397	10
6	Jed-Forest	14	4	0	10	217	509	8
7	Heriot's FP	14	3	0	11	224	416	6
8	Stirling County	14	2	1	11	220	524	5

HEINEKEN NATIONAL LEAGUE

1996-97 Divison One Champions: Pontypridd

Heineken National League Divison One:

		P	W	D	L	F	A	T	Bon	Pts
1	Pontypridd	22	20	0	2	944	334	124	22	62
2	Swansea	22	14	0	8	879	471	128	22	50
3	Llanelli	22	16	2	4	789	351	111	16	50
4	Cardiff	22	14	1	7	750	543	99	12	41
5	Bridgend	22	10	1	11	604	527	79	10	31
6	Newport	22	12	2	8	541	632	71	5	31
7	Ebbw Vale	22	12	2	8	431	552	50	4	30
8	Neath	22	10	0	12	524	603	74	9	29
9	Dunvant	22	10	2	10	524	601	69	5	27
10	Caerphilly	22	2	0	20	422	801	59	10	14
11	Treorchy	22	3	0	19	413	825	57	4	10
12	Newbridge	22	4	0	18	358	939	45	0	8

INSURANCE CORP ALL-IRELAND LEAGUE

1996-97 Division One Champions: Shannon

Insurance Corp All Ireland League Division One:

		P	W	D	L	F	A	Pts
1	Shannon	13	12	0	1	362	193	24
2	Lansdowne	13	9	0	4	349	184	18
3	Terenure College	13	9	0	4	301	179	18
4	St Mary's College	13	8	1	4	305	279	17
5	Ballymena	13	8	0	5	258	247	16
6	Cork Constitution	13	7	1	6	299	252	14
7	Garryowen	13	7	0	6	287	283	14
8	Blackrock College	13	7	0	6	288	288	14
9	Young Munster	13	6	0	7	233	274	12
10	Dungannon	13	5	0	8	324	344	10
11	Old Crescent	13	4	0	9	239	281	8
12	Old Belvedere	13	4	0	9	193	287	8
13	Old Wesley	13	3	0	10	206	327	6
14	Instonians	13	1	0	12	182	408	2

CIS COUNTY CHAMPIONSHIP FINAL
Apr 19 Twickenham
Cumbria 21-13 Somerset
Cumbria: Tries: Bell, Milnes. Conversion: Scott
Penalties: Scott 3
Somerset: Tries: Rees, King. Penalty: Edmonds

SWALEC CUP FINAL
Apr 26 Cardiff Arms Park
Cardiff 33-26 Swansea
Cardiff: Tries: Walker, Thomas, Hall. Conversions: Jarvis 3. Penalties: Jarvis 4
Swansea: Tries: Taylor 2, Moore, penalty try. Conversions: Williams 3

PILKINGTON CUP FINAL
May 10 Twickenham
Leicester 9-3 Sale
Leicester: Penalties: Stransky .
Sale: Penalty: Mannix

SRU TENNENTS CUP FINAL
May 10 Murrayfield
Melrose 31-23 Boroughmuir
Melrose: Tries: Shepherd 3, Moncrieff. Conversion: Shepherd. Penalties: Shepherd 3
Boroughmuir: Tries: McLean 2, Wyllie. Conversion: Aitken. Penalties: Aitken 2

MIDDLESEX SEVENS FINAL
May 17 Twickenham
Barbarians 57-5 Saracens

SANYO CUP
May 24 Twickenham
Wasps 31-52 Sanyo World XV
Wasps: Tries: Logan 2, Roiser, White. Conversions: Rees 4. Penalty: Rees
Sanyo World XV: Tries: Serevi 3, Vunibaka 2, Campese, Ofahengaue, Sella. Conversions: Viars 6

BRITISH LIONS IN SOUTH AFRICA
Jun 21 **First Test** Cape Town
South Africa 16-25 British Isles
South Africa: Tries: du Randt, Bennett. Penalties: Lubbe, Honiball
British Isles: Dawson, Tait. Penalties: Jenkins 5
Jun 28 **Second Test** Durban
South Africa 15-18 British Isles
South Africa: Tries: van der Westhuizen, Montgomery, Joubert
British Isles: Penalties: Jenkins 5. Drop Goal: Guscott
Jul 5 **Third Test** Johannesburg
South Africa 35-16 British Isles
South Africa: Tries: van der Westhuizen, Montgomery, Snyman, Rossouw. Conversions: de Beer 2, Honiball
Penalties: de Beer 3
British Isles: Try: Dawson. Conversion: Jenkins. Penalties: Jenkins 3
British Isles won series 2-1

SKIING

ALPINE WORLD CHAMPIONSHIP

Men

Overall
1 Luc Alphand ... FRA
2 Kjetil André Aamodt ... NOR
3 Josef Strobl ... AUT

Downhill
1 Luc Alphand ... FRA
2 Kristian Ghedina ... ITA
3 Fritz Strobl ... AUT

Super-G
1 Luc Alphand ... FRA
2 Josep Strobl ... AUT
3 Andreas Schiffer ... AUT

Giant Slalom
1 Michael von Gruenigen ... SUI
2 Kjetil André Aamodt ... NOR
3 Hans Knaus ... AUT

Slalom
1 Thomas Sykora ... AUT
2 Thomas Stangassinger ... AUT
3 Finn Christian Jagge ... NOR

Women

Overall
1 Pernilla Wilberg ... SWE
2 Katja Seizinger ... GER
3 Hilde Gerg ... GER

Downhill
1 Renate Goetscl ... AUT
2 Heidi Zurbriggen ... SUI
3 Warwara Zelenskaja ... RUS

Super-G
1 Hilde Gerg ... GER
2 Katja Seizinger ... GER
3 Pernilla Wilberg ... SWE

Giant Slalom
1 Deborah Campagnoli ... ITA
2 Katja Seizinger ... GER
3 Anita Wachter ... AUT

Slalom
1 Pernilla Wilberg ... SWE
2 Claudia Riegler ... NZL
3 Deborah Campagnoli ... ITA

SNOOKER

EMBASSY WORLD CHAMPIONSHIP
Apr 19-May 5 Crucible Theatre, Sheffield
Champion: Ken Doherty (Ireland)
Final:
Ken Doherty beat Stephen Hendry (Scotland) 18-12
Frame scores
Doherty first: 67-7; 5-117; 0-106; 77-13; 78-9; 75-51; 69-11; 0-122; 12-76; 89-32; 62-55; 57-43; 65-13; 85-50; 47-74; 60-28; 23-70; 71-24; 4-110; 86-0; 85-16; 59-45; 0-137; 12-75; 30-61; 0-114; 57-61; 82-23; 69-19; 71-49

SQUASH

DUNLOP EUROPEAN TEAM CHAMPIONSHIP
April 23-27 Odense, Denmark

Men's Final
England 4 Wales 0
M Cairns beat A Gough 9-3, 8-10, 3-9, 9-4, 9-6
P Johnson beat D Evans 9-5, 9-5, 9-5
S Meads beat G Davies 10-9; 9-5; 9-7
N Taylor beat M benjamin 9-1; 9-1; 9-0)

Women' Final
England 3 Germany 0
E Wright beat S Schoone 9-6, 9-6, 9-5
L Charman beat S Baum 9-5, 9-3, 9-2
J Martin beat K Beriere 9-0, 9-1, 9-1

WORLD OPEN CHAMPIONSHIP
November 1-9 Kuala Lumpar

Men's Semi-Finals
R Eyles AUS beat P Marshall ENG 10-15, 15-8, 15-8, 15-6
P Nicol SCO beat A Gough WAL 15-13, 15-8, 15-15

Final
R Eyles AUS beat P Nicol SCO 15-11, 15-12, 15-12

SWIMMING

EUROPEAN CHAMPIONSHIP
August 13-24 Seville

Selected Men's Finals

50m Freestyle
1 A Popov ... RUS ... 22.30
2 M Foster ... GBR ... 22.53
3 J Sicot ... FRA ... 22.78

200m Butterfly
1 F Esposito ... FRA ... 1:57.24
2 D Silantiev ... UKR ... 1:58.48
3 S Parry ... GBR ... 1:58.78

200m Freestyle
1 P Palmer ... GBR ... 1:48.85
2 M Rosolino ... ITA ... 1:49.02
3 B Szabados ... HUN ... 1:49.98
4 J Salter ... GBR ... 1:49.99

400m Freestyle
1 E Brembilla ... ITA ... 3:45.96
2 M Rosolino ... ITA ... 3:48.11
3 P Palmer ... GBR ... 3:50.03

1500m Freestyle
1 E Brembilla ... ITA ... 14:58.65
2 I Snitko ... UKR ... 15:07.85
3 D Zavgorodny ... UKR ... 15:19.28
4 G Smith ... GBR ... 15:22.11

4x200m Freestyle Relay
1 Great Britain ... 7:17.56
(P Palmer, A Clayton, G Meadows, J Salter)
2 Holland ... 7:17.84
3 Germany ... 7:18.86

Selected Women's Finals

200m Freestyle
1 M De Bruin ... IRE ... 1.59.93
2 N Chemezova ... RUS ... 1:59.97
3 C Potec ... ROM ... 2:00.17
4 K Pickering ... GBR ... 2:01.02

200m Butterfly
1 M Pelaez ... SPA ... 2:10.25
2 M De Bruin ... IRE ... 2:10.88
3 M Jacobsen ... DEN ... 2:11.97

400m Freestyle
1 D Hase ... GER ... 4:09.58
2 M De Bruin ... IRE ... 4:10.50
3 K Kielgass ... GER ... 4:10.89

400m Medley
1 M De Bruin ... IRE ... 4:42.08
2 Y Klochkova ... UKR ... 4:43.07
3 H Cerna ... CZR ... 4:44.05

4x100m Medley Relay
1 Germany ... 4:07.73
2 Russia ... 4:09.04
3 Great Britain ... 4:10.31
(S Price, J King, C Foot, K Pickering)

TABLE TENNIS

WORLD TEAM CHAMPIONSHIP
Apr 29-30 Manchester

Men's Final
China 3-1 France

Women's Final
China 3-0 North Korea

MEN'S WORLD CHAMPIONSHIP
Oct 24-26 Nimes

Singles Final
Z Primorac ... CRO beat K Linghui ... CHI
21-19; 22-20; 21-13

TENNIS

AUSTRALIAN OPEN
Jan 12-26 Melbourne

Men's Singles
P Sampras ... USA beat C Moya ... SPA
6-2, 6-3, 6-3

Women's Singles
M Hingis ... SUI beat M Pierce ... FRA
6-2, 6-2

Men's Doubles
M Woodforde ... AUS and T Woodbridge ... AUS
beat
S Lareau ... CAN and A O'Brien ... USA
4-6, 7-5, 7-5, 6-3

Women's Doubles
M Hingis ... SUI and N Zvereva ... BLR
beat
L Davenport ... USA and L Raymond ... USA
6-2, 6-2

Mixed Doubles
M Bollegraf ... NED and R Leach ... USA
beat
L Neiland ... LAT and JL de Jager ... RSA
6-3, 6-7 (5-7), 7-5

FRENCH OPEN
May 26-Jun8 Roland Garros

Men's Singles
G Kuerten ... BRA beat S Bruguera ... SPA
6-3, 6-4, 6-2

Women's Singles
I Majoli ... CRO beat M Hingis ... SUI
6-4, 6-2

Men's Doubles
Y Kafelnikov ... RUS and D Vacek ... CZE
beat
M Woodforde ... AUS and T Woodbridge ... AUS
7-6 (14-12), 4-6, 6-3

Women's Doubles
G Fernandez ... USA and N Zvereva ... BLR
beat
MJ Fernandez ... USA and L Raymond ... USA
6-2, 6-3

Mixed Doubles
R Hiraki ... JAP and M Bhupathi ... IND
beat
L Raymond ... USA and P Galbraith ... USA
6-4, 6-1

WIMBLEDON
June 23- July 6 London

Men's Singles
P Sampras ... USA beat C Pioline ... FRA
6-4, 6-2, 6-4

Women's Singles
M Hingis ... SUI beat J Novotna ... CZE
2-6, 6-3, 6-3

Men's Doubles
T Woodbridge ... AUS and M Woodforde ... AUS
beat
J Eltingh ... NED and P Haarhuis ... NED
7-6, 7-6, 5-7, 6-3

Women's Doubles
G Fernandez ... USA and N Zvereva ... BLR
beat
N Arendt ... USA and M Bollegraf ... NED
7-6, 6-4

Mixed Doubles
C Suk ... CZE and H Sukova ... CZE
beat
A Olhovskiy ... RUS and L Neiland ... LAT
4-6, 6-3, 6-4

US OPEN
Aug 25 - Sep 7 Flushing Meadow, NY

Men's Singles
P Rafter ... AUS beat G Rusedski ... GBR
6-3, 6-2, 4-6, 7-5

Women's Singles
M Hingis ... SUI beat V Williams ... USA
6-0, 6-4

Men's Doubles
Y Kafelnikov ... RUS and D Vacek ... CZE
beat
J Biorkman ... SWE and N Kulti ... SWE
7-6 (10-8), 6-3

Women's Doubles
L Davenport ... USA and J Novotna ... CZE
beat
G Fernandez ... USA and N Zvereva ... BLR
6-3, 6-4

Mixed Doubles
M Bollegraf ... NED and R Leach ... USA
beat
M Paz ... ARG and P Albano ... ARG
3-6, 7-5, 7-6 (7-3)

FED CUP FINAL
Oct 4-5 Netherlands

Netherlands 1-4 France

Singles
M Pierce ... FRA beat M Overmans ... NED
6-4, 6-1
S Testud ... FRA beat B S'-McCarthy ... NED
6-4, 4-6, 6-3
B S'-McCarthy ... NED beat M Pierce ... FRA
4-6, 6-3, 6-4
S Testud ... FRA beat M Overmans ... NED
0-6, 6-3, 6-3

Doubles
N Tauziat ... FRA and A Fusai ... FRA
beat
M Bollegraf ... NED and C Vis ... NED
6-3, 6-4

YACHTING

WHITBREAD ROUND THE WORLD RACE

First Leg – Southampton to Cape Town
Sept 21-Oct 26

				d	h	m	pts
1	EF Language	P Cayard	SWE	29	16	54	125
2	Merit Cup	G Dalton	MON	30	12	20	110
3	Innovation Kvaemer	K Frostad	NOR	30	40	09	97
4	Silk Cut	L Smith	GBR	31	14	17	84
5	Chessie Racing	M Fischer	USA	32	06	12	72
6	Toshiba	C Dickson	USA	32	15	23	60
7	America's Challenge	R Field	USA	32	18	52	48
8	Swedish Match	G Krantz	SWE	33	01	14	36
9	EF Education	C Guillou	SWE	34	01	28	24
10	Brunel Sunergy	H Bouscholte	NED	35	13	42	12

GENERAL

English Sports Council
Tel: 0171 273 1500
Fax: 0171 383 5740

United Kingdom Sports Council
Tel: 0171 380 8000
Fax: 0171 380 0927

AEROBATICS

British Aerobatic Association
Tel: 0121 554 2117
Fax: 0121 235 2769

Federation Aeronautique Internationale
Tel: + 33 1 49 54 38 92
Fax: + 33 1 49 54 38 88
Website: http://www.fai.org/

AMERICAN FOOTBALL

British American Football Ass. Senior League
Tel: 01205 363522
Fax: 01205 358139

National Football League
Tel: + 1 212 450 2000
Fax: + 1 212 681 7599
Website: http://www.nfl.com

World League Of American Football
Tel: 0171 335 1995
Fax: 0171 499 8098
Website: http://www.worldleague.com

ANGLING

Confederation Internationale De La Peche Sportive
Tel: + 39 6 36858239
Fax: + 39 6 368 58109

National Federation Of Anglers
Tel: 01283 734735
Fax: 01283 734799

Salmon And Trout Association
Tel: 0171 283 5838
Fax: 0171 929 1389

ARCHERY

English Field Archery Society
Tel: 01905 358957
Fax: 01905 358957
Website: http://www.fieldarcher.com

Federation Internationale De Tir A L'Arc
Tel: + 41 21 614 3050
Fax: + 41 21 614 3055
Website: http://www.archery.org

Grand National Archery Society
Tel: 01203 696631
Fax: 01203 419662

ATHLETICS

AAA Of England
Tel: 0121 440 5000
Fax: 0121 440 0555

British Athletic Federation
Tel: 0121 440 5000
Fax: 0121 440 0555
Website: http://www.british-athletics.co.uk

International Amateur Athletic Federation
Tel: + 377 93 10 88 88
Fax: + 377 93 15 95 15
Website: http://www.iaaf.org/

BADMINTON

Badminton Association Of England
Tel: 01908 568822
Fax: 01908 566922

International Badminton Federation
Tel: 01242 23 49 04
Fax: 01242 22 10 30
Website: http://www.intbadfed.org

Scottish Badminton Union
Tel: 0141 445 1218
Fax: 0141 425 1218

Welsh Badminton Union
Tel: 01222 222 082
Fax: 01222 394 282

BASEBALL

Major League Baseball
Tel: + 1 212 339 7800
Fax: + 1 212 593 7138
Website: http://www.majorleaguebaseball.com

British Baseball Federation
Tel: 01482 643551
Fax: 01482 640224

International Baseball Association
Tel: + 41 21 311 18 63
Fax: + 41 21 311 18 64
Website: http://www.monviso2.alpcom.it/digesu

National League Of Professional Baseball Clubs
Tel: + 1 212 339 7700
Fax: + 1 212 935 5069
Website: http://www.majorleague baseball.com

The American League Of Professional Baseball Clubs
Tel: + 1 212 339 7600
Fax: + 1 212 593 7138
Website: http://www.majorleaguebaseball.com

BASKETBALL

Basketball League
Tel: 0121 749 1355
Fax: 0121 749 5355

Budweiser League
Tel: 0121 308 3505
Fax: 0121 308 5506

English Basketball Association
Tel: 0113 2 36 11 66
Fax: 0113 2 36 10 22

BRITISH CLUBS

Birmingham Bullets
Tel: 0121 246 6022
Fax: 0121 246 6033

Chester Jets
Tel: 0151 356 2616
Fax: 0151 355 2373

Crystal Palace
Tel: 0181 776 7755
Fax: 0181 676 8754

Derby Storm
Tel: 01332 340 484
Fax: 01332 340 484

Leicester Riders
Tel: 0116 270 3761

Leopards
Tel: 0171 491 7676
Fax: 0171 491 7572

London Towers
Tel: 0171 722 0109
Fax: 0171 586 1422

Manchester Giants
Tel: 0161 950 7000
Fax: 0161 950 7007

Newcastle Eagles
Tel: 0191 528 4804
Fax: 0191 488 0900

Sheffield Sharks
Tel: 0114 257 1994
Fax: 0114 257 1993

Thames Valley Tigers
Tel: 01344 300 185
Fax: 01344 409 855

Watford Royals
Tel: 01442 825 760
Fax: 01442 381 992

Worthing Bears
Tel: 01903 213 806
Fax: 01903 236 552

BMX BIKE

English BMX Association
Tel: 0181 813 2838
Fax: 0181 813 2838

BOWLS

English Bowling Association
Tel: 01903 820222
Fax: 01903 820444

English Indoor Bowling Association
Tel: 01664 481 900
Fax: 01664 481 901

English Womens Indoor Bowling Association
Tel: 01604 494 163
Fax: 01604 494 434

World Bowls Board
Tel: 01903 247468
Fax: 01903 502616

BOXING

International Amateur Boxing Association
Tel: + 49 30 423 6766
Fax: + 49 30 423 5943

Amateur Boxing Association
Tel: 0181 778 0251
Fax: 0181 778 9324

CANOEING

British Canoe Union
Tel: 0115 982 1100
Fax: 0115 982 1797

International Canoe Federation
Tel: + 36 1 363 48 32
Fax: + 36 1 157 56 43
Website:http://www.worldsport.com/sports/canoeing/home.html

CHESS

International Chess Federation
Tel: + 41 21 310 3900
Fax: + 41 21 310 3905

British Chess Federation
Tel: 01424 442500
Fax: 01424 718372

CRICKET

Board Of Control For Cricket In Sri Lanka
Tel: + 941 1 697 405
Fax: + 941 1 691 439

New Zealand Cricket Inc.
Tel: + 64 3 366 2964
Fax: + 64 3 365 7491

England & Wales Cricket Board
Tel: 0171 432 1200
Fax: 0171 289 5619

The Board Of Control For Cricket In India
Tel: + 91 265 431 122
Fax: + 91 802 200 010

The Board Of Control For Cricket In Pakistan
Tel: + 92 42 877 817
Fax: + 92 42 5711860

The International Cricket Council
Tel: 0171 2661818
Fax: 0171 266 1777
Website:http://lords.msn.com/admin/email/con − s05.htm

United Cricket Board Of South Africa
Tel: + 27 11 880 2810
Fax: + 27 11 880 6578
Website: http://www-rsa.cricket.org

West Indies Cricket Board Of Control
Tel: + 1 268 460 5462
Fax: + 1 268 460 5452

Womens Cricket Association
Tel: 0121 440 0520
Fax: 0121 446 6344

Zimbabwe Cricket Union
Tel: + 263 4 729370
Fax: + 263 4 729370

Australian Cricket Board
Tel: + 61 3 654 3977
Fax: + 61 3 654 8103
Website: http://www.acb.com.au

BRITISH CLUBS

Derbyshire CCC
Tel: 01332 383 211
Fax: 01332 290 251

Durham CCC
Tel: 0191 387 1717
Fax: 0191 387 1616

Essex CCC
Tel: 01245 252 420
Fax: 01245 491 607

Glamorgan CCC
Tel: 01222 343 478
Fax: 01222 377 044
Website: http://www.cricket.org:8003/glamorgan – ccc

Gloucestershire CCC
Tel: 0117 924 5216
Fax: 0117 924 1193

Hampshire CCC
Tel: 01703 333 788
Fax: 01703 330 121

Kent CCC
Tel: 01227 456 886
Fax: 01227 762 168
Website: http://www.kentnet.co.uk/kent – ccc

Lancashire CCC
Tel: 0161 282 4000
Fax: 0161 282 4100

Leicestershire CCC
Tel: 0116 283 1880
Fax: 0116 244 0363

Middlesex CCC
Tel: 0171 289 1300
Fax: 0171 289 5831

Northamptonshire CCC
Tel: 01604 232 917
Fax: 01604 232 855

Nottinghamshire CCC
Tel: 0115 982 1525
Fax: 0115 945 5730

Somerset CCC
Tel: 01823 272 946
Fax: 01823 332 395

Surrey CCC
Tel: 0171 582 6660
Fax: 0171 735 7769

Sussex CCC
Tel: 01273 732 161
Fax: 01273 771 549

Warwickshire CCC
Tel: 0121 466 4777
Fax: 0121 446 4544
Website: http://www.warwickshireccc.org.uk

Worcestershire CCC
Tel: 01905 748 474
Fax: 01905 748 005

Yorkshire CCC
Tel: 0113 278 7394
Fax: 0113 278 4099
Website: http://www.yorkshireccc.org.uk

CROQUET

International Croquet Association
Tel: 0171 736 3148
Fax: 0171 789 6066

The Croquet Association
Tel: 0171 736 3148
Fax: 0171 736 3148

CYCLING

British Cycling Federation
Tel: 0161 230 2301
Fax: 0161 231 0591

Cyclists Touring Club
Tel: 01483 417217
Fax: 01483 426994

Road Time Trials Council
Tel: 0161 766 5787
Fax: 0161 796 2396

Union Cycliste Internationale
Tel: + 41 21 622 05 80
Fax: + 41 21 622 05 88
Website: http://www.uci.ch

DARTS

British Darts Organisation - HQ
Tel: 0181 883 5544/5
Fax: 0181 883 0109

World Darts Federation
Tel: 0181 883 5055
Fax: 0181 883 0109

DISABLED

British Blind Sport
Tel: 01788 536142
Fax: 01788 536 676

British Sports Association For The Disabled
Tel: 0171 490 4919
Fax: 0171 490 4914

Cerebral Palsy Sport
Tel: 01602 401202
Fax: 01602 402984

International Paralympic Committee
Tel: + 32 5038 9340
Fax: + 32 5 039 0119
Website: http://info.lut.ac.uk/research/paad/ipc/ipc.html

International Blind Sports Association
Tel: + 33 1 40 31 45 00
Fax: + 33 1 40 31 45 42
Website: http://www.ibsa.es

Special Olympics International
Tel: + 1 202 628 36 30
Fax: + 1 202 824 02 00
Website: http://www.specialolympics.org

DRAGON BOAT RACING

British Dragon Boat Racing Association
Tel: 0171 930 2296
Fax: 0171 930 4777

EQUESTRIAN

British Equestrian Federation
Tel: 01203 696697
Fax: 01203 696484

Federation Equestre Internationale
Tel: + 41 21 312 5656
Fax: + 41 21 312 8677
Website: http://www.bcm.nl/fei/calender/calender.html

FENCING

Amateur Fencing Association
Tel: 0181 742 3032
Fax: 0181 742 3033
Website: http://www.netlink.co.uk/users/afa

Federation Internationale D'escrime
Tel: + 41 21 3203115
Fax: + 41 21 3203116
Website: http://www.calvacom.fr/fie/

FIELD HOCKEY

Federation Internationale De Hockey
Tel: + 32 2 219 4537
Fax: + 32 2 219 2761
Website: http://www.fihockey.org

The Hockey Association
Tel: 01908 689 290
Fax: 01908 689 286

FOOTBALL

FEDERATIONS AND ASSOCIATIONS

Federation Internationale De Football Association
Tel: + 41 1 384 9595
Fax: + 41 1 384 9696
Website: http://www.fifa.com

The Football Association
Tel: 0171 262 4542
Fax: 0171 402 0486

The Football Association Of Wales
Tel: 01222 37 23 25
Fax: 01222 34 39 61

The Football League Limited
Tel: 01253 729421
Fax: 01253 724786

The Irish Football Association
Tel: 01232 66 94 58
Fax: 01232 66 76 20

The Scottish Football Association
Tel: 0141 332 6372
Fax: 0141 332 7559

The Scottish Football League
Tel: 0141 248 3844
Fax: 0141 221 7450

U.E.F.A
Tel: + 41 22 994 44 44
Fax: + 41 22 994 44 88

The Football Association Of Ireland
Tel: + 353 1 676 6864
Fax: + 353 1 661 0931

PREMIER LEAGUE CLUBS

Arsenal Football Club
Tel: 0171 704 4000
Fax: 0171 704 4001
Website: http://www.arsenal.co.uk

Aston Villa Football Club
Tel: 0121 327 2299
Fax: 0121 322 2107

Barnsley Football Club
Tel: 01226 211 211
Fax: 01226 211 444

Blackburn Rovers Football Club
Tel: 01254 698 888
Fax: 01254 671 042
Website: http://www.rovers.co.uk

Bolton Wanderers Football Club
Tel: 01204 389 200
Fax: 01204 382 334
Website: http://www.boltonwfc.co.uk

Chelsea Football Club
Tel: 0171 385 5545
Fax: 0171 381 4831
Website: http://www.chelseafc.co.uk

Coventry City Football Club
Tel: 01203 234 000
Fax: 01203 234 099
Website: http://www.ccfc.co.uk

Crystal Palace Football Club
Tel: 0181 771 8841
Fax: 0181 653 4708

Derby County Football Club
Tel: 01332 202 202
Fax: 01332 293 514

Everton Football Club
Tel: 0151 330 2200
Fax: 0151 286 9112
Website: http://www.evertonfc.com

Leeds United Football Club
Tel: 0113 226 1155
Fax: 0113 226 6056
Website: http://www.lufc.co.uk

Leicester City Football Club
Tel: 0116 291 5232
Fax: 0116 291 1249
Website: http://www.lcfc.co.uk

Liverpool Football Club
Tel: 0151 263 2361
Fax: 0151 260 8813

Manchester United Football Club
Tel: 0161 872 1661
Fax: 0161 876 5502
Website: http://www.sky.co.uk

Newcastle United Football Club
Tel: 0191 201 8400
Fax: 0191 201 8600
Website: http://www.newcastle-utd.co.uk

Sheffield Wednesday Football Club
Tel: 0114 221 2121
Fax: 0114 221 2122

Southampton Football Club
Tel: 01703 220 505
Fax: 01703 330 360
Website: http://www.soton.ac.uk

Tottenham Hotspur Football Club
Tel: 0181 365 5000
Fax: 0181 365 5005
Website: http://www.spurs.co.uk

West Ham United Football Club
Tel: 0181 548 2748
Fax: 0181 548 2758
Website: http://www.westhamunited.co.uk

Wimbledon Football Club
Tel: 0181 771 2233
Fax: 0181 768 0641

(CONTINUED)

DIRECTORY

FOOTBALL

SCOTTISH LEAGUE CLUBS

Aberdeen Football Club
Tel: 01224 632 328
Fax: 01224 644 173

Celtic Football Club
Tel: 0141 556 2611
Fax: 0141 551 8106
Website: http://www.celtic.co.uk

Dundee United Football Club
Tel: 01382 833 126
Fax: 01382 889 398

Dunfermline Football Club
Tel: 01383 724 295
Fax: 01383 723 468

Heart of Midlothian Football Club
Tel: 0131 337 6132
Fax: 0131 346 0699
Website: http://www.hearts.co.uk

Motherwell Football Club
Tel: 01698 333 333
Fax: 01698 276 333

Rangers Football Club
Tel: 0141 427 8500
Fax: 0141 427 2676

St Johnstone Football Club
Tel: 01738 626 961
Fax: 01738 625 771

Hibernian Football Club
Tel: 0131 661 2159
Fax: 0131 659 6488
Website: http://www.hibs.co.uk

Kilmarnock Football Club
Tel: 01563 525 184
Fax: 01563 522 181

GAELIC FOOTBALL

Gaelic Athletic Association
Tel: 00 353 1 836 3222
Fax: 00 353 1 836 3420

GLIDING

British Gliding Association
Tel: 0181 579 1813
Fax: 0181 840 2117

GOLF

Council Of National Golf Unions
Tel: 01704 872164
Fax: 01704 833028

English Golf Union
Tel: 01526 354 500
Fax: 01526 354 020

Ladies Golf Union
Tel: 01334 75811
Fax: 01334 72818

PGA European Tour
Tel: 01344 842881
Fax: 01344 842929

USA PGA Tour
Tel: + 1 904 285 3700
Fax: + 1 904 285 7913

The Professional Golfers Association -UK HQ
Tel: 01675 470333
Fax: 01675 470674

The Professional Golfers Association Of America
Tel: + 1 561 624 8400
Fax: + 1 561 629 8484
Website: http://www.pga.com

Womens PGA & European Golf Tour
Tel: 01625 611444
Fax: 01625 610406

GREYHOUND RACING

National Greyhound Racing Club
Tel: 0171 267 9256
Fax: 0171 482 1023

GYMNASTICS

British Amateur Gymnastics Association
Tel: 01952 820330
Fax: 01952 820326
Website: http://www.baga.co.uk

Federation Internationale De Gymnastique
Tel: + 41 32 494 64 10
Fax: + 41 32 494 64 19
Website: http://www.worldsport.com/sports/gymnastics/home.html

HANDBALL

British Handball Association
Tel: 01706 229354
Fax: 01706 229 354

International Handball Federation
Tel: + 41 61 272 1300
Fax: + 41 61 272 1344
Website: http://www.worldsport.com/sports/handball/home.html

HORSE-RACING

International Racing Bureau
Tel: 01638 668881
Fax: 01638 665032

British Horse-Racing Board
Tel: 0171 396 0011
Fax: 0171 935 3626

ICE HOCKEY

British Ice Hockey Association
Tel: 01202 303946
Fax: 01202 398005

International Ice Hockey Federation
Tel: + 41 1289 8600
Fax: ⎮ 41 1 289 8620
Website: http://www.iihf.com/

CLUBS

Ayr Scottish Eagles
Tel: 01292 678 822
Fax: 01292 678 833

Basingstoke Bisons
Tel: 01256 355 266
Fax: 01256 357 367

Bracknell Bees
Tel: 01344 860 033
Fax: 01344 860 023

Cardiff Devils
Tel: 01222 397 198
Fax: 01222 397 160
Website: http://www.cwtc.co.uk/devils

Manchester Storm
Tel: 0161 950 4000
Fax: 0161 950 6000

Newcastle Cobras
Tel: 0191 260 5000
Fax: 0191 260 2200

Nottingham Panthers
Tel: 0115 948 4526
Fax: 0115 941 3103
Website: http://www.ccc.nottingham.ac.uk/nozjs

Sheffield Steelers
Tel: 0114 256 2002
Fax: 0114 256 1605
Website: http://www.steelers.co.uk

JUDO

British Judo association
Tel: 0116 255 9669
Fax: 0116 255 9660
Website: http://www.ijf.org

International Judo Federation
Tel: + 82 2 759-6936
Fax: + 82 2 754-1075
Website: http://www.ijf.org/

KARATE

World Karate Federation
Tel: + 33 1 4395 4200
Fax: + 33 1 4543 8984

LIFE SAVING

Federation Internationale De Sauvetage Aquatique
Tel: + 32 16 35 35 00
Fax: + 32 16 35 01 02

NETBALL

All England Netball Association
Tel: 01462 442344
Fax: 01462 442343

International Federation Of Netball Associations
Tel: 0121 678 7878
Fax: 0121 440 24 08
Website: http://www.netball.org

MOTORBOATING

Union Internationale Motonautique
Tel: + 33 4 92 05 25 22
Fax: + 33 4 92 05 25 23

MOTORCYCLING

Auto Cycle Union
Tel: 01788 540519
Fax: 01788 573 585

Federation Internationale Motocycliste
Tel: + 41 22 950 9500
Fax: + 41 22 950 9501

MOTORSPORT

Federation Internationale Du Sport Automobile
Tel: + 33.1 43 12 44 55
Fax: + 33 114312 4466

R.A.C. Motor Sports Association
Tel: 01753 681736
Fax: 01753 682938

BRITISH CIRCUITS

Brands Hatch
Tel: 01474 872 331
Fax: 01474 874 766

Donington Park
Tel: 01332 810 048
Fax: 01332 850 422

Silverstone
Tel: 01327 857 271
Fax: 01327 857 663

Thruxton
Tel: 01264 772 696
Fax: 01264 773 794

Knockhill
Tel: 01383 723 337
Fax: 01383 620167

Snetterton
Tel: 01953 887 303
Fax: 01953 888220

MOUNTAIN BIKE

British Mountain Bike Federation
Tel: 0161 223 2244
Fax: 0161 231 0592

POLO

Hurlingham Polo Association
Tel: 01869 350044
Fax: 01869 350625

International Polo Federation
Tel: + 1 310 557-9259
Fax: + 1 310 472-5220

RUGBY LEAGUE

British Amateur Rugby League Association
Tel: 01484 544131
Fax: 01484 519 985

International Board Secretary
Tel: + 64 9 378 8388
Fax: + 64 9 378 1060

Rugby Football League
Tel: 0113 232 9111
Fax: 0113 232 3666
Website: http://www.sporting-life.com/rleague

CLUBS

Bradford Bulls
Tel: 01274 733 899
Fax: 01274 724 730
Website: http://www.bradfordbulls.co.uk

Castleford Tigers
Tel: 01977 552 674
Fax: 01977 578 007

Leeds Rhinos
Tel: 0113 278 6181
Fax: 0113 275 4284
Website: http://www.sporting-life.com

Halifax Blue Sox
Tel: 01422 250 600
Fax: 01422 251 666

London Broncos
Tel: 0181 410 5000
Fax: 0181 410 5001
Website: http://www.hoppanet.com/broncos

Hull Sharks
Tel: 01482 290 40
Fax: 01482 203 38

Huddersfield Giants
Tel: 01484 530 710
Fax: 01484 531 712

Sheffield Eagles
Tel: 0114 261 0326
Fax: 0114 261 0303

St Helens
Tel: 01744 236 97
Fax: 01744 451 302
Website: http://saints.merseyworld.com

Salford Reds
Tel: 0161 737 6363
Fax: 0161 745 8272
Website: http://www.reds.co.uk

Warrington Wolves
Tel: 01925 635 338
Fax: 01925 571 744

Wigan Warriors
Tel: 01942 231 321
Fax: 01942 820 111

RUGBY UNION

International Rugby Football Board
Tel: +353 1662 5444
Fax: +353 1676 9334
Website: http://www.irfb.com

The French Rugby Union
Tel: +33 1 53 211515
Fax: +33 1 4526 1919

The Irish Rugby Union
Tel: +353 1 668 4601
Fax: +353 1 660 5640

The Rugby Football Union
Tel: 0181 892 8161
Fax: 0181 892 9816

The Scottish Rugby Union
Tel: 0131 346 5000
Fax: 0131 313 2810

The Welsh Rugby Union
Tel: 01222 390111
Fax: 01222 378472

CLUBS

Bath Rugby Football Club
Tel: 01225 325 200
Fax: 01225 325 201
Website: http://www.bathrugby.co.uk

Bristol Rugby Football Club
Tel: 0117 908 5500
Fax: 0117 908 5530

Gloucester Rugby Football Club
Tel: 01452 381 087
Fax: 01452 383 321
Website: http://www.glawster.demon.co.uk

Harlequins Rugby Football Club
Tel: 0181 410 6000
Fax: 0181 410 6001
Website: http://www.quins.co.uk

Leicester Rugby Football Club
Tel: 0116 254 1607
Fax: 0116 285 4766
Website: http://www.le.ac.uk/leicester/
tigers/index

Newcastle Rugby Football Club
Tel: 0191 214 5588
Fax: 0191 214 0488

Northampton Rugby Football Club
Tel: 01604 751 543
Fax: 01604 599 110

Richmond Rugby Football Club
Tel: 0181 332 7112
Fax: 0181 332 7113
Website: http://richmond.uk.oracle.com

Sale Rugby Football Club
Tel: 0161 973 6348
Fax: 0161 969 4124

Saracens Rugby Football Club
Tel: 01923 496 200
Fax: 01923 496 201
Website: http://www.saracens-rfu.co.uk

London Irish Rugby Football Club
Tel: 01932 783 034
Fax: 01932 784 462

Wasps Rugby Football Club
Tel: 0181 743 0262
Fax: 0181 740 2508

ROWING

Amateur Rowing Association
Tel: 0181 748 3632
Fax: 0181 741 4658

Federation Internationale Des Societies D'aviron
Tel: +41 21 617 8373
Fax: +41 21 617 8375
Website: http://erebus.rutgers.edu/ronchen/
fisa.html

SKATING

International Skating Union
Tel: +41 81 410 06 00
Fax: +41 81 410 06 06
Website: http://virtserv.interhop.net/isu/

National Skating Association of Great Britain
Tel: 0171 253 3824
Fax: 0171 490 2589

SKIING

British Ski Federation
Tel: 01506 884343
Fax: 01506 882952
Website: http://alpha.communicata.co.uk/
BSF/homepage.

Federation Internationale de Ski
Tel: +41 33 244 6161
Fax: +41 33 243 5353
Website: http://www.zip.com.au/birdman/
fis.html

SLEDDOG

International Federation of Sleddog Sports
Tel: +1 208 232 5130
Fax: +1 208 234 1608

SPEEDWAY

British Cycle Speedway Council
Tel: 01508 493 880
Fax: 01508 493 880

Speedway Control Board Ltd
Tel: 01788 540096
Fax: 01788 552 308
Website: http://www.british-speedway.co.uk

SQUASH

World Squash Federation
Tel: 01424 42 92 45
Fax: 01424 42 92 50
Website: http://www.squash.org

Squash Rackets Association
Tel: 0181 746 1616
Fax: 0181 746 0580

SWIMMING

Amateur Swimming Association
Tel: 01509 618700
Fax: 01509 610720

Federation Internationale De Natation Amateur
Tel: +41 21 312 6602
Fax: +41 21 312 6610
Website: http://www.fina.org

TABLE TENNIS

English Table Tennis Association
Tel: 01424 722525
Fax: 01424 422103

International Table Tennis Federation
Tel: 01424 721 414
Fax: 01424 431 871
Website: http://www.ittf.com

TAEKWONDO

The World Taekwondo Federation
Tel: +82 2 566 2505
Fax: +82 2 / 553 4728
Website: http://www.wtf.or.kr/

British Taekwondo Council
Tel: 01895 420 722

TENNIS

International Tennis Federation
Tel: 0171 381 80 60
Fax: 0171 381 39 89
Website: http://www.itftennis.com/

Lawn Tennis Association
Tel: 0171 381 7000
Fax: 0171 381 5965
Website: http://www.itftennis.com

Corel WTA Tour
Tel: 01642 463 020
Fax: 01642 463 020
Website: http://www.corelwtatour.com/

ATP Tour
Tel: 0171 352 3852
Fax: 0171 376 7213
Website: http://www.atptour.com

TRIATHLON

International Triathlon Union
Tel: +1 604 926 7250
Fax: +1 604 926 7260
Website: http://triathlon.org

British Triathlon Federation
Tel: 01530 414 234
Fax: 01530 560 279

TUG-OF-WAR

Tug-Of-War Association
Tel: 01494 783057
Fax: 01494 792040

Tug-Of-War International Federation
Tel: +1 608 879 2869
Fax: +1 608 879 2103

VOLLEYBALL

English Volleyball Association
Tel: 01602 816324
Fax: 01602 455429

International Volleyball Federation
Tel: +41 21 320 89 32
Fax: +41 21 320 88 65
Website: http://www.fivb.ch/

WEIGHTLIFTING

British Amateur Weightlifting Association
Tel: 01865 200339
Fax: 01865 790 096

International Weightlifting Federation
Tel: +36 1 1318153
Fax: +36 1 153 01 99
Website: http://www.worldsport.com/sports/
weightlifting/home.html

WRESTLING

British Amateur Wrestling Association
Tel: 0161 832 9209
Fax: 0161 833 1120

Federation Internationale Des Luttes Associees
Tel: +41 21 312 8426
Fax: +41 21 323 6073
Website: http://www.uni-leipzig.de/iat/
fila/fila1.htm

YACHTING

International Sailing Federation
Tel: 01703 635111
Fax: 01703 635789
Website: http://www.sailing.org

Royal Yachting Association
Tel: 01703 627400
Fax: 01703 629924

Sportcal International

The Daily Telegraph Sport Diary and Yearbook 1998 is the essential guide for all sports enthusiats who want to know when an event is taking place and how to buy tickets. It is the perfect reference to what's going on in 1998. But what happens when an event changes date or has yet to be confirmed?
The answer is **Sportcal International.**

Sportcal International is a constantly updated sports events information system with all the latest news on when and where events are taking place. Covering over 14,000 national and international sports events from now until the year 2007, it really is the most comprehensive guide to the future world of sport.

If you are a newspaper journalist or television broadcaster you can be constantly kept in touch with all the latest events information through Sportcal Global Communications' full range of services provided on a subscription basis.

For the real sports enthusiasts, Sportcal Global Communications have recently introduced a monthly fax report service providing all the latest information straight to your home or office for less than £10 per month.

As all events listed in The Daily Telegraph Sport Diary and Yearbook 1998 have been provided by Sportcal International, why not check out the latest information on sport either by visiting Sportcal Global Communications' Online Internat site or by signing up to one of our subscription services.

Contact us at:
Sportcal Global Communications Ltd, Hill Place House,
55a High Street, Wimbledon Village, London SW19 5BA
Telephone: 0181 944 8786
Fax: 0181 944 8740
email: info@sportcal.co.uk
internet: http://www.sportcal.co.uk

CONVERSION FORMULAE

		Distance	1 Kilometre =	
			0·62137	Land Miles United Kingdom
			0·53961	Nautical Miles United Kingdom
			0·53996	Nautical Miles International

To Convert	M'ply By	To Convert	M'ply By	To Convert	M'ply By	To Convert	M'ply By
Inches to C'metres	2.5400	Sq Metres to Sq Feet	10.7600	Cu Feet to Cu Metres	0.0283	Ounces to Grams	28.3500
C'metres to Inches	0.3937	Sq Feet to Sq Metres	0.0929	Cu Metres to Cu Feet	35.3100	Grams to Ounces	0.0353
Feet to Metres	0.3048	Sq Yards to Sq Metres	0.8361	Cu Yards to Cu Metres	0.7646	Pounds to Grams	453.6000
Metres to Feet	3.2810	Sq Metres to Sq Yards	1.1960	Cu Metres to Cu Yards	1.3080	Grams to Pounds	0.0022
Yards to Metres	0.9144	Sq Miles to Sq K'metres	2.5900	Cu Ins to Litres	0.0163	Pounds to K'grams	0.4536
Metres to Yards	1.0940	Sq K'metres to Sq Miles	0.3861	Litres to Cu Ins	61.0300	K'grams to Pounds	2.2050
Miles to Kilometres	1.6090	Acres to Hectares	0.4047	Gallons to Litres	4.5460	Tons to K'grams	1016.0000
Kilometres to Miles	0.6214	Hectares to Acres	2.4710	Litres to Gallons	0.2200	K'grams to Tons	0.0009
Sq Ins to Sq C'ms	6.4520	Cu Ins to Cu C'ms	16.3900	Grains to Grams	0.0648		
Sq C'ms to Sq Ins	0.1550	Cu C'ms to Cu Ins	0.0610	Grams to Grains	15.4300		

CONVERSIONS FOR USE IN THE USA

Metric to US
Litres x 2.1134 = US Pints
Litres x 0.2642 = US Galls
Hectolitres x 26.417 = US Galls
Hectolitres x 2.838 = US Bushels
Cu Metres x 264.172 = US Galls

(UK Equivalent)
(1 x US Pint = 0.8327 UK Pint)
(1 x US Gall = 6.6616 UK Pints)
(H'litres x 21.997 = UK Galls)
(H'litres x 2.750 = UK Bushels)
(Cu Metres x 219.969 = UK Galls)

Litres per 100 K'metres x 0.00425 = US Gallons per mile
1 Barrel of oil = 42 US Gallons = 34.97 UK Galls = 0.159 Cu Metres

Clothing: Men's shoe sizes: US are 1 size larger than UK equivalent
Women's shoe sizes: US are 1½ sizes larger than UK equivalent
Men's clothing – similar sizes to UK but women's = 2 sizes smaller in US

WORLD TIMES
Note: Based on GMT at 12.00 hours compared with Local Standard Time

Place	Location	Time	Place	Location	Time	Place	Location	Time
Adelaide	S Australia	21.30	Jerusalem	Israel	14.00	Yangon/Rangoon	Myanmar/Burma	18.30
Amsterdam	Netherlands	13.00	Lagos	Nigeria	13.00	Riyadh	Saudi Arabia	15.30
Athens	Greece	14.00	Lisbon	Portugal	12.00	Rio de Janeiro	Brazil	9.00
Auckland	New Zealand	24.00	Madeira		12.00	Rome	Italy	13.00
Berlin	Germany	13.00	Madras	India	17.30	San Francisco	USA	4.00
Bombay/Calcutta	India	17.30	Madrid	Spain	13.00	Santiago	Chile	8.00
Brindisi	Italy	13.00	Malta		13.00	St John's	Newfoundland	8.30
Brussels	Belgium	13.00	Manama	Bahrain	15.00	St Louis	USA	6.00
Bucharest	Romania	14.00	Melbourne	Australia	22.00	St Petersburg	Russia	15.00
Budapest	Hungary	13.00	Montreal	Canada	7.00	Singapore		20.00
Buenos Aires	Argentina	9.00	Moscow	Russia	15.00	Stockholm	Sweden	13.00
Cairo	Egypt	14.00	New York	USA	7.00	Suez	Egypt	14.00
Cape Town	South Africa	14.00	Oslo	Norway	13.00	Sydney	Australia	22.00
Chicago/New Orleans	USA	6.00	Ottawa	Canada	7.00	Tokyo	Japan	21.00
Copenhagen	Denmark	13.00	Panama		7.00	Toronto	Canada	7.00
Geneva	Switzerland	13.00	Paris	France	13.00	Vancouver	Canada	4.00
Gibraltar		13.00	Peking	China	20.00	Vienna	Austria	13.00
Helsinki	Finland	14.00	Perth	W Australia	20.00	Winnipeg	Canada	6.00
Hong Kong		20.00	Prague	Czech Rep.	13.00	Yokohama	Japan	21.00
Istanbul	Turkey	15.00	Quebec	Canada	7.00			

INTERNATIONAL PAPER SIZES

BLED WORK OR EXTRA TRIMS

Size	Millimetres	Inches
SRA0	900 x 1280	35.43 x 50.39
SRA1	640 x 900	25.20 x 35.43
SRA2	450 x 640	17.72 x 25.20

TRIMMED SIZES

Size	Millimetres	Inches
2A	1189 x 1682	46.81 x 66.22
A0	841 x 1189	33.11 x 46.81

Size	Millimetres	Inches
A1	594 x 841	23.39 x 33.11
A2	420 x 594	16.54 x 23.39
A3	297 x 420	11.69 x 16.54
A4	210 x 297	8.27 x 11.69
A5	148 x 210	5.83 x 8.27
A6	105 x 148	4.13 x 5.83
A7	74 x 105	2.91 x 4.13

COUNTRY	CAPITAL	LANGUAGE	CURRENCY	CODE (00+)	COUNTRY	CAPITAL	LANGUAGE	CURRENCY	CODE (00+)
Algeria	Algiers	Arabic	Dinar (DZD)	213	Luxembourg	Luxembourg	Fre./German	Franc (LUF)	352
Argentina	Buenos Aires	Spanish	Peso (ARS)	54	Madagascar	Antananarivo	Malagasy/Fre.	Franc (MGF)	261
Australia	Canberra	English	Dollar (AUD)	61	Malawi	Lilongwe	Chichewa/Eng.	Kwacha (MWK)	265
Austria	Vienna	German	Schilling (ATS)	43	Malaysia	Kuala Lumpur	Bahasa Malay	Ringgit (MYR)	60
Bahrain	Manama	Arabic	Dinar (BHD)	973	Mauritania	Nouakchott	Fre./Arabic	Ouguiya (MRO)	222
Bangladesh	Dhaka	Bengali	Taka (BDT)	880	Mexico	Mexico City	Spanish	Peso (MXN)	52
Belgium	Brussels	French/Dutch	Franc (BEF)	32	Morocco	Rabat	Arabic	Dirham (MAD)	212
Bolivia	La Paz	Spanish	Boliviano (BOB)	591	Mozambique	Maputo	Portuguese	Metical (MZM)	258
Brazil	Brasilia	Portuguese	Real (BRL)	55	Netherlands	Amsterdam	Dutch	Guilder (NLG)	31
Bulgaria	Sofia	Bulgarian	Lev (BGL)	359	New Zealand	Wellington	English	Dollar (NZD)	64
Cameroon	Yaoundé	Fre./Eng.	Franc (XAF)	237	Nicaragua	Managua	Spanish	Cordoba (NIO)	505
Canada	Ottawa	Eng./Fre.	Dollar (CAD)	1	Niger	Niamey	French	Franc (XOF)	227
Chile	Santiago	Spanish	Peso (CLP)	56	Nigeria	Abuja	English	Naira (NGN)	234
China	Beijing	Chinese	Ren Min Bi Yuan (CNY)	86	Norway	Oslo	Norwegian	Krone (NOK)	47
Colombia	Bogotá	Spanish	Peso (COP)	57	Oman	Muscat	Arabic	Rial (OMR)	968
Costa Rica	San José	Spanish	Colon (CRC)	506	Pakistan	Islamabad	Urdu/English	Rupee (PKR)	92
Cuba	Havana	Spanish	Peso (CUP)	53	Panama	Panama City	Spanish	Balboa (PAB)	507
Czech Rep	Prague	Czech	Koruna (CZK)	42	Paraguay	Asunción	Spanish	Guarani (PYG)	595
Denmark	Copenhagen	Danish	Krone (DKK)	45	Peru	Lima	Spanish	New Sol (PES)	51
Ecuador	Quito	Spanish	Sucre (ECS)	593	Philippines	Manila	Filipino/Eng.	Peso (PHP)	63
Egypt	Cairo	Arabic	Pound (EGP)	20	Poland	Warsaw	Polish	Zloty (PLN)	48
Estonia	Tallinn	Estonian	Kroon (EEK)	372	Portugal	Lisbon	Portuguese	Escudo (PTE)	351
Finland	Helsinki	Finnish	Markka (FIM)	358	Qatar	Doha	Arabic	Riyal (QAR)	974
France	Paris	French	Franc (FRF)	33	Romania	Bucharest	Romanian	Lei (ROL)	40
Gabon	Libreville	French	Franc (XAF)	241	Russian Fed.	Moscow	Russian	Rouble (RUR)	7
Germany	Berlin	German	Deutsche Mark (DEM)	49	Saudi Arabia	Riyadh	Arabic	Riyal (SAR)	966
Ghana	Accra	English	Cedi (GHC)	233	Senegal	Dakar	French	Franc (XOF)	221
Greece	Athens	Greek	Drachma (GRD)	30	Singapore	Singapore	Malay/Mandarin	Dollar (SGD)	65
Guatemala	Guatemala City	Spanish	Quetzal (GTQ)	502	Slovakia	Bratislava	Slovak	Koruna (SKK)	42
Hungary	Budapest	Magyar	Forint (HUF)	36	Somalia	Mogadishu	Somali	Shilling (SOS)	252
Iceland	Reykjavik	Icelandic	Krona (ISK)	354	South Africa	Cape Town	Afrikaans/Eng.	Rand (ZAR)	27
India	New Delhi	Hindi/Eng.	Rupee (INR)	91	Spain	Madrid	Spanish	Peseta (ESP)	34
Indonesia	Jakarta	Bahasa Ind.	Rupiah (IDR)	62	Sri Lanka	Colombo	Sinhala/Tamil	Rupee (LKR)	94
Iran	Tehran	Farsi	Rial (IRR)	98	Sudan	Khartoum	Arabic/Eng.	Dinar (SDD)	249
Iraq	Baghdad	Arabic	Dinar (IQD)	964	Sweden	Stockholm	Swedish	Krona (SEK)	46
Ireland (Eire)	Dublin	Eng./Irish	Pound (IEP)	353	Switzerland	Berne	Ger./Fre./Ital.	Franc (CHF)	41
Israel	Jerusalem	Hebrew/Arabic	Shekel (ILS)	972	Syrian Rep	Damascus	Arabic	Pound (SYP)	963
Italy	Rome	Italian	Lira (ITL)	39	Taiwan	Taipei	Mandarin	Dollar (TWD)	886
Jamaica	Kingston	English	Dollar (JMD)	1 809	Tanzania	Dar-es-Salaam	Kiswahili/Eng.	Shilling (TZS)	255
Japan	Tokyo	Japanese	Yen (JPY)	81	Thailand	Bangkok	Thai	Baht (THB)	66
Jordan	Amman	Arabic	Dinar (JOD)	962	Tunisia	Tunis	Arabic/Fre.	Dinar (TND)	216
Kenya	Nairobi	Kiswahili/Eng.	Shilling (KES)	254	Turkey	Ankara	Turkish	Lira (TRL)	90
Korea Dem. Rep.	Pyongyang	Korean	Won (KPW)	850	Uganda	Kampala	English	Shilling (UGS)	256
Korea Rep. of	Seoul	Korean	Won (KRW)	82	UAE	Abu Dhabi	Arabic	Dirham (AED)	971
Kuwait	Kuwait	Arabic	Dinar (KWD)	965	USA	Washington	English	Dollar (USD)	1
Latvia	Riga	Latvian	Lats (LVL)	371	Uruguay	Montevideo	Spanish	Peso (UYU)	598
Lebanon	Beirut	Arabic	Pound (LBP)	961	Venezuela	Caracas	Spanish	Bolivar (VEB)	58
Libya	Tripoli	Arabic	Dinar (LYD)	218	Zaire	Kinshasa	French	Zaire (ZRN)	243
Lithuania	Vilnius	Lithuanian	Litas (LTL)	370	Zambia	Lusaka	English	Kwacha (ZMK)	260

UK ROAD DISTANCE CHART

Note: Shortest practical routes by road for business use.

	YORK	SOUTHAMPTON	SHEFFIELD	PORTSMOUTH	OXFORD	NOTTINGHAM	NORWICH	NEWCASTLE	MANCHESTER	LONDON	LIVERPOOL	LEEDS	INVERNESS	GLASGOW	EXETER	EDINBURGH	DOVER	DERBY	CARDIFF	BRISTOL	BIRMINGHAM	ABERYSTWYTH	ABERDEEN
ABERDEEN	307	538	347	552	473	379	480	228	333	492	335	314	107	141	565	121	563	384	493	490	411	440	—
ABERYSTWYTH	195	198	156	218	157	156	271	259	131	212	105	171	477	321	199	320	285	140	110	124	116	—	440
BIRMINGHAM	129	128	76	141	63	49	161	204	81	111	90	110	448	292	164	290	185	40	102	88	—	116	411
BRISTOL	217	74	164	94	70	137	209	288	162	114	161	196	527	371	75	369	189	127	44	—	88	124	490
CARDIFF	231	118	178	138	104	151	235	301	173	150	165	208	530	374	120	373	228	142	—	44	102	110	493
DERBY	88	154	37	175	90	16	139	161	59	123	81	70	419	270	203	263	196	—	142	127	40	140	384
DOVER	264	143	229	131	129	196	156	343	257	74	270	257	600	466	244	442	—	196	228	189	185	285	563
EDINBURGH	186	418	227	431	353	259	360	107	213	372	214	193	158	45	444	—	442	263	373	369	290	320	121
EXETER	292	107	240	124	141	213	282	364	238	170	237	271	602	446	—	444	244	203	120	75	164	199	565
GLASGOW	210	419	241	432	354	279	383	265	214	389	216	211	167	—	446	45	466	270	374	371	292	321	141
INVERNESS	344	575	385	589	511	416	517	265	371	529	372	351	—	167	602	158	600	419	530	527	448	477	107
LEEDS	25	229	34	242	164	70	174	94	41	191	73	—	351	211	271	193	257	70	208	196	110	171	314
LIVERPOOL	97	217	72	231	153	99	217	155	34	198	—	73	372	216	237	214	270	81	165	161	90	105	335
LONDON	194	77	160	71	56	123	112	274	184	—	198	191	529	389	170	372	74	123	150	114	111	212	492
MANCHESTER	65	208	38	222	144	71	185	131	—	184	34	41	371	214	238	213	257	59	173	162	81	131	333
NEWCASTLE	82	319	128	332	254	159	260	—	131	274	155	94	265	145	364	107	343	161	301	288	204	259	228
NORWICH	181	190	146	184	141	123	—	260	185	112	217	174	517	383	282	360	156	139	235	209	161	271	480
NOTTINGHAM	80	160	38	173	95	—	123	159	71	123	99	70	416	279	213	259	196	16	151	137	49	156	379
OXFORD	174	65	130	78	—	95	141	254	144	56	153	164	511	354	141	353	129	90	104	70	63	157	473
PORTSMOUTH	252	17	208	—	78	173	184	332	222	71	231	242	589	432	124	431	131	175	138	94	141	218	552
SHEFFIELD	53	195	—	208	130	38	146	128	38	160	72	34	385	241	240	227	229	37	178	164	76	156	347
SOUTHAMPTON	239	—	195	17	65	160	190	319	208	77	217	229	575	419	107	418	143	154	118	74	128	198	538
YORK	—	239	53	252	174	80	181	82	65	194	97	25	344	210	292	186	264	88	231	217	129	195	307

AIRLINES - RESERVATIONS

Aer Lingus	0645 737747	American Airlines	0181-572 5555
Aeroflot	0171-355 2233	Austrian Airlines	0171-439 4144
Aerolineas Argentinas	0171-494 1001	British Airways	0345 222 111
Air Canada	0990 247 226	British Midland	0345 554 554
Air France	0181-742 6600	British West Indian	0181-577 1100
Air India	01753-684828	Cathay Pacific	0171-747 8888
Air Malta	0181-785 3177	Cyprus Airways	0171-388 5411
Air Portugal TAP	0171-828 0262	Finnair	0171-408 1222
Air UK	0345 666777	Iberia	0171-830 0011
Air Zimbabwe	0171-491 0009	Japan Airlines	0171-408 1000
Alitalia	0171-602 7111	Kenya Airways	0171-409 0277

KLM	0181-750 9200	SAS	0171-734 4020
Lufthansa	0345 737747	Singapore Airlines	0181-747 0007
Malaysian Airlines	0181-341 2020	Sudan	0171-499 8101
Middle East Airlines	0171-493 5681	Swissair	0171-439 4144
Monarch Airlines	01582 398333	Turkish Airlines	0171-499 4499
Olympic Airways	0171-409 3400	Thai International	0171-499 9113
Pakistan International	0171-734 5544	Trans World (TWA)	0171-439 0707
Polish Airlines (LOT)	0171-580 5037	Varig Brazilian	0171-287 3131
Qantas	0345 747767	Virgin Atlantic	01293 747747
Sabena	0181-780 1444		
Saudi Arabian	0181-995 7777		

SEA LINKS/EUROTUNNEL - RESERVATIONS

Brittany Ferries	0990 360360	Irish Ferries	0990 171717	Sally (UK)	01843 595522	Le Shuttle	0990 353 535
Colour Line	0191 2961313	North Sea Ferries	01482 377177	Scandinavian Seaways	0171-409 6060		
Hoverspeed/Seacat	01304 240241	P & O European Ferries	0990 980980	Stena Line	01233 647047		

TEMPERATURE - SPEEDS - TYRE PRESSURES

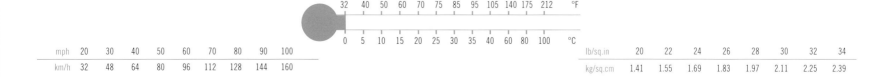

°F	32	40	50	60	70	75	85	95	105	140	175	212
°C	0	5	10	15	20	25	30	35	40	60	80	100

mph	20	30	40	50	60	70	80	90	100
km/h	32	48	64	80	96	112	128	144	160

lb/sq.in	20	22	24	26	28	30	32	34
kg/sq.cm	1.41	1.55	1.69	1.83	1.97	2.11	2.25	2.39

ADDRESS BOOK

NAME	ADDRESS	NUMBERS
	telephone	
	fax	
	mobile	
	e-mail	
	telephone	
	fax	
	mobile	
	e-mail	
	telephone	
	fax	
	mobile	
	e-mail	
	telephone	
	fax	
	mobile	
	e-mail	
	telephone	
	fax	
	mobile	
	e-mail	
	telephone	
	fax	
	mobile	
	e-mail	
	telephone	
	fax	
	mobile	
	e-mail	
	telephone	
	fax	
	mobile	
	e-mail	

NAME	ADDRESS		NUMBERS
		telephone	
		fax	
		mobile	
		e-mail	
		telephone	
		fax	
		mobile	
		e-mail	
		telephone	
		fax	
		mobile	
		e-mail	
		telephone	
		fax	
		mobile	
		e-mail	
		telephone	
		fax	
		mobile	
		e-mail	
		telephone	
		fax	
		mobile	
		e-mail	
		telephone	
		fax	
		mobile	
		e-mail	
		telephone	
		fax	
		mobile	
		e-mail	

ADDRESS BOOK

NAME	ADDRESS		NUMBERS
		telephone	
		fax	
		mobile	
		e-mail	
		telephone	
		fax	
		mobile	
		e-mail	
		telephone	
		fax	
		mobile	
		e-mail	
		telephone	
		fax	
		mobile	
		e-mail	
		telephone	
		fax	
		mobile	
		e-mail	
		telephone	
		fax	
		mobile	
		e-mail	
		telephone	
		fax	
		mobile	
		e-mail	
		telephone	
		fax	
		mobile	
		e-mail	

NAME	ADDRESS	NUMBERS
		telephone
		fax
		mobile
		e-mail
		telephone
		fax
		mobile
		e-mail
		telephone
		fax
		mobile
		e-mail
		telephone
		fax
		mobile
		e-mail
		telephone
		fax
		mobile
		e-mail
		telephone
		fax
		mobile
		e-mail
		telephone
		fax
		mobile
		e-mail
		telephone
		fax
		mobile
		e-mail

ACKNOWLEDGEMENTS

Edited and compiled by: David Welch and Martin Smith
Conceived and produced for William Clowes Limited by: Jonathan Hayden
Project Manager: Alison Locke
Art direction, design and artwork by: Fiona Andreanelli, Janfranco Caro and Rachel Godfrey at Wherefore Art?

With grateful thanks to:
Members of the Daily Telegraph Sports Department: Russell Cheyne, Patrick Miles, Nicky McGovern, Joanna Lloyd
and all the writers and photographers

Despite every effort on the part of the publisher to ensure the accuracy of dates or other information compiled for this
diary, we cannot accept any responsibility for errors that may have occurred. At time of going to press some dates and
information are still provisional.

First published by **CLOWES** works in 1997
Text and Pictures © The Daily Telegraph
Design © Clowes Group
ISBN: 0 85194 103 6
Printed and bound in Great Britain by: Clowes Group, Beccles, England

TRANSPORT MAPS

National Rail Enquiries   0345 484950

British Rail International   0171-834 2345

Eurostar   01233 617575

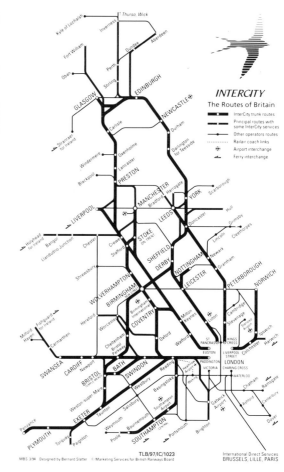

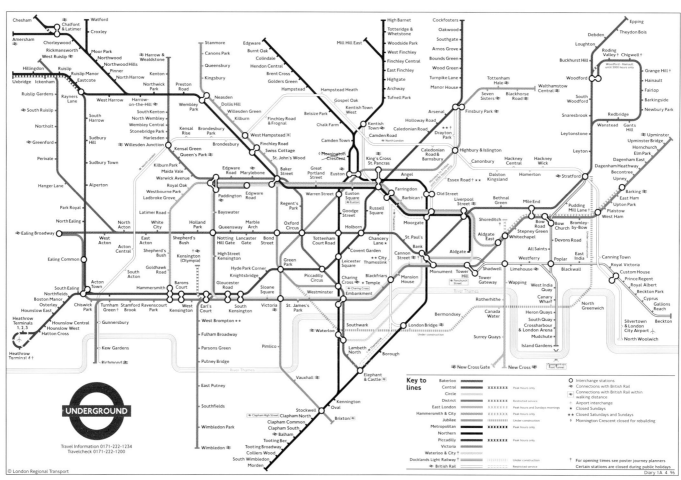

CONTENTS

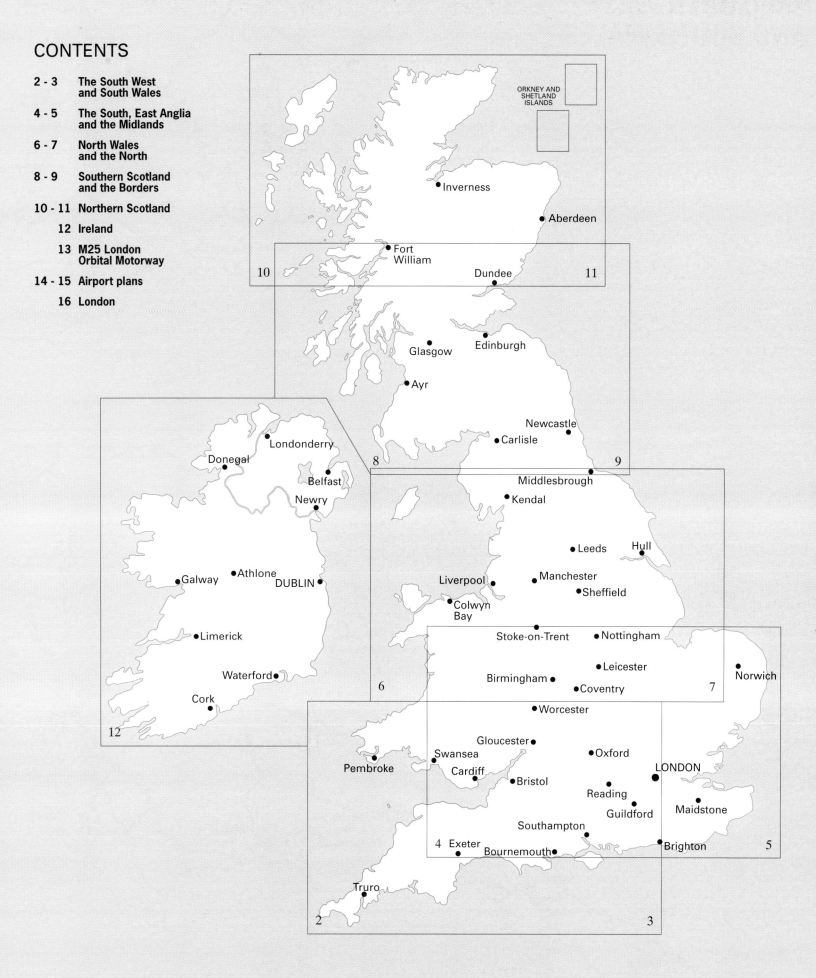

ORKNEY AND
SHETLAND
ISLANDS

10

11

● Inverness

● Aberdeen

Fort
William ●

Dundee ●

8

Glasgow ●

Edinburgh ●

Ayr ●

Newcastle ●

Carlisle ●

9

Donegal ●

Londonderry ●

Belfast ●

Newry ●

Middlesbrough ●

Kendal ●

Leeds ●   Hull ●

Galway ●   Athlone ●
DUBLIN ●

Liverpool ●   Manchester ●

Colwyn
Bay ●

Sheffield ●

6

Stoke-on-Trent ●   Nottingham ●

Limerick ●

Leicester ●

Birmingham ●   Coventry ●

7   Norwich ●

Waterford ●

Worcester ●

Cork ●

Gloucester ●

12

Swansea ●

Oxford ●

Pembroke ●

Cardiff ●

Bristol ●

LONDON ●

Reading ●

Guildford ●   Maidstone ●

Southampton ●

Brighton ●   5

4   Exeter ●

Bournemouth ●

Truro ●

2   3

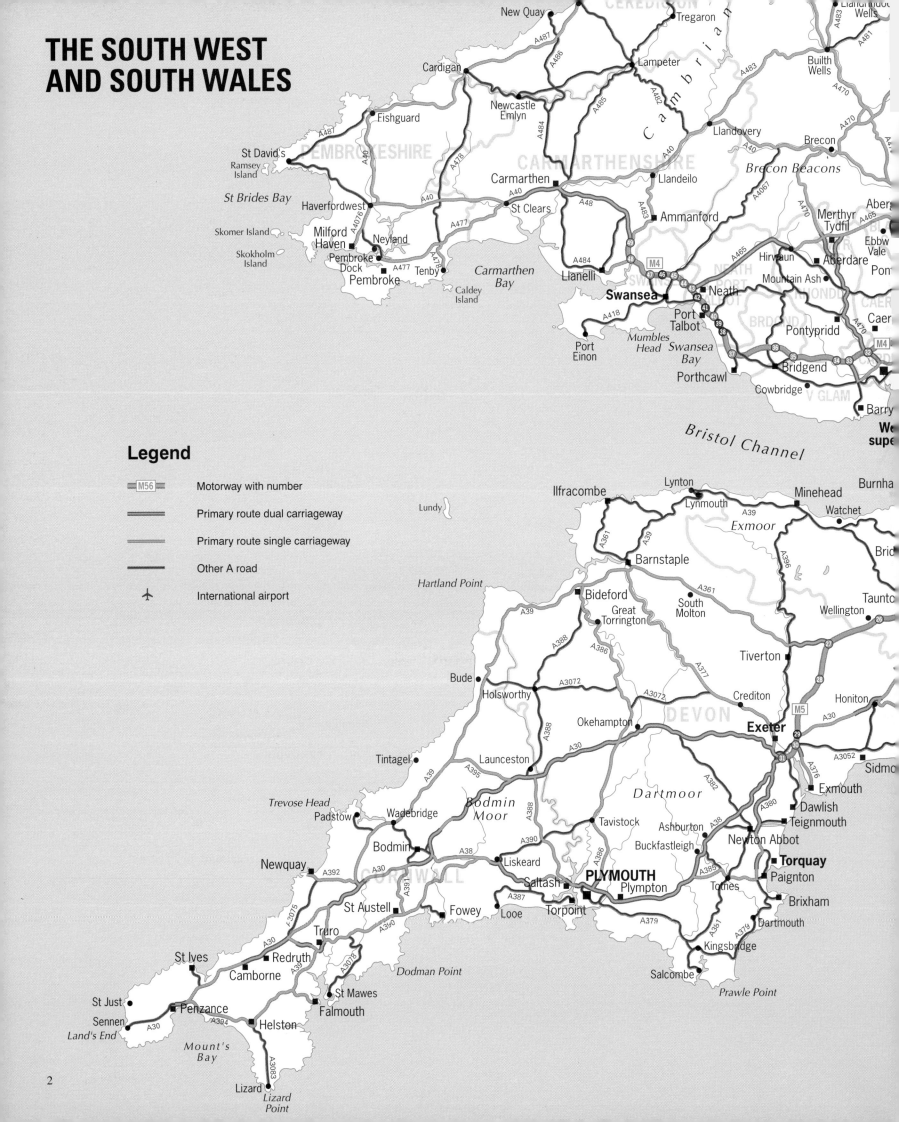

THE SOUTH WEST AND SOUTH WALES

Legend

M56	Motorway with number
	Primary route dual carriageway
	Primary route single carriageway
	Other A road
✈	International airport

New Quay
Tregaron
Llandrindod Wells
Cardigan
Lampeter
Builth Wells
Newcastle Emlyn
Fishguard
Llandovery
Brecon
St David's
Ramsey Island
Carmarthen
Llandeilo
Brecon Beacons
St Brides Bay
Haverfordwest
St Clears
Aberg
Merthyr Tydfil
Skomer Island
Milford Haven
Neyland
Ammanford
Ebbw Vale
Skokholm Island
Pembroke Dock
Pembroke
Tenby
Caldey Island
Llanelli
Carmarthen Bay
Swansea
Hirwaun
Mountain Ash
Aberdare
Neath
Port Talbot
Port Einon
Mumbles Head
Swansea Bay
Pontypridd
Caer
Porthcawl
Bridgend
Cowbridge
V GLAM
Barry
Bristol Channel
We super

Lynton
Minehead
Burnha
Ilfracombe
Lynmouth
Watchet
Exmoor
Lundy
Bri
Barnstaple
Taunto
Hartland Point
Bideford
South Molton
Great Torrington
Wellington
Bude
Tiverton
Holsworthy
Crediton
Honiton
Okehampton
Exeter
Tintagel
Launceston
Sidmo
Dartmoor
Exmouth
Trevose Head
Tavistock
Dawlish
Padstow
Wadebridge
Bodmin Moor
Ashburton
Teignmouth
Newquay
Bodmin
Buckfastleigh
Newton Abbot
Liskeard
PLYMOUTH
Torquay
St Austell
Saltash
Plympton
Paignton
Fowey
Torpoint
Totnes
Brixham
Looe
Truro
Dartmouth
Redruth
Kingsbridge
St Ives
Camborne
St Mawes
Dodman Point
Salcombe
St Just
Penzance
Falmouth
Prawle Point
Sennen
Helston
Land's End
Mount's Bay
Lizard
Lizard Point

2

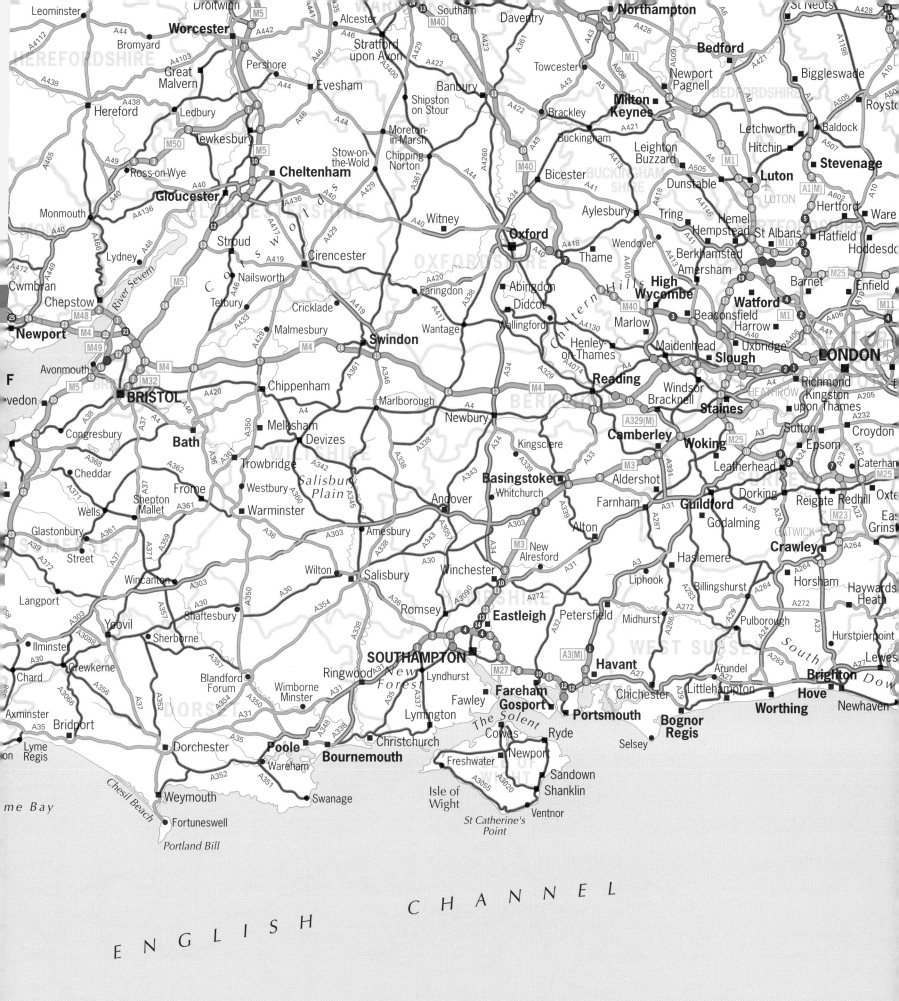

ENGLISH CHANNEL

| 0 | 10 | 20 | 30 miles |
| 0 | 10 | 20 | 30 | 40 kilometres |

3

THE SOUTH, EAST ANGLIA AND THE MIDLANDS

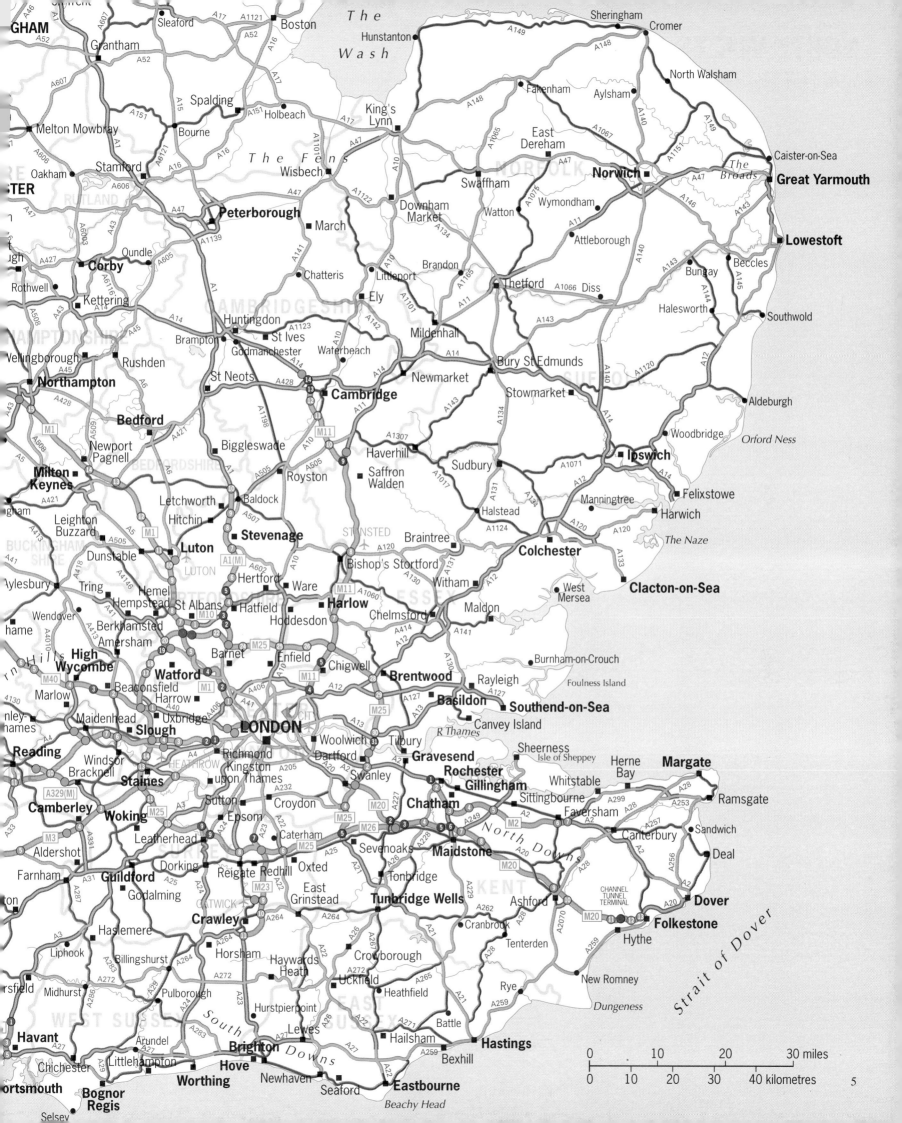

NORTH WALES AND THE NORTH

North Head
Whitehaven
Egremont

CUMBRIA
Brough
Lake District
Ambleside
Coniston
Windermere
Kendal
Hawes
Yorksh
Sedbergh

Point of Ayre
A17
Isle of Man
Ramsey
Maughold Head
A3
Peel
A4
Laxey
A2
A1
A3
A5
Douglas
Port Erin
Castletown

Irish Sea

Dreswick Point

ISLE OF MAN

Millom
Ulverston
Kirkby Lonsdale
Settle

Barrow-in-Furness
Isle of Walney
Grange-over-Sands
Carnforth
Morecambe
Heysham
Lancaster

Fleetwood
Garstang
Clitheroe

Blackpool
Kirkham
Padiham
Burn
Nels
Preston
Accrington
Lytham St Anne's
Blackburn
Leyland
Darwen
Rawtenst
Southport
Chorley
Rochdal
Ormskirk
Bolton
Bury
Formby
Skelmersdale
Wigan
Mid
Kirkby
Oldha
Crosby
St Helens
Salford
MAN
Bootle
LIVERPOOL
Sale
Wallasey
Warrington
Cheadle
Birkenhead
Altrincham
MANCHE
Bebington
Widnes
Knutsford
Wilmslow
Runcorn
Frodsham
Northwich
Macclesf
Ellesmere Port
Holmes Chapel
Chester
Middlewich
Bid
Sandbach
A527
Crewe
Kidsgro
Newcastle-under-Lyme
STO
Wrexham
Nantwich

Carmel Head
Amlwch
Great Ormes Head
Prestatyn
Holyhead
Anglesey
Llandudno
Colwyn Bay
Rhyl
River Dee
Holy Island
Beaumaris
Conwy
Abergele
Holywell
ISLE OF ANGLESEY
Menai Bridge
Bangor
St Asaph
Flint
Bethesda
Denbigh
Queensferry
Caernarfon
Mold
Caernarfon Bay
Llanberis
Ruthin
Betws-y-coed
CONWY
DENBIGHSHIRE

Ffestiniog
Whitchurch
Llangollen
Market Drayton
Porthmadog
Bala
Ruabon
Lleyn Peninsula
Pwllheli
Llangollen
Oswestry
Abersoch
GWYNEDD
Newport
Bardsey Island
Welshpool
Barmouth
Dolgellau
Shrewsbury
Mallwyd
Telford
Aberdyfi
Machynlleth
WOLVERHAMPTON
Cardigan Bay
Church Stretton
Bridgnorth
West Brom
Dudley
Stourbridge
Aberystwyth
Newtown
Kiddermimster
Llangurig
Ludlow
Rhayader

6

SOUTHERN SCOTLAND AND THE BORDERS

Tiree

Coll

Tobermory

Isle of Mull

Ulva

Iona

Fionnphort

Lochaline

Craignure

Lismore

Oban

Connel

Fort William

Glencoe

Ballachulish

Portnacroish

Sound of Mull

Loch Linnhe

Firth of Lorne

Killin

Tyndrum

Lochearnhead

Crianlarich

ARGYLL AND BUTE

Colonsay

Oronsay

Scarba

Luing

Inveraray

Strachur

Tarbet

Callander

Dunblane

STIRLING

Stirling

Denny

Ardlussa

Lochgilphead

Helensburgh

Dunoon

Gourock

Greenock

Port Glasgow

Alexandria

Dumbarton

Kilsyth

Kirkintilloch

Cum

Clydebank

GLASGOW

GLASGOW

Aird

Jura

Port Askaig

Islay

Coul Point

Tighnabruaich

Tarbert

Kennacraig

Rothesay

Largs

Johnstone

Paisley

Hamilton

Mothe

East Kilbride

Larkhall

LANA

Port Ellen

Gigha

Tayinloan

Kintyre

Sound of Bute

Kilbrannan Sound

Millport

Kilbirnie

Ardrossan

Kilwinning

Strathaven

NORTH AYRSHIRE

Kilmarnock

Lesmahagow

Arran

Brodick

Holy I

Firth of Clyde

Irvine

Troon

Prestwick

Ayr

Mauchline

EAST AYRSHIRE

Cumnock

Campbeltown

Mull of Kintyre

Ailsa Craig

Girvan

SOUTH AYRSHIRE

Maybole

Dalmellington

New Cumnock

Souther

New Galloway

DUMFRI AND GALLOWAY

North Channel

Cairnryan

Loch Ryan

Newton Stewart

Castle Douglas

Stranraer

Portpatrick

Luce Bay

Whithorn

Wigtown Bay

Kirkcudbright

Abbey Head

Drummore

Mull of Galloway

Burrow Head

Pitlochry

A924

Dunkeld

Blairgowrie

Kirriemuir

Brechin
A90
A935
● Montrose

ANGUS

A926
A932

Forfar

Lunan Bay

Coupar Angus
A94
A90

D KINROSS
DUNDEE CITY

A933

Arbroath

● Carnoustie

Dundee

Newport-on-Tay

Firth of Tay

Perth
A90

A823
A91

Bridge
of Earn

M90

St Andrews Bay

St Andrews

Cupar
A91

A914 (A92)

A915

Fife Ness

Glenrothes

A917

Elie

Isle of May

Kinross
A92

FIFE

M90

A977

Buckhaven

Kirkcaldy

Cowdenbeath

Dunfermline

rangemouth

Bo'ness

Inverkeithing
South Queensferry

Firth of Forth

North Berwick
A198

EDINBURGH

Linlithgow

EAST
LOTHIAN

A1

Dunbar

Musselburgh

Haddington

St Abb's Head

Livingston

Dalkeith

A1107

Bonnyrigg

WEST
LOTHIAN

MIDLOTHIAN

Penicuik

Eyemouth

A68

N O R T H

S E A

A70

A702

A703

A7

A6105

Berwick-upon-Tweed

Biggar

Peebles

Lammermuir Hills

A721

A73

A72

Uplands

A697

A6112

A698

Coldstream

Holy Island

A708

Galashiels

A8089

Kelso

A1

BORDERS
(SCOTTISH)

Selkirk

Wooler

Abington

Jedburgh

The Cheviot Hills

74(M)

Hawick

A68

A697

Alnwick

A6088

A1

A1068

Moffat

Amble

A74

NORTHUMBERLAND

Otterburn

Lochmaben

Langholm

Ashington
Newbiggin-
by-the-Sea

Lockerbie

Morpeth

A1

Bedlington

A74(M)

A696

Blyth

Dumfries

A68

Whitley Bay

Longtown

Ponteland

Tynemouth

A75

Annan

Gretna

Gosforth
South Shields

Corbridge
A69

NEWCASTLE UPON TYNE

y Firth

Wigton

A689

Brampton

Haltwhistle

Hexham
A695

Jarrow

Gateshead

A6

Carlisle

A69

A1

SUNDERLAND

A596

A68

A692

A963

Washington

Maryport

A595

Alston

Consett

Stanley

Houghton
le Spring

A19

Chester-le-
Street

A686

A697

M6

Durham

Peterlee

A167

A689

Crook

A1(M)

ington

Cockermouth

Keswick

Penrith

CUMBRIA

A66

A66

Bishop Auckland

A688

Spennymoor

Hartlepool

A689

Newton
Aycliffe

**Stockton-
on-Tees**

Barnard
Castle

A688

Redcar

Middlesbrough

9

NORTHERN SCOTLAND

0   10   20   30 miles
0 10 20 30 40 kilometres

Cape Wrath

Whiten Head

Rudha Rhoshanais
(Butt of Lewis)

Port Nis
(Port of Ness)

Durness

A857

Ton

Tolsta Head

A838

Handa Island

Gallan Head

WESTERN
ISLES

Steornabhagh
(Stornoway)

Broad Bay

Point of
Stoer

A894

A838

Altnaharra

A858

Eye Peninsula

Unapool

A836

Scarp

A859

Isle of
Lewis

The Minch

Lochinver

A837

Lairg

Tairbeart
(Tarbert)

Shiant
Islands

Summer
Isles

A835

A837

Toe
Head

Harris

Greenstone
Point

Ullapool

Highlands

Bo
Bri

Pabbay

Sound of Harris

Rudha
Reidh

Uibhist a Tuath
(North Uist)

The Little Minch

A832

Gairloch

Alness

A835

Loch nam Madadh
(Lochmaddy)

A867

Uig

Dunvegan
Head

Rona

Kinlochewe

A832

Garve

A832

Dingwall

Beinn na Faoghla
(Benbecula)

A87 (A856)

Sound of Raasay

Inner Sound

Achnasheen

A896

A890

Torridon

A9

HIGHLAND

Inverness

Dunvegan

Portree

A863

Raasay

West

Uibhist a Deas
(South Uist)

A865

Rudha Hallagro

Scalpay

Lochcarron

A831

Loch Baghasdail
(Lochboisdale)

Isle of
Skye

Soay

Stromeferry

Cannich

Drumnadrochit

A82

Kyle of Lochalsh

A87
(A850)

Kyleakin

Dornie

Sound of Barra

Eriskay

Cuillin

Shiel Bridge

Invermoriston

Mona
Moun

Barra

A888

Canna

A851

A87

Highland

Bagh a Chaisteil
(Castlebay)

Rum

Ardvasar

Sound of Sleat

A887

A87

Invergarry

K
Newtonm

Mingulay

Eigg

Mallaig

North

Laggan

Muck

Sound of Arisaig

A830

Spean Bridge

A86

Dalwhinnie

A82

Inner Hebrides

Fort William

Gram

A861

Glencoe

Tobermory

Ballachulish

A82

Coll

A884

Loch Linnhe

Portnacroish

Sound of Mull

Lochaline

A828

Tiree

Lismore

Killin

Craignure

Oban

Connel

Tyndrum

A827

Ulva

Isle of Mull

A85

IRELAND

0 10 20 30 40 50 miles

North Channel

Carndonagh   Portrush   Ballycastle
Buncrana   Coleraine   Cushendall
Londonderry   Limavady   A37
A2   Ballymoney
Dungloe   Letterkenny   N13   LONDONDERRY   A26   Ballymena   Larne
DONEGAL   Dungiven   A6   M2   A36   A2
Ballybofey   Strabane   Newtown-
Malin Moore   Newtownstewart   Magherafelt   Randalstown   abbey   Carrickfergus
NORTHERN   A29   Antrim   Bangor
Killybegs   Donegal   Omagh   A505   Cookstown   BELFAST   Newtownards
Ballyshannon   IRELAND   A5   Lisburn
TYRONE   Portadown   M1   Lurgan   A7   Portaferry
N15   Invinestown   Ballygawley   Craigavon   Downpatrick
Manorhamilton   FERMANAGH   Enniskillen   A4   Armagh   A1   Clough
Belmullet   N18   Monaghan   N2   Newcastle
Bangor   Sligo   A32   A28   Newry   A1
Erris   Ballina   N16   Clones   Carrickmacross   Dundalk
SLIGO   Boyle   Carrick-on-   Cavan   N2   LOUTH   Irish
N17   N4   Shannon   N3   N1
Castlebar   Charlestown   Kells   Drogheda   Sea
Westport   N5   Longford   Edgeworthstown   Navan   N1   Balbriggan
Claremorris   Roscommon   Delvin   N4   N2   Ashbourne
Clifden   N17   Ballygar   Mullingar   Dunshaughlin   N3   Portmarnock
GALWAY   Roscommon   Kinnegad   Maynooth   M1
Athlone   Kilbeggan   M4   DUBLIN
Kilronan   Athenry   N6   Ballinasloe   N6   Tullamore   M7   DUN Laoghaire
Galway   Loughrea   OFFALY   Kildare   Naas   M9   Bray
Kinvarra   Gort   Cloghan   Birr   Kilcullen   M11   Greystones
Ballyvaghan   Portlaoise   LAOIS   N7   Wicklow
Ennistymon   CLARE   Roscrea   N7   N9   Rathdrum
Ennis   Nenagh   Durrow   Carlow   Tullow   N11   Arklow
Kilkee   Newmarket   Templemore   N8   Ballyragget   Ballon
Kilrush   on Fergus   Thurles   Urlingford   Kilkenny   Muine   Gorey
Limerick   TIPPERARY   Bheag
Tarbert   LIMERICK   N24   Cashel   N9   Enniscorthy
Listowel   Newcastle   Croom   Tipperary   New Ross   N25   Rosslare
Abbeyfeale   West   Rath Luirc   Cahir   Clonmel   N24   Wexford   Harbour
Tralee   Mitchelstown   N8   Carrick-on-   Waterford
KERRY   Castleisland   Mallow   Fermoy   Suir   N25   Tramore
Dingle   Killorglin   Killarney   Lismore   Dungarvan
Cahersiveen   Kenmare   N22   Macroom   Rathcormack   Youghal
Waterville   Sneem   N25   Midleton
Cork   Cobh
Bantry   Bandon   Kinsale
Clonakilty
Schull   Castletownshend

Mouth of the Shannon

IRISH REPUBLIC

St George's Channel

12

M25 LONDON ORBITAL MOTORWAY

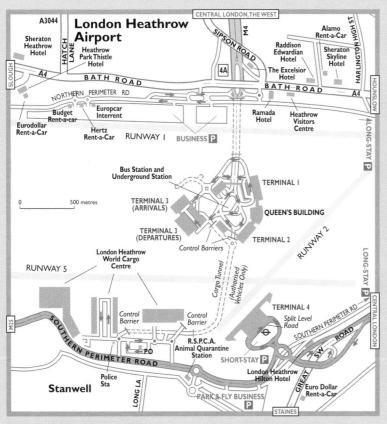

London Heathrow Airport – 16 miles west of London

Telephone: 0181 759 4321
Parking: Short-stay, long-stay and business parking available. For charge details tel: 0800 844844
Public Transport: Coach, bus and London Underground
There are several 4-star and 3-star hotels within easy reach of the airport, and car hire facilities are available

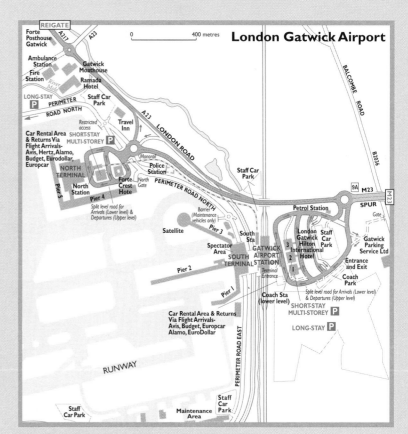

London Gatwick Airport – 35 miles south of London

Telephone: 01293 535353
Parking: Short-stay and long-stay parking available at both the North and South terminals. For charge details tel: 01293 502390 (short-stay) and either 0800 128128 or 01293 569222 (long-stay)
Public Transport: Coach, bus and rail. There are several 4-star and 3-star hotels within easy reach of the airport, and car hire facilities are available

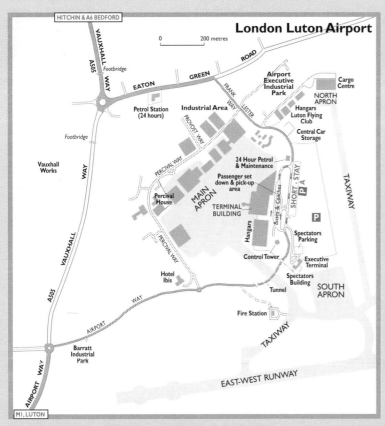

London Luton Airport – 33 miles north of London

Telephone: 01582 405100
Parking: Short-stay and long-stay open air parking available
Public Transport: Coach, bus and rail
There is one 2-star hotel at the airport and several 3-star hotels within easy reach of the airport. Car hire facilities are available

London Stansted Airport – 38 miles north-east of London

Telephone: 01279 680500
Parking: Short-stay and long-stay open-air parking available. For charge details tel: 01279 662373
Public Transport: Coach, bus and a direct rail link to London on the 'Stansted Skytrain'
There are several 4-star and 3-star hotels within easy reach of the airport, and car hire facilities are available

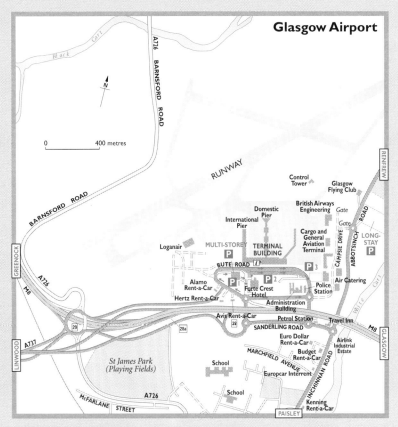

Glasgow Airport

Glasgow Airport – 8 miles west of Glasgow

Telephone: 0141 887 1111
Parking: Short-stay and long-stay parking is available, mostly open-air. For charge details tel: 0141 889 2751
Public Transport: Regular coach services operate between central Glasgow and Edinburgh
There are several 3-star hotels within easy reach of the airport, and car hire facilities are available

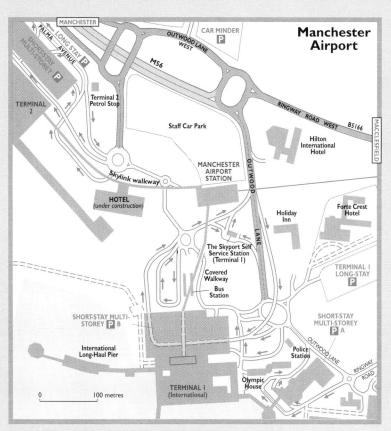

Manchester Airport

Manchester Airport – 10 miles south of Manchester

Telephone: 0161 489 3000
Parking: Short-stay and long-stay parking available.
Public Transport: Bus, coach and rail. Manchester airport railway station connects with the Rail network
There are several 4-star and 3-star hotels within easy reach of the airport, and car hire facilities are available

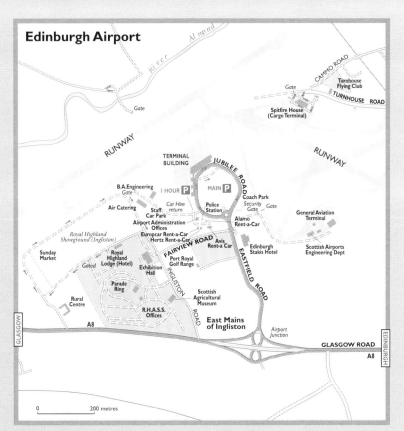

Edinburgh Airport

Edinburgh Airport – 7 miles west of Edinburgh

Telephone: 0131 333 1000
Parking: Open-air parking is available. For charge details tel: 0131 344 3197
Public Transport: Regular coach services operate between central Edinburgh and Glasgow
There is one 4-star and several 3-star hotels within easy reach of the airport, and car hire facilities are available

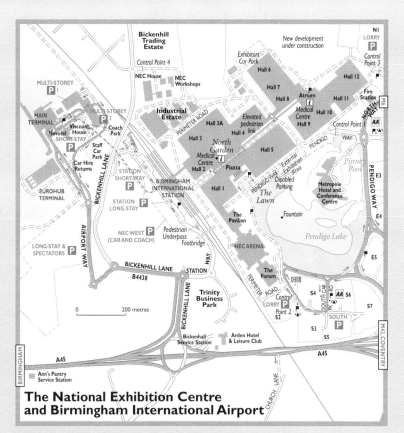

The National Exhibition Centre and Birmingham International Airport

Birmingham International Airport – 8 miles east of of Birmingham

Telephone: 0121 767 5511 (Main Terminal), 0121 767 7502 (Eurohub Terminal)
Parking: Short-stay and long-stay parking available
For charge details tel: 0121 767 7861
Public Transport: Shuttle-bus service to Birmingham International railway station and the NEC.
There are several 3-star hotels within easy reach of the airport, and car hire facilities are available

CENTRAL LONDON

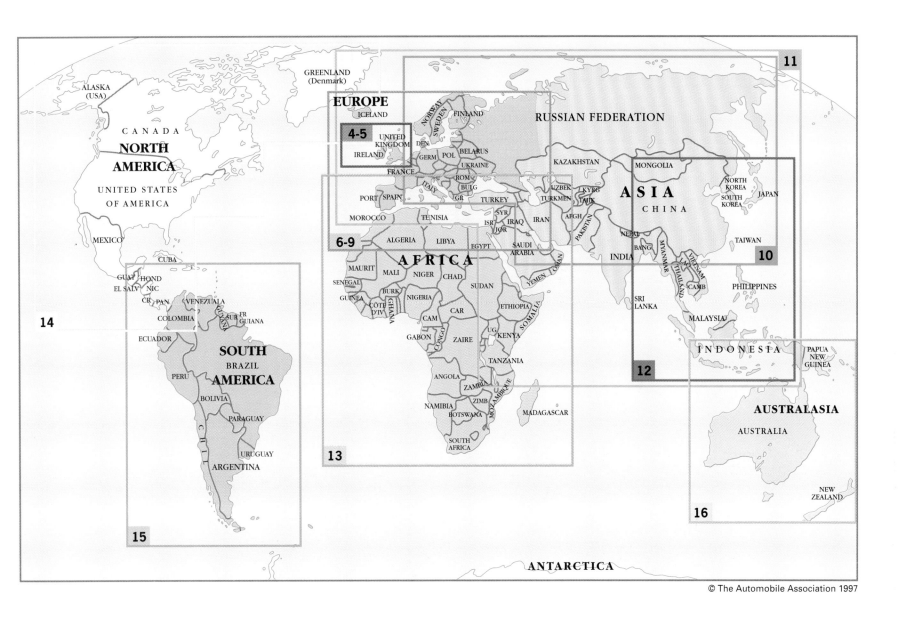

© The Automobile Association 1997

1	**Key to map pages**	
2-3	**The World**	
4-5	**Great Britain**	
6	**Western Europe**	
7	**Northern Europe**	
8-9	**Europe**	
10	**Russian Federation**	

11	**Asia**
12	**The Far East**
13	**Africa**
14	**North America**
15	**South America**
16	**Australasia**

Over 6000m
5000 - 6000m
4000 - 5000m
3000 - 4000m
2000 - 3000m
1000 - 2000m
500 - 1000m
200 - 500m
0 - 200m
Below sea level

The World

GREENLAND
(Denmark)

AR

ALASKA (USA)
Anchorage

Arctic Circle

Iceland
Godthåb
Reykjavik
Faroe
(Den

C A N A D A

UNITED
KINGDOM
Glasg

Edmonton

Vancouver
Winnipeg
Québec
Ottawa Montréal
Toronto
Dublin
REP OF
IRELAND

Seattle
Chicago
Detroit
Boston
New York
Philadelphia

PORTUGAL
Lisboa

Denver
St Louis
Washington

San Francisco
UNITED STATES
OF AMERICA

Azores
(Port)

Los Angeles
Dallas
Madeira
(Port)
Rabat

Houston
New Orleans
Bermuda (UK)

MOROCCO

MEXICO
Gulf of
Mexico
Miami

Canary Is
(Sp)

Tropic of Cancer

WESTERN
SAHARA

Hawaiian Is
(USA)
La Habana
BAHAMAS
A T L A N T I C

Ad Dakhla

Mexico
City
CUBA
DOMINICAN
REPUBLIC

MAURITANIA

JAMAICA HAITI
Puerto Rico (USA)
BELIZE
GUATEMALA
Belmopan
Kingston
ANTIGUA

Nouakchott

Guatemala
City
HONDURAS
Caribbean
DOMINICA

CAPE VERDE
SENEGAL

EL SALVADOR
Tegucigalpa
Sea
ST LUCIA
BARBADOS

THE GAMBIA
Dakar

NICARAGUA
ST VINCENT
GRENADA

GUINEA-BISSAU
Bamako

Managua
Panamá
City
TRINIDAD &
TOBAGO

Conakry
GUINEA

San José
Caracas
Freetown

COSTA RICA
PANAMA
VENEZUELA
Georgetown
Paramaribo
SIERRA LEONE
CÔT
IVO

Monrovia
Abidja

Bogotá
Cayenne
LIBERIA

O C E A N

Palmyra Is
(USA)
P A C I F I C
COLOMBIA
GUYAN SURIN Fr Guiana
(Fr)

0° Equator
Quito

Galapagos Is
(Ecuador)
ECUADOR
Manaus

Guayaquil
Belém

Phoenix Is

B R A Z I L
Ascension I
(UK)

Tokelau Is
Marquesas Is
(Fr)
Recife

PERU

W SAMOA
O C E A N
Lima
Salvador
St Helena
(UK)

Society
Is (Fr)
Tuamotu
Archipelago
(Fr)
La Paz
Brasilia

TONGA
Tahiti
BOLIVIA

Rarotonga
Rio de Janeiro

Tropic of Capricorn
PARAGUA
São Paulo

Pitcairn I
(UK)
Easter I
(Chile)
Asunción

Juan Fernandez
Is (Chile)
Rosario
Porto Alegre

Kermadec Is
(NZ)
ARGENTINA
URUGUAY
Montevideo
Tristan da Cunha
(UK)

Santiago
Buenos
Aires
Bahia Blanca

Gough I
(UK)

Chatham Is
(NZ)
Falkland Is (UK)
S Georgia
(UK)

Antarctic Circle
BRITISH ANTARCTIC TERRITORY

ROSS DEPENDENCY (NZ)

AND : ANDORRA
AR : ARMENIA
AUS : AUSTRIA
AZ : AZERBAIJAN
BAN : BANGLEDESH
BEL : BELGIUM
B-H : BOSNIA-HERZEGOVINA
C : CROATIA
CR : CZECH REPUBLIC
EQ GU : EQUATORIAL GUINEA
GEO : GEORGIA
H : HUNGARY
L : LIECHTENSTEIN
LUX : LUXEMBOURG
LEB : LEBANON
M : MOLDAVIA
MA : MALTA
MAC : MACEDONIA
MON : MONACO
NETH : NETHERLANDS
S : SLOVENIA
SL : SLOVAKIA
SM : SAN MARINO
UAE : UNITED ARAB EMIRATES
YUG : YUGOSLAVIA

RUSSIAN FEDERATION

OCEAN

NORWAY
SWEDEN
FINLAND
Helsinki
Stockholm
Oslo
ESTONIA
København
LATVIA
ARK
erdam
Amsterdam
GERMANY
Berlin
Warszawa
POLAND
BELARUS
Praha
Kiyev
Wien
UKRAINE
ITALY
Roma
ALBANIA
BULGARIA
GREECE
Athina
Tunis
TUNISIA
Tarābulus
Banghāzi
LIBYA
EGYPT
El Qāhira
Arkhangel'sk
Sankt Peterburg
Moskva
Yekaterinburg
Omsk
Novosibirsk
KAZAKHSTAN
Aral Sea
Ulaanbaatar
MONGOLIA
Alma Ata
Tashkent
Bishkek
KYRGYZSTAN
UZBEKISTAN
Dushanbe
TAJIKISTAN
Baku
TURKMENISTAN
Tbilisi
GEO
Ashgabat
Tehrān
AZ
Kābul
AFGHANISTAN
SYRIA
Dimashq
Baghdād
IRAQ
IRAN
Amman
JORDAN
Yerushalayim
ISRAEL
LEB
CYPRUS
Istanbul
Ankara
TURKEY
Islamabad
PAKISTAN
Lahore
Kathmandu
NEPAL
Delhi
BHUTAN
KUWAIT
QATAR
BAHRAIN
UAE
Ar Riyād
SAUDI ARABIA
Mecca
Masqat
OMAN
Karachi
Ahmadabad
Calcutta
Dhaka
BURMA
(MYANMAR)
Bombay
INDIA
Hyderabad
Madras
SRI LANKA
Colombo
MALDIVES

CHINA
Shenyang
N KOREA
Beijing
P'yŏngyang
Sŏul
S KOREA
JAPAN
Tōkyō
Ōsaka
Chongqing
Wuhan
Nanjing
Shanghai
T'ai-pei
Guangzhou
Hong Kong
TAIWAN
Hanoi
LAOS
Viangchan
Rangoon
THAILAND
VIETNAM
Bangkok
CAMBODIA
Phnom
Penh
Ho Chi Minh
Ho Chi Minh

PACIFIC
Aleutian
Is (USA)
Tropic of Cancer
Wake I
(USA)
Northern
Marianas
(USA)
OCEAN
MARSHALL
IS
Palau
(USA)
FEDERATED STATES
OF MICRONESIA
PHILIPPINES
Quezon City
Manila
KIRIBATI
Equator 0°
NAURU

NIGER
CHAD
Niamey
N'Djamena
SUDAN
El Khartûm
San'ā
Asmera
ERITREA
YEMEN
DJIBOUTI
Adīs Ābeba
ETHIOPIA
NIGERIA
Lagos
CENTRAL
AFRICAN
REPUBLIC
CAMEROON
Yaoundé
Bangui
EQ
GU
Libreville
GABON
TOMÉ
ÍNCIPE
CO
CABINDA
Brazzaville
Kinshasa
ZAÏRE
UGANDA
Kampala
RWANDA
Kigali
BURUNDI
Bujumbura
KENYA
Nairobi
Dodoma
TANZANIA
Dar es Salaam
SOMALIA
Muqdisho
SEYCHELLES

MALAYSIA
Kuala Lumpur
BRUNEI
SINGAPORE
INDONESIA
Jakarta
Surabaya
PAPUA
NEW
GUINEA
Port Moresby
SOLOMON
IS
TUVALU
VANUATU
FIJI

Luanda
ANGOLA
ZAMBIA
Lusaka
MALAWI
Lilongwe
Harare
ZIMBABWE
NAMIBIA
BOTSWANA
Windhoek
MOZAMBIQUE
MADAGASCAR
Antananarivo
MAURITIUS
RÉUNION
Gaborone
Pretoria
Johannesburg
Maputo
Mbabane
SWAZILAND
REP OF
LESOTHO
Maseru
Durban
SOUTH AFRICA
Cape Town

INDIAN

OCEAN

New
Caledonia
(Fr)
Tropic of Capricorn
Darwin
AUSTRALIA
Brisbane
Perth
Adelaide
Sydney
Canberra
Melbourne
Auckland
Hobart
NEW
ZEALAND
Wellington

St Paul I
(Fr)
Amsterdam I (Fr)
Crozet Is
(Fr)
Kerguelen Is
(Fr)
Heard I
(Aust)

NORWEGIAN DEPENDENCY
AUSTRALIAN ANTARCTIC TERRITORY
TERRE ADÉLIE (FR)
AUS ANT TERRITORY
ROSS DEPENDENCY (NZ)
Antarctic Circle

0	1000	2000	3000	4000 kms
0	500	1000	1500	2000	2500 miles

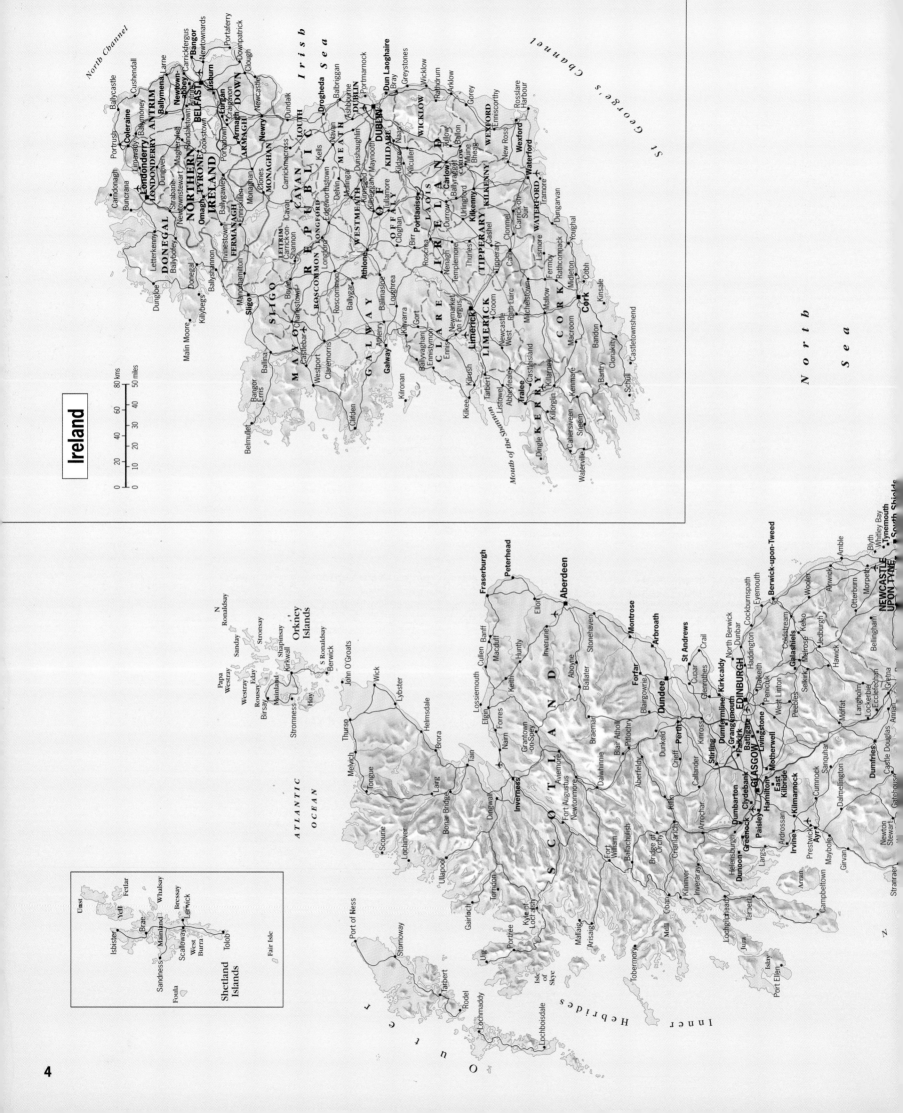

Ireland

80 kms
50 miles
60
40
40
30
20
20
10
0
0

North Channel

Ballycastle
Portrush
Coleraine
Cushendall
Larne
Carndonagh
Buncrana
Limavady Ballymoney
LONDONDERRY
Newtownstewart
Strabane
Dungiven
Magherafelt
ANTRIM
Ballymena
Newtown-
abbey
Carrickfergus
Bangor
Portaferry
Newtownards
BELFAST
Portadown
Cookstown
Lurgan
Lisburn
DOWN
Downpatrick
Clough
Newcastle
Letterkenny
NORTHERN
Omagh **TYRONE**
IRELAND
Portadown
Armagh
ARMAGH
Newry
Dunloe
Killybegs
Donegal
DONEGAL
Ballygawley
FERMANAGH
Enniskillen
Monaghan
Clones
MONAGHAN
Carrickmacross
Dundalk
Newcastle
Malin Moore
Ballyshannon
Manorhamilton
LEITRIM
Cootehill
Cavan
CAVAN
LONGFORD
Kells
LOUTH
Drogheda
Balbriggan
Portmarnock
Ballina
SLIGO
Sligo
Carrick-on-
Shannon
ROSCOMMON
Longford
Edgeworthstown
Delvin
MEATH
Navan
Dunshaughlin
DUBLIN
Dun Laoghaire
Bray
Greystones
Bangor
Erris
Belmullet
Charlestown
Boyle
Castlerea
Roscommon
WESTMEATH
Mullingar
Maynooth
DUBLIN
Wicklow
Westport
MAYO
Castlebar
Ballyhaunis
Athlone
Moate
Edenderry
Clonard
Kilcock
Naas
KILDARE
Kilcullen
WICKLOW
Rathdrum
Claremorris
Ballinasloe
Birr
Tullamore
OFFALY
Kildare
LAOIS
Portlaoise
Stradbally
Arklow
Clifden
Ballygar
Loughrea
Roscrea
Clophan
Carlow
Ballon
Gorey
GALWAY
Galway
Athenry
Gort
Nenagh
Templemore
Durrow
Muine
Bheag
KILKENNY
Enniscorthy
Kilronan
Ballyvaghan
Kinvarra
CLARE
Ennistymon
Ennis
Newmarket-
on-Fergus
TIPPERARY
Thurles
Kilkenny
Urlingford
Callan
WEXFORD
Wexford
Rosslare
Harbour
LIMERICK
Limerick
Cashel
Clonmel
Carrick-on-
Suir
WATERFORD
New Ross
Kilkee
Kilrush
Tarbert
Croom
Rath-Luirc
Cahir
Waterford
Tramore
Listowel
Castleisland
Newcastle
West
Michelstown
Lismore
Dungarvan
Kilkee
Abbeyfeale
Mallow
Fermoy
Rathcormack
Youghal
Dingle
Tralee
Castleisland
Killorglin
KERRY
Killarney
Macroom
CORK
Cork
Midleton
Cobh
Mouth of the Shannon
Cahersiveen
Sneem
Kenmare
Bantry
Bandon
Kinsale
Waterville
Schull
Clonakilty
Castletownshend

Irish Sea
St George's Channel

North Sea

SCOTLAND

Fraserburgh
Peterhead
Aberdeen
N
Ronaldsay
Orkney
Islands
S
Ronaldsay
Kirkwall
John O'Groats
Wick
Lybster
Cullen
Banff
Macduff
Elgin
Keith
Huntly
Ellon
Stonehaven
Lossiemouth
Inverurie
Montrose
Arbroath
Thurso
Melvich
Helmsdale
Brora
Nairn
Forres
Grantown-
on-Spey
Aviemore
Ballater
Braemar
Aboyne
Blairgowrie
Forfar
Dundee
St Andrews
Crail
Tongue
Lairg
Dingwall
Inverness
Fort
Augustus
Newtonmore
Dalwhinnie
Blair Atholl
Pitlochry
Aberfeldy
Perth
Cupar
Glenrothes
Kirkcaldy
North Berwick
Dunbar
Scourie
Ullapool
Bonar Bridge
Kinloch
Kingussie
Crieff
Callander
Stirling
Dunfermline
Grangemouth
EDINBURGH
Haddington
Cockburnspath
Eyemouth
Gairloch
Torridon
Fort
William
Fort
Augustus
Arrochar
Dumbarton
GLASGOW
Clydebank
Falkirk
Bathgate
Livingstone
Dalkeith
West Linton
Peebles
Selkirk
Galashiels
Melrose
Coldstream
Kelso
Jedburgh
Berwick-upon-Tweed
Kyle of
Lochalsh
Portree
Isle
of
Skye
Mallaig
Arisaig
Ballachulish
Bridge of
Orchy
Crianlarich
Inveraray
Helensburgh
Greenock
Paisley
Hamilton
Motherwell
East
Kilbride
Strathaven
Lanark
Biggar
Moffat
Langholm
Hawick
Bellingham
Uig
Tobermory
Oban
Lochgilphead
Dunoon
Largs
Ayr
Kilmarnock
Cumnock
Sanquhar
Lockerbie
Ecclefechan
Annan
Gretna
Rodel
Isle
of
Mull
Jura
Kilberry
Inverary
Ardrossan
Irvine
Prestwick
Troon
Maybole
Dalmellington
New Galloway
Dumfries
Lochmaddy
Lochboisdale
Islay
Port Ellen
Jura
Campbeltown
Girvan
Newton
Stewart
Castle Douglas
Dalbeattie
Gatehouse
Stranraer

ATLANTIC OCEAN
Inner Hebrides
Outer Hebrides

Port of Ness
Stornoway

Uist
Yell
Fetlar
Whalsay
Bressay
Lerwick
Isbister
Brae
Scalloway
West
Burra
Tolob
Sandness
Mainland
Foula
Shetland
Islands
Fair Isle
Papa
Westray
Westray
Eday
Rousay
Shapinsay
Stronsay
Sanday
Birsay
Mainland
Hoy
Stromness
Berwick

Alnwick
Amble
Blyth
Whitley Bay
Tynemouth
South Shields
NEWCASTLE
UPON TYNE
Morpeth
Otterburn
Wooler
Rothbury
Ponteland

4

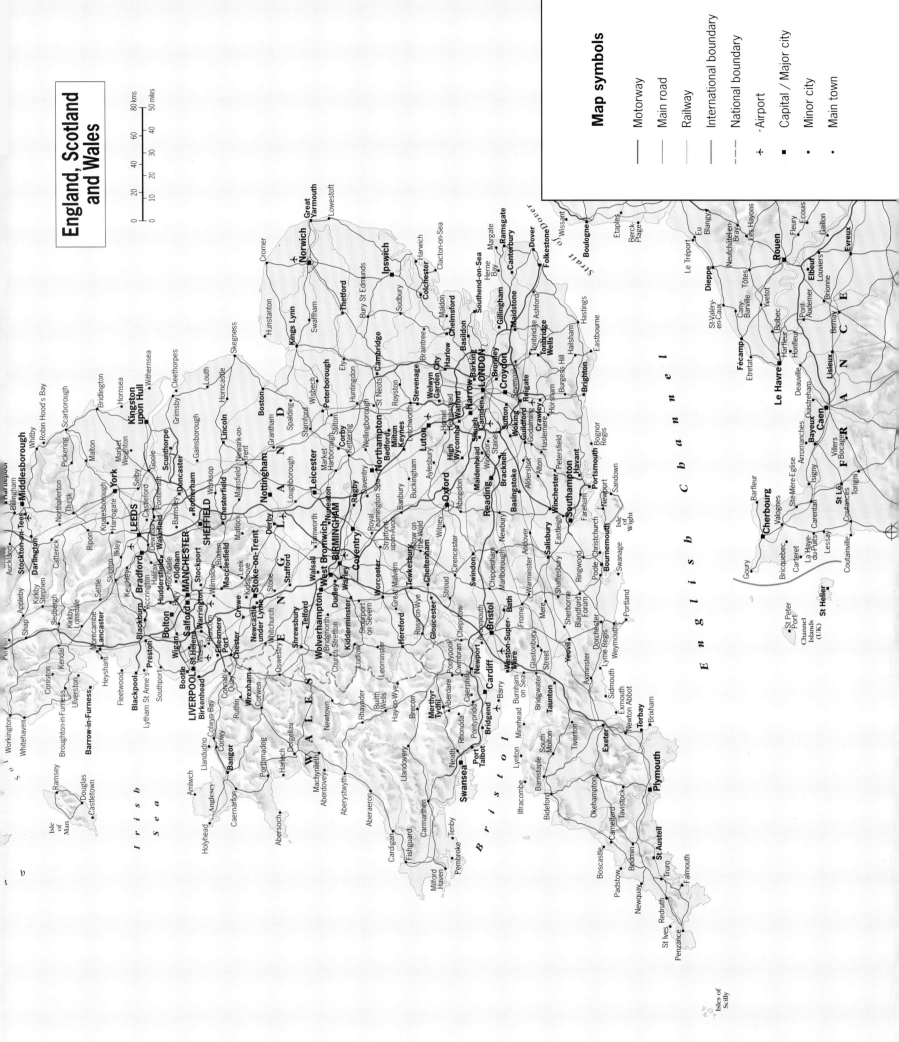

England, Scotland and Wales

Russian Federation

10

ARCTIC OCEAN

Bering Sea

Bering Strait

Chukchi Sea

East Siberian Sea

Laptev Sea

Kara Sea

Barents Sea

White Sea

North Sea

Baltic Sea

Gulf of Bothnia

Sea of Okhotsk

Sea of Japan

Yellow Sea

East China Sea

Black Sea

Caspian Sea

The Gulf

Gulf of Oman

RUSSIAN FEDERATION

NORWAY
SWEDEN
FINLAND
DENMARK
GERMANY
POLAND
BELARUS
UKRAINE
LITHUANIA
LATVIA
ESTONIA
MOLDAVIA
ROMANIA
SLOVAKIA

KAZAKHSTAN
UZBEKISTAN
TURKMENISTAN
KYRGYZSTAN
TAJIKISTAN
MONGOLIA
CHINA
JAPAN
NORTH KOREA
SOUTH KOREA

GEORGIA
ARMENIA
AZERBAIJAN
TURKEY
IRAN
IRAQ
SYRIA
KUWAIT
SAUDI ARABIA
QATAR
BAHRAIN
UNITED ARAB EMIRATES
OMAN
AFGHANISTAN
PAKISTAN
INDIA
NEPAL

OSLO
STOCKHOLM
HELSINKI
KØBENHAVN
BERLIN
HAMBURG
WARSZAWA
MINSK
KIYEV
MOSKVA
Sankt Peterburg
NIZHNIY NOVGOROD
RIGA
TALLINN
VILNIUS

TOKYO
PYONGYANG
SEOUL
BEIJING
SHANGHAI
TAI-PEI
ULAANBAATAR
TASHKENT
BISHKEK
ALMA ATA
DUSHANBE
ASHKHABAD
TEHRAN
BAKU
TBILISI
YEREVAN
BAGHDAD
KUWAIT
DOHA
ABU DHABI
MASQAT
KABUL
ISLAMABAD
NEW DELHI
KATHMANDU
KARACHI

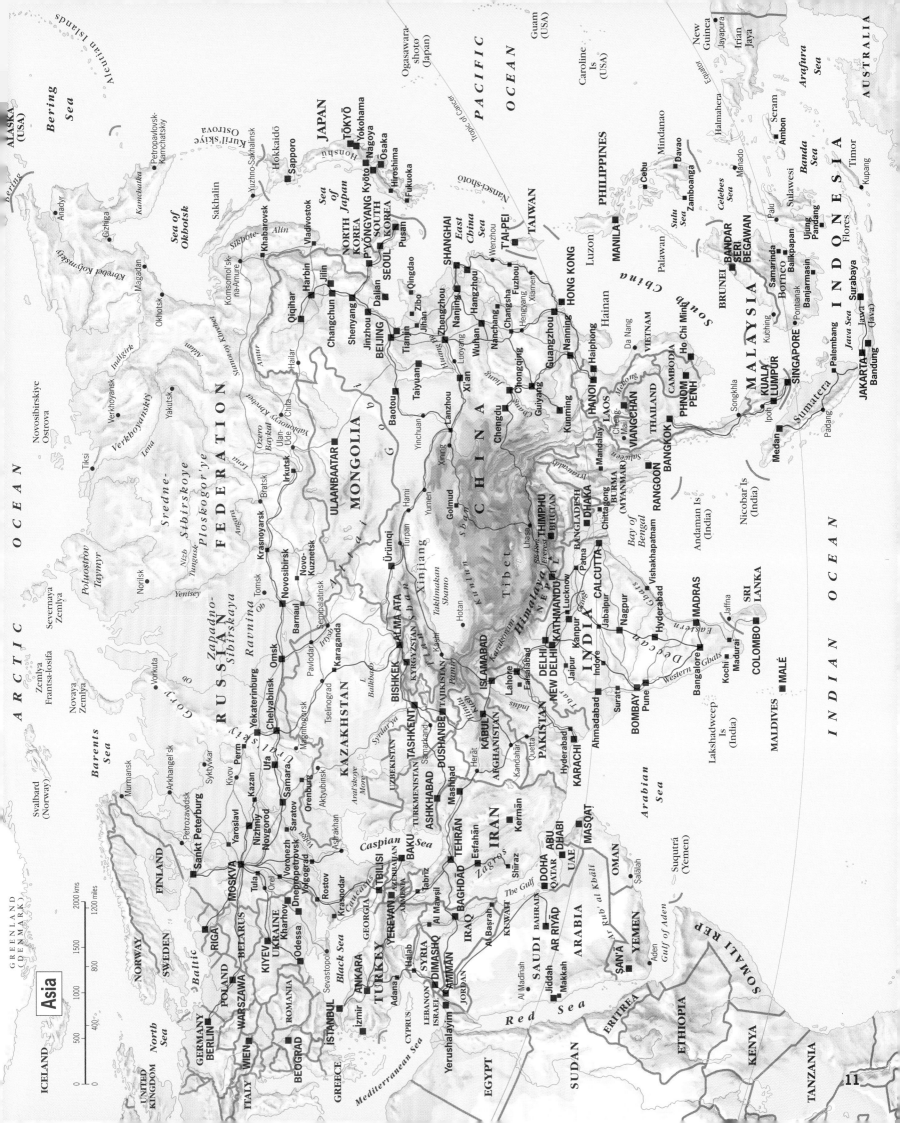

Asia

The Far East

Africa

FRANCE
BERN AUSTRIA BUDAPEST KISHIN'OV RUSSIAN
Bay of SWITZ HUNGARY MOLDAVIA FEDERATION
Biscay LJUBLJANA ROMANIA
ZAGREB BEOGRAD BUCUREŞTI
PORTUGAL SARAJEVO SOFIA Black Sea UZBEKISTAN
BULGARIA Istanbul TBILISI
MADRID ROMA ALBANIA SKOPJE GEORGIA BAKU TURKMENISTAN
SPAIN TIRANĖ GREECE YEREVAN ASHKHABAD
LISBOA Mallorca TUNIS ATHÍNA ANKARA ARMENIA AZERB
Sardegna TURKEY
Tanger Oran ALGER Annaba Malta CYPRUS SYRIA TEHRĀN
RABAT Constantine TUNIS Sea BAYRŪT DIMASHQ BAGHDĀD IRAN
Casablanca Fez TUNISIA Sfax Gulf of El Iskandarîya LEB IRAQ
Meknès TARĀBULUS Sirte Bûr ISRAEL AMMAN KUWAIT KUWAIT
Marrakesh 4165m Al Baydā' EL QAHÎRA Saîd JORDAN
MOROCCO Ouargla Banghāzî El Faiyûm YERUSHALAYIM
El Minya BAHRAIN ABU
Islas Canarias Suez SAUDI ARABIA QATAR DHABI
Madeira ALGERIA Sabhā EGYPT Asyût AR RIYĀD DOHA UAE
Tropic of Cancer Aswân Nile OMAN
Ad Dakhla WESTERN SAHARA LIBYA Red Lake Bûr
Atar Ahagg Nasser Sūdān
MAURITANIA Tamanrasset Tibesti S U D A N ERITREA YEMEN
NOUAKCHOTT Néma 3415m Mits'iwa SAN'Ā'
St Louis MALI NIGER Emi Koussi Omdurman ASMERA 4620m
DAKAR Tombouctou CHAD EL KHARTŪM Ras Dashen
SENEGAL Tahoua Abéché El Fâsher DJIBOUTI
Kaolack Zinder Lake El Obeid Dirē Dawa DJIBOUTI
THE BAMAKO Chad Berbera
GAMBIA NIAMEY Kano ADĪS ĀBEBA
BANJUL GUINEA- BURKINA Maiduguri N'DJAMENA White ETHIOPIA
BISSAU BISSAU OUAGADOUGOU Kaduna Nile Blue Nile
Bobo NIGERIA CENTRAL Juba SOMALIA
CONAKRY Dioulasso BENIN ABUJA AFRICAN REPUBLIC Bangassou Lake
SIERRA GHANA Ilorin Turkana
FREETOWN LEONE CÔTE Kumasi PORTO Ibadan BANGUI Buta KENYA
Bo D'IVOIRE NOVO Lagos CAMEROON 4095m UGANDA 4321m 5200m
MONROVIA Bouaké LOMÉ Enugu Doula Kisangani Mt Elgon Kirinyaga
LIBERIA YAMOUSSOUKRO ACCRA Port 4095m 5110m KAMPALA Kisumu MUQDISHO
Abidjan Takoradi Harcourt YAOUNDÉ Douala Ruwenzori Lake
Gulf of Guinea Bioko EQUAT GUINEA Zaïre Mbandaka 4507m Victoria NAIROBI
Equator SÃO TOMÉ & PRINCIPE BATA CONGO Karisimbi RWANDA Kismaayo
LIBREVILLE GABON ZAIRE KIGALI Mwanza NDIAN
Francevile BRAZZAVILLE BUKAVU BURUNDI 5895m Mombassa
Pointe-Noire KINSHASHA Kananga BUJUMBURA Kilimanjaro Tanga OCEAN
CABINDA Matadi Mbuji-Mayi Lake DODOMA Pemba SEYCHELLES
SOUTH Tanganyika Zanzibar
LUANDA TANZANIA Dar es Salaam
Ascension ATLANTIC ANGOLA Kolwezi Likasi Kasama Mafia Aldabra
Lobito Mbeya
OCEAN Benguela Huambo Ndola Lake COMOROS Antsiranana
Namibe Menongue LILONGWE Nyasa Pemba
St Helena ZAMBIA MALAWI
LUSAKA Blantyre MOZAMBIQUE MADAGASCAR ANTANANARIVO
Livingstone Zambezi Quelimane Mauritius
HARARE Réunion
Grootfontein Okavango ZIMBABWE Beira Toamasina
Delta Gweru
NAMIBIA Francistown Bulawayo Fianarantsoa
WINDHOEK BOTSWANA Limpopo Toliara
Tropic of Capricorn Walvis Bay Pietersburg Inhambane
GABORONE PRETORIA
Lüderitz Keetmanshoop Johannesburg SWAZ MAPUTO
Kimberley MBABANE
Springbok Orange Bloemfontein MASERU Pietermaritzburg
REPUBLIC OF LESOTHO 3482m Durban
SOUTH AFRICA East London
Cape Town Port Elizabeth

North America

0 400 800 1200 kms
0 200 400 600 miles

Chukchi Sea
ARCTIC OCEAN

Bering Sea
Bering Str

C Barrow
• Barrow

Nome • Seward Pen
Prudhoe Bay

Beaufort Sea

ALASKA (USA)

Yuko • Fort Yukon
Fairbanks •
Inuvik •

Brooks Range

6194m ▲ Mt McKinley
Alaska Range

Anchorage
Seward

6050m ▲ Mt Logan
Whitehorse

Kodiak I

Gulf of Alaska

Bristol Bay
Alaska Pen

Juneau

Alexander Archipelago

Mackenzie Mts
Mackenzie

Hay River •

Queen Elizabeth Islands

Ellesmere I

GREENLAND (Denmark)

Thule •

Greenland Sea

Faroe Is

ICELAND
2118m Vatnajökull

REYKJAVIK

Denmark Strait

Parry Islands
McClure Str
Devon I
Lancaster Sound

Banks I

Baffin Bay

Victoria I

Pr of Wales I
Somerset I
Spence Bay
Melville Pen

Baker Lake •
Southampton I
Foxe Basin

Baffin Island

C Dyer

Davis Strait

C Farewell

GODTHÅB

Thelo
Bac

Great Bear Lake

Great Slave Lake

Chesterfield Inlet •

Port Harrison •

Hudson Bay

Belcher Is

Churchill •

Ungava Bay

Hudson Strait

C Chidley

Nain •

Hamilton Inlet

Labrador Plateau

Gander •

St John's •

Reindeer L
L Athabasca

Peace River

C A N A D A

Nelson

Scheffervile •

Labrador City •

C Bauld

Newfoundland

Prince Rupert
Queen Charlotte Is

Queen Charlotte Sd

Vancouver I

Prince George
3954m Mt Robson

Peace River •
Edmonton •

Saskatchewan

James Bay
Fort George •

Severn

Sept Iles •

Port aux Basques

Sydney
C Breton I

4042m ▲ Mt Waddington

Kamloops •
Fraser

Calgary •
Saskatoon •
Yorkton •

L Winnipeg
Albany

Laurentian Mts
St Lawrence
Pr Edward I
Moncton •

Rocky Mountains

Regina •

Lethbridge •

Winnipeg ■

Thunder Bay •

Quebec ■

St John •
Halifax •
C Sable

Vancouver ■
Victoria

Seattle ■
Spokane •

4392m ▲ Mt Rainier

Columbia

Butte •

Billings •

Fargo •

Duluth •

L Superior

Sault Ste Marie

Sudbury •

Montréal
OTTAWA ■

Portland •
Providence •
Boston ■

Portland ■
Yellowston

Missouri

Minneapolis ■ St Paul

L Huron
L Michigan
Toronto ■
Hamilton
Buffalo

C Sable

PACIFIC OCEAN

4371m ▲ Mt Shasta

Snak

Great Salt L

Sioux City •

Milwaukee ■
Detroit

CHICAGO

Cleveland
L Erie
Pittsburgh •

NEW YORK
PHILADELPHIA ■

ATLANTIC OCEAN

Sacramento ■

Great Basin

Salt Lake City

Cheyenne •

Omaha •
Des Moines •

Columbus •

Baltimore •
WASHINGTON

San Francisco ■
San José ■

4418m ▲ Mt Whitney

Denver ■

UNITED STATES

OF

St Louis •

Indianapolis ■
Cincinnati •

Richmond •
Norfolk •

4399m Mt Elbert

Platte

Louisville •

Sierra Nevada

Fresno •
Las Vegas •

Colorado Plateau

AMERICA

Kansas City ■

Obi

Nashville •

Charlotte •

C Hatteras

Bermuda (UK)

San Bernardino •

Grand Canyon

Santa Fe •
Pueblo •

Wichita •

Ozark Plateau

Memphis •

Atlanta ■

Charleston •

LOS ANGELES ■

Phoenix •
Yuma •
Gila

Albuquerque •
Amarillo •

Oklahoma City ■
Little Rock •

Birmingham •

Savannah •

San Diego ■

Tucson •

El Paso •

Fort Worth •

Dallas ■
Jackson •

Montgomery •

Jacksonville •

Tropic of Cancer

Guadalupe (Mex)

Ciudad Juárez ■

Waco •
Austin •

Beaumont •

Red

New Orleans ■

Orlando •

Tampa •
St Petersburg

BAHAMAS

Baja California

Hermosillo •

San Antonio ■
Houston

Fort Lauderdale •

Miami ■

NASSAU ■

C San Lucas

Golfo de California

Chihuahua •

Ciudad Obregón •

Sierra Madre

Monterrey ■
Torreón •

Rio Grande

Gulf of Mexico

Straits of Florida

LA HABANA ■
Santa Clara •
Camagüey •

CUBA

Santiago de Cuba •

San Juan •
DOMINICAN REPUBLIC

HAITI

Puerto Rico (USA)

JAMAICA
KINGSTON ■

PORT-AU-PRINCE

SANTO DOMINGO

Mazatlán •

San Luis Potosí •

Tampico •

MEXICO

Léon •

MEXICO CITY ■

Guadalajara ■
Morelia •

Puebla •

5452m Popocatépetl

Bahía de Campeche

Mérida •
Yucatán
Campeche •

Yucatán Channel

Caribbean Sea

Curaçao (Neth)

Revillagigedo Is (Mex)

Acapulco •

Oaxaca •

Villahermosa •

Comitán •

Veracruz •

BELMOPAN
BELIZE

Gulf of Honduras

HONDURAS
TEGUCIGALPA ■

Santa Marta •

CARACAS ■

GUATEMALA
GUATEMALA CITY ■

SAN SALVADOR
EL SALVADOR

NICARAGUA

Barranquilla •
Cartagena •

Maracaibo •

VENEZUELA

MANAGUA ■

Limón •

Colón •
PANAMÁ

SAN JOSE
COSTA RICA

PANAMÁ

Golfo de Panamá

Medellín •

Cúcuta •
San Cristóbal •

Bucaramanga •

BOGOTÁ
COLOMBIA

Coco (CR)

Jane's

AIRLINES &
AIRLINERS

AIRLINES &
AIRLINERS

Collins

JEREMY FLACK

In the UK for information please contact:
HarperCollinsPublishers
77-85 Fulham Palace Road
Hammersmith
London W6 8JB

Visit the book lover's website: www.**fire**and**water**.com

In the USA for imformation please contact:
HarperCollinsPublishers
10 East 53rd Street
New York
NY 10022

www.harpercollins.com

Jane's Information Group
www.janes.com

First published in Great Britain by HarperCollinsPublishers 2003

1 3 5 7 9 10 8 6 4 2

© Jeremy Flack 2003
Jeremy Flack asserts the moral right to be identified as the author of this work

ISBN 000715174-8

Printed and bound by Bath Press, England

Acknowledgements

I would like to thank Airbus, Bae Systems, BN Historians Collection,
Bombardier, Dornier, EADS, Embraer, Rolls Royce and SAAB,
especially Francoise Maenhaut and Bénédicte Bastid plus John Belanger, David
Dorman, Keith Faulkner, Mike Johnson, David McIntosh, Baldur Sveinsson as
well as Sam Ward who were all a great help. I would also like to thank the
various airlines that responded to my requests for information. I would also
like to give a big thank you to my long suffering wife Julie who has helped and
supported me through yet another of these projects.

Contents

ABOVE: *A320 cockpit (Airbus)*

Introduction

The whole airline industry is going through a major upheaval and we have seen major upsets with airline fortunes that one would not have considered a few years ago. So much is being quoted as either pre- or post-September 11th but unfavourable winds had already been blowing for some time and-been for some airlines, it was just going to be a matter of time before their real problems surfaced.

While travel agents have traditionally provided passengers with their travel arrangements, computer technology has enabled direct access to the airlines. Most airlines have leapt on this bandwagon as it enables them to cut out the 'middle-man' and often offer customers better rates. This has obviously affected travel agents' business. The result will be that those that survive will be the ones that provide a better service, especially for package deals and for customers who are not so computer orientated.

For those travellers who like to be able to put their own holiday package together, the internet enables an easy entry into the travel industry. Simply keying in a destination will produce huge numbers of potential suppliers of tickets. Most are travel agents who have taken on this technology while others may simply be small companies with a number of terminals specialising in selling tickets.

In this book I have selected most of the world's major and national airlines. I have provided information to enable direct contact with airlines to help select the best carrier for passenger needs. The web sites listed usually give direct access to airline timetables and also any special offers.

It should be noted that while airline web sites should be secure, the usual security precautions should be taken. Neither the author nor the publisher can accept any responsibility for any problems encountered in using any of the web sites listed.

For anyone with concerns with security at their destination there are three web sites worth looking at:-

British Foreign and Commonwealth Office;
www.fco.gov.uk/travel/countryadvice.asp

US Department of State;
http://travel.state.gov/travel_warnings.html

Canadian Department of Foreign Affairs and International Trade;
http://voyage.dfait-maeci.gc.ca/destinations/menu

I have also included details of the airline's history as well as the fleet. These have seen major turbulence since September 11th, 2001 when the worst atrocity in the history of aviation and terrorism were brought together.

The effect of these acts of terrorism were not only immediate, with thousands of innocent people killed, but also long-lasting in terms of passenger loss. While understandable, the effect of the US administration closing down US airspace did little more than spread the tragedy wider.

The airline business had been entering a downward period during the late 90s with much of the problem caused by itself. The continual get bigger syndrome can only go so far. Without passenger levels to sustain it, the accountants' ideal of increasing profit year on year at any cost will cause service levels to drop in the desperate need to achieve the impossible.

A substantial number of airlines were starting to enter some form of financial difficulties and it was only going to need a small hiccup to cause them problems. September 11th was no hiccup - it was a major catastrophe. Inevitably passenger levels dropped immediately but closing down the whole network placed an immediate strain on every US airline or airline that operated services to the US.

What had been needed for some time and, it could be argued had been a victim of cost cutting, was an effective level of security. The Western way of life has its pitfalls. We all want to live in a free society but this does leave us open to abuse by those that oppose our ideals. The current increased security, which still took a long time to implement, should have been in place ten years previously. Cockpit security doors and more effective screening of passengers and their

baggage should have been a matter of course.

While understandable, the close down of US airspace brought home the current deficiencies in the system and, in my opinion, increased the problem of passenger loss. The result was that the big airlines which had become heavy in administration and unable to react to passenger needs had already lost vast sums of money during the close down but were also unable to react quickly enough when they found that they had few passengers. The result was a huge lay-off of staff. While this was nothing compared to the families who had lost members in the Twin Towers and on the aircraft, to the airline staff that were laid off in an industry which had no jobs, the future was also bad. The Government came in with its Loan Guarantee Programme through the Air Transportation Safety and System Stabilization Act which was signed on September 22nd to make US$10 billion available in Federal credit. This was obviously a help to the US airlines, saving many from closing down completely, but left many non-US airlines disadvantaged to a greater or lesser degree.

The most affected airlines have been US airlines plus those with routes to and from the US. During 2002 most of these airlines have struggled through and are seeing passenger numbers gradually increase although many are still not back to their original rates. Despite the events of September 11th, airline travel remains the safest form of travel. It is unfortunate that when any airline accident occurs anywhere in the world, it invariably become headline news. If newspapers or TV catalogued every car crash in the world, they would produce a huge list but it doesn't put us off using the car.

An interesting phenomenon has been the growth of the low-cost flights. By cutting out the extras that are supplied by the mainstream airlines, a number of small existing or new start-up airlines are operating with rapidly increasing passenger levels. The massive growth of easyJet and Ryanair, for instance, is something that the mainstream airlines could only dream of. This is

good news for the airline industry if they attract new customers to airline travel but not so good if they have simply taken them from the larger airlines. It will be interesting to see how long they are able to maintain some of the very low fares.

Boeing currently appears to be in a bit of a wilderness. Having put its super 747X on hold, it is investing a substantial amount of resources into its Sonic Cruiser programme. With the "Boeing's position is that speed matters" being quoted by the programme manager at Farnborough 2002, it would appear now that it may have realised that the European aircraft industry had gone down that route back in the 60s. Concorde first flew in March 1969 as the European prestige airliner project compared with the Boeing 747 which first flew in February 1969. Each was targeted at different markets - small quantities of passengers at supersonic speed vs large number at subsonic speed. The result was a few Concordes ordered compared to some 1,400 747. With Airbus going ahead with the A380 and its order book growing, perhaps Boeing has realised that an aircraft that will have a potential fuel premium will not be required by airlines in sufficient numbers to make it viable. Although faster, the speed margin will not be great enough to make journey times that much shorter compared with time wasted getting to and waiting at the airport. This is reinforced with the passenger cross-section seeing a reduction in the numbers of premium paying business passengers and a substantial growth in the low fare traveller. Boeing now appears to be looking towards a "Super Efficient Airplane" for the future.

The Airbus vs Boeing battle for orders appears to be getting progressively more in favour of Airbus with 300 placed compared with 251 for Boeing in 2002. When one takes into account cancellations for existing orders, the figures put Boeing even further behind. With sales producing profits, Boeing appear to be at a disadvantage.

For the purpose of this book I have defined a regional airline to being one that operates in specific regions (ie North

America, Central America, South America, Europe, Africa, Middle East, Far East, Asia plus Pacific and Australia). An international airline is one that flies from one region to another. Only 100% owned subsidiary airlines are listed.

ABOVE: *The Airbus family of airliners out sells its main competitor in 2002 (Airbus)*

BELOW: *Ryanair continues to expand in the low-cost market (Ryanair)*

Adria Airways

Registered name: Adria Aviopromet

Country: Slovenia

Region: Europe

Address: Kuzmiceva 7
         1000 Ljubljana

Tel: 00386 1 369 10 00

Fax: 00386 1 436 92 33

Web site: www.adria.si

Main operational base: Ljubljana

STATUS

IATA scheduled and charter carrier

National Flag Carrier

Employees: 574

Passengers per year: 690,000 (2001)

ICAO code: ADR

IATA code: JP

SERVICES

International / Regional / Passenger
Charter / Cargo

International routes: Austria, Bosnia,
Croatia, Cyprus, France, Germany, Israel,
Russia, Switzerland, Turkey, UK

ALLIANCES / CODE SHARES

Air France, Austrian Airlines, Croatia
Airlines, Lufthansa

FLEET

A320 - 3, CRJ200LR - 4

Adria Airways was originally formed as Adria Aviopromet in 1961 as a charter airline operating flights with DC-6s primarily between a number of European airports to the tourist resorts along the Adriatic coast. The name changed to Inex-Adria Aviopromet following an association with Interexport in 1968, however this ended in 1986 and the airline's name changed to the current Adria Airways. The DC-6s were replaced with DC-9s and a DC-8 was subsequently leased for the long-haul routes. During the mid-1970s five MD-80s were purchased and the acceptance of its application to join IATA led to a steady expansion of the airlines business.

Following the declaration of independence of Slovenia in 1991 Adria Airways

ABOVE: *Adria Airways CRJ200LR, S5-AAD (C/n 7166). (Bombardier)*

became the national airline of Slovenia. In 1994 a pair of the STOL DHC-7s enabled operation into a number of airports previously considered too small for its jet airliners. However, the charter business had reduced dramatically due to conflict in the region and resulted in shedding six of the fleet of thirteen aircraft. Fortunately, the scheduled side of the business remained strong, even expanding. As a result three Airbus A320 were acquired followed later by three Canadair CRJ 200LRs in 1998, the latter replacing the DC-9s and DHC-7s. This led to a more environmentally friendly fleet as well as improving passenger comfort.

Aegean Airlines

Country: Greece

Region: Europe

Address: 572 Vouliagmenis Avenue
         Afgiroupoulis
         Athens 16451

Tel: 0030 1 99 88 350

Fax: 0030 1 995 7598

Web site: www.aegeanair.com

Main operational base: Athens

RIGHT: *Aegean Airlines BAe.146 RJ100. (BAe Systems)*

STATUS
Regional carrier
Employees: 636
Passengers per year: 1,286,000 (2001)
ICAO code: AEE
IATA code: A3

SERVICES
Regional / Domestic / Passenger / Charter
International routes: Germany*, France*, Italy*, UK* (*code share)

ALLIANCES / CODE SHARES
Cronus A/1

FLEET
ATR 72-200 - 3, RJ100 - 6, Learjet 552

Aegean Airlines came into being in 1970 as a general aviation operator but in 1992 it was granted an Air Operators Certificate.

In 1994 the Vassilakis Group gained control of Aegean Airlines and started a charter business.

In 1998 Aegean Airlines commenced domestic scheduled services on four routes, in 2000 merging with Air Greece and in 2001 with Cronus.

Aer Lingus

Registered name: Aer Lingus plc
Country: Ireland
Region: Europe
Address:　PO Box 18
　　　　　　　Head Office Building
　　　　　　　Dublin Airport
　　　　　　　Dublin
Tel: 00353 1 886 22 22
Fax: 00353 1 886 38 32
Web site: www.aerlingus.ie
Stockholder: The Aer Lingus Group plc
Main operational base: Dublin

STATUS
IATA scheduled international carrier
National Flag Carrier
Employees: 6,500
Passengers per year: 6,655,000 (2001)
ICAO code: EIN
IATA code: EI

SERVICES
International / Regional / Domestic
Passenger / Cargo
International routes: Belgium, France, Germany, Italy, Netherlands, Spain, UK, USA

ALLIANCES / CODE SHARES
Oneworld / KLM

OWNED SUBSIDIARY AIRLINES
Air Lingus Commuter

FLEET
A320-200 - 6, A321-200 - 6, A330-200 - 3, A330-300 - 5, 737-448 - 5, 737-548 - 8, BAe 146-300 - 8.
On order: A319 - 4 2003.

Aer Lingus Teoranta was incorporated on May 22nd, 1936, as a state-owned enterprise and began operations five days later with a de Havilland DH 84 Dragon from Baldonnel (Dublin) to Bristol. In 1938 a DH.84B Dragon Express was added and a DH.89 Dragon Rapide replaced the original DH.84. In 1939 a pair of Lockheed 14 monoplanes were added to the existing biplane fleet. The following year the Aer Lingus operation was moved to the newly constructed Dublin Airport at Collinstown and the first of two new DC-3s was delivered. These were used to maintain the Dublin to Liverpool airlink throughout the war.

ABOVE: *Aer Lingus A320-214, EI-CVA (1242) with the Airbus test registrstion F-WWITT. (Airbus)*

In 1945 the London link was resumed and two new DC-3s as well as several surplus military C-47s were added to the fleet. Paris and Shannon were added to the list of destinations using the DC-3s and DH.86Bs. When a shortage of DC-3 spares threatened the operation a fleet of seven Vickers Vikings were ordered and used to modernise the fleet. However, they proved to be uneconomical and were disposed of in less than two years of starting operation.

In 1947 Aer Lingus commenced a series of new routes into Europe spreading as far as Rome. An association with Aerlinte Eireann led to a transatlantic service being offered which was operated with five Lockheed Constellations ordered by Aerlinte Eireann. However, they were short

Aer Lingus

lived due to the cost. This resulted in the closure of Aerlinte Eireann and the sale of the Constellations.

The Bristol 170 Freighters were acquired in 1952 and the first of four Vickers Viscounts arrived in March 1954. The turboprop Viscount proved a popular aircraft and more were added to the fleet through to the late 60s. Five F-27 Friendships arrived in 1958, to replace the DC-3s, with a further pair in 1966.

A second attempt to operate a transatlantic route was tried in 1958 with leased Super Constellations. Carvair conversions of the DC-4 were introduced from 1963 to replace the Bristol Freighters that were primarily used to transport race horses around Europe.

In 1960 Aer Lingus entered the jet age with the first of three 720s which were used on the transatlantic route, replacing the Super Constellations. 707s arrived from 1965 to replace the 720s. The first 737 arrived in March 1969 and in 1971 the first of two 747s was delivered.

Aer Lingus Commuter was formed in 1983 initially operating the Short SD360 on low-density routes. Fokker 50s were bought to replace these together with BAe146s.

In 1993 Aer Lingus Group plc was established with Aer Lingus plc to operate the intra-European air services and Aer Linte Eireann plc (subsequently renamed Aer Lingus Shannon plc) to operate the transat-

ABOVE: *Aer Lingus A330-301, EI-CRK (070). (Airbus)*

ABOVE: *Aer Lingus A321-211, EI-CPF (991). (Jeremy Flack/API)*

ABOVE: *Aer Lingus 737-548, EI-CDC (24968). (Jeremy Flack/API)*

lantic service. Several years of heavy loss making led to a restructure of the business rationalising the assets and making some disposals. Some cash injection by the Irish Government, which owns the equity, led to a reduction in the debt burden and to Aer

Lingus returning to profit. In June 2000 Aer Lingus became a member of the Oneworld Alliance. Hit badly by the events of September 11, the airline has made even greater strides with its restructure which has helped in the recovery.

Aero California

Registered name: Aero California SSA
Country: Mexico
Region: Central America & Caribbean
Address: Aquiles Serdan #1995
          La Paz
          Baja California Sur, 23000
Tel: 0052 112 266 55
Fax: 0052 112 539 93

STATUS

IATA scheduled carrier
Employees: 2,800
Passengers per year: 1,108,000 (2001)

ICAO code: SER
IATA code: JR

SERVICES

International / Regional / Domestic
Passenger / Cargo
International routes: USA

ALLIANCES / CODE SHARES

American A/1

FLEET

DC-9-15 - 8, DC-9-32 - 6

Aero California started in 1960 as an air taxi business based at La Paz with Cessna twins and Beech 18s. During the early 1980s, DC-3s were acquired and used for domestic charters. Scheduled services commenced between La Paz, Tijuana and Hermosillo with Convair 340s in the early 1980s and, as the service grew, a DC-9 was added in 1982. By 1995, Aero California had upgraded to an all DC-9 fleet and has steadily progressed to become Mexico's fourth largest airline.

Aero Continente

Country: Peru
Region: South America
Address: Avenue Jose Pardo 651
Lima, L-18
Lima
Tel: 0051 1 242 46 20
Fax: 0051 1 446 76 38
Web site: www.aerocontinente.com

STATUS

Scheduled carrier
National Flag Carrier
Employees: 700
Passengers per year: 1,223,000 (2001)
ICAO code: ACQ
IATA code: N6

SERVICES

International / Regional / Domestic
Passenger / Charter
International routes: Chile, Panama, USA

OWNED SUBSIDIARY AIRLINES

Aero Continente Chile (49%), Aviandina

FLEET

An-32 -1, 727-100 - 5, 737-100 - 2, 737-200 - 2, 737-200Adv - 3, 757-200 - 1, Jetstream 31 - 1, F-27J - 2, F-28 Fellowship 1000 - 1, L.1011 Tristar - 1, L.1011 Tristar 100 – 2

Aero Continente was formed on January 4th, 1992, when tax incentives were being granted to encourage decentralised business. Initial operations were in support of the oil exploration business. The first service was flown by a 737 on 25th May 1992. Initial operations were based on the requirements of Occidental Petroleum Corporation with aircraft being leased out when not required.

Eventually Aero Continente began its own scheduled service with its fleet of one 727 and three 737s. With an emphasis being placed on punctuality together with efficiency and security, the number of routes have expanded and have brought about a steady increase in passenger numbers.

During 2002 Aero Continente ran a roller-coaster with a bid to take a 70% share in Ecuadoriana being rejected. Around the same time the Chilean division of Aero Continente was being declared bankrupt in Chile following the jailing of four of its executives for money laundering, pilots on strike and the authorities suspending its operations.

Aero Continente claimed that although they denied the accusations they were so compromised that, much as it was regretted, the operation in Peru had to be closed down. In August a judge released the four executives and the charges were dropped! In the meantime Aero Continente was making a $100m offer for Aerolineas Argentinas which was being considered by the ailing airline with debts reaching $900m.

Aeroflot Russian Airlines

Registered name: Aeroflot Russian Airlines JSC
Country: Russian Federation
Region: Asia
Address: 37/9 Leningradsky Prospect
9 Block
Moscow 125167
Tel: 007 095 155 66 43
Fax: 007 095 752 90 28
Web site: www.aeroflot.ru
Main operational base: Moscow

STATUS

IATA scheduled international carrier
National Flag Carrier
Employees: 15,352
Passengers per year: 5,831,000 (2001)
ICAO code: AFL
IATA code: SU

SERVICES

International / Regional / Domestic
Passenger / Cargo
International routes: Angola, Austria, Armenia, Azerbaijan, Belgium, China, Croatia, Cuba, Cyprus, Czech, Denmark, Egypt, Estonia, Finland, France, Greece, Georgia, Germany, Hungary, India, Iran, Ireland, Italy, Japan, Jordan, Kazakhstan, Kyrgyzstan, Latvia, Lebanon, Lithuania, Luxembourg, Macedonia, Malta, Mongolia, Nepal, Netherlands, Norway, Poland, Portugal, Romania, Serbia, Singapore, South Korea, Slovakia, Slovenia, Spain, Sweden, Switzerland, Syria, Thailand, Tunisia, Turkey, UAE, UK, Ukraine, USA, Vietnam

ABOVE: *Aeroflot A310-304, F-OGQU (646). (Airbus)*

ALLIANCES / CODE SHARES

Air France, Air-India, Armenian Airliners, Austrian Airlines, CSA Czech Airline,

Aeroflot Russian Airlines

LEFT: *Aeroflot 767-3Y0ER, EI-CKD (C/n 26205), is leased from GECAS and remains on the Irish register. (Jane's)*

Cubana de Aviacion, Cyprus Airways, Estonian Air, Finnair, LOT, Malev, Pulkovo, Royal Jordanian, TAROM, Uzbekistan Airways

FLEET

A310-300 - 11, 737-400 - 10, 767-300ER - 4, 777-200ER - 2, DC-10-30F - 1, Il-62M - 12, Il-76TD - 10, Il-86 - 15, Il-96-300 6, Tu-134A/A-3 - 16, Tu-154M - 24
On order: A319 / A320 - 18, Il-96 – 19

Aeroflot was established by the Soviet Government in March 1923 as the national flag carrier and named Dorbolet. Initial aircraft operated were modified ex-military aircraft and in July 1923 the first domestic scheduled service was flown. In 1929 it merged with Ukvozduchput to form Dobroflot that was reorganised in February 1932 and renamed Aeroflot. At its peak Aeroflot was the world's largest airline with some 4,000 aircraft and estimated staff levels between 400,000 and 500,000. In addition to conventional scheduled and charter, passenger and cargo services Aeroflot offered a wide range of other aviation services including crop-spraying, survey, fishery and ice reconnaissance, forest firefighting and aeromedical services. Aeroflot had concentrated on the domestic market with only a limited number of flights outside the eastern bloc. The jet airliner was introduced in 1956 with the Tu-104 and in 1958 development of an international network commenced.

The Tu-114 was the largest airliner at the time and was developed from the Tu-20 Bear bomber. It entered service with Aeroflot in April 1961. The Tu-124 was a development of the Tu-104 and entered service in 1962. September 1967 saw the introduction into service of the Tu-134. Looking very similar to the 727 the Tu-154 was first delivered to Aeroflot in 1971 but did not enter scheduled service until February 1972.

Supersonic cargo flights commenced with the Tu-144 on 26th December 1975 and a passenger service was inaugurated on 1st November 1977. However, both were suspended in 1978 following an accident. In 1980 Aeroflot was designated the general carrier for the XXII Olympic Games which was held in Moscow. Following the break-up of the Soviet Union, Aeroflot commenced a capital reconstruction and became a public company the following year. The government has retained 51% under its control and the balance is owned by Russian and international institutional and private investors. To reflect the changes the airline was named Aeroflot - Russian International Airlines on the 28th July 1992.The huge old Aeroflot had been broken up into around 160 components with most regions forming their own airlines. Although significantly smaller, Aeroflot remained the largest airline in the former Soviet Union but emerged as a leaner and fitter organisation. A first for Aeroflot was the introduction of foreign airliner types in 1992 - the Airbus A310 led the way followed by the 767 two years later. The Ilyushin Il-96 was introduced into service in 1994, representing the first Russian airliner built to Western noise standards, while a DC-10 was leased the following year for cargo operations.

Aeroflot has completed a corporate and financial reorganisation and currently works closely with Air France. On 24th June

LEFT: *Aeroflot Il-86, RE-86067 (C/n 51483203034). (Jeremy Flack/API)*

2000 its name was changed once again to Aeroflot - Russian Airlines. Aeroflot plans to join the Sky Team Alliance which includes Air France, Delta Airlines, Korean Air and Air Mexico.

The US Government approved a US$1bn loan to Aeroflot to enable it to buy a fleet of 20 Il-76s that will be equipped with Pratt & Whitney engines and Rockwell avionics. There was strong disapproval voiced by Boeing and other US aircraft manufacturers who would not benefit and saw this as a subsidy for a foreign manufacturer. However, the US Government maintains the agreement will provide many US jobs and is an opportunity for the US to enter the Russian market.

ABOVE: *Aeroflot Tu-134A, RA65760. (Jeremy Flack/API)*

Aeroflot-Don

Registered name: Aeroflot-Don JSC
Country: Russian Federation
Region: Asia
Address: 272 Sholokhov Avenue
344009 Rostov-on-Don
Tel: 007 8632 52 50 79
Fax: 007 8632 52 05 67
Web site: www.glomanet.com/aeroflot-don/
Stockholder: Aereoflot Group
Main operational base: Rostov-on-Don

STATUS
Scheduled charter and cargo carrier
Employees: 950
Passengers per year: 400,000 (2001)
ICAO code: DNV
IATA code: D9

SERVICES
Regional / Domestic / Passenger Charter / Cargo
International routes: Russia and CIS (some 80 destinations)

FLEET
An-12 - 2, Tu-134A-3 - 6, Tu-154B-2 - 8, Tu-154M - 2, Tu-204 - 2, Yak-40 – 3

Don Civil Aviation was originally formed in 1925 and operated as the major airline operating out of Rostov-on-Don airport.

It was absorbed into Aeroflot. However, in April 2000 it re-emerged as Aeroflot-Don to operate as a subsidiary of the Aeroflot Group.

Aeroflot-Don now operates is own schedule of domestic and international services as well as charter service.

Aerolineas Argentinas

Registered name: Aerolineas Argentinas SA
Country: Argentina
Region: South America
Address: Bouchard 547
9th Floor
Buenos Aires 1106
Tel: 0054 11 43 17 30 00
Fax: 0054 11 43 20 21 16
Web site: www.aerolineas.com.ar
Main operational base: Buenos Aires

STATUS
IATA scheduled international and domestic carrier
National Flag Carrier
Employees: 5,197
Passengers per year: 1,876,000 (2001)
ICAO code: ARG
IATA code: AR

SERVICES
International / Regional / Domestic Passenger / Cargo
International routes: Australia, Bolivia, Colombia, Chile, Cuba, Mexico, New Zealand, Paraguay, Peru, Spain, Uruguay, USA, Venezuela

ALLIANCES / CODE SHARES
Qantas Airways

FLEET
A340-200 - 4, A340-300 - 2, 737-200 - 1, 737-200 Advanced - 20, 747-200B - 9, Jetstream 32EP - 3 (Operated as Aerolineas Argentinas Express), MD-83 - 1, MD-88 - 5
On Order: A340-600- 6 for delivery from 2002

Aerolineas Argentinas

Aerolineas Argentinas was formed on May 14th, 1949, by the Argentine Government to take over four existing independent airlines to develop a co-ordinated domestic and international service. The four local airlines were Flota Aerea Mercante Argentina (FAMA), Aviacion del Litoral Fluvial Argentino (ALFA), Zonas Oeste y Norte de Aerolineas Argentinas (ZONDA) and Aeroposta Argentina of which the last originated in 1928. FAMA, which was formed in 1946, was the largest and had been the Argentine Flag carrier and was operating a route to London with its DC-4s. Aerolineas Argentinas commenced its operations with an enlarging domestic and international network.

Jet transport was introduced by Aerolineas Argentinas with the de Havilland Comet in May 1959 and the Caravelle in 1962 on the domestic and regional routes. 707 deliveries commenced towards the end of 1966.

The 1970s saw a steady expansion in the Aerolineas Argentinas service. In 1970 the first of nine 737s were delivered and the first two of three F-27 Friendships arrived in 1975 with the first 747 the following year. 727s were also added to the fleet with the first example being delivered in 1978. In 1980 Aerolineas Argentinas used its 747s to commence an Argentina to New Zealand service. Aerolineas Argentinas has been trying to attract international investment but has had to rely on government support as business dropped. Rationalisation has resulted in parts of the business being sold including Aerolineas Argentinas Express which was bought by Brazil's TAM Group in 2001. In 2002 Aero Continente made a $100m offer for Aerolineas Argentinas which was being considered by the ailing airline which had debts now reaching $900m.

Aerolineas Centrales de Columbia (ACES)

Country: Colombia
Region: South America
Address:　　Calle 49 50-21
　　　　　　　Piso 34
　　　　　　　Edificio del Cafe
　　　　　　　Medellin,
Tel: 0057 4 251 7500
Fax: 0057 4 511 22 37
Web site: www.acescolombia.com or www.aces.com
Main operational base: Bogota Eldorado

STATUS

Passenger and cargo carrier
Employees: 1,425
Passengers per year: 2,135,000 (2001)
ICAO code: AES
IATA code: VX

SERVICES

International / Regional / Domestic
Passenger / Charter / Cargo

ABOVE: *Aces ATR 42-320, HK-3684X (C/n 284). (ATR)*

International routes: Dominican Republic Ecuador, Peru, Puerto Rico, USA

ALLIANCES / CODE SHARES

Continental Airlines

FLEET

A320-200 - 5, ATR 42-320 - 4, ATR 42-500 - 6, 727-200 - 4, DHC-6 Twin Otter 300 - 9
On Order: A320 - 3

Aerolineas Centrales de Colombia was formed on August 30th, 1971, operating the Saunders ST-27 turboprop variant of the de Havilland Heron on domestic routes. Twin Otters were added to enable route expansion.

During 1981 the 727 was added and international charters commenced in 1986. The following year the ST-27s were being replaced with F-27 Friendships although they gave way to the ATR 42 in 1991. At the

same time the 727-100s were replaced by the improved 727-200s. These enabled scheduled services to commence to Miami.

During the late 90s ACES took delivery of A320s enabling it to meet the increasing demand for its service as Colombia's second largest airline.

On 28th February 2002 ACES announced the signature of an agreement for the integration of its services with those of Avianca and SAM.

Aeroméxico

Registered name: Aerovias de Mexico
Country: Mexico
Region: South America
Address: Avenue Paseo de la Reforma 445
Piso 12 Torre A, Colonia Cuauhtemoc
Mexico City, 06500
Tel: 0052 5 133 40 05
Fax: 0052 5 133 46 17
Web site: www.aeromexico.com
Main operational base: Mexico City

STATUS

IATA scheduled carrier
National Flag Carrier
Employees: 6,458
Passengers per year: 9,475,000 (2001)
ICAO code: AMX
IATA code: AM

SERVICES

International / Regional / Domestic
Passenger / Cargo
International routes: Brazil, Chile, France, Peru, Spain, USA

ALLIANCES / CODE SHARES

SkyTeam / AeroCaribe, AeroMar, LanChile, Mexicana

FLEET

757-200 - 8, 767-200ER - 4, 767-300ER - 1, DC-9-31 - 3, DC-9-32 - 14, MD-82 - 13, MD-83 - 8, MD-87 - 5, MD-88 - 10, SAAB 340 - 9, Metro 23 / 11 - 23
On order: 737-700 - 15 to replace DC-9s

Aeroméxico was initially formed on September 15th, 1934, as Aeronaves de Mexico with the original Pan American as a major shareholder. During the 50s and 60s four other airlines were merged into Aeronaves de Mexico before the Mexican Government nationalised the airline in July 1959. During this period DC-3s, DC-4s and Constellations were operated with DC-6s being added a little later.

The Bristol Britannia was used to open a Mexico City-New York service in December 1957 and the first DC-8 was introduced in 1964. The DC-9s entered service from 1967. In 1970 the Mexican Government reorganised and rationalised the eight domestic operators into a co-ordinated system under the control of Aeronaves de Mexico. In

ABOVE: *Aeroméxico 767-283ER, XA-TOJ (C/n 24727). (Aeroméxico)*

February 1972 the name of Aeronaves de Mexico was changed to Aeroméxico.

In 1974 the first two DC-10s were delivered and by the mid-1980s AeroMexico was operating an all McDonnell Douglas fleet.

In 1998 Aeroméxico ceased trading after financial difficulties. However, it was restarted shortly after, with private investors, as Aerovias de Mexico and continues to operate as Aeroméxico.

In 1992 Aeroméxico became the first South American Airline to operate a frequent flyer programme and in 1999 was the first again to offer an e-ticket system.

Aeropostal – LAV

Registered name: Lineas Aeropostal Venezolana
Country: Venezuela
Region: South America
Address: Polar Oeste
         22nd Floor
         Plaza Caracas
         Caracas
Tel: 0058 2 708 62 11
Fax: 0058 2 782 63 23
Web site: www.aeropostal.com
Main operational base: Caracas

STATUS

Scheduled international, domestic and charter carrier
Employees: 2,167

Passengers per year: 2,167,000 (1999)
ICAO code: LAV
IATA code: LV

SERVICES

International / Regional
Domestic / Passenger
International routes: Aruba, Barbados, Brazil, Colombia, Dominican Republic Ecuador, Havana, Peru, San Tome, Trinidad & Tobago, USA

FLEET

DC-9-32 - 6, DC-9-51 - 12, 727-200Adv - 5

The origins of Aeropostal LAV can be traced back to 1933 when Linea Aeropostal Venezolana was formed by the Venezuelan Government to take over from the French Compagnie Générale Aéropostale (formed 1930) and operated Latécoére 28s.

In 1951 Aeropostal took over TACA de Venezuela. The international schedules were transferred to VIASA in 1960.

In 1994, Aeropostal ceased operations. However, the assets were acquired by Aeron Aviation Resources and Airfinans. The business was reorganised and, in 1997, was reformed flying primarily domestic schedules together with some international services.

Air 2000

Registered name: Air 2000 Ltd
Country: UK
Region: Europe
Address: Commonwealth House
         Chicago Avenue
         Manchester Airport
         M90 3DP
Tel: 0044 161 489 0321
Fax: 0044 161 908 2288
Web site: www.air2000.com
Stockholder: First Choice Holidays plc
Main operational base: Manchester

STATUS

Scheduled and charter carrier
Employees: 2,319
Passengers per year: 6,938,000 (2001) including charter
ICAO code: AMM
IATA code: DP

SERVICES

International / Regional / Passenger Charter / Cargo
International routes: Cyprus, Portugal, Spain

FLEET

A320-200 - 6, A321-200 - 6, 757-200 - 19, 767-300ER - 3

On order: A320-200 - 1 for 2004, 757-200 - 1 for April 2004

Air 2000 was launched on 11 April, 1987, and commenced operations in May with a pair of 757s as a new holiday charter airline out of Manchester Airport.

In 1988 First Choice Holidays acquired Unijet and its subsidiary Leisure International Airways that was then amalgamated with Air 2000. In January 1999, Air 2000 installed life-saving defibrillators on its aircraft.

In April 2000 an announcement was made that Air 2000 was going to commence scheduled services and the first was flown in

ABOVE: *Air 2000 A-320-212, G-OOAP (C/n 1306). (Airbus)*

July that year to Cyprus. With the charter business accounting for about 66%, Air 2000 flew almost seven million passengers in 2000 that took it to being the fourth largest UK airline in respect of passengers carried. It also operated with one of the highest load factors in the world.

A fleet renewal programme was announced in March 2001 with up to eight 767s to be acquired.

In August 2001, Air 2000 celebrated its one millionth flying hour since it commenced operation.

Air Algérie

Country: Algeria
Region: Africa
Address: 1 Place Maurice Audin, Algiers
Tel: 00213 21 74 24 26
Fax: 00213 21 74 44 25
Web site: www.airalgerie.dz
Main operational base: Algiers

ABOVE: *Air Algérie A310-203, 7T-VJC (C/n 291) during test flight with Airbus test registration F-WZED.(Airbus)*

STATUS

IATA scheduled carrier
National Flag Carrier
Employees: 8,696
Passengers per year: 3,577,000 (2001)
ICAO code: DAH
IATA code: AH

SERVICES

International / Regional / Domestic
Passenger / Cargo
International routes: Belgium, Burkina, Cote D'Ivoire, Egypt, France, Germany, Italy, Jordan, Lebanon, Libya, Mali, Mauritania, Niger, Poland, Russia, Saudi Arabia, Senegal, Spain, Syria, Switzerland, Tunisia, Turkey, UAE, UK

FLEET

A310-203 - 2, 727-200 - 9, 737-200 - 24, 737-600 - 5, 737 -800 - 7, 767-300 -3, F-27 Mk 400 - 7, L-100-30 Hercules - 2 (Operated for Algerian Air Force)
On order: 737-600 - 5

The origins of Air Algérie date back to 1946 with the forming of the non-scheduled operator Compagnie Générale de Transports Aériens (CGTA). It had gradually established a service operating several routes to France. In 1953 it was merged with Compagnie Air Transport, that was offering a similar service, to rationalise their operations. These were operated from 1960 with the Caravelle. Air Algérie was designated the national carrier in 1963 and became wholly government owned in 1972.

In May 1972 Société de Travail Aérien, which provided a domestic service as well as air taxi, agricultural and aeromedical services became a subsidiary of Air Algérie. It subsequently was absorbed into Air Algérie.

Air Algérie operates the C-130 Hercules which were also operated on behalf of the Algerian Air Force.

Air Atlanta Icelandic

Registered name: Flugfelagid Atlanta hf
Country: Iceland
Region: Europe
Address: Atlanta House, PO Box 80
270 Mosfellsbaer
Tel: 00354 515 77 00
Fax: 00354 515 77 66
Web site: www.atlanta.is

ABOVE: *Air Atlanta Icelandic 747-341, TF-ATH (C/n 24106). (Baldur Sveinsson, via API)*

STATUS

International passenger + cargo carrier
Employees: 1,400
ICAO code: ABD
IATA code: CC

SERVICES

International / Regional / Passenger
Charter / Cargo
International routes: Denmark, France, Spain, UK

FLEET

747-200 / 300 - 13, 767-200 / 300 - 8

Atlanta Icelandic Air Transport was started on 10 February, 1986, after Eagle Air ceased trading. It was formed by Armgrimur Johannson, who had been Eagle Air's chief pilot, to provide charters and lease aircraft on demand. It also operated scheduled services for other airlines on contract.

Gradually the older 747s and Tristars have been replaced with more modern 747s and 767s with 757s probably to be added in the near future.

Air Baltic

Registered name: Air Baltic Corporation A/S

Country: Latvia

Region: Europe

Address: Riga International Airport

Riga

LV-1053

Tel: 00371 7 20 70 69

Fax: 00371 7 20 73 69

Web site: www.airbaltic.com

Main operational base: Riga International Airport

ABOVE: *Air Baltic Fokker 50, YL-BAT (C/n 20163). (Air Baltic)*

STATUS

IATA scheduled and charter passenger + cargo carrier

National Flag Carrier

Employees: 290

Passengers per year: 248,700 (2001)

ICAO code: BTI

IATA code: BT

SERVICES

International / Regional / Passenger Charter / Cargo

International routes: Belarus*, Belgium*, Czech*, Denmark, Finland, Germany, Hungary, Lithuania, Luxembourg*, Netherlands*, Norway*, Poland*, Russia*, Slovakia*, Sweden, Switzerland, UK, Ukraine (*code share with SAS)

ALLIANCES / CODE SHARES

Estonian Air, SAS

FLEET

RJ70 - 3, Fokker 50 - 3

The origin of Air Baltic dates back to 1992 when Baltic International was formed with DC-9s and Tu-134s. In 1995 Latvio-Latvian Airlines developed problems and the two were merged to form Air Baltic and re-equipped with SAAB 340s.

Ownership of Air Baltic is primarily 51% by the Latvian Privatisation Agency and 29% SAS and it had been declared the national airline of Latvia.

Air Berlin

Registered name: Air Berlin GmbH & Co Luftverkehrs AG

Country: Germany

Region: Europe

Address: Saatwinkler Damm 42-43

D-13627 Berlin

Tel: 0049 30 34 34 10 01

Fax: 0049 30 34 34 10 09

Web site: www.airberlin.com

Main operational base: Berlin

ABOVE: *Air Berlin 737-88J, D-ABAN (C/n 28068). (Air Berlin)*

STATUS

Scheduled and charter carrier

Employees: 1,540

Passengers per year: 5,500,000 (2001)

ICAO code: BER

IATA code: AB

SERVICES

International / Regional / Domestic Passenger / Charter

International routes: Italy, Portugal, Greece, Morocco, Spain, Turkey, UK

FLEET

737-400 - 5, 737-800 - 24

Aircraft movements into Berlin were restricted after WW2 and then the Cold War, to aircraft of the Allies only. As a result Air Berlin Inc was formed in July 1978 in Oregon, USA. The first flight was made on April 28th, 1979, from Berlin to Palma de Mallorca with a leased 707.

The 707 was replaced with a pair of 737-200s which in turn started to give way to 737-300s in 1982.

When the occupation of Berlin ended the Allies lost their access privileges. This meant that Air Berlin had to lose the US identity and gain a German majority shareholding to remain in business. As a result, Air Berlin GmbH & Co Luftverkehrs AG was launched on 16 April 1991 and established its HQ at Tegel.

The move was good for Air Berlin which saw its numbers of annual passengers carried rapidly rise from 1.04 million in 1994 through 2.04 million in 1998 and 3 million in 1999 to 5.5 million in 2001.

In recent years Air Berlin has found it advantageous to regularly replace its aircraft to the extent that their average age is now under two years. This enables technology to be of the latest standards and engine noise emissions and fuel economies are the best available. With reduced maintenance this enables Air Berlin to achieve good

operating costs while considering the environment.

With this aim, the existing 737-400s are being replaced by 737-800s that have 17 more seats and fly a greater range faster but save 10% in fuel.

Air Berlin was also the first German holiday airline to install, voluntarily, the TCAS

ABOVE: *Air Berlin 737-88J, D-ABAF (C/n 30878). (Air Berlin)*

anti-collision system in its aircraft. Air Berlin was also the first airline to install winglets to the wings of its 737-800s that enable a faster rate of climb and result in greater fuel efficiency.

Air Botswana

Country: Botswana
Region: Africa
Address: Head Office Building
Sir Seretse Khama Airport
PO Box 92, Gaborone
Tel: 00267 35 28 12
Fax: 00267 37 48 02
Web site: www.airbotswana.co.bw
Main operational base: Sir Seretse Khama Airport

STATUS

IATA scheduled regional and domestic carrier
National Flag Carrier
Employees: 295
Passengers per year: 168,000 (2001)
ICAO code: BOT
IATA code: BP

SERVICES

Regional / Domestic / Passenger / Cargo
International routes: South Africa, Zimbabwe

FLEET

ATR 42-500 - 3

Air Botswana came into being in 1972 as a result of the demise of Botswana Airways. Initial aircraft operated were the Britten Norman Islander and Fokker F-27 Friendship later to be replaced by HS748 and Viscounts. However, the airline struggled, relying on government support to keep it operational.

In 1988 the airline became the government-owned national carrier known as Air Botswana Corporation. In 1994 the airline was restructured and recapitalised with a view to privatisation. ATR 72s were leased from the manufacturer to replace the existing older types being operated and have since been purchased. A substantial maintenance base was established at Sir Seretse

ABOVE: *Air Botswana ATR 42-500 . (ATR)*

Khama Airport that attracts contract work from other ATR operators in Kenya, Malawi, Tanzania and Zambia. In April 2001 the International Finance Corporation was appointed to advise on privatisation proposals. However, the slow-down in the airline business, compounded by the events of 11 September has temporarily put the plan on hold. An optimistic plan now hopes to conclude the privatisation by May 2003.

Air Botswana managed to increase its portion of the market and accounted for 38% of passengers entering or departing Botswana in 2001 compared with 23% in 1995.

Air Burkina

Country: Burkina Faso
Region: Africa
Address: PO Box 1459
Avenue Loudun
Ouagadougou
Tel: 00226 31 53 24
Fax: 00226 31 48 80
Main operational base: Ouagadougou

STATUS

Scheduled international and domestic carrier
National Flag Carrier
Employees: 82
ICAO code: VBW
IATA code: 2J

SERVICES

Regional / Domestic / Passenger
International routes: Benin, Burkina Faso, Cote D'Ivoire, Mali, Niger, Togo

FLEET

EMB110P2 Bandeirante - 1, F-28
Fellowship 4000 - 1

Air Burkina was originally formed as Air Volta on March 17th, 1967, with assistance from Air Afrique and UTA. In 1985 Air Volta was renamed Air Burkina after the name of the country which had also changed name from Upper Volta to Burkina Faso.

Air Burundi

Country: Burundi
Region: Africa
Address: PO Box 2460
40 Avenue du Commerce
Bujumbura
Tel: 00257 22 44 85
Fax: 00257 22 34 52
Main operational base: Bujumbura

STATUS

National Flag Carrier
ICAO code: PBU
IATA code: 8Y

SERVICES

Domestic / Passenger

FLEET

DHC-6 Twin Otter 300, 1900C-1

Air Burundi origins date to April 1971 when Société de Transports Aériens du Burundi (STAB) was formed with three DC-3s from France - two of which were ex-French AF. In addition to its transport role, STAB used light aircraft for spraying insecticides.

In 1975 STAB was renamed Air Burundi and the following year an ex-Air France Caravelle was received which has since been retired.

Aircalin

Registered name: Air Calédonie International SA
Country: New Caledonia
Region: Australia & Pacific
Address: 8 rue Frederic-Surleau
PO Box 3736
Noumea
98846
Tel: 00687 26 55 00
Fax: 00687 27 27 72
Web site: www.aircalin.nc
Main operational base: Noumea

STATUS

IATA regional carrier
National Flag Carrier
Employees: 201
Passengers per year: 287,000 (2001)
ICAO code: CDI
IATA code: SB

ABOVE: *Aircalin A310-325, F-OHPX (C/n 672). (Airbus)*

SERVICES

International / Regional / Domestic
Passenger / Cargo
International routes: Australia, Fiji, Japan,
New Zealand, Tahiti, Wallis & Futuna
Islands, Vanuatu

ALLIANCES/CODE SHARES

Air Pacific, Air Vanuatu, Qantas

FLEET

A310-325 - 1, 737-300 - 1, DHC-6 Twin
Otter 300 - 1. **On Order:** A330-200 - 2

Air Calédonie International was formed in
September 1983 to provide an air link with
Australia and New Zealand. Its initial service to Melbourne was operated using
capacity on a Qantas 747s while a Brisbane-
Port Vila-Wallis and Nadi service was operated with a leased 737. A Caravelle was
leased in 1984 and due to its success one
was purchased the following year.

A Twin Otter was added to provide a
Wallis-Futuna service during 1987 while in
1988 the Caravelle was retired and replaced
by a leased 737. Having successfully operated the 737, a new one was purchased in

1989. During January 1995 Air Calédonie
International chartered a DC-10 for 14
months from AOM for the New Zealand
service. August 1995 saw Air Calédonie
International designated as the official carrier for the New Caledonia and Wallis teams
for the 10th Pacific Games in Tahiti. The
following year the 737 appeared in a new
colour scheme while the airline became a
member of IATA. Delivery of an Airbus
A310 was taken in March 2000 with its first
route flown to Japan later that month, while
in December the first service to the USA
was offered to Los Angeles.

Air Canada

Country: Canada
Region: North America
Address: Air Canada Centre
PO Box 14000, St Laurent
Quebec H4Y 1H4
Tel: 001 514 422 50 00
Web site: www.aircanada.ca
Stockholder: Air Canada Group
Main operational base: Toronto

STATUS

IATA scheduled and charter carrier
National Flag Carrier
Employees: 33,200
Passengers per year: 23,100,000 (2001)
ICAO code: ACA
IATA code: AC

SERVICES

International / Regional / Domestic
Passenger / Charter / Cargo
International routes: Antigua & Barbuda,
Argentina, Australia, Bahamas, Barbados,
Bermuda, Brazil, China, Denmark, France,
Germany, Guadeloupe, Haiti, India, Israel,
Jamaica, Japan, Martinique, Mexico, St
Lucia, S Korea, Switzerland, Taiwan,
Trinidad & Tobago, UK, USA

ALLIANCES / CODE SHARES

Star Alliance / Air Jamaica, Alitalia, Atlantic
Coast Airlines, Delta A/L, EVA Airways,

Korean Air Lines, Mexicana, Royal
Jordanian, Spanair

OWNED SUBSIDIARY AIRLINES

Air Canada Jazz

FLEET

A319-100 - 46, A320-200 - 50 (6 operated by
Tango), A321-200 - 13, A330-300 - 8, A340-
300 - 10, A340-500 - 2, 1900D - 5 (operated
by Jazz), 737-200 - 3 (operated by Tango),
747-400 - 4, 747-400 Combi - 3, 767-200 - 11,
767-200ER - 5, 767-300ER - 35 (4 being withdrawn), BAe 146-200 - 10 (operated by
Tango), CRJ100 - Qty -10, CRJ200 - 8 (operated by Jazz), DHC-8 Dash 8-100 - 54 (oper-

ABOVE: *Air Canada A319-114, C-FYCK (C/n 691)
during test flight with Airbus test registration D-AVYP.
(Airbus)*

ated by Jazz), DHC-8 Dash 8-300 - 18 (operated by Jazz), F-28 Fellowship 1000 - 30
(being phased out)
On order: A319-100 - 2 for 2003, A320-200 -
6 for 2003 & 2004, A340-600 - 3 for 2004,
1900D - 8 (for Jazz)

Air Canada was formed on 10 April, 1937,
as Trans-Canada Airlines (TCA) as a subsidiary of the Canadian National Railway
Co. It flew its first scheduled route between
Vancouver and Seattle on 1st September
1937, using a Lockheed 10 carrying mail

Air Canada

and two passengers. Lockheed 14s were subsequently added to the fleet.

TCA operated flights to Europe during WW2 in support of the Canadian forces with Lancastrians.

Post-war operations utilised DC-3s on the domestic network which were soon joined by Canadian-built DC-4 North Stars for the scheduled transatlantic routes.

Having been designated the national flag carrier, TCA steadily enlarged its routes and fleet. Super Constellations were added in 1954 and it became the first operator of a turboprop aircraft with the introduction of the Vickers Viscount in April 1955. TCA found this a popular aircraft and a total of 51 were operated, remaining in service until 1974. TCA entered the jet age with the arrival of the DC-8 in 1960. The first Vickers Vanguard arrived in December 1960 and DC-9s entered service during April 1966. In the meantime, TCA was renamed Air Canada on January 1, 1965.

In 1966 Air Canada became the first North American carrier to offer a service to the Soviet Union.

Air Canada began a 747 service in April 1971 following the delivery of its first example in March of that year. March 1973 saw the arrival of another widebody airliner in the form of the L1011 Tristar.

Air Canada became a separate business in 1977 and a fully private corporation in 1989.

In 1997 Air Canada issued a letter of intent for five A330s and three A340s with options on a further 20 to replace the older 747s. This was to be the first phase of a fleet renewal programme. Phase two would include additional A340s and the third a further batch to replace the 747-400s. Also in May 1997 Air Canada became a founder member of the Star Alliance.

Air Canada acquired Canadian Airlines International in 2000 making it become the twelfth largest airline.

A bizarre survey was compiled during 2000 for an international development bank to help it avoid booking its employees on potentially unsafe airlines. Following a complex survey that combines the accident history with 10 other safety factors, including management structure, fleet composition and safety regulations, Air Canada was identified as being the world's safest airline.

ABOVE: *Air Canada A320-211, C-FFWN (C/n 159) in 65th anniversary colours. (Air Canada)*

In 2001 Air Canada introduced the first non-stop flight from North America to India. This was flown on a polar route with an A340. In November, Tango was formed as a low-cost carrier based at Toronto.

In January 2002, Air Canada Regional Inc was formed and combined the four regional airlines - AirBC, Air Nova, Air Ontario and Canadian Regional. With this complete the new regional carrier, named Air Canada Jazz, commenced operations in March 2002 and now serves some 80 destinations with 122 aircraft. A further low-cost carrier called Zip was also formed to operate in Western Canada out of Calgary.

BELOW: *Air Canada A340-313, C-FTNQ (C/n 088). (Airbus)*

Air Caraibes

Registered name: Air Caraibes SA
Country: Guadeloupe
Region: Central America & Caribbean
Address: Immeuble Le Caducée
Morne Vergain, 97139 Abymes
Le Lamentin
Tel: 00590 82 47 34
Fax: 00590 82 47 49
Web site: www.aircaraibes.com
Stockholder: Groupe Dubreuil
Main operational base: Point-a-Pitre

STATUS

IATA scheduled passenger and cargo carrier
National Flag Carrier
Employees: 450
Passengers per year: 660,000 (2000)
ICAO code: AGU
IATA code: TX

SERVICES

International / Regional / Domestic
Passenger / Charter
International routes: Dominica, Dominican Republic, Martinique, Netherlands Antilles, Puerto Rico, St Lucia

ALLIANCES / CODE SHARES

Carib Sky Alliance / Air France

FLEET

ATR 42-500 - 2, ATR 72-500 - 2, 208 Caravan - 4, Do 228-212 - 4, ERJ-145 - 2

Air Caraibes originally started out in 1969 as Air Guadeloupe. In August 1994 a change in ownership resulted in the name changing to Société Nouvelle Air Guadeloupe. In 2000, Air Guadeloupe was

ABOVE: *Air Caraibes ATR 72-512. (ATR)*

merged with subsidiaries - Air Martinique (formed in 1974), Air Saint Martin and Air Saint Barthelemy (formed 1981), later renamed Air Caraibes.

Air China

Registered name: China Aviation Company
Country: China
Region: Far East
Address: Jing Xin Building, JIA-2
Dong San Huan North Road
Beijing, 100027
Tel: 008610 66016667
Fax: 008610 64662835
Web site: www.air-china.co.uk or
www.airchina.com.cn
Main operational base: Beijing

STATUS

IATA scheduled international passenger and cargo
National Flag Carrier
Employees: 12,000
Passengers per year: 9,275,000 (2001)
ICAO code: CCA
IATA code: CA

SERVICES

International / Regional / Domestic
Passenger / Cargo
International routes: Australia, Canada, Denmark, France, Germany, India,

ABOVE: *Air China A340-313x. (Airbus)*

Indonesia, Italy, Japan, Mongolia, Myanmar, Russia, Singapore, South Korea, Sweden, Switzerland, Thailand, UAE, UK, USA

ALLIANCES / CODE SHARES

Air France, Austrian Airlines, British Midland, Finnair, Lufthansa, Northwest, SAS, Swiss, Tarom

FLEET

A340-300, BAe 146-100 - 4, 737-300 - 19, 737-800 - 9, 747-200B - 2, 747-200F - 2, 747-400 - 5, 747-400 SCD - 5, 767-200ER - 6, 767-300ER - 4, 777-200 - 10, Y-7 - 5
On order: A318 - 8, A340 - 3, 737-800 - 35, 777-200 - 12

Air China

Air China was originally formed as part of the Civil Aviation Administration of China (CAAC) that commenced operations in November 1949. In 1988 CAAC, which was responsible for most aspects of aviation in China, began establishing nine separate airlines such as Air China that was formed on July 1st, 1988, from the Beijing Division. Initial aircraft were supplied from the CAAC fleet but all new acquisitions were of Western aircraft much centred on the 737 although the larger 747, and more recently the 777 were also included. Most recently Air China has ordered the Airbus A318 and 340.

In 1993 Air China was granted independent trade group status and was the largest air transport group in China. Development progressed largely with the assistance of Lufthansa and Asiana and future growth is also branching into other areas including tourism.

The general downturn in the Far East economies during the second half of the 90s largely bypassed China due to the limited quantity of international business. However, the airlines were very much exposed and suffered badly. After several years of losses CAAC stepped in, initially banning discounting and aircraft lease renewals. In 2002 a reform plan, which had been rumoured for several years, was announced. The result of the reform will see Air China - already the largest airline in China - and the China Southwest Aviation Company merging to become the China International Aviation Company. As the new airline is established so the external administration links will be cut.

Air Europa

Registered name: Air Europa Lineas Aereas, SA
Country: Spain
Region: Europe
Address: Centro Empresarial Globalia
PO Box 132
E - 07620 Llucmajor
Tel: 0034 971 17 83 67
Fax: 0034 971 17 81 21
Web site: www.air-europa.com

STATUS

Scheduled domestic and international + charter passenger carrier
Employees: 2,080
Passengers per year: 6,329,000 (2001)
ICAO code: AEA
IATA code: UX

SERVICES

International / Regional / Domestic Passenger / Charter
International routes: Cuba, Dominican Republic, France, Portugal, Switzerland, UK, USA

ALLIANCES / CODE SHARES

Continental, Malev, TAP

FLEET

737-300 - 5, 737-400 - 8 (2 leased out), 737-800 - 10, 757-200 - 6, 767-300ER - 3

Air Europa was originally formed in 1984 as Air España. It commenced charter operations in 1986 with 737s for the holiday market, especially the British International Leisure Group (ILG) who had a 25% share holding.

In 1991 ILG collapsed and a group of Spanish businessmen stepped in led by Jose Hildago. Development has been rapid across the market and the Airlines of Europe Group now hold a substantial portfolio of tour operators and travel agencies with the Hildago family holding some 71% of the equity.

In 1993, following the implementation of EU legislation, Air Europa became the first private Spanish airline to operate a domestic scheduled service initially using BAe ATPs followed shortly after by an international service.

Air Europe SpA

Registered name: Soc. Air Europe SpA
Country: Italy
Region: Europe
Address: Via Carlo Noe 3
I - 21013 Gallarate, Varese
Tel: 0039 0331 71 31 11
Fax: 0039 0331 71 38 45
Web site: www.aireurope.it

RIGHT: *Air Europe Spa A320-214, I-PEKA (C/n 1134). (Airbus)*

STATUS

Scheduled and charter passenger carrier

Employees: 725

Passengers per year: 5,575,000 (1998)

ICAO code: AEL

IATA code: PE

SERVICES

International / Regional / Domestic
Passenger / Charter

International routes: Cuba, France, Guadeloupe, Havana, Jamaica, Mauritius, Montego Bay, Nice, Pointe-A-Pitre

FLEET

A320-200 - 5, 767-300ER - 4, 777-200IGW - 2

Air Europe was initially formed in 1989 as part of the Airlines of Europe prior to being acquired by Italian interests. It was equipped with a 767 to fly charters and it was 1997 before a scheduled service was operated.

The first Air Europe scheduled service was to Cuba followed by Mauritius and Jamaica.

The SAir Group took a 49.9% shareholding in TEGEL in November 1998 which controlled Air Europe.

Air Europe joined the Qualifyer Group in April 1999 and now also operates scheduled domestic services.

Air France

Registered name: Air France, LLC

Country: France

Region: Europe

Address: 45 rue de Paris
F - 95747 Roissy Charles de Gaulle
Cedex Paris

Tel: 0033 1 41 56 56 00

Fax: 0033 1 41 56 84 19

Web site: www.airfrance.com

Main operational base: Paris Charles de Gaulle Airport

STATUS

IATA scheduled international passenger and cargo carrier

National Flag Carrier

Employees: 70,156

Passengers per year: 43,300,000 (2001)

ICAO code: AFR

IATA code: AF

BELOW: *Air France 737-228 Advc, F-GBYD (C/n 23003). (Jeremy Flack/API)*

SERVICES

International / Regional / Domestic
Passenger / Cargo

International routes: Angola, Argentina, Austria, Belgium, Benin, Brazil, Bulgaria, Burkina Faso, Cameroon, Central African Republic, Chad, Colombia, Congo, Cote D'Ivoire, Croatia, Cuba, Czech, Democratic Republic of Congo, Denmark, Djibouti, Dominican Republic, Egypt, Finland, Gabon, Germany, Greece,

Air France

Guadeloupe, Guatemala, Guinea, Haiti, Honduras, Hungary, India, Ireland, Israel, Italy, Jordan, Latvia, Lebanon, Luxembourg, Madagascar, Mali, Martinique, Mauritania, Mauritius, Mexico, Morocco, New Caledonia, Nicaragua, Netherlands, Niger, Nigeria, Norway, Poland, Portugal, Romania, Russia, St Lucia, Saudi Arabia, Senegal, Serbia, Slovakia, Slovenia, South Africa, Spain, Sweden, Switzerland, Syria, Tahiti, Togo, Tunisia, Turkey, UAE, UK, Ukraine, USA, Venezuela

ALLIANCES / CODE SHARES

SkyTeam /Aeromexico, Alitalia, CSA, Delta A/l, Korean A/l

OWNED SUBSIDIARY AIRLINES

Regional Airlines, Brit Air, City Jet

FLEET

A319-100 - 39, A320-100 / 200 - 61, A321-100 / 200 - 17, A330-200 - 5, A340-300 /300E - 22, Concorde 101 - 5 (1 withdrawn), 737-300 / 500 - 36 (1 withdrawn), 747-200 / 300 - 13, 747-200F - 12 (Air France Cargo), 747-400 - 13, 767-300ER - 5 (1 withdrawn), 777-200ER / 300 – 23
On order: A318 - 15 for delivery from 2003, A319 - 2, A321-200 - 4, A330-200 - 9, A380-800 - 10 for delivery from 2006, 747-

BELOW: *Air France A330-203, F-GZCA (C/n 422). (Airbus)*

400F - 5, 777-300 - 15 for delivery from 2004

Air France was considered to have formed on August 30th, 1933, when SCELA (which had only formed in May that year from the merging of four existing airlines - Air Orient, Air Union, CIDNA and SGTA) purchased the assets of the bankrupt Compagnie Aeropostale. This resulted in SCELA having a fleet of 259 aircraft of 35 different types. With France having a large number of colonies throughout the world, the airline put these aircraft to good work.

Having been suspended during WW2 and its fleet effectively destroyed, the remaining structure of SCELA was nation-

ABOVE: *Air France Concorde 101. (Air France)*

alised after the end of the war. On 1st January 1946 Société National Air France became the operating name of the restructured SCELA and rapidly progressed in re-establishing its pre-war network. On 24th June 1946 Constellations were flown to inaugurate services to New York and South America. The French Languedoc plus American DC-3s and DC-4s were flown on other routes. Later Super Constellations were operated. In June 1948 the airline's name changed to Compagnie Nationale Air France when it was incorporated by the French Government. Air France entered the jet age with the de Havilland Comet when it flew its first scheduled route to Beirut via Rome on 26th August 1953. The French Caravelle entered service in May 1959 and the 707 in February 1960.

A variety of airliners from several manufacturers were operated in various numbers and for varying lengths of time. Some were conventional in design while others were not. The Breguet 763 Provence Deux Points with its double deck configuration was certainly one of the latter and was operated into the 70s. Other types included the 727, CV-990, F-27 Friendship and Viscount.

Air France has had a close association with Airbus right from the early days of the

company and introduced the A300 into its network in 1974. The airline became the launch customer for the Airbus A320 in 1981 and repeated the decision with the A318 in 1999.

The first Concorde supersonic service was flown on 21st January 1976 from Paris with a simultaneous take-off by a British Airways example at Heathrow.

In 1990 Air France absorbed UTA (formed 1963) and Air Inter (formed 1954) in 1997.

In 1999 Air France underwent a partial privatisation. A global alliance was signed in conjunction with Delta Air Lines and Aeroméxico which led to the new SkyTeam Alliance which was established the following year.

In July 2000, Air France suffered a major disaster when one of its Concorde's struck a piece of debris from a previously departing DC-10 at Charles De Gaulle airport. The piece of metal punctured the wing and the

fuel ignited causing it to crash just minutes into its flight with a total loss of life. Both British and French Concordes were grounded. However, after major modifications they returned to service. Air France announced the merger of three of its domestic subsidiaries in 2001 – Flandre Air, Proteus Airlines and Regional Airlines – into one airline Regional with a combined fleet of over 80 aircraft.

ABOVE: *Air France A320-211, F-GFKI (C/n 062). (Jeremy Flack/API)*

The French Government announced plans to further privatise Air France with the decision to reduce its stake of 54% to around 20% which would enable the airline more freedom to proceed further with its fleet modernisation.

Air Gabon

Registered name: Compagne Nationale Air Gabon
Country: Gabon
Region: Africa
Address: PO Box 2206,
              Leon Mba International Airport
              Libreville
Tel: 00241 73 21 97
Fax: 00241 73 01 11
Main operational base: Libreville

ABOVE: *Air Gabon ATR 72. (ATR)*

STATUS

IATA domestic carrier
National Flag Carrier
Employees: 1,394
Passengers per year: 374,000 (2001)
ICAO code: AGN
IATA code: GN

SERVICES

International / Regional / Domestic Passenger / Cargo
International routes: Angola, Belgium, Benin, Cameroon, Central African Republic, Congo, Cote D'Ivoire, Democratic Republic of Congo, Equatorial Guinea, France, Italy, Kenya, Mali, Nigeria, Sao Tome & Principe, Senegal, South Africa, Switzerland, Togo, UAE, UK

ALLIANCES/CODE SHARES

Inter Air

Air Gabon

FLEET
ATR 72-200 - 1, 727-200 - 1, 737-200 - 1, 737-300 - 1, 737-400 - 1, 747-200 - 1, 767-200ER - 1

Air Gabon can trace its origins back to 1951 when Compagnie Aerienne Gabonaise was formed. Compagnie Aerienne Gabonaise was designated the national flag carrier in July 1968. The name changed to Société Nationale Transgabon. However, when the Gabonese Goverment decided to pull out of Air Afrique in 1977 this airline was renamed Air Gabon on 1st of June 1977.

Equipped with four F-28 Fellowships, of which one was operated for the Gabonese Government, Air Gabon operated a domestic and regional service to various parts of Africa. A 737 and a 747 were delivered in 1978 which enabled some international routes to be started and reached as far as Paris. By the 1990s, Air Gabon was suffering from a cumulative debt problem and required some assistance in the short term. In addition, its aircraft were getting rather long in the tooth and needed replacing. This was particularly the case as the national airline, Air Gabon, handled over half of the 800,000 passengers flying in and out of Libreville and had established a reasonable customer base. This was being achieved with just three passenger aircraft while a further one was being used for freight only.

Air Gabon tried desperately hard to get its house in order to make it attractive for privatisation.

In 2001, having achieved privatisation, Air Gabon placed an order for two 737-700s, a 747-400 Combi and a 767-300 with a 737-300 and a 737-400 leased temporarily as an interim measure.

Air Greenland

Registered name: Groenlandsfly AS
Country: Greenland
Region: Europe
Address: PO Box 1012
Nuuk / Godthaab
DK-3900
Tel: 00299 34 34 34
Fax: 00299 32 72 88
Web site: www.greenlandair.gl

STATUS

Scheduled and charter carrier
National Flag Carrier
Employees: 543

Passengers per year: 444,000 (2001)
ICAO code: GRL
IATA code: GL

SERVICES

International / Regional / Domestic
Passenger / Charter / Cargo
International routes: Canada, Denmark, Iceland

FLEET

A330-200 - 1, AS.350B2 Ecureuil - 5, 757-200 - 1, King Air 200 - 1, 212 - 4, DHC-6 Twin Otter 300 - 2, DHC-7 Dash 7-100 - 6, MD500 - 4, S-61N - 4

Groenlandsfly AS was formed in November 1960 by SAS and the mining company Kryolitselskabet to provide support to economic life in an environmentally difficult and often hostile part of the world. The airline became a pioneer in providing a scheduled helicopter service. In addition to air taxi and normal charter business, Groenlandsfly AS is often involved in providing specialist tasking in support of the various local industries as well as providing air ambulance and search and rescue services.

In 1962 the Greenland Home Rule Government and Danish Government became co-owners. A DC-6B was added to the fleet during the early 80s enabling international as well as local charters to be flown. This was replaced by DHC-7s and in 1998 a 757 was added to the fleet enabling scheduled routes to Canada, Denmark and Iceland to be offered.

In 2002 the name of the airline was changed from Groenlandsfly AS to Air Greenland. In October of that year SAS withdrew its route to Greenland, leaving Air Greenland as the sole operator to Denmark.

LEFT: *Air Greenland A330-223, OY-GRN (C/n 230). (Airbus)*

Air-India

Registered name: Air-India Ltd
Country: India
Region: Asia
Address: Air-India Building
Nariman Point,
Mumbai 400 021
Tel: 0091 22 202 41 42
Fax: 0091 22 204 85 21
Web site: www.airindia.com
Main operational base: Mumbai Airport
(Bombay)

STATUS

Government owned
National Flag Carrier
Employees: 16,375
Passengers per year: 3,125,000 (2001)
ICAO code: AIC
IATA code: AI

SERVICES

International / Domestic
Passenger / Cargo
International routes: Austria*, China,
Bahrain, Denmark*, France, Germany*,
Indonesia, Japan, Kenya, Kuwait, Malaysia,
Mauritius*, Netherlands*, Nigeria*,
Oman, Russia, S Korea*, Saudi Arabia,
Singapore, Switzerland*, Thailand,
Tanzania, UAE, UK, USA

ALLIANCES / CODE SHARES

Aeroflot, Air France, Air Mauritius, Asiana
Airlines, Austrian Airlines, Bellview
Airlines, Emirates, Indian Airlines, Kuwait,
Lufthansa, Malaysia Airlines, SAS, Silk Air,
Singapore Airlines, Swiss Air Transport,
Thai Airways, Virgin Atlantic

OWNED SUBSIDIARY AIRLINES

Air-India Charters Ltd

FLEET

A310-300 - 17, 747-200B - 4, 747-300C - 2,
747-400 - 7

The origins of Air-India can be traced back
to the 1930s when a British barnstorming
pilot by the name of Nevill Vintcent met a
young Indian pilot J.R.D Tata - the first to
get an A-licence in India.

ABOVE: *Air-India A310-304, VT-EJJ (C/n 392). (Airbus)*

Having seen the potential for air travel in India, Vintcent and Tata gained the support of Sir Dorab Tata - Chairman of Tata Sons. Eventually government support was gained and Tata Airlines formed. On 15th October 1932, the first commercial flight was made with a de Havilland Puss Moth from Karachi to Bombay with a load of mail in the hands of Mr Tata. Steadily the business grew and additional aircraft were acquired in the form of a Leopard Moth, Waco, DH.86, DH.89 and Stinson Trimotors. Tata Airlines benefited greatly from the Empire Airmail Scheme from 1938.

The scheme was suspended following the outbreak of war and the government requisitioned the DH.89s. Later Beech 18s and DC-2s were loaded plus DC-3s towards the end of the war.

Once it was over, Tata was allotted four surplus DC-3s by the US. Further examples were also bought. With the experience amassed and the now much enlarged fleet, Tata was converted to a PLC and renamed Air-India in 1946. At the same time it became the national flag carrier for international routes. In 1948 Air-India International was formed jointly by Air-India and the Indian Government to concentrate on the international routes. The Constellations were ordered and commenced operations with a flight from Bombay to London on 8th June 1948.

The post-war boom, with cheap aircraft available, had seen a plethora of airlines with 21 registered. As their financial positions deteriorated during the early 1950s the Indian Government decided to nation-

BELOW: *Air-India 747-437 (C/n 28094) (Jeremy Flack/API).*

Air-India

alise air travel. On 1st August 1953, eight domestic airlines were merged to form Indian Airlines while Air-India International would continue to operate the international schedules. 'International' was dropped in 1962. Aircraft operated by Air-India have included the Super Constellation, the 707 that brought the airline into the jet age with its arrival in February 1960 plus the 747 and DC-8. Air-India scheduled routes continued

to expand especially to the Middle East following the oil boom.

During the 1980s Air-India ordered three Airbus A300s followed by A310s and more 747s while additional 747s were ordered in the 1990s and five A310s leased in 2000/1.

In 1990 Air-India was involved in the airlifting of 110,000 stranded Indian nationals from Amman to Mumbai that was recorded as the largest evacuation of civilians accord-

ing to the 1993 Guinness Book of World Records.

Air-India had been registered as Air-India Ltd in 1994. It remained totally government owned until 2001 when it was privatised along with Indian Airlines.

The last two A300s operated were gifted to Ariana Afghan Airlines in November 2002. It is currently looking to upgrade its present fleet.

Air Jamaica

Registered name: Air Jamaica Holdings, Ltd
Country: Jamaica
Region: Central America & Caribbean
Address: 72-76 Harbour Street
  Kingston
Tel: 001 876 922 34 60
Fax: 001 876 967 31 25
Web site: www.airjamaica.com
Main operational base: Montego Bay

STATUS

IATA scheduled carrier
National Flag Carrier
Employees: 1,737
Passengers per year: 1,900,000 (2001)
ICAO code: AJM
IATA code: JM

SERVICES

International / Regional / Domestic
Passenger / Cargo
International routes: Antigua & Barbuda, Bahamas, Cayman Islands, Cuba, Grenada, Netherlands Antilles, St Lucia, UK, USA

ALLIANCES / CODE SHARES

Delta Airlines, Air Canada

FLEET

A310 - 4, A320-200 - 10, A321-200 - 3, A340-300 - 3, DHC-6 Twin Otter - 2 (operated by Air Jamaica Express), DHC-8 Dash 8-100 - 6 (operated by Air Jamaica Express)

Air Jamaica was formed in October 1968 by the Jamaican Government with assistance from Air Canada. Initial routes were flown to Miami and New York.

Gradually, Air Jamaica's network expanded with new routes being introduced and included Canada and Europe in addition to extra services around the Caribbean.

In 1980 the Jamaican Government bought up Air Canada's minority holding. However, in 1994, following lengthy discussions, Air Jamaica was privatised. The national airline status was retained.

Following privatisation, Air Jamaica underwent a livery change that was applied to the ground based part of the business as well as the aircraft.

Air Jamaica Express was established as a subsidiary on 1st November 1995 to fly domestic passengers as well as to some of the local islands.

Air Jamaica had focussed on customer service and a continual programme of improvements is being implemented. An interesting recent introduction was that of check-in desks at major hotels enabling customers more relaxation prior to flights.

BELOW: *Air Jamaica A321-211, 5-Y-JMH with Airbus test registration D-AVZU. (Airbus)*

Air Macau

Registered name: Air Macau Ltd
Country: China
Region: Far East
Address: 693 Avenida da Praia Grande
Edificio Tai Wah 5, 8-12 Andar
Macau
Tel: 00853 396 68 88
Fax: 00853 396 68 66
Web site: www.airmacau.com.mo
Main operational base: Macau

STATUS

Scheduled regional carrier
Employees: 688
Passengers per year: 1,520,500 (2001)
ICAO code: AMU
IATA code: NX

SERVICES

Regional / Domestic
Passenger / Cargo
International routes: Philippines, Singapore, Taiwan, Thailand, S Korea

FLEET

A319 - 2, A320-200 - 3, A321-100 - 5, 757-200 -1
On order: A319-100 - 4 for delivery in 2003

ABOVE: *Air Macau A321-131, B-MAA (C/n 550) still with previous registration CS-MAA. (Airbus)*

Air Macau was established on September 13th, 1995, and commenced operations on the 9th November serving Peking and Shanghai with its single aircraft.

Macau is China's southern gateway and has seen Air Macau grow rapidly to provide a service of 180 round-trips per week to fourteen destinations.

Air Macau is 51% owned by China National Aviation Corp (Macau) Co Ltd. The logo on the tail is a combination of the lotus flower - the symbol of Macau - and a dove - the international symbol for peace.

Air Madagascar

Country: Madagascar
Region: Africa
Address: 31 Avenue de l'Independance
BP 437
Antananarivo
Tel: 00261 20 222 22 22
Fax: 00261 20 223 37 60
Web site: www.airmadagascar.info
Main operational base: Antananarivo

STATUS

IATA scheduled carrier
National Flag Carrier
Employees: 1,220
Passengers per year: 624,000 (2001)
ICAO code: MDG
IATA code: MD

SERVICES

International / Regional / Domestic
Passenger / Cargo
International routes: Comoro Islands, France, Italy, Kenya, Mauritius, Reunion, Seychelles, South Africa

ALLIANCES / CODE SHARES

Air Austral, Air Inter

FLEET

ATR 42-320 - 3, 737-200 - 1, 737-200Adv - 1, 737-300 - 1, 747-200B (SCD) - 1, 767-300ER - 1, DHC-6 Twin Otter 300 - 4

Air Madagascar was formed on January 1st, 1962, following independence from France two years earlier. The airline was established by the new Malagasy Republic Government (51%) with the assistance of Air France who had a 40% stake. Initial services were flown with a DC-7C which was owned and crewed by TAI.

Gradually, a mixed fleet was established comprising of light aircraft for local charter, a substantial fleet of twin-engined transports including Twin Otters and HS748s that were used to provide a domestic service replacing DC-3s and DC-4s. In addition, the original DC-7 was replaced with their own 707 and 737s and a 747 for medium and long-haul schedules.

Gradually the lighter end of the fleet was withdrawn and services concentrated on the medium to long-haul operation and the three ATR 42s used for the domestic routes.

Air Malawi

Country: Malawi
Region: Africa
Address: Robins Road
            PO Box 84, Blantyre
Tel: 00265 62 08 11
Fax: 00265 62 00 42
Web site: www.airmalawi.net
Main operational base: Blantyre

RIGHT: *Air Malawi ATR 42-320, 7Q-YKQ (C/n 236) (ATR)*

STATUS

IATA scheduled passenger carrier
National Flag Carrier
Employees: 550
Passengers per year: 118,000 (2001)
ICAO code: AML
IATA code: QM

BELOW: *Air Malawi 737-33A (C/n 25056) (T. J. Walker/API)*

SERVICES

International / Regional
Domestic / Passenger
International routes: Kenya, South Africa, Tanzania, UAE, Zambia, Zimbabwe

ALLIANCES / CODE SHARES

Air Tanzania, Air Zimbabwe, Kenya Airways

FLEET

ATR 42-320 - 1, 737-300 - 1, 208B Caravan - 1

The current Air Malawi was formed on September 1st, 1967, to replace a previous airline of the same name. The previous Air Malawi was established in March 1964 as a subsidiary of the Central African Airways Corporation (CAA) following the country's independence and operated DC-3s.

The Malawi Government formed Air Malawi as its national airline with a pair of Vickers Viscounts to which a number of BAC 1-11s were later added. A VC10 was operated in the second half of the 1970s to provide a service to London.

Since then, Air Malawi has operated a variety of airliners including the Do.228, HS748, Islander, King Air, Skyvan and a 747SP

Air Mali

Registered name: Air Mali SA
Country: Mali
Region: Africa
Address: BP2690
            Bamaku
Tel: 00223 22 9394
Fax: 00223 22 9403
Main operational base: Bamako Airport

STATUS

Scheduled domestic and charter carrier
National Flag Carrier
Passengers per year: 15,000 (1994)

ICAO code: MLI
IATA code: L9

SERVICES

Regional / Domestic / Passenger
Charter / Cargo
International routes: Cote D'Ivoire, Senegal

FLEET

An-24RV - 1, DC-8-92 - 1, Let-410UVP-E - 3, F-28 Fellowship - 1, Yak-42 - 1

Air Mali is the second airline to have that name. The first was formed on October 27th, 1960, as Mali's national airline. It was equipped with three ex-BEA DC-3s that were presented by the British Government.

Following independence and the government forming strong links with the Soviet Union, replacement aircraft were sourced from them. These included the An-24 and Il-18. The current Air Mali was formed on 22nd October 1993 and has seen a more mixed fleet with 727, 737, BAe146 and Twin Otters being operated at various times.

In 2002, the Egyptian Airline AMC bought a 49% stake in Air Mali bringing their expertise as well as three aircraft.

Air Malta

STATUS

IATA scheduled and charter carrier
National Flag Carrier
Employees: 1,500
Passengers per year: 1,646,000 (2001)
(includes charters)
ICAO code: AMC
IATA code: KM

SERVICES

International / Regional / Passenger
Charter / Cargo
International routes: Austria, Belgium,
Bulgaria, Cyprus, Egypt, France, Germany,
Greece, Ireland, Italy, Libya, Morocco,
Netherlands, Norway, Russia, Spain,
Sweden, Switzerland, Tunisia, Turkey, UK

OWNED SUBSIDIARY AIRLINES

Malta Air Charter, AZZURRAair

FLEET

A320-200 - 4, 737-200Adv - 2, 737-300 - 7

Air Malta was established by a Resolution of Malta's House of Representatives on March 21st 1973 and registered on the 30th. Its purpose was to participate in and further develop the island's tourism business that was an important part of Malta's economy. Initial operations commenced on April 1st to various parts of Europe and Libya with a pair of 720s to which three more were subsequently added. In March 1982 three 737s were ordered for delivery the following March. Within six months Air Malta had established a world record of 14.9 hours per day utilisation although it has surpassed this since. An additional three 737s were purchased in August 1986 followed by another and an A320 in 1987 – the latter being delivered in August 1990. Two of the 720s were disposed of in 1987 and two years later an additional A320 was ordered together with an additional three 737s. In 1989 the last remaining 720 was retired.

As a temporary measure, an ATP was leased for 18 months in October 1992 for short-haul operations to Catania, Monastir, Palermo and Tunis. This and four of the 737s were replaced with four Avro RJ70s that were delivered during September 1994. A major commitment came in January 1994 to cargo operations with the opening of the Air Malta Cargo Systems and Transhipment Centre. This used the old passenger terminal that had been vacated with the opening of the new one. This was suitably restructured for its new role.

ABOVE: *Air Malta A320-211, 9H-ABP (C/n 112) (Jeremy Flack/API)*

Air Malta continues to develop its core business with the tourism market and has established an effective engineering and training side to its operation able to offer these services to other operators. In addition, the Air Malta Group owns a number of hotels as well as other tourist accommodation and catering. Malta Air Charter was established to operate an inter-island helicopter service with Mi-17s. In July 1996 Air Malta was a major player in getting AZZURRAair off the ground in Italy. As part of deal Air Malta leased four RJ70s from its own fleet. In December 1997 approval was given by Malta's House of Representatives for Air Malta to become a plc and the share capital was raised from Lm5 million to Lm35 million.

In June 2002 Air Malta and Lufthansa Technik AG formed a new joint venture. Starting in January 2003, Lufthansa Technik Malta will perform C-Checks on the complete range of Boeing 737 and Airbus A320 family aircraft for Lufthansa German Airlines, Air Malta and third parties. Air Malta is in the process of a current fleet modernisation programme. In July 2002 an agreement was concluded to replace the whole fleet with 12 new airliners from the Airbus A320 family over a four and a half year period.

Air Marshall Islands

ABOVE: *Air Marshall Islands SAAB 2000, V7-9508 (C/n 017) (SAAB)*

Registered name: Air Marshall Islands, Inc
Country: Marshall Islands
Region: Australia & Pacific
Address: PO Box 1319
Majuro
MH 96960
Tel: 00692 625 37 31
Fax: 00692 625 37 30
Main operational base: Majuro

STATUS

IATA scheduled Passenger + cargo carrier
National Flag Carrier
Employees: 183
Passengers per year: 23,000 (1997)
ICAO code: MRS
IATA code: CW

SERVICES

Regional / Domestic / Passenger
Charter / Cargo
International routes: Fiji, Kiribati, Tuvalu

FLEET

Do.228-201 - 2, Saab 2000 - 1, HS748 - 1

Air Marshall Islands was formed in 1980 as the Airline of the Marshall Islands. It was the national carrier for the Republic of the Marshall Islands which had become independent the previous year. Initial services were with two GAF Nomads to which an HS748 was subsequently added.

During the late 80s a DC-8 combi was leased mainly to offer a freight service as far as the USA until it was returned in 1996. In 1990 Airline of the Marshall Islands was renamed Air Marshall Islands. Two SAAB 2000s were acquired in the mid-1990s.

Air Marshall Islands operates a domestic service which provides air access to 27 of the 29 atolls that make up the Republic. A variety of other services is also operated including air ambulance and aeromedical as well as maritime surveillance.

Air Mauritanie

Country: Mauritania
Region: Africa
Address: PO Box 41, Nouakchott
Tel: 00222 25 22 11
Fax: 00222 25 38 15
Web site: www.airmauritanie.mr
Main operational base: Nouakchott

STATUS

Scheduled passenger carrier
National Flag Carrier
Employees: 350
Passengers per year: 109,000 (2001)
ICAO code: MRT
IATA code: MR

SERVICES

Regional / Domestic / Passenger
International routes: Gambia, Mauritania, Morocco, Senegal, Spain (Canary Is)

FLEET

ATR 42 - 2, BN-2T Islander - 1, F-28 Fellowship 4000 - 1, PA-31T Cheyenne II - 1, 737-700 - 1

ABOVE: *Air Mauritanie ATR 42 with ATR test registration F-OKMS (ATR)*

Air Mauritanie was formed in September 1962. The airline was established to take over and develop limited services that were operated by Air France and Union Aeromaritime de Transport (UAT). The first operations commenced in October 1963 with technical assistance and an F-27 Friendship from Spantax. Gradually the fleet has been modernised with ATR 42 and F-28 Fellowship being acquired. In May 2002 Air Mauritanie added a leased 737.

Air Mauritius

Registered name: Air Mauritius Ltd
Country: Mauritius
Region: Africa
Address: Air Mauritius Centre
President John Kennedy Street
Port Louis
Tel: 00230 207 70 70
Fax: 00230 208 83 31
Web site: www.airmauritius.com
Main operational base: SS Ramgoolam

STATUS

IATA scheduled international carrier
National Flag Carrier
Employees: 1,796
Passengers per year: 999,000 (2001)
ICAO code: MAU
IATA code: MK

SERVICES

International / Regional / Domestic
Passenger / Cargo
International routes: Australia, Austria,
Belgium, China, France, Germany, India,
Italy, Kenya, Madagascar, Malaysia,
Mauritius, Reunion, Seychelles, Singapore,
South Africa, Switzerland, UAE, UK

ALLIANCES / CODE SHARES

Air France, Air Seychelles, Air-India

FLEET

A319-100 - 2, A340-300 - 5, ATR 42-500 - 2,
ATR 72-500 - 1, 206B JetRanger - 3, 767-
200ER - 2

Air Mauritius was originally founded in
June 1967 to develop an airlink with the
nearby island of Reunion. Operations did
not commence until 1972.

A 707 was acquired to commence services
onto mainland Africa and they eventually
reached as far as London, helping to boost

ABOVE: *Air Mauritius A319-112, 3B-NBF (C/n 1592) m
with airbus test registration D-AVYX (Airbus)*

the island's tourist trade.

Air Mauritius has operated several different aircraft types over the years including a
pair of Twin Otters for domestic services
and 747SPs for long haul. Despite various
dips in regional economics, Air Mauritius
has continued to provide a steadily increasing capacity to a sought-after tourist resort.

Air Moldova

Country: Moldova
Region: Europe
Address: Chisinau International Airport
MD-2026
Tel: 00373 2 52 51 77
Fax: 00373 2 52 60 73
Web site: www.airmoldova.md or
www.airmoldova.com
Main operational base: Chisinau International
Airport

STATUS

International scheduled and charter passenger + cargo carrier

National Flag Carrier
Employees: 585
Passengers per year: 137,000 (2001)
ICAO code: MLD
IATA code: 9U

SERVICES

International / Regional / Passenger
Charter / Cargo
International routes: Austria, Cyprus,
Czech, France, Greece, Lebanon, Romania,
Russia, Turkey

ALLIANCES / CODE SHARES

Transaero A/l

FLEET

An-24 - 4, An-26B - 2, EMB.120RT Brasilia -
1, ERJ-145 - 1, Tu-134A - 5, Yak-40 - 1
On order: ERJ-145 - 2 + 2 options

Air Moldova was formed in January 1992 by
the Moldovan state following its independence. Prior to that Moldova was part of the
Soviet Union with its civil air services operated by a division of Aeroflot. It was initially
equipped with ex-Aeroflot Tu-154s.

In June 2000 the issued ordinary share
capital was increased to US$5.3 million and
40% of the equity was purchased by the
German Unistar Ventures GmbH.

Air Moldova International

Registered name: Air Moldova International SA
Country: Moldova
Region: Europe
Address: Hotel, 4th Floor
Chisinau International Airport
2026
Tel: 003732 52 64 11
Fax: 003732 52 64 14
Web site: www.ami.md
Main operational base: Chisinau International Airport

STATUS
Scheduled passenger + cargo carrier
Employees: 120
ICAO code: MLV
IATA code: RM

SERVICES
Regional / Passenger / Cargo
International routes: Germany, Ukraine

FLEET
An-24 - 1, Yak-42D - 2

Air Moldova International was established on April 1st, 1995, as a privately owned airline operating the Yak-40 and Yak-42 for passenger services and an An-24 for freight.

In October 1996, Air Moldova International became the first Moldovan airline to become a member of IATA and joined IATC the following January.

Air Namibia

Country: Namibia
Region: Africa
Address: PO Box 731
Windhoek 9000
Tel: 00264 61 299 61 51
Fax: 00264 61 299 61 79
Web site: www.airnamibia.com.na
Main operational base: Windhoek

STATUS
IATA international, regional and domestic carrier
National Flag Carrier
Employees: 479
Passengers per year: 238,000 (2001)
ICAO code: NMB
IATA code: SW

SERVICES
International / Regional / Domestic Passenger / Cargo
International routes: Angola, Botswana, Germany, South Africa, UK, Zimbabwe

ALLIANCES / CODE SHARES
Comair, TAAG

FLEET
737-200Adv - 1, 747-400C - 1,
F-28 Mk.3000 - 2

Air Namibia was originally formed as Southwest Air Transport in 1946 and commenced services two years later operating DC-3s. The airline became NamibAir in 1978 and, following Namibia's independence, it became the country's national airline.

Services slowly expanded with much of its operation centred on providing a link with SAA flights operating in and out of Windhoek.

Following the acquisition of a 747SP, NamibAir commenced international services in 1990 which were to reach as far as London.

NamibAir was renamed Air Namibia in 1993. Until 1998 Air Namibia had been owned by Trans Namib – a state owned holding company. Although still state owned, Air Namibia has now become a separate company.

Air Nauru

Registered name: Nauru Air Corporation
Country: Nauru
Region: Australia & Pacific
Address: PO Box 40
        Civic Centre
        Yaren District
Tel: 00674 444 31 41
Fax: 00674 444 37 05
Web site: www.airnauru.com.au
Main operational base: Nauru

STATUS

Scheduled passenger and cargo carrier
National Flag Carrier
Employees: 71
Passengers per year: 164,000 (2001)
ICAO code: RON
IATA code: ON

SERVICES

Regional / Passenger / Cargo
International routes: Australia, Fiji, Guam, Kiribati, Micronesia, Nadi, Philippines

FLEET

737-400 - 1

Air Nauru was formed on February 14th, 1970 by the Nauru Government as their national regional carrier, initially operating a Dassault Falcon 20 from Nauru to Brisbane.

An F28 Fellowship replaced the Falcon in 1972 as the demand and routes expanded. This was replaced, in turn, by a 737 and two 727s during the mid-1970s.

A downturn in passengers in the early 90s led to a major reorganisation of Air Nauru services with all but the most profitable routes being cut. This led, in turn, to a reappraisal of aircraft requirements and

ABOVE: *Air Nauru 737-217C, C2-RN3 (C/n 21073 (Bob Clegg/API)*

resulted in the four jets being replaced with a single new 737 in 1993.

In July 1996 Air Nauru became Air Nauru Corporation to raise the image although it remained government owned.

In February 2001 the Australian Civil Aviation Safety Authority grounded Air Nauru's 737 due to operational reasons. The airline took steps to resolve this and the suspension of its Air Operators Certificate was lifted two weeks later.

Air New Zealand

Registered name: Air New Zealand Ltd
Country: New Zealand
Region: Australia & Pacific
Address: Quay Tower
        29 Customs Street West
        Private Bag 92007
        Auckland 1
Tel: 0064 9 336 24 00
Fax: 0064 9 336 24 01
Web site: www.airnewzealand.com
Main operational base: Auckland

STATUS

IATA scheduled passenger carrier
National Flag Carrier
Employees: 9,500
Passengers per year: 8,829,000 (2001)
ICAO code: ANZ
IATA code: NZ

SERVICES

International / Regional / Domestic
Passenger / Cargo
International routes: Australia, Austria*, China, Cook Islands, France*, Germany*, Fiji, Hawaii, Japan, London, Mexico*, New

ABOVE: *Air New Zealand 737-300 (Air New Zealand)*

Caledonia, Samoa, Singapore, Switzerland*, Tahiti, Tonga, Taiwan, UK, USA (* code share)

Air New Zealand

LEFT: *Air New Zealand Boeing 747-419, ZK-NBT (C/n 24855) (Air New Zealand)*

RIGHT: *Air New Zealand Link ATR 72-212A, ZK0MCF (C/n 600) operated by Mount Cook Airline (Air New Zealand)*

ALLIANCES / CODE SHARES

Star Alliance / Air Canada, BMI, JAL, Lufthansa, Mexicana, Singapore A/l, United A/l

OWNED SUBSIDIARY AIRLINES

Mount Cook, Eagle Airways, Freedom Air, Safe Air

FLEET

737-200Adv - 1, 737-300 - 14, 747-400 - 8, 767-200ER - 4, 767-300ER - 9, ATR 72-500 - 12 (operated by Mount Cook)
On order: A320 15 + 20 options for delivery from Sept 2003, 9 737-300s as they are replaced.

The origins of Air New Zealand date back to August 1939 with the incorporation of the Tasman Empire Airways Ltd (TEAL). Equipped with three Short S.30 Empire Class flying boats the first service was flown on April 30th 1940 between Auckland and Sydney with 10 passengers and took ten hours.

During the war, TEAL undertook a number of special charters and reconnaissance flights to Fiji, Hawaii, New Caledonia, Samoa and Tonga.

In 1946, the first of the Tasman Class flying boats was delivered, while a couple of surplus PBY-5 Catalinas were acquired for training purposes.

The Tasman flying boats were grounded for four months in 1948 due to engine problems and the service was operated by leased DC-4s. The following year the first Short Solent flying boat was delivered while the last converted military Sandringham was retired towards the end of the year.

The birth of the legendary Coral Route was seen in 1941, from Auckland via Fiji and the Cook Islands to Tahiti. In June that year TEAL commenced operation of a Christchurch - Melbourne service with a DC-4 chartered from Qantas. When BCPA (British Commonwealth Pacific Airlines) was liquidated in 1953, three DC-6s were transferred to TEAL to enable the transtasman and Hibiscus service to be continued.

In December 1953 Queen Elizabeth II was flown by TEAL from Suva to Lautoka and return, then to on to Tonga. This was the first time that the any of the Royal Family had been flown by a commercial airline.

TEAL received its first Lockheed Electra in 1959 and in September 1960, TEAL operated its last Solent flying boat service. This was then delivered to the Museum of Transport and Technology in Auckland. In December the first Fokker F-27 Friendship arrived.

On April 28th 1961 the New Zealand Government announced that it would be purchasing Australia's 50% share of TEAL making it the sole owner. The following month, the DC-6s were taken over by the RNZAF for use as military transports.

An order was placed in September 1963 for the purchase of three DC-8s. Their arrival took TEAL into the jet age and they were used to inaugurate the Auckland-Los Angeles service in December 1965.

On April 1st 1965 TEAL was renamed Air New Zealand.

The first of three 737s were delivered during September 1968. In September 1970 an order was placed for three DC-10s (subsequently increased to five) and they entered service from February 1973. Meanwhile, in May 1972 the last Electra service had been flown and the type withdrawn.

On April 1st 1978 National Airways Corporation (formed April 1947) was merged with Air New Zealand.

In June 1979 the US FAA withdrew the DC-10 type certificate which immediately grounded all DC-10s. Pan Am 747s were chartered to move 1,000 passengers that were stranded. However, later that month the DC-10 services were reinstated. Sadly, a DC-10 was lost on a sightseeing flight over Antarctica in November with all on board lost as the result of flying into a mountain.

The first Air New Zealand 747 was delivered in May 1981 and commenced commercial service in June and was used largely to replace the DC-10.

In April 1984 Air New Zealand commenced a 747 Auckland-London service with a single stop in Los Angeles. The following June Air New Zealand announced revenue exceeding NZ$1bn for the first time. In July, Air New Zealand announced that it was taking a 77% stake in Mount Cook Group while in September the first

ABOVE: *Air New Zealand 767-219ER, ZK-NBA (C/n 233326) (Jane's)*

767 was delivered.

Air New Zealand announced another record with its highest ever profits before tax of NZ$210.5 million for 1986/7.

The New Zealand Government announced the 100% sale of Air New Zealand in December 1988. However, it retained a Kiwi share which ensured that New Zealanders retain the majority stake. The sale generated NZ$600 million for the government.

In December 1990 the last F-27 Friendship was withdrawn.

The first of seven ATR 72s entered service in November 1995 with Mount Cook Airline under the Air New Zealand Link banner. Three months later they replaced the HS748 which had been operated by Mount Cook for 27 years.

Air New Zealand entered into an agreement in September 1996 to purchase 50% of Ansett Holdings giving them a greater access to Australia.

In November 1996 Her Majesty Queen Elizabeth II arrived in Auckland aboard an Air New Zealand 747 to attend the Commonwealth Heads of Government Conference. This was the first time that a reigning British monarch had flown on a scheduled commercial flight.

In April 2000, approval was given for the purchase of the remaining 50% of Ansett Holdings while Singapore Airlines purchased Brierley Investments B shares which increased their stake in Air New Zealand to 25%.

In December 2000, safety inspections lead to the voluntary grounding of six of the Ansett 767s causing significant disruptions. Just prior to the following Easter weekend Ansett advised CASA that it had discovered pylon cracks in some of its 767s. All ten of the fleet were immediately grounded. For the second time in just a few months ANZ had to cope with major disruptions at peak passenger times.

In early September Ansett Group was reported to be losing in the region of NZ$1.3m per day. As a result, the sale of Ansett Australia was negotiated with Qantas. However, following the terrorist attacks on September 11 and the announcement by ANZ of a NZ$1.425bn loss, mainly due to Ansett and the Qantas withdrawal of their interest in the purchase; Air New Zealand had little option but to place Ansett Australia into voluntary administration which it did on September 14th.

The New Zealand Government announced a NZ$855 million loan in the form of an equity investment to help recapitalise Air New Zealand resulting in it becoming an 82% shareholder. A major restructuring of the airline was rapidly implemented.

Three of the four BAe146 were withdrawn and the 737-200s retired.

As recovery progressed and passenger levels started to return, Air New Zealand became the 110th Airbus customer for the A320 with an order in 2002 for 15 aircraft to replace 767s and 737-300s.

As 2002 drew to a close, Air New Zealand and Qantas confirmed that they were entering into an agreement whereby Qantas would take a 22.5% shareholding in ANZ. In addition, they will be introducing new codeshare arrangements. Besides the obvious important cash boost for ANZ, these arrangements will enable both airlines to make better use of their resources rather than the previous large number of uneconomic duplicated services.

Air Niugini

Country: Papua New Guinea

Region: Australia & Pacific

Address: ANG House
      Jacksons Airport
      PO Box 7186, Boroko

Tel: +675 327 32 00

Fax: 00675 327 34 82

Web site: www.airniugini.com.pg

Main operational base: Port Moresby /
Jacksons Airport

STATUS

Scheduled passenger carrier

National Flag Carrier

Employees: 1,968

Passengers per year: 1,191,000 (2001)

ICAO code: ANG

IATA code: PX

SERVICES

International / Regional / Domestic
Passenger / Charter / Cargo

International routes: Australia, China,
Indonesia, Philippines, Singapore,
Solomon Islands

ALLIANCES / CODE SHARES

Qantas

FLEET

767-300 - 1, DHC-8 Dash 8-200 - 2,
F-28 Fellowship 1000 - 5,
F-28 Fellowship 4000 - 3

Air Niugini was formed in 1973 by the Government of Papua New Guinea in co-operation with Qantas and TAA operating a number of DC-3s and F-27 Friendships.

Papua New Guinea became independent in 1975 and the government, which initially held 60% of the shareholding, bought up the balance the following year and declared Air Niugini the national airline. In 1977 the first of eight F-28 Fellowships arrived. Gradually the routes expanded and had included Singapore and Sydney by 1975. In 1980 a pair of 707s was acquired allowing

ABOVE: *Air Niugini A310-324, P2-ANA with airbus test registration F-WWCA (Airbus)*

longer routes to be achieved.

In 1984 a leased Airbus A300 arrived to replace the 707s followed by an A310 in 1989. A leased 767 was added to the fleet in August 2002 and replaced the A310.

In addition to the international services, Air Niugini operates to some 100 airstrips around the country and provides a scheduled service to the 20 main centres.

Air Nostrum 'Iberia Regional'

Country: Spain

Region: Europe

Address: Avenida Comarques del Pais Valencia 2
      Zona de Servicio del
      aeropuerto de Valencia
      E-46930 Quart de Poblet, Valencia

Tel: 0034 96 196 02 00

Fax: 0034 96 196 02 09

Web site: www.airnostrum.es

Main operational base: Valencia

STATUS

Scheduled and charter passenger carrier

Employees: 1,440

Passengers per year: 2,803,000 (2001)

ICAO code: ANS

IATA code: VW

SERVICES

International / Regional / Domestic
Passenger / Charter

International routes: France, Germany,
Italy, Morocco*, Portugal, Switzerland, UK
(*code share with Iberia)

ALLIANCES / CODE SHARES

Air France, Iberia

OWNED SUBSIDIARY AIRLINES

Binter Mediterraneo, Denim Air

FLEET

ATR 72-500 - 5, CRJ200 - 15, DHC-8 Dash
8-Q300 - 15 (leased to Denim Air), Fokker
50 - 19

On order: CRJ200 - 10, DHC-8 Dash 8-
Q300 - 4 on order for Denim Air

Air Nostrum was formed in 1994 and commenced operation in December. By 1996, Air Nostrum had a fleet of ten Fokker 50s and had carried 406,674 passengers.

The careful selection of routes and services to match the customers needs have enabled this growth to continue at a spectac-

ular rate. In 1997, a franchise agreement was signed with the Iberia Group that resulted in a beneficial deal for both airlines. With their aircraft painted in the Iberia colours, Air Nostrum benefited from the corporate identity associated with Iberia and by co-ordinating their services were able to provide a good

feeder service for passengers requiring connection to international services. Air Nostrum acquired Binter Mediterraneo for $4.1m in 2001 from Iberia.

BELOW: *Air Nostrum ATR 72-212A (ATR)*

Air Pacific

Registered name: Air Pacific Ltd
Country: Fiji
Region: Australia & Pacific
Address: Private Mail Bag
PO Box 9266, Nadi Airport
Tel: 00679 72 07 77
Fax: 00679 72 05 12
Web site: www.airpacific.com
Main operational base: Nadi Airport

STATUS

IATA scheduled regional carrier
National Flag Carrier
Employees: 766
Passengers per year: 327,000 (2001)
ICAO code: FJI
IATA code: FJ

SERVICES

International / Regional / Domestic
Passenger / Cargo

International routes: Australia, Canada, Japan, New Caledonia, New Zealand, Samoa, Solomon Islands, Tahiti, Tonga, USA, Vanuatu

ALLIANCES / CODE SHARES

Air Caledonie, Air Vanuatu, American A/l, Qantas

FLEET

737-700 - 1, 737-800 - 1, 747-200B - 1, 767-300ER - 1

The origins of Air Pacific date back to 1947 when an Australian aviator named Harold Gatty registered Katafaga Estates. Regular domestic services commenced in 1951. Known as Fiji Airways, a variety of aircraft was operated over the following twenty years including the de Havilland Dragon Rapide, Heron and Drover, DC-3, Turbo-Beaver and HS748.

The name changed to Air Pacific in 1972 and the fleet standarised on the BAC 1-11 and the HS748. These aircraft enabled an improved service to be offered with the increased range available.

In 1974 a service commenced to Auckland and another to Brisbane via Noumea the following year.

A DC-10 was acquired in 1983 that was used to inaugurate a service to Honolulu from Nadi.

In 1998, Qantas increased its equity in Air Pacific to 46.05%. The Fiji Government holds 51%.

Two 737s were delivered in 1999 but one was returned the following year along with a second 747 due to political crises and an ensuing dramatic decline in tourism.

Air Pacific announced its first loss in 14 years in 2001 and was undergoing a restructuring of its operation to adjust to the change in passenger levels.

Air Sénégal International

Registered name: Air Sénégal International
Country: Senegal
Region: Africa
Address: 45 Avenue Albert Sarraut
BP 8010
Dakar
Tel: 00221 823 62 69
Fax: 00221 820 00 33
Web site: www.air-senegal-international.com
Main operational base: Yoff Airport

STATUS

Scheduled and non-scheduled regional
National Flag Carrier
Employees: 135
Passengers per year: n/a
ICAO code: DSB
IATA code: DS

SERVICES

International / Regional / Domestic
Passenger / Cargo
International routes: Cape Verde, France,
Gambia, Guinea, Guinea Bissau, Mali,
Mauritania, Morocco, Spain

FLEET

737-500 - 1, 737-700 - 1, DHC-8 Dash 8-
Q300 - 1
On order: 737-500 - 2

Air Sénégal was originally formed as Ardic
Aviation in November 1962.

Ardic Aviation was nationalised in 1971
and renamed Air Sénégal.

Over the years, the airline has operated a
variety of different aircraft which include the
DC-3, DHC-6 Twin Otter, F-27 Friendship,
and HS748. In addition, a number of Aztec
and Pawnee aircraft were used for
charter/taxi flights and agricultural services.

More recently, Air Sénégal has concentrated on domestic and short-haul international routes to neighboring countries.

Now known as Air Sénégal International
the airline is jointly owned by the
Government of Senegal and Royal Air
Maroc, the latter being the major stock
holder.

BELOW: *Air Sénégal International DHC-8 (Bombardier)*

Air Seychelles

Registered name: Air Seychelles Ltd
Country: Seychelles
Region: Africa
Address: Victoria House
Victoria, PO Box 386
Mahé
Tel: 00248 38 10 00
Fax: 00248 22 43 05
Web site: www.airseychelles.net
Main operational base: Mahé

STATUS

IATA scheduled and domestic carrier
National Flag Carrier
Employees: 608
Passengers per year: 420,000 (2001)
ICAO code: SEY
IATA code: HM

SERVICES

International / Regional / Domestic
Passenger / Charter / Cargo
International routes: France, Germany,
India, Italy, Kenya, Mauritius, Reunion,
Singapore, South Africa, Switzerland, UAE,
UK

ALLIANCES / CODE SHARES

Air Austral, Air France, Air Mauritius.

FLEET

737-700 - 1, 767-300ER - 2, BN-2A-Islander -
1, DHC-6 Twin Otter 300 - 4, SD360 - 1

RIGHT: *Air Seychelles BN-2A, S7-AAA Islander (C/n 540).*
(BN Historians Collection)

Air Seychelles was originally formed on September 15th, 1977, from the merger of Air Mahé and Inter Island Airways and became the national carrier. It was initially equipped with Britten Norman Islanders and Trislanders.

In 1983 an expansion plan was put into operation using a chartered DC-10 to commence international routes to London and Frankfurt. This was subsequently replaced by an A300 and the network enlarged.

The expansion was successful and as a result an order was placed for 767-200s and 707s were used as a stop-gap until the 767s were delivered.

Air Seychelles currently uses its Islander and Twin Otters for island hopping while the 737 and 767s provide the medium- and long-range capabilities.

Air St Pierre

Registered name: Air St Pierre SA
Country: St Pierre et Miquelon
Region: Central America & Caribbean
Address: 18 Rue Albert Briand
PO Box 4225, F-97500
Tel: 00508 41 00 00
Fax: 00508 41 00 02
Web site: www.airsaintpierre.com
Main operational base: Pamandzi

BELOW: *Air St Pierre ATR 42-320, F0OHGL (C/n 323) (ATR)*

STATUS

Scheduled international passenger and charter carrier
Employees: 38
ICAO code: SPM
IATA code: PJ

SERVICES

Regional / Passenger
International routes: Canada

FLEET

ATR 42-320 - 1, PA-31-350 Chieftain - 1

Air St Pierre was formed on March 6th, 1964, and initially shared a DC-3 with Eastern Provincial Airways.

An Aztec was acquired in 1965 followed by another twelve months later. A Beech 18 was used during the early 70s and in 1976 the DC-3 was replaced by an HS748 that was operated as a pooled aircraft with EPA. A Chieftain was acquired in 1981 and a second HS748 in 1990.

An ATR 42 was acquired in January 1994 that replaced the two HS748s that were sold to an African operator.

Air Tahiti Nui

Registered name: Air Tahiti Nui
Country: Tahiti
Region: Australia & Pacific
Address: Dexter Building
Paul Gaugin St
PO Box 1673
Papeete
Tel: 00689 86 60 92
Fax: 00689 86 6072
Web site: www.airtahiti-nui.pf
Main operational base: Papeete

STATUS

Scheduled passenger carrier
National Flag Carrier
Employees: 139
Passengers per year: 909,000 (2001)
ICAO code:
IATA code: TN

SERVICES

International / Passenger
International routes: Japan, USA

ALLIANCES / CODE SHARES

Qantas

FLEET

A340-200 - 1
A340-300 - 2

Air Tahiti Nui was formed on October 31st 1996, as a long-haul airline owned by local interests including the French Polynesia Government (10%), to operate long-haul schedules.

Air Tahiti Nui works closely with Air France and has acquired an ex-Sabena A340-300 which is leased to Air Tahiti Nui by ILFC. It is used to provide a scheduled service to Los Angeles

BELOW: *Air Tahiti Nui A340-211, F-OITN (C/n 031) (Airbus)*

Air Tanzania

Registered name: Air Tanzania Corporation
Country: Tanzania
Region: Africa
Address: ATC House
Ohio St
PO Box 543
Dar-es-Salaam
Tel: 00255 51 11 02 45
Fax: 00255 51 11 31 14
Web site: www.mwebmarketplace.co.za/airtan/
Main operational base: Dar-es-Salaam International Airport

STATUS

IATA scheduled passenger carrier
National Flag Carrier
Employees: 642
Passengers per year: 178,000 (2001)
ICAO code: ATC
IATA code: TC

SERVICES

Regional / Domestic / Passenger / Cargo
International routes: Burundi, Kenya, Malawi, Rwanda, South Africa, Uganda, Zambia, Zimbabwe

FLEET

737-200C - 2, F-27 Mk.600 - 3 (1 grounded)

Air Tanzania was formed on June 1st, 1977, as a government-owned airline to develop domestic, regional and international services. This followed the collapse of East African Airways (EAA) in January 1977 after which an interim emergency service was arranged.

Air Tanzania was initially equipped with the F-27 Friendship and 737s were added shortly after.

In February 1998 the Government of Tanzania invited interested parties to register their interest prior to the opening of negotiations leading to privatisation. In November 1998 SAA was believed to be the successful bidder.

Air Vanuatu

Registered name: Air Vanuatu (Operations) Ltd
Country: Vanuatu
Region: Australia & Pacific
Address: Air Vanuatu House
Rue de Paris
PO Box 148
Port Vila
Tel: 00678 238 38
Fax: 00678 256 26
Web site:
www.pacificislands.com/airlines/vanuatu.html
Main operational base: Port Vila

STATUS

IATA scheduled international carrier
National Flag Carrier
Employees: 180
Passengers per year: 120,900 (2000)
ICAO code: AVN
IATA code: NF

SERVICES

Regional / Passenger / Cargo
International routes: Australia, Fiji, New
Caledonia, New Zealand

ALLIANCES / CODE SHARES

Air Caledonie, Air Pacific, Qantas,
Solomon A/l

FLEET

737-300 - 1, DHC-8 Dash 8-100 - 1

Air Vanuatu was formed in 1981 by the
Vanuatu Government in conjunction with
Ansett airlines. Operations commenced in
September 1981 using a 737.

Air Vanuatu has been responsible for a
major increase in the number of tourists visiting Vanuatu. Qantas provides most crew
training plus maintenance and ground handling while in Australia.

The domestic airline Vanair, which acts as
the marketing arm for the Government of
Vanuatu, merged with Air Vanuatu in April
2001.

Air Zimbabwe

Registered name: Air Zimbabwe
Country: Zimbabwe
Region: Africa
Address: PO Box AP1
Harare Airport, Harare
Tel: 00263 457 51 11
Fax: 00263 457 50 53
Web site: www.air.zim.co.zw
Main operational base: Harare Airport

STATUS

IATA scheduled international and domes-
tic passenger carrier
National Flag Carrier
Employees: 1,950
Passengers per year: 308,000 (2001)
ICAO code: AZW
IATA code: UM

SERVICES

International / Regional / Domestic
Passenger / Cargo
International routes: Australia, Cyprus,
Germany, Kenya, Malawi, Mauritius,
Mozambique, Namibia, South Africa,
Tanzania, UK, Zambia

FLEET

737-200Adv - 3, 767-200ER - 2, BAe 146-200
- 1

Air Zimbabwe can trace its history back to
September 1st, 1967, when Air Rhodesia
was formed after the dissolution of Central
African Airways.

Air Rhodesia changed its name to Air
Zimbabwe Rhodesia in 1978 before becoming Air Zimbabwe in April 1980 following
independence.

In 1983 Air Zimbabwe acquired the cargo
carrier Affretair.

Aircraft operated have included the DC-
3, Viscount, 707 and 737 which were flown
to various destinations around Africa with a
few routes to Europe and Australia.
However, the fluid political situation in

ABOVE: *Air Zimbabwe BAe 146-200, Z-WPD (C/n E2065)*
(David McIntosh/BAe systems)

Africa has meant that these have always
been in a state of flux. During the late 1980s
and early 1990s an effort was made to modernise the fleet. The 767s replaced the 707s
and BAe146 and Fokker 50s were acquired
for the short haul.

The more recent internal political problems have caused Air Zimbabwe increasing
operational difficulties. The Heathrow-
Victoria Fall service was suspended in
November 2001 and a number of the other
services are uncertain.

Alaska Airlines

Registered name: Alaska Airlines, Inc
Country: USA
Region: North America
Address: PO Box 68900
Seattle
Washington
Tel: 001 206 433 32 00
Fax: 001 206 433 33 79
Web site: www.alaskaair.com
Stockholder: Alaska Airlines Group
Main operational base: Seattle

STATUS

IATA scheduled passenger carrier
Employees: 11,025
Passengers per year: 13,668,000 (2001)
ICAO code: ASA
IATA code: AS

SERVICES

Regional / Domestic
Passenger / Cargo
International routes: Canada, Mexico

ALLIANCES / CODE SHARES

American A/l, American Eagle,
Continental A/l, ERA Avn, Hawaiian A/l,
Helijet Int, Horizon Air, KLM, LanChile,
Northwest A/l, Penair, Qantas

FLEET

737-200C - 9, 737-400 - 40, 737-700 - 19,
737-900 - 11, MD-82 / 83 - 32

The history of Alaska Airlines can be traced back to 1932 when Mac McGee commenced flying three Stinsons between Anchorage and Bristol Bay in Alaska as McGee Airways.

In 1934 a merger with Star Air Service created Alaska's largest airline with 22 aircraft. In 1937 Alaska Interior Airlines was bought and the Star side of the business sold to a group led by one of its former pilots – Don Goodman.

The Civil Aeronautics Authority was set up in 1938 to regulate airlines which brought an end to much of the ad-hoc true bush-flying.

Don Goodman registered his business Star Air Lines and managed to get most of the routes that it applied for. During 1942 three smaller local carriers were purchased and the name changed to Alaska Star Airlines becoming Alaska Airlines in 1944.

At the end of the war the charter business significantly outgrew the scheduled services and Alaska Airlines made the most of it. Amongst some of the largest operations

that it took part in were the Korean War, Berlin Airlift and the carriage of refugees to Israel using surplus military aircraft.

Two more local carriers were purchased in 1950. The bubble burst on free-for-all overseas charters following new government legislation. However, in 1951 Alaska Airlines was awarded the coveted Anchorage and Fairbanks routes to Seattle.

By the time Charlie Willis arrived in 1957 as chairman and CEO, Alaska Airlines was starting to come together financially.

The old DC-3s were being replaced by DC-6s and Convair 340s. Charters were being flown to Russia and it became the first airline to show in-flight movies.

Another first was the introduction of the C-130 Hercules to support the oil business and in the mid-1960s it entered the jet age with the arrival of the 727. These were to gradually provide the backbone of Alaska Airlines and enable an expansion of its route network. Mergers continued with Southeast Airlines, Alaska Coastal-Ellis and Cordova in 1968.

However, bad times were round the cor-

BELOW: *Alaska Airlines 737-290C Advc, N743AS (C/n 21821) (Jeremy Flack/API)*

ner and by 1972 Alaska Airlines was in danger of going under. A new management team was put in place and service improved enabling the company to just pull through declaring a small profit for 1973.

Alaska Airlines had been pushing for deregulation that eventually came in 1979. For Alaska Airlines this was the way ahead as it struggled with services to 11 cities with ten aircraft.

A slow but steady expansion ensued as opportunities arose. Services south extended down to Southern California and at last revenue and profits soared. The Air Alaska Group was formed in 1985 and Horizon Air and Jet American Airlines were bought the following year. A service into Mexico was introduced in 1988.

The deregulation had brought with it competition resulting in the lowering of fares. Alaska Airlines managed to quickly implement a streamlining of its cost structure and increased the utilisation of its fleet. The result was that it was able to offer better rates than most of its competitors

especially along the West Coast.

Alaska Airlines suffered a setback with the loss of one of its aircraft but a rationalisation of its fleet and an order for 11 of the new 737-900, for which Alaska Airlines was the launch customer, have seen it bounce back. The first of these new 737s were delivered in May 2001.

As part of Alaska Airlines use of the latest technology, a counterless check-in was pre-

ABOVE: *Alsaka Airlines operate the MD-82 and MD-83 (Alaska Airlines)*

viewed in 2002. Passengers will be able to obtain the boarding pass from a machine and only need to go to an agent if they have baggage. The planned opening of this system is 2004.

Alitalia

Registered name: Alitalia-Linee Aeree Italiane SpA
Country: Italy
Region: Europe
Address: Centro Direzionale
       Via Alessandro Marchetti 111
       Rome, I-00148
Tel: 0039 06 656 22020
Fax: 0039 06 656 24733
Web site: www.alitalia.it
Main operational base: Roma-Fiuminico

STATUS

IATA scheduled international and domestic carrier
National Flag Carrier
Employees: 18,465
Passengers per year: 24,737,000 (2001)
ICAO code: AZANOV
IATA code: AZ

SERVICES

International / Regional / Domestic Passenger / Cargo
International routes: Albania, Algeria, Argentina, Australia*, Austria, Belgium, Bahrain*, Brazil, Bulgaria, Canada*, Chile*, Cyprus, Croatia*, Czech, Denmark,

ABOVE: *Alitalia A320-214, I-BIKE (C/n 999) (Airbus)*

Egypt, France, Germany, Ghana, Greece, Hungary, India, Iran, Ireland, Israel, Japan, Jordan, Kenya*, Korea, Lebanon, Libya, Malta, Morocco, Netherlands, Nigeria,

Alitalia

LEFT: *Alitalia MD-82, I-DACV (C/n 53056) (Jeremy Flack/API)*

Poland, Portugal, Romania, Russia, Saudi Arabia, Senegal, Seychelles*, Singapore*, Slovakia, South Africa, Spain, Sweden, Switzerland, Syria, Tunisia, Turkey, UAE, UK, USA, Venezuela (* code shares)

ALLIANCES / CODE SHARES

Skyteam / Air Canada, Azzurrair, Croatia A/l, Cyprus A/l, JAL, LOT, Malev, Meridiana, Minerva, Qantas, Tarom, Uzbezistan A/w, Varig, Volare

OWNED SUBSIDIARY AIRLINES

Alitalia TeamAlitalia ExpressEurofly

FLEET

A320-200 - 11, A321-100 - 23, ATR 42 - 6, ATR 72-200 - 4 (Operated by Alitalia Express), ATR 72-500 - 6(Operated by Alitalia Express), DC-9-82 - 89   (20 operated by Alitalia Express), 767-300ER - 12 (1 sub-leased to Eurofly), 777-200ER - 1, ERJ-145 - 8 (Operated by Alitalia Express), MD-11 - 3, MD-11C - 5
On order: A319 - 12, 777-200ER - 5, ERJ-170 - 6 + 6 options (to replace DC-9s)

The origins of Alitalia date back to September 16th, 1946, when Aerolinee Italiane Internazional was formed, assisted by British European Airways. The first service was flown by a Fiat G.12 Alcione from Turin to Rome. Savoia-Marchetti SM.95 and Lancastrians were added a little later.

At the same time, Linee Aeree Italiane (LAI) was also formed with assistance from TWA and equipped with DC-4s.

Both airlines developed an extensive domestic network and were increasingly in competition with each other. In 1957, it was decided that a merger was necessary and the resulting airline was named Alitalia-LAI on September 1st.

By this time the merged fleet numbered 37 and included the DC-3, DC-6, DC-7, Convair 340 and 440 plus Viscount. Alitalia joined the jet set with its first DC-8 in April 1960 followed by the Caravelle in May 1960. The domestic airline Aero Trasporti Italiani (ATI) was formed by Alitalia to operate the domestic routes. By this time the merged fleet included the DC-3, DC-6, DC-7, Convair 340 and 440 plus Viscount. The first Caravelle entered service on May 23rd

1960 on the Rome-London route. This was followed the next month with a DC-8 to New York. These were followed some years later by the DC-9 in 1967 which gradually replaced the Caravelle.

The charter and domestic airline Aero Trasporti Italiani (ATI) was formed by Alitalia in 1963 to take over routes previously operated by Societa Aerea Mediterranea (SAM). Wide-bodied aircraft were the next advance with the 747 in June 1970 and DC-10 in February 1973. The 727s entered service with Alitalia in 1976 followed by the A300s in June 1980.

During the early 1980s, a fleet rationalisation saw the phasing out of the DC-8s, disposal of the DC-10s and beginning of DC-9 and 727 replacements with the MD-80 from 1984.

New aircraft continued to arrive during the 1990s with MD-11s in 1991, the Airbus A321 in 1994 and 767 in 1995. ATI was absorbed into Alitalia in 1994 but a subsequent decision was made to split Alitalia in 1997 into two divisions – Alitalia Express for short and medium haul and Alitalia for long haul.

During the end of the 1990s the Italian Government injected some capital into Alitalia which it owned and which had suffered several years of loss. With a more solid financial base, Alitalia has now been privatised. In July 2001, Alitalia joined the Skyteam alliance.

BELOW: *Alitalia A321-111, I-BIXU (C/n 434) with the Airbus test registration F-WWID. (Airbus)*

All Nippon Airways/ANA

Registered name: All Nippon Airways Co Ltd.

Country: Japan

Region: Far East

Address: 3-5-10 Haneda Airport
Ota-ku, Tokyo 144-0041

Tel: 00813 57 5656 75

Fax: 00813 57 5656 79

Web site: www.ana.co.jp

Stockholder: ANA Group

Main operational base: Haneda Airport

STATUS

IATA scheduled international carrier

Employees: 13,000

Passengers per year: 43,700,000 (2001)

ICAO code: ANA

IATA code: NH

SERVICES

International / Regional / Domestic
Charter / Cargo

International routes: China, France, Germany, Korea, Singapore, Thailand, UK, USA, Vietnam

OWNED SUBSIDIARY AIRLINES

Air Nippon, Air Japan

FLEET

A320 - 25, A321 - 7 (to be retired by the end of 2006), 747-100 - 9 (to be retired by the end of 2006), 747-200 - 3 (to be retired by the end of 2006), 747-400 - 23, 767-200 - 10 (to be retired by the end of 2006), 767-300 - 42, 767-300ER - 6 (Operated jointly with Nippon Cargo Airlines), 767-300F - 1 (Operated jointly with Nippon Cargo Airlines), 777-200 - 16, 777-300 - 5

On order: 767-300ER - 12 in 2003 / 06, 777-300 - 7 for delivery in 2003 / 06, 777-300ER - 3 for delivery in 2004 / 2005

All Nippon Airways ancestry dates back to December 27th, 1952, with the establishment of Nippon Helicopter and Far East Airlines. Although they were separate operations they worked closely together until 1957 when the decision was made to merge. The result was All Nippon Airways Co Ltd (ANA).

ABOVE: *All Nippon Airways A320-211, JA8386 (C/n 0170) (Airbus)*

ANA slowly embarked on a programme of expansion of the number of scheduled domestic routes flown. Although ANA had been flying international charters since 1971, none was scheduled. In 1986 ANA entered a new era with its first overseas route from Tokyo to Guam. Following the success of this first overseas route ANA has steadily expanded its international scheduled routes reaching out through Asia and across to Europe and the USA.

Early operations were flown with Convair 240 and 340 piston-powered airliners which were gradually replaced with the Viscount and F-27 Friendship turbo props in the early 1960s. ANA entered the jet age with 727s in the mid-1960s and the 747 and Tristar wide-bodies followed in the 1970s. The 767s and Airbus A300 were added during the 1980s. By offering a quality service ANA expansion has been impressive and enabled it to climb into the world's top ten airlines in terms of passengers flown.

In October 1999 ANA became a full member of the Star Alliance. In addition to its 20 overseas routes ANA serves 34 domestic routes which, together with others in the group account for around 50% of the domestic market. In 2002 ANA announced a programme to rationalise its fleet which will come into effect during 2004/6. The eight 747-100s, two 747-200s, eight 767-200s and seven A321s will be retired gradually by the end of fiscal year 2006. These will have made way for five 777-300 and nine 767-300ER that have been ordered for delivery over the same period. These aircraft are more efficient and will have a lower maintenance requirement as well as reducing the number of types operated – all of which will reduce their operating costs.

BELOW: *All Nippon Airways 747-481, JA8097 (C/n 25135) (Jeremy Flack/API)*

America West Airlines

Registered name: America West Airlines, Inc
Country: USA
Region: North America
Address: 111 West Rio Salado Parkway
Tempe
Arizona
AZ 85281
Tel: 001 480 693 57 29
Fax: 001 480 693 55 46
Web site: www.americawest.com
Stockholder: America West Holdings Corporation
Main operational base: Pheonix - Sky Harbor International

STATUS

IATA scheduled passenger and cargo carrier

Employees: 14,000
Passengers per year: 19,576,000 (2001)
ICAO code: AWE
IATA code: HP

SERVICES

International / Regional / Domestic Passenger / Cargo
International routes: Mexico

ALLIANCES / CODE SHARES

Air China, Air Midwest A/l, Big Sky A/l, BA, Chautauqua A/l, EVA A/w, Hawaiian A/l, Mesa A/l, Northwest A/l

FLEET

A319-100 - 32, A320-200 - 49, 737-200Adv - 10, 737-300 - 39, 757-200 - 13,
CRJ700 - 3 (America West Express),
CRJ200 - 25 (America West Express),
ERJ-145 - 7 (America West Express),
DHC-8 Dash-8 - 11 (America West Express)
On order: A318-100 -15 for delivery from 2003, A320-200 – 8

America West Airlines came into being during February 1981 and commenced operations on August 1st 1983 with three aircraft and 280 employees. It grew rapidly to the extent that it achieved a major-airline status by 1990 with annual revenue of more than US$1 billion.

ABOVE: *America West Airlines A319-132, N801AW (C/n 889) (Airbus)*

America West Airlines is the USA's eighth largest commercial air carrier. It provides a scheduled passenger and cargo service to around 90 destinations across North America from its three hubs at Pheonix, Arizona, Las Vegas, Nevada and Columbus, Ohio. Following difficulties caused by the disaster of September 11th, America West Airlines received US$380 million federal loan guarantee under the Air Transportation Safety and Stabilisation Act.

BELOW: *America West Express CRJ700 operated by Dester Sun Airlines (Bombardier)*

American Airlines

Country: USA
Region: North America
Address: PO Box 619616
Dallas-Fort Worth Airport
Texas 75261-96
Tel: 001 817 963 12 34
Fax: 001 817 967 38 16
Web site: www.amr.com
Stockholder: AMR Corporation
Main operational base: Dallas / Fort Worth

STATUS

IATA scheduled passenger carrier
Employees: 114,363
Passengers per year: 80,654,000 (2001)
ICAO code: AAL
IATA code: AA

SERVICES

International / Regional / Domestic
Passenger / Cargo
International routes: Argentina, Antigua &
Barbuda, Aruba, Belgium, Barbados,
Belize, Bermuda, Brazil, Canada, Cayman
Islands, Chile, Colombia, Costa Rica,
Dominican Republic, Ecuador, France,
Germany, Guatemala, Haiti, Honduras,
Italy, Jamaica, Japan, Mexico, Netherlands
Antilles, Nicaragua, Panama, Paraguay,
Peru, Puerto Rico, Spain, Sweden,
Switzerland, Trinidad & Tobago, Turks &
Caicos Islands, UK, Uruguay, Venezuela,
Virgin Islands (US)

ALLIANCES / CODE SHARES

Oneworld / Aer Lingus, Aero California,
Air Pacific, Alaska Airlines, China Eastern,
EVA Airways, Gulf Air, Hawaiian A/l, JAL,
LOT, Singapore A/l, Siss, TACA, TAM,
TAP, THY

OWNED SUBSIDIARY AIRLINES

American Eagle

FLEET

A300-605R - 34,737-800 - 77, 757-200 - 150,
767-200 - 8, 767-300ER - 49, 767-200ER - 21,
777-200ER - 43, Fokker 100 - 74 (to be
retired 2003 - 2005), MD-11 - 3 (not in
service), MD-82 / MD-83 - 362

On order: 737-800 - 40, 757-200 - 2, 777-200ER - 4 for delivery into 2003

ABOVE: *American Airlines 757-223, N639AA (C/n 24597) (Rolls Royce)*

The origins of American Airlines date back to the mid-1920s when a number of fledgling aviation companies were being established to fly US mail around the country. In 1929 the Aviation Corporation was formed to acquire some of these companies - one of which was Robertson Aircraft Corporation of Missouri. The chief pilot for Robertson was Charles A Lindeburgh who had made their first mail flight in a DH.4 on April 15th, 1926.

The subsidiaries of Aviation Corporation were incorporated into American Airways Inc in 1930 and in 1934 American Airways Inc became American Airlines.

American Airlines became the first airline to fly the DC-3 commercially when it entered service on June 25th 1936. By the end of the decade it had expanded to the extent that it had become the largest US domestic air carrier in terms of revenue passenger miles. In February 1937 American Airlines carried its millionth passenger.

During the war, half of its fleet was transferred to the military along with the crews.

During 1944 American Airlines introduced the first domestic scheduled freight service using the DC-3. As they became available DC-4s, DC-6As and DC-7s were added to the fleet.

America operated American Overseas Airlines (AOA) from 1945 to 1950 providing routes into several European countries. AOA had been formed by a merger of American Airlines international division with American Export Airlines. AOA merged with Pan American World Airways in 1950.

With the aircraft manufacturers keen to keep some production running after the end of the war a number of new airlines competed for business. In 1948 American Airlines took delivery of its first DC-6 and Convair 240. By 1948 American became the first US airline to operate a completely post-war fleet of pressurised passenger airliners. A Family Fare Plan was introduced to provide families with a discount when flying together. A scheduled coach service was provided which offered a more economical alternative to first class.

American Airlines

ABOVE: *American Airlines 757-223, N635AA (C/n 24593) (American Airlines)*

Non-stop transcontinental services were pioneered in 1953 with the DC-7 and became jet operated in January 1959 with the introduction of the 707. At the same time the Lockheed Electra entered service followed by the Convair 990 in 1962.

Commencing in late 1959, American Airlines and IBM teamed up to introduce SABRE (Semi-Automated Business Research Environment) - the largest data processing system for business use. By 1964, the SABRE network was in coast-to-coast use. It became the second largest real-time data processing system after that of the US Government.

New airliners continued to be added to American Airlines fleet to replace obsolete older types with the 727 arriving in 1964 followed by the 747 in 1966 and DC-10 in 1968.

The DC 7 was American Airline's last operational piston aircraft and the final flight was made in December 1966.

A merger with Trans Caribbean Airways in 1970 extended American Airlines network into the Caribbean; that was further increased in 1975 with acquisitions from Pan American.

American Airlines began marketing the SABRE system to travel agents in 1975 while in April it introduced the Super Saver fare. Initially this popular discount fare was only available on the New York to California route but soon spread across the North American network.

Following US airline deregulation in 1978, American Airlines commenced a major route expansion and the following year moved its headquarters from New York to Dallas, Texas.

The rapidly rising fuel costs signalled the end for the gas-guzzling 707s, all of which had been retired by August 1981.

American Airlines carried its 500 millionth passenger in 1983 and commenced its first 767 service. A new hub was established at Chicago while in May 1983, a transatlantic service was re-established between Dallas/Fort Worth and London/Gatwick. As part of a reorganisation, AMR Corporation was formed to become the parent company for American Airlines.

In 1983 the first MD-80 was delivered and agreement was announced that American Airlines was going to exchange its 747s for Pan Am's DC-10s.

The American Eagle network of regional airlines was established in 1984 enabling smaller cities to link up with the American Airlines network. Conversely, the specialised 747 cargo fleet was retired and the emphasis placed on smaller shipments which could be carried in the bellies of scheduled passenger services.

To compete with the low cost airlines that came into being following deregulation, American Airlines introduced the Ultimate Super Saver fare in 1985 that offered passengers up to 70% discounts and the Senior SAAVers Club which offered discounts to senior citizens.

By now, the SABRE processing system was in use by over 10,000 travel agents to make their reservations. Such was the strategic importance to the industry of SABRE that American Airlines completed an underground fire and earthquake proof facility. This was to house what had become the world's largest private real-time computer network and travel information database and was located at Tulsa, Okla in 1987. By 1998, SABRE could be accessed via the PC.

A second-day door-to-door freight service was introduced in 1985 utilising hold capacity available in its passenger aircraft. By 1998 this had been developed sufficiently to enable a next-day service to be offered.

American Airlines opened a new hub in Nashville in April 1986 followed by another at San Juan in November. The Sky Chefs airline catering subsidiary was sold in 1986 while Air California (Air Cal) was acquired.

The first A300-600ER was acquired in 1988 for the Caribbean routes and the 757 entered service the following year. Another new hub - the seventh - was opened at Miami in September 1989.

American Airlines added new services into Latin America during 1990 following the acquisition of routes from Eastern Airlines.

To preserve some of its history, the American Airlines C R Smith Museum was established in July 1993 within its new headquarters complex at Fort Worth.

American Airlines acquired Reno Air in 1998 and in September announced the establishment of the Oneworld alliance with four other airlines. The multi-million dollar programme was designed to raise the standard of global air travel.

The 777s and 737-800s entered service in 1999. A programme of fitting defibrillators

into all aircraft was completed and American Airlines became the first airline to offer in-flight DVD video players on scheduled flights.

As part of a passenger comfort promotion the 'More Room Throughout Coach' was instigated for which two rows of seats were removed to increase leg room throughout the coach cabin. This was subsequently extended to increase leg room in the first class cabin.

In 2001, American Airlines announced that it was to purchase substantially all of the assets of the bankrupt TWA which was completed by April. This was a move that secured its position as the world's largest airline. A subsequent announcement gave plans for the early retirement of 19 DC-9s, 12 727s, four MD-11s and one Fokker 100.

While American Airlines had been moving ahead nothing could prepare it for what was just around the corner.

The hijacking of AA011 and AA077 on September 11th 2001 and the crashing of them into the World Trade Centre in New York and Pentagon in Washington along with the other hijackings and the loss of thousands of lives will ensure that the date will never be forgotten the world over.

This act of terrorism has also had a lasting effect on the world's airlines causing an

immediate grounding of all US domestic fights and inbound international flights to the US. This and the following drop in airline passenger levels caused major economic difficulties.

Unfortunately, for American Airlines it didn't stop there. Two months later on November 12th the tail broke off one of their A300s shortly after take-off.

As a result more aircraft were retired, the new ex-TWA 717s were returned to the manufacture and announcements of 15,000 personnel cuts still resulted in a US$1.8 billion loss in 2001 from a US$813 million profit the previous year.

ABOVE: *American Airlines MD-82, N467AA (C/n 49596) (Jeremy Flack/API)*

While airlines contemplate a number of scenarios – operational or emergency – to enable plans to be rehearsed, very little could have been prepared for the devastation caused by a handful of terrorists on September 11th.

Within a few minutes of taking off from Boston, just before 8 am the hijackers took control of an American Airlines 767 to LA

BELOW: *American Airlines 777-223ER, N790AN(C/n 30251) (Jeremy Flack/API)*

American Airlines

with 81 passengers aboard. A minute later another 767 operated by United Airlines also took off and was hijacked. Both then headed to New York where they were crashed into the Twin Towers within 20 minutes of each other with devastating results and huge loss of life.

A second United airliner took off just after 8 am and crashed near Pittsburgh. The fourth aircraft to be hijacked was an American Airlines 757 which took off from Washington Dulles at 8.10 am and crashed into the Pentagon.

The effect on American Airlines just kept getting worse. The numbing loss of two of their airliners was followed by the grounding of all US aviation. When this was relaxed - passenger levels had dropped to below economic levels on many routes.

Unfortunately for American it kept going. On November 12th, an A300-600 took off from New York's JFK airport with some 250 passengers and crew and broke up just minutes into its flight.

With many routes suspended, aircraft grounded and workforce cut the overheads remain still high and despite a US$15 billion aid package approved by Bush to help the airline industry this was proving too great a hurdle. In hindsight, the purchase of TWA for US$742m plus their debts of US$3.5 billion was perhaps not such a good move.

In November 2002, American Airlines and British Airways applied to the US DOT for regulatory approval to establish a code share between the two airlines. However, the airline continues to struggle with its huge debt.

American Eagle Airlines

Country: USA
Region: North America
Address: PO Box 619616
   DFW International Airport
   Texas 75261-96
Tel: 001 817 967 1295
Fax: 001 817 967 3902
Web site: www.aa.com
Stockholder: AMR Corporation
Main operational base: DFW International Airport

ABOVE: *American Eagle Airlines ERJ-135KL N800AE (C/n 145425) (Jane's)*

STATUS

Scheduled regional carrier
Employees: 13,915
Passengers per year: 11,995,000 (2001)
ICAO code: AAL
IATA code: AA

SERVICES

International / Regional / Domestic Passenger / Cargo
International routes: Anguilla, Antigua & Barbuda, Bahamas, Barbados, Canada, Dominica, Dominican Republic, Grenada, Guadeloupe, Netherlands Antilles, Puerto Rico, St Kitts & Nevis, St Lucia, St Vincent & Grenadines, Trinidad & Tobago, Virgin Islands

ALLIANCES / CODE SHARES

Alaska A/l, Continental A/l, Hawaiian A/l, Midwest A/l

FLEET

CRJ700 - 1, ERJ-135 - 40, ERJ-140 - 15, ERJ-145LR - 44, ATR 42-300 - 30, ATR 72-200 - 8, ATR 72-212 - 23, ATR 72-500 -12, 340B - 66 (to retire as leases end), 340B+ - 25 (to retire as leases end)
On Order: ATR 72-500 - 42, CRJ700 - 24 + 25 options, ERJ-140 - 124 + 25 options, ERJ-145LR - 17

In 1984, American Airlines established the American Eagle system to form a network of regional airlines offering a high level service from small communities to large cities enabling connection to and from American Airlines.

Early agreements were signed in 1984 by Metro Airlines (formed 1966) and Chaparral Airlines (formed 1975). These were followed by Avair (formed 1979), Simmons Airlines (formed 1978) in 1985, Air Midwest (formed 1965), Command Airways (formed 1966) and Wings West (formed 1975) in 1986.

During 1996 American Eagle rationalised its route network around six hubs - Chicago O'Hare, Dallas / Fort Worth, Los Angeles, Miami, New York JFK, and San Juan. In addition, further code share agreements were made with Hawaiian Airlines, Reno Air and Southwest Airlines. American Airlines announced that American Eagle would acquire small regional jets. In March 1999 the acquisition of Business Express (formed 1984) was completed and the airline absorbed into American Airlines. This resulted in the addition of two further hubs to the network - New York La Guardia and Boston. The first of the regional jets - an Embraer ERJ-135 - was delivered in 1999. This was joined by the ERJ-140 in 2001 and ERJ-145.

AMERICAN EAGLE AIRLINES

American Trans Air/ATA

Registered name: American Trans Air Inc
Country: USA
Region: North America
Address: 7337 West Washington Street
Indianapolis
Indiana 46231
Tel: 001 317 247 40 00
Fax: 001 317 240 7091
Web site: www.ata.com
Stockholder: ATA Holdings Corp
Main operational base: Indianapolis

STATUS

Scheduled and charter passenger carrier
Passengers per year: 8,635,000 (2001)
ICAO code: AMT
IATA code: TZ

SERVICES

International / Regional / Domestic
Passenger / Charter
International routes: Aruba, Cayman
Islands, Hawaii, Jamaica, Mexico

OWNED SUBSIDIARY AIRLINES

ATA Execujet, Chicago Express

FLEET

737-800 - 39, 757-200 - 17, 757-300 - 10,
L.1011 Tristar 50 - 10, L.1011 Tristar 500 - 6

American Trans Air was originally formed by John Mikelsons in August 1973 with a leased 720B. It was set up to fly members of the Ambassadair Travel Club on vacation packages.

An additional 720 was acquired in 1978 and following the deregulation of the airline industry in 1978, an application was made to change the airline's status.

American Trans Air was certified as a common-air carrier in 1981 which enables it to operate commercial charters. As a result ATA acquired eight more 707s.

With this successful formula ATA rapidly expanded and the following year had built up a staff level of 320 and ended the year with a turnover of $30.5 million. In 1984 AmTran Inc was formed as a holding company for Ambassadair, ATA and future sub-

sidiaries. In the meantime the 707s were sold and replaced with 727s.

The following year, a number of Tristars were added to the fleet making it the largest charter carrier in North America. The American 'Inc Magazine' named AmTran as the seventh largest private company in the US.

In 1986 ATA commenced its first scheduled service between Indianapolis and Ft Myers, Florida.

With an ever-increasing fleet size, ATA opened a Maintenance and Engineering Centre at Indianapolis Airport in 1988. ATA Execujet was established in 1989 to provide small jet charters and 757s were added to the main fleet.

A contract in 1991 to assist the DoD with transportation to the Middle East for Operation Desert Storm led to 494 missions during which 108,000 military personnel were carried.

ATA became the first airline to obtain FAA certification in 1992 for 180-minute ETOPS operation with the 757 which enabled a greater over water capability. A Chicago-Midway service was inaugurated and 500,000 passengers were carried in the first year.

During 1986 ATA opened a maintenance facility at Chicago. ATA Connection was launched with Chicago Express Airlines to provide feeder links to the Chicago operation. The 727-100s were sold off and replaced with 727-200s in 1993. The follow-

ABOVE: *American Trans Air L. 1011-385 Tristar 50, N186AT (1074) (Jeremy Flack/API)*

ing year ATA concluded an arrangement with the largest Hawaiian tour operator - Pleasant Hawaiian Holidays - which resulted in a number of scheduled services to the Island.

ATA continued to expand its scheduled services and at the same time bought Chicago Express in 1999 as well as adding several travel businesses to its portfolio. By the end of the year, annual revenue exceeded $1 billion for the first time.

US Department of Transportation reclassified ATA as a major carrier in 2000. The number of scheduled routes continued to expand, including overseas destinations by the end of 2001.

ATA became the first carrier to receive the 737-800 with the performance-enhancing winglets when the first of 39 was delivered in June 2001.

The terrorist attack on September 11th hit virtually all US air travel. Shortly after the attack, ATA announced a 20% reduction in its scheduled services and retired the 727 fleet by end of October.

During 2002 ATA and ATA Connection announce new services. They applied to the US Government for a loan guarantee of $148.5m to assist in securing $165m in private financing. ATA was one of the few airlines not to have been hit badly in the business downturn.

Ariana Afghan Airlines

Registered name: Ariana Afghan Airlines Co Ltd

Country: Afghanistan

Region: Asia

Address: PO Box 76
Ansari Watt,
Kabul

Tel: 00873 762 52 38 44/45

Fax: 00873 762 52 38 46

Web site: www.flyariana.com/

Main operational base: Kabul

STATUS

IATA scheduled carrier

National Flag Carrier

Employees: 950

Passengers per year: 1,023,000 (1999)

ICAO code: AFG

IATA code: FG

SERVICES

International / Regional

Domestic / Passenger

FLEET

A300B4-203 -3, An-24RV - 5, 727-100C - 1,
727-100C -1, 727-200 Advanced -1

Aryana Airlines was originally formed on January 27th, 1955, as a domestic carrier with a DC-3 by the Afghan Government. This was achieved with the support of Transoceanic Airways of the USA with a DC-3. Pan Am took a 49% stake in 1956 and enabled Ariana Afghan Airlines to commence international operations with DC-4s and later DC-6s. In 1967 Bakhtar Afghan Airlines Ariana was formed to operate the domestic routes. Ariana Afghan entered the jet age with a 727 that it used on the European routes.

In 1979 the 727 was replaced with a DC-10 but this was damaged during the Soviet invasion later that year. Russian aircraft joined Ariana Afghan in the form of An-24, An-26, Tu-154 and Yak-40. However, international flights were restricted to Russia and eastern European destinations mainly in support of the military.

Pan Am had withdrawn its support as internal security broke down and Ariana Afghan ceased operations in 1985.

ABOVE: *Ariana Afghan Airlines An-24, YA-DAM (C/n 57310404) (Jeremy Flack/API)*

Operations recommenced in 1988 in a limited form but eventually most of its fleet had been damaged or destroyed. Ariana Afghan limped on but following the events of September 11th and the US-led invasion the airline was restricted to internal flights.

By this time the fleet was down to one 727 and an An-24. Considering the resources available a tremendous effort was made to get and keep these two aircraft airworthy and a limited service was operated. A second 727 was acquired and in November 2002 two A300s were gifted to Ariana Afghan Airlines as they became surplus.

Asiana Airlines

Country: Korea

Region: Asia

Address: Asiana Building, 2-ka
Hoehyun-Dong
PO Box 142, Chung -ku
Seoul

Tel: 0082 2 669 38 54

Fax: 0082 2 669 38 60

Web site: flyasiana.com

Stockholder: Kumho Group

Main operational base: Incheon Airport

STATUS

International and domestic scheduled passenger carrier

National Flag Carrier

Employees: 5,804

Passengers per year: 11,924,000 (2001)

ICAO code: AAR

IATA code: OZ

SERVICES

International / Regional / Domestic
Passenger / Cargo

International routes: Australia, China, Germany, India, Japan, Kazakhstan, Philippines, Russia, Singapore, Thailand, USA, Uzbekistan, Vietnam

ALLIANCES / CODE SHARES

American A/1, Qantas, THY

FLEET

A321-100 - 3, A321-200 - 5, A330-200 - 8, A330-300 - 10, 737-400 - 22, 737-500 - 3, 747-400 - 12, 767-300 - 4, 767-300ER - 8, 777-200 - 4

Asiana was formed by the Kumho Group on February 17th, 1988, and commenced a

domestic service in South Korea in December, with 737s, as South Korea's second national airline. Asiana took delivery of its first 767 in 1990 followed by 747s in 1992. The first international service by Asiana was inaugurated in 1990 to Japan with Hong Kong and Taiwan added later that year.

Asiana signed an order for 18 A321s in 1996 and the following year added six more A330s to the ten already on order.

By the end of the 1990s, Asiana had become the largest foreign carrier in China and Japan.

Asiana added a leased 777 to its fleet in February 2001 to increase fleet capacity for Southeast Asia and trans-Pacific routes.

ABOVE: *Asiana Airlines A321-131, HL7588 (C/n 771) (Airbus)*

Atlantic Airways

Registered name: Atlantic Airways (Faroe Islands) Ltd
Country: Denmark (Faroe Is)
Region: Europe
Address: Vagar Airport
FO-380 Sorvagur,
Faroe Islands
Tel: 00298 34 10 00
Fax: 00298 34 10 01
Web site: www.atlantic.fo
Main operational base: Vágar

STATUS

Scheduled passenger carrier
National Flag Carrier
Employees: 75
Passengers per year: 98,000 (2001)
ICAO code: FLI
IATA code: RC

SERVICES

Regional / Domestic / Passenger Charter / Cargo
International routes: Denmark, Iceland, Norway, UK

ALLIANCES / CODE SHARES

Air Iceland

FLEET

BAe 146-200A - 2 (1 leased out), Bell 212 - 1, Bell 412 - 2

Atlantic Airways was formed in November 1987 as a partnership between the Faroe Island Government and Cimber Air. It was established to serve the Faroes to Copenhagen route with a BAe146.

Various attempts were made to increase passenger levels with additional flights to Denmark, UK and Norway but with a small indigenous population and it not being a big tourist attraction it was an uphill battle. The oil exploration business has produced some business and some routes were targeted to try to gain business.

Some of the flights were dropped but those that were retained caused a stretch in available capacity. Although this required an additional aircraft the trade was seasonal and dropped off in the winter, reaching a point where a second aircraft ceased to be viable. An aircraft was leased from Malmo and passenger numbers steadily rose. When Debonair folded in September 1999, one of its BAe146s was purchased. Being the low

period it was leased out and returned to Atlantic Airways the following spring. A Bell 212 is used to carry passengers and cargo around the island especially when the weather makes it difficult by sea.

In 2001 Atlantic Airways introduced a Search And Rescue (SAR) service with a Bell 412. At the same time a new livery was introduced together with a fresh logo. This has included an internal upgrade with leather seats and a little extra leg room which has cost a couple of seats.

As business continued to grow, Atlantic Airways was looking forward with a plan to buy an Avro RJX. However, as BAE Systems decided not to put this aircraft into production, it has to consider an alternative. The A318 / A319, 737 or Embraer 170 / 190 are all possibilities but it is probable that an RJ85 / RJ100 will be acquired.

BELOW: *Atlantic Airways BAe. 146, OY-CRG (C/n E2075) (BAe systems)*

Atlantic Coast Airlines

Country: USA
Region: North America
Address: 45200 Business Court
Dulles
Virginia 20166
Tel: 001 703 650 60 00
Fax: 001 703 650 62 99
Web site: www.atlanticcoast.com
Main operational base: Dulles

STATUS

Scheduled and charter carrier
Employees: 4,000
Passengers per year: 4,937,000 (2001)
ICAO code: BLR
IATA code: DH

SERVICES

Domestic / Passenger
International routes: Domestic only

ALLIANCES / CODE SHARES

Air Canada, Delta A/L, Lufthansa, SAS,
United A/L

FLEET

CRJ200 - 60, 328Jet - 33
On order: CRJ200 36 + 80 options

ABOVE: *Atlantic Coast Airlines 328Jet operated as Delta Connection (Dornier)*

Atlantic Coast Airlines was formed on December 15th, 1989, as the Atlantic Coast Division of WestAir (formed 1972).

WestAir was a United Express partner operating out of Los Angeles and San Francisco. Presidential Airways, also a United Express partner and operating the East coast was experiencing financial difficulties which in December 1989 turned out to be terminal. With just 11 days available, WestAir were asked to put together a new operation at Washington Dulles. With three Brasilias and the Jetstream 32s to cover six destinations they managed to cover the service on time.

WestairAir continued with the service but in 1991 it too was suffering some financial difficulties and decided to sell the Atlantic Coast Division.

The operation was bought by a group, headed by Mr Acker, and named Atlantic Coast Airlines (ACA) for which shares were first offered publically in 1993. The Brasilias were sold and DHC-Dash 8s operated for a while. However, the BAE Jetstream proved popular and a fleet of 28 Jetstream J32 and J41s was established. These were phased out in 2001.

ACA decided that the time was right for it to get into the jet age. As a consequence the Canadair Regional Jet was ordered. When the first one arrived in 1997 United had still not approved the new type to fly its customers. However, by April 2004 it is expected that 154 will have been delivered.

In October 1999, a sister airline was established by Atlantic Coast Airlines Holdings – Atlantic Coast Jet – which would provide a similar service for Delta Connection. In 2001 ACA and ACJ were combined to operate as Atlantic Coast Airlines. As part of the US Government assistance to airlines in difficulty after the terrorist atrocities on September 11th, ACA received US$9.7m in loan guarantees. A total of 32 Fairchild Dornier 328Jets were ordered and received for use on the Delta Connection operation. However, with the manufacturer, Fairchild Dornier, struggling to stave off bankruptcy after only two were delivered, the balance of 30 ordered for the United Express part of the business was cancelled. An order for a further 25 CRJ200s was placed in June 2002. The two 328Jets delivered were passed on to the private charter arm of ACA.

LEFT: *Atlantic Coast Airlines CRJ200 operated as United Express (Bombardier)*

Atlantic Southeast Airlines/Delta Connection

Registered name: Atlantic Southeast Airlines Inc
Country: USA
Region: North America
Address: 100 Hartsfield Centre Parkway
Suite 800
Atlanta
Georgia 30354
Tel: 001 404 766 14 00
Fax: 001 404 209 01 62
Web site: www.flyasa-air.com
Stockholder: Delta Air Lines Inc
Main operational base: Atlanta

STATUS

Scheduled domestic passenger carrier
Employees: 5,000
Passengers per year: 6,600,000 (2001)
ICAO code: ASE
IATA code: EV

SERVICES

Regional / Domestic
Passenger / Cargo
International routes: Mexico, Canada

ALLIANCES / CODE SHARES

Sky Team / China Southern A/l, CSA, Royal Air Maroc, Skywest A/l, SAA

FLEET

ATR 72-210 - 19, CRJ100 - 10, CRJ200 - 66, CRJ700 - 7
On order: CRJ200 - 7 +127 options, CRJ700 - 24 +83 options

Atlantic Southeast Airlines (ASA) was incorporated on March 12th, 1979, and commenced operations on June 27th. The first service was flown from Atlanta to Columbus, Georgia with a DHC-6 Twin Otter. The first of 12 Bandeirantes were added in 1981, plus the first of five DHC-7 Dash 7 a year later. Following completion of the initial stock offering in 1982, Southeastern Airlines was acquired in 1983, ASA became the world's first customer for the Brasilia with an order for 33 aircraft for delivery in 1985 and received the first of eight Short SD360s.

Following an agreement with Delta Air Lines in June, ASA commenced its first ser-

ABOVE: *Atlantic South East Airlines CRJ200 operated as Delta Connection (Bombardier)*

vice as a Delta Connection operator on December 15th.

Delta Air Lines announced in May 1986 that it was to invest in ASA with the purchase of 2,665,000 common shares. With business expanding ASA terminated its operations from Memphis to concentrate on Dallas/Fort Worth.

The ATR 72 entered service in June 1994 and the first jet service was in May 1995 using the BAe146.

In January 1997 ASA placed an order for 30 Canadair Regional Jets (CRJ) and the first entered service in October. The following year, a further order for another 27 CRJs was placed.

ASA became a wholly owned subsidiary of Delta in May 1999. During the following March, an order for 104 CRJs was announced which would be shared between ASA and its Delta Connection partner Comair. The order is planned for comple-

tion by 2004 and includes options for a further 396.

ASA broke from its purely domestic role in June when it commenced a service to Toronto in Canada. Another to Monterrey in Mexico followed in October. On December 26th, ASA flew its 6 millionth passenger that year breaking all previous records.

Delta Air Lines was a sponsor of the 2002 Olympic Games and ASA did its bit by flying the Olympic flame from Miami to Mobile in one of the CRJs. The first CRJ700 was received in January 2002 and entered service in April with operations out of the Atlanta hub. The steady expansion of the ASA network resulted in the introduction to its 100th city - Cincinnati - on September 1st 2002.

Austrian Airlines

Registered name: Austrian Airlines
Österreichische Luftverkehrs AG
Country: Austria
Region: Europe
Address: Fontanastrasse 1, A-1107 Vienna
Tel: 0043 5 17 89
Fax: 0043 1 688 55 05
Web site: www.austrianairlines.com or
www.aua.com
Stockholder: Austrian Airlines Group
Main operational base: Vienna

STATUS

IATA international passenger + cargo
carrier
National Flag Carrier
Employees: 7,752
Passengers per year: 3,768,000 (2001)
ICAO code: AUA
IATA code: OS

SERVICES

International / Regional / Domestic
Passenger / Charter / Cargo
International routes: Albania, Armenia,
Australia, Belarus, Belgium, Bosnia
Herzegovina, Bulgaria, Canada, China,
Croatia, Cyprus, Czech, Denmark, Egypt,
Estonia, Finland, France, Georgia,
Germany, Greece, Hungary, India,
Indonesia, Iran, Israel, Italy, Kenya, Japan,
Jordan, Kosovo, Latvia, Lebanon, Libya,
Lithuania, Luxemburg, Nepal, Malaysia,
Maldives, Moldova, Morocco, Netherlands,
Norway, Poland, Romania, Russia, Serbia,
Slovakia, Slovenia, Spain, Sri Lanka,
Sweden, Switzerland, Syria, Thailand,
Turkey, UAE, UK, Ukraine, USA

ALLIANCES / CODE SHARES

Star Alliance

OWNED SUBSIDIARY AIRLINES

Tyrolean Airways, Rheintalflug, Lauda Air -
99%

FLEET

A321 - 6, A320 - 8, A330-200 - 4, A340-200 -
2, A340-300 - 2, MD-82 - 3, MD-83 - 2, MD-
87 - 4, Fokker 70 - 6

On order: A320 - 6, 737-800 - 2, 777 - 2,
DHC-8, Dash 8-400Q - 3, CRJ200ER - 4, ERJ-
145 - 1

ABOVE: *Austrian Airlines A340-212, OE-LAG (C/n 075)*
(Airbus)

Austria claims to have operated the world's first international scheduled air service when on March 31st 1918, a regular mail service was flown from Vienna to Krakow, Lvov and Kiev.

Österreichische Luftverkehrs AG was originally formed in May 1923 and operated until 1938 when it was liquidated and incorporated into Deutsche Lufthansa. During this period it had flown 4.7 million miles and safely carried some 120,000 passengers.

After World War Two the Allies did not allow civil aviation activities until the State Treaty was signed in 1955.

Plans for two new airlines were being proposed - Air Austria and Austriana Airways. However, these plans were merged and resulted in Österreichische Luftverkehrs AG which was formed again on September 30th 1957. Initially it chartered four Vickers Viscount turboprop airliners from Fred Olsen and commenced operations on March 31st 1958. In 1960 deliveries of its own six Viscounts commenced. In February 1963 Austrian Airlines entered the jet age with the arrival of the first of five of the French Caravelle airliners that entered service in April. Until this point all the opera-

tions had been international but in May the first domestic service was flown with the venerable DC-3. The DC-3s were replaced by a pair of HS748s in 1966. On April 1st 1968 Austrian Airlines commenced its Vienna to New York service that routed via Brussels. This service was operated in co-operation with Sabena from whom a 707 had been chartered. However, passenger numbers were badly miscalculated and after two years the service terminated.

On June 18th 1971 the first of nine DC-9s was delivered to replace the Viscounts. It was the first year that Austrian Airlines had posted a net profit - ATS 8.6 million.

A technical co-operation agreement was signed in 1972 with Swissair in which maintenance for the DC-9 would be shared and a new base set up at Vienna airport.

In October 1977 Austrian Airlines placed another order for a new model of the DC-9, the MD-81 that entered service in September 1980.

In 1978 Austrian Airlines expanded into the leisure industry when it invested in a number of hotel and catering businesses. In December 1984 four MD-87s were ordered with two options and the following year two Fokker 50s were also ordered with two options.

In 1988 24.2% of the state-owned share capital was offered to the public via the Vienna stock market and Swissair took 3% which was raised to 8% the following year. In addition Nippon Airways acquired 3.5% holding after the Austrian Airlines share was made available. In 1990 this was raised further to 10% and 9% respectively.

In December 1988 the first of four Airbus A310s was delivered and the following April the sixth MD-87 order was changed to an MD-83. In September an order for a fifth Fokker was placed.

The year for the big spend was 1990 which started slowly in September with a repeat for a single MD-83 followed in October by another order with Airbus for 13 A320 / A321 for delivery from 1996 and options on a further 13 aircraft. This ATS 22 billion order was the largest ever in Austrian aviation.

The orders continued in 1991 with one for a single Fokker 50 and two of the long-range A340.

Passenger levels had continued to rise and in 1992 the annual figures exceeded the three million mark for the first time.

In 1994 Austrian Airlines announced that it was going to purchase shares of other airlines when it bought 42.85% of the Austrian domestic Tyrolean Airways shares.

Orders for new aircraft continued in 1995 with four Fokker 70 and options for a further four placed in January. In December two more A340s were ordered along with three Fokker 70s. In the meantime the original two A340s had been delivered and were already in service.

In 1996 the first route was flown to Moscow with the A321 which coincided with a new corporate makeover with new uniforms for the air and ground staff as well as colour for the aircraft. Towards the end of the year four Airbus A330s were ordered to replace the A310s.

Airline acquisition continues with 36% of Lauda Air in 1997 along with an increase in its Tyrolean share to 85.6% - reaching 100% in 1999. The Lauda share was increased to 54.6% in 2001 and is now 100%. 1998 saw the inaugural flight to New York with the A330 and additional orders for another A321 and six A320s. Profits continue and have reached ATS 189.4 million - the best ever for Austrian Airlines.

ABOVE: *Austrian Airlines A321-111, OE-LBB (C/n 570) with Austrian Millenium Anniversary Colours (Airbus)*

Another record with annual passenger levels passing the 8 million mark came in 1999. In 2000 Austrian Airlines became a member of the Star Alliance and the last of its A310s was retired.

An announcement of the takeover of 100% of Rheintalflug shares by Austrian Airlines came in 2001.

The Austrian Government came to the aid of Austrian Airlines following the September 11th atrocity by providing temporary underwriting for war risk insurance. Although the tragedy affected Austrian Airlines it had been in good health and passenger figures are rising steadily once again.

BELOW: *Austrian Airlines A330-223, OE-LAP 9C/n 317) with the airbus test registration F-WWYQ (Airbus)*

Avianca

A V I A N C A

Registered name: Aerovias Nacionales de Colombia SA

Country: Colombia

Region: South America

Address: Avenida Eldorado No. 93-30
Santa Fe de Bogotá

Tel: 0057 1 413 95 11

Fax: 0057 1 263 73 76

Web site: www.avianca.com.co or www.avianca.com

Main operational base: Bogotá

ABOVE: *Avianca 767-284ER, N988AN (C/n 24742) Leased from Pacific AirCorp and opertating with a US registration (Jeremy Flack/API)*

STATUS

IATA scheduled carrier

National Flag Carrier

Employees: 3,608

Passengers per year: 4,493,000 (2001)

ICAO code: AVA

IATA code: AV

SERVICES

International / Regional / Domestic

Passenger / Cargo

International routes: Argentina, Brazil, Chile, Ecuador, France, Germany, Mexico, Panama, Spain, Peru, UK, USA, Venezuela

ALLIANCES / CODE SHARES

Air France, TACA, TAROM

OWNED SUBSIDIARY AIRLINES

SAM Colombia (Sociedad Aeronautica de Medellin Consolidad SA), Helicol (Helicopteros Nacionales de Colombia SA)

FLEET

727-200Adv - 1, 757-200 - 4, 767-200ER - 3, 767-300ER - 1, Fokker 50 - 10, MD-83 - 13

Avianca has one of the longest records of unbroken scheduled service. It was formed on December 5th, 1919, as Sociedad Colombo-Alermana de Transportes Aereos (SCADTA) by German and Colombian businessmen. The first service did not commence until September 1921 when a Junkers F13 seaplane was flown from Bogotá to Barranquilla.

In 1931 Pan American took an 80% stake in SCADTA and in 1933 merged the small domestic carrier Servicio Aereo Colombiano. Around the same time the name of SCADTA was changed to Avianca. In 1941 Aerovias Ramales Colombianos was taken over and from August 1946 Avianca operated a domestic service for the Ecuadorian Government.

International routes commenced with DC-4s stretching to Europe subsequently being replaced with Constellations. In 1951, following the ending of the Ecuadorial arrangement, Avianca decided to strengthen its own domestic operation and took over Lineas Aereas Nacionales (LANSA) together with its substantial network.

During the 1960s Avianca took delivery of 707 and 727 jet airliners adding 747s and 757s during the 1980s. On February 28th 2002 Avianca announced that Avianca, SAM and ACES would be integrated. Ownership would by held jointly by Valores Bavaria and the Federation of Coffee Growers as equal partners.

AzzurraAir

Registered name: AzzurraAir

Country: Italy

Region: Europe

Address: Via Paleocapa 3/D
I-24122 Bergamo

Tel: 0039 035 416 03 11

Fax: 0039 035 416 03 00

Web site: www.azzurraair.it

Stockholder: Gallarate

Main operational base: Bergamo

STATUS

IATA scheduled international, domestic and charter carrier

Employees: 400+

Passengers per year: 1,201,852 (2001) - Includes charters

ICAO code: AZI

IATA code: ZS

SERVICES

Regional / Domestic / Passenger

Charter / Cargo

International routes: Denmark, Greece, Germany, Netherlands, Portugal, Spain, Sweden

ALLIANCES / CODE SHARES

Alitalia

FLEET

737-700 - 5, RJ70 - 4, RJ85 - 3

AZZURRAAir was formed by Air Malta on December 20th, 1995, with BAe146s to operate from Bergamo to London, Munich and Paris.

When Air Malta decided to reduce its part in AZZURRAAir after a year of operation, Alitalia entered into a collaborative agreement in 1998. This has led to AZZURRAAir flying its aircraft on behalf of Alitalia.

RIGHT: *AzzurraAir Avro RJ85, EI-CNI (C/n E2299) (David McIntosh/BAe)*

Bahamasair

Registered name: Bahamasair Holding Ltd
Country: Bahamas
Region: Central America & Caribbean
Address: Windsor Field
P.O.Box N 4881
Nassau
Tel: 001 242 377 84 51
Fax: 001 242 377 74 09
Web site: www.bahamasair.com
Main operational base: Nassau

STATUS

Scheduled passenger carrier
National Flag Carrier
Employees: 750
Passengers per year: 1,593,000 (2001)
ICAO code: BHS
IATA code: UP

SERVICES

International / Regional / Domestic
Passenger / Cargo
International routes: USA, Turks & Caicos

FLEET

737-300 - 2, DHC-8 Dash 8 - 5

Bahamasair was formed, with assistance from BOAC, on June 18th, 1973, as the national airline for the Bahamas, which had just received independence.

Services commenced straight away with the DC-3 operating the routes of Flamingo Airlines and Out Island Airways which had been acquired. The BAC 1-11 and HS748 were operated shortly after, together with several Aero Commanders and Short SD360s later on. The Bahamas Government took complete control of Bahamasair in 1980.

The 1-11s have given way to the 737 while the HS748 have been replaced by Dash 8.

A fresh company image, including aircraft colour schemes, was instigated following a change in the Board of Directors and management team in 2000.

RIGHT: *Bahamasair DHC-8 Dash 8 (Bombardier)*

Bangkok Airways

Registered name: Bangkok Airways CI Ltd
Country: Thailand
Region: Asia
Address: 60 Queen Sirkit National Convention
Centre
New Rattadpisek Rd
Klongtoey
Bangkok 10110
Tel: 0066 2 229 34 56
Fax: 0066 2 229 34 54
Web site: www.bangkokair.com
Main operational base: Bangkok

STATUS

Scheduled carrier
Employees: 777
Passengers per year: 751,400 (1999)
ICAO code: BKP
IATA code: PG

SERVICES

International / Regional / Domestic
Passenger / Charter
International routes: Cambodia, China,
Laos, Singapore, Vietnam,

ALLIANCES / CODE SHARES

Siem Ream Int.

FLEET

ATR 72-200 - 8, ATR 72-500 - 2, 717-200 - 4

ABOVE: *Bangkok Airways ATR 72-212A, HS-PGL (C/n 670) (Via Avaireps)*

Bangkok Airways initially began operating in 1968 as Sahakol Air operating a privately owned air taxi service with a ten-seat twin-engined Tradewind. A substantial part of these early operations was in support of the oil and gas exploration business. In 1986 the name was changed to Bangkok Airways about which time tourism to Thailand began to increase and this was reflected in the expanding number of routes. In 2000, Bangkok Airways became the first Asian airline to operate the Boeing 717 when it took delivery of the first of two on lease from Pembroke Capital.

Bangkok Airways also own the airports at Samui and Sukhotai, these two being joined by Trad in December 2002.

Belavia

Registered name: Belavia Belarussian Airlines
Country: Belarus
Region: Europe
Address: Nemiga 14
Minsk
220004
Tel: 00375 172 28 22 90
Fax: 00375 172 29 23 83
Web site: www.belavia.net
Main operational base: Minsk National Airport

STATUS

National Flag Carrier
Passengers per year: 313,000 (2001)
ICAO code: BRU
IATA code: B2

RIGHT: *Belavia Tu-154M, EW-85706 (Jane's)*

SERVICES

International / Passenger
Charter / Cargo
International routes: Austria, Cyprus, Germany, Ireland, Israel, Italy, Kazakhstan, Poland, Russia, Turkey, UK, Ukraine, Uzbekistan

ALLIANCES / CODE SHARES

Scheduled and charter passenger + cargo carrier

FLEET

Tu-134A - 16, Tu-134A-3 - 2, Tu-154B-2 - 15, Tu-154M - 5

Belavia was formed on March 5th, 1996, by the Belorussian Government when the local Aeroflot Division was nationalised and renamed.

Although Belarus had a history of air transport dating back 60 years, most of this was dominated by Aeroflot. The current

fleet comprises the aircraft from the local Aeroflot division.

As the national airline and with Minsk as its base, Belavia is steadily increasing its network of routes throughout Europe.

Biman Bangladesh Airlines

Registered name: Bangladesh Biman Corporation
Country: Bangladesh
Region: Asia
Address: Balaka
Zia International Airport
Kurmitola, Dhaka 1206
Tel: 00880 2 89 73 86
Fax: 00880 2 89 30 05
Web site: www.bangladeshonline.com/biman/
Main operational base: Zia International Airport

STATUS

IATA scheduled carrier
National Flag Carrier
Employees: 5,536
Passengers per year: 1,450,000 (2001)

ICAO code: BBC
IATA code: BG

SERVICES

International / Regional / Domestic
Passenger / Cargo
International routes: Bahrain, Belgium, China, France, Germany, India, Italy, Japan, Kuwait, Malaysia, Myanmar, Nepal, Oman, Saudi Arabia, Singapore, Thailand, UAE, UK, USA

ALLIANCES / CODE SHARES

Scheduled passenger + cargo carrier

FLEET

A310-300 - 3, ATP - 2, DC-10-30 - 5, F-27 Mk.4000 - 3

ABOVE: *Bangladesh Airlines A310-325, S2-ADE (C/n 698) with Airbus test registration F-WWCF (Airbus)*

Air Bangladesh was formed on January 4th, 1972, with a DC-3 but the name was changed to Biman Bangladesh Airlines before operations as the national flag carrier commenced a month later. The ex-military Dakota was joined shortly after by F-27 Friendships and 707s. These enabled Biman Bangladesh Airlines to establish a number of routes in the Far East and as far as London to the west. Biman Bangladesh Airlines took delivery of the first of three DC-10s in 1983. Three more were subsequently added together with four A310s for the long and medium haul routes. F-28 Fellowships and BAe ATPs have replaced the F-27s for the domestic services.

Binter Canarias

Registered name: Binter Canarias SA
Country: Spain
Region: Europe
Address: Aeropuerto de Gran Canaria
Parcela 9
del Zima
E-35230
Tel: 0034 9 28 57 96 01
Fax: 0034 9 28 57 96 04
Web site: www.bintercanarias.com
Stockholder: Hisperia de Inversions Aéreas, S.A.
Main operational base: Aeropuerto de Gran Canaria

STATUS
Scheduled regional carrier
Employees: 298
Passengers per year: 2,200,000 (2001)
ICAO code: IBB
IATA code: NT

SERVICES
Regional / Domestic / Passenger
International routes: Portugal

FLEET
ATR 72-200 - 9, ATR 72-500 - 2

Binter Canarias was founded on February 18th, 1988, as a subsidiary of Grupo Iberia. It commenced operations on March 26th as a regional carrier on the Canary archipelago flying four CN-235s.

Six ATR 72s were gradually added to the fleet as the routes expanded to link Gran Canaria, Tenerife, La Palma and Fuerteventura, followed by Lanzarote and El Hierro.

Three DC-9s were leased from Iberia and operated between 1995 and 1998.

Binter Canarias underwent a reorganisation in 1996 and a further three ATR 72 were ordered for delivery the following year. Another two were ordered in 1999.

The CN235 were withdrawn in 1997.

By now Binter was equipped with a fleet of ATR 72s; however, a BAe ATP was leased from British World Airlines to help cover the peak months of the Spring and Summer during 2001 to help operate the extensive inter island service.

The entire equity of Binter Canarias was sold to a consortium of island investors in March 2002.

LEFT: *Binter Canarias ATR 72-212A (C/n 582) also sporting the ATR test registration F-WWEL (EADS)*

bmi British Midland

Registered name: British Midland Airways Ltd
Country: UK
Region: Europe
Address: Donnington Hall
Castle Donnington
Derby, DE74 2SB
Tel: 0044 1332 85 40 00
Fax: 0044 1332 85 46 62
Web site: www.flybmi.com
Stockholder: British Midland PLC.
Main operational base: East Midlands Airport

STATUS
IATA scheduled and charter passenger carrier
Employees: 4,575

Passengers per year: 6,730,000 (2001)
ICAO code: BMA
IATA code: BD

SERVICES
International / Regional / Domestic Passenger / Charter / Cargo
International routes: Belgium, Denmark, Germany, Ireland, Italy, Netherlands, Spain, USA

ALLIANCES / CODE SHARES
Star Alliance / Air France, Aurigly Air Service, Malaysia A/l, South African Aw, TAO, Virgin Atlantic Aw

OWNED SUBSIDIARY AIRLINES
bmi regional, bmibaby.

FLEET
A320-200 - 10, A321-100 - 10, A330-200 - 4 (1 leased to SAA), 737-300 - 2, 737-400 - 1, 737 500 - 8, ERJ-135 - 2, ERJ-145 - 9, Fokker 100 - 6, Fokker 70 - 3
On order: A320-200 - 2 (plus 1 option), ERJ-135 - 2, ERJ-145 - 2 (plus 5 options)

British Midland commenced life as Air Schools Ltd in 1938 and specialised in pilot instruction for the RAF who desperately needed new pilots for the war that was

rapidly approaching.

As the military established major training programmes in the USA and around the Commonwealth the need for the British Midland service declined. The de Havilland Rapides were used to provide ad hoc passenger and cargo service.

Derby Aviation was formed in 1949 at Burnaston, near Derby, to operate passenger charter services. It commenced its first scheduled service in July 1953. These were flown from Wolverhampton to Jersey via Birmingham using the Handley Page Marathon and DC-3.

The same year the flying instruction for the RAF ended.

Derby Aviation was renamed in 1959 as Derby Airways and again in October 1964 as British Midlands Airways (BMA). About the same time saw the introduction of the familiar blue and white scheme associated with British Midland.

In 1965 BMA moved from the grass airfield to the new East Midlands Airport. This enabled larger aircraft to be operated into Europe. The first Viscount was delivered in 1967 which replaced the Argonauts and DC-3s. BMA was acquired by the banking and investment group Minster Assets in 1968.

BMA entered the jet age when the BAC 1-11 entered service in early 1970 for European charters but these were short-lived. During the 1970s BMA acquired a number of 707s that it leased out to other airlines, especially to newly starting carriers who were unable to purchase their own aircraft. This was referred to as its 'Instant Airline' programme. Transatlantic charter flights were operated from 1974 for British Caledonian and in 1978 BMA and British Airways agreed to some route swapping in which BMA gained a number of domestic routes in exchange for the Birmingham to Brussels and Frankfurt routes.

A number of BMA directors purchased the principal shareholding from Minster Assets in 1974 and in 1979 annual passengers carried passed the million mark. In the same year BMA was awarded the Queen's Award for Export Achievement for the 'Instant Airline' programme. It had assisted 25 carriers get started and earned £40 million in foreign exchange.

ABOVE: *bmi A320-232, G-MIDV (C/n 1383) (Airbus)*

BMA commenced its first scheduled service in April 1980 from Leeds / Bradford to Heathrow. The following year BMA launched a programme to get into the 1982 holiday market with the introduction of flights from East Midlands to 10 Mediterranean resorts.

Following an initial rejection by the CAA, BMA obtained approval to operate Heathrow to Edinburgh and Glasgow services. These were in direct competition with British Airways and the first commenced in 1982.

BMA changed title to British Midland in

BELOW: *bmi 737-36N, G-ECAS (C/n 28554) in their previous British Midland International clour (Jeremy Flack/API)*

bmi British Midland

LEFT: *bmi Fokker 100, G-BVJD (C/n 11503) in the colours prior to that on the 737 on the previous page (Jeremy Flack/API)*

1985 and modified its colour scheme.

SAS announced it was taking a 24.9% share in BM worth £25 million in 1988 which it increased to 35% in 1992 and 40% in 1994.

The Diamond EuroClass was introduced in 1993 to provide the business class with a separate cabin and addition in flight services was introduced on European routes and subsequently extended to most regional routes.

In 1997, British Midland placed a $1 billion order for 11 A320s and nine A321s - the largest UK order that had so far been placed with Airbus. This was followed by a $500 million order with Embraer for its regional jets in 1998.

An announcement was made that Lufthansa was to take a stake in British Midland by purchasing half of the SAS 40%.

As a result, British Midland joined the Star Alliance in July 2000. Meanwhile, a $1.9 billion order is placed for four A330-200s.

During 2001 plans were announced regarding the retiring of the 737s and the possible replacement of the Fokker 50 with A318.

British Midland underwent a re-branding in 2001 and changed its name to bmi British Midland. At the same time new international services to Washington and Chicago was launched with A330s. BM Commuter was renamed British Midland Regional Ltd and commenced trading as bmi regional.

bmi increased its order with Embraer in 2001 from eight to 10 ERJ145s and from two to four of the ERJ135s.

bmi had been lobbying for a number of years against the regulations that restricted the number of transatlantic operators, reducing competition and allowing higher fares. In December 2001, the US Department of Justice (DOJ) accepted that United's application to add bmi British Midland to its existing antitrust immunity with Lufthansa, SAS, and Austrian Group posed no risk to competition.

An announcement by bmi in January 2002 gave details of the launch of a new low-cost no-frills airline - bmibaby. Initially equipped with two of its own 737s, the new airline was designed to offer high frequency services to various Mediterranean destinations with fares starting at £25 one way. However, its success has resulted in the expansion of routes to over 30 destinations from its hubs at East Midlands and Cardiff with another hub possible for 2003.

Over the years British Midland has been an innovative airline being at the front with a number of new services. These have ranged from vegetarian meals on UK domestic routes in 1992, internet booking and payment in 1995 and installing Tempus 2000 – an integrated telemedicine service – added to long-haul routes.

In October 2002 the BBW Partnership sold 10% of the British Midland PLC shares to Lufthansa bringing its holding up to 30% less one share. SAS retains 20% while BBW maintains overall control with 50% plus one share.

Braathens

Registered name: Braathens ASA
Country: Norway
Region: Europe
Address: Oksenoyveien 3
PO Box 55
Fornebu N-1330
Tel: 0047 67 59 70 00
Fax: 0047 67 58 06 63
Web site: www.braathens.no
Stockholder: SAS Group
Main operational base: Gardermoen, Oslo

STATUS

IATA scheduled and charter carrier
Employees: 2,200
Passengers per year: 5,757,000 (2001)
ICAO code: BRA
IATA code: BU

SERVICES

Regional / Domestic / Passenger Charter / Cargo
International routes: France, Ireland, Italy, Spain, UK

FLEET

737-400 - 5, 737-500 - 15, 737-700 - 7

Braathens was originally formed on March 28th, 1946, as the charter element of the Braathens Shipping Company and commenced operations in February 1947 with the intention of serving the Norwegian fleet throughout the world. A scheduled service was inaugurated by Braathens in 1949 using a DC-4 flying from Oslo to Hong Kong taking four days. A route to Venezuela via

Iceland followed which resulted in the name being amended by the addition of SAFE (South American and Far East).

Norwegian Government policy put a halt to these international routes and plans for any new ones when it decided all international services would be provided by the national carrier - SAS.

As a result, Braathens SAFE continued to develop its domestic scheduled operations that commenced in 1952 with the de Havilland Heron. These have been the subject of Braathens core business together with the original charter business.

The Herons were replaced by F-27 Friendships. Braathens SAFE entered the jet age with its first two 737s in January 1969 and has standardised on this type apart from a short period in 1984 with a pair of 767s which it found uneconomical.

Braathens SAFE acquired 50% of

Transwede in 1996 and the balance at the end of the following year to be renamed Braathens Sweden. In 1998, Malmo Aviation was also acquired and the two operate an integrated service with the latter now named Braathens Malmo.

In December 2001, SAS acquired the

ABOVE: *Braathens 737-705, LN-TUI (C/n 29094) (Braathens)*

entire stockholding and the name returned to Braathens.

British Airways

Registered name: British Airways plc
Country: UK
Region: Europe
Address: Waterside
PO Box 365
Harmondsworth, UB7 0GB
Tel: 0044 208 875 95 51 (Local 08457 79 99 77)
Fax: 0044 208 562 99 30
Web site: www.britishairways.com
Main operational base: London Heathrow + Gatwick

STATUS

IATA scheduled international and domestic + charter carrier
National Flag Carrier
Employees: 62,175
Passengers per year: 38,575,000 (2001)
ICAO code: BAW
IATA code: BA

SERVICES

International / Regional / Domestic
Passenger / Charter (one off only) / Cargo
International routes: Antigua & Barbuda,
Argentina*, Armenia*, Australia*, Austria*, Azerbaijan*, Bahamas, Bahrain, Barbados, Belgium*, Bermuda, Brazil, Bulgaria, Cayman Islands, Canada, China, Chile*, Colombia, Cyprus, Czech, Denmark*, Djibouti*, Egypt, Eritrea*, Estonia*, Ethiopia*, Finland, France, Georgia*, Germany, Gibraltar*, Ghana, Greece, Grenada, Hungary, India, Iran*, Ireland*, Israel, Italy, Jamaica, Japan, Kazakhstan*, Kenya*, Kosovo, Kuwait, Kyrgyzstan*, Latvia*, Lebanon*, Libya, Luxembourg, Malaysia, Mexico, Malawi, Mauritius,

Morocco*, Netherlands, New Zealand*, Nigeria, Norway*, Oman, Peru*, Poland*, Portugal*, Romania, Russia, St Lucia, Saudi Arabia, Serbia, Seychelles, Singapore*, South Africa*, Spain*, Sudan*, Sweden*, Switzerland*, Syria*, Tanzania, Thailand*, Trinidad & Tobago, Tunisia, Turkey, Turks & Caicos Islands, Uganda, Ukraine, UAE, USA, Uzbekistan*, Venezuela, Zambia*, Zimbabwe* (*code share)

BELOW: *British Airways A319-131, G-EUPA (C/n 1082) (Jane's)*

British Airways

LEFT: *British Airways Concorde 102, G-BOAF (C/n 100-016) British Airways*

ABOVE: *British Airways 747-436, G-BNLJ (C/n 24052) with one of the previous 'ethnic' tail schemes (Jeremy Flack/API)*

ALLIANCES / CODE SHARES

Oneworld / America West, British Mediterranean, GB Airways, Emirates, LOT, Swiss

OWNED SUBSIDIARY AIRLINES

British Airways CitiExpress, Deutsche BA

FLEET

A319 - 33, A320 - 13, BAe 146 - 5, Concorde - 7, 737-400 - 31, 737-500 - 10, 747-400 - 56, 757-200 - 23, 767-300 - 21, 777-200 - 45, ERJ-145 - 29, RJ100 - 16
On order: A318 - 6, A319 - 6

The origins of British Airways can be traced back to August 25th, 1919, when Air Transport and Travel (AT&T) was formed. The initial service was to Paris with a DH-4A and was followed by other continental routes.

AT&T, which had become Daimler Airways, together with Instone, Handley Page and British Air Maritime Navigation were merged in 1924 to form Imperial Airways. This was to be the flag carrier to develop international service.

A private airline named British Airways was formed in 1935 from a number of small operations and based at Gatwick. It competed directly with Imperial Airways on European routes.

Following a British Government review, Imperial Airways and British Airways were merged in 1939 to form the state-owned British Overseas Airways Corporation (BOAC).

Imperial Airways had operated a wide range of aircraft, from various sources, such as the de Havilland 86, Fokker F.12, Junkers Ju52 and Lockheed 10 Electra.

Unable to operate a normal service during the war, BOAC continued to fly a makeshift operation providing capacity wherever needed. In the early days this could be flying troops or armaments, collecting ball bearings from Sweden or moving aircrews across the Atlantic to ferry aircraft back. Although they had BOAC logos, flying unarmed camouflaged aircraft often on military business, they suffered numerous losses from German combat aircraft.

As the war progressed, BOAC established a fleet of flying boats and commenced a series of long-haul communications routes. A number of converted military aircraft were introduced in the form of Halifax Lancasters, Liberators, Mosquitos, Warwicks and Whitleys. A number of transports such as the C-47 Dakota and York were also used.

After the war BOAC flew the long-haul routes around the world apart from South America. These routes were flown by British South American Airways (BSAA) until 1949 when it was merged into BOAC.

Constellations and Sandringhams augmented the C-47s, Lancastrians, Sunderlands and Yorks. Meanwhile British European Airways Corporation had been formed on August 1st, 1946 to operate the domestic and European routes initially as a division within BOAC. In February 1947 BEA was nationalised in its own right along with 14 other small pre-war airlines that had provided the pre-war domestic network but had run down during the war. Over the next two decades a plethora of aircraft types were operated by BOAC including the British Solent flying boat and the Hermes, the Canadian Argonaut (an improved DC-4 with British Merlin engines) and the American Stratocruiser. The first de Havilland Comet took BOAC into the jet age in 1951 with the service commencing the following year. Three were lost in various accidents that were explainable.

RIGHT: *British Airwyas 757-236, G-BIKR (C/n 22189) (Jeremy Flack/API)*

However, when one broke up departing from Rome in 1954 the aircraft was grounded in a blaze of publicity. A second was subsequently lost which resulted in the manufacturer – de Havilland – loosing its market lead to the 707.

More important to BOAC, it was now short of aircraft by some 20% of its current and planned fleet. As a result many routes had to be cut.

Aircraft were hurriedly acquired including DC-7 and Super Constellation. The Britannia arrived in the mid-1950s followed by the 707 and the revised Comet 4 in 1958 - seven years after the original. The VC10, which entered service with BOAC in 1964, represented a leap forward in the jet airliner both in passenger comfort and range. Their introduction saw the demise of the

BELOW: *British Airways RJ100, G-BZAT (C/n E3320) operated as CityFlyer Express. (David McIntosh/BAE)*

Comet and Britannia.

The first of the 747 wide-body 'jumbo jets' arrived in 1969 and enabled a major increase in capacity. In 1974, BEA and BOAC were merged to form British Airways (BA). This initially led to financial losses while adjustments were made but the pioneering spirit prevailed and in January 1976 Concorde entered service.

BA was privatised in 1987 and subsequently acquired British Caledonian Airways which was merged in April 1988.

A new type for BA joined the fleet in the form of the BAe ATP that entered service in January 1989 on regional routes while the 747-400 commenced on long-haul in July. In February 1990 the 767 entered service.

A $4.3 billion order was announced in August 1991 for 15 - 777s plus 24 - 747-400s and 11 - ATPs plus options.

British Airways

ABOVE: *British Airways Citiespress ERJ145EU (C/n 145300) (Jane's)*

CityFlyer Express (formed 1991) was acquired in 1999 after having been operating as British Airways Express since 1993. During the mid-1990s a new image was created for BA which resulted in the removal of the traditional Union flag on the tail for a series of ethnic artworks. It had lost its national identity and simultaneously passenger numbers dropped. BA is placed fifth largest on the list of cargo airlines although it does not operate any pure freight aircraft. British Airways World Cargo was established as a separate full profit centre and exclusively purchases all the belly-hold cargo space throughout the fleet. In addition it has arrangements with JAL, Singapore Airlines, Korean Air Lines and EVA airways. Further capacity is acquired as required. BA purchased British Regional Airlines Group (BRAL - formed March 1991) in May 2001 and entered negotiation with KLM over a possible merger.

A co-ordinated return to service of Concorde in November with Air France was made after modifications following the crash of the Air France aircraft in July 2000. In early October 2001 the various subsidiary regional airlines (BRAL, Brymon (commenced operations in 1972) and Manx Airlines (originally formed 1947 and reformed 1982) were integrated to form British Airways CitiExpress. This creates Europe's second largest regional airline which will carry an estimated 5 million passengers a year with its 92 aircraft.

British Airways – Comair

Registered name: Comair Ltd
Country: South Africa
Region: Africa
Address: PO Box 7015
              Bonaero Park 1622
Tel: 0027 11 921 01 11
Fax: 0027 11 973 16 58
Web site: www.ba.co.za
Main operational base: Johannesburg
International Airport

STATUS

IATA scheduled regional and domestic carrier

Employees: 791
Passengers per year: 1,287,000 (2001)
ICAO code: CAW
IATA code: MN

SERVICES

Regional / Domestic
Passenger / Cargo
International routes: Namibia, Zambia, Zimbabwe

ALLIANCES / CODE SHARES

Air Namibia, BA

OWNED SUBSIDIARY AIRLINES

Kalula

FLEET

727-200Adv - 6, 737-200 - 10, 737-400 - 2

Comair was registered as Commercial Air Services (Pty) in 1943 by three members of the South African Air Force. As colleagues in the North African desert during the war they discussed the idea of creating a charter airline.

The first operation was on July 14th 1946 and a variety of work was undertaken including air taxi as well as maintenance.

Its first scheduled service commenced in 1949 linking Johannesburg with Welkom. The routes were steadily expanded and passenger numbers grew.

The name was changed to Commercial Airways in November 1967.

Early equipment included the ex-military C-47 / DC-3 Dakotas to which the Cessna 401 and 404 were subsequently added. The first F-27 Friendship arrived in 1976 and they gradually replaced the Dakotas. These brought about a substantial increase in passenger numbers with their increased comfort.

By 1992 Comair was operating the main domestic routes and carried 100,000 passengers. A franchise agreement was signed with British Airways in October 1996. This resulted in the BA brand name being used to create a higher-profile awareness although all the services were provided by Comair. The first aircraft flew in BA colours later that month. By the end of the year around 1 million passengers had been carried. Comair became a public listed company in July 1998.

A low-cost subsidiary - Kalula - was launched in August 2001.

A five year contract was signed with SAA at the end of October 2002 to provide maintenance for Comair's fleet of 737s.

British Mediterranean Airways

Registered name: British Mediterranean Airways Ltd
Country: UK
Region: Europe
Address: Cirrus House, Bedfont Road
London Heathrow Airport
Staines, TW19 7NL
Tel: 0044 (0)1784 26 63 00
Fax: 0044 (0)1784 26 63 54
Web site: www.britishmediterranean.com
Stockholder: British Airways
Main operational base: London Heathrow

ABOVE: *British Mediterranean Airways A320-232, G-MEDE (C/n 1194) (British Mediterranean Airways)*

STATUS
Scheduled carrier
Employees: 380
Passengers per year: 211,500 (2001)
ICAO code: LAJ
IATA code: KJ

SERVICES
International / Passenger / Cargo
International routes: Armenia, Azerbaijan, Egypt, Ethiopia, Georgia, Iran, Jordan, Kazakhstan, Kyrgyzstan, Lebanon, Syria, Uzbekistan

ALLIANCES / CODE SHARES
Oneworld

FLEET
A320-200 - 2, A321-200 - 2

British Mediterranean Airways was formed in 1994 and commenced operations on October 28th of that year providing a service to Beirut with an A320.

Following a failed attempt in 1996, a franchise partnership was agreed in 1997 resulting in British Mediterranean Airways operating as the sole UK carrier to Amman, Beirut and Damascus. As a result, the aircraft markings were changed to the standard BA scheme.

As additional routes to the Middle East, Asia and Africa were added so the fleet has expanded with A321s and further A320s and, in 2002, A321s.

BELOW: *British Mediterranean Airways Airbus A321-231, G-MEDG (C/n 1711) (British Mediterranean Airways)*

BWIA British West Indies Airways

Registered name: BWIA West Indies Airways Ltd
Country: Trinidad & Tobago
Region: Central America & Caribbean
Address: Administration Building
Piarco International Airport
PO Box 604
Port of Spain
Tel: 001 868 669 30 00
Fax: 001 868 669 15 20
Web site: www.bwee.com
Main operational base: Port of Spain - Piarco International

STATUS
IATA scheduled international carrier
National Flag Carrier
Employees: 2,510
Passengers per year: 1,129,000 (2001)
ICAO code: BWA
IATA code: BW

SERVICES
International / Regional
Passenger / Cargo
International routes: Antigua, Canada, Grenada, Jamaica, Netherlands Antilles, St Lucia, UK, USA, Venezuela

ALLIANCES / CODE SHARES
United A/l

OWNED SUBSIDIARY AIRLINES
BWee Express

FLEET
A340-300 - 2, 737-800 - 6, DHC-8 Dash 8-Q300 - 2, L.1011 Tristar 600 - 1, MD-83 - 2

British West Indian Airways was formed in 1939 to provide an airlink to the islands of Trinidad and Tobago. For this they operated a Lockheed Lodestar.

BWIA British West Indies Airways

In 1948 BWIA was sold to British South American Airways. However, the link between the islands continued to operate as BWIA. The following year BSAA was absorbed into BOAC. BWIA continued to operate as a subsidiary and was equipped with Viscounts for regional routes. By the 1960s, in an expanded role, Britannias were operated for the international link to London that was routed via New York.

The Goverment of Trinidad and Tobago bought shares and took complete ownership in the mid-1960s. Around the same time the Viscounts were replaced with 727s and 707s were introduced for longer routes.

In 1980 BWIA was merged with the domestic Trinidad and Tobago Air Service and renamed BWIA International. As the national carrier a new type was introduced

ABOVE: *British West Indies Airways L1011 Tristar 500, 9Y-TGN (C/n 1191) (Jane's)*

in the form of the Tristar.

On February 2nd 1995 BWIA was privatised although the government retained 33.5% of the company. However, the financial health of BWIA has suffered along with many of the world's airlines. As a result it is currently looking to rationalise its fleet.

Cameroon Airlines

Country: Cameroon
Region: Africa
Address: 3 Avenue General de Gaulle
PO Box 4092
Douala
Tel: 00237 42 01 11
Fax: 00237 42 25 13
Web site: www.camairsa.co.za
Main operational base: Douala

STATUS
IATA scheduled international and domestic carrier
National Flag Carrier
Employees: 1,476

Passengers per year: 247,000 (2001)
ICAO code: UYC
IATA code: UY

SERVICES
International / Regional / Domestic
Passenger / Cargo
International routes: Benin, Burundi, Chad, Congo, Cote D'Ivoire, Democratic Republic of Congo, Equatorial Guinea, France, Gabon, Kenya, Nigeria, Rwanda, South Africa, UK, Zimbabwe

FLEET
737-200 - 1, 737-300 - 2, 767-200 - 1, 767-300ER - 1, CRJ200 - 1, CRJ700 - 1, HS748 - 1

Cameroon Airlines was formed with the assistance of Air France on July 26th, 1971, following the Cameroon Government decision to withdraw from Air Afrique. Initial equipment was two 737s.

Services commenced in November and soon included domestic and regional routes. A 707, acquired in November 1972, enabled international routes into Europe. The 707 was replaced in the early 80s with a 747 and three HS748s acquired for short-haul routes.

Cathay Pacific Airways

Registered name: Cathay Pacific Airways Ltd
Country: China
Region: Far East
Address: 35/F, Two Pacific Place
    88 Queensway
    Hong Kong
Tel: 00852 27 47 50 00
Fax: 00852 28 10 65 63
Web site: www.cathaypacific.com
Main operational base: Chep Lap Kok

STATUS

IATA scheduled international passenger carrier

Employees: 14,500
Passengers per year: 11,300,000 (2001)
ICAO code: CPA
IATA code: CX

SERVICES

International / Regional
Passenger / Cargo

International routes: Australia, Bahrain, China, France, Germany, India, Indonesia, Italy, Japan*, Malaysia, Netherlands, New Zealand, Philippines*, S Korea, Saudi Arabia, Singapore, South Africa*, Sri Lanka, Taiwan, Thailand, Turkey, UAE, UK*, USA, Vietnam (*code share)

ALLIANCES / CODE SHARES

OneWorld /AHK Air Hong Kong, JAL, Malaysia A/1, PAL, SAA, THY

OWNED SUBSIDIARY AIRLINES

Air Hong Kong

FLEET

A330-300 - 23, A340-300 - 15, A340-600 - 3, 747-200F - 7 (3 leased to AHK - 2 not in service), 747-300 - 6 (all but one leased out), 747-400 - 17, 747-400F - 5, 777-200 - 5, 777-300 - 7
On order: A330-300 - 3, 777-300 - 3

Cathay Pacific Airways was formed on September 24th, 1946, and operated primarily a charter passenger and freight service using DC-3s. As the result of an agreement, Cathay operated to the south of Hong Kong while Hong Kong Airways operated to the north. The Swire Group became a major shareholder in 1948 and two Catalinas were added to the seven DC-3s to enable service to reach across to the Philippines, Singapore and Thailand.

The DC-4, DC-6 and Lockheed Electra were added in turn while the Cathay route network continued to expand rapidly. In 1959 Cathay acquired Hong Kong Airways that enabled it to operate not only into China but other potentially lucrative routes including Japan.

Cathay entered the jet age with the Convair 880s in 1962 which were subsequently replaced by 707s from 1971.

Service to Australia commenced in 1974 while the first Tristar was received in August 1975.

Cathay eventually managed to obtain approval for a route to link with London in 1980 which it operated with the newly received 747s. Cathay retired its last Tristar in October 1996 which had been the work-horse of the fleet for 21 years.

In 1998 Cathay recorded its first loss brought about by the economic collapse of several of the regional economies. Following an HQ move and consolidation, which enabled a reduction in staff by about 5,000, and an upturn in the Asian economy, profits and the success of the Oneworld alliance had turned to $641 million by 2000.

Cathay was one of the first airlines to complete an upgrade to its First Class cabins in the long-haul jets. In addition to the seats which easily recline into a full-length bed, personal TV / video units allow selection from a range of 45 films with hold and replay facility. Emails can be sent to anywhere in the world and catering offers 'a la carte' or buffet to be cooked at a time to suit the passengers.

The effects of September 11th were far reaching and Cathay suffered difficulties which were worse that 1998. This time the traditional 13th month bonus was cut as were a number of routes and frequencies. Six aircraft were also grounded. However, this time there were no job cuts.

The United Nations Children's Fund (UNICEF) presented Cathay with its "Leadership for Children" award in June 2002 because of the airline collecting unused currency from passengers that was donated to UNICEF. Over the past decade nearly US$5 million has been donated. Towards the end of 2002 passengers and freight levels start to improve again.

BELOW: *Cathay Pacific Airways 747-367, B-HIK (C/n 23534) with its original Hong Kong registration VR-HIK (Jeremy Flack/API)*

Cayman Airways

Registered name: Cayman Airways Ltd
Country: Cayman Islands
Region: Central America & Caribbean
Address: PO Box 1101 GT
Grand Cayman
Tel: 001 345 949 82 00
Fax: 001 345 949 76 07
Web site: www.caymanairways.com
Main operational base: Owen Roberts Airport

STATUS
Scheduled passenger and cargo carrier
National Flag Carrier
Employees: 320
Passengers per year: 297,000 (2001)
ICAO code: CAY
IATA code: KX

SERVICES
International / Regional / Domestic
Passenger / Cargo
International routes: Jamaica, USA,

ALLIANCES / CODE SHARES
United A/l

FLEET
737-200 - 3

Cayman Airways was formed in July 1968 as a successor to Cayman Brac Airways (formed 1955) - a LACSA subsidiary. It was 51% owned by the Cayman Government and 49% LACSA and continued to operate the two Cayman Brac BAC 1-11s and Islanders.

Cayman Airways was nationalised in 1977.

During the early 1980s a DC-6 was acquired for the freight role. The BAC 1-11s were replaced with a pair of 727s in 1982 and the Islander replaced with a Shorts 330.

By the mid-1990s the 727s were getting long in the tooth and were initially replaced with 737-400s but these were subsequently changed to the -200 model.

China Airlines

Registered name: China Airlines Ltd
Country: Taiwan
Region: Far East
Address: 131, Sec. 3,
3, Nankng East Road, Taipei,
Tel: 00886 2 27 15 22 33
Fax: 00886 2 25 14 57 54
Web site: www.china-airlines.com
Main operational base: Taipei and Kaohsiung

STATUS
Scheduled international and domestic
passenger + cargo carrier
Employees: 9,356
Passengers per year: 7,972,000 (2001)
ICAO code: CAL
IATA code: CI

SERVICES
International / Regional / Domestic
Passenger / Charter / Cargo
International routes: Australia, Canada, Germany, Guam, Hong Kong, India, Indonesia, Italy, Japan, Malaysia,

Netherlands, Philippines, Singapore, Thailand, UAE, USA, Vietnam

ALLIANCES / CODE SHARES
Garuda Indonesia, Vietnam A/l

OWNED SUBSIDIARY AIRLINES
CAL-Dynasty International Inc (inc CAL-Dynasty Aircraft Leasing Corp), Mandarin Airlines Ltd

FLEET
A300-600R - 12, A340-300 - 5, 737-800 - 11, 747-200F – 2, 747-400 - 13, 747-400F - 12
On order: 737-800 - 2 for delivery 4/2004,

BELOW: *China Airlines A340 (Airbus)*

A340-300 - 2 for delivery 7/2003 and 6/2004 + 1 option, 747-400F - 3 for delivery 7/2004, 8/2004 and 3/2007

China Airlines was founded on December 16th, 1959, by a group of retired air force specialists who pooled their savings. This was the first airline owned by Chinese and comprised 26 employees and two PBY Catalina flying boats.

In 1961 China Airlines was asked to parachute supplies into Laos. The following year war erupted in Vietnam and the airline was contracted to fly for the Vietnamese Government. From small beginnings this work enabled China Airlines to gradually establish a solid financial base. In 1962 a domestic scheduled service commenced and in 1965 it was designated the national carrier. The following year the first international route was flown to Saigon (now named Ho Chi Minh City) during which time it was operating C-46s, C-47s and Constellations.

The arrival of its first jet – a 727 – in March 1967 saw the commencement of the commercial scheduled service with modern aircraft. Routes to Hong Kong and Japan were inaugurated and these expanded and additional aircraft were purchased.

In 1968 Civil Air Transport was suspended. China Airlines took the opportunity to take over its domestic rights and added three YS-11s although one was lost in an accident.

In 1975 China Airlines leased its first 747 that it bought the following year and then took delivery of more over the next few years. In June 1982 the first of four Airbus A300s were delivered. In December 1982 a 767 was delivered and a route to Europe commenced the following year. New 747-400s and MD-11s arrived in the early 1990s to replace some of the earlier long-range models while 737s were added later for the shorter routes. After several years preparatory work China Airlines shares were offered for sale in 1993 and it became Taiwan's first publicly traded airline.

China Airlines underwent a revision of its corporate image that resulted in a new colour scheme for its fleet in 1995.

In May 2002 China Airlines suffered the loss of one of the 747s that broke up mysteriously in flight off the Taiwanese coast with all 225 on-board killed. This came at a bad time for China Airlines which had just about recovered from the most recent of a total of 12 fatal accidents that it had suffered since 1969.

China Eastern Airlines

Registered name: China Eastern Airlines Corporation Ltd
Country: China
Region: Far East
Address: 2550 Hongqiao Road
    Hong Qiao International Airport
    Shanghai 200335
Tel: 0086 21 62 68 62 68
Fax: 0086 21 62 68 61 16
Web site: www.ce-air.com
Main operational base: Hong Qiao Airport (Shanghai)

RIGHT: *China Eastern A300-605R, B-2318 (C/n 707) with Airbus test registration F-WWAU (Airbus)*

STATUS

IATA scheduled passenger carrier
Employees: 12,675
Passengers per year: 10,371,000 (2001)
ICAO code: CES
IATA code: MU

SERVICES

International / Regional / Domestic Passenger / Cargo
International routes: Australia, France, Germany, Japan, S Korea, Singapore, Spain, Thailand, USA

ALLIANCES / CODE SHARES

Air France, All Nippon Aw, American A/l, Asiana, JAL, Korean A/l, Qantas

FLEET

A300-600R - 10, A319 - 8, A320-200 - 17, A340-300 - 5, 737-300 - 6, 737-700 - 4, 747-200F - 1, MD-11 - 3 (options to convert to MD-11F), MD-11F - 3, MD-82 - 2, MD - 1, MD-90-30 - 9
On order: A319 - 2, A320-200 - 17 for delivery through 2005

China Eastern Airlines was originally part of the Civil Aviation Administration of China (CAAC) that provided all the airline services in China. Several Regional Administrations evolved which provided their service in specific parts of the county.

China Eastern Airlines

By 1991 these regions had developed further and the CAAC control released. China Eastern Airlines was originally formed from the CAAC Shanghai Division in 1988 as the China Eastern Air Group. It was equipped with MD-82s inherited from the CAAC to which MD-11s were added in 1993. These enabled routes to Europe and the USA to commence.

In 1997, China Eastern was listed on the Hong Kong Stock Exchange, New York Stock Exchange and Shanghai Stock Exchange.

Already the third largest Chinese air carrier, the airline continued to expand and, in June 2001, acquired Air Great Wall. It had been actively negotiating with China Yunnan and China Northwest concerning mergers that finally came into being when they were confirmed in 2002 as part of a reform of Chinese civil aviation.

ABOVE: *China Eastern A319-112, B-2331 (C/n 1285) (Jane's)*

China Northern Airlines

Registered name: China Northern Aviation Company
Country: China
Region: Far East
Address: Dongta Airport
Shenyang City
Liaoning Province
110043
Tel: 0086 24 88 29 44 35
Fax: 0086 24 88 29 44 32
Web site: www.cna.ln.cniinfo.net
Main operational base: Shenyang-Taoxin

STATUS

IATA scheduled carrier
Employees: 6,847
Passengers per year: 5,535,000 (2001)
ICAO code: CBF
IATA code: CJ

SERVICES

International / Regional / Domestic
Passenger / Cargo
International routes: N Korea, S Korea, Russia,

ALLIANCES / CODE SHARES

China Southern A/l, Korean A/l

FLEET

A300-600R - 6, A321 - 2, MD-82 - 6, MD-82 - 2, MD-90-30 - 11, MD-82 - 24, Y-7-100 - 11
On order: A300-600R - 9 (options), A321 - 8

China Northern was originally part of the Civil Aviation Administration of China (CAAC) that provided all the airline services in China. Several Regional Administrations evolved and these provided their service in specific parts of the country. Gradually, these regions had developed further and the CAAC released sufficient control to establish nine separate airlines. Sadly, in July 2002

BELOW: *China Northern A300-622R, B-2315 (C/n 733) (Airbus)*

China Northern lost one of it's MD-82s when it crashed into Dalian Bay with the loss of all 112 passengers and aircrew. In 2002 further reform of the Chinese civil aviation was announced. The plan was to separate the enterprise of the airline from the administration and create just three airlines.

As a result, China Northern Airlines, which was previously CAAC Shenyang region until 1990, will be merged with Xinjiang Aviation to form China South Aviation Group Corp. Once the merger is complete the three new airlines will cut their ties with the General Administration of Civil Aviation of China.

China Northwest Airlines

Registered name: China Northwest Aviation Company
Country: China
Region: Far East
Address: Xiguan Airport
2 Feng Hao Rd
Xian City
Shaanxi Province 710082
Tel: 0086 29 870 22 99
Fax: 0086 29 426 16 22
Web site: www.cnwa.com
Main operational base: Xiguan Airport

STATUS
IATA scheduled and charter passenger + cargo carrier
Employees: 4,000
Passengers per year: 3,444,100 (2001)
ICAO code: CNW
IATA code: WH

BELOW: *China Northwest Airlines BAe.146-300, B-2720 (C/nE3219) (BAe systems)*

SERVICES
Regional / Domestic / Passenger Charter / Cargo
International routes: Japan

FLEET
A300-600R - 3, A310-222 - 3, A320-200 - 13, BAe 146-100 - 3, BAe 146-300 - 8, Y-5 - 12, Tu-154M - 9

ABOVE: *China Northwest Airlines BAe. 146-300, B2720 (C/n E3219) (BAe systems)*

The development of China Northwest is similar to that of China Northern although the transition of China Northwest happened in 1989.

As a result of the reforms China Northwest will be merged into China East Aviation Group Corp together with China Yunnan Aviation Company.

China Southern Airlines

LEFT: *China Southern A320-232, B-2342 (C/n 696) with Airbus test registration F-WWII) (Airbus)*

Registered name: China Southern Airlines Co Ltd
Country: China
Region: Far East
Address: Baiyun International Airport
Guangzhou
Tel: 0086 20 86 12 34 27 / 68 18 18
Fax: 0086 20 86 64 46 23
Web site: www.cs-air.com/en
Stockholder: China Southern Airlines Group
Main operational base: Baiyun International Airport

STATUS

IATA scheduled passenger carrier
Employees: 17,725
Passengers per year: 19,120,000 (2001)
ICAO code: CSN
IATA code: CZ

SERVICES

International / Regional / Domestic
Passenger / Charter / Cargo
International routes: Australia, Cambodia,
Indonesia, Japan, Malaysia, Netherlands,
Philippines, Russia, South Korea,
Singapore, Thailand, USA, Vietnam

ALLIANCES / CODE SHARES

Asiana, China Northern A/1, China
Yunnan A/1, Delta A/1, Garuda, Japan Air
System, KLM, Vietnam A/1

FLEET

SA365N Dauphin 2 - 2, A319-100 - 4, A320-
200 - 20, 737-300 - 22, 737-500 - 12, 737-800
- 4, 747-400F - 2, 757-200 - 22, 777-200ER -
9, S-76A - 3
On order: 737-800 - 16 (to replace older
737s), 777-200 - 1

The development of China Southern is similar to that of China Northern although the
transition of China Northwest happened in
1989.

China Southern was granted the authority to not only develop its domestic market
but also international routes. However, to
stop competing with the other carriers,
each was allocated different destinations. It
was equipped with a fleet of 737s to which
757s and 767s were added. In 1993 the airline status changed once more with it being
granted further freedom of operation as an

'autonomous aviation enterprise'. In 1997,
34.8% of the state-owned share capital was
offered to the public. China Southern
received the first of 20 A320s in 1992 and it
entered service in June. The next new type
to arrive was the 777 at the end of 1995.

As other airlines emerged, alliances were
contemplated which were to its advantage,
such as that with Guizhou Airlines in 1998
or acquisition of Zhongyuan in 2000.

In October 2001 China Aviation Supplies
Import & Export Corporation (CASC)
placed an order for 30 737-800s of which 20
were for China Southern.

China Southern has strived to offer a
good and attractive service which was
reflected in only a small dip in passengers
carried following the events of September
11th. Following lengthy discussions, in
February 2002 it was announced that a
merger proposal had been approved which
involved China's nine major carriers. China
Northern and Xinjiang Airlines would be
merged into China Southern. The separate
identity of each would be retained for the
short term but would eventually all take on
the China Southern identity. Each of the
other airlines operates a mixture of
Western aircraft including A300, A321, MD-
82, MD-90, 737, 757 and ATR 72, and
Russian aircraft including - Mi-8, Mi-17, Il-
86, Il-96 and Tu-154. A few Chinese types
are also included such as the Y-5 and Y-7.
Once the merger has settled down it is
inevitable that some of these aircraft will be
disposed of as the fleet is rationalised.
However, China Southern will remain the
largest airline in China.

In October 2003 China Southern's main
base of operation, including its headquarters, will move to a new large airport north
of Baiyun.

As a result of the reforms announced in
2002, China Northwest will be merged into
China East Aviation Group Corp together
with China Yunnan Aviation Company.

China Southwest Airlines

Registered name: China Southwest Aviation Company
Country: China
Region: Far East
Address: Shuangliu Airport
Chengdu
Sichuan
Tel: 0086 28 558 14 66
Fax: 0086 28 558 26 30
Web site: www.cswa.com
Main operational base: Shuangliu Airport

STATUS

IATA Scheduled Passenger Carrier
Employees: 7,000
Passengers per year: 5,355,000 (2001)
ICAO code: CXN
IATA code: SZ

SERVICES

Regional / Domestic
Passenger / Cargo
International routes: Laos, Nepal, Singapore, Thailand

FLEET

A340-300 - 6, 737-300 - 20, 737-600 - 6, 757-200 - 10, Harbin Yunshuji Y-12II - 4, Tu-154M - 5, Y-7-100 - 3

The development of China Southwest is similar to that of China Northern although the transition of China Southwest happened in October 1987.

As a result of the reforms China Southwest, that was originally the CAAC Chengdu Region, will be incorporated into China International Aviation Company.

Comair/Delta Connection

Registered name: Comair Inc
Country: USA
Region: North America
Address: PO Box 75021
Cincinnati / Northern Kentucky Airport
Cincinnati, Ohio 45275
Tel: 001 859 767 25 50
Fax: 001 859 767 29 69
Web site: www.fly-comair.com
Stockholder: Delta Air Lines
Main operational base: Cincinnati

SSTATUS

Scheduled passenger carrier
Employees: 4,700
Passengers per year: 4,766,000 (2001)
ICAO code: COM
IATA code: OH

SERVICES

International / Regional
Domestic / Passenger
International routes: Canada, Bahamas

FLEET

CRJ100LR - 128, CRJ700 - 3, EMB 120 Brasilia - 9
On order: CRJ700 - 17

Comair was founded in April 1977 by the father and son team Raymond and David Mueller. It was initially equipped with three Piper Navajos that were flown on scheduled routes linking Cincinnati, Cleveland, Detroit and Akron-Canton.

As business expanded Piper Chieftains were added. With further expansion envi-

ABOVE: *Comair CRJ700 being operated as Delta Connection (Bombardier)*

sioned Comair went public to finance the acquisition of a fleet of the Brazilian Bandeirante. The steady growth of Comair attracted the attention of Delta Air Lines. In 1984 Comair was designated a Delta Connection carrier and in 1986 Delta took 22% of the common stock. At the same time Comair started Comair Jet Express to provide on demand charter. Comair also became the first US airline to operate the 30 seat SAAB 340.

In 1987 Comair and Delta developed a new hub in Orlando which greatly enhanced their opportunities.

Growth continued and in 1988 more

Comair/Delta Connection

Brazilian aircraft in the form of the 30 seat Brasilia were purchased. The following year the Comair Aviation Academy was established to become the only flight training school to be operated by an airline.

In 1990 Comair was voted as Regional Airline of the Year by Air Transport World for its growth and maturation.

The growth continued and in 1993 Comair became the launch customer for the Canadair Regional Jet - the first regional carrier to offer a jet service. The following year

Comair opened its 53 gate Concourse C at Cincinnati/Northern Kentucky International Airport, the largest ever designed exclusively for a regional carrier.

All of these expansion plans were paying off - in 1997 over 5.4 million passengers were carried. In 1998 a US$40m expansion of the still almost new Concourse C was undertaken. During 2000 Comair was acquired for approximately US$1.8bn to become the wholly owned subsidiary of Delta. It took delivery of the 100th CRJ which enabled the Cincinnati hub to

become an all-jet operation. Passenger levels continued to rise with over 8 million carried in 2000.

In 2001, further expansion of the Concourse C led to the waiting areas to nearly double over that of the original construction. Comair Jet Express was renamed Delta AirElite Business Jets for corporate charters.

Comair took delivery of a CRJ on January 23rd 2002 in a special 25th Anniversary colour scheme.

Continental Airlines

Registered name: Continental Airlines, Inc
Country: USA
Region: North America
Address: 1600 Smith Street
Houston
Texas 77002
Tel: 001 713 324 50 00
Fax: 001 713 324 20 87
Web site: www.continental.com
Main operational base: Houston

STATUS

IATA scheduled international carrier
Employees: 48,000
Passengers per year: 44,238,000 (2001)
ICAO code: COA
IATA code: CO

SERVICES

International / Regional / Domestic Passenger / Cargo

International routes: Antigua & Barbuda, Aruba, Australia, Bahamas, Belgium, Belize, Bermuda, Brazil, Canada, Cayman Islands, China, Colombia, Costa Rica, Dominican Republic, Ecuador, El Salvador, France, Germany, Grand Cayman, Guam, Guatemala, Honduras, Indonesia, Ireland, Israel, Italy, Jamaica, Japan, Mexico, Netherlands, Netherlands Antilles, Nicaragua, Panama, Peru, Philippines, Portugal, Puerto Rico, Peru, Spain, Switzerland, Taiwan, UK, Venezuela, Virgin Islands

ALLIANCES / CODE SHARES

Air China, Air Europa, Alaska A/l, American Eagle, Commutair, COPA, EVA Aw, flybe, Gulfstream Int A/l, Hawaiian A/l, KLM, Northwest A/l, Pinacle A/l, Virgin Atlantic Aw

OWNED SUBSIDIARY AIRLINES

Continental Micronesia

FLEET

1900 - 15 (operated by Continental Connection), 737-300 - 57 (1 to be withdrawn in 2003), 737-500 - 65 (2 to be withdrawn in 2003), 737-700 - 36, 737-800 - 77, 737-900 - 15, 757-200 - 41, 757-300 - 4, 767-200ER - 10, 767-400ER - 16, 777-200ER - 18, MD-81/-82/-83 - 30
On Order: 737-700 - 15 (+ 24 options), 737-800 - 38 (+35 options), 737-900 - (12

ABOVE: *Continental Airlines 737-924, N79402 (C/n 30119) (Jeremy Flack/API)*

options), 757-300 - 11 (+ 11 options), 767-200ER - (2 options), 777-200ER - (3 options)

Continental can trace its roots back to the South West Division of the Varney Speed Lines. It began flying from El Paso, Texas on July 15th, 1934, using three Lockheed Vegas.

The main division of Varney Speed Lines had commenced operations in 1926 but was taken over by what led to United Airlines in 1930.

Renamed Varney Air Transport in December 1934, the name was changed again on July 1st 1937 to Continental Airlines. The route network expanded to

cover Kansas, New Mexico, Oklahoma and Texas.

During World War Two, Continental built the Denver Modification Centre where the B-17 Flying Fortress and B-29 Superfortress were prepared for the USAAF.

The Pioneer Airlines was purchased in 1954 with extended routes into Texas and New Mexico.

May 1957 saw Continental commence a trunk route linking Chicago and Los Angeles via Denver and Kansas with a DC-7. This was replaced with the Vickers Viscount which entered service the following May.

The 707 took Continental into the jet age with the first operations commencing in June 1959 and the following year unveiled a revised colour scheme as part of a new corporate identity.

The first 727 was delivered in June 1967 and Air Micronesia was formed with assistance from Continental in 1968. During the Vietnam war Continental undertook a substantial number of charters on behalf of the US Military. In September 1965 Continental Air Services was formed and based in Laos for specialised charters.

Continental commenced operation of wide-body airliners with the 747s in 1970 and DC-10s in 1972 and, as a result, the Continental route network underwent a significant expansion. This included new routes to Australia and New Zealand from Los Angeles. By the 1980s it had ratio-

nalised on just the 727s and DC-10s. Texas Air Corporation (TAC) acquired a controlling interest in Continental in October 1982, merged with its subsidiary - Texas International Airlines. This created a fleet of 112 aircraft and the headquarters moved to Houston.

Financial difficulties forced Continental to seek protection under Chapter 11 provisions in September 1983 but it emerged in 1987 following capital reconstruction.

Having already acquired New York Air, TAC purchased People Express and Frontier Airlines in 1986 which were incorporated into Continental during February making it the third largest US airline.

Financial difficulties due to rising fuel costs forced Continental to seek protection

ABOVE: *Continental Airlines Boeing 757 with New York in the background (Jeremy Flack/API)*

under Chapter 11 provisions once more in December 1990 but it emerged in 1993 following capital reconstruction with a US$450 million investment by Air Canada.

A new livery was introduced in February 1991. A massive order for 92 aircraft was placed in 1993 for 737s, 757s, 767s and 777s.

During 1995 efforts were made to improve Continental performance and it achieved best on-time and baggage handler several months running. By the end of the year it announced that it had earned its

BELOW: *Continental Airlines 777-244ER, N78002 (C/n 27578) (Continental)*

Continental Airlines

largest ever profit (US$224) million. Plans were announced in 1997 to order 35 767s and 777s followed by 15 737-900s and 10 767s the following year. In the meantime, Continental declared that it had another bumper year with a US$640 million profit for 1997. Also during 1998 new routes were inaugurated to Ireland, Scotland and the first 777s were received, ready to offer a non-stop service to Japan at the turn of the year.

Continental was ranked as the No 1 US major airline in terms of customer satisfaction for long distance flights in a study by Frequent Flyer magazine in May 1999 that it repeated the following year.

Continental Airlines is the only major airline to operate a hub in the New York City metropolitan area. It operates out of New York Liberty International Airport which is just 16 miles (25 km) from downtown Manhattan. After six consecutive years of profit, Continental reported a net loss of US$95 million for 2001 following the terrorist atrocities of September 11th resulting in substantial cuts in routes and staff. It was allocated a Stabilisation Act grant of US$417m and remains the fifth largest airline in terms of passenger traffic and is finding passenger levels steadily rising.

Continental has announced plans to establish a new hub at Luis Muniz Marin International Airport in San Juan, Puerto Rico, to compete with American Airlines which is already there.

While the regional airlines have a more favourable outlook, Continental has sold 47% of its holding in its subsidiary Expressjet with a view to selling all of it.

Continental Micronesia

Registered name: Continental Micronesia Inc
Country: USA
Region: Central America & Caribbean
Address: PO Box 8778-S
 862 South Marine Drive
 Tamuning 96931, Guam
Tel: 00671 647 65 95
Fax: 00671 649 65 88
Web site: www.continental.com
Stockholder: Continental Airlines Inc
Main operational base: Guam

STATUS
Scheduled carrier
Employees: 1,873

Passengers per year: 1,381,000 (2001)
ICAO code: CMI
IATA code: CS

SERVICES
International / Domestic / Passenger Charter / Cargo
International routes: Australia, China, Indonesia, Japan, Mariana Islands, Marshall Islands, Micronesia, Philippines

FLEET
737-800 - 9 (leased from Continental Airlines)

Continental Micronesia was originally formed in 1966 as Air Micronesia by the United Micronesian Development Association (UMDA), Continental Airlines and Aloha Airlines. Scheduled services commenced in May 1968.

Air Micronesia was established to provide inter-island service between the US Trust Territory of Micronesia, Territory of Guam and the Commonwealth of Northern Mariana Islands. In 1993 the name was changed to Continental Micronesia. Continental became the sole shareholder of Continental Micronesia in July 1997.

COPA Airlines

Registered name: Compania Panamena de Aviacion SA
Country: Country: Panama
Region: Central America & Caribbean
Address: Avenue Justo Arosemena y Calle 39
 PO Box 1572, Panama 1
Tel: 00507 227 45 51
Fax: 00507 227 19 52
Web site: www.copaair.com
Main operational base: Tocumen International

STATUS
Scheduled carrier
National Flag Carrier
Employees: 2,200

Passengers per year: 1,772,000 (2001)
ICAO code: CMP
ATA code: CM

SERVICES
International / Regional / Domestic Passenger / Cargo
International routes: Argentina, Brazil, Colombia, Cuba, Dominican Republic, Ecuador, Guatemala, Honduras, Jamaica, Haiti, Nicaragua, Panama, Peru, Puerto Rico, USA, Venezuela

ALLIANCES/CODE SHARES
Contininental A/l

FLEET
737-200Adv - 11 (2 are cargo only), 737-700 - 12
On order: 737-800 - 2

Compania Panamena de Aviacion (COPA) was formed as Panama's national airline on June 21st, 1944, with assistance from Pan Am.

Domestic services commenced in 1947 with the DC-3 / C-47. These were later augmented with the Lockheed Electra and later still the 727. COPA Airlines now operates a 737 fleet and is owned by Panamanian and US interests.

Corsair

Registered name: Corse Air International
Country: France
Region: Europe
Address: 2 avenue Charles Lindbergh
F-94636 Rungis Cedex
Tel: 0033 1 49 79 49 59
Fax: 0033 1 49 79 49 68
Web site: www.corsair.fr
Stockholder: TUI AG
Main operational base: Paris-Orly

STATUS

Scheduled and charter passenger carrier
Employees: 1,229
Passengers per year: 2,175,000 (2001)
ICAO code: CRL
IATA code: SS

SERVICES

International / Passenger / Charter
International routes: Cote D'Ivoire, Djibouti, Egypt, French Guiana, Greece, Guadeloupe, Ireland, Israel, Italy, Martinique, Morocco, New Caledonia, Portugal, Tahiti, Thailand, Togo, Tunisia, Turkey, UK, USA

ABOVE: *Corsair Airlines A330-243, F-HCAT (C/n 285) (Airbus)*

FLEET

A330-200 - 2, 737-200Adv - 1, 737-400 - 2, 747-100 - 1, 747-200B - 2, 747-300 - 2, 747SP - 1, DC-10-30 - 1

Corsair was originally formed as Corse Air International in 1981. Operations commenced in July with Caravelles linking Paris-Orly with Malta and spread to other parts of Europe and the Mediterranean.

The Caravelles have given away to the 737s and a 747 was added to provide long haul capacity.

The name of Corse Air was changed to Corsair in 1971 following the addition of a new business partner - the French tour operator - New Frontiers.

Although most airlines suffered to a greater or lesser degree following the terrorist attacks on September 11th, Corsair was the only French airline to have remained in the black

Croatia Airlines

Registered name: Croatia Airlines
Country: Croatia
Region: Europe
Address: Savska cesta 41
10000 Zagreb
Tel: 00385 1 616 00 66
Fax: 00385 1 617 68 45
Web site: www.croatiaairlines.hr or
www.ctn.hr/ctn/index-en.html or
www.ctn.tel.hr/ctn/index-en.html
Main operational base: Zagreb

STATUS

IATA scheduled and charter carrier
National Flag Carrier
Employees: 830
Passengers per year: 1,242,000 (2001)
ICAO code: CTN
IATA code: OU

ABOVE: *Croatia Airlines A319-112, 9A-CTG (C/n 767) (Airbus)*

SERVICES

International / Regional / Domestic
Passenger / Charter / Cargo
International routes: Austria, Belgium, Bosnia Herzegovina, Czech, Denmark, France, Germany, Israel, Italy, Macedonia, Netherlands, Russia, Spain, Switzerland, Turkey, UK

Croatia Airlines

ALLIANCES / CODE SHARES

Adria, Air France, Alitalia, CSA, Iberia, Lufthansa, Malaysia A/l, THY

FLEET

A319-100 - 4, A320-200 - 3, ATR 42-300 - 3

Croatia Airlines was initially formed on July 29th 1989 as Zagreb Airlines and commenced operations on August 7th with a Cessna 402. The name was changed to Croatia Airlines on May 5th, 1991 and provided a service from Zagreb and Split with ex-Adria MD-82 following the break up of the former Yugoslavia. Some 737s were added in 1992 and routes to parts of Europe started the following year. 1993 saw the delivery of a pair of ATR 42s that were used for domestic routes.

ABOVE: *Croatia Airlines ATR 42*

Croatia Airlines became the first airline to offer a scheduled service to war-damaged Sarajevo in 1996.

Airbus A320s began to arrive in 1997 and A319s the following year while the 737s were sold.

In 2002 a second BAe146 was ordered from Flightline on a one-year lease.

CSA Czech Airlines

Registered name: CSA Czech Airlines
Country: Czech Republic
Region: Europe
Address: Kolejni 55012
 Prague 6, CZ 160 00, Prague
Tel: 00420 2 20 11 11 11
Fax: 00420 2 20 56 22 66
Web site: www.czech-airlines.com
Main operational base: Prague-Ruzyne

STATUS

IATA scheduled international and charter carrier
National Flag Carrier
Employees: 3,971
Passengers per year: 2,877,000 (2001)
ICAO code: CSA
IATA code: OK

SERVICES

International / Regional / Domestic
Passenger / Charter / Cargo
International routes: Austria, Bahrain, Belgium, Bulgaria, Canada, Croatia, Cyprus, Denmark, Egypt, Finland, France, Germany, Greece, Hungary, Ireland, Israel, Italy, Latvia, Lebanon, Lithuania, Malta*, Netherlands, Norway, Poland, Romania, Russia, Serbia, Slovakia, Slovenia, Spain, Sri Lanka, Sweden, Syria, Switzerland, Turkey, UAE, UK, Ukraine, USA (*code share)

ALLIANCES / CODE SHARES

Skyteam / Air Malta, Continental A/l, KLM, Lufthansa, Olympic Aw, TAROM, Transaero A/l, THY, Yugoslav A/l

FLEET

A310-300 - 2, ATR 42-320 - 3, ATR 42-400 - 2, ATR 72-202 - 4, 737-400 - 9, 737-500 - 10

ABOVE: *Czech Airlines ATR 42-420, OK-AFE (C/n 487) (ATR)*

CSA / Ceskoslovenske Statni Aerolinie was founded on July 19th 1923 as the national airline for Czechoslovakia. Its first operations with Aero A-14 biplanes started on October 28th. International services commenced in July 1930 with the Aero A-23. Throughout the 1930s a steady expansion progressed with Airspeed Envoys and Savoia Marchetti S-73s until March 15th 1939 with the outbreak of war. CSA was then absorbed into Lufthansa.

Once the war ended CSA, together with CLS and SLAS, were merged into the new CSA that formed on September 15th 1945. Initially it was equipped with the Il-12, the Li-2 (a Russian C-47) and Aero A-45 from 1949. CSA struggled to re-establish its previously held market share.

CSA entered the jet age in 1957 with the Tu-104 but was still adding piston airliners to the fleet in the form of the Il-14. Deliveries of the turboprop Il-18 began in 1960.

Czechoslovak-built LET L410s were bought to provide some of the short-haul domestic capacity while Russian Il-62 and Tu-134 provided the long-range capability from the late 1960s and early 1970s respectively. A number of the small Yak-40 were added to the fleet from 1974 and the larger Tu-154 in 1988.

With the relaxation of restrictive relations with the West, CSA was eventually permitted to buy non-eastern bloc aircraft. As a

ABOVE: *Czech Airlines 737-45S, OK-FGR (C/n 28477) (Jeremy Flack/API)*

result in 1991 the first of two A310s was delivered. This was followed by ATR 72s and 737s the following year and ATR 42s in 1996.

The airline changed its name to CSA Czech Airlines following the break-up of the Czechoslovak Federation. Although

obviously hit by the immediate downturn in business in 2001 CSA claims to have been one of the few airlines to have remained in the black in 2001.

Cubana

Registered name: Cubana de Aviacion
Country: Cuba
Region: Central America & Caribbean
Address: Calle 23 No.64
            esq a infanta
            Vedado
            Havana
Tel: 0053 7 33 49 49 / 50
Fax: 0053 7 33 40 56
Web site: www.cubana.cu
Main operational base: Havana

STATUS

IATA scheduled carrier
National Flag Carrier
Employees: 2,955
Passengers per year: 944,000 (2001)
ICAO code: CUB
IATA code: CU

SERVICES

International / Regional / Domestic
Passenger / Charter / Cargo

International routes: Belgium, Canada, Czech, France, Germany, Guyana, Jamaica, Mexico, Nicaragua, Panama, Russia, Spain

ALLIANCES / CODE SHARES

Aeroflot, Spanair

FLEET

An-24RV - 8, An-26 - 13, Il-62M - 3, Il-76MD - 1, Yak-40 - 3, Yak-42 - 3

Cubana was formed from the Curtiss Aviation Group on October 8th, 1929, as Cubana de Aviación Curtiss SA. Operations commenced the following year with the Ford 5-AT-C Trimotor to which the Sikorsky S-38s were added.

This airline was acquired by Pan American and the name changed to Compañía Nacional Cubana de Aviación SA. The Lockheed Electra was added in 1935 and flights began to other Caribbean islands during the early 1940s.

The airline name changed to Compañía

Cubana de Aviación SA in March 1944 and was a founder member of ICAO in November and IATA the following April. The DC-3 was added to the fleet in 1945 followed by a number of types over the next years. These included the Constellation, Super Constellation, DC-4, C-46, Britannia and Viscount which enabled routes to be flown not only to Mexico and the USA but as far as Madrid in Spain.

Following the emergence of the Communist Government in 1959, the airline was nationalised and renamed Empresa Consolidada Cubana de Aviación. The fleet was replaced with aircraft supplied by the Soviet Union. These and subsequent aircraft included the An-12, An-24, An-26, Il-14, Il-18, Il-62, Il-76 Tu-154, Yak-40 and Yak-42.

More recently, the fleet has reduced in size and has seen the re-introduction of Western aircraft in the form of the DC-10 and F-27 Friendship although these are no longer believed to be operated.

Cyprus Airways

Registered name: Cyprus Airways Ltd
Country: Cyprus
Region: Europe
Address: 21 Alkeou Str. 2404 Engomi
P.O.Box 21903
CY-1514 Nicosia
Tel: 00357 22 66 30 54
Fax: 00357 22 66 31 67
Web site: www.cyprusair.com
Stockholder: Cyprus Airways Group
Main operational base: Larnaca International
Airport

STATUS

IATA scheduled passenger carrier
National Flag Carrier
Employees: 11,841
Passengers per year: 1,503,400 (2001)
ICAO code: CYP
IATA code: CY

SERVICES

International / Regional / Passenger
Charter / Cargo
International routes: Austria, Bahrain,
Belgium, Egypt, France, Germany, Greece,
Hungary, Israel, Italy, Jordan, Lebanon,
Netherlands, Poland, Russia, Saudi Arabia,
Switzerland, Syria, UAE, UK

ALLIANCES / CODE SHARES

Aeroflot, Alitalia, El-Al, Gulf Air, KLM,
LOT, Syrianair

OWNED SUBSIDIARY AIRLINES

Eurocypria Airlines

FLEET

A310-203 - 3, A310-204 - 1, A319-100 - 2,
A320 200 - 10, A330-200 - 2

Cyprus Airlines was formed on September 24th, 1947, as a joint venture between the Cypriot Government, BEA and some private investors and equipped with DC-3s.

BEA Elizabethans then Viscounts were operated for and on behalf of Cyprus Airways until the arrival of ex-BEA Tridents in September 1969. One of the Tridents was damaged beyond repair at Nicosia Airport during the invasion of Cyprus by Turkish forces in 1974 that left Nicosia permanently closed. It was seven months before any kind of service was able to resume to

ABOVE: *Cyprus Airways A310-204, 5B-DAX (C/n 486) in old colour-scheme (Airbus)*

Larnaca. The Tridents were replaced by BAC 1-11s that remained in service for only a short time. 707s also arrived in 1975. These remained in service until 1984 when they were replaced by A310s. During the early 1990s Cyprus Airways underwent a restructuring and revised corporate images. This included re-designed and improved interiors to the aircraft. Eurocypria Airlines was formed as a subsidiary in 1991 to operate charter flights.

When an A320 returned from lease with Eurocypria in 2002, the airliner was painted in yet another new colour scheme.

BELOW: *Cyprus Airlines A319, 5B-DBO (C/n 1729) in new colour-scheme (Airbus)*

Daallo Airlines

Registered name: Daallo Airlines
Country: Djibouti
Region: Middle East
Address: Al Khaleej Road,
Al Firdons Hotel Bldg,
Ground Floor, PO Box 12197
Deira-DUBAI-U.A.E
Tel: 00971 4 73 38 08
Fax: 00971 4 73 44 64
Web site: www.daallo.com

STATUS

Scheduled and charter passenger + cargo carrier

Employees: 60
ICAO code: DAO
IATA code: D3

SERVICES

International / Regional
Domestic / Passenger
International routes: Djibouti, Ethiopia, France, Kenya, Saudi Arabia, Somalia

FLEET

An-24 - 1, 757-200 - 1, Il-18 - 1, Let-410UVP - 1, Tu-154 - 1

Daallo Airlines commenced operations in 1992 with a single Cessna following the demise of Somali Airlines and Air Djibouti during the civil war.

From these humble beginnings, Daallo Airlines has grown and now has a fleet of ten aircraft. Daallo Airlines is privately owned by two directors. Although registered in Djibouti where they have a local office, their head office is in the UAE. It has been in profit since its inception.

A European Djibouti-Paris route was inaugurated by Daallo Airlines in June 2001.

dba

Registered name: Deutsche BA
Luftfahrtgesellschaft GmbH
Country: Germany
Region: Europe
Address: Wartungsalle 13
Munich Airport, D-85356
Tel: 0049 89 97 59 15 00
Fax: 0049 89 97 59 15 03
Web site: www.flydba.com
Stockholder: British Airways
Main operational base: Munich

STATUS

IATA scheduled and charter passenger carrier
Employees: 861
Passengers per year: 3,300,000 (2001)
ICAO code: BAG
IATA code: DI

SERVICES

Regional / Domestic
Passenger / Charter

FLEET

737-300 - 16

dba was originally formed as Delta Air in 1978 and commenced operations in April to provide scheduled and charter services. Aircraft operated were the King Air, Twin Otter and Cheyenne. Delta Air was

ABOVE: dba 737-31S, D-ADBV (C/n 29266) (dba)

acquired in 1992 by a consortium headed by British Airways (49%) and two banks. Subsequently, BA acquired the whole equity. During this period the name changed to Deutsche BA and the carrier operated as a high-service, low-cost airline with 737s. Deutsche BA underwent a restructuring programme in 1996 to cut the losses that it had been suffering. It cut a number of unprofitable international routes while expanding some of its domestic routes. The SAAB 340A and 2000 were sold followed by the Fokker 100s the following year. Despite these efforts, with rising fuel costs and a weakened Euro, Deutsche BA continued to make a loss. BA agreed to sell the airline to easyJet; however, in April 2002, Deutsche BA was re-launched as the no-frills airline dba. The colour scheme was changed and dba soon achieved an increased load factor and increased its market share.

Delta Air Lines

Registered name: Delta Air Lines Inc
Country: USA
Region: North America
Address: Box 20706
   Hartsfield
   Atlanta
   Georgia 30320-60
Tel: 001 404 715 26 00
Fax: 001 404 767 84 99
Web site: www.delta.com
Main operational base: Atlanta

STATUS

IATA scheduled international passenger
carrier
Employees: 72,470
Passengers per year: 104,943,000 (2001)
ICAO code: DAL
IATA code: DL

SERVICES

International / Regional / Domestic
Passenger / Cargo
International routes: Aruba, Austria,
Bahamas, Belgium, Brazil, Canada,
Cayman Islands, Colombia, Denmark,
Czech, Germany, Greece, India, Ireland,
Italy, Japan, Mexico, Netherlands, Panama,
Peru, Poland, Russia, Spain, Switzerland,
Turkey, UK, Venezuela, Virgin Islands

ALLIANCES / CODE SHARES

Skyteam / Aeropostal, Air Jamaica, Atlantic
Coast A/l, Atlantic Southeast A/l, China
Southern A/l, Malaysian A/l, Royal Air
Maroc, Singapore A/l, Southwest A/l, SAA

OWNED SUBSIDIARY AIRLINES

ASA Holdings (parent of Atlantic
Southeast Airlines) Comair Holdings Inc
(parent of Comair)

FLEET

727-200Adv - 27 (All sold - deliveries to end
2003), 737-200Adv - 52, 737-300 - 17, 737-
800 - 69, 757-200 - 121, 767-200 - 15, 767-
300 - 28, 767-300ER - 59, 767-400ER - 21,
777-200 - 8, MD-88 - 120, MD-90-30 - 16
On order: 737 - 61 + 321 options, 757-200 -
62 options, 767-300 - 10 options, 767-
400ER - 28 options, 777-200 - 35

The origin of Delta Air Lines can be traced
back to May 30th 1924 when Huff Daland
Dusters was founded as the first aerial crop
dusting organisation with a pair of Jennys.
In 1928 the company was renamed Delta
Air Service. The following year Delta
carried its first passengers on a route from
Dallas, Texas to Jackson, Mississippi using
Travel Air S-6000B.

The end of the mail contract forced the

cessation of passenger services but these
were resumed in 1934 with operations as
Delta Air Lines. Various aircraft were added
to the fleet during the 1930s including the
Stinson Model A and Lockheed 10 followed
by the DC-2 and DC-3 in 1940.

Delta helped in the war effort by modifying over 1,000 aircraft, overhauling engines
and training USAAF pilots and mechanics.
In 1945 Delta received the National Safety
Council Award for flying over 300 million
passenger miles over ten years without a single fatality. This was repeated in 1947 for
500 million passenger miles.

In 1953 Chicago and Southern Airlines
merged with Delta and was named Delta-
C&S for the next two years. Delta pioneered
the hub and spoke system in 1955 with
small scheduled airliners carrying passengers to the hub airports for connection to
long-haul Delta flights. The following year,
radar was fitted in the noses of the whole
Delta fleet.

The jet age arrived with Delta when the
DC-8 was introduced into service in 1959
and the Convair 880 the following year.
These airliners were used to operate trans-
continental and inter-continental services.

The first DC-9 service commenced in 1965 and the following year the crop-dusting division closed. In commemoration of this, and as a memorial to CE Woolman, the Delta founder who died in 1966, a reconditioned 1925 Huff Daland Duster was donated to the Smithsonian Museum.

The Delta Express commenced operating a low-fare service in October 1966 with 737s. The 747s joined Delta's all-jet fleet and commenced operation in 1970. In 1972 Northeast Airlines merged with Delta and the 727s entered service followed by the Tristar the following year.

Delta achieved a world record in 1979 when it became the first airline to board 1 million passengers in a single month at Atlanta.

Having suffered a financial loss in 1982, Delta employees raised $30 million in payroll deductions to purchase its first 767 that was named 'The Spirit of Delta'.

Delta merged with Western Airlines in 1987 to become the fourth largest US carrier and fifth largest world carrier. It also commenced its first transpacific route flying from Altanta to Tokyo via Portland.

The MD-11 entered service in 1990 and Delta joined 23 other airlines in the Civil Reserve Air Fleet to transport military personnel and cargo to the Middle East for Desert Storm.

Delta purchased virtually all of the Pan Am routes as well as the Pan Am Shuttle, in the largest ever acquisition of flights.

ABOVE: *Delta Air Lines 727-232, N532DA (C/n 22045)* *(Jeremy Flack/API)*

During 1997, Delta became the first airline to board over 100 million passengers in a year. Routes were expanded into Latin America, a new aircraft livery was introduced and the 777s ordered.

The remaining 78% of issue stock of Comair Holdings was acquired in October 1999.

The SkyTeam alliance was launched in 2000 with AeroMexico, Air France and Korean Air. In the same year, the Delta Connection airlines Atlantic Southeast Airlines (ASA) and Comair were acquired. The largest regional jet order was placed on their behalf for 500 aircraft for which a new aircraft livery was launched. A record 120 million passengers were carried.

Although it retains joint operating arrangements, the Delta stake in SkyWest Airlines was sold in October 2001 for US$125 million.

As with most airlines, Delta suffered a major reduction in business following the events of September 11th, recording its first loss in six years. These resulted in vital major cost savings and grounding of the 15 MD-11s and deferred delivery of new 737s scheduled for 2003 / 4 deliveries. Included were redundancy plans for up to 13,000 employees with 7,000 to 8,000 announced that October. It initially received US$346 million from the US Government out of a possible total of US$600 million compensation.

LEFT: *Delta Air Lines 757-232, N671DN (C/n 25332)* *(Jane's)*

Dragonair

Registered name: Hong Kong Dragon Airlines Ltd
Country: China
Region: Far East
Address: Dragonair House
            11 Tung Fai Road
            Hong Kong International Airport
            Lantau
Tel: 00852 31 93 31 93
Fax: 00852 31 93 31 94
Web site: www.dragonair.com
Stockholder: Hong Kong Macau International
Investment Co
Main operational base: Chek Lap Kok

SERVICES

Regional / Domestic / Passenger
Charter / Cargo
International routes: Bangladesh, Brunei,
Cambodia, Japan, Malaysia, Nepal,
Thailand

ALLIANCES / CODE SHARES

Royal Brunei A/l

FLEET

A320-200 - 8, A321-200 - 4, A330-300 - 8,
747-300F - 2
On order: A320-200 - 3, A321-200 - 2, A330-
300 - 1

ABOVE: *Dragonair A321-231, B-HTE (C/n 1024) with
the Airbus test registration D-AVZO (Airbus)*

Dragonair was founded in May 1985 and
commenced operations in July by flying a
737 from Kai Tak to Kota Kinabalu in
Malaysia.

Steadily, new routes were added into
China and various nearby countries.
Additional 737s were acquired as demand
required.

Cathay Pacific Airways and its parent
company, Swire Pacific, bought a 35% stake
in Dragonair in January 1990, while CITIC
Hong Kong which holds a 12.5% interest in
Cathay Pacific, acquired a 38% share.
These were increased to 43% and 46%
respectively later on that year.

A Lockheed Tristar was leased from
Cathay Pacific in April 1990 for use on the
Beijing and Shanghai routes. It also signed
an agreement with the ABACUS travel
agency distribution system in Asia which

gave it greater access. The first Dragonair
A320 arrived in March 1993 to begin the
replacement of the five 737s. In 1994 a leasing agreement was signed with ILFC for two
A330s for delivery the following year.

The China National Aviation
Corporation (Group) Ltd. (CNAC Group)
purchased a 35.86% interest in Dragonair
in April 1996 and became the largest shareholder. CITIC Pacific retained 28.50%,
Swire/Cathay Pacific 25.50% and the Chao
Family 5.02%.

Dragonair and Dah Chong Hong established a joint venture to provide repair and
maintenance services on ground support
equipment at Chek Lap Kok - the new international airport for Hong Kong.

An order for two A320s was announced in
October 1996, with options for five more.
At the same time lease of another A330 was
confirmed and an additional example
ordered the following January. In August
agreements were signed to replace its
owned A320 with upgraded models. At the

same time, the two leased A320s were to be
replaced by the larger A321.

Dragonair operated the last scheduled service into Kai Tak in July 1998.

Approval was given in February 2000 for all
regular Dragonair charter flights into China
to be converted to scheduled services. As a
result an order was placed with Airbus for five
A320s and three A330s plus options for a further two A330s. In addition, an A321 and
A330 were leased from ILFC. The scheduled
services commenced towards the end of
March and the new aircraft started being
delivered the following month.

In June, Dragonair moved its headquarters
to Dragonair House at the new airport of
Chek Lap Kok.

The success of Dragonair's introduction of
its cargo service with the 747 in July resulted
in the purchase of a further two aircraft from
Singapore Airlines in October.

Druk Air

Registered name: Royal Bhutan Airlines
Country: Bhutan
Region: Asia
Address: PO Box 209
        Thimphu
Tel: 00975 2 32 28 25
Fax: 00975 2 32 27 75
Web site: www.drukair.com.bt/
Main operational base: Paro

STATUS

Scheduled passenger carrier
National Flag Carrier
Employees: 145
ICAO code: DRK
IATA code: KB

SERVICES

Regional / Domestic / Passenger
International routes: Bangladesh, India, Nepal, Thailand

FLEET

BAe 146-100 - 2

Druk Air was formed by the Bhutan Government on April 5th, 1981, and commenced operations in January 1983 with a Dornier 228 that extended to India and Bangladesh.

With a population of around 600,000, tourism is a vital part of the Bhutan econo-

ABOVE: *Durk Air BAe 146. (BAe)*

my. This resulted in a pair of BAe146s being added to the fleet and enabled additional destinations to be serviced.

easyJet

Registered name: EasyJet Airline Ltd
Country: UK
Region: Europe
Address: easyLand
        London Luton Airport
        Luton, LU2 9LS
Tel: 0044 1582 600 00 00
Fax: 0044 1582 44 33 55
Web site: www.easyjet.com
Stockholder: Go Fly Ltd

STATUS

Scheduled carrier
Employees: 2,000
Passengers per year: 7,115,000 (2001)
ICAO code: EZY
IATA code: U2

SERVICES

Regional / Domestic / Passenger
International routes: France, Greece,

Netherlands, Spain, Switzerland

FLEET

737-300 - 18, 737-700 – 17
On order: 737-700 - 16 for delivery up to 2004 + 30 options

ABOVE: *easyJet 737-33V, G-EZYP (C/n 29340) (easyJet)*

The budget airline easyJet was formed on October 18th 1995 by Stellios Haji-Ioannou. It commenced operations the fol-

easyJet

lowing month with a service from Luton to Glasgow using a 737. More domestic and regional routes were soon added. A stake was made in TEA Basel by the holding company in March 1998 which resulted in the subsequent name change to easyJet Switzerland.

Shares in easyJet were launched on the Stock Market in November 2000 that resulted in 25% being taken up by investors. The rest was held by the Haji-Ioannou family (64%) and airline staff (11%).

While most of the 'normal' fare carriers were suffering badly from the effects of September 11th, many of the 'low-cost' airlines were having good times, easyJet was certainly continuing to grow.

An announcement was made by easyJet in May 2002 that it had entered in negotiations to purchase the whole of Go (Go commenced operations in May 1998) at a cost of £374 million. With the formal agreements completed, the integration of the two airlines followed. A number of dupli-

cated routes were cut and some 10,000 ticketed passengers required transferring. A revised crew roster was drawn up but, with what was later admitted to be a shortage of trained staff, this caused chaos.

In an interesting development, city investors pushed for the stepping down of Stellios Haji-Ioannou, whose drive built up easyJet from nothing to the multi-million pound business of which the family now owned 22%.

easyJet Switzerland

Registered name: EasyJet Switzerland SA
Country: Switzerland
Region: Europe
Address: 5 Route de l'Aeroport
              CH-1214 Geneva 15
Tel: 0041 22 717 88 20
Fax: 0041 22 788 27 00
Main operational base: Basle

ICAO code: EZS
IATA code: BH

SERVICES
Regional / Passenger
International routes: France, Netherlands, Spain, UK

FLEET
737-300 - 5 leased from easyJet

easyJet Switzerland was originally formed as TEA Basel on May 18th 1988 and commenced operations in March 1989 flying Zurich to Lisbon with a 737. With the

demise of the TEA charter group in the early 1990s, TEA Basel survived and was renamed TEA Switzerland in 1994. TEA Switzerland provided a variety of services to various airlines over the following years including wet leases of its 737s. In addition several subsidiaries were established including TEA Cyprus and TEA Hellas.

Following its taking a stake in March 1998, TEA Switzerland became an associate of easyJet and began to operate a low-cost service in November. The airline name was changed to easyJet Switzerland and established its base in Geneva. A service to Luton commenced the following January.

STATUS
Scheduled carrier
Employees: 280
Passengers per year: 1,200,000 (2001)

EgyptAir

Registered name: EgyptAir
Country: Egypt
Region: Africa
Address: New Administration Complex
              Airport Road
              Cairo
Tel: 0020 2 26/ 47 00
Fax: 0020 2 696 46 27
Web site: www.egyptair.com.eg
Main operational base: Cairo

STATUS
IATA scheduled international carrier
National Flag Carrier
Employees: 8,993

Passengers per year: 4,895,000 (2001)
ICAO code: MSR
IATA code: MS

SERVICES
International / Regional / Domestic
Passenger / Cargo
International routes: Algeria, Australia, Austria, Bahrain, Belgium, Morocco, Cote D'Ivoire, Cyprus, Denmark, Eritrea, Ethiopia, France, Gaza Strip, Germany, Ghana, Greece, Hungary, India, Italy, Jordan, Kenya, Kuwait, Lebanon, Malta, Netherlands, Nigeria, Oman, Russia, Saudi Arabia, South Africa, Spain, Sudan, Sweden, Switzerland, Syria, Tanzania,

Tunisia, Turkey, UAE, Uganda, UK, Ukraine, USA, Yemen, Zimbabwe

ALLIANCES / CODE SHARES
Malaysian A/l, Olympic Aw, Philippine A/l

OWNED SUBSIDIARY AIRLINES
Air Sinai

FLEET
A300-600R - 7, A318-200 - 5, A320-200 - 7, A321-200 - 4, A340-200 - 3, A340-600 - 5, 737-500 - 5, 747-300 - 2, 777-200ER - 5

EgyptAir was originally formed on June 6th 1932 as Misr Airwork by the Misr Bank with

assistance from Airwork. Initial aircraft included the de Havilland Dragon and domestic services commenced the following July. The first international route was flown to Lydda and Haifa commenced in 1934 with additional routes being slowly added.

Once the war ended, Misr Airwork commenced a rapid degree of expansion and in 1949 became fully government owned with the name being amended to Misrair SAE in 1949. Operational aircraft still included a Rapide as well as the Beech 18, Sud-Est Languedoc and eight Vickers Viking.

The Vickers Viscount entered service in 1956 and was used to fly international routes that eventually linked with London.

Misrair SAE was merged with Syrian Airways in January 1961 to form United Arab Airways (UAA). However, this was short lived and Syria withdrew. UAA continued as an international Egyptian airline with the Comet followed by a number of Soviet types including An-24s, Il-18s, Il-62s and Tu-154s. In 1968 a return to Western aircraft saw the 707 followed by the 737 in 1976. Domestic services continued to be operated under the Misrair name.

UAA was renamed EgyptAir on October 10th 1971 following the country's name to the Arab Republic of Egypt. An A300 was leased in 1977 and a number of models have been added since.

During the late 1970s, EgyptAir undertook a major survey which formed the basis of a restructure plan to re-establish the airline. With new finance in place eight A300s were ordered in September 1980. Three F-27 Friendships were also acquired for the domestic routes.

Having achieved the aim of getting EgyptAir back on stream, a new round of spending followed in which it effectively replaced the whole of its fleet with orders for 737s, a 747, 767s, 777s, A300-600s, A320s, A321s and A340s. This huge commitment concluded with an order for three A318s in April 1999 to replace the remaining 737-200s at a total cost of some US$3,112 million.

ABOVE: *Egyptair A340-212, SU-GBM (C/n 156) (Airbus)*

In October 1999 EgyptAir 990 crashed with the loss of 217 lives. The NTSB board cited the co-pilot as being the cause by deliberately crashing the 767 while the airline strongly refuted this claiming a malfunction.

In May 2002 the airline sadly suffered another loss when a 737-500 hit a hill during approach to Tunis in bad weather.

EgyptAir is currently planning to add new services to Canada, China and Malaysia.

BELOW: *Egyptair 777-266ER. SU-GBS (C/n 2845) (Jeremy Flack/API)*

El Al

Registered name: El Al Israel Airlines
Country: Israel
Region: Middle East
Address: Ben Gurion International Airport
Tel Aviv 70100
Tel: 00972 3 971 61 11
Fax: 00972 3 972 14 42 or 971 60 40
Web site: www.elal.co.il
Main operational base: Tel Aviv / Ben Gurion

ABOVE: *El Al 747-258B, 4X-AXC (C/n 20704) (Jeremy Flack/API)*

STATUS

IATA scheduled international carrier
National Flag Carrier
Passengers per year: 2,963,000 (2001)
ICAO code: ELY
IATA code: LY

SERVICES

International / Regional / Passenger
Charter / Cargo

ALLIANCES / CODE SHARES

Cyprus A/l, Delta A/L, Iberia, LOT, Thai
Int A/l

FLEET

737-700 - 2, 737-800 - 3, 747-400 - 4, 757-200
- 5, 767-200 - 6, 777-200ER - 3
On order: 777-200 - 1

El Al was formed on November 15th, 1948, as the national airline of the newly formed state of Israel although an inaugural flight was made in September to fly the country's first president from Geneva to Israel. Services commenced the following year with flights to Paris and Rome using DC-4 / C-54s and the C-46 Commandos.

A route commenced to South Africa in 1950 and another to New York the following year with newly acquired Constellations.

El Al accepted delivery of the first of four Bristol Britannias in 1957 that were used on European and the New York routes. However, their transatlantic use was short-lived with the arrival of a leased 707 in 1961. It is with the 707 that El Al set a world record for the longest non-stop commercial flight of 5,760 statute miles in 9 hours 33 minutes on its first service to New York. The 707s were augmented with a number of 720s. The first of many 747s was delivered in May 1971 and they were used initially on the transatlantic routes. During 1982 El Al suffered financial difficulties that resulted in a four-month suspension of operations. The Israeli Government ban on all Saturday services – the Jewish Sabbath – did not help in its recovery, nor the high level of security costs incurred.

In 1984, El Al flew the first commercial international flight with the 767 on a Montreal / Tel Aviv service. During Operation Solomon in May 1991, a total of 1,087 Ethiopian Jews were flown from Addis Ababa in a 747. A plan to privatise El Al was postponed in 1997 and was to be reviewed in 2003. However, the unresolved political position continues to be a cause of difficulties for the airline which still operates at a loss. With tourism cut by nearly 50% together with the high security overheads and only a six-day operation the privatisation will proceed in the near future. The surface-to-air missile (SAM) attack on an Arkia 757 in 2002 by terrorists in Kenya will not have helped.

Emirates

Registered name: Emirates UAE
Country: United Arab Emirates
Region: Middle East
Address: PO Box 686, Duba
Dubai
Tel: 00971 4 295 11 11
Fax: 00971 4 295 58 17
Web site: www.emirates.com
Main operational base: Dubai

STATUS

IATA international carrier
National Flag Carrier
Employees: 9,063
Passengers per year: 6,765,000 (2001)
ICAO code: UAE
IATA code: EK

SERVICES

International / Regional / Domestic
Passenger / Cargo
International routes: Australia, Bahrain, Bangladesh, China, Cyprus, France, Germany, Greece, India, Indonesia, Iran, Italy, Jordan, Kuwait, Lebanon, Maldives, Malta, Oman, Pakistan, Saudi Arabia, Sri Lanka, Sweden, Switzerland, Syria, Thailand, Turkey, UAE, UK, Yemen

ABOVE: *Emirates 777 21H, A6 EMI (C/n 27250) (Jeremy Flack/API)*

ALLIANCES / CODE SHARES

Air-India, BA, Continental Aw, Deutsche BA, SAA, SriLankan A/l, Thai Aw Int, United A/l

FLEET

A300-605R - 1, A310-308 - 1, A330-200 - 23, 777-200 - 9, 777-300 - 5

On order: A340-500 - 6, A340-600 - 8 for delivery 2000 to 2004 + 10 options, A380-800 - 22 for delivery from 2006 + 10 options, 777 - 25

Emirates was formed in May 1985 by the Dubai Government with a leased A300 from Pakistan Airlines (PIA). The first service was flown to Karachi in October 1985. Early services were flown with a leased 737 from Pakistan Airlines (PIA) and an A300.

New routes were steadily added and the fleet increased with additional A300s, A310s and a 727 with a 777 introduced in 1996.

Emirates announced an order for 16 A330s in November 1996 with options for a further seven. These were to replace the A300 and A320 fleet which had provided the backbone of the Emirates operation.

ABOVE: *Emirates A330-243 (Airbus)*

During 2001 Emirates brought out its answer to the, then, recent publicity about deep vein thrombosis when it announced that it was going to issue each passenger with an aerogym. This inflatable pad enables exercise that stimulates blood flow to the leg muscles without causing disturbance to fellow passengers.

Emirates was fortunate in that it is one of only a few airlines that does not seem to have been hit financially as a result of September 11th although its schedules were reduced briefly and soon restored. Since then it has seen passenger levels continue to rise and US$15 billion of orders

was announced at the Dubai Air Show in 2001. This was in line with Emirates' plans for the future, to increase the fleet from its current strength to over 100 by 2010, that will also require a doubling of staff.

Part of its success may be in the quality of its service, with all A310 customers having access to six TV channels and 18 on the A330s and 777s. Business Class has a 50-title film library to watch in their personal video player.

Estonian Air

Registered name: Estonian Air
Country: Estonia
Region: Europe
Address: 13 Lennujaama St
Tallinn 11101
Tel: 00372 640 11 00
Fax: 00372 601 60 92
Web site: www.estonian-air.ee
Main operational base: Tallinn

STATUS

IATA scheduled and charter passenger + cargo carrier.

National Flag Carrier
Employees: 383
Passengers per year: 272,500 (2001)
ICAO code: ELL
IATA code: OV

SERVICES

Regional / Domestic / Passenger
Charter / Cargo
International routes: Denmark, Estonia, Germany, Latvia, Lithuania, Russia, Sweden, UK, Ukraine

ALLIANCES / CODE SHARES

Aeroflot, Aerosvit, AirBaltic, SAS

FLEET

737-500 - 2, Fokker 50 - 2

Estonian Air was formed on December 12th 1991 by the newly formed Estonian Government from the local division of Aeroflot. It was initially equipped with the An-12, Tu-134 and Yak-40.

Approval for the airline to be partially privatised was given in 1995 with 66% of the equity made available to private investors. Maersk successfully bid for 49% and assisted in providing a pair of 737s that were followed by a pair of Fokker 50 a little later.

Ethiopian Airlines

Registered name: Ethiopian Airlines Enterprise
Country: Ethiopia
Region: Asia
Address: PO Box 1755
Bole International Airport
Addis Ababa
Tel: 00251 1 61 22 22
Fax: 00251 1 61 14 74
Web site: www.flyethiopian.com
http://www.ethiopianairlines.com/
Main operational base: Bole International Airport

STATUS

IATA scheduled carrier
National Flag Carrier

Employees: 3,891
Passengers per year: 965,500 (2001)
ICAO code: ETH
IATA code: ET

SERVICES

International / Regional / Domestic
Passenger / Charter / Cargo
International routes: Angola, Burundi, Chad, China, Congo, Congo Republic, Cote D'Ivoire, Denmark, Djibouti, Egypt, Germany, Ghana, India, Israel, Italy, Kenya, Lebanon, Malawi, Netherlands, Nigeria, Pakistan, Rwanda, Saudi Arabia, Somalia, South Africa, Sudan, Tanzania, Thailand, UAE, Uganda, UK, USA, Virgin Is, Yemen, Zambia, Zimbabwe

ABOVE: *Ethiopian Airlines 767-260ER (T. W. Walker/API)*

ALLIANCES / CODE SHARES

Ghana Aw

FLEET

ATR 42-300 - 2, 737-200Adv - 2, 757-200 - 4, 757-200F - 1, 767-200ER - 2 (to be replaced by 767-300ER, 767-300 - 1, 767-300ER - 2, DHC-6 Twin Otter 300 - 3, Fokker 50 - 5, L-100-30 Hercules - 2, Ag-CAT - 7, Turbo Thrush - 2
On order: 737-700 - 6 for delivery 2002/3 + 5 options, 767-300ER - 6 for delivery 2002/3, 777 - 3

Ethiopian Airlines was formed in December 1945 with assistance from TWA and equipped with five C-47 / DC-3s. The first service was from Addis Ababa to Cairo in April 1946. More international routes followed, as did domestic routes to isolated parts of the country.

By the 1980s, Ethiopian Airlines was operating a jet fleet of 720s plus one 707. Some 727s, 737s and 767s were later added together with DHC-6 Twin Otters and the ATR 42. An Ethiopian Airlines 767 was the subject of a hijack in November 1996 during a flight from Addis Ababa to Nairobi. As fuel ran out the pilot attempted to land on the sea in shallow water near Grande Comore. Unfortunately the aircraft broke up into large sections but rescuers were able to reach the wreck quickly and 48 of

the 175 passengers were saved. In addition to its normal airline services, Ethiopian Airlines operates a number of light aircraft for pilot training as well as some agricultural aircraft that are used for crop spraying.

ABOVE: *Ehtiopian Airlines 50-120, ET-AKS (C/n 20328) (T.W. Walker/API)*

EVA Airways

Registered name: EVA Airways Corporation
Country: Taiwan
Region: Far East
Address: EVA Air Building
    376 Hsin-nan Rd, Sec 1, Taipei 338
Tel: 00886 2 85 00 25 20
Fax: 00886 2 25 15 91 71
Web site: www.evaair.com.tw
Stockholder: Evergreen Group
Main operational base: Taipei

STATUS

Scheduled international passenger + cargo carrier.
Employees: 4,981
Passengers per year: 4,186,000 (2001)
ICAO code: EVA
IATA code: BR

SERVICES

International / Regional / Domestic Passenger / Charter / Cargo
International routes: Austria, Australia, Belgium, Canada, China, France, India, Indonesia, Japan, Malaysia, Netherlands, New Zealand, Philippines, Singapore, Taiwan, Thailand, UAE, UK, USA, Vietnam

ALLIANCES / CODE SHARES

Air Canada, Air New Zealand, Air Nippon, Air Orient, America West A/l, American A/l, BA, Continental A/l, Qantas

FLEET

747-400 -15, 747-400F - 2, 767-200 - 4, 767-300ER - 4, MD-11 - 3, MD-11F - 9
On order: A330-200 - 8, 747-400F - 3, 777-200/300 - 7 +8 options
EVA Airways was formed on April 7th, 1989, by the shipping company Evergreen Group and commenced its first scheduled service on July 1st, 1991.

ABOVE: *Computer aided photo of an EVA Airways A340-500 (Airbus)*

In 1997, EVA Airways entered into an agreement with Continental to share operating services.

In 2001 EVA Airways suffered its worst loss since 1994 (US$89 million) although this was better than it had forecast. This was considered to have been due to the significant size of its cargo business. As a result the three passenger-carrying MD-11s were to be modified to freighters.

ExpressJet Airlines/Continental Express

Registered name: New ExpressJet Airlines, Inc
Country: USA
Region: North America
Address: 1600 Smith St
Houston
TX 77002
Tel: 001 713 324 26 39
Fax: 001 713 324 44 20
Web site: www.expressjet.com
Stockholder: ExpressJet Holdings, Inc
Main operational base: Houston

LEFT: *ExpressJet Airlines ErJ-135 (foreground) and ERJ-145 operate as Continental Express for Continental Airlines (Continental)*

STATUS

Scheduled regional commuter carrier
Employees: 5,500
Passengers per year: 3,388,000 (2001)
ICAO code: BTA
IATA code: CO

SERVICES

Regional / Domestic / Passenger
Cargo
International routes: Mexico

ALLIANCES / CODE SHARES

Northwest A/l

FLEET

ERJ-135 - 30, ERJ-145 - 140, ERJ-145ER - 44, ERJ-145XR - 18
On Order: ERJ-145XR - 86 for delivery in 2003 onwards + 100 options

ExpressJet was originally formed as Vercoa Air Service in 1956 and became Britt Airways in 1968. Operations commenced as Continental Express in January 1989 which was later acquired by Continental.

ExpressJet Airlines provides the whole of the regional capacity for Continental operating out of its hubs at Houston, Cleveland and Newark covering some 110 cities.

ExpressJet became the launch customer for the new Embraer ERJ-145XR regional jet. It took delivery of the first two of its 104 firm orders in December 1996 following aircraft certification by the US Federal Aviation Administration.

ExpressJet underwent a transfer in April 2002. Continental sold 30 million shares to establish New ExpressJet Airlines Inc. The assets, equipment and personnel of ExpressJet were then transferred to the new airline that then changed its name to ExpressJet Airlines.

Finnair

LEFT: *Finnair A319-112, OH-LVB (C/n 1107) (Airbus)*

Registered name: Finnair O/Y
Country: Finland
Region: Europe
Address: Tietotie 11 A
Helsinki-Vantaa Airport
Helsinki FIN-0105
Tel: 00358 9 818 81
Fax: 00358 9 818 44 01
Web site: www.finnair.com and www.finnair.fi
Stockholder: The Finnair Group
Main operational base: Helsinki-Vantaa Airport

STATUS

IATA scheduled and charter carrier
National Flag Carrier
Employees: 9,038
Passengers per year: 7,540,000 (2001)
ICAO code: FIN
IATA code: AY

SERVICES

International / Regional / Domestic
Passenger / Charter / Cargo

International routes: Austria, Belgium, China, Cyprus, Czech, Denmark, Estonia, France, Germany, Greece, Hungary, Ireland, Italy, Japan, Latvia, Lithuania, Netherlands, Norway, Poland, Russia, Singapore, Spain, Sweden, Switzerland, Thailand, UK, USA

ALLIANCES / CODE SHARES

Oneworld / Air France, Air Littoral, Lithuanian A/l, Luxair, SN Brussels A/l, TAP, Ukraine Int A/l

FLEET

A319-112 - 4, A320-214 - 7, A321-211 - 4, ATR 72 - 9, 757-200 - 7, DC-9-51 - 8, MD-11 - 5, MD-82 / MD-83 - 16
On order: A319-112 - 4 + 2 options, A320-214 - 6 + 2 options, A321-211 - 1 + 2 options

ABOVE: *Finnair A321-211, OH-LZB (C/n 961) (Jeremy Flack/API)*

Finnair was originally founded on September 12th, 1923, as Aero O/Y and commenced operation the following March with Junkers F.13 float-planes linking Helsinki with Tallinn in Estonia. Later these were joined by a G 24 followed by five Ju-52s and a pair of Dragon Rapides.

Operations were limited during the war with civil aviation placed under military control and the Rapides transferred to the Air Force and two DC-2s acquired in 1940. Of 3,900 passengers carried during the war, 1,500 were children evacuated to Sweden. However, the Finnish Government assisted in getting Aero O/Y operating again in 1946 by taking a majority stake (70%). Eight surplus C-47s were acquired of which six were converted for airline use. This enabled a network to be re-established using these and the Ju-52s with aircraft marked as Finnish Air Lines. However, it was slow and it was 1954 before a service to London and Paris commenced. The holding of the Olympic Games in Finland had provided a useful boost.

Convair 340s, and later 440s, began to replace the ex-military DC-3s and the air-line started using the name Finnair in its new corporate image.

Negotiations with its Soviet neighbours, Aeroflot, led to it being the first post-war non-communist carrier to be permitted to operate a route to Moscow in 1956. The jet age reached Finnair in April 1960 with its first Caravelle schedule and it became the first Super Caravelle operator in 1964. Aero O/Y formally changed name to Finnair in 1968. Polar-Air Oy was established as a subsidiary for charter operations in 1969. A holding was taken in Kar-Air in 1962 that resulted in most of the charter business being transferred from Polar-Air.

A service with a DC-8 commenced in May 1969 linking Helsinki with New York via Copenhagen and Amsterdam. During the 1970s Finnair widened its business base with acquisitions of hotels and travel agencies.

The DC-9 was ordered in September 1970 and entered service for the short-haul routes in 1972. This was followed by orders for the DC-10, placed in December, for the long-haul services. This DC-10 was fitted with an additional fuel tank that enabled it to be the first and only airline to fly from Western Europe to Tokyo direct. Five years later, it was flying to China direct.

Finnaviation was established as a subsidiary in 1979 with Bandeirante. The following year, the Convair 440s were withdrawn from service and replaced with F-27 Friendships for domestic destinations unsuitable for jet operations.

The Aero Oy title was revived in 1982 - this time as a subsidiary - for technical services and leasing operations. In April 1983 Finnair flew its last scheduled Caravelle service. During 1986 an order was placed for five ATR 72 turboprop airliners and received its first two A300s.

Finnair became the first operator of the MD-11 in December 1990. In 1997 orders were placed for Airbus A219s, A320s and A321s for use on its European routes with the first A321s arriving in January 1999.

Finnair joined the Oneworld alliance in 1999.

FlyBe

ABOVE: *FlyBe DHC-8 Q400 (Bombardier)*

Registered name: FlyBE
Country: UK
Region: Europe
Address: Exeter International Airport
Exeter, EX5 2BD
Tel: 0044 1392 36 66 99
Fax: 0044 1392 36 61 51
Web site: www.flybe.com
Stockholder:
Main operational base: Exeter

STATUS

Scheduled and charter carrier
Employees: 1,779
Passengers per year: 2,573,000 (2001)
ICAO code: BEE
IATA code: BE

SERVICES

Regional / Domestic / Passenger
Charter / Cargo
International routes: Belgium, France*,
Ireland, Netherlands (*code share)

ALLIANCES / CODE SHARES

Air France, Continental A/l, Scot Aw, VLM

FLEET

BAe 146-100 - 1, BAe 146-200 - 7, BAe 146-300 - 5, CRJ200 - 4, DHC-8 Dash 8-Q200 - 3, DHC-8 Dash 8-Q300 - 6, DHC-8 Dash 8-Q400 - 2
On order: DHC-8 Dash 8-Q400 - 2

FlyBe was originally formed as Jersey European Airways (JEA) on November 1st, 1979. JEA comprised the Jersey-based Intra Airways and the passenger element of Express Air Services. Initial aircraft were DC-3s, Heralds and Viscounts.

Following a change in direction the fleet changed with Bandeirantes, Islanders and Twin Otters replacing the larger aircraft during the early 1980s. SD330s were subsequently added followed by the SD360 and HS748.

Walkersteel Group, which also owned the charter airline Spacegrand, acquired JEA in 1983 and the two airlines were formally merged under Jersey European Airways title in 1985.

The arrival of a pair of F-27 Friendships in 1988 for the Channel Island service saw growth in the route. A new corporate image resulted in a fresh colour scheme for the fleet. JEA gained its first route into London - Gatwick from Guernesy in 1991 plus another from Jersey shortly after. This resulted in six more F-27s being acquired in 1991 and the first BAe 146 added in 1993 with a further six added to the fleet a little later. These were to be operated on the London to Belfast, Belfast to Birmingham and Channel Islands services.

Code share agreements with Air Inter in 1995 and franchise routes with Air France in 1996 saw the JEA network expanding into Europe. At the same time the BAe 146 Business Class saw an enhancement with leather seats as well as improved booking and checking in facilities.

A new London base in the form of London City enabled further expansion and 11 DHC-8s were ordered.

JEA was renamed British European on June 1st, 2000 and became FlyBe on July 18th, 2002. During this period a policy of a two-type fleet was established resulting in a current fleet of BAe 146s, DHC-8s and CRJ200s with plans to dispose of the CRJs.

The aims of FlyBe are to take the best elements of the budget airline with the service of the traditional airline. It has entered a code share agreement with Continental Airlines and provides US connections through Birmingham and Gatwick.

Frontier Airlines

Registered name: Frontier Airlines Inc
Country: USA
Region: North America
Address: 7001 Tower Rd
Denver
Colorado 80249-31
Tel: 001 720 374 42 00
Fax: 001 720 374 46 21
Web site: www.frontierairlines.com
Main operational base: Denver

ABOVE: *Frontier 737-3M8, N303FL (C/n 25039) (Jeremy Flack/API)*

STATUS

Scheduled carrier
Employees: 2,479
Passengers per year: 3,017,000 (2001)
ICAO code: FFT
IATA code: F9

SERVICES

Domestic / Passenger / Cargo
International routes: Domestic only

ALLIANCES / CODE SHARES

Great Lakes Avn, Mesa Air Gp

OWNED SUBSIDIARY AIRLINES

Frontier Jet Express

FLEET

A319-100 - 13, 737-200Adv - 5, 737-300 - 17
On order: A318-100 - 6, A319-100 - 16 (3 for delivery in 2003 replacing 737s)

The original Frontier Airlines was formed in 1946 but ceased operations as such following its acquisition by People Express.

The name was resurrected and operations for the new Frontier Airlines commenced in July 1994. Although based at Denver, as with the original airline, the operating similarity stopped there in that the new airline was established as a low-fare operation.

The opportunity was taken following the downsizing of an existing Denver operation. A management group of the former Frontier Airlines saw the opportunity with a number of service gaps and established itself at the new Denver International Airport.

During the late 1990s Frontier Airlines implemented a programme that will see all the 737s replaced by an all-Airbus fleet operating a mixture of A318s and A319s. By the time the programme is complete it is anticipated that there will be a total of between 36 and 45 of the A320 family by 2005.

Frontier Airlines saw a steady and continued increase in annual passenger levels until September 2001. The sudden drop in passenger numbers forced a number of the scheduled services to be cut.

In June 2002, Frontier Airlines filed an application for a US$70 million loan with 85% guaranteed by the US Government under the ATSB provisions.

Frontier Airlines has entered a code share with Mesa Air Group, flying as Frontier JetExpress. Frontier currently operates a domestic service to 37 cities. Most of its jets feature a 21 ft high artwork of a wild animal on the tail.

Garuda Indonesian Airways

Registered name: Garuda Indonesian PT
Country: Indonesia
Region: Asia
Address: Garuda Indonesia Building
5th Floor
Jalan Merdeka Selatan 13
Jakarta 10110
Tel: 0062 21 231 26 12
Fax: 0062 21 381 14 86
Web site: www.garuda-indonesia.com
Main operational base: Jakarta

STATUS

IATA scheduled passenger + cargo carrier
National Flag Carrier
Employees: 9,086
Passengers per year: 6,478,000 (2001)
ICAO code: GIA
IATA code: GA

SERVICES

International / Regional / Domestic
Passenger / Cargo
International routes: Australia, China, Germany, Japan, Malaysia, Netherlands, New Zealand, Saudi Arabia, S Korea, Singapore, Thailand, UK

ALLIANCES / CODE SHARES

China A/l, Malaysia A/l

FLEET

A330-300 - 6, 737-300 - 7, 737-400 - 14, 737-500 - 5, 747-200 - 4, 747-400 - 3, 777-200 - 6, DC-10-30 - 5, F-28 Mk.4000 - 2 (operated by Citilink)
On order: A330-300 - 3, 747-400 - 5+6 options

Garuda Airlines was formed on March 31st, 1950 by the government with KLM as joint

Garuda Indonesian Airways

ABOVE: *Garuda Indonesian Airways 747-2U3B, PK-GSC (C/n 22248) (Jeremy Flack/API)*

shareholders to succeed from KLM's Inter-Island Division. However, the first flight was flown on January 26th. Initial services were operated with DC-3s and Catalinas and by the end of the year the fleet comprised an impressive 22 DC-3s, 8 Catalinas and 8 Convair 240s. Eight Convair 340s and 14 de Havilland Herons were added in 1953.

Garuda was nationalised in 1954 and the first international route was flown to Singapore. The Catalinas were withdrawn in 1955 and the following year the airline flew its first service to Mecca for pilgrims.

The Lockheed Electra entered service in 1961 enabling new routes to commence to Hong Kong and Tokyo.

Garuda entered the jet age with the Convair 990 in September 1963 that enabled new routes to be operated. By 1965 they extended as far as Amsterdam. DC-8s were also added from 1966.

The Fokker F-27 Friendship entered service in 1969 on domestic routes plus a pair of DC-9s. In 1971, the first pair of an eventual fleet of 33 F-28 Fellowships, entered service making it the world's largest user of the type. The year 1976 saw the arrival of the first wide-body airliner in the form of the DC-10 that was joined by 747s in 1980. Garuda acquired the domestic airline Merapati Nusantara Airlines (formed September 1962) in October 1978. Merapati would later take over the Garuda domestic fleet and continue in its own name leaving Garuda to concentrate on international routes. A number of different types were added to the Garuda fleet during the 1980s ranging from the Airbus A300 and A300-600 through 737-300s and -400s and McDonnell Douglas MD-11s. This enabled a reorganisation of the operation and a rationalisation.

Garuda launched its own low-cost airline - Citilink in July 2001 operating F-28s. The sudden slowdown in the Far East economies in the late 1990s saw difficult times for Garuda. Having already dropped its USA routes, the events of September 11th did not cause undue difficulties for the airline although the rapid growth in the number of domestic airlines does pose a problem. Plans are in hand for a partial privatisation in 2004.

GB Airways

Registered name: GB Airways Ltd
Country: UK
Region: Europe
Address: The Beehive
Gatwick Airport
West Sussex, RH6 0LA
Tel: 0044 1293 66 42 39
Fax: 0044 1293 66 42 18
Web site: www.gbairways.com
Stockholder: Bland Group
Main operational base: London - Gatwick

ABOVE: *GB Airways A320-231 operates in BA colours with small GB name on the nose (GB Airways)*

STATUS

International scheduled passenger + cargo carrier

Employees: 755
Passengers per year: 1,303,200 (2001)
ICAO code: GBL
IATA code: GT

SERVICES

International / Regional / Passenger Charter / Cargo
International routes: France, Gibraltar, Malta, Morocco, Portugal, Spain, Tunisia

ALLIANCES / CODE SHARES

Iberia

FLEET

A320-200 - 5, A321-200 - 2, 737-300 - 4
On order: A320 / A321s - 4 for Spring / Summer 2003

GB Airways was originally formed as Gibair in 1931 as part of the Gibraltar Shipping Company and equipped with a Saro Windhoever flying boat. After only two months the operation was suspended.

The name of Gibair was resurrected in May 1947 when a new airline was established and the original route to Tangiers subsequently resurrected in conjunction with BEA. A Viscount entered service in 1974.

The name was changed to GB Airways in November 1981 and it became a BA franchise partner in February 1995. This saw the disappearance of its own aircraft colour-scheme as it took the BA corporate identity. This arrangement was renewed for a further eight years in 2000.

In March 1999 GB Airways had two causes to celebrate. Not only had it been based in the UK for 10 years but more importantly, it had carried over 1 million passengers in a 12 month period for the first time. The following March saw GB Airways commence its first schedule into France to Nantes. In May the first of the A320 / A321 fleet arrived. By the end of 2003 the 737s will have been replaced.

Ghana Airways

ABOVE: *Ghana Airways DC-10-30, 9G-ANA (C/n 48286) (Jeremy Flack/API)*

Registered name: Ghana Airways Ltd
Country: Ghana
Region: Africa
Address: Ghana Airways House
                  Ghana Airways Avenue
                  Airport Residential Area
                  PO Box 1636, Accra
Tel: 00233 21 77 33 21 / 42 / 35
Fax: 00233 21 77 70 78 / 77 33 16
Main operational base: Accra

STATUS

IATA scheduled passenger carrier
National Flag Carrier
Employees: 1,364
Passengers per year: 308,000 (2001)
ICAO code: GHA
IATA code: GH

SERVICES

International / Regional / Passenger
Cargo
International routes: Benin, Burkina Faso, Cote D'Ivoire, Ethiopia, Gambia, Germany, Guinea, Italy, Liberia, Nigeria, Senegal, South Africa, UK, USA, Zimbabwe

ALLIANCES / CODE SHARES

Ethiopian A/l, Nigeria A/l, SAA

FLEET

A320 - 1, DC-10-30 -4, DC-9-51 - 2

Ghana Airways was originally formed on July 4th, 1958, in conjunction with BOAC (40%) to take over the operations of the West African Airways Corporation. First operations were flown with an ex-BOAC Stratocruiser.

Ghana Airways became fully nationalised in 1961 and acquired a mixed fleet that included Russian An-12s and Il-18s as well as British Britannias and Viscounts. By the mid-1960s they were being replaced by a VC.10 for long-haul and HS748 plus F-28s for the domestic services.

A DC-9 arrived in 1978 and a DC-10 replaced the VC.10 in the early 1980s. One of the DC-9s suffered a wheels-up landing in November 2000 reducing the number operated from three to two.

It is understood that following a partnership deal with Nationwide airlines of South Africa and the Government of Ghana, Ghana Airways will become known as Ghana Nationwide. This is subject to signature and also requires a solution to the airlines existing debt that had totalled US$160 million.

Gulf Air

Registered name: Gulf Air Ltd
Country: Bahrain
Region: Middle East
Address: PO Box 138
    Manama
Tel: 00973 32 22 00
Fax: 00973 33 85 55
Web site: www.gulfairco.com
Main operational base: Bahrain

STATUS

IATA scheduled passenger carrier
National Flag Carrier
Employees: 4,948
Passengers per year: 5,252,000 (2001)
ICAO code: GFA
IATA code: GF

SERVICES

International / Regional / Domestic
Passenger / Charter / Cargo
International routes: Bangladesh, China,
Cyprus, Egypt, France, Germany, India,
Indonesia, Iran, Jordan, India, Kenya,
Kuwait, Lebanon, Malaysia, Morocco,
Nepal, Pakistan, Philippines, Saudi Arabia,
Sri Lanka, Singapore, Sudan, Syria,
Tanzania, Thailand, Turkey, UAE, Uganda,
UK, Yemen

ALLIANCES / CODE SHARES

Air-India, American A/l, Cyprus Aw, PAL,
Royal Air Maroc, Saudi Arabian A/l

FLEET

A320-200 - 10, A330-200 - 6, 767-300ER - 10

Formed on March 24th 1950 as Gulf
Aviation Co Ltd equipped with Avro Ansons
and headquartered in Bahrain. Initial operations were little more than sight seeing trips.
Gradually a commuter service emerged
between Bahrain, Doha and Dhahran. A de
Havilland Dove and an Auster were later
added to the fleet and helped to operate
contracts with oil companies.

BELOW: *Gulf Air A330-243, A40-KB (C/n 281) (Airbus)*

During the 1950s, BOAC became a major
shareholder of Gulf Aviation with an operating capital injection plus supplying pilots
and technicians. Some de Havilland
Herons were added to the fleet. This
enabled further expansion of its Middle
East network to include Abu Dhabi, Kuwait,
Muscat and Sharjah.

F-27 Friendships replaced the older aircraft in 1968 and Gulf Air entered the jet
age with the arrival of its first BAC 1-11 in
1969.

In 1973/4 the entire share capital was
acquired equally by the governments of Abu
Dhabi, Bahrain, Oman and Qatar. The airline changed its name to the current Gulf
Air and it was established as the national carrier for each member country. Vickers
VC.10s were ordered and began to be delivered from 1974 enabling new long-haul
routes to be operated. The VC.10s were
replaced with Tristars from 1976 and 737s
the following year. More recently new types
have been added in the form of the 767s in
1988, A320s in 1992 and A340s in 1994.

Following the expansion of the Gulf Air
route network, annual passenger levels
broke the 5 million mark for the first time
in 1995. Prestigious services are expensive
and Gulf Air was offering an extensive quality service that could be sustained during
the booming oil days. However, the late
1990s saw a shrinking market that became
progressively more difficult for the airline.

Gulf Air had been struggling for a while
and the September 11th attack has
exacerbated this. With debts of around
$800 million a cash injection of $160million
in 2001 was followed by a further $80mil-
lion in 2002 by the states of Abu Dhabi,
Bahrain and Oman. However, the fourth
partner has decided to withdraw. In the
meantime a restructure programme is in
the process of being implemented to
reduce costs. This has included cutting
routes to Australia as well as Athens and
Milan and disposing of its fleet of five
A340s.

LEFT: *Gulf Air 767-3P6ER, A40-GY (C/n 26234) (Jeremy
Flack/API)*

Hapag-Lloyd Flug

Registered name: Hapag-Lloyd Flugesellschaft mbH
Country: Germany
Region: Europe
Address: Flughafenstrasse 10
              D-30855 Langenhagen
Tel: 0049 511 97 27 0
Fax: 0049 511 97 27 341
Web site: www.hlf.de
Stockholder: TUI AG
Main operational base: Hanover

ABOVE: *Hapag-Lloyd A310-204, D-AHLV (C/n 430) in their old colours (Jane's)*

STATUS

Scheduled and charter passenger carrier
Employees: 2,262
Passengers per year: 7,082,000 (2001)
ICAO code: HLF
IATA code: HF

SERVICES

International / Regional / Passenger
Charter
International routes: Spain, Greece, Italy,
Morocco, Portugal, Turkey, Tunisia

FLEET

A310-200 - 4, 737-800 - 29

ABOVE: *Hapag-Lloyd 737-8K5, D-AHLP (C/n 32905) in their new colours (Hapag-Lloyd)*

The origins of Hapag-Lloyd can be traced back to 1910 when the Hamburg-America Line (HAPAG) was handling airship passengers for Deutsche Luftschiffahrts AG.

In 1923 HAPAG and North German Lloyd set up Deutsche Aero Lloyd, which in 1926 merged with Junkers Luftverkehr to form Deutsche Luft Hansa resulting in the ending of the HAPAG name with aviation but not for ever.

Hapag-Lloyd was founded on June 20th 1972 by the shipping company of the same name and commenced operations on March 31st to Ibiza from Hamburg with a 727.

Bavaria-Germanair was acquired in 1979 with its BAC 1-11s. The first A300s arrived the same year and were operated until replaced by the A310s and 737s by the end of the 1980s.

The latest addition to the fleet was the 737-800s of which the first of 29 arrived in 1998.

Hawaiian Air

Registered name: Hawaiian Airlines Inc
Country: USA
Region: Central America & Caribbean
Address: PO Box 30008
              Honolulu
              Hawaii
              HI 96820
Tel: 001 808 835 37 00
Fax: 001 808 835 36 90
Web site: www.hawaiianair.com
Main operational base: Honolulu

STATUS

Scheduled passenger carrier
Employees: 3,491
Passengers per year: 5,886,000 (2000)
ICAO code: HAL
IATA code: HA

SERVICES

International / Regional / Domestic
Passenger / Charter / Cargo
International routes: American Samoa,
Hawaii, Tahiti, USA

ALLIANCES / CODE SHARES

American A/l, American Eagle A/l,
Continental A/l, Northwest A/l, Virgin
Atlantic Aw

FLEET

717-200 -13,767-300ER - 11, DC-10-10 - 5*,
DC-10-30 - 2*
On order: 717-200 - 7 options, 767-300ER -
5 for delivery 2002/3 (*DC-10s to be
replaced by 767-300ER by end of 2003)

Hawaiian Air

Hawaiian Air was originally formed on January 30th, 1929, as Inter Island Airways. The first service commenced in November using a pair of eight-seat Sikorsky S-36 flying boats, operating services between the islands.

Inter Island Airways operated mail contracts during the 1930s, adding the larger 16-seat S-43 flying boats in 1935. The airline commenced scheduled services in 1939.

The name was changed to Hawaiian Air in October 1941 and withdrew the S-43s in favour of the DC-3. During the war years, the airline provided an aerial lifeline to the neighbouring islands. Convair 340s were introduced in 1952 followed by a DC-6 in 1958.

Hawaiian Air entered the jet age with the arrival of the first DC-9 in 1966 and reduced travel time between the islands to between 20 and 30 minutes. Short SD330 were

added for domestic services in the mid-1970s while Lockheed Electras were also added mainly for cargo operations.

Three DC-8s were operated on charters from 1984 and five Lockheed Tristars were acquired during 1985 for long-haul scheduled passenger and charter operations. DHC-7s were added to the fleet to operate on domestic services.

Hawaiian Air began an association with American Airlines in 1994 when it converted its computer system to their SABRE system. In addition, the Tristars were replaced with DC-10s which would be maintained by American Airlines.

More recently, the 717s have gradually replaced the DC-9s that have formed the backbone of Hawaiian Airlines.

Hawaiian Air operates predominantly in the tourist sector which has lower margins. Hawaiian suffered financial difficulties dur-

ing the early 1990s but re-emerged from a voluntary Chapter 11 in 1974 with creditor holding 67.8% ownership and employees 16.8%.

Since their difficulties, Hawaiian have steadily improved their position and arranged several code share agreements with US airlines. A proposed merger with Aloha Airlines in December 2001 did not proceed.

As with most US airlines, Hawaiian suffered following the terrorist activity on September 11th but was granted US$38.8 million aid.

All of the DC-9s were replaced by 717s and the last example was donated to the University of Hawaii and Honolulu for use in their Aerospace Training Centre. In October 2001 Hawaiian began taking delivery of the 16 767s which will have replaced the DC-10 fleet by the end of 2003.

Horizon Air

Registered name: Horizon Air
Country: USA
Region: North America
Address: PO Box 48309, Seattle, Washington 98148

Seattle
Washington 98148
Tel: 001 206 241 67 57
Fax: 001 206 431 46 96
Web site: www.horizonair.com
Stockholder: Alaska Air Group Inc
Main operational base: Seattle

ABOVE: *Horizon Air DHC-8 Dash 8 Q-202 with a Q-401 tail in the foreground (Bombardier)*

STATUS
Scheduled passenger carrier
Employees: 4,038
Passengers per year: 4,668,000 (2001)
ICAO code: QXE
IATA code: QX

SERVICES
Regional / Domestic / Passenger
Cargo
International routes: Canada

ALLIANCES / CODE SHARES
Alaska A/l, Continental A/l, Helijet Int, KLM, Northwest A/l

FLEET
CRJ700 - 30, DHC-8 Dash 8-100 -9, DHC-8 Dash 8-Q200 - 28, DHC-8 Dash 8-Q400 - 12, F-28 Mk 4000 - 15
On order: CRJ700 - 16, DHC-8 Dash 8-Q200 - 35, DHC-8 Dash 8-Q400 - 3

Horizon Air was formed in September 1981 with two Fairchild built F-27 Friendships.

The airline was established following the Airline Deregulation Act of 1979 when a number of routes were abandoned by the larger airlines. Having realised that there were a number of routes without a service, yet a sufficiently potential market, Milt

Kuilt founded Horizon Air together with a group of venture capitalists.

Initially routes operated by Horizon Air were between Yakima, Pasco and Seattle, however, these services grew rapidly. In 1982 Air Oregon was acquired along with Transwestern Airlines the following year.

Horizon became a public company in 1984 and the funds raised enabled debts to be cleared and created a fund to purchase new aircraft. As with many small successful businesses, Horizon attracted the attention of some larger airlines. Eventually, the Alaska Air Group Inc acquired the airline. While it has been allowed to remain independently managed, it has gained some competitive advantages by being linked to Alaska Airlines. These include connections and the frequent flyer Mileage Plan.

The Dash 8 Q200s replaced the earlier 100 models from 1997 for operation on the

short routes while the new CRJ700s have the greater range. The terrorist action caused problems for Horizon which reacted by cutting its schedule by 20% after what had been a zero growth year. Combined with the late delivery of the CRJ700s to

ABOVE: *Horizon Air DHC-8 Dash 8 Q-401 N406QX (C/n 4048) (Bombardier)*

replace the old F-28s resulted in an overall net loss for 2001 of US$5.8 million.

Iberia

Registered name: Lineas Aéreas de España
Country: Spain
Region: Europe
Address: Calle Velazquez 130
         Madrid E28006
Tel: 0034 91 587 87 87
Fax: 0034 91 587 73 29
Web site: www.iberia.com
Stockholder: Iberia Group
Main operational base: Madrid and Barcelona

STATUS

IATA scheduled passenger carrier
National Flag Carrier
Employees: 28,320
Passengers per year: 27,298,000 (2001)
ICAO code: IBE
IATA code: IB

SERVICES

International / Regional / Domestic
Passenger / Cargo
International routes: Austria, Argentina, Belgium, Brazil, Colombia, Cuba, Czech, Denmark, Dominican Republic, Ecuador, Egypt, Equatorial Guinea, Finland*, France, Germany, Greece, Guatemala, Honduras, Ireland, Israel, Italy, Japan*, Jordan*, Mexico, Morocco, Netherlands, Nicaragua, Norway, Panama, Paraguay*, Peru, Poland, Portugal, Senegal, South Africa, Sweden, Switzerland, Syria*, Thailand*, Turkey, Ukraine*, Uruguay*, UK, USA, Venezuela (*code share)

ABOVE: *Iberia A319-112, EC-HGR (C/n 1154) (Airbus)*

ALLIANCES / CODE SHARES

Oneworld / Air France, American Falcon, CSA, El Al, JAL, LOT, Royal Air Maroc, Royal Jordanian, Syrian Arab, TAM, TAP, TAROM, Ukraine International A/l

Iberia

FLEET

A319-100 - 4, A320-200 - 58, A321-100 - 4,
A340-200 - 8, A340-300 - 7, 747-200B - 5,
757-200 - 18, DC-8-62F - 2, MD-87 - 24, MD-88 - 13

On order: A319-100 - 9 options, A320-200 -
12 for 2003 - 2006 delivery + 8 options,
A321-100 - 12 for 2003 - 2005 delivery + 11
options, A340-300 - 1, A340-600 - 3 for
delivery from 6/2003 + 2 options - to
replace 747-300s

Iberia was originally formed in July 1927
and commenced operations in December
with a service linking Barcelona and
Madrid.

The following year a merger with CETA
and Union Aerea Espana resulted in an airline named Compana de Lineas Aereas
Subvencionadas SA (CLASSA) which flew
its first service from Madrid to Seville with a
Junkers aircraft.

During the 1930s CLASSA continued to
develop its route network and in 1937 the
name reverted to Iberia. Despite its claim to
be neutral, the 49% ownership by Luft
Hansa resulted in operating difficulties during the war. However, after the war Iberia, as
with many other airlines, took advantage of
the surplus and cheap C-47s / DC-3s. DC-4s
were acquired in 1946 and enabled a service
to Buenos Aires. In 1954 Super
Constellations arrived for the New York

route to be replaced by DC-8s in 1961.
Caravelles began to arrive the following year
for European routes. As the routes continued to expand, DC-9s arrived in 1967 and
gradually replaced the Caravelles. The first
of six small F-27 Friendships were also
acquired for routes where the existing aircraft were too large. At the other end of the
scale 747s were ordered for longer routes
and deliveries commenced in 1970. The
first of 37 727s entered service in April 1972
followed by DC-10s the following year.
Airbus A300s were delivered from March
1981 onwards. By the late 1980s Iberia had
rationalised on A300s, 727s, 747s and DC-9s.

Iberia experienced the beginnings of
financial difficulties in 1994. Having spent a
number of years running at a loss, Iberia
implemented a reconstruction plan to run
over 2000 - 2003. A group holding company
was created to manage four separate oper-

ating companies covering aircraft maintenance, handling, freight and systems.

Iberia was privatised in April 2001 and
was one of only a few European airlines to
have produced a profit that year. This was
due in part to the reconstruction plan.
When passenger levels dropped dramatically after September 11th a further rationalisation programme was quickly put in place.
This included staff levels that were cut by
2,500, cancelling of all wet-lease contracts
and a freeze on new deliveries. In addition
Binter Canarias was sold. This quick reaction saved the company from the problems
suffered by many others.

ABOVE: *Iberia A340-313x, EC-HGU (C/n 318) (Iberia)*

BELOW: *Iberia A320-211, EC-GRH (C/n 146) (Jeremy
Flack/API)*

Icelandair

Registered name: Flugleider HF
Country: Iceland
Region: Europe
Address: Reykjavik Airport
101 Reykjavik
Tel: 00354 505 03 00
Fax: 00354 505 03 50
Web site: www.icelandair.com
Main operational base: Reykjavik

ABOVE: *Icelandair 757-208, TF-FIH (C/n 24739) (Baldur Sveinsson)*

STATUS

IATA scheduled passenger carrier
National Flag Carrier
Employees: 1,337
Passengers per year: 1,358,000 (2001)
ICAO code: ICE
IATA code: FI

SERVICES

International / Regional / Passenger
Charter / Cargo
International routes: Austria*, Belgium*,
Denmark, Finland*, France, Germany,
Ireland*, Netherlands, Norway, Sweden*,
Switzerland*, UK, USA (*code share)

ALLIANCES / CODE SHARES

SAS

OWNED SUBSIDIARY AIRLINES

Air Iceland

FLEET

737-300F - 1, 737-400 - 1, 757-200ER - 9, 757-200F - 1, 757-300ER - 1
On order: 757-300ER - 1

Icelandair was originally formed as Flugfelag Akureyrar in 1937 operating domestic services with a Waco YKS floatplane.

In 1940 the airline was renamed Flugfelag Islands. As demand grew by inhabitants in remote locations a second domestic airline - Loftleidir - was formed in 1944.

In the meantime, Flugfelag had leased a 14-seat Liberator to establish a service to Glasgow and a DC-3 for another to Copenhagen.

The first F-27 Friendship was delivered in 1965 while the 727 brought Icelandair into the jet age with its first aircraft delivered in 1967.

Icelandair was formed in 1973 by the merging of Flugfelag Islands and Loftleidir although they continued to retain their identities until October 1979.

The arrival of the first DC-8 in 1982 enabled long-haul services to commence. These included many new European as well as transatlantic destinations.

More recently, 737s and 757s have enabled a continued expansion of their services. In 1997 Air Iceland was formed to operate the domestic and some selected short-haul routes.

The reliance on transitory passengers caused it to suffer more than most European airlines after September 11th. With the loss of some 25% of its transatlantic schedules, the airline concentrated on consolidation and cost cutting. Icelandair Charter and Leasing was established and two aircraft have been allocated to cargo services.

Indian Airlines/IAC

Registered name: Indian Airlines Limited
Country: India
Region: Asia
Address: Airlines House
113 Gurdwara Rakabganj Road
New Delhi 110001
Tel: 0091 11 371 05 30
Fax: 0091 11 371 45 46
Web site: www.indian-airlines.nic.in
Main operational base: Chennai, Delhi, Kolcotta and Mumbai

STATUS

IATA scheduled passenger + cargo carrier
Employees: 19,671
Passengers per year: 5,780,000 (2001)
ICAO code: IAC
IATA code: IC

SERVICES

International / Regional / Domestic
Passenger / Charter / Cargo
International routes: Bahrain, Bangladesh,
Kuwait, Malaysia, Maldives, Myanmar, Nepal, Oman, Singapore, Sri Lanka, Thailand, UAE

ALLIANCES / CODE SHARES

Air-India, SriLankan A/l

OWNED SUBSIDIARY AIRLINES

Alliance Air

FLEET

A300B2-101 - 3, A300B4-203 - 4, A320-200 - 34, 737-200Adv - 11 (operated by Alliance Airlines), Do 228-200 - 3

Indian Airlines/IAC

ABOVE: *Indian Airlines A320-231, VY-EPB (C/n 045) (Airbus)*

Indian Airlines was established on May 28th, 1953, by the Indian Government. It was formed to take over the operations of eight private airlines as part of the nationalisation of Indian air transport to operate domestic and regional services. The airlines concerned were Air-India Ltd, Air Services of India Ltd, Airways (India) Ltd, Bharat Airways Ltd, Deccan Airways Ltd, Himalayan Aviation Ltd, Indian National Airways Ltd and Kalinga Airlines. Operations commenced with a fleet of 99 aircraft on August 1st. However, due to the scale of the merger, each of the airlines continued to operate with its own identities for a while before being fully merged. The fleet mainly comprised of DC-3s, DC-4s and Vickers Vikings and many had seen better days and so a replacement plan was soon put together.

The first Vickers Viscount entered service in October 1957 followed by the F-27 Friendships in May 1961. Indian Airlines entered the jet age with the arrival of the first Caravelle in November 1963 which commenced operations the following February. These three types provided the majority of the fleet for the next few years.

Hindustan Aeronautics produced the Hawker Siddeley HS748 under licence in India and Indian Airlines took delivery of its first example in June 1967. A 737 arrived in November 1970 and as deliveries progressed they replaced the Caravelles. Indian Airlines received its first wide-body airliner in the form of an A300 in October 1976, which entered service in the December.

Alliance Air was formed as a subsidiary in 1996 operating 737s. Indian Airlines has established itself as the largest regional airline in Asia.

Although Indian Airlines has been suffering a series of losses these are not particularly related to September 11th. It has lost some 60% of the domestic market which is partially due to the older aircraft encountering mechanical problems which result in flight delays although this did improve in 2001.

Indian Airlines wishes to upgrade its fleet and the Indian Government has been trying to find a strategic partner. This has proved to be difficult due to the size of investment required.

Iran Air

Registered name: The Airline of the Islamic Republic of Iran
Country: Iran
Region: Middle East
Address: Iran Air Building
Mehrabad International Airport
PO Box 13185-775, Tehran
Tel: 0098 21 979 11 11
Fax: 0090 21 600 32 48
Web site: www.iranair.org
Main operational base: Tehran

STATUS

IATA Scheduled and charter carrier
National Flag Carrier
Employees: 9,439

Passengers per year: 7,894,000 (2001)
ICAO code: IRA
IATA code: IR

SERVICES

International / Regional / Domestic
Passenger / Charter / Cargo
International routes: Austria, Azerbaijan, Bahrain, China, Cyprus, Denmark, France, Germany, Greece, Italy, Kazakhstan, Kuwait, Lebanon, Malaysia, Netherlands, Norway, Japan, Russia, Saudi Arabia, Sweden, Syria, Turkey, UAE, UK, Uzbekistan

ALLIANCES / CODE SHARES

Malaysia Airlines

FLEET

A300-600R - 2, A300B2-203 - 4, A310-200 - 5, A310-300 - 1, 727-100 - 2, 727-200Adv - 4, 737-200 - 3, 747-100 - 1, 747-200 - 2, 747SP - 5, Fokker 100 - 5

The origins of Iran Air can be traced back to December 1944 when Iranian Airways was formed and commenced domestic operations in May 1945 using DC-3s.

The first scheduled service was operated from Teheran to Meshed in May 1946 and led to a steady expansion of routes to many Middle East cities with its fleet of 17 aircraft plus one to Paris.

Iran Airways acquired the domestic carrier - Eagle Airlines - in 1949 with its de

Havilland Dove. The 1950s saw DC-4s, Convair 240s and Vickers Viscounts being added to the fleet. In the meantime, Persian Air Services formed in 1954 to operate a cargo service with chartered Avro Yorks.

The Iranian Government merged and nationalised Iran Airways and Persian Air Services in 1962 as Iran Air.

Iran Air entered the jet age during the 1960s with the 707s and 727s for services into Europe and Russia. These services were followed by the 737s and 747s in the 1970s with the latter being used to inaugurate a service to New York. Although the 707s have been retired, a number of the others airliners remain in service.

The rise in influence of Ayatollah Khomeini in 1979 and the demise of the Shah saw a dramatic change in Iran Air schedules. The extensive international routes were cut with over 100 international departures reduced to under 30 although the domestic operation was largely untouched.

This was followed by conflict with Iraq

ABOVE: *Iran Air 747-286B SCD, EP-IAH (C/n 21218) (Jeremy Flack/API)*

which caused suspension of a number of services.

The first Airbus - an A300 - entered service in March 1980 and Fokker 100s were acquired in 1990/1 for use on domestic and regional routes.

Iran Air proposes to replace the older aircraft in its fleet while the Iranian Government is considering part-privatisation of the airline.

Iraqi Airways

Registered name: Iraqi Airways
Country: Iraq
Region: Middle East
Address: Baghdad International Airport

Tel: 00964 886 39 99
Fax: 00964 886 58 08
Main operational base: Baghdad

STATUS

IATA scheduled passenger carrier
National Flag Carrier
ICAO code: IAW
IATA code: IA

SERVICES

Domestic / Passenger / Cargo

FLEET

707-300C - 2, 727-200Adv - 6, 737-200C - 2, 747-200C - 3

Iraqi Airways was formed in December 1945 by the government as a subsidiary of Iraqi State Railways. It commenced operations with de Havilland Rapides the following month flying a service from Baghdad to Basra.

International services had commenced by the end of the year with DC-3s to various cities throughout the Middle East. Over the next couple of years these had extended into Europe.

The first of five Vickers Viscounts was delivered in 1955. Subsequent aircraft were mainly sourced from the Soviet Union and included An-12s, An-24s, Tu-124s and later Il-76s although some 707s, 737s and 747s were also delivered in the mid-1970s.

The conflict with Iran saw a number of services suspended but they were totally suspended during the Gulf War following an invasion of Kuwait.

Iraqi Airways remains embargoed by a United Nations resolution. Domestic services were temporarily recommenced in November 2000. It is uncertain how many aircraft survived the Gulf Wars and of those, how many will return to service.

Japan Airlines/JAL

Registered name: Japan Airlines Company Ltd
Country: Japan
Region: Far East
Address: The JAL Building
4-11, Higashi-shinagawa 2-chome
Shinagawa-ku
Tokyo 140-8637
Tel: 0081 3 54 60 31 21
Fax: 0081 3 54 60 39 36
Web site: www.jal
Stockholder: JAL Group
Main operational base: Tokyo - Haneda and Narita

STATUS

IATA scheduled international passenger + cargo carrier.
Employees: 16,486
Passengers per year: 37,183,000 (2001)
ICAO code: JAL
IATA code: JL

SERVICES

International / Regional / Domestic Passenger / Cargo
International routes: Australia, Brazil, China, Denmark*, France, Germany, Guam, India, Indonesia, Italy, Malaysia*, Mariana Islands, Mexico, Netherlands, New Caledonia*, New Zealand*, Philippines, Russia, S Korea, Singapore, Spain*, Sweden*, Switzerland, Thailand, Turkey*, UK, USA, Vietnam

ALLIANCES / CODE SHARES

Air France, Air New Zealand, Alitalia, American A/l, BA, Cathay Pacific Aw, China Eastern, Iberia, Malaysia A/l, Northwest A/l, Qantas, Thai Aw Int, THY

OWNED SUBSIDIARY AIRLINES

JAL Express, JAL Ways, Japan Airlines System, Japan Asia Airways, Japan Transocean Air

FLEET

737-400 - 23 (some operated by others in group), 747-100 - 4, 747-200 - 20, 747-300 - 13, 747-400 - 42, 767-200 - 3, 767-300 - 17, 777-200 - 5, 777-300 - 7, DC-10-40 - 9
On order: 747-400 - 3, 747-300 - 4, 777-200 - 16, 777-300 - 8

All Japanese civil aviation was banned after the end of WW2. However, permission was granted by the Supreme Commander - Allied Forces to form Japanese Air Lines on August 1st, 1951. A proviso stipulated that no Japanese pilots were to be used. Early services were operated using Martin 202s followed by DC-4s leased from Northwest Airlines.

The airline was reorganised in October 1953 with the Japanese Government taking a 50% stake. As part of the change, the airline name was amended to Japan Air Lines. Orders were placed for DC-4s and DC-6s while the Beech 18 and de Havilland Heron were acquired for domestic routes.

JAL's first international service was flown to San Francisco with its DC-6s in February 1954 routed via Wake Is and Honolulu. Further services commenced to Far East locations.

JAL entered the jet age in 1960 when a service commenced to Paris in April in association with Air France. Its first own jet was a DC-8 that was delivered in July and was used to provide a service to San Francisco from August 1960. These aircraft were unusual in that their interior was custom tailored to recreate the atmosphere of a fine Japanese home. JAL introduced the oshibori to passengers – the steaming hot towels – a service now replicated by many other airlines. As capacity allowed, new routes were added extending to the Middle East and Europe. In 1965 a new treaty with the US allowed JAL to fly from San Francisco to New York which then opened new routes to Europe.

Japan Air Lines (JAA) was established as a subsidiary of JAL in March 1974 to look after its service to Taiwan. JAL became privatised once again in November 1987 when

BELOW: *Japan Airlines 767-346, JA8266 (C/n 23966) (Jeremy Flack/API)*

the Japanese Government sold its remaining 34.5% stake. In 1990 JAL purchased a 5% stake in DHL that it increased to 25% in 1992.

A number of changes were made to JAL subsidiary airlines during the 1990s. The regional airline J-Air was reorganised to operate a scheduled service from Hiroshima and currently operates Jetstreams and CRJ200s. Japan Air Charter was renamed JAL Ways, operated low-cost scheduled services and operated 747s and DC-10s. Japan Asia Airways operates services to Taiwan plus some limited domestic routes with 747s, 767s and DC-10s.

Besides the airline business, JAL has established a variety of other subsidiaries to broaden its business base. Some are closely linked businesses such as hotels and tour companies for the tourism market and over 300 other subsidiaries and affiliates.

JAL underwent a revision of its corporate image in 1989 part of which was the change

ABOVE: *JAL 747-446, JA8089 (C/n 26342) (Jeremy Flack/API)*

of the name from Japan Air Lines to Japan Airlines. In November 2001, JAL announced the full merger with Japan Air Systems which was due to be completed by the end of 2002.

JAT - Yugoslav Airlines

Registered name: JAT - Yugoslav Airlines
Country: Yugoslavia - Serbia
Region: Europe
Address: Bulevar Umetnosti 16
11070 Belgrade
Tel: 00381 11 311 42 22
Fax: 00381 11 311 28 53
Web site: www.jat.com
Main operational base: Belgrade

STATUS

IATA international and domestic scheduled carrier
National Flag Carrier
Employees: 4,952
Passengers per year: 995,000 (2001)
ICAO code: JAT
IATA code: JU

SERVICES

International / Regional / Domestic
Passenger / Charter / Cargo
International routes: Austria, Belgium,

Bosnia Herzegovina, Bulgaria, Czech, Cyprus, Denmark, Egypt, France, Germany, Greece, Italy, Lebanon, Libya, Malta, Macedonia, Netherlands, Russia, Sweden, Switzerland, Syria, Tunisia, Turkey, UAE, UK

ALLIANCES / CODE SHARES

Air Srpska, CSA

ABOVE: *JAT-Yugoslav Airlines ATR 72-201, YU-ALN (C/n 180) (Jeremy Flack/API)*

FLEET

ATR 72-202 - 3, 727-200 - 8, 737-300 - 9, DC-9-32 - 9, DC-10-30 - 1
On order: A319-100 - 8 for delivery from 2007

JAT - Yugoslav Airlines

The origins of JAT - Yugoslav Airlines can be traced back to June 1927 when Aeroput was formed.

The airline Jugoslovenski Aerotransport (JAT) was re-established after WW2 by the Yugoslav Government in 1946 with Ju-52s to replace the service previously being provided by its military forces.

DC-3s were added to the fleet which enabled service to commence to neighbouring countries as well as its domestic schedules.

The split with the Soviet Union caused a temporary suspension of services in 1949. During the 1950s Convair 340s, 440s and DC-6s were progressively added to the fleet to provide ever expanding European routes. Il-14s were acquired in 1957 to replace the older types on the domestic services.

The jet age arrived 1963 with the entry into service of Caravelles which were joined by DC-9s in 1973 and 727s in 1974 enabling disposal of the Caravelles. The 707s had also entered service during the early 1970s and enabled expansion of the long-haul routes as far as Australia. The DC-10s marked their entry into the wide-body airliners in 1978.

Civil operations were suspended once more in 1992 and control of JAT was taken by Serbia. A few services were operated from 1995; however, these were not to last for long and in 1998 all international flights were halted.

In 1999 JAT signed a preliminary order with Airbus for eight A319s but this was put on hold with the troubles in the region and the imposition of UN sanctions.

Once these sanctions were dropped JAT quickly re-established services. This is despite having a debt of around $350 million as the government is providing guarantees until it is properly back on its feet.

BELOW: *JAT-Yugoslav Airlines 737-3H9 YU-ANV (C/n 24140) (Jeremy Flack/API)*

JetBlue Airways

Registered name: JetBlue Airways Corporation
Country: USA
Region: North America
Address: 80-82 Kew Gardens Rd
Kew Gardens
New York 11415
Tel: 001 718 286 79 00
Fax: 001 718 286 79 50
Web site: www.jetblue.com
Main operational base: New York JFK

STATUS

Domestic carrier
Employees: 2,116
Passengers per year: 3,117,000 (2001)

ICAO code:
IATA code: B6

SERVICES

Regional / Domestic / Passenger
International routes: Puerto Rico

FLEET

A320 - 36
On order: A320 - 48 for delivery from 2003 + 48 options

JetBlue was incorporated in August 1998 and made its first scheduled flight on 11th February 2000 from New York's JFK to Fort Lauderdale, FL. Operating Airbus 320s, a total of 123 have been ordered of which 36 had been delivered by the end of 2002 increasing to 50 by the end of 2003.

Despite the downturn in the airline business, the low-cost JetBlue has found an expanding market for its services. Initially operating predominantly along the US west coast, the routes are now expanding across to the east coast with its 162-seat airliners. Although the ticket costs are low this is not reflected in the service. It is the first airline to offer live 24-channel satellite TV free to all customers with seatback monitors. All seats are outfitted with leather. In addition to the satellite TV JetBlue has introduced many firsts to raise the standards of passen-

ger comfort and safety. It was the only airline to broadcast the Olympic Games live at every seat. The first US airline to introduce the "paperless cockpit", the first airline to operate a 100% e-ticket, the first US airline to install bullet-proof doors across its whole fleet and the first airline to install security cameras in the passenger cabin. Many of these features are still unique to JetBlue.

Such is the success of the JetBlue opera-

tion that in June 2002 it reported an 86% seat take up. As a result it has asked Airbus to consider a stretch to the fuselage length to increase the number of available seats.

With the demise of National Airlines in November 2002 JetBlue brought forward its plans for a JFK to Las Vegas service starting in November.

JetBlue has firmly bucked the recent trend of many airlines and is operating with the

ABOVE: *JetBlue A320-232, N507JB (C/n 1240) with Airbus test registration F-WWP (Airbus)*

high load factors, high utilization and low seat mile costs that some can only dream of. With quality of service top of the agenda the expansion of passenger numbers has shown that the huge initial order for the A320 was right and deliveries continue with a new delivery approximately every month.

Kenya Airways

Registered name: Kenya Airways Ltd
Country: Kenya
Region: Africa
Address: Embakasi Airport
P.O Box 19002, Nairobi
Tel: 00254 2 32822653
Fax: 00254 2 823545
Web site: www.kenya-airways.com
Stockholder: Kenya Airways Group
Main operational base: Nairobi

STATUS

IATA scheduled international carrier
National Flag Carrier
Employees: 3,500
Passengers per year: 1,411,000 (2001)
ICAO code: KQA
IATA code: KQ

SERVICES

International / Regional / Domestic
Passenger / Cargo
International routes: Burundi, Congo Democratic Republic, Cote D'Ivoire, Denmark, Egypt, Ethiopia, India, Malawi, Netherlands, Nigeria, Pakistan, Rwanda, Seychelles, South Africa, Sudan, Tanzania, UAE, Uganda, UK, Zambia, Zimbabwe

ALLIANCES / CODE SHARES

Tanzania

OWNED SUBSIDIARY AIRLINES

Kenya Flamingo Airlines

FLEET

A310-300 - 2, 737-200 - 2, 737-300 - 4, 737-700 - 2, 767-300ER - 3

On order: 767-400ER - 3 for delivery from 4/2004, 777-200ER - 3

Air Kenya was formed on January 22nd 1977 following the break-up of the consortium airline East African Airways. Several ex-EAA aircraft entered service with Air Kenya. A daily flight to London-Frankfurt-Rome-Athens-Nairobi service commenced in February initially with a leased 707 from British Midland Airways.

Kenya Airways then ordered its own 707s and the first of four arrived in 1978 along with a leased 720. Ex-EAA F-27s were used for domestic routes while the DC-9 was leased out.

In 1986 two Airbus A310s were delivered followed shortly after by 737s. In the same year, the Government announced its inten-

Kenya Airways

tion to privatise Kenya Airways.

Air Kenya had been operated at a loss for a while and suffered from a steadily rising debt. In 1990 the Kenyan Government established a committee to resolve these difficulties. In 1995 KLM was selected as a strategic partner and as a result it acquired a 26% shareholding. Since the privatisation in 1996, passenger and cargo traffic have seen a steady growth and it is the only airline on the African continent that has been successfully privatised. One of the A310s was lost shortly after take-off from Abidjan in January 2000 when it crashed into the sea with the loss of 169 passengers and crew.

Kenya Airways has established itself as a major scheduled carrier on domestic, inter-African and international routes to Europe and the Middle East. Such is that success that it has been awarded Regional Airline

and African Airline of the Year for several years running.

ABOVE: *Kenya Airways A310-304 (Airbus)*

Khalifa Airways

Registered name: Khalifa Airways
Country: Algeria
Region: Africa
Address: Lot No 5
                Base equipee
                Dar el Beida, Algiers
Tel: 00213 2 50 66 78
Fax: 00213 2 50 63 70
Web site: www.khalifaairways-dz.com
Stockholder: Groupe Khalifa
Main operational base: Algiers

STATUS

Scheduled domestic and international carrier
ICAO code: KZW
IATA code: K6

SERVICES

International / Regional / Domestic Passenger
International routes: France, Germany, South Africa, Spain, UAE, UK

OWNED SUBSIDIARY AIRLINES

Antinea Airlines

FLEET

A300B4 - 1, A310-300 - 7, A319-100 - 8, A320-200 - 2, A330-300 - 2, A340-300 - 3, ATR 42-300 - 4, ATR 72-500 - 12, 737-400 - 3, 737-800 - 2, 777 - 200 - 2
On order: A340-500 - 3, A330-200 - 5, A320-200 - 10

Khalifa Airways is a privately owned airline that was formed in June 1999 and commenced operations in August.

Khalifa Airways took delivery of its first ATR 72 in October 2000. This was the first of seven ATRs that had been ordered of which four were second-hand ATR 42s and the remaining three new ATR 72s, all seven were

ABOVE: *Khalifa Airways A310-324, F-OHPY (C/n 449) (Airbus)*

delivered by the end of 2000. A further 10 ATR 72s were ordered in March 2001.

An order for 18 Airbus aircraft was placed in March 2001. These were for three A340-500s, five A330-200s and 10 A320s. As an interim, it took delivery of two leased A320s in April for use on new services to Istanbul and Dubai.

Khalifa Airways signed a five year lease for two 777s in October 2002 for delivery the following November and December. These aircraft are for use on the African, European and transatlantic routes.

KLM Royal Dutch Airlines

Registered name: Koninklijke Luchtvaart Maatschappij NV
Country: Netherlands
Region: Europe
Address: PO Box 7700
Schiphol Amsterdam Airport
NL-1117
Tel: 0031 20 649 91 23
Fax: 0031 20 648 80 96
Web site: www.klm.com
Main operational base: Schiphol

STATUS

IATA scheduled international carrier
National Flag Carrier
Employees: 30,253
Passengers per year: 16,079,000 (2001)
ICAO code: KLM
IATA code: KL

SERVICES

International / Regional / Domestic
Passenger / Cargo
International routes: Aruba, Austria, Australia*, Bahrain, Belgium, Brazil, Canada, China, Cote D'Ivoire, Cyprus*, Czech, Denmark, Ecuador, Egypt, Finland, France, Germany, Ghana, Greece, Hungary, India, Indonesia, Iran, Ireland*, Israel, Italy, Japan, Jordan, Kazakhstan, Kenya, Kuwait, Lebanon, Libya, Lithuania*, Luxemburg, Malaysia, Mexico, Morocco*, Netherlands, Netherlands Antilles, Nigeria, Norway, Oman, Peru, Philippines, Poland, Portugal, Romania, Russia, S Korea, Saudi Arabia, Singapore, South Africa, Spain, Surinam, Syria, Sweden, Switzerland, Taiwan, Tanzania, Thailand, Turkey, UAE, UK, Ukraine, USA, Venezuela (*code shares)

ALLIANCES / CODE SHARES

Ael Lingus, Alaska A/l, China Southern A/l, Continental A/l, CSA, Cyprus Aw, Eurowings, Horizon Air, Lithuanian A/l, Malaysia A/l, Malev, Northwest A/l, Pinnacle A/l, Surinam Aw, Transavia A/l, Ukraine Int A/l

OWNED SUBSIDIARY AIRLINES

KLM Cityhopper, KLM Helikopters, KLM UK, Martinair

FLEET

737-300 - 15, 737-400 - 14, 737-800 - 13, 737-900 - 4, 747-300 - 2 (to be replaced with 777-200ERs), 747-300M - 8 (to be replaced with 777-200ERs), 747-300SF (SCD) - 2 (to be replaced with 777-200ERs), 747-400 - 5, 747-400ERF - 3, 747-400M (SCD) - 16, 767-300ER - 12, MD-11 - 10
On order: A330-200 - 6 for 2005+ delivery + 18 options, 747-400ERF - 3 for delivery late 2003, 747-400M (SCD) - 3, 777-200ER - 10 for delivery late 2003

KLM is the world's oldest airline still operating under its own name. Formed on October 7th, 1919, Royal patronage was bestowed upon it that December by Queen Wilhelmina of The Netherlands and granted it the right to bear the 'Royal' title. Thus, KLM Royal Dutch Airlines commenced the oldest scheduled route when it started flying to London from Amsterdam in a de Havilland DH.16 on May 17th, 1920.

KLM ordered its first Fokker airliner in 1921 - an F-II. In 1924 a Fokker F-VII operated a pioneering flight to Indonesia. However, the flight took 55 days due to engine problems but proved that it was possible. After some more trials in 1928, an inaugural scheduled service commenced in September 1929.

BELOW: *KLM 747-406 SCd, PH-BFD (C/n 24001)(Jane's)*

KLM Royal Dutch Airlines

ABOVE: *KLM 737-406, PH-BTA (C/n 25412) (Jeremy Flack/API)*

KLM became the first European airline to operate the Douglas DC-2 when the first one arrived in 1934. Koene Dirk Parmentier successfully captained one of the DC-2s in the London - Melbourne Race. At the same time a Fokker F.XVIII was flown to Curacao for the first time. The DC-2s were followed by the DC-3 in 1936.

During WW2, KLM had 'Holland' painted on the fuselages to identify it as a neutral country. It managed to maintain a number of routes and established a new one to the USA.

With the war over, KLM was anxious to re-establish all of its old routes. An ex-military C-54 was used to provide a service to Indonesia while a new DC-4 flew an inaugural flight to New York in May 1946. KLM was the first European airline to re-open the link to New York. The entry into KLM service of the DC-6 enabled new routes to be established to South America, Santiago and Mexico. More new types were added including the Super Constellation in 1955, Vickers Viscount in 1957, DC-7 in 1958 and Lockheed Electra in 1959.

Delivery of the first DC-8 in March 1960 took KLM into the jet age. In 1964 it became the first European airline to take delivery of a DC-8F freighter.

The establishment of KLM Helicopters in 1965 proved fruitful when in 1968 it began to operate flights to the oil rigs in the North Sea.

Having placed an order for six 747s, KLM took delivery of its first wide-bodied airliner in January 1971, followed by the DC-10 at the end of 1972.

KLM introduced its FFF-Class (Full Fare Facilities) in 1974 in which passengers were provided with enhanced facilities for a premium fare - a forerunner to Business Class.

In March 1977 a KLM 747 was involved in a major disaster when it struck a taxiing Pan Am 747 during its take off at Tenerife.

During the 1980s, KLM took delivery of its first A310 and 737 which were to gradually replace the DC-9s. KLM was awarded the 'Airline of the Year' by Air Transport World in 1985. It was granted immunity from US anti-trust legislation by the US Department of Transportation with Northwest Airlines enabling a closer alliance and took a 20% equity share. Also, in 1989 its first 747-400 was delivered.

In 1992 the active regional subsidiary, NLM Cityhopper was merged with Netherlines and renamed KLM Cityhopper. The fleet was enhanced with the addition of 20 new Fokker 50 and SAAB 340b airliners to its existing F-28 Fellowships. KLM took delivery of its first MD-11 in 1994 followed by the 767 in 1995.

KLM sold its 20% stake in Northwest in 1998 and took stakes in a number of other domestic and international airlines. A long-term alliance agreement was struck with Alitalia but this was revoked in 2000. Later that year the Netherlands Government sold all its remaining Common Shares and Preference Shares - having already reduced its stake to 11%. However, it retained the 'A' Preference Shares and Priority Shares. It also retains the right to acquire the majority shareholding through the issue of 'B' Preference Shares should the need ever arise. During 2000, KLM and British Airways were in discussions about a full merger but these were broken off after a few months. The horrifying events of September 11th caused KLM to cut capacity by 15%, to lay off 1,500 staff and put a further 10,000 on reduced hours. However, by the following Summer the figures were only a little down on the previous year. Despite this, KLM is currently undergoing a fleet replacement programme that is aimed at reducing the number of types operated by the intercontinental fleet to the A330s, 747s and 777s.

In 2001, KLM was showing interest in buying Go from British Airways to merge with its own low-cost airline Buzz, but this did not proceed.

In a pilot project KLM has introduced a catalogue of high-quality consumer goods for passengers from which they could order through cabin attendants, by post or via the KLM website. Members of the Flying Dutchman loyalty programme can earn FD points for every article purchased and also be able to use FD points to cover part of the purchase costs. These goods will not attract duty free status.

KLM began displaying its web site address on the side of some of its aircraft from July 2002.

KLM UK

STATUS

IATA scheduled passenger carrier
Employees: 2,848
Passengers per year: 3,871,000 (2001)
ICAO code: UKA
IATA code: UK

SERVICES

Regional / Domestic / Passenger
Charter / Cargo
International routes: Belgium, Finland,
France, Germany, Italy, Netherlands,
Norway, Spain, Switzerland

ALLIANCES / CODE SHARES

KLM, Northwest A/l, VLM

FLEET

ATR 72-200 - 5, BAe 146-300 - 10, Fokker 50
- 9, Fokker 100 - 17
On order: Fokker 100 - 2

KLM UK was formed on January 30th 1998
from Air UK. Before that, Air UK was the
result of a merger on 16th January 1980
between Air Anglia and British Island
Airways. BIA also brought with it its subsidiaries in the form of Air Westward and
Air Wales (formed May 29th 1979).

The initial Air UK fleet comprised BAC 1-
11s, Embraer EMB-110 Bandeirantes,
Fokker F-27 Friendships and Handley Page
Heralds. With a number of sub-variants this
mixed fleet was a result of the merger but
rationalisation saw the Bandeirantes and
Heralds being retired, the former being

ABOVE: *KLM UK BAe. 146-300, G-UKAC (C/n E. 3142)
prior to formation of buzz, which was subsequently sold to
Ryanair (BAe systems)*

replaced by the Short 360.

In November 1982 Air UK and BMI jointly launched Manx Airlines to operate the
Isle of Man services. They had failed to
profit on this route when operating dupli-
cate services in competition.

In 1987 KLM took an interest in Air UK
and purchased 14.9% shareholding that
had risen to 30% by the following year. The
1988 summer season commenced with a
pair of leased 737s. The operation was successful and four new 400 series were
ordered.

Buzz was established as a low-cost off-
shoot of KLM UK but sold to Ryanair in
early 2003.

KLM UK continues to offer the service
which took Air UK to becoming the third
largest scheduled British airline while having the security of being part of a larger
group.

Korean Air

K
O
R
E
A
N

A
I
R

Registered name: Korean Air Lines Co Ltd
Country: Korea - South
Region: Asia
Address: 1370, Gonghang-Dong
  Gangseo
  Seoul
Tel: 0082 2 656 71 14 or 751 75 07
Fax: 0082 2 656 71 69 or 751 73 86
Web site: www.koreanair.com
Stockholder: Hanjin Group
Main operational base: Seoul

STATUS

National Flag Carrier
Employees: 15,959
Passengers per year: 21,638,000 (2001)
ICAO code: KAL
IATA code: KE

SERVICES

International / Regional / Domestic
Passenger / Cargo

International routes: Australia, Belgium, Brazil, Canada, China, Denmark, Egypt, Fiji, France, Germany, India, Indonesia, Italy, Japan, Mariana Islands, Malaysia, Mongolia, Netherlands, New Zealand, Philippines, Russia, Singapore, Switzerland, Thailand, UAE, UK, USA, Vietnam

ALLIANCES / CODE SHARES

Skyteam / Air France, Alitalia, China Eastern A/l, Delta A/l, Garuda A/l, Malaysia A/l, Vietnam A/l

FLEET

A300-622R - 16, A330-200 - 3, A330-300 - 13, 737-800 - 14, 737-900 - 4, 747-200F - 2, 747-200F - 5, 747-300B - 1, 747-300M - 1, 747-400 - 27, 747-400C (SCD) - 1, 747-400F (SCD) - 6, 777-200ER - 6, 777-300 - 4, Fokker 100 - 10, MD-11F - 4, MD-83 - 3, MD-83 - 1
On order: A330-300 - 3, 737-900 - 12

Korean Air was formed in June 1962 by the South Korean Government as Korean Air Lines (KAL) to succeed Korean National Airlines which dated back to 1948.

Domestic services were initially provided with Fokker F-27 Friendships. DC-9s were acquired in July 1967 and three routes to Japan were gradually established but the airline was running at a loss.

In 1969 KAL was acquired by the Hanjin Transport Group, despite the previous losses that were being incurred, the 720s were purchased and new routes established reversing the airlines fortunes. KAL commenced wide-body operations with the 747s in 1973 followed by the DC-10s and A300s in 1978. Route expansion took place to

ABOVE: *Korean Air A300B4-622R, HL7293 (C/n 554) (Jeremy Flack/API)*

international destinations ranging from USA to Europe.

KAL has placed great emphasis on passenger service for which it received a number of awards. More importantly, it has raised the KAL stature to being among the world's top twenty airlines for several years.

In addition, KAL operates its own flying training school, which produces high-quality graduates, plus a Maintenance Division. Such is the quality of the maintenance that Pratt & Whitney gave honours to KAL for achieving a 100% record for zero in-flight shutdowns and despatch rates due to engine maintenance.

KAL suffered a substantial financial loss in 2001 which was due to a number of factors besides the September 11th tragedy. These included the rise in oil prices and the adverse dollar exchange rate against the won. However, they are now returning to profit once again.

KAL operates a continual programme of aircraft renewal with new A330-300s, 737-800s and 900s, 747-400s and 777-200s delivered over the last few years. These, and future deliveries, will replace the older MD-11, MD-82 and MD-83 and Fokker 100 airliners.

KrasAir

Registered name: Krasnoyarsk Airlines
Country: Russia
Region: Asia
Address: Krasnoyarsk Airport
Krasnoyarsk 663020
Tel: 007 3912 23 63 66
Fax: 007 3912 66 02 05
Web site: www.krasair.ru
Main operational base: Krasnoyarsk

STATUS

International and domestic scheduled and charter + cargo carrier
Passengers per year: 1,027,000 (2001)
ICAO code: KJC
IATA code: 7B

SERVICES

International / Domestic / Passenger Charter / Cargo
International routes: China, Cyprus, Germany, Greece, Moldova, Thailand, Turkey, UAE, Ukraine

ALLIANCES / CODE SHARES

Aeroflot, Transaero A/1

FLEET

Il-62 - 5, Il-76T - 8, Il-76TD - 3, Il-86 - 4, Tu-134 - 4, Tu-154B -7, Tu-154M - 11, Tu-204 - 2, Yak-40 - 5

KrasAir was originally formed as the Krasnoyarsk Division of Aeroflot in 1950. In 1982 it became Krasnoyarsk Airlines and was merged with Achinsk Avia to form KrasAir in 1995.

KrasAir continued to operate the Russian-built aircraft although a couple of DC-10s were leased during the mid-1990s.

During 2000 KrasAir took delivery of its first new aircraft for a number of years in the form of a Tu-204 of which it had two on order plus two options. However, doubts about deliveries of the two, which were becoming protracted, led KrasAir to look at leasing 767s. As Russia's third largest airline, with rapidly increasing passenger levels, sufficient capacity was becoming a problem.

An announcement was made in September 2002 that KrasAir was planning to lease eight DC-9s although import duties and some runway strengths were causing difficulties.

Kuwait Airways

Registered name: Kuwait Airways Corporation
Country: Kuwait
Region: Middle East
Address: Kuwait International Airport
PO Box 394, 13004 Safat
Tel: 00965 434 55 55
Fax: 00965 431 41 18
Web site: www.kuwait-airways.com
Main operational base: Kuwait International Airport

STATUS

IATA scheduled international carrier
National Flag Carrier
Employees: 4,324
Passengers per year: 2,108,000 (2001)
ICAO code: KAC
IATA code: KU

SERVICES

International / Regional / Passenger Charter / Cargo

ABOVE: *Kuwait Airways A300-605R, 9K-AMC (C/n699) (Airbus)*

International routes: Bahrain, Bangladesh, Cyprus, Egypt, France, Germany, Greece, India, Indonesia, Italy, Jordan, Lebanon, Morocco, Netherlands, Oman, Philippines, Saudi Arabia, Singapore, Sri Lanka, Switzerland, Syria, Thailand, UAE, UK, USA

Kuwait Airways

ABOVE: *Kuwait Airways 747-269B, 9K - ADC (C/n 21543) (Jeremy Flack/API)*

ALLIANCES / CODE SHARES

Air-India, Olympic Aw

FLEET

A300-600R - 5, A310-300 - 3, A320-200 - 3, A340-300 - 4, 777-200ER - 2

Kuwait Airways was formed in March 1953 as Kuwait National Airways and began operations with a DC-3 in 1954.

New routes were added to Bahrain and Cairo and in 1957 the name was changed to Kuwait Airways Corporation.

Management of KAC was contracted to BOAC for five years in June 1958 and Vickers Viscounts replaced the DC-3s. The following year the local charter airline British International Airlines - a BOAC subsidiary was merged into KAC.

The Comet introduced KAC to the jet age with the delivery of the first improved model 4C in January 1963 and was used on the London Route. The first Trident was delivered in March 1966 and used on regional schedules.

The arrival of the first of a total of eight 707s arrived in November 1968 and became the mainstay of the long-haul fleet until delivery of its first 747 in July 1978.

The Tridents were replaced with four 727s from 1980 and were subsequently joined by the A300s, A310s and 767s during the mid-1980s.

A total of 15 Kuwait Airways airliners was destroyed during the Iraqi invasion at the beginning of the Gulf War along with most of their facilities. At the end of the war these were replaced and are equipped with the latest entertainment systems.

Kyrgyzstan Airlines

Registered name: Kyrgyzstan Aba Zholdoru
Country: Kyrgyzstan
Region: Asia
Address: Manas Airport
   Bishkek 720062
Tel: 00996 3312 44 51 32
Fax: 00996 3312 257162
Web site: www.kyrgyzstanairlines.kg/
Main operational base: Manas Airport

ABOVE: *Kyrgyzstan Airlines A320-231 F-OHGA (C/n 478) (Airbus)*

STATUS

Scheduled and charter passenger + cargo carrier

National Flag Carrier

Passengers per year: 176,000 (2001)
ICAO code: KGA
IATA code: K2

SERVICES

International / Regional / Passenger Charter / Cargo
International routes: China, Germany, India, Kazakhstan, Russia, Turkey, Uzbekistan

ALLIANCES / CODE SHARES

Indian A/l

FLEET

A320-200 - 1, An-26B - 1, An-28 - 1, Il-76TD - 1, Mi-8 - 6, Mi-8MTV-1 - 4
On order: A319-100 -2 for delivery from 2002

Kyrgyzstan Airlines was originally formed as the Kyrgyzstan Division of Aeroflot.

It split from Aeroflot in 1992 with state support as Kyrgyzstan Airlines.

LACSA

Registered name: Lineas Aéreas Costaricenses SA
Country: Costa Rica
Region: Central America & Caribbean
Address: PO Box 1531-1000, San Jose
Tel: 00506 290 27 27
Fax: 00506 232 41 78
Web site: www.centralamerica.com/cr/lacsa
Stockholder: TACA Group
Main operational base: San Jose

ABOVE: *LACSA A320-232, N981LR (C/n 558) (Airbus)*

STATUS

IATA scheduled international carrier
National Flag Carrier
Employees: 904
Passengers per year: 631,000 (2001)
ICAO code: LRC
IATA code: LR

SERVICES

International / Regional / Domestic
Passenger / Charter /Cargo
International routes: Chile, Colombia, Cuba, Ecuador, El Salvador, Guatemala, Honduras, Mexico, Nicaragua, Panama, Peru, USA, Venezuela

ALLIANCES / CODE SHARES

Avianaca, SAM Colombia, TACA Int

FLEET

A320-200 - 5, 737-200-3

LACSA was formed on October 17th, 1945 by the Costa Rican Government with assistance from Pan American Airways. Domestic operations commenced with DC-3s and C-46s in 1946.

The first international service was flown to Miami in 1951 and was designated the national flag carrier, by which time DC-6s had been added to the fleet.

The BAC 1-11s brought LACSA into the jet age in 1967. These enabled routes to be flown into South America and were replaced by the 727s during the early 1980s enabling destinations even further south.

While a Lockheed Electra and DC-8 have been used for their cargo service, the 727s have given way to 737s and A320s and LACSA is now part of the TACA Group.

LAM (Linhas Aéreas de Moçambique)

Registered name: Linhas Aéreas de Moçambique
Country: Mozambique
Region: Africa
Address: PO Box 2060
Maputo
Tel: 00258 1 46 51 43
Fax: 00258 1 46 51 34
Web site: www.lam.co.mz
Main operational base: Luanda

STATUS

IATA scheduled international carrier
National Flag Carrier
Employees: 1,153
Passengers per year: 266,000 (2001)
ICAO code: LAM
IATA code: TM

SERVICES

International / Regional / Domestic
Passenger / Charter / Cargo
International routes: Portugal, South Africa, Zimbabwe

ALLIANCES / CODE SHARES

TAP

FLEET

737-200 - 3, 767-200ER - 1, King Air 200C - 2, 402C Utililiner II - 5, 212-200 Aviocar - 4, Fokker 100 - 1, P.68C - 4, TB.200 Tobago-1

LAM (Linhas Aéreas de Moçambique) can trace its ancestry back to August 1936 when it was formed as Direccao de Exploracao dos Transp Aéreos (DETA). It was then a division of the Ports and Railways services and operated aircraft as diverse as the Ju-52 and de Havilland Gipsy Moth. It helped to provide easy connections to neighbouring countries. At the end of WW2 ex-military C-47s were available at rock bottom prices and DETA took advantage to obtain some newer aircraft for its fleet. These were subsequently replaced by F-27 Friendships, 737s, Il-62s, returning to 737s by the 1990s.

In 1980, following Independence from Portugal, the name of DETA was changed to LAM - Mozambique Airlines. As a government-owned airline it continued to operate as such until December 1998 when it gained its own independence and was transformed into a Limited Company. The state still holds 80% of the shares with the balance of 20% being held by employees of the airline.

LAM operated services to various parts of Africa and Europe but by the mid-1990s the European flights had been reduced to Lisbon only.

LanChile Airlines

OWNED SUBSIDIARY AIRLINES

LanExpress Inc

FLEET

A320-200 - 10, A340-300 - 4, 737-200Adv - 21, 737-200C - 1, 767-300ER - 12, 767-300ER (F) - 6, DC-8-71F - 4

On order: A320-200 - 15 + 20 options (replacing 737-200s), A340 - 3 + 14 options (replacing 767-300s)

ABOVE: *LanChile A340-313X (Airbus)*

Registered name: Linea Aerea Nacional de Chile
Country: Chile
Region: South America
Address: Avienda Americo Vespucio Sur 901
Renca
Santiago
Tel: 0056 2 565 25 25
Fax: 0056 2 565 28 17
Web site: www.lanchile.com
Main Operational base: Santiago

STATUS

IATA scheduled international carrier
National Flag Carrier
Employees: 5,352
Passengers per year: 5,234,000 (2001)
ICAO code: ICAO code: LAN
IATA code: IATA code: LA

SERVICES

International / Regional / Domestic
Passenger / Cargo
International routes: Argentina, Brazil, Colombia, Dominican Republic, Ecuador, Germany, Mexico, Paraguay, Peru, Spain, Tahiti, Uruguay, USA, Venezuela

ALLIANCES / CODE SHARES

OneWorld / AeroMexico, Alaska A/l, American A/l, Canadian A/l, Iberia

LanChile can trace its ancestry back to March 5th 1929 when operations commenced as Linea Aeropostal Santiago-Arica. This followed the successful request by the Chief of Army Services - Commander Arturo Merino Benitez - to the Chilean president to form a national air transport company.

Initially de Havilland Moths were used to carry mail and passengers. Early operations were successful and the 12-seat Ford 5-AT-C was acquired and, despite the primitive operating conditions, 800 passengers were carried in the first year. This increased to over 5,000 by the end of 1930.

On July 21st 1932 the military operation became the government-owned Linea Aerea Nacional. In 1936 a boost to its credibility was given when an air-bridge was established between Chillan and Santiago

to transport emergency supplies and casualties following a major earthquake. This effort saved many lives.

New aircraft delivered included the Lockheed 10 Electra and C-60 Lodestars and an Air Hostess Service was created to look after the passengers. In 1946 a fleet of 21 DC-3s enabled routes to cover the whole country. The Martin 202 enabled international routes to expand further while the de Havilland Dove was introduced for domestic use. During the mid-1950s the DC-6 was introduced increasing further expansion of its routes including the first to the Antarctic. In 1958 this expansion included a Santiago to Miami service.

The LanChile entry into the jet age was with the French-built Caravelle. In 1967 the 707 was introduced, operating as far as New York, while the HS.748 was ordered for domestic use.

The steady acquisition of new aircraft and progressive expansion led to new routes which by this time included Australia and Europe as well as the Easter Islands and Tahiti together with numerous destinations throughout South America.

The programme continued with a 737 and

DC-10 although the latter was replaced with 767s in 1986. A 747 was leased for peak demand while BAe146s were ordered for domestic operations in 1989. About the same time the Chilean Government partially privatised LanChile with full privatisation being achieved on May 26th 1994. Around the same time LanChile commenced an acquisition programme with Fast Air Courier SA in May followed by LanExpress in August. In November approval was given for LanChile to buy Ladeco which had commenced as an air taxi company and expanded into domestic operations. It was totally absorbed by 2001.

During 1995/6 LanChile experienced the third highest growth of any airline in the world with a 44.8% increase in its sales. This impressive growth enabled continued expansion with an increased regularity of service on a number of routes. Following record profits, improvements to the fleet

continued with additional 767s, improved passenger seating and overall improvements including its airport facilities. As a result another financial record with a 79.5% increase in operating income was reported for 1997. The improvements continued with the plan to position the airline as one of the world's top ten in terms of service, quality and efficiency.

LanChile also operates a cargo service that has seen healthy expansion resulting in the changing of one of the 767s for a 747. During the first month of operation this freighter achieved approximately 500 flight hours with an average factor achieved of over 90%. They have more recently been granted a concession by the Miami authorities to develop a 17-hectare cargo complex at the airport.

In 1998 LanChile was invited to join the Oneworld alliance. Plans to upgrade the fleet have proceeded with orders for twenty

A320s followed by seven A340s.

The LanChile investment has not only been restricted to its fleet and infrastructure but also to its staff. In 2000 an alliance was formed with Fererico Santa Maria Technical University to form an Aeronautic Sciences Acadamy (ACA). The university would provide professional training in most aspects of the aviation industry. In January 2001 LanChile came to the rescue of LanPeru which had suspended its operation a few months earlier because of a financial crisis. Following a restructure LanPeru was able resume a normal service which includes a number of the LanChile-style improved service.

In line with most other airlines the event of September 11th had an immediate effect on LanChile with a cut back in operations by 10% and staff by 5%.

In 2002 LanChile revealed plans to establish a new carrier in Ecuador LanEcuador.

Lao Aviation

Registered name: Lao Aviation
Country: Laos
Region: Asia
Address: BP 41692
 Rue Pan Kham
 Vientiane
Tel: 00856 21 21 20 50
Fax: 00856 21 21 20 56
Web site: www.lao-aviation.com
Main operational base: Vientiane

STATUS

Scheduled international and domestic carrier.
National Flag Carrier
Employees: 416
Passengers per year: 211,000 (2001)
ICAO code: LAO
IATA code: QV

SERVICES

Regional / Domestic / Passenger
International routes: Cambodia, China, Thailand, Vietnam

FLEET

ATR 72-202 - 2, An-24RV - 1, 737-200Adv - 1, Y-12 - 6, Mi-8 - 1, Y-7-100C - 3

Lao Aviation was formed in December 1975 as a result of the merger of Royal Air Lao and Lao Airlines into the Civil Aviation Co that had been operated by Pathet Lao.

Lao Aviation operated a number of aircraft types left behind by US forces at the end of the Vietnam war including C-47s, C-54s, C-130 Hercules and Sikorsky S-58s plus a Vickers Viscount. However, spares were a

ABOVE: *Lao Aviation ATR 72-320, F-OGQV (C/n 306) with ATR test registration F-WWEF (ATR)*

problem and these aircraft slowly became unserviceable.

Gradually a new fleet was assembled with Chinese-built Yun-7s and Yun-12s that were Russian designs by Antonov. One of the Y-12s was lost in October 2000 when it crashed into a mountain with the loss of 8 lives.

An ATR 42 and 737 were leased for a while but returned when the financial crisis hit Asia. Since then Lao Aviation purchased an ATR 72 in 2001 and has leased another.

Lauda Air

Registered name: Lauda Air
Country: Austria
Region: Europe
Address: PO Box 56
               Vienna Airport A-1300, Vienna
Tel: 0043 1 700 00
Fax: 0043 1 700 07 90 15
Web site: www.laudaair.com
Stockholder: Austrian Airlines Group
Main operational base: Vienna

ABOVE: *Lauda Air 767-3Z9ER, OE-LAX (C/n 27095) (Jane's)*

STATUS

IATA scheduled and charter carrier
Employees: 1,709
Passengers per year: 1,124,000 (2001)
ICAO code: LDA
IATA code: NG

SERVICES

International / Regional / Passenger
Charter / Cargo
International routes: Australia, Bulgaria,
Estonia, Italy, Latvia, Lithuania, Malaysia,
Morocco, Thailand, Spain, Turkey, USA

ALLIANCES / CODE SHARES

Star Alliance / Malaysia A/l

BELOW: *Lauda Air CRJ-200 (Bombardier)*

FLEET

737-300 - 2, 737-400 - 2, 737-600 - 2, 737-700
- 2, 737-800 - 2, 767-300ER - 4, 777-200 - 2,
CRJ100LR - 4

Lauda Air was established by the world
champion racing driver - Niki Lauda - in
April 1979 and commenced operations in
May. It was formed to operate charter and
inclusive-tour flights and operated a number of regular flights for Klagenfurt - a leading tour operator.

Initially a pair of F-27 Friendships was
operated and was subsequently joined by a
pair of leased Romanian-built BAC 1-11s
from TAROM and eventually replaced with
737s in the mid-1980s.

Lauda Air was licensed to commence scheduled domestic services in 1987 which was
extended to international routes in 1990. This
enabled Lauda Air to commence service to
the Far East and Australia operating a 767.

Niki Lauda resigned as chairman in 2000
after a protracted and bitter argument with
the majority shareholders - Austrian Airlines.

LIAT

Registered name: Leeward Islands Air Transport
(1974) Ltd
Country: Antigua & Barbuda
Region: Central America & Caribbean
Address: PO Box 819
V C Bird International Airport,
Saint Johns, Antigua
Tel: 001 268 480 56 00
Fax: 001 268 480 56 35
Web site: www.liatairline.com
Main operational base: V C Bird International
Airport

ABOVE: *LIAT DHC-8 Dash 8-300 (Bombardier)*

STATUS

Scheduled regional passenger carrier
Employees: 951
Passengers per year: 1,369,000 (2001)
ICAO code: LIA
IATA code: LI

SERVICES

Regional / Passenger / Cargo
International routes: Anguilla, Barbados,
Dominica, Grenada, Guadeloupe,
Martinique, Montserrat, Netherlands
Antilles, St Kitts & Nevis, St Vincent &
Grenadines, Trinidad & Tobago, Virgin
Islands

ALLIANCES / CODE SHARES

CaribSky Alliance / BWIA West Indies A/l

FLEET

DHC-8 Dash 8-100 - 9, DHC-8 Dash 8-300 - 3

The original Leeward Islands Air Transport
was established in 1959 and acquired by
Court Line in 1971. It was subsequently
bankrupted with the failure of Court Line.

The current LIAT was formed on
September 20th, 1974, to continue the inter-
island transport between most of the eastern
Caribbean territories. It was equipped with a
mixed fleet of HS748s, Islanders, Trislanders
and Twin Otters. This vital means of communication is necessary to support business
and tourism.

Because of the short stages between destinations the operating costs are high and it
is difficult to achieve a profit. When Court
Line went bankrupt the loss was widely felt
in the region because there was no alternative operator. As a result eleven of the local
governments formed a consortium,
acquired the net assets and then re-established the airline with some expansion of

the service. The fleet has since been rationalised on the Dash 8.

Around the same time, three major
Caribbean airlines created a comprehen-
sive network of air services for the
Caribbean. They named the association the
CaribSky Alliance and the founder mem-
bers were LIAT, Windward Islands Airways
(Winair) and Air Caraibes. Other airlines
have also joined including Trans Island
Airways (TIA), Carib Aviation, Tyden Air
and CAT.

Between them, the CaribSky Alliance carries some 1.4 million passengers per year to
46 destinations with 690 daily flights
throughout the Caribbean.

In 1995, BWIA acquired a 29% share in
LIAT.

Libyan Arab Airlines

Registered name: Jamahiriya Libyan Arab
Airlines
Country: Libya
Region: Africa
Address: PO Box 2555
Haiti Street
Triploi G.S.P.L.A.
Tel: 00218 21 60 20 93 / 60 88 60
Fax: 00218 22 309 70
Web site: www.aaco.org/midfrm/lybiandown.asp
Main operational base: Tripoli

STATUS

International and domestic passenger +
cargo carrier
National Flag Carrier
Passengers per year: 584,000 (2001)
ICAO code: LAA
IATA code: LN

SERVICES

International / Regional / Domestic
Passenger
International routes: Algeria, Austria,

Egypt, Italy, Jordan, Netherlands, Sudan,
UAE, UK

FLEET

A300-600R - 2, A310-200 - 2, 727 - 9

The history of Libyan Arab Airlines can be
traced back to 1964 when the Libyan
Government established Royal Libyan
Airlines to succeed Libiavia.

In 1965 Royal Libyan Airlines was
renamed Kingdom of Libya Airlines prior

Libyan Arab Airlines

to scheduled services commencing, initially using Caravelles.

The Kingdom of Libya Airlines was renamed Libyan Arab Airlines on September 1st, 1969.

A substantial domestic and international network of routes was gradually established mainly with F-27 Friendships and 737s.

Following an increase in world terrorism, of which a number of trails led back to

Libya, the US launched a strike on various Libyan targets and UN sanctions were imposed in 1992.

The sanctions were relaxed in 1999 and now the Libyan Arab Airlines fleet is in urgent need of modernisation after the period of political isolation. An approach was made to Airbus for new aircraft. However, with a number of components of US origin and Airbus unable to obtain the necessary Washington approval, an order for an estimated $1.5 billion for A320s, A330s and A340s was stalled. However, a few Airbus types are being operated after having been leased through Royal Jordanian Airlines.

As a result, Libyan Arab Airlines is looking to Russian and Ukrainian manufacturers as a source and some of the 727s have been offered for sale.

Lithuanian Airlines

Registered name: Lietuvos Avialinja
Country: Lithuania
Region: Europe
Address: A Gustaieio 4,
Vilnius 2038
Tel: 00370 2 30 60 17
Fax: 00370 2 26 68 28
Web site: www.lal.lt
Main operational base: Vilnius

STATUS

IATA scheduled and charter carrier
National Flag Carrier
Employees: 911
Passengers per year: 256,000 (2001)
ICAO code: LIL
IATA code: TE

SERVICES

Regional / Domestic / Passenger
Charter / Cargo
International routes: Denmark, Estonia, Finland, France, Germany, Netherlands, Poland, Russia, Spain, Sweden, UK, Ukraine

ALLIANCES / CODE SHARES

Air Ukraine, CSA, Finnair, Iberia, KLM, LOT

OWNED SUBSIDIARY AIRLINES

Air Lithuania

FLEET

737-200 - 2, 737-300 - 2, SAAB 2000 - 3
The origins of Lithuanian Airlines date back to 1938 with the formation of Lietuvos oro linijos with two Percival Q-6s. However, it was absorbed into Aeroflot in 1941 during the occupation by the Soviet Union.

It was re-formed on September 20th 1991 just prior to independence from the Soviet Union. Initially equipped with ex-Aeroflot An-24, Tu-134 and Yak-42 types, it was only months before the Lithuanian national airline signed a lease for its first 737 that December. As these increased in number,

so the larger Russian aircraft were withdrawn.

During the early 1990s Lithuanian Airlines route network rapidly expanded adding new destinations to Moscow, Warsaw, Berlin, Frankfurt, Copenhagen and London in 1991 alone.

In July 1995, Lithuanian Airlines was reorganised from being state owned to become a joint stock company and a further two 737s were acquired.

In February 1997, the Lithuanian Government declared its proposal to privatise Lithuanian Airlines and Air Lithuania - both of which were state owned. On August 1st, Air Lithuania was made a subsidiary of Lithuanian Airlines and an order was placed for an ATR 42.

The first SAAB 2000 was delivered in November 1999 and entered service a few days later on the Vilnius - Stockholm route. A proposal to privatise Lithuanian Airlines nearly came to a head in 2000 but was it was decided to postpone the event until the general economic situation improved. Lithuanian Airlines sold its last two Yak-42s in March 2002 to a Russian customer and completed the transition of its fleet to all Western aircraft.

Lithuanian Airlines plans to continue expanding its routes with CIS countries, Finland, Germany, Scandinavia, UK and US being high on the list of priorities.

Lloyd Aero Boliviano/LAB

Registered name: Lloyd Aéreo Boliviano SA
Country: Bolivia
Region: South America
Address: Jorge Wilstermann Airport
PO Box 132, Cochabamba
Tel: 00591 4 425 07 36 / 37 / 38
Fax: 00591 4 425 07 66
Web site: www.labairlines.com
Main operational base: Cochabamba

STATUS

IATA scheduled international and domestic passenger + cargo carrier
Employees: 1,392
Passengers per year: 1,502,100 (2001)
ICAO code: LLB
IATA code: LB

SERVICES

International / Regional / Domestic Passenger / Cargo
International routes: Argentina, Brazil, Chile, Colombia, Mexico, Panama, Paraguay, Peru, Venezuela

FLEET

A310-304 - 1, 727-100 - 2, 727-100C - 1, 727-200Adv - 4, 737-300 - 1, F-27 Mk.200 - 1

Lloyd Aero Boliviano was originally formed on September 15th 1925 by private investors, supported by the government operating a Junkers F-13. These investors were German residents, which resulted in a number of German-built aircraft being operated by the airline. These included the Ju-52 and Ju-86. Initially, LAB only operated domestic flights but from 1930 it commenced an international service.

Lloyd Aero Boliviano was nationalised in 1941 with Braniff taking a 13.41% stake. US aircraft then began to appear in the fleet commencing with the Lockheed Lodestar followed by the C-46s, DC-4s and DC-6s after the war ended.

LAB took delivery of a Lockheed Electra in 1968 followed by the first two of six of the Fairchild Hiller version of the F-27 Friendship - the FH-227s in 1969.

LAB entered the jet age following delivery of its first 727 in 1970, followed by a number more from the mid-1970s plus a 707 in 1977 and another in 1981.

Lloyd Aero Boliviano was privatised again in 1992 when Iberia attempted a take over, but this failed. In 1995 VASP took a 50% shareholding which it increased to 95% in 1998. However, when VASP was declared bankrupt in 2001, LAB was sold to private Bolivian interests.

LOT - Polish Airlines

Registered name: LOT - Polish Airlines
Country: Poland
Region: Europe
Address: 17 Stycznia St, PL-00-906 Warsaw
Tel: 0048 22 606 61 11
Fax: 0048 22 606 60 60
Web site: www.lot.com
Stockholder: Polskie Linie Lotnicze LOT SA
Main operational base: Warsaw

STATUS

IATA scheduled international carrier
National Flag Carrier
Employees: 3,993
Passengers per year: 2,801,000 (2001)
ICAO code: LOT
IATA code: LO

SERVICES

International / Regional / Domestic Passenger / Charter / Cargo
International routes: Austria, Belgium, Bulgaria, Croatia, Czech, Denmark, Estonia, Finland, France, Netherlands, Germany, Greece, Hungary, Israel, Italy, Latvia, Lebanon, Lithuania, Norway, Romania, Russia, Serbia, Slovakia, Spain, Sweden, Switzerland, Turkey, UK, Ukraine, USA

ALLIANCES/CODE SHARES

Star Alliance / Aeroflot, Air France, Alitalia, American A/l, BA, CSA, Cyprus Aw, Finnair, Iberia, Lufthansa, Malev

OWNED SUBSIDIARY AIRLINES

EuroLOT

FLEET

ATR 42-300 - 5 (operated by EuroLOT),
ATR 72 - 8 (operated by EuroLOT),

LOT - Polish Airlines

LEFT: *LOT - Polish Airlines 737-500 (Jeremy Flack/API)*

737-300- 2, 737-400- 7, 737-500 - 10, 737-800 -
2, 767-200ER - 2, 767-300ER - 3, ERJ-145 - 14
On order: ATR 42-500 - 5 (to replace the
300s), 737-800 - 2ERJ-145 - 1

LOT was originally established as the state
airline Aerolot by the Polish Government
on January 1st 1929, from Aerolloyd that
was formed in 1922. It was formed by the
merging of Aerolot and Aero TZ (founded
1922). It began operations during March of
that year as Linje Lotnicze LOT becoming
Polskie Linje Lotnicze LOT in 1929.

LOT became a full member of IATA in
1931 and worked hard to expand its network
for which it purchased 10 Fokker FV.IIbs. By
1939 it was flying to 26 countries and operat-

ing Lockheed 10s and 14s as well as DC-2s
and Ju-52s. The name was changed slightly
to Polskie Linie Lotnicze LOT. During 1938
route proving was undertaken in South
America including carrying mail ready for a
new service to commence in 1940.

However, operations were suspended
during the war and 16 of the fleet of 26 aircraft detained in Romania and all the
hangars and airport buildings destroyed.

In 1945 LOT Polish Airlines looked to re-
establish its old network, this time with 10
surplus military Li-2s and nine DC-3s. These
were gradually replaced by five Il-12s and 13
Il-14s while the first of an order for eight
turboprop Il-18s entered service in 1962. In
1957, three Convair 240s arrived and in

1962 LOT took delivery of three ex-British
United Vickers Viscounts which was an
interesting departure from the normally
solidly Soviet aircraft types operated by the
Eastern European airlines. In addition,
these aircraft enabled LOT to commence
international services outside Europe once
more which began with a route to Cairo.

A substantial expansion in the fleet started in 1966 when the first An-26 was delivered followed by the jet-powered Tu-134 in
1968 replacing some of the Il-18s. The
arrival of the Il-62s in 1972 enabled the
more distant destinations to be added and a
New York schedule commenced in 1973.
More Middle East and Far East routes followed and in 1978 a revised colour scheme
for the aircraft was introduced.

During the 1980s and early 1990s the
country was in turmoil. During 1981 some
airlines suspended their services to
Warsaw and in December all flights were
suspended when martial law was imposed.
This was relaxed at the end of 1982 and
gradually flights resumed, returning to
USA in 1985. The Solidarnosc movement

BELOW: *Euro LOT ATR 42-320, SP-EDE (C/n 031)
(ATR)*

continued to force the resignation of the communist government and Soviet domination. Once achieved, Poland attempted to reach for a Western style economy during the early 1990s but has found it painful on the way. Meanwhile the Il-18s and Tu-154s were withdrawn in 1986 and the Tu-154 entered service. In 1988 a decision was made to operate Western aircraft - LOT was the first airline in Central and Eastern Europe to do so. An order was placed for a pair of 737s. They entered service the following year and LOT flew the highest number of passengers in one year that it had ever done - 2.3 million.

New aircraft continue to be added to the fleet with the first ATR 72 in 1991 and 737 in 1992 and, according to a report prepared for IATA, in 1994 LOT had the youngest fleet of all airlines.

In 1992 LOT became a Joint Stock Company and subsequently underwent partial privatisation in 1999.

From the mid-1990s LOT has won a number of awards including a US one for advertising in which the slogan "Poland is free. The flight very reasonable" was displayed.

On December 19th 1996, EuroLot was formed as a subsidiary of LOT to operate the domestic schedules.

LOT placed an order for two 737s in 1996 by which time the whole fleet comprised Western airliners. This was followed by its first order for eight of the ERJ-145s in 1999.

Later that year, the privatisation of LOT commenced with a sale of 25% of the shares to the SAirGroup. The events of September 11th had two effects on LOT. Initially, reduced passenger levels on top of the already higher fuel prices forced LOT to cut services and reduce staff levels. With a US$160 million loss filed at the end of the year, a further share issue was made for a

government cash injection resulting in the state treasury owning 67.96%, SAirGroup 25.1% and the balance of 6.94% held by LOT employees.

Worse was to come when the SAirGroup filed for bankruptcy. Fortunately LOT had already been implementing a cost-cutting exercise due to the financial climate prior to September. This meant that a number of strategies were already in place and overall record passenger levels for 2001 have enabled LOT to struggle through. With the termination of the Qualifyer Alliance in February 2002, LOT entered into a code-share agreement with Lufthansa and joined the Star Alliance a few months later and has since ordered new ATR 42s to replace the older models.

LTU International Airways

Registered name: LTU Lufttransport-Unternehmen GmbH

Country: Germany

Region: Europe

Address: Flughafen Halle 8
D-40474 Dusseldorf

Tel: 0049 211 9418 888

Fax: 0049 211 9418 881

Web site: www.ltu.com

Stockholder: LTU Group

Main operational base: Dusseldorf

STATUS

IATA international scheduled and charter passenger carrier
National Flag Carrier
Employees: 2,300
Passengers per year: 7,400,000 (2001)
ICAO code: LTU
IATA code: LT

SERVICES

International / Domestic / Passenger Charter / Cargo

International routes: Bulgaria, Canada, Cuba, Dominican Rep, Egypt, Greece, Iceland, Italy, Kenya, Maldives, Mexico, Morocco, Namibia, Portugal, Sri Lanka, South Africa, Spain, Thailand, Tunisia, Turkey, USA

FLEET

A320-200 - 9, A321-200 - 1, A330-200 - 7, A330-300 - 3, 757-200 - 6
On order: A320-200 - 2 + 4 options for A320s or A321s

ABOVE: *LTU A320-214, D-ALTB (C/n 1385) (Airbus)*

LTU was established on May 5th 1955, with Vickers Vikings as Lufttransport-Unternehmen but later became known by its initials. The de Havilland Dove was acquired in 1957.

The DC-4s and Nord 262s entered service in 1958 and although LTU was formed as a charter airline it was undertaking some scheduled services for Lufthansa by 1960.

LTU International Airways

LTU's first F-27 Friendship entered service in 1961 followed by the French Caravelle taking them into the jet age in 1965. These were replaced with the F-28 Fellowships from 1969.

The first wide-body airliner to serve with LTU was the Tristar in 1973 followed by the MD-11 in 1991- a year after a scheduled service had commenced to the USA.

In the meantime, 757s were delivered in 1984. These were transferred to the sister airline LTE, when it was formed in 1987 to operate charters from Spain, and LTS which had been formed in 1983. These were followed by 767s in 1989.

LTU began to use Airbus airliners with the A330 in 1995 and although the 737 entered service for a short while in 1999, plus the A320, the airline is moving towards an all Airbus fleet with the A321 being delivered in 2001 together with more A330s.

ABOVE: *LTU 757-2G5ER. D-AMUY (C/n 24176) (Jane's)*

Lufthansa German Airlines

Registered name: Deutsche Lufthansa AG
Country: Germany
Region: Europe
Address: Von-Gablenz-Strasse 2-6
Cologne D-50679
Tel: 0049 221 82 60
Fax: 0049 221 826 38 18
Web site: www.lufthansa.com
Stockholder: Lufthansa Group
Main operational base: Frankfurt and Munich

STATUS

IATA scheduled international carrier
National Flag Carrier
Employees: 33,983
Passengers per year: 45,700,000 (2001)
ICAO code: DLH
IATA code: LH

BELOW: *Lufthansa A340-211 D-AIBF (C/n 006) with Airbus test registration F-WWBE (Airbus)*

SERVICES

International / Regional / Domestic
Passenger / Cargo
International routes: Argentina, Austria, Azerbaijan, Belarus, Belgium, Bosnia Herzegovina, Brazil, Bulgaria, Canada, Chile, China, Cote D'Ivoire, Croatia, Cyprus, Czech, Denmark, Egypt, Eritrea, Ethiopia, Finland, France, Germany, Ghana, Greece, Hungary, India, Indonesia, Iran, Ireland, Italy, Japan, Jordan, Kazakhstan, Kuwait, Latvia, Libya, Lebanon, Lithuania, Macedonia, Malta, Mexico, Morocco, Netherlands, Nigeria, Norway, Oman, Philippines, Poland, Portugal, Romania, Russia, Saudi Arabia, Serbia, Singapore, South Africa, South Korea, Spain, Sudan, Switzerland, Sweden, Thailand, Tunisia, Turkey, Turkmenistan, UAE, UK, Ukraine, USA, Venezuela, Vietnam, Yemen

ALLIANCES/CODE SHARES

Star Alliance / Adria Aw, Air Canada, Air China, AirDolomiti, Air New Zealand, Air One, All Nippon Aw, Augsburg Aw, Austrian A/l, bmi british midland, Cimber Air, Cirrus A/l, CityLine, Contact Air, Croatia A/l, Czech A/l, Deutsche Bahn

AG, Eurowings, LaudaAir, Luxair, LOT, MaerskAir, Mexicana, Scandinavian A/l, Singapore A/l, South African Aw, Spanair, Thai Aw, Tyrolean Aw, United A/l, Varig

OWNED SUBSIDIARY AIRLINES

Lufthansa Cargo, Lufthansa Cityline GmbH

FLEET

A300-600 - 14, A310-300 - 6, A319-100 - 20, A320-200 - 36, A321-100 - 26, A340-200 - 6, A340-300 - 28, 737-300 - 32, 737-300QC - 7, 737-400 - 7, 737-500 - 30, 747-200B - 8, 747-400 - 30, BBJ-1 - 1

On order: A300-600 - 1, A320-200 - 2, A330-300 - 10, A340-600 - 10, A380-800 - 15

Lufthansa was established on January 6th 1926 as Deutsche Luft Hansa Aktiengesellschaft using a Fokker Grulich FII. It was formed from the merger of Deutsche Aero Lloyd (DAL) and Junkers Luftverkehr. The current logo is a combination of the crane from DAL (which was originally designed in 1919) and the blue and yellow house-colours from Junkers Luftverkehr. Scheduled flights began on April 6th 1926 with a fleet comprised 162 aircraft of 18 different types.

Lufthansa bought a stake in the German-Russian Dereluft airline in 1926 and was influential in the founding of Iberia in Spain, Syndicato Condor in Brazil and Eurasia in China. In 1934 Lufthansa inaugurated the first transatlantic scheduled airmail service to South America as well as experimenting with a North Atlantic service. Service was also flown to Bangkok in the east. Types operated included the Dornier flying boats, Fw-200 Ju-52s, Ju-86s and Ju-90s, some of which were to play a significant military role during the war. By 1939 it had become the largest airline in Europe and was carrying in the region of 250,000 passengers a year.

During the war Lufthansa flights were restricted to just a few European countries

ABOVE: *Lufthansa 747-430, D-ABVA (C/n 23817) (Lufthansa)*

BELOW: *Lufthansa 737-330, D-ABXT (C/n 24281) (Lufthansa)*

Lufthansa German Airlines

ABOVE: *Lufthansa CityLine RJ85, D-AVRF (C/n E2269) with BAe test registration G-JAYV (Jeremy Flack/API)*

and once the war ended the Allies stopped Germany from any flying activities. As a result Lufthansa went into receivership and was wound up and struck off the Berlin commercial register.

In 1951 a working committee was set up to prepare for the resumption of air traffic in Germany. Aktiengesellschaft für Luftverkehrsbedarf (Luftag) was established in Cologne on January 6th 1953. Orders were placed for four Super Constellations and four Convair 340s. The name was changed to Deutsche Lufthansa Aktiengesellschaft in 1954 and a scheduled service resumed on April 1st 1955, initially flying domestic routes.

In October 1958 Lufthansa received the first of 11 Vickers Viscount turboprop airliners and, in 1960, the 707s brought the jet age in to fly scheduled services to the USA. 720s arrived shortly after.

Lufthansa was the first European customer for the 727 with which it commenced medium-range hauls in 1964. It led again with the 737s that were used for short-haul routes. The arrival of the first three 747s for Lufthansa, in 1970, was followed by DC-10s from 1973 and A300s from 1976.

In 1990 - 45 years after the war ended - Lufthansa was allowed to resume a scheduled service to Berlin.

During the early 1990s Lufthansa suffered its worst crisis following German reunification. An urgent restructuring was undertaken. This resulted in the airline, which was largely owned by the state, being privatised stage by stage and various non-airline businesses sold off.

In 1997, Lufthansa created the Star Alliance along with Air Canada, SAS, Thai Airways and United Airlines to become the first multilateral airline grouping.

Lufthansa business was severely hit by the September 11th disaster and cut services and staff levels with net profits for 2000 of US$606 million dropping to a loss of US$557 million. This has been exasperated by the loss-making LSG Sky Chefs subsidiary. However, a year later the passenger levels are seen to be returning and improved operating practices are expected to take it back into the black.

In June 2002 Lufthansa re-established a route to the USA with a scheduled service between Dusseldorf and Newark operating a BBJ-1. The service is aimed specifically at Business Class passengers and is fitted in a 48-seat configuration.

Luxair

Registered name: Luxair SA
Country: Luxembourg
Region: Europe
Address: Luxembourg Airport
             L-2987
Tel: 00352 47 98 42 81
Fax: 00352 47 98 42 89
Web site: www.luxair.lu
Main operational base: Luxembourg Airport

STATUS

Scheduled and charter carrier
National Flag Carrier
Employees: 2,120
Passengers per year: 1,142,000 (2001)

ABOVE: *Luxair 737-5C9, LX-LGP (C/n 26439) (Luxair)*

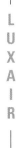

Luxembour being the seat of several important European institutions it was felt that the airline and its services should be improved. A reorganisation followed in 1961 and the airline emerged as Luxair - Société Luxembourgeoise de Navigation Aérienne and commenced its scheduled services the following year with a leased F-27 Friendship.

The new Luxair saw rapid growth and one year later purchased its own F-27. Another followed and by 1967 a fleet of three were being operated plus a Vickers Viscount. These were later replaced with Fokker 50s and EMB-Brasilias.

Luxair entered the jet age with the arrival of the first two Caravelles in March 1972 and a third in May of that year. In 1977 the first of two 737s arrived and an order for two EMJ-135 regional jets was placed with the Brazilian manufacturer Embraer. The following year an additional five ERJ-145s were ordered and deliveries commenced in August 1998. They have been designated "Eurojet" by Luxair.

While a sizeable part of Luxair's turnover is generated by the inclusive tour market, of which the majority are flown to the Mediterranean, the majority is earned from scheduled business traffic.

In November 2002 a Fokker 50 was lost - sadly with 20 fatalities - Luxair's first accident in 40 years of operation.

ABOVE: *Fokker 50, LX-LGE (C/n 20180) (Luxair)*

ICAO code: LGL
IATA code: LG

SERVICES

International / Regional / Passenger Cargo
International routes: Austria, Denmark, France, Germany, Greece, Ireland, Italy, Malta, Morocco, Portugal, Spain, Sweden, Switzerland, Tunisia, Turkey, UK

ALLIANCES/CODE SHARES

Air France, Lufthansa, Tyrolean, VLM A/1

FLEET

737-400 - 2, 737-500 - 3, ERJ-145 - 8, Fokker 50 - 3

Originally formed in 1948 as the Luxembourg Airlines Company. With the evolving European Community and

Macedonian Airlines/MAT

Registered name: Macedonian Airlines JSC
Country: Macedonia
Region: Europe
Address: Partizanski Odredi 17A
Skopje 9100
Tel: 00389 9 11 63 33
Fax: 00389 9 122 95 76
Web site: www.mat.com.mk
Main operational base: Skopje

STATUS

IATA scheduled and charter passenger + cargo carrier
National Flag Carrier
ICAO code: MAK
IATA code: IN

SERVICES

Regional / Domestic / Passenger Charter / Cargo
International routes: Belgium, Denmark, Germany, Italy, Netherlands, Sweden, Switzerland

FLEET

737-300 - 2, DC-9-30 - 2

Macedonian Airlines was formed on January 16th 1994 and operated its first scheduled flight on June 23rd from Skopje to Zurich using a 737.

Macedonian Airlines was granted the status of being the National flag carrier for Macedonia in 2000 and has already carried over 1 million passengers.

Maersk Air

Registered name: Maersk Air A/S
Country: Denmark
Region: Europe
Address: Copenhagen Airport South
DK-2791 Dragoer
Tel: 0045 32 31 44 44
Fax: 0045 32 31 44 90
Web site: www.maersk-air.com
Stockholder: A P Moller Group
Main operational base: Copenhagen

STATUS

Scheduled and charter passenger + cargo carrier
National Flag Carrier
Employees: 1,252
Passengers per year: 2,098,000 (2001)
ICAO code: DAN
IATA code: DM

SERVICES

International / Regional / Domestic
Passenger / Charter / Cargo
International routes: Belgium, Egypt, France, Germany, Greece, Ireland, Italy, Netherlands, Norway, Portugal, Sweden, Switzerland, Turkey, UK

ALLIANCES/CODE SHARES

Air France, SAS

OWNED SUBSIDIARY AIRLINES

Maersk Air Ltd, Maersk Helicopters, Star Air A/S

BELOW: *Maersk Air Ltd CRJ700 (Bombardier)*

FLEET

737-300 - 2, 737-500SP - 15, 737-700 - 7, CRJ200LR - 5 (Maersk Air Ltd), CRJ700 - 5 (Maersk Air Ltd), Fokker 50 - 2 (leased to Air Estonia)
On order: 737-700 - 1

Maersk Air was formed in 1969 as part of the AP Moller Group. The Moller Group has its origins dating back to 1904 with the setting up of a shipping business which currently operates some 250 vessels.

Maersk Air was established principally as a charter operator with F-27 Friendships and an HS125. As the inclusive tours market was developed, 720s were added to the fleet from 1972 to enable greater distances to be served.

The 737s began to enter service with Maersk from 1976 and replaced the older aircraft to provide the backbone of the fleet with newer models subsequently being added.

Maersk Air Ltd was formed as a subsidiary

ABOVE: *Maersk Air 737-7L9, OY-APP (C/n 29234) (Maersk Air)*

in 1993 following the split of the merged Brymon Airways and Birmingham European. The latter had been formed as Birmingham Executive Airways in 1983 and was acquired by Maersk while Brymon became a subsidiary of British Airways.

In the meantime, Birmingham Executive Airways had been formed in 1983 with Jetstream 31s. Such was the quality of its service that the following year it operated several services on behalf of British Airways.

Birmingham Executive Airways was acquired by the Plimsoll Line - a subsidiary of Maersk Air - together with British Airways and private interests in 1988 and renamed Birmingham European Airways. Brymon merged briefly but split after only a year to become a wholly owned subsidiary of BA. The Maersk Group then acquired the whole airline in 1993 and it was renamed Maersk Air Ltd. This was the first European airline to be wholly operated by a foreign company. Maersk Air Ltd currently operates as a BA franchisee.

The BAC 1-11s that were introduced in 1989 were replaced by the CRJ100 from 1998 to which CRJ700s were added in 2001 and the Maersk UK fleet of all CRJs are painted in BA colours.

Meanwhile, Maersk Air continues to operate its fleet of 737s on charter and scheduled services and is also in the business of leasing aircraft to other airlines.

Malaysia Airlines

Registered name: Malaysian Airline System
Berhad (MAS)
Country: Malaysia
Region: Asia
Address: 33rd Floor
Bangunan MAS
Jalan Sultan Ismail
50250 Kuala Lumpur
Tel: 0060 3 21 61 05 55
Fax: 0060 3 21 61 34 72
Web site: www.malaysiaairlines.com.my
Main operational base: Kuala Lumpur Int Airport

STATUS

IATA scheduled carrier
National Flag Carrier
Employees: 21,661
Passengers per year: 15,734,000 (2001)
ICAO code: MAS
IATA code: MH

SERVICES

International / Regional / Domestic
Passenger / Charter / Cargo
International routes: Australia, Austria,
Bangladesh, Brunei, Cambodia, China,
Denmark, Egypt, Finland*, France,
Germany, India, Indonesia, Iran, Ireland,
Italy, Japan, Jordan*, Lebanon, Maldives,
Mauritius, Myanmar, Netherlands,
Norway*, Pakistan, Philippines, Saudi
Arabia, Singapore, South Africa, South
Korea, Sri Lanka, Sweden*, Taiwan,
Thailand, Turkey, UAE, UK, USA,
Uzbekistan, Vietnam (*code share)

ALLIANCES/CODE SHARES

Air-India, bmi, Cathay Pacific Aw, Egyptair,
Garuda, KLM, Korean A/l, Lauda Air,
MEA, Northwest A/l, PAL, Qatar Aw, Royal
Brunei A/l, Royal Jordanian, SriLankan,
Uzbekistan Aw, Virgin Atlantic Aw

FLEET

A330-300 - 9, 737-400 - 39, 737-700 (BBJ) -
1, 747-200B (F) - 4, 747-300 - 1, 747-400 -
18, 777-200IGW - 13, DHC-6 Twin Otter
300 - 6, Fokker 50 - 10
On order: 747-400 - 2, 777-200IGW - 3,
A380 - 6

The origin of Malaysia Airlines dates back
to a joint initiative between the Steamship
Company of Liverpool, the Straits
Company of Singapore and Imperial
Airways to operate between Penang and
Singapore. This led to the incorporation of
Malaysian Airways Ltd (MAL) on October
12th 1937.

Due to the war, MAL did not carry its first
passenger until April 2nd 1947 when an
Airspeed Consul flew from Singapore to
Kuala Lumpur.

With services expanding domestically
and regionally, extra capacity was acquired
in the form of the DC-3.

Following the independence of Malaysia
in 1957, assisted by BOAC and QANTAS,
the government of the Federation of
Malaya, Singapore and the Territory of

ABOVE: *Malaysia Airlines A330-322, 9M-MKC (C/n
069) (Airbus)*

North Borneo launched MAL as a public
limited company becoming Malaysian
Airlines Ltd. This provided new resources
that enabled it to add five Beavers and a
Douglas DC-4 to the fleet.

The DC-4 enabled a route to Hong Kong
to be inaugurated and started its longer
routes. This continued with the addition of
a Viscount in 1959 plus a Super
Constellation and the first of a fleet of
Bristol Britannias the following year.

The year 1963 saw the amalgamation of
Borneo Airways with MAL as part of a trans-

BELOW: *Malaysia Airlines 747-4H6, 9M-MHO (C/n
25126) (Malaysia Airlines)*

Malaysia Airlines

port integration plan. Five F-27 Friendships were acquired. The Governments of Malaysia and Singapore became the majority shareholders in MAL in 1966 at a time when the de Havilland Comet was introduced. Following the formation of Singapore in 1967, MAL was renamed Malaysia-Singapore Airlines (MSA). Three 707s were delivered together with an additional two Friendships to increase capacity for the additional routes that were now spreading into Australia.

The Malaysia / Singapore partnership was dissolved in 1971 and MSA was renamed Malaysia Airlines Berhad in April which was further changed to Malaysian Airline System Berhad (MAS).

During May 1973 MAS carried its millionth passenger but such was the growth that the second millionth was carried by the end of the year. Routes continued to expand reaching out into the Middle East and as far as London.

Computerisation was taken on by MAS and during 1976 it managed to incorporate the whole of its operation. The arrival of the first DC-10 brought with it a large increase in capacity allowing additional routes to Europe.

During the mid-1980s MAS was privatised, services to the USA were introduced and, in October 1987, MAS was renamed Malaysia Airlines.

In 1991, a RN9.6 billion fleet investment saw orders for A330 and Fokker 50 airliners and MD-11 freighters. A further large investment was announced in 1996 for 15 777s and 10 747s. When the first 777 was delivered on April 2nd 1997 it broke two world records. The first was for the longest non-stop record (Seattle-Kuala Lumpur) and the second was for the speed recorded for the journey.

In April 2001 Malaysia Airlines became the first airline to fly a twin-engined commercial jet through the newly opened polar routes.

This enabled a significant time saving.

Malaysia Airlines has been operating at a loss for a number of years and has been undertaking a restructuring that includes disposal of a number of surplus assets. As a result the accumulated debt should be substantially reduced. The domestic routes have been a major loss maker for Malaysian Airlines and in January 2002 the Malaysian Government announced that it would split the international and domestic services into two groups that would be run separately. Tune Air which had acquired Malaysia's second national carrier - Air Asia - in 2001 announced in 2002 that it would be prepared to manage and operate the domestic services.

At the begining of 2003, Malaysian Airlines announced an order for six A380s which could be worth US$1.5 billion. With this order Malaysian became the 10th airline to order the 550 seat airliner which it anticipates will enter service in 2007.

Malév Hungarian Airlines

Registered name: Malev Hungarian Airlines plc
Country: Hungary
Region: Europe
Address: Roosevelt Terrace 2
     Budapest H-1051
Tel: 0036 1 235 35 35
Fax: 0036 1 266 26 85
Web site: www.malev.hu

STATUS

IATA scheduled international carrier
National Flag Carrier
Employees: 2,615
Passengers per year: 2,075,000 (2001)
ICAO code: MAH
IATA code: MA

ABOVE: *Malév Hungarian Airlines CRJ200, HA-LNA (C/n 7676) (Bombardier)*

SERVICES

International / Regional / Domestic
Passenger / Charter / Cargo
International routes: Albania, Austria, Belgium, Bosnia Herzegovina, Bulgaria,

Croatia, Cyprus, Czech, Denmark, Egypt, Finland, France, Germany, Greece, Ireland, Israel, Italy, Latvia, Lebanon, Libya, Macedonia, Netherlands, Norway, Poland, Romania, Russia, Spain, Sweden, Switzerland, Turkey, UK, Ukraine, USA

ALLIANCES/CODE SHARES
Aeroflot, Aerosvit, Air Europa, Air France, Alitalia, Austrian A/l, LOT, Northwest A/l, Siss, TAROM

FLEET
737-300 - 7, 737-400 - 6, 737-500 - 2, 767-200ER - 2, CRJ200ER - 2 (operated by Malev Express), Fokker 70 - 6
On order: 737-600 - 6 for delivery from 2/2003, 737-700 - 7 for delivery from 2/2003, 737-800 - 5 for delivery from 2/2003, CRJ200/700 - 2 for delivery in 2004 +6 options (for Malev Express)

Aviation services in Hungary were among the first in the world with the Aero Joint

Stock Company formed in June 1919. Military courier aircraft of the Austro-Hungarian monarchy delivered airmail from July 1918. Some of these had airmail stamps affixed and have become highly valued by philatelists.

A number of airlines were established during the 1920s and by 1928, when Malert was formed, some 10,000 passengers and 1 million kg of cargo had been carried. Malert operated Ju-52s and SM-75s during the 1930s to provide services to various foreign cities. However, Malert and those other surviving Hungarian airlines were effectively destroyed during WW2.

Mászovlet was formed as a joint Hungarian-Soviet (50-50) venture on March 29th 1946 with the remaining Malert staff. Initially, the airline was equipped with five Li-2s followed by three PO-2s in September. The first operations commenced on October 15th. An Aero 45 was acquired in 1940 and from 1950 the PO-2s were used to deliver mail to provincial

ABOVE: *Malév Hungarian Airlines 737-2QB, HA-LEA (C/n 21735) (Jeremy Flack/API)*

towns. Delivery was rather primitive in that the mailbags would be thrown overboard when the aircraft was above the designated point. This enabled a substantial number of deliveries to be made on each flight. Following trials, PO-2s were also used for crop spraying from the mid-1950s. On November 6th 1954, Mászovlet announced the end of the Hungarian-Soviet agreement. However, as the airline had been successful, the Hungarian Government bought the Soviet share and Mászovlet was renamed Malév Hungarian Air Transport Company. Li-2s continued to be operated on their domestic routes.

During the 1956 Revolution, Malév ferried Red Cross aid from Vienna. However, all operations were halted for three months following Soviet occupation. By the end of 1956 the fleet comprised eight Li-2s. Following the decision to establish routes

Malév Hungarian Airlines

outside Hungary, Malév took delivery of the first of three Il-14s in 1957 with a further five the following year. A number of ex-Hungarian AF Li-2s were also added to the fleet to use for its cargo operation. The arrival of Il-18s in 1960 enabled longer routes to be flown. Trouble was on the horizon for Malév. Hungary had been devastated by the ravages of war when the airline was formed and any kind of communication was difficult. By the 1960s the situation had changed. The time taken by land was competing on the relatively short domestic routes. With revenues failing to match costs and with state aid gradually reducing, Malév was running up serious debts. This was compounded by the withdrawal of the Li-2s in 1963 and the inability of the Il-14s to operate from a number of the small airfields. The domestic service, having been suspended during the winter months for a number of years, was terminated by Malév in 1968.

In 1968, four Tu-134s were ordered and the first was delivered that December taking Malév into the jetage. They commenced service the following April. Malév was admitted to ICAO later that year and the surviving Il-14s were sold in 1970.

Three larger Tu-154s were ordered in 1972 and entered service with Malév in 1973 with a further three ordered the following year. They gradually replaced the Il-18s on the passenger services from 1976 although the old turboprop proved suitable for cargo following conversion.

In 1984, with annual passenger levels now regularly exceeding one million, Malév became the 125th full-right member of IATA.

Malév operations went from strength to strength but it was finding that the Tu-154, its fleet, was struggling to match the operating costs and quality of service of the Western types operated by most other airlines. In November 1988 the first of Malév's leased 737s arrived and the following year the Il-18s were finally withdrawn along with the first of the Tu-134s. Also in 1988 TNT-Malév Express Cargo took delivery of its first BAe146 which was flown and operated by Malév air and ground personnel.

In 1993 two 767s entered service for use on long-haul operations and commenced a Budapest-New York scheduled service. By 1995 a total of 12 737s were on strength and this enabled the withdrawal of the rest of the Tupolev airliners from scheduled passenger operations. On June 30th 1992 Malev became a public limited company and has since become fully independent from state control.

The entry into service of the Fokker 70 in December 1995 and the withdrawal of the last Tu-134s and Tu-154s have allowed Malév to operate a modern Western fleet and at last be able to compete equally with other European airlines.

It is currently modernising its fleet by leasing two 737-600s, six 737-700s and two 737-800s from ILFC to replace the existing fifteen older 737-300s, -400s and -500s that were already on lease.

In addition, subsidiary Malev Express commenced operations with a leased CRJ100 between Prague and Budapest in July 2002. It has since taken delivery of CRJ200s.

Mandarin Airlines

Registered name: Mandarin Airlines Ltd
Country: Taiwan
Region: Far East
Address: 13F, 134 Min Sheng East Road
 Taipei 105
Tel: 00886 2 27 17 11 88
Fax: 00886 2 27 17 07 16
Web site: www.mandarin-airlines.com
Main operational base: Taipei

STATUS

Scheduled and charter carrier
Employees: 658
ICAO code: MDA
IATA code: AE

SERVICES

Regional / Domestic / Passenger
Cargo

International routes: Cambodia, Indonesia, Japan, Laos, Malaysia, Mariana Islands, Myanmar, North Korea, Philippines, South Korea, Thailand

FLEET

737-800 - 3, Do 228 - 3, Fokker 100 - 2, Fokker 50 - 7

Mandarin Airlines was formed on June 1st, 1991, as a joint venture between China Airlines and the Koos Group. Operations commenced in October establishing routes to Sydney and Vancouver and became the first Taiwanese airline to fly direct to Australia and Canada.

China Airlines acquired the Koos shareholding of Mandarin Airlines in October 1992 although the airline remained autonomous.

Mandarin Airlines merged with Formosa Airlines (formed 1966) in August 1999. This was a domestic airline in which China Airlines already had a 42% shareholding, acquired in 1996.

This enabled Mandarin Airlines to establish a strong domestic schedule as well as developing its regional ones. As these schedules expanded to most countries in the region, it was decided to transfer the two long-haul routes to Australia and Canada to China Airlines. Despite the original plan to operate international routes, Mandarin Airlines had developed a strong domestic and regional route and it was considered that this was where its best future lay.

Martinair Holland

Registered name: Martinair Holland NV
Country: Netherlands
Region: Europe
Address: PO Box 7507
Schiphol Airport
NL-1118
Tel: 0031 20 601 12 22
Fax: 0031 20 601 13 86
Web site: www.martinair.com
Stockholder: KLM

STATUS

Scheduled and charter passenger + cargo
carrier
Employees: 3,070
Passengers per year: 2,121,000 (1999)
ICAO code: MPH
IATA code: MP

SERVICES

International / Passenger / Charter
Cargo
International routes: Canada, Cuba,
Dominican Republic, Jamaica, Mexico,
Netherlands Antilles, Puerto Rico, USA

ALLIANCES/SHARE CODES

Air ALM

FLEET

A320 - 2, 747-200C - 2, 747-200F - 1, 757-
200 - 1, 767-300ER - 5, MD-11CF - 4, MD-
11F - 2
On order: A320 - 2 options

Martinair Holland was originally formed as
Martin's Air Charter on May 24th 1958,
operating various light aircraft to undertake banner flying and joy-rides.

Martin's Air Charter took over Veen's Air
Service (formed 1962) and Fairways
Rotterdam (formed 1964). Aircraft were
leased according to requirements.

As with many successful small companies,
Martin's Air Charter attracted the interest
of the larger airlines. An association was
made with KLM that resulted in larger aircraft being made available including DC-6s
and a DC-8. The name was changed to
Martinair Holland in April 1968.

A subsidiary, Luchtreclamebedrijf

ABOVE: *Martinair Holland A320-203, PH-MCX (Airbus)*

Nederland Reclamair NV, was formed to
continue the original light aircraft services
while Martinair continued to expand into
the business of worldwide passenger and
cargo charters.

The first DC-9 was acquired in 1969 along
with an F-28 Fellowship. These were followed by four of the wide-body DC-10s during the 1970s.

The DC-9s were replaced by MD-80s during the early 1980s and MD-11s replaced
the DC-10s. 747s were subsequently added
to increase capacity along with A320s and
767s.

The association with KLM continued with
50% of the share being owned by the major
airline and there were a number of
rumours about their possible integration of
services. However, it was made clear that
this would not be happening in the short
term after the EC advised that approval
would not be easy.

Merpati Nusantara Airlines

Registered name: PT Merpati Nusantara Airlines
Country: Indonesia
Region: Asia
Address: Jalan Angkasa Blok B 15 Kav 2-3
Jakarta Pusat
PO Box 1323
Jakarta 10720
Tel: 0062 21 654 88 88
Fax: 0062 21 654 06 20
Web site: www.merpati.co.id
Main operational base: Jakarta

STATUS

Scheduled and charter passenger + cargo carrier
National Flag Carrier
Employees: 4,503
Passengers per year: 1,741,000 (2001)
ICAO code: MNA
IATA code: MZ

SERVICES

International / Regional / Domestic
Passenger / Charter / Cargo
International routes: Australia, Malaysia, Singapore

FLEET

737-200 - 7, DHC-6 Twin Otter 300 - 8, Fokker 100 - 3, F-27 Mk.500 - 7, F-28 Mk.4000 - 22, CN212-200 Aviocar - 10, CN235-200 - 12
On order: CN235-200 - 12, N-250-100 - 15

Merpati Nusantara Airlines was formed on September 6th 1962, as PN Merpati Nusantara by the Indonesian Government to take over domestic schedules previously operated by the military. Operations commenced with four ex-military DHC-Otters and two C-47s.

The Dutch-controlled De Kroonduif was handed over to Garuda in 1963 about the time that Irian Jaya was handed to the Indonesians by the Netherlands. Garuda considered itself to be an international carrier; these routes were passed to the Merpati along with an additional three C-47s, two Twin Pioneers and a Beaver.

PN Merpati Nusantara was split into two regions in 1969 - Merpati Irian Barat and Merpati Operasi Barat including Java, Kalimantan, Sulawesi and Nusa Tenggara. This didn't last long and shortly afterwards the airline was renamed Merpati Nusantara Airlines.

In 1971 it became PT Merpati Nusantara Airlines. Opportunities were taken to expand business with charter flights for the hajj, transmigration programmes as well as the ever-increasing tourists. BAC 1-11s were used on the Manila - Denpasar (Bali) route while a 707 flew Los Angeles - Denpasar.

Merpati was absorbed into Garuda Indonesian Airlines in October 1978 but continues to operate under its own name. It has expanded its domestic schedules to include Australia and Malaysia.

In August 1996, Merpati commenced a Jakarta - Melbourne service following which the Indonesian Government decided that Merpati should be considered an independent carrier and in April 1997 it was split from Garuda. Sadly, Merpati has suffered seventeen accidents over the last ten years. However, this is a country with difficult terrain and sometimes very violent tropical storms. While some of the accidents have been minor, eight have resulted in fatalities, the most recent being in March 2001 when an F-27 Friendship flew into a mountain while on a training flight killing all three crew.

Mesa Air Group

Registered name: Mesa Air Group Inc
Country: USA
Region: North America
Address: 410 North 44th St
Suite 700, Phoenix
Arizona 85008
Tel: 001 602 685 40 00
Fax: 001 602 685 43 50
Web site: www.mesa-air.com
Main operational base: Phoenix

STATUS

Scheduled regional passenger carrier
Employees: 3,000
Passengers per year: 4,789,000 (2001)
ICAO code: MSE
IATA code: YV

SERVICES

Regional / Domestic / Passenger
Cargo
International routes: Canada, Mexico

ALLIANCES/CODE SHARES

America West Express, Frontier A/l, Midwest Express, US Airways

ABOVE: *CCAir DHC-8 Dash 8 102 in US Airways Express colours (Bombardier)*

OWNED SUBSIDIARY AIRLINES

Mesa Airlines, Air Midwest, CCAir

FLEET

CRJ200 - 52 (operated as America West

Express & US Airways Express), CRJ-700 - 4, DHC-8 Dash 8-200 - 17 (operated as US Airways Express & Mesa Airlines), ERJ-145 -29 (operated as US Airways Express), 1900D - 22 (operated as America West Express & US Airways Express), Jetstream 32 - 9 (operated as US Airways Express)
On order: CRJ700 - 16, CRJ900 - 20, ERJ-135/145 - 60

Mesa was formed in August 1982 by Larry Risley and has rapidly grown with a revenue of US$11 million in the late 1980s to over US$350 million in 1994.

Mesa acquired the assets of Aspen Airways / United Express in 1990, Air Midwest / US Air Express in 1991, West Air / United Express in 1993 and Crown Airways in 1994.

Mesa experienced some financial problems in the mid-1990s and lost United Airlines as a partner. As a result, the previous Chairman and CEO Jonathan Ornstein returned and made a complete overhaul of the Mesa organisation to return the airline to profit and re-establish the confidence of passengers and partners.

The Mesa Air Group owns and oversees three airline divisions.

Mesa Jet operates CRJ200s and ERJ145s as US Airways Express at the Philadelphia, Charlotte and Washington DC hubs.

CRJ200s are also operated as America West Express at the Phoenix and Columbus hubs.

Air Midwest (formed 1965) was acquired in 1991 and operates a fleet of 1900Ds. These are split between the US Airways Express hubs of Tampa, Pittsburgh and Philadelphia, America West Express in Phoenix and Mesa Airlines at Albuquerque.

CCAir (formed 1979) was acquired in 1999 and operated a fleet of Jetstream 32 and DHC-8 Dash 8s as US Airways Express from the Charlotte hub. CCAir ceased flying on November 4th 2002 and there are no plans to resume operations.

ABOVE: *Mesa CRJ700 in America West Express colours with Bombardier test registration C-FZVM (Bombardier)*

Also in November 2002, Mesa returned 12 1900Ds to Raytheon with a further three during early 2003.

In 2001 Mesa became the first airline to order the CRJ900 when the contract for 20 was finalised on July 25th. The first deliveries are scheduled for 2003. It is expected that by 2004 there will be a total of 108 CRJs in the fleet. A letter of intent was issued with US Airways for the next batch of 50 RJs in November 2002.

Mexicana

Registered name: Compañía Mexicana de Aviación, SA de CV
Country: Mexico
Region: Central America & Caribbean
Address: Col Del Valle
 03100 Mexico City
Tel: 0052 5 448 30 00
Fax: 0052 5 687 87 86
Web site: www.mexicana.com
Stockholder: Cintra
Main operational base: Mexico City

STATUS

IATA international scheduled and charter passenger + cargo carrier
National Flag Carrier
Employees: 6,934
Passengers per year: 8,699,000 (2001)
ICAO code: MXA
IATA code: MX

SERVICES

International / Regional / Domestic Passenger / Charter / Cargo
International routes: Argentina, Canada, Colombia, Cuba, Guatemala, Panama, USA, Venezuela

ALLIANCES/CODE SHARES

Star Alliance / Aeromar, Aeromexico, Air Canada, Air New Zealand, ANA, Lufthansa, United Airlines, Varig

FLEET

A319 - 6, A320-200 - 23, 757-200 - 1, 757-200ER - 7, Fokker 100 - 12

Mexicana was originally formed on July 12th 1921, as Compañía Mexicana de Transportación Aérea (CMTA) and is the fourth largest airline in the world.

The name was changed to Mexicana Airlines in August 1924. Operations under

Mexicana

the new title were made delivering payrolls to remote oil fields due to the vulnerability of land routes to bandits. Subsequently, mail and passenger services were added.

Pan Am took control of the Mexicana stock in 1929 which resulted not only in the first international route to the USA but it also became the first airline to provide a service in connecting two foreign destinations Brownsville and Guatemala.

During the 1930s Mexicana operated five Ford Tri-motors, eight Fairchild FC2s, three Fokker F.X and a Keystone plus two Stearman for mail transfer and pilot training. Meanwhile the network of services expanded to include El Salvador, Costa Rica and Cuba, as well as to Los Angeles.

Mexicana added new aircraft to the fleet as they became available with the DC-2s, DC-3s and DC-4s which provided ever increasing levels of range and passenger comfort.

Keeping up the association with Douglas, the DC-6 entered service in the early 1950s which introduced pressurisation to further improve comfort. The Mexicana Airlines Flight Attendant School opened in 1955 not only to train the attendants to look after passengers in flight but also to be able to manage and control emergency situations

and able to perform first aid on passengers and crew.

Mexicana entered the jet-age with the arrival of the first of five de Havilland Comet 4Cs that entered service in July 1960 on the Mexico City to Los Angeles route.

The 1960s were a tough time for Mexicana with strong competition on both its domestic and international routes. Such was the situation that the airline was on the verge of bankruptcy in 1967. However, following a change of management and a complete overhaul Mexicana not only survived but came back stronger than ever before. The first examples of a substantial fleet of 727s were leased.

The Pan Am stock was bought back in January 1968 to become 100% Mexican once again. New routes continued to be added along with 727s so that the fleet included 19 by the second half of the 1970s and passenger levels exceeded over 3 million a year.

The first wide-body DC-10 was delivered in July 1981 and the following year the Mexican Government took 54% of the stock. However, ownership of Mexicana returned to the private sector during the early 1990s following the formation of the Falcon Group. A programme was initiated

ABOVE: *Mexicana A320-231, N225RX (C/n 225) (Airbus)*

to raise the airline's image with the Airbus A320 and Fokker 100 together with revised markings.

AeroCaribe was formed by private investors in 1975 but was bought by Mexicana in 1990 to operate as a subsidiary.

757s were subsequently added to the fleet and code sharing agreements formalised with United Airlines, Lufthansa, Air Canada, Varig and Air New Zealand.

Mexicana became a member of the Star Alliance in July 2000 and continued to grow with around 800 destinations.

The ownership of Mexicana changed again with it coming under the control of the government holding company Cintra along with Aeroméxico. Movements to re-privatise were made in 2001 but domestic politics were making it difficult and it finally stopped with the events of September 11th. The Mexican Government came to its rescue with aid to assist with the soaring insurance premiums.

Although a loss was incurred for 2001, Mexicana has continued with its fleet renewal programme, replacing the last of the 727s with A319s and A320s.

Middle East Airlines – MEA

Registered name: Middle East Airlines - Air Liban
Country: Lebanon
Region: Middle East
Address: PO Box 206
              Beirut Airport, Beirut
Tel: 00961 1 62 88 88
Fax: 00961 1 62 92 60
Web site: www.mea.com.lb
Main operational base: Beirut

STATUS

IATA scheduled international carrier
National Flag Carrier
Employees: 3,456
Passengers per year: 817,000 (2001)
ICAO code: MEA
IATA code: ME

SERVICES

International / Regional
Passenger / Charter / Cargo
International routes: Australia, Cote D'Ivoire, Cyprus, Egypt, France, Germany, Ghana, Greece, Iran, Italy, Jordan, Kuwait, Nigeria, Saudi Arabia, Sri Lanka, Switzerland, Turkey, UAE, UK

ALLIANCES/CODE SHARES

Air France, Malaysia A/l

FLEET

A300-600R - 1, A310-200 - 3, A320-200 - 3, A321-200 - 2, A330-200 - 3

Middle East Airlines (MEA) was formed on May 31st, 1945 as Middle East Airlines Company SA. It commenced regular operations in January 1946 with de Havilland Rapides.

Having carried nearly 9,000 passengers in the first year, DC-3s were purchased and routes established to Turkey and Middle East destinations.

In 1949, Pan American took a 36% shareholding and additional DC-3s were acquired. Pan Am broke with MEA in early 1955 but BOAC took a 38.5% stake later in the year which enabled the airline to obtain new aircraft in the form of the Vickers Viscount.

The de Havilland Comet was ordered by MEA in 1960 and its four aircraft entered service from January 1961 although some were leased from BOAC prior to this. Later that year BOAC sold its share in MEA to Lebanese shareholders.

MEA formed an association with Air Liban in June 1963 that resulted in further development of its combined route network. More Caravelles were acquired to join the couple already being operated by Air Liban and options placed in 1965 for two of the Anglo-French supersonic Concorde airliners that were being developed at the time. The two airlines formally merged in November 1965. Due to its interests in Air Liban, Air France ended up with a 30% holding in the new MEA.

More capacity was leased in the form of 707s and VC10s during 1967 and new 707s acquired the following year.

On December 28th, 1968 disaster struck the airline when Israeli Commandos attacked Beirut airport and destroyed a 707, two Caravelles, three Comets, a VC10 and a Viscount. The following year Lebanese International Airways (formed 1956), which had lost all of its aircraft in the Beirut raid, was absorbed into MEA. Some Convair 990s were acquired from American

Airlines the following year but replaced with 720s during the early 1970s.

Despite the political turmoil in Lebanon, including the closure of Beirut Airport, MEA managed to continue operating limited schedules as well as providing charter and leasing services by working from bases which were established outside Lebanon.

New 747s were acquired in 1975 but were leased after a short use. However, the 707 and 720 fleet was becoming old and had limited appeal to other airlines so by the late 1980s replacements were being sought.

The A310-222s were the first to be received and commenced operations in 1992 on the European routes. These were followed by the A320-232s and A321-231s which began to be operated from January and May 1997 respectively on short-haul routes around the Middle East. An A300-605R was acquired in 2001 and is operated

ABOVE: *Middle East Airlines A321-131, F-OHMP (C/n 668) with Airbus test registration D-AVZN (Airbus)*

on the medium and long-haul routes into Africa.

MEA took delivery of three A330s, on lease from ILFC, during the first half of 2003 to operate these higher-capacity airliners on any of its routes as required.

Midwest Express Airlines

Registered name: Midwest Express Airlines Inc
Country: USA
Region: North America
Address: 6744 South Howell Avenue
Oak Creek, Wisconsin 53154
Tel: 001 414 570 40 00
Fax: 001 414 570 99 22
Web site: www.midwestexpress.com
Stockholder: Midwest Express Holdings
Main operational base: Milwaukee

STATUS

Scheduled passenger + cargo carrier
Employees: 2,868
Passengers per year: 2,031,000 (2001)
ICAO code: MEP
IATA code: YX

SERVICES

Domestic / Passenger / Cargo
International routes: Domestic only

ALLIANCES/CODE SHARES

Air Midwest, American Eagle

FLEET

1900D - 15 (operated by Midwest Express Connection), DC-9-10 - 8, DC-9-30 - 16, 328Jet - 8 (operated by Midwest Express Connection), 717-200 - 5, MD-81 / 82 - 6, MD-88 – 2
On order: 717-200 - 15, ERJ-140ER - 20 (for Midwest Express Connection)

Midwest Express Airlines was formed in 1983 as a subsidiary of the Kimberly-Clark Corporation and commenced operation in June 1984 with DC-9s. Prior to this Kimberly-Clark provided a corporate air service for their executives and engineers to travel between their HQ and the various mills. This had commenced in 1948 and led to K-C Aviation in 1969. They also maintained other corporate aircraft.

Following the US Airline Deregulation Act of 1978, K-C Aviation was developed with support from the parent company to maximise its expertise which resulted in Midwest Express Airlines.

Subsequently, Midwest Express became a subsidiary of Midwest Express Holdings which was owned by Kimberly-Clark and Astral Aviation which owned Skyways Airlines.

In September 1995, 80% of the issued common stock of Midwest Express Holdings was offered on the market followed by the remaining Kimberly-Clark equity by mid-1996.

Midwest Express was ranked the No 1 Domestic Airline by the 2001 Zagat Airline Survey.

The events of September 11th caused Midwest Express to cut capacity by 15% and 450 jobs. Some schedules were transferred to Skyways. Despite this, a loss of US$38 million was incurred. However, the results of 2002 saw its passenger numbers increase despite costs such as fuel and insurance rising.

Another blow to forward planning was the cancellation of the Fairchild Dornier 428Jet. Some 328s were received for use by the Midwest Express Connection operator Skyways Aviation.

An order for 25 717s was placed in April 2001 in a US$940 million deal which includes options for a further 25 aircraft. Initial deliveries during 2003 are to expand capacity but will also be used to replace the DC-9s.

Moldavian Airlines

Registered name: Moldavian Airlines SA
Country: Moldova
Region: Europe
Address: MD-2026
Chisinau Airport
Chisinau
Tel: 00373 2 52 93 56
Fax: 00373 2 52 50 64
Web site: www.mdv.md
Main operational base: Kishinev

STATUS

Scheduled and charter passenger + cargo carrier
National Flag Carrier
Employees: 174
Passengers per year: 34,000 (2000)
ICAO code: MDV
IATA code: 2M

SERVICES

International / Regional
Passenger / Charter / Cargo
International routes: Hungary, Russia

FLEET

340B-3

ABOVE: *Moldavian Airlines SAAB 340, ER_ASA, HB-AKP (C/n 168) (SAAB)*

Moldavian Airlines was established on August 20th 1994 as Moldova's first private airline. Initially operating a leased Yak-42 from the Ukraine which retained its origi-

nal Aeroflot colour-scheme but with Moldavian Airlines titles. A scheduled service was flown to Moscow's Domodedovo airport that provided good connection to Siberia.

A pair of Yak-40s was purchased in 1995 to replace the leased Yak-42. The following year, a Tu-134 was added to the fleet.

In 1997 Moldavian Airlines completed a reappraisal of its services and decided that, if it was to expand its routes into Europe, the old Soviet aircraft would need to be replaced with modern Western aircraft. The SAAB 340 was selected as being an ideal type for their operation and the first example was leased from Crossair in 1997.

In 1999 Moldavian Airlines became a member of IATA, and in addition to the scheduled services, a number of regular charter flights were instigated to Antalya, Turkmenbashi, Bucharest, Lisbon and Debrecen amongst others.

Moldavian Airlines has finally replaced the last of its old aircraft with three SAAB 340s making it the first Moldavian airline to operate a wholly Western fleet of aircraft.

Monarch Airlines

Registered name: Monarch Airlines Ltd
Country: UK
Region: Europe
Address: Prospect House, Prospect Way
London Luton Airport
Beds, LU2 9NU
Tel: 0044 1582 40 00 00
Fax: 0044 1582 41 10 00
Web site: www.flymonarch.com
Main operational base: Luton

STATUS
International scheduled and non-scheduled passenger carrier
Employees: 2,708
Passengers per year: 4,878,000 (2001)*
includes charter
ICAO code: MON
IATA code: ZB

SERVICES
Regional / Passenger / Charter
Cargo
International routes: Gibraltar, Spain

FLEET
A300-605R - 4, A320-200 - 4, A321-200 - 5, A330-200 - 2, 757-200 - 7

ABOVE: *Monarch 757-2T7, G-DRJC (C/n 23895) (Jeremy Flack /API)*

Monarch was founded on June 5th 1967 to act as the carrier for the Cosmos holiday tour business together with a charter ser-

BELOW: *Monarch A321-231, G-OZBE (C/n 1707) (Monarch)*

Monarch Airlines

vice. Operations commenced in April 1968 with two Bristol Britannias.

By 1969 the fleet had grown to six aircraft and 250,000 passengers a year were being carried. The Britannias were replaced in the early 1970s with 1-11s and 720s to provide short- and long-haul capacity and, by 1976, operated an all-jet fleet.

During the 1980s, 737s were added to replace the 1-11s and 757s for the 720s. In 1981 one million passengers were carried for the first time. With extra capacity required for some routes, a DC-10 was subsequently added. Applications were placed for scheduled route licences in 1985 and these began operating the following year as the Monarch Crown Service.

Monarch ordered four A330s in July 1997 that entered service in 1999. It became the first UK airline to operate both the wide-body A330 and single-aisle A320 family.

The Crown Service was renamed Monarch Scheduled in March 2002 and a revised livery was applied to the aircraft. In addition to the scheduled services to Spain, Monarch operates an extensive charter service reaching across the Atlantic, into Africa and to the Far East which accounts for around 85% of its business.

Mongolian Airlines/MIAT

Registered name: Mongolyn Irgeniy Agaaryn Teever
Country: Mongolia
Region: Asia
Address: MIAT Building, Buyant-Ukhaa 45
          Ulaanbaatar 210134
Tel: 00976 1 265 49
Fax: 00976 1 37 99 73
Web site: www.miat.com
Main operational base: Ulaan Baatar

STATUS

Scheduled and charter carrier
National Flag Carrier
Employees: 900
Passengers per year: 258,000 (2001)
ICAO code: MGL
IATA code: OM

SERVICES

International / Regional / Domestic
Passenger / Charter / Cargo
International routes: China, Germany, Japan, Russia, S Korea, Turkey

FLEET

A310-300 - 1, An-2 - 30, An-24B / RV - 8, An-26 - 3, An-30 - 1, 727-200 - 2, 737-800 - 1, Mi-8 - 2

Mongolian Airlines was originally formed in 1956 as Air Mongol - MIAT with the assistance of Aeroflot. It commenced operations in July with Li-2s and aircrew supplied by Aeroflot.

An extensive domestic network was established and additional services developed in the form of air ambulance and agricultural spraying. Some international routes were established to Russia to connect to the Aeroflot network.

MIAT took delivery of its first 737-800 in July 2000 as part of a plan to replace the older existing types with Western airliners.

ABOVE: *Mongolian Airlines/MIAT An-26 (Mongolian Airlines)*

BELOW: *Mongolian Airlines/MIAT 737-8CX (C/n 32364) (Mongolian Airlines)*

Myanmar Airways International

Registered name: Myanmar Airways International
Country: Myanmar
Region: Asia
Address: 08-02 Sakura Tower
339 Bogyoke Aung San Road
Yangon
Tel: 00951 25 52 60
Fax: 00951 25 53 05
Web site: www.maiair.com
Main operational base: Yangon

STATUS

International carrier
National Flag Carrier
Passengers per year: 414,000 (2001)
ICAO code: UBA
IATA code: UB

SERVICES

Regional / Passenger / Cargo
International routes: China, Indonesia, Malaysia, Singapore, Thailand

FLEET

737-300 - 3

Myanmar Airways International can trace its origins back to August 1st 1948. This was shortly after the Union of Burma was established on independence from British control. The new Burmese Government established an airline that was named the Union of Burma Airways.

Initially equipped with DC-3s, the Union of Burma Airways slowly developed a domestic network until 1950 when it launched its first international routes to East Pakistan (now Bangladesh) and Thailand.

The first of three Vickers Viscounts was delivered in July 1957 followed by Fokker F-27 Friendships in 1963. Additional models were added to the fleet through to 1976. These enabled more international routes to reach India and Nepal and even as far as Hong Kong.

A 727 was acquired in 1970 and operated until 1976 when it was replaced with three Fokker F-28 Fellowships. DHC-6 Twin Otters were also acquired for short-range domestic operations into difficult airfields.

In December 1972 the name of the airline had been changed to Burma Airways Corporation and in 1989 it changed once more to Myanmar Airways reflecting the name change of the country to the Union of Myanmar.

In 1993 Myanmar Airways was split in two with a new airline named Myanmar Airways International established by the Myanmar Government with Brunei and Singaporean interests to operate the international routes.

A 757 was leased from Royal Brunei Airlines and schedules included services to China, Indonesia, Malaysia and Singapore.

The 757 was returned in 1994 and a pair of 737s was leased from Malaysian Airlines. In 1998 the Myanmar Government took full control of the airline.

The Singaporean Region Air was selected as a foreign partner in January 2001 and has taken a 49% stake in Myanmar Airways International with the balance held by Myanmar Interests Including Myanmar Airways. In July 2001 Myanmar took delivery of an A321 on lease but was returned in 2002.

On April 22nd 2002 the Myanmar Airways International IATA code was changed from UB to 8M.

Nigeria Airways

Registered name: Nigeria Airways Ltd
Country: Nigeria
Region: Africa
Address: PO Box 136
Airways House
Murtala Mohameed Airport
Ikeja, Lagos
Tel: 00234 1 497 08 27
Fax: 00234 1 497 08 29
Main operational base: Lagos

STATUS

IATA international scheduled and charter carrier
National Flag Carrier
Employees: 3,593
ICAO code: NGA
IATA code: WT

SERVICES

International / Regional / Domestic
Passenger / Cargo
International routes: Benin, Cameroon, Congo Democratic Republic, Cote D'Ivoire, Gabon, Gambia, Ghana, Guinea, Kenya, Saudi Arabia, Togo, UAE

ALLIANCES/CODE SHARES

British Aw, Ghana Aw, SAA

FLEET

737-200Adv - 2

Nigeria Airways was formed on August 23rd, 1958 as West Africa Airways Corporation (Nigeria) and commenced operations in October. It was established by the Nigerian Government to take over the Nigerian domestic services of the WAAC which had been operating since 1946.

Before long it was offering international services that were operated by BOAC initially using the Stratocruiser but later by Britannia, Comet, 707 and then VC10.

Meanwhile, WAAC (Nigeria) was nationalised in March 1961 and Fokker F-27 Friendships entered service on domestic routes in 1963.

International routes commenced with an ex-BOAC VC10 in 1969. WAAC (Nigeria) was renamed Nigeria Airways in January 1971 although it had been referred to as such for some time before that. Later that year a 707 was acquired for the expanding international routes while Fokker F-28 Fellowships began to arrive in 1973. With passengers increasing, Nigeria Airways entered into wide-body operations with the delivery of its first DC-10 in October 1976.

Nigeria Airways

Nigeria has been the scene of much deep-rooted conflict over the years and in 1993 the US banned Nigeria Airways flights into New York. The ban was not lifted until May 1999 although services did not resume until 2001 following a joint venture with South African Airlines.

British Airways increased the number of flights to Lagos from December 1999 in conjunction with Nigeria Airways which was allocated a number of seats on each flight.

An announcement was made in August 2001 that the Lagos to London route would be resumed using a 747 together with other services to the Middle East. However, the British CAA banned Nigerian Airways 747 from flying into London. The aircraft, which was leased from Air Djibouti had given cause for concern over safety. This was the second occasion that the airline had been banned. Previously, in 1997, the airline had to suspend schedules when it was alleged that it was operating without insurance. Although the ban was lifted the following year Nigeria Airways was unable to operate the route due to a lack of aircraft and debts that amounted to US$60 million.

As a result of the British safety ban, the Nigerian Aviation Minister sacked the airline's managing director.

The SAA and Nigeria Airways code share agreement broke down in early 2002. Talks to reconcile the problems commenced towards the end of the year. A further separate announcement was made regarding a government investigation into the alleged misappropriation of US$400 million of airline funds.

Nigeria Airways is a sad shadow of its former self with civil unrest and corruption having taken its toll. This reduced the airline, from the early 1980s when it was the fastest growing airline in Africa carrying some 800,000 passengers in its 30+ aircraft to the current fleet of two.

Plans for the future by the government are to get the airline back to a fully operational state with a clean slate with a view to privatisation.

Northwest Airlines

Registered name: Northwest Airlines Inc
Country: USA
Region: North America
Address: Minneapolis /
St Paul International Airport
5101 Northwest Drive
St Paul, Minnesota
Tel: 001 612 726 21 11
Fax: 001 612 726 20 14
Web site: www.nwa.com
Main operational base:
Minneapolis / St Paul International

ABOVE: *Northwest Airlines A320-212, N348NW (C/n 410) (Jeremy Flack/API)*

STATUS

International scheduled carrier
Employees: 45,000
Passengers per year: 54,100,000 (2001)
ICAO code: NWA
IATA code: NW

SERVICES

International / Regional / Domestic Passenger / Cargo
International routes: Bermuda, Canada, China, Cayman Islands, France, Germany, Guam, Jamaica, Japan, Mariana Islands, Mexico, Netherlands, Netherlands Antilles, Philippines, S Korea, Singapore, Taiwan, Thailand, UK

ALLIANCES/CODE SHARES

Air China, Alaska A/l, America West A/l, American Eagle, Big Sky A/l, Continental A/l, Continental Express, Gulfstream Int A/l, Hawaiian A/l, Horizon Air, JAS, KLM Cityhopper, KLM Exel, KLM, KLM UK, Malaysia A/l, Malev, Mesaba A/l, Pacific Islands Avn, Pinnacle A/l, Transavia A/l

FLEET

A319-100 - 42, A320-200 - 74, 747-200 - 20, 747-400 - 16, 757-200 - 56, 757-300 - 5, CRJ200LR - 43 (operated by Pinnacle), RJ85 - 36 (operated by Mesaba), DC-9-10 - 9, DC-9-30 - 114, DC-9-40 - 12, DC-9-50 - 35, DC-10-30 /-30 (ER) - 24 (to be replaced by A330-300), 340A - 43 (operated by Mesaba and Pinnacle), 340B / B+ - 61 (operated by Mesaba and Pinnacle)
On order: A319-100 - 36 + 25 options, A320-200 - 10 + 16 options, A330-300 - 24 for delivery 2003-6 + 36 options, 747-400 - 2 options, 757-300 - 10 for delivery to 2004 + 17 options

ABOVE: *Northwest Airlines DC-9-51, N774NC (C/n 47776) (Jeremy Flack/API)*

Northwest Airlines history can be traced back to September 1st 1926 when Col Lewit Brittin founded Northwest Airways. It was based at Speedway Flying Field which is the site of the current Minneapolis / St Paul International Airport. Equipped with a Thomas Morse Scout and a Curtiss Oriole, the first service flown was airmail to Chicago on October 1st. The following month a Stinson Detroiter was purchased enabling passengers to be carried in the first closed-cabin commercial plane. However, it was the following July before the first paying passenger was carried.

As Northwest expanded its routes, more aircraft were added including the Ford Tri-Motor in September 1928 with a capacity for 14 passengers.

The following year Northwest changed hands and the US Government adopted the Northwest 'US Air Mail' logo for all air mail operators.

Northwest moved its operation to nearby St Paul's Holoman Field in July 1930 where it built the first radio ground station.

On April 16th 1934 Northwest Airways was re-incorporated as Northwest Airlines

and the twin-engined Lockheed 10 Electra was added to the fleet towards the end of the year.

During 1938, Northwest assisted the Mayo Clinic to develop a practical oxygen mask. This enabled high-altitude flying which permitted a service to operate over the Rocky Mountains. The following year the first DC-3 entered service along with Northwest's first stewardess.

In 1941 Northwest common stock was publicly traded for the first time. However, the war in Europe was well underway and Northwest undertook various government services which saw employment soar from 881 to 10,439. Half of Northwest's fleet was commandeered which resulted in many ser-

vices being suspended. The engineering centre was tasked with modification of bombers.

The Douglas DC-4 entered service with Northwest in June 1945 and on July 15th 1947 the Northwest Orient service to Tokyo, Seoul, Shanghai and Manila was inaugurated. The following year the colour-scheme was modified to include an all red tail 'trade mark' which remains an easy airline identifier today.

The first Boeing 377 Stratocruiser was delivered in August 1949. This was an adaptation of the B-29 Superfortress bomber

BELOW: *Northwest Airlines 747-451, N667US (C/n 24222) (Jeremy Flack/API)*

Northwest Airlines

with an added bulbous fuselage for passengers. It featured lounges for relaxation on long flights.

The Douglas DC-6 was added to the fleet in September 1954 along with L-1048 Constellation the following January. Northwest became the first airline to operate in the Pacific region and to Alaska without government subsidy.

During 1957 Northwest pioneered the forecasting of clear air turbulence (CAT). Meanwhile the DC-7C entered service followed by the turboprop Lockheed L-188 Electra in June 1959.

On July 8th 1960 Northwest entered the jet age following the inauguration of the first service with the Douglas DC-8. By November it had become an all-jet fleet with the retirement of the last DC-3s. These had been replaced by US licence-built turboprop Fokker F-27s, built by Fairchild.

Northwest was presented with the Flight Safety Foundation safety award for its work on turbulence search in 1964. Around the same time the 727 was added to the fleet. In 1970 the first of the wide-body airliners arrived in the form of the 747 followed by the DC-10 in 1972.

In February 1979, Northwest launched its first transatlantic cargo service to Scotland followed by passenger services to Scandinavia in March.

Northwest announced a partnership in December 1984 with Mesaba to form Northwest Airlink which commenced operation the following May. In January 1986, Northwest announced a US$884 million agreement to acquire Republic Airlines which was formed on July 1st 1979 by the merging of North Central Airlines and Southern Airways. They absorbed Hughes Airwest the following year.

Northwest became the first airline to ban smoking in April 1988 and in June began trials of an airborne video system while in September trials of the Traffic Alert and Collision Avoidance System (TCAS) began.

Northwest became the launch customer for the 747-400 in January 1989 while in June the investment group Wings Holdings bought the company shares valuing Northwest at US$3.5 billion thus making it a private corporation.

Northwest ordered its first non-US built airliner in 1990 - the Airbus A320 and by the following year had become the world's

ABOVE: *Northwest Airlink CRJ200LR, N8432A (C/n 7432) operated by Express Airlines (Bombardier)*

largest operator with 32 of the type. In an interesting promotion Northwest announced that on-time arrivals are guaranteed at 18 southern airports with free round-trip tickets if the flights are late. According to a US Department of Transportation consumer report, Northwest had the best on-time performance amongst the seven largest US airlines in 1990.

1993 saw the association of Northwest and KLM and the development of a number of agreements to enable customers to connect between the two carriers more effectively. This was the beginnings of what was to be the world's first airline alliance. A similar agreement was signed with Alaska Airlines in 1995.

The largest ever annual Northwest net profit of US$536.1 million was announced for 1996. This was repeated in 1997 with profits of US$597 million.

An order for 50 Airbus A319s was placed during October 1997 with deliveries commencing in 1999. Also in 1999 Northwest

and Continental began a co-operation on domestic flights. An order for 54 CRJ200 regional jets was signed in February 1999 for domestic operations along with options for up to 70 more. A further massive re-equipment programme was put in place in January 2001. Orders were placed for 24 A330-300s, six A319s as well as 20 757-300s and two 747-400s with deliveries spread over 2002 through to 2006.

In 2000 Northwest was shown to be the best on-time airline for the tenth consecu-tive year. Following the terrorist attack on September 11th, Northwest announced a reduction in capacity of 20% and a staff reduction of 10,000. In the end this was reduced to less than 8,500 but the previous net profit of US$256 million was turned to a net loss of US$423 million. By October 17th a flight deck security door had been fitted to all aircraft in the fleet.

During 2002 it deferred delivery of the 22 Airbus narrow-bodies scheduled for 2003 although the A319s continued and should all be in service by the end of 2003.

Northwest Airlines has a feeder network comprising Northwest Airlink operated by Express Airlines and Northwest Airlink and Northwest JetLink operated by Mesaba Airlines. Express Airlines was operated as a subsidiary but has been sold and renamed Pinnacle Airlines. Prior to September 11th Northwest was proposing to take over Mesaba in which it has a 28% interest. This plan has been dropped.

Olympic Airways

Registered name: Olympic Airways Ltd
Country: Greece
Region: Europe
Address: 96-100 Syngrou Avenue
Athens
GR-117 41
Tel: 0030 1 926 91 11
Fax: 0030 1 926 71 54
Web site: www.olympic-airways.gr
Stockholder: Olympic Airways Group
Main operational base: Athens - Spata

STATUS

IATA international scheduled carrier
National Flag Carrier
Employees: 8,227
Passengers per year: 6,403,000 (1998)
ICAO code: OAL
IATA code: OA

SERVICES

International / Regional / Domestic
Passenger / Charter / Cargo
International routes: Albania, Australia, Belgium, Brazil*, Bulgaria, Canada, Cyprus, Denmark, Egypt, France, Germany, Hungary, Israel, Italy, Jordan, Kuwait, Netherlands, Portugal*, Romania, Russia, Saudi Arabia*, Serbia, South Africa, Spain, Switzerland, Thailand, Turkey, UAE, UK, Ukraine*, USA (*code share)

ALLIANCES/CODE SHARES

CSA, Egyptair, Kuwait Aw, TAP

OWNED SUBSIDIARY AIRLINES

Olympic Aviation, Macedonian Airlines

FLEET

A300-605R - 3, A340-300-4, 737-200 - 11, 737 300 - 2, 737 400 - 13 (3 leased to Macedonian Airlines)
On order: 737-800 - 4 for delivery from 2000

Olympic Airways was formed by the merg-ing of TAE / Technical and Air Enterprises Co (formed 1935) and Hellas on April 6th 1957, operating 14 DC-3s. Owned by Aristotle Onassis, he had been given an assurance by the Greek Government that he would have a 50-year guarantee of being designated the sole national airline as well as a monopoly of domestic routes.

DC-4s and DC-6s were added to the fleet which enabled longer international routes.

In 1960 Olympic Airways entered the jet age with the de Havilland Comet of which five were purchased to replace the DC-6s. They were initially operated on the Athens to London route followed by the Middle East and lasted through to the end of the decade.

During the mid-1960s Olympic Airways scheduled services were reaching out to the USA and Africa with 707s. In October 1967 Olympic formed its Department of Light Aircraft that provided charter, leasing and training as well as operation of various smaller aircraft. In August 1971 the

BELOW: *Olympic Airways A300B4-102, SX-BEE (C/n 103) (Jeremy Flack/API)*

Olympic Airways

Department was formed into Olympic Aviation and currently has a fleet of 20 aircraft including 717s.

727s had replaced the Comets towards the end of the 1960s on the European routes and the first of six YS-11s arrived in 1970 to be used on domestic routes to replace the vintage DC-3s. Some ex-military C-47s continued to operate in the cargo role where the larger doors were invaluable.

Investment in new aircraft proceeded and the first of seven 720s were delivered in February 1972 followed by two 747s in 1973. The network was expanding and during the early 1970s the schedules included Asia and Australia, but with overexpansion substantial losses were being incurred which led to Onassis suspending operations in 1974 and the airline was grounded. However, on January 1st 1975, the Greek Government stepped in enabling operations to commence again. More new aircraft were added to the fleet with first three 737s operated by Olympic delivered in 1976 followed by its first Airbus in the form a pair of A300s in 1979. During the 1980s another six A300s were added to the fleet along with two 747s and five 737s. New computer systems were commissioned for check-in and reserva-

tions. It was anticipated that the Hermes reservation system would save the airline in the region of US$2.5 million per year.

More new aircraft continued to be acquired during the 1990s with six 737s being followed by two A300-600s and four A340s. However, Olympic Airways had been encountering troubled times for a few years and attempts continued to resolve these financial difficulties. Disputed alleged illegal state aid was reported to the European Commission by the Hellenic Air Carriers Association and investigated. In June 1999 a 30 month agreement was entered into with

ABOVE: *Olympic Aviation ATR 42-312, SX-BIA (C/n 169) (ATR)*

LEFT: *Olympic Airways A340-313X, SX-DFA (C/n 235) (Airbus)*

BA whereby it would provide a consultancy team that would manage the airline leading to BA taking an equity share. However, the events of September 11th stopped this and pushed it teetering towards the edge.

A review of operations has resulted in a number of cost-cutting-actions. In March 2002 a number of loss-making international routes in and out of Thessaloniki were suspended. During September Olympic issued an Invitation to Tender for six surplus 737-400s and another for nine 737-200s the following month. In November 2002 Olympic suspended its schedule to Australia that had become increasingly uneconomic.

The Greek Government has been in discussion with several airlines regarding partial privatisation and the Greek airline Axon Airlines appears to be the preferred bidder. With a total debt believed to be over US$250 million and EC rules preventing state subsidies, following two unsuccessful restructuring attempts, hopes for a takeover or cash injection now look increasingly gloomy.

Oman Air

Registered name: Oman Aviation Services Co (SAO)
Country: Sultanate of Oman
Region: Middle East
Address: P.O.Box 58
Seeb International Airport
Postal Code 111
Tel: 00968 51 96 16
Fax: 00968 51 07 71
Web site: www.oman-air.com
Stockholder: Oman Aviation Services Group
Main operational base: Muscat

STATUS

Scheduled and charter carrier
National Flag Carrier
Employees: 2,500
Passengers per year: 730,000 (2001)
ICAO code: OAS
IATA code: WY

SERVICES

International / Regional / Domestic
Passenger / Charter (Domestic) / Cargo
International routes: Egypt, India, Kenya,
Kuwait, Lebanon, Pakistan, Qatar, Saudi
Arabia, Sri Lanka, Tanzania, UAE

ALLIANCES/CODE SHARES

Gulf Air, Kenya Aw, Sri Lankan A/l, Swiss

FLEET

737-700 - 3, 737-800 - 1, ATR 42-500-2
On order: 737-700 - 1 for delivery 5.2004

Oman Air originated as Oman Aviation on
May 20th, 1981, operating light aircraft and
helicopter charters mainly in support of the
oil companies. An F-27 Friendship was
delivered in 1981 followed by two more in
1982 and a further one the following year.

ABOVE: *Oman Air 737-8Q8, A40-BN (C/n 30652)
(Oman Air)*

Oman Air was formed on March 20th
1993 and has steadily developed by offering
a quality service to an ever-increasing network of international destinations. While a
pair of A310s was previously operated,
these, the F-27s and the older 737s have
been retired and Oman Air now operates a
modern fleet of ATR 42s and 737NGs which
have been painted in new markings with
the Khanjar on the tail.

Pakistan International Airlines/PIA

Registered name: Pakistan International Airlines
Corporation
Country: Pakistan
Region: Asia
Address: PIA Building
Quaid-e-Azam International Airport
Karachi 75200
Tel: 0092 21 457 20 11
Fax: 0092 21 457 22 25
Web site: www.piac.com.pk
Main operational base: Karachi

STATUS

IATA scheduled international carrier
National Flag Carrier
Employees: 17,766
Passengers per year: 4,877,000 (2001)
ICAO code: PIA
IATA code: PK

SERVICES

International / Regional / Domestic
Passenger / Charter / Cargo
International routes: Bahrain, Bangladesh,
Canada, China, Denmark, France, Greece,
India, Indonesia, Italy, Japan, Kuwait,
Libya, Malaysia, Nepal, Netherlands,

ABOVE: *Pakistan International Airlines 747-217B, AP-
BCO (C/n 20927) (PIA)*

Norway, Oman, Philippines, Saudi Arabia,
Singapore, Sri Lanka, Turkey, UAE, UK,
USA, Uzbekistan

Pakistan International Airlines/PIA

FLEET

A300B4-200 - 8, A310-300 - 6, 737-300 - 7, 747-200 - 4, 747-300 - 6, DHC-6 Twin Otter 300 - 2, F-27 Mk.200-11

On order: 777-200LR-2, 777-200ER - 3, 777-300ER-3

Pakistan International Airlines was originally formed as Orient Airways on October 23rd 1946 by Mr A M Ispahani at the request of Mr Mohammed Ali Jinnah - the first Governor-General of Pakistan to link East and West Pakistan. About to be established, the new Islamic state was split in two with some 1,000 miles between them. Four DC-3s were acquired and operations commenced in June 1947.

Orient Airways was soon tied up with relief operations and transporting of the populus between Karachi and Delhi, assisted by BOAC. By the end of 1949 the airline had established its first scheduled routes and had a fleet of 10 DC-3s and three Convair 340s and these were rapidly becoming insufficient.

As a private company, Orient Airways had limited resources but had developed good experience. So when the Pakistani Government decided to form a national air-line Orient was naturally invited to participate. The result was the establishment, on March 11th 1955, of the state-owned Pakistan International Airlines (PIA) into which Orient had been merged. Amongst much controversy within the country was the inauguration of the first international scheduled service to London via Cairo and Rome. Although the country has limited resources, it was considered that there was a strong need to provide this service for expatriates. It was quickly justified by earning substantial foreign exchange that enabled the financing of more aircraft.

In 1956 orders were placed for two Super Constellations and five Vickers Viscounts for delivery in 1959. In March 1960 PIA entered the jet-age with its first 707 service and became the first Asian airline to operate a jet. A service linking Karachi to New York commenced the following year.

Orders were placed for additional aircraft including 720s, F-27 Friendships and even three Sikorsky S-61 helicopters. The S-61s were operated during the early 1960s and carried over 70,000 scheduled passengers in 1963. Unfortunately a couple of accidents brought this otherwise successful service to an end in 1966.

ABOVE: *Pakistan International Airlines F-27-200, AP-BDB, (C/n 10292) (PIA)*

PIA was keen to make its mark, so in 1962 it planned to establish a speed record between London and Karachi. With a good upper altitude wind forecast FAI observers were invited on the flight. The flight was completed in 6 hours 43 min - a record which still stands.

In 1964 PIA became the first non-communist airline to fly into China when it commenced a schedule to Shanghai via Canton.

During the war between India and Pakistan in 1965, PIA aircraft were used for support and operated a number of flights for the armed services.

During the mid-1960s the Viscounts were exchanged for Tridents, while the air hostesses caused a stir when they appeared in a new uniform designed by Pierre Cardin. Computers were introduced into PIA - the first in Pakistan.

During the early 1970s, an agreement was signed with Libyan authorities enabling PIA to operate domestic services in Libya. Wide-body operations commenced in 1974 with the delivery of three DC-10s that were fol-

lowed by a couple of 747s in 1976. Another pair of 747s was received in 1980 together with four A300s.

PIA was rated as the leading and most efficient airline during the 1981 annual Hajj operation. New schedules were added to Abu Dhabi and Dubai. The following year a record operating surplus was announced for the third time in seven years. This time it was for Rs 441 million. In 1984, PIA established a feeder service with 737s and for the first time its revenue exceeded Rs 10 billion. In 1987 a new service to Toronto was inaugurated while the following year the DHC-6 Twin Otter entered service for domestic services between Muzaffarabad and Rawalakot. Female pilots started flying passenger flights for the first time in 1989.

PIA financial strength continues to grow with another record revenue of R2 20 billion creating a Rs 1.58 billion record operating surplus in 1991. More new routes were steadily added during the 1990s to Europe, the Middle East, Far East while

ABOVE: *Pakistan Internaional Airlines DHC-6 Twin Otter 300, AP-BCG (C/n 725) (PIA)*

USA and Canada schedules were rerouted via Shannon rather than other European airports to reduce costs. in 1999.

Palestinian

Registered name: Palestinian Airlines
Country: Palestine
Region: Middle East
Address: P.O. Box 4043
        Jamel Abd El-Nasser St
        Gaza
Tel: 00970 8 284 8888
Fax: 00970 8 284 8884
Web site: www.palairlines.com
Main operational base: Gaza

STATUS

Regional passenger + cargo carrier
National Flag Carrier
Employees: 342
ICAO code: PNW
IATA code: PF

SERVICES

International / Passenger / Charter
International routes: Cyprus, Egypt, Jordan, Qatar, Saudi Arabia, Turkey, UAE

FLEET

727-177 - 1, Fokker 50 - 2, DHC-8 Dash 8-Q300 - 2 (leased out)
On order: CRJ200 - 2

Palestinian Airlines was established by the Palestinian Government in July 1994 as the national airline. The first service was flown on January 10th 1997 to carry pilgrims from Port Said Airport in Egypt to Jeddah. Two Fokker 50s carried a total of 325 pilgrims on seven return flights.

On November 27th 1998, operations were transferred to Gaza International Airport. In August 2001, Palestinian Airlines flew from Al-Arish Airport to

ABOVE: *Palestinian DHC-8 Dash 8-315, SU-YAN (C/n 549) (Bombardier)*

Damascus to conclude bilateral agreements to pave the way for regular schedules between Palestine and Syria. However, due to the harsh prevailing political situation currently facing Palestine, the airline is not operating normally and future prospects are not clear although a scheduled service from Al-Arish to Amman is being operated.

Philippine Airlines/PAL

ABOVE: *Philippine Airlines A340-313X (Airbus)*

Registered name: Philippine Airlines Inc
Country: Philippines
Region: Asia
Address: PAL Centre Building
Legaspi St, Legaspi Village
Makati City
Tel: 0063 2 817 12 34
Fax: 0063 2 813 67 15
Web site: www.philippineairlines.com
Main operational base: Manila

STATUS

IATA scheduled passenger carrier
National Flag Carrier
Employees: 7,220
Passengers per year: 5,748,000 (2001)
ICAO code: PAL
IATA code: PR

SERVICES

International / Regional / Domestic
Passenger / Cargo
International routes: Australia, China, Indonesia, Japan, S Korea, Saudi Arabia, Singapore, Taiwan, Thailand, USA, Vietnam

ALLIANCES/CODE SHARES

Cathay Pacific Aw, Egyptair, Garuda, Gulf Air, Malaysia A/l

FLEET

A320-200 - 3, A330-300 - 8, A340-300 - 4, 737-300 - 7, 737-400 - 3, 747-200 - 3, 747-400 - 4

Philippine Airlines was formed on February 26th, 1941 by local industrialists and commenced operations in March with a Beech 18 from Manila and Baguio. It took over the routes that had previously been operated by the Philippine Aerial Taxi Company (PATCO) (formed 1931) which had been declared bankrupt in July 1940.

WW2 disrupted services within a few months but they were returned in February 1946 with a DC-3. Having been given National Carrier status in November 1946, a schedule to Los Angeles commenced the following month with a DC-4.

By May 1947 PAL was operating a network of 32 domestic destinations and then took over its main competitor - Far East Air Transport Inc (FEATI). In August, Commercial Air Lines Inc (CALI) was also absorbed resulting in PAL becoming the only domestic carrier. It was also operating 12 international schedules.

By 1954 passenger levels had dropped substantially and a number of traffic rights were lost which resulted in all international routes being suspended apart from the one to Hong Kong. PAL concentrated on its domestic schedules and took delivery of its first Viscount in May 1957 which it used on the Hong Kong service. Convair 340s were gradually replaced by the more efficient turboprops and the DC-3s retired with the arrival of the F-27 Friendships, from 1960.

Philippine Airlines chartered 707s from Pan Am in December 1961 prior to attempting another international route in 1962.

BAC 1-11s were acquired for domestic and regional routes in 1966 and HS748s began to replace the F-27s from 1967. Most of the surviving F-27s were transferred to the Philippine AF in 1971. Philippine Airlines underwent a partial privatisation in March 1992 when 67% of the equity was acquired by PR Holdings.

The Pacific region economic downturn resulted in a substantial reduction in passenger levels and caused several years of losses. As a result, Philippine Airways filed a Rehabilitation Plan with the Philippine Securities and Exchange Commission (SEC) in June 1998. This required a significant fleet reduction as well as other assets and personnel and a restructuring of the route network. Subsequently, PAL filed for bankruptcy protection and negotiated to continue operations. A ten-year rehabilitation plan was approved by the SEC to be conducted under its supervision.

Philippine Airlines planned to achieve listing on the Philippine Stock Exchange but this has been abandoned for the time being. Having recorded a loss in 2001, Philippine law requires it to maintain a profit for three consecutive years before it can apply again.

Piedmont Airlines/US Air Express

Registered name: Piedmont Airlines Inc

Country: USA

Region: North America

Address: Salisbury / Ocean City
Wicomico Regional Airport
5443 Airport Terminal Road
Salisbury, MD-21804

Tel: 001 410 742 29 96

Fax: 001 410 742 40 69

Web site: www.piedmont-airlines.com

Stockholder: US Airways Group Inc

Main operational base: Salisbury

STATUS

Scheduled passenger carrier

Employees: 1,983

Passengers per year: 3,287,000 (2001)

ICAO code: PDT

IATA code: US

SERVICES

International / Regional / Domestic
Passenger

International routes: Bahamas, Canada.

FLEET

DHC-8 Dash 8-100 - 43, DHC-8 Dash 8-200 - 19, DHC-8 Dash 8-300-9

Piedmont Airlines was originally formed in 1931 as Henson Aviation by an aviation pioneer - Richard A. Henson - who was previously a Fairchild Aircraft test pilot.

Activities commenced as a fixed-base operation at Hagerstown, Maryland.

In 1962 Henson Aviation instigated a scheduled passenger service between Hagerstown and Washington National as the Hagerstown Commuter. Once established, the company concentrated its efforts on the scheduled service; this has certainly paid off.

Henson became the first Allegheny Commuter when it commenced the Hagerstown - Washington - Baltimore schedule on November 15th, 1967. This was the first of the code-share agreements that were to soon become the 'norm'. Henson purchased the Beech 99 turboprop for the operation and a year later had replaced Allegheny at Salisbury. A network was established to link Salisbury with Philadelphia as well as Baltimore and Washington National.

The fleet continued to grow with more Beech 99s and in 1977 four Shorts 330s were purchased. Later that year the millionth passenger had been carried.

Henson ordered the 50-seat DHC-7 Dash 7 in 1979 which helped to move the airline up the scale. In 1981, Henson was named as Airline of the year by Air Transport World.

The outstanding growth of Henson soon came to the attention of other airlines and in 1983 Piedmont purchased the booming airline. However, Henson had to withdraw from the Allegheny operation which was providing the feeder service to US Air and revert purely to Henson.

With the pace ever quickening, and pleased with the Canadair Dash 7s, more aircraft were ordered including the improved Dash 8. Following repeat orders they were to become one of the largest operators of the type.

During 1985 the 5 millionth passenger was carried and in 1986 over 1 million were carried in that year alone. This helped the network expansion to snowball from the original Maryland into the surrounding states, then spreading south into the lucrative holiday state of Florida and the Bahamas.

By 1987 Henson was reaching 38 cities and USAir became interested in the operation. This time however, USAir purchased Henson and Piedmont with Piedmont being merged into USAir.

Prior to this, Piedmont had been formed on July 2nd, 1940. It began scheduled services in February 1948 with DC-3s and the network expanded throughout Kentucky, North Carolina and Virginia using a substantial fleet which included NAMC YS-11s,

BELOW: *Piedmont Airlines DHC-8 Dash-8-10, N909HA (C/n 018) operating in US Air Express colours (Bombardier)*

Piedmont Airlines/US Air Express

737s, 727s and F-28 Fellowships amongst others.

The Henson Beech 99s were retired in 1987 and the SD330s in 1989. In the meantime, the 33 Dash 7s and Dash 8s were repainted in the markings of USAir Express. In 1993 Henson Aviation was renamed Piedmont Airlines while USAir became US Airways in 1997. This resulted in the new Piedmont and the other USAir Express carriers all being painted in a new colour-scheme and marked US Airways Express.

Such was the growth in the US Airways Express operation that US Airways was finding it difficult to operate its own operation as well as the Express carriers. Initially, ground and passenger handling duties were handed over. A large portion of the operation was later handled by the carriers at six major hubs.

Piedmont handling duties were taken over at Charlottesville, Key West, Lynchburg, Newport News, Tallahassee and White Plains and in 1997 took over operations in Baltimore, Tampa and Washington National.

Piedmont continued with the fleet rationalisation with the Dash 7 being retired along with some of the older Dash 8s during the late 1990s so that by 2000 57 Dash 8s were being operated and carrying some 3 million passengers per year. While the US regional carriers were reaching a plateau during the early 1990s, Piedmont was looking for new business areas. Towards the end of 2000 it took over the ground handling operation at Ottawa in Canada. Henson / Piedmont was always near the front of innovation and some of this has been recognised by the authorities. The FAA presented Piedmont with a Team Spirit Award in recognition of its proactive strategic action in promoting the Safer Skies Agenda across the industry. It was the first regional airline to be certified for use of the TCAS anti-collision system. It received the FAA's distinguished 2000 Diamond Certificate of Excellence for its proactive role in aircraft maintenance training of the ground engineers.

PLUNA

Registered name: Primeras Lineas Uruguayas de Navegacion Aérea
Nationality: Uruguay
Region: South America
Address: Puntas de Santiago 1604
CP 11500
Montevideo
Tel: 00598 2 604 22 44
Fax: 00598 2 604 22 60
Web site: www.pluna.com.uy
Main operational base: Montevideo

STATUS

IATA scheduled passenger carrier
National Flag Carrier
Employees: 635
Passengers per year: 625,400 (1999)
ICAO code: PUA
IATA code: PU

SERVICES

International / Regional / Domestic
Passenger / Charter / Cargo
International routes: Argentina, Brazil, Chile, Paraguay, Spain, Uruguay.

ALLIANCES / CODE SHARES

Rio-Sul, VARIG.

FLEET

737-200Adv - 3, 737-300 - 1, 767-200 - 1, DC-10-30 - 1

PLUNA was formed on November 20th, 1936 by two young brothers Jorge and Alberto Marquez Vaeza. It was equipped with a pair of de Havilland DH.90 Dragonfly five-seat biplanes and commenced services between Montevideo, Salto and Paysandu in the northwest region of Uruguay. By the end of its first year it had carried some 2,600 passengers and a substantial amount of freight and mail.

Operations were suspended during WW2 but, when it ended, the Uruguayan Government initially took an 83% stake in the airline followed by total ownership in 1951.

The first international flight linked the cities of Montevideo with Porto Alegre in Brazil in May 1948 and a number of other new domestic and international routes spread across South America due to the poor means of any alternative transport.

DC-3s were in use from the mid-40s and subsequently joined by de Havilland Herons. The first three Viscounts arrived during the late 50s with more subsequently added to the fleet, replacing the DC-3s.

PLUNA entered the jet-age with the delivery of a 737 in December 1969 but it was damaged later the following year. It was repaired and returned to service but sold soon after. The first of three 727s arrived in August 1978 but were not successful and were replaced by more 737s.

The first European route was Montevideo to Madrid via Buenos Aires in 1981, with 707s.

In 1986 a 767 owned by VARIG was jointly operated initially on the service to Santiago de Chile then on other long-haul routes while 737s were used for domestic and regional services.

The 767 was replaced with a DC-10 from the early 90s and was subsequently leased to and operated solely by PLUNA. A new livery was applied to the fleet apart from one of the 737s which had an ethnic scheme applied which had been designed by Uruguay's best known contemporary artist - Carlos Paez Vilaro.

In June 1995, the government released 51% of the shares and the airline was renamed PLUNA Uruguayan Airlines.

In December 2002 PLUNA received its own 767 followed by a newer 737. These aircraft will enable increased frequencies of flight to be operated.

Polynesian Airlines

Registered name: Polynesian Ltd
Country: Western Samoa
Region: Australia & Pacific
Address: 2nd Floor, NPF Building
PO Box 599
Beach Road
Apia
Tel: 00685 212 61
Fax: 00685 200 23
Web site: www.polynesianairlines.co.nz
Main operational base: Apia

STATUS

IATA international scheduled carrier
National Flag Carrier
Employees: 310
Passengers per year: 173,000 (2001)
ICAO code: PAO
IATA code: PH

SERVICES

International / Regional / Domestic
Passenger / Charter / Cargo
International routes: American Samoa,
Australia, Fiji, New Zealand, USA

ALLIANCES/CODE SHARES

Air New Zealand, Air Pacific, Air Tahiti
Nui, Mount Cook A/l, Qantas, Royal
Tongan A/l

FLEET

737-800 - 2, BN-2A-8 Islander - 1, DHC-6
Twin Otter 300 - 2

Polynesian Airlines was formed in 1959 by a group of local businessmen led by Australian Sir Reginald Barnewell to provide a link between the independent state of Samoa and the American Samoa. A Hunting Percival Prince was purchased and operations commenced in August 1959.

Polynesian Airlines was granted permits to commence scheduled operations between Apia and Pago Pago in March 1960. The following year two more Princes were acquired.

In 1962, following the formation of Western Samoa, the airline leased a DC-3 from TEAL which became the first Samoan-registered aircraft. The schedules were extended to include Fiji, Kingdom of Tonga and Wallis Islands in 1964 and a second DC-3 purchased. This enabled the Princes to be retired.

The Government of Samoa took a controlling stake in Polynesian Airlines in 1971 and designated it as its flag carrier. The following year two Hawker Siddeley HS748s were added to the fleet.

Polynesian Airlines became a member of the International Air Transport Association (IATA) in 1973 and subscribed to an airline teleprinter network in 1975. This resulted in an improved relationship with other airlines and a more efficient passenger reservation system.

In 1977 a BN-2 Islander was added to the fleet along with a Cessna 172 for short hops and charters. However, 1978 saw a major progression with the arrival of its first 737 which pushed it into the jet-age. This leased aircraft, which was crewed by Air New Zealand personnel, enabled a new schedule

BELOW: *Polynesian Airlines BN-2A Islander, 5W-FAF (109) (BN Historians Collection)*

Polynesian Airlines

to Auckland to commence. Later in the year the network had expanded to include the Wallis Islands and Tahiti.

Also in 1978, a second Islander and a GAF G-22 Nomad were acquired for domestic services and in 1981 a new 737 was purchased.

By this time the airline was encountering competition from other airlines that were also operating in the region and the new 737 was not really earning its keep. The government arranged for the 737 to be sold and leased back to the airline. The following year a five-year management contract was signed with Ansett Australia.

In 1984, Polynesian Airlines added Sydney to its network and a GAF N22 Nomad was presented to Samoa by the Australian Government and added to the fleet.

Having transferred its reservation system onto the Ansett Ansamatic system and pleased with the management contract, a 10 year extension was agreed and signed.

A new route to Brisbane commenced in 1990 but was dropped later that year.

Ansett Australia obtained authorisation to commence its own international schedules in 1992. Unfortunately, this meant it under new Australian aviation laws that they could no longer service the contract with Polynesian Airlines and so it was cancelled.

Polynesian Airlines continued under local management and added new routes to Honolulu and Los Angeles while a 767 had been added to the fleet together with a DHC-6 Twin Otter by the end of 1993.

Sadly this rapid expansion proved too much for the Polynesian airline's finances with further increased pressure from competition, especially in the operation to the US.

In August 1994 a new management team was created to try to rescue the airline. As a result, the fleet was reduced to a single 737, Islander and Twin Otter.

In February 1995, an agreement was signed with Air New Zealand which included a variety of relationships including code-sharing. Polynesian Airlines also transferred its reservation system onto the ANZ CARINA system. It also increased the computerisation of its systems enabling automated ticketing.

The service to Honolulu resumed in December 1995 under a code-share with ANZ and a second Twin Otter was added to the fleet. More services were resumed the following spring including Nadi and Fiji plus Los Angeles in February 1997 - the latter being another code-share with ANZ.

1999 saw Polynesian Airlines entering a new agreement, this time with Qantas which resulted in adoption of the QUBE reservation system.

A 737NG was acquired in November 2000 which provided greater efficiency, more passengers and less fuel. A second 737NG was added to the fleet in September 2001.

PSA Airlines/US Airways Express

Registered name: PSA Airlines Inc
Country: USA
Region: North America
Address: 3400 Terminal Drive
 Vandalia
 Ohio 45377
Tel: 001 937 454 11 16
Fax: 001 937 454 58 28
Web site: www.psaairlines.com
Stockholder: US Airways Group
Main operational base: Vandalia

STATUS

Scheduled passenger carrier
Employees: 1,274
Passengers per year: 1,173,000 (2001)
ICAO code: JIA
IATA code: US

SERVICES

Regional / Domestic / Passenger
Cargo
International routes: Canada

FLEET

328-100-30

The origins of the current PSA can be traced back to Vee Neal Airlines which was formed in 1979 by Vee Neal Frey as an FBO with a Cessna 402 at Latrobe, PA.

Vee Neal commenced a scheduled service to Pittsburgh in May 1980 and was allocated the IATA code TF.

Following the US airline deregulation various proposals were put together to establish an airline at Erie, PA following the reduction of services there. Attempts to get these off the ground during the early 1980s failed.

When USAir announced that it was to suspend its direct schedule to Chicago in April 1983, an additional incentive was created. A new proposal to raise venture capital to expand Vee Airlines was put together by local businessmen and approved.

Six British Aerospace Jetstream 31s were ordered for the airline that was renamed

Jetstream International Airlines (JIA) and launched in December 1983 once the first two aircraft arrived. The Jetstream was selected due to its speed for the distances to be flown making them relatively short flights. The aircraft was pressurised and was comfortable for the passenger.

JIA moved to Erie in 1984 and a series of schedules developed to various cities. However, this stretching caused some financial difficulties so JIA became an affiliate of Piedmont Airlines linking Erie with Piedmont's Baltimore and Dayton hubs. Despite this, JIA was still experiencing problems and, in mid-1986, Piedmont made an offer for JIA. As a result JIA became a subsidiary in August 1986.

Following USAir's acquisition of Piedmont in November 1987, JIA began operating as Allegheny Commuter in April 1988 out of the USAir hub at Philadelphia. This was in addition to the feed that it was already operating into the Piedmont hubs.

On July 1st, 1988, JIA became a wholly

owned subsidiary of the USAir Group. In June 1989 it replaced the service that had been operated into Indianapolis by Air Kentucky after it had filed for bankruptcy.

From August 5th, 1989, JIA began operating all its flights as USAir Express following the full integration of Piedmont into USAir.

An agreement was finalised in November 1991 for the lease of seven of the Brazilian 28-seat EMB-120 Brasilia. The first of these entered service in January 1992 on the Indianapolis - Milwaukee route. A further two were added in 1993 which were fitted with 30 seats.

On October 18th, 1993, JIA temporarily replaced the USAir Express West Coast operation, StateWest. Five of its Jetstreams were relocated and the operation was successfully run until January 1994.

In February 1994 JIA began operating the USAir Express facility at Pittsburgh. Here it was the dominant Express carrier in the USAir fortress hub operating 100 daily departures.

Jetstream and Dornier completed an agreement to lease 20 32-seat 328 Jet airliners with options on more in October 1994. The first one arrived in November and entered service in February the following year and by the time that the 20th arrived in March 1996 JIA was totally equipped with the 328. The last of the Brasilia were retired in July 1995 and the last Jetstream 31 in March 1996.

On November 1st 1995 USAir decided that Jetstream International Airlines would be renamed PSA.

This was a re-use of the airline name as Pacific Southwest Airlines (PSA) had originally been formed on May 6th 1949, initially with DC-3s then DC-4s, Electras, DC-6s. It expanded during the mid-1960s with 727s, DC-9s and 737s all the time operating low-cost schedules in the southwest USA. During the 1980s the 727s gave way to BAe146s.

USAir Group bought PSA in 1987 from the PS Group for US$400 million. PSA was absorbed into USAir and its identity lost.

In the meantime a further order for five Dornier 328s was placed by the new PSA in January 1996 and delivery of these commenced in August of that year.

USAir changed its name to US Airways in February 1997 which meant that PSA had to change the name on its aircraft to US Airways Express.

In December 2001, PSA concluded a further agreement for the leasing of an additional five Dornier 328s of which the last was delivered in May 2002.

While PSA suffered with reduced passengers after September 11th, the US Airways Group was hit badly with a net loss of nearly US$2 billion. On August 11th, 2002 it filed for voluntary petition for reorganisation under Chapter 11 of the Bankruptcy Code.

Pulkovo Airlines

Registered name: Pulkovo Aviation Enterprise
Country: Russia
Region: Asia
Address: Pilotov Str, 18 / 4
Pulkovo International Airport
St Petersburg 196210
Tel: 007 812 324 34 46
Fax: 007 812 324 36 40
Web site: www.eng.pulkovo.ru
Main operational base: St Petersburg – Pulkovo

ABOVE: *Pulkovo Airlines Tu-154M, RA-85771, (C/n 93A-953) (Jeremy Flack/API)*

STATUS

Scheduled and charter passenger + cargo carrier
Employees: 7,000
Passengers per year: 1,878,000 (2001)
ICAO code: PLK
IATA code: Z8

SERVICES

International / Regional / Domestic Passenger / Charter / Cargo
International routes: Austria, Belgium, Bulgaria, Cyprus, Czech, Denmark, Finland, France, Germany, Greece, Hungary, Ireland, Israel, Italy, Luxemburg, Netherlands, Norway, Poland, Spain, Sweden, Switzerland, UK

FLEET

Il-86 - 8, Tu-134 - 11, Tu-154B - 13, Tu-154M - 10, Tu-204- 1

The origin of Pulkovo Airlines date back to June 24th 1932 as part of Aeroflot with the arrival of two aircraft at Leningrad after flights from Moscow.

A variety of Russian-built aircraft were operated in the early days including the U-

Pulkovo Airlines

2, R-1, R-5, Sh-2 G-5, PS-40 and PS-84 to provide a mainly mail and newspaper delivery and cargo service but passengers were also carried. In 1939, the first service to Murmansk enabled newspapers to be read for the first time inside the Arctic Circle on the same day as published in Moscow.

In January 1941 Leningrad to Moscow became a scheduled service. The arrival of German aircraft over Leningrad on June 22nd came as a shock to the inhabitants whose newspapers, delivered that day, made no mention of the war. Aviation suddenly became vital to the city during the 900 day siege which commenced in September 1941 with all civilian aircraft and crews put to military use.

When the siege of Leningrad ended in

January 1944 the transport aircraft reverted to a civil role. Aeroflot opened an agency and in 1945 some 12,000 passengers were carried in addition to substantial quantities of cargo. Gradually, the pre-war routes were restored.

The old aircraft were replaced by new types such as the Antonov An-2 and Ilyushin Il-12 and Il-14. These were augmented with the turboprop Il-18 and, in March 1959, the Northern Administration, which became the Leningrad Division of Aeroflot, entered the jet-age with the arrival of the Tu-104.

The Antonov An-24 and Yakovlev Yak-40 entered service in 1965 followed by the Tu-124 and Tu-134. Over the next ten years the passenger levels rapidly increased resulting in more aircraft deliveries in the form of

the Yak-42 and Tu-154 plus the An-12 for the cargo role. The wide-bodied Il-86 airliner entered service in 1983.

A national Wings of Russia competition was first held in 1998 in which 30 Russian carriers took part. Pulkovo won the Regular Domestic Carrier of the Year and took third place in the Regular International Carrier of the Year. Pulkovo Airport, which is owned by state-owned Pulkovo Aviation Enterprise, also won the Airport of the Year and these titles have continued to be held.

Sadly, fourteen Pulkovo aircrew were lost when one of its Il-86s crashed due to stabiliser problems while taking off from Moscow airport. Two air hostesses survived the accident which happened on July 28th, 2002; no passengers were being carried.

Qantas Airways

Registered name: Qantas Airways Ltd
Country: Australia
Region: Australia & Pacific
Address: Qantas Centre
203 Coward St
Mascot
Sydney
NSW 2020
Tel: 0061 2 96 91 36 36
Fax: 0061 2 96 91 33 39
Web site: www.qantas.com.au
Main operational base: Sydney

STATUS

IATA scheduled international carrier
National Flag Carrier
Employees: 31,000
Passengers per year: 20,193,000 (2001)
ICAO code: QFA
IATA code: QF

SERVICES

International / Regional / Domestic
Passenger / Cargo
International routes: Argentina*, Austria*, Canada, Chile*, China, Denmark*, Fiji*, Finland, France, Germany, Hawaii, Indonesia, Italy, Japan, Netherlands*, New

Caledonia, New Zealand, Norway, Papua New Guinea, Philippines, Singapore, South Africa, South Korea*, Sweden*, Switzerland*, Tahiti, Taiwan, Thailand, UK*, USA, Vanuatu, Vietnam, Western Samoa, Zimbabwe (*code share)

ALLIANCES/CODE SHARES

OneWorld / Aerolineas Argentinas, Air Caledonie Int, Air Niugini, Air Pacific, Air Tahiti Nui, Air Vanuatu, Alaska A/l, Alitalia, Asiana A/l, China Easten A/l, EVA

ABOVE: *Qantas Airways A330-201, VH-EBA (C/n 508) with Airbus test registration F-WWKM (Airbus)*

Aw, JAL, Norfolk Jet Express, Oregon Pacific, Polynesian A/l, Solomon A/l, SAA, Vietnam A/l

OWNED SUBSIDIARY AIRLINES

Airlink Australia, Australian Airlines, Eastern Australia Airlines, Impulse Airlines, Southern Australian Airlines, Sunstate Airlines

FLEET

A330-200 - 1, 717-200 - 14 (operated as QantasLink), 737-300 - 17, 737-400 - 22, 737-800 - 15, 747-300 - 6, 747-400 - 25, 747-400ER - 6, 767-200ER - 7, 767-300ER - 29, BAe 146-100 - 6 (operated as QantasLink), BAe 146-200 - 9 (operated as QantasLink), BAe 146-300 - 2 (operated as QantasLink), 1900D Airliner - 13 (operated as QantasLink), DHC-8 Dash 8-Q100 - 20 (operated as QantasLink), DHC-8 Dash 8-Q200 - 4 (operated as QantasLink), DHC-8 Dash 8-Q300 - 4 (operated as QantasLink), SD360 - 4 (operated as QantasLink).
On order: A330-200/300 - 12, A380-100 12 for delivery between 2006 and 2011, 737-800 - 60 options, DHC-8 Dash 8-Q300 - 2 (operated as QantasLink)

Qantas was originally formed as the Western Queensland Auto Aero Service by a group of ex-WW1 pioneer aviators and the first aircraft ordered on August 19th, 1920. Papers were later drawn up on November 16th, 1920 establishing the business and registering it as the Queensland and Northern Territory Aerial Services (QANTAS). Initial operations were pleasure trips and air taxi flights using ex-military Avro 504 and a Be2C.

The first scheduled passenger flight was on November 2nd with 84-year old Alexander Kennedy. He had agreed to invest in the airline and joined the provisional board on the condition that he had the first ticket. Scheduled services continued carrying mail and passengers.

In 1926, Qantas licence-built its own de Havilland DH.50.

Qantas was a key player in the development of Australian aviation. The first flying doctor service was operated in 1928 for the Reverend John Flynn's Australian Inland Mission. In 1931 it flew a link to Darwin to deliver mail to the Imperial Airways service to the UK. This resulted in the formation of Qantas Empire Airways Ltd with Imperial Airways holding 50% and the regular Australia-UK mail service.

The first Qantas aircraft to fly out of Australia was a de Havilland DH-86 to Singapore in February 1935 which carried passengers there two months later. Such was the demand that the Short C Class Empire flying boat was subsequently introduced. In July 1938 they were used to inaugurate the Sydney - Southampton route.

During WW2, Qantas was involved often on the front line with its unarmed aircraft. It helped in the evacuation of personnel at risk of being captured by the Japanese. Japanese Zeros shot down one flying boat that was evacuating women and children from Surabaya. By March 1942 three of its

10 flying boats had been destroyed by the Japanese and a further two lost in accidents while flying in support of the war effort. Qantas crews continued dropping supplies at tree-top heights in New Guinea on top of maintaining the regular link to the UK until the Japanese advances forced this to be suspended in 1943.

The cutting of the UK link brought about a daring plan. A 5,625km route was established by Catalina to provide a link to Allied forces in Ceylon (now Sri Lanka). This became the longest non-stop regular passenger flight ever attempted in the world. The crew had to use celestial navigation and maintain radio silence as enemy aircraft patrolled much of the route. Such was the range that only 69kg of diplomatic and armed forces mail plus three passengers could be carried on flights that could last from 28 to 32 hours depending on the weather.

A total of 271 of these missions were flown and 648 passengers carried and each were given a certificate entitling them to member of 'The Rare and Secret Order of the Double Sunrise' as they had been airborne for more than 24 hours.

Qantas Airways

ABOVE: *Qantas Airlink BAe 146-200, VH-NJH (C/n E2178) (BAe systems)*

After the war Qantas expanded rapidly with the Catalina and Sandringham flying boats, DC-3s and DC-4s although the Lancastrians and Short Hythes were being phased out. Nationalised in 1947, the airline took delivery of its first pressurised Constellation. This enabled a Sydney-London route to be operated and the service commenced that December.

During 1949 the Trans-Australia Airlines (TAA) took over the Queensland and Northern Territory networks and Flying Doctor Service from Qantas.

Qantas continued to expand its network with a Super Constellation service commencing to San Francisco and Vancouver in October 1953. The Olympic flame was flown from Athens to Darwin in 1956 enroute to Melbourne.

Qantas entered the jet age with its first 707 in 1959 - the first non-US airline to own a 707. This led to the routes being further expanded during the 1960s.

Two Super Constellations took off on January 14th 1958 in opposite directions to inaugurate the Qantas round-the-world service. They both returned six days later and subsequently resulted in eight such flights per week being scheduled.

The name was changed to Qantas Airways on August 1st 1967.

The first of a substantial fleet of 747s was delivered in July 1971. Following the devastation of Darwin by Cyclone Tracy in 1974, a total of 673 passengers was evacuated on one of the flights. In 1979 the last 707 was retired, resulting in Qantas being the only airline in the world to operate only the 747s.

The 767s were added in 1985. In August 1989 the first 747-400 was delivered and set a world distance record for a commercial jet flying from Sydney to London non-stop - a record that was not broken until 1993. A far cry from the Kangaroo Route that Qantas helped to establish in 1935 that required five aircraft types from three airlines making 42 refuelling stops as well as two railways. Time taken cut from 14 days to just over 20 hours.

Following deregulation of the Australian domestic airline industry in 1990, the Australian Government announced that it was to sell Australian Airlines and 49% of Qantas. It also removed the barrier between the international and domestic operators. This gave Qantas the opportunity to return to providing a domestic service.

The Qantas bid of $A400 million was accepted in June 1992 by the government which also decided to sell the whole of Qantas. The British Airways bid of $A665 million for 25% was accepted and completed in March 1993, with full privatisation being achieved in July 1995. BA subsequently reduced its holding to 21.4% in 2001.

Qantas acquired four regional subsidiaries - Australian Airlink, Eastern Australia Airlines, Southern Australia Airlines and Sunstate Airlines. In 2001 they were rebranded as QantasLink. In November, Impulse was purchased and added to the operation with eight 717s.

An A$1.5 billion order for 15 new 737-800s was announced in October 2001 to meet the demand created by the collapse of Ansett Airlines.

Qantas was not hit as badly as most airlines due to the failure of Ansett which produced a 40% increase in domestic passenger levels. International levels dropped

BELOW: *Qantas Link DHC-8 Dash 8-102, VH-TQF (C/n 067) operated by Eastern Australia Airlines (Bombardier)*

though, producing a small loss for that part of the business. Besides the additional fuel and insurance costs, Qantas operating, have risen steeply due to the need to acquire additional aircraft to service the extra domestic passengers.

The first 737-800 entered service in February 2002 and the world's first 747-400ER in October while in March the sec-ond of two 747SP was retired. In addition, six more 717s were added to the QantasLink fleet in April to provide non-stop schedules to various Queensland cities, and took the total up 76 aircraft.

Qantas announced plans in 2002 to re-establish Australian Airlines as a low-cost leisure carrier. The first schedule was flown on October 27th to Japan. Other schedules include Singapore, Taiwan and Hong Kong. This was initially with four 767s but with plans to increase to 12 within their first two years of operation.

Qantas took delivery of its first A330 in December 2002 which will be followed by 12 more over the next three years for domestic operations.

Qatar Airways

Registered name: Qatar Airways
Country: Qatar
Region: Middle East
Address: Qatar Airways Tower
PO Box 22550, Doha
Tel: 00974 449 60 00
Fax: 00974 462 15 33
Web site: www.qatarairways.com
Main operational base: Doha

STATUS

Scheduled carrier
National Flag Carrier
Employees: 2,100
Passengers per year: 1,528,000 (2001)
ICAO code: QTR
IATA code: QR

SERVICES

International / Regional
Passenger / Charter / Cargo
International routes: Austria, Bahrain, Bangladesh, Egypt, France, Germany, India, Indonesia, Italy, Japan, Jordan, Kuwait, Lebanon, Malaysia, Maldives, Morocco, Nepal, Netherlands, Oman, Pakistan, Philippines, Saudi Arabia, Sri Lanka, Sudan, Sweden, Switzerland, Syria, Thailand, UAE, UK

ALLIANCES/CODE SHARES

Lufthansa, Malaysia A/l

FLEET

A300-622R - 7 (to be replaced by A330s), A320-200 - 8, A330-200 - 4, ACJ319 - 1

(operated on behalf of Qatar Amiri flight)
On order: A320-200 - 7 for 2004 delivery, A330-200 - 1 for 2/2004 delivery, A380-100 - 2

Qatar Airways was formed by Sheik Hamad Ali Jabor Al-Thani on 22nd November 1993 and commenced operations in January 1994 with 747s. It is now owned entirely by Qatari investors.

A new A330 joined the Qatar fleet in May 2002. This was the first of four aircraft in a US$560 million order for the aircraft which is configured for 238 passengers and includes state of the art entertainment sys-

BELOW: *Qatar Airways A319-133XD, A7-HHJ (C/n 1335) (Airbus)*

Qatar Airways

ABOVE: *Qatar Airways A319CJ (Airbus)*

which is already constructing a new international airport at Doha at the cost of US$1 billion. This is due to be completed in time for the Asian Games in 2006.

Destinations continue to be added to its network with seven new ones in 2002 and 2003 with a target total of 50 in 2004. Capacity has been increased with the new A320 and A330s with the Airbus A380 expected for delivery in 2008. Qatar was the launch customer for the new 'super' airliner. Qatar Airways also has an ACJ319 corporate jet that is available for charter.

Qatar has a 25% stake in Gulf Air.

BELOW: *Qatar Airways A330-203, A7-ACB (C/n 489) (Jeremy Flack/API)*

tems as well as the latest in comfort seating.

Qatar Airways has been increasing its schedules to India and, with four of the metro airports being privatised, it has been showing interest in investing in one or more of them.

This not a new venture for Qatar Airways,

Rio-Sul

Registered name: Rio-Sul Servicios Aéreos Regionais
Country: Brazil
Region: South America
Address: Avenue Rio Branco 85/10
Rio de Janeiro RJ, 20040-00
Tel: 0055 21 263 25 65
Fax: 0055 21 253 20 44
Web site: www.voeriosul.com.br

STATUS

Scheduled domestic carrier
Employees: 2,228
Passengers per year: 3,935,000 (2001)
ICAO code: RSL
IATA code: SL

SERVICES

Domestic / Passenger / Cargo
International routes: Domestic only

ALLIANCES/CODE SHARES

Nordeste

FLEET

737-500 - 15, 737-700 - 2, EMB.120RT
Brasilia - 8, ERJ-145 - 14

Rio-Sul was originally formed as Top Taxi Aereo as an air taxi operator with the Sabreliner and Navajo Chieftain.

Rio-Sul was established as a regional carrier on August 24th, 1976 following a Brazilian Government plan for domestic route development. This was undertaken,

in conjunction with VARIG, in the southern part of the country of which one of the states is Rio Grande do Sul. A fleet of EBB-110 Bandeirante was acquired and the service commenced in September.

As passenger levels grew a pair of F-27 Friendships was acquired in the first half of 1982 with another later in the year. Another pair was added to the fleet in the mid-1980s.

In 1995, Rio-Sul acquired Nordeste (formed June 1976) which gave it a ready-made domestic network to the north of the country.

Supported by VARIG, which has a 52% stake, Rio-Sul has managed to develop a substantial network which now includes 737s and ERJ-145 in its fleet.

Royal Air Maroc

Registered name: Compagnie Nationale de Transports Aériens
Country: Morocco
Region: Africa
Address: Anfa Airport
Casablanca
Tel: 00212 2 91 20 00
Fax: 00212 2 91 07 07
Web site: www.royalairmaroc.com/ver_en/
Main operational base: Casablanca

STATUS

International scheduled carrier
National Flag Carrier
Employees: 5,420
Passengers per year: 3,750,000 (2001)
ICAO code: RAM
IATA code: AT

SERVICES

International / Regional / Domestic
Passenger / Charter / Cargo
International routes: Belgium, Canada, Cote D'Ivoire, Egypt, France, Gabon, Germany, Guinea, Italy, Mali, Mauritania, Netherlands, Niger, Saudi Arabia, Senegal, Spain, Switzerland, UAE, UK, USA

ALLIANCES/CODE SHARES

Air France, Delta Air Lines, Gulf Air, Iberia, Tunisair

FLEET

ATR 42 - 2, 737-200Adv - 2, 737-400 - 7, 737-500 - 6, 737-700 - 4, 737-800 - 8, 747-200B (SCD) - 1, 747-400 - 1, 757-200 - 2, 767-300ER - 2
On order: A321-200 - 4 for delivery late 2003, 737-700 - 1, 737-800 - 1

Royal Air Maroc was originally formed on June 28th, 1953, with the merger of Compagnie Cherifienne d'Aviation (Air Atlas - formed 1946) and Societe Avia Maroc Ligne Aerienne (Air Maroc - formed 1947). The new airline was called Compagnie Cherifienne de Transports Aeriens (CGTA) (Air Atlas-Air Maroc). Initial services were operated with Ju-52s with DC-3s and Constellations being added later.

ABOVE: *Royal Air Maroc ATR 42-300, CN-CDT (C/n 127) (ATR)*

After Morocco's independence from France and largely from Spain in 1956, CGTA was renamed Royal Air Maroc the following year.

The Caravelle brought RAM into the jet age in 1960. It commenced schedule service in May on the Casablanca - Paris route.

The 727s and first 707 were added to the fleet in 1970, followed by 737s in 1976 and the 747s in 1978.

The end of the decade saw fuel and adverse exchange rates combine to increase operating costs. However, RAM managed to cushion these effects with an efficiency programme that cut other costs as well as managing to increase passenger levels.

RAM underwent an extensive fleet renewal review which resulted in orders being placed in 2000 for an additional four A321-200s and 20 737-700/800s - half being firm orders and the other options. These are for delivery spread from 2003 to 2013. Deliveries of the new 737NGs will initially replace the older 737 models.

An agreement was concluded with the Senegalese Government for the formation of Air Sénégal International of which RAM provided 51% of the capital. Early plans to progress towards privatisation were abandoned following the events of September 11th 2001.

BELOW: *Royal Air Maroc 737-8B6, CN-RNK (C/n 28981) (Jeremy Flack/API)*

Royal Brunei Airlines

ABOVE: *Royal Brunei Airlines 767-33AER, V8-RBF (C/n 23453) (Royal Brunei Airlines)*

Registered name: Royal Brunei Airlines

Country: Brunei

Region: Asia

Address: PO Box 737

Bandar Seri Begwan

BS 8671

Tel: 00673 2 24 05 00

Fax: 00673 2 24 47 37

Web site: www.bruneiair.com

Main operational base: Brunei International Airport

STATUS

IATA scheduled carrier

National Flag Carrier

Employees: 3,047

Passengers per year: 1,242,000 (2001)

ICAO code: RBA

IATA code: BI

SERVICES

International / Regional / Passenger Cargo

International routes: Australia, China, India, Indonesia, Kuwait, Malaysia, Philippines, Saudi Arabia, Singapore, Taiwan, Thailand, UAE

ALLIANCES/CODE SHARES

BMI, Dragonair, Malaysia A/l, United A/l

FLEET

757-200ER - 2, 767-300ER - 8 (1 on lease to Royal Tongan Airlines)

On order: A319-100 - 2

Royal Brunei Airlines was formed on November 18th, 1974, by the government of Negara Brunei Darussalam, as the national carrier. Two 737s were purchased and the first schedule flown in March 1975.

New routes were quickly established to Hong Kong, Malaysia, Philippines and Thailand during 1976 and 1977. Additional 737s were purchased in 1980 which enabled another route to Malaysia as well as new ones to Australia and Indonesia.

The arrival of the first of three wide-body 757s dramatically increased the capability of Royal Brunei Airlines. New routes commenced to Taiwan in 1986, Dubai in 1988 and Frankfurt in 1990.

Such was the success of Royal Brunei Airlines that the 737s were sold and replaced by 767s the first of which was delivered in June 1990. The delivery flight was flown from Seattle to Mombasa/Nairobi and took 17 hours and 51 minutes. This was a world distance record for a civil twin-engined airliner, that lasted for almost ten years, when it was taken by a 777.

The 767s enabled the route network to be expanded significantly ranging from London to Perth. Others new routes included destinations in Europe, Middle East, and Asia although a few were later suspended.

Royal Jordanian Airlines

Registered name: Royal Jordanian plc
Country: Jordan
Region: Middle East
Address: Housing Bank Commercial Centre
PO Box 302
Amman
Tel: 00962 6 560 28 92
Fax: 00962 6 567 62 85
Web site: www.rja.com.jo
Main operational base: Amman

STATUS

IATA scheduled international carrier
National Flag Carrier
Employees: 3,569
Passengers per year: 1,178,000 (2001)
ICAO code: RJA
IATA code: RJ

SERVICES

International / Regional / Domestic
Passenger / Charter / Cargo
International routes: Austria, Bahrain, Belgium, Cyprus, Egypt, France, Germany, Greece, India, Indonesia, Ireland, Israel*, Italy, Kuwait, Libya, Lebanon, Malaysia, Morocco, Netherlands, Oman, Pakistan, Palestine*, Russia, Saudi Arabia, Spain, Sri Lanka, Sudan, Switzerland, Syria, Tunisia, Turkey, Thailand, UAE, UK, USA, Yemen
(* Operated by Royal Wings)

ALLIANCES/CODE SHARES

Aeroflot, Air-Canada, Air-India, Austrian A/l, Iberia, Malaysia A/l, SriLankan A/l, Syrian Arab A/l

OWNED SUBSIDIARY AIRLINES

Royal Wings

FLEET

A310-300 - 7 (1 converted to freighter), A320-200 - 5, A340-200 - 2, 707-300C - 2

Royal Jordanian Airlines was formed by royal decree on December 8th, 1963 as Alia - The Royal Jordanian Airline after the king's daughter. It succeeded Jordan Airways which itself had replaced Air Jordan two years previously. Scheduled ser-

ABOVE: *Royal Jordanian Airlines A310-304, JY-AGK (C/n 573) (Jeremy Flack/API)*

vices commenced on December 15th with a pair of ex-Royal Jordanian AF Handley Page Heralds.

A DC-7 was quickly added to the fleet but in 1965 a leap forward in capability and stature was made with the arrival of tits first Caravelle jet airliner that was flown on the Amman - London route.

The London schedule was taken over by the 707s following delivery of the first in 1971. In 1974 Jordanian World Airways was formed as a subsidiary to operate the charter flights. Initially 707s were taken from the parent airline as required although some were subsequently acquired for its own use as the business developed.

A 720 was delivered in 1972 followed by three 727s in 1974. Wide-body airline's followed with a pair of 747s in 1977 plus another in 1981 plus the first of 10 Tristars.

The airline was renamed Royal Jordanian Airlines in 1986.

The Gulf War badly affected the airline with the fleet grounded for two months. Most of the fleet sat at Maastricht and Vienna and one flight per day was allowed into Amman. Once the war ended and aircraft were allowed to fly normally, however, the passenger levels remained low and took two years to return to something like normal. As a result, the airline's financial position had deteriorated badly and took some time to recover.

Privatisation plans have been ongoing for some years and a number of non-core activities have been sold but following September 2001 the plans were put on hold. However, in February 2002 the government gave RJA exclusive international rights for a period of four years, restricting other Jordanian operators to charter operations. This was to provide stability for the airline while the privatisation moves forward once more.

BELOW: *Royal Jordanian Airlines 707-323C, JY-AEC (C/n 18949) in old colours (Jeremy Flack/API)*

Royal Nepal Airlines

Registered name: Royal Nepal Airlines Corporation
Country: Nepal
Region: Asia
Address: RNAC Building
PO Box 401, Kantipath
Kathmandu
Tel: 00977 1 22 07 57
Fax: 00977 1 22 53 48
Web site: www.royalnepal.com
Main operational base: Kathmandu

ABOVE: *Royal Nepal Airlines HS.748 Series 200, 9N-AAU (C/n 1671) (BAe Regional)*

STATUS

Scheduled international and domestic carrier
National Flag Carrier
Employees: 1,988
Passengers per year: 641,000 (2001)
ICAO code: RNA
IATA code: RA

SERVICES

International / Regional / Domestic
Passenger / Cargo
International routes: China, France, Germany, India, Japan, Singapore, Thailand, UK

FLEET

757-200 - 2, HS748 Srs.2A - 2, DHC-6 Twin Otter 300 - 7

Royal Nepal Airways was formed on July 1st 1958 by the Nepalese Government. It was established to take over the routes that had previously been flown by Indian Airlines since the early 1950s. Initially operating a leased DC-3, the new national airline operated various domestic routes while Indian Airlines conducted international ones until 1960 when Royal Nepal commenced operating these as well.

A variety of aircraft has been operated by Royal Nepal Airlines including PC-6 Turbo Porters, A310s and 727s while current types include a small fleet of the DHC-6 Twin Otters with a good STOL performance and 757s for the longer international routes.

The HS748 also proved useful for the higher-volume domestic services but their current status is uncertain.

Being such a mountainous country, aviation provided a vital means of travel to many remote parts and assisted in encouraging tourism. However, it does pose difficulties. In July 2000, a Twin Otter was lost along with 25 passengers and crew.

Unfortunately, for a small country an airline is an expensive operation and relies heavily on tourism to keep it viable. In 2002 the management was looking for a potential collaborator to enter into a joint venture to enable Royal Nepal Airlines to survive.

Royal Tongan Airlines

Registered name: Royal Tongan Airlines
Country: Tonga
Region: Australia & Pacific
Address: Royco Building
Fatafehi Road, Private Bag 9
Nuku'alofa
Tel: 00676 23 414
Fax: 00676 24 056
Web site: www.royaltonganairlines.com
Main operational base: Tongatapu

ICAO code: HRH
IATA code: WR

SERVICES

International / Regional / Domestic
Passenger / Charter / Cargo
International routes: Australia, Fiji, New Zealand, Tonga, Western Samoa

ALLIANCES/CODE SHARES

Air New Zealand

STATUS

IATA international and domestic carrier
National Flag Carrier
Employees: 126

FLEET

737-300 - 1*, 757-200 - 1, DHC-6 Twin Otter 300 - 2, SD360 - 1, Y-12-1 - 1
(*Joint leased with Air Pacific)

Royal Tongan Airlines was originally formed as the Friendly Island Airways by the Government of Tonga and began domestic services as the national carrier on December 14th 1985 operating a BN-2A Islander and an 212 Aviocar.

In 1989, two Twin Otters were leased to replace the Islander and Aviocar. In 1991 The Friendly Island Airways was renamed Royal Tongan Airlines and a 737 was leased to commence international services. Subsequently an HS748 was leased from Mount Cook Airlines for a service to Niue. An agreement with Air New Zealand allowed for additional capacity to be bought and sold on flights to New Zealand.

In addition Royal Tongan can purchase seats on its flights to Los Angeles. Another agreement with Air Pacific provides for the joint lease of a replacement 737 and a Qantas 747.

The HS748 has since been sold and replaced with a Short SD360. Following delivery of a leased 757 from Royal Brunei Airlines in November 2002, the weekly scheduled Nuku'alofa - Auckland service resumed and a new route to Sydney and Hawaii was established.

ABOVE: *Royal Tongan 757-2M6ER, V8-RBB (C/n 23453) (Royal Tongan)*

Ryanair

Registered name: Ryanair Ltd
Country: Ireland
Region: Europe
Address: Corporate Head Office
             Dublin Airport
             Co Dublin
Tel: 00353 1 812 12 12
Fax: 00353 1 844 44 01
Web site: www.ryanair.com

STATUS

IATA scheduled international carrier
Employees: 1,476
Passengers per year: 7,400,000 (2001)
ICAO code: RYR
IATA code: FR

SERVICES

Regional / Domestic / Passenger
International routes: Denmark, France, Italy, Norway, Sweden, UK

FLEET

737-200Adv - 21, 737-800 - 33.
On order: 737-800 - 117 for delivery 2003-10

Ryanair was formed in 1985 initially flying weekday schedules between Eire and Luton Airport with BAC 1-11s and also offering an air-taxi service with a Bandeirante.

In 1986 London European Airways (formed 1983) was acquired which enabled services to be operated through to Amsterdam and Brussels.

In 1994 ex-Britannia Airways and Transavia 737-200s started to replace the 1-11s. This was the beginning of the ever-expanding number of the type in various model forms.

By 2001, Ryanair had become less reliant on commission paid travel agencies. According to the airline, it was only accounting for 8% of ticket sales. It also increased the number of direct purchase customers who bought tickets via the web to two thirds.

In February 2001 Ryanair announced that it had negotiated for Brussels

BELOW: *Ryanair 737-8AS, EI-CSA (C/n 29916) (Ryanair)*

Ryanair

Charleroi Airport to be its new European hub with a plan of up to 30 departures per day. It also offered new shares to help fund the 737 orders that were to be delivered over the next couple of years. Some £70.4 million of shares were four times oversubscribed. As a result, a further £15 million were issued.

In February 2002 Ryanair opened a second European hub at Frankfurt.

By offering a low-cost service Ryanair rapidly expanded the passenger base but this caused it problems.

During 2002 Ryanair encountered diffi-culty in maintaining some of its schedules due to staff shortages. With the low-cost operations the passenger increase was plac-ing a strain on the operation and two routes were scrapped (Belfast-Edinburgh and Belfast-Glasgow). A new rostering system worsened the problem when it left aircrews out of position.

During September a major promotion offered seats on selected flights for just 1p plus taxes

After a huge effort the situation was back to normal by the end of the year with record passenger numbers carried (14.5 million). This may be a high figure as the Ryanair numbering system does include no shows which together with the major pro-motion will have provided a boost.

In early 2003, Ryan acquired the KLM low-cost carrier Buzz for £15 million. Orders were also increased for the 737-800 by anoth-er 22 aircraft for delivery during 2004/5. This latest order meant that 250 737-800s had been ordered by Ryanair since January 2002 of which half were firm orders.

Plans are also in hand to expand into Sweden and Spain and to develop its Italian market.

Saudi Arabian Airlines

Registered name: Saudi Arabian Airlines
Country: Saudi Arabia
Region: Middle East
Address: PO Box 620
Jeddah
21231
Tel: 00966 2 686 00 00
Fax: 00966 2 686 45 52
Web site: www.saudiairlines.com or
www.saudiaairlines.com xxx
Main operational base: Jeddah

STATUS

IATA scheduled international carrier
National Flag Carrier
Employees: 24,262
Passengers per year: 12,835,000 (2001)
ICAO code: SVASDI
IATA code: SV

SERVICES

International / Regional / Domestic
Passenger / Charter / Cargo
International routes: Algeria, Bahrain, Bangladesh, Egypt, Eritrea, Ethiopia, France, Germany, Greece, India, Indonesia, Iran, Italy, Jordan, Kenya, Kuwait, Lebanon, Malaysia, Morocco, Oman, Pakistan, Philippines, Senegal, Singapore, South Africa, Sri Lanka, Sudan, Switzerland, Syria, Thailand, Tunisia, Turkey, UAE, UK, USA, Yemen

FLEET

A300-600 - 11, 707-300C - 2 (owned by Saudi Government), 737-200 - 8 (1 owned by Saudi Government), 747-100 - 9, 747-200F - 1, 747-300 - 11 (1 owned by Saudi Government), 747-400 - 5, 747SP - 3 (1 owned by Saudi Government), 777-200ER - 23, A36 Bonanza - 6 (for training), Falcon 900 - 2 (owned by Saudi Government), DHC-6 Twin Otter 300 - 1 (owned by Saudi Government), Gulfstream II - 4 (3 owned by Saudi Government), Gulfstream III - 3 (owned by Saudi Government), Gulfstream IV - 6 (owned by Saudi Government), L.1011 TriStar 500 - 2 (owned by Saudi Government), MD-11F - 4, MD-90-30 - 29, PA-28-181 Archer II - 8 (for training)

Saudi Arabian Airlines was originally gov-ernment formed on May 25th, 1945 with assistance from TWA. It was equipped with a DC-3 presented to King Abdul Aziz by President Franklin D Roosevelt and domes-tic operations commenced shortly after. Two DC-3s were acquired a few months later.

Saudi Arabian Airlines first scheduled domestic service commenced in March 1947 and international routes were soon being operated to various countries in the Middle East.

The first of five Bristol 170 Wayfarer transports were delivered in 1949. With the nose comprising a large clam-shell type door, large size freight could be carried including cars, in addition to passengers.

By 1952 five DC-4s were added to the Saudi Arabian Airlines fleet which was oper-ating 13 DC-3s and four Lockheed Lodestars as well as the Wayfarers. These were followed by Convair 340s in 1954 that were eventually used to provide a daily Jeddah - Riyadh service from 1959.

Saudi Arabian Airlines entered the jet-age with the arrival of the two 720s in December 1961. They entered service the following March and Saudi Arabian was the first Middle East airline to operate a com-mercial jet airliner.

Saudi Arabian Airlines was made a corpo-ration by royal decree in 1963. A pair of DC-6 were acquired the following year and a third the year after that. These allowed more distant destinations to be flown including Khartoum and Bombay.

More jets were added to the fleet with DC-9s arriving in 1967 enabling many new routes to North Africa and Europe - many being staged through Beirut. The following year two 707s were acquired and used to provide scheduled services to London.

In 1972 the name was changed to Saudia and the aircraft painted in new colours. More new aircraft arrived in the form of five 737s which replaced the old DC-3s and 340s as well as the DC-9s.

ABOVE: *Saudi A300B4-620, HZ-AJF (C/n 312) (Airbus)*

More new routes continued to be added to the 49 already being scheduled. In 1974 these were to Paris and Muscat as well as a direct Medina - Karachi service. Later that year orders were placed for the first two Lockheed Tristar airliners. Eventually, 20 of these wide-body airliners were to serve with the airline.

The last of the DC-3s were replaced with a couple of the US licence-built F-27 Friendships from 1975 while a couple more 707s were ordered and the first of the Tristars was delivered.

In 1977 the first of an initial five 747s arrived, boosting capacity further. In a joint operation with Pan Am, a non-stop Dharan - New York service commenced in February 1979 with 747SPs.

Fokker F-28 Fellowships replaced the F-27s in 1980 and the arrival in 1981 of its own 747SP enabled Saudia to commence a Jeddah - New York service.

Saudia was the launch customer for the Airbus A300-600 and the first of eleven were delivered in May 1984.

A fleet modernisation programme was signed in October 1995 for a total of 61 aircraft comprising 5 747s, 23 777s, 4 MD-11s and 29 MD-90s worth in the region of US$6 billion.

1996 saw a new corporate image introduced and the name reverted to Saudi Arabian Airlines. By 1998 the new airliners were being delivered and entering service. More new routes were introduced to Alexandria, Athens and Milan.

Saudia Catering which produces meals not only for Saudi Arabian Airlines but also 50 other international airlines produced some 13.5 million meals in 2000.

The first stage on the path to privatisation was signed in October 2000. By August 2001 all the new aircraft had been delivered and further extensions to the scheduled network added the destinations of Dhaka and Mumbai. With one of the most modern fleets in the world, Saudi Arabian Airlines was already reaping the benefits, but no sooner was the airline impressively placed to move forward than the events of September 11th struck. Probably because of the modernisation the effects on the airline were not so great with passenger numbers staying around level.

Plans for privatisation continue with a target date of 2004 / 5.

In addition to the airline operation, Saudi Arabian Airlines operates a number of VIP aircraft on behalf of the Saudi Arabian Government. A small fleet of light aircraft are also maintained for training purposes. A number of C-130 Hercules have also been operated in conjunction with the Saudi Air Force as flying hospitals within the country.

Scandinavian Airlines System/SAS

Registered name: SAS Danmark / SAS Norge / SAS Sverige

Country: Denmark / Norway / Sweden

Region: Europe

Address: Frosundaviks Alle 1

Stockholm S-19587

Tel: 0046 8 797 00 00

Fax: 0046 8 797 15 15

Web site: www.scandinavian.net

Stockholder: SAS AB

Main operational base: Copenhagen, Oslo and Stockholm

STATUS

IATA scheduled international carrier

National Flag Carrier

Employees: 31,035

Passengers per year: 23,063,000 (2001)

ICAO code: SAS

IATA code: SK

SERVICES

International / Regional / Domestic

Passenger / Cargo

International routes: Austria, Belgium, China, Czech, Denmark, Estonia, Finland, France, Germany, Hungary, Ireland, Italy, Japan, Lithuania, Netherlands, Norway, Poland, Russia, Singapore, Spain, Sweden, Switzerland, Thailand, UK, USA

ALLIANCES/CODE SHARES

Star Alliance / AirBaltic, Estonian Air, Icelandair, Maersk Air, Spanair

OWNED SUBSIDIARY AIRLINES

SAS Cargo, SAS Commuter, Air Botnia Wideroe, Braathens, ASA

FLEET

A321-200 - 6, A330-300 - 2, A340-300 - 7, 737-600 - 32, 737-700 - 6, 737-800 - 17, 767-300ER - 7 (being replaced by A330 / A340), DHC-8 Dash 8-Q400 - 24 (Operated by SAS Commuter), F-28 Fellowship Mk.4000 - 8 (Operated by SAS Commuter), Fokker 50 - 9 (Operated by SAS Commuter), MD-81 - 19, MD-82 - 28, MD-83 - 2, MD-87 - 15, MD-90-30 - 8

On order: A321-200 - 6, A330-300 - 2, 737-800 - 4

Scandinavian Airlines System came into being on 1st August 1946 following pressure from private enterprise to merge the three existing national airlines of Denmark, Sweden and Norway. These were Det Danske Luftfartselskab AB / DDL of Denmark (which was formed in 1918), Det Norske Luftfartselskap / DNL of Norway and Svensk Interkontinental Lufttrafik AB / SLA and Aktiebolaget Aerotransport / ABA of Sweden. National ownership of SAS was divided approximately in the ratio 2:2:3 with 50% of each privately owned and 50% owned by the respective governments.

SAS initially took over the more modern of the aircraft types operated by the previous airlines and commenced operations with seven DC-4s. DC-3s, Ju-52 and Convair 340s, together with two Sandringham flying boats, were joined by 12 DC-6s from 1948. These were followed by SAAB 90 Scanias, Convair 440s and DC-7s and the Caravelle eventually taking SAS into the jet age in 1959. Some Convair CV990s was operated as a stopgap until the DC-8 was in service in 1960. A number of DC-8 variants were operated including the stretched 200-seat DC-8-63. A BAC 1-11 was leased for a few months in 1967/8 to provide extra capacity while initial delivery of the DC-9 fleet was awaited.

In February 1968 the first DC-9 entered service with SAS. This was a -41 model with a 1.87m (6ft 4in) fuselage stretch, used on

BELOW: *SAS 737-638, SE-DNM (C/n 28288) (SAS)*

the Middle East and European routes. The DC-9-21 with a shorter range was designated for the domestic routes. During 1969 Turi Widerøe joined SAS as the first female pilot in a major Western airline.

The 747s arrived in February 1971, DC-10s in 1974 and the Caravelles retired. Four A300s were ordered and delivered in the late 1970s but their operation was short lived due to the downturn in passenger traffic. Smaller MD-80s were ordered to replace some of the older DC-9s. MD-87s arrived in the 1990s along with 767s and F-28 Fellowships.

In the mid-1980s SAS was listed among the top 20 airlines but that was not to last following a major downturn in business. As a result SAS decided to concentrate its activities on the core business of air transport and all non-related enterprises were sold off. A major re-focusing on the passenger enabled a turnaround.

In 1988 nine 767s were ordered followed by 61 MD-80s. In 1995 SAS placed its largest order ever for 41 737-600s. In May 1997 SAS became a founder member of the Star Alliance. Later that year it took a 29% stake in the Widerøe Flyveselskap which it increased to 66.2% the following year. It also acquired Air Botnia of Finland, increasing further its extensive shareholding in other airlines.

In September 1998 SAS announced another change to its corporate identity with a new scheme for its aircraft, and new uniforms, which were implemented the following year. 1999 also saw the retirement of the F-28 Fellowships.

Being one of the largest operators of the DC-9 / MD-80 family outside USA, SAS performs the complete range of overhaul and maintenance on these aircraft. However, the fleet is on the wane with the last -21 model retired in October 2000 and the last -41 scheduled to be withdrawn in 2003.

Rivals SAS and Maersk were the subject of a European Commission investigation over cartel-building where it was alleged that they were dividing key routes between them. SAS was fined US$36.7 million but were to appeal.

The events of September 11th hit SAS but a recovery plan was quickly instigated. Some 20 aircraft were grounded plus new aircraft deliveries rescheduled and staff levels dropped by approximately 1,000.

ABOVE: *SAS A340-313X, SE-REA (C/n 413) which has since been re-registered LN-RKF (Airbus)*

Although painful, the 12% cut has enabled SAS to survive better than many.

However, in October 2001 an SAS MD 80 was taking off at Linate Airport near Milan. As it accelerated down the runway in thick fog conditions, a small light aircraft taxied onto the runway. The pilot tried to swerve to miss the Cessna at the last moment but unfortunately it skidded out of control into a building, 110 passengers and crew died in the accident.

SAS withdrew its service to Greenland in November 2002 after 50 years of operation following strong competition from the national carrier Air Greenland.

BELOW: *SAS Commuter Dash 8 Q400 (Bombardier)*

Siberia Airlines

Registered name: Siberia Airlines JSC

Country: Russia – General

Region: Asia

Address: Siberia Airlines Headquarters

Frunze str., 4

Novosibirsk 630091

Tel: 007 3832 22 68 30

Fax: 007 3832 22 19 31

Web site: www.sibair.ru

Main operational base: Tolmachevo

(Novosibirsk)

STATUS

IATA scheduled and charter passenger + cargo carrier

Employees: 4,257

Passengers per year: 1,919,000 (2001)

ICAO code: SBI

IATA code: S7

SERVICES

International / Regional / Domestic Passenger / Charter / Cargo

International routes: Armenia, Azerbaijan, China, Germany, Israel, Korea, Turkey, UAE, Uzbekistan, Yakutsk

ALLIANCES/CODE SHARES

Armavia

FLEET

Il-86 - 10, Tu-154B - 10, Tu-154M - 18, Tu-204-100 - 2

Siberia Airlines was originally formed as the Novosibirsk-Tolmachevo division of Aeroflot.

Following the fragmentation of Aeroflot, Siberia Airlines was established in May 1992 at Tolmachevo airport at Novosibirsk. This was the largest airport in eastern Russia.

The growth in the number of airlines caused serious problems for the first few years as these airlines competed for passengers. Siberia Airlines realised that it needed more than seats on aeroplanes to attract customers and in 1998 a new management was installed.

Almost immediately the customers recognised that they were the airline's priority which was a considerable change from the old days. As a result passenger levels with Siberia Airlines started to rise and continued.

By 2001 the passenger levels were beginning to stabilise with little opportunity to increase on the existing routes. One of the main obstacles for future growth was the lack of a connection to Moscow. Initially, an alliance was formed with Vnukovo Airlines to co-ordinate schedules. However, Vnukovo was not in good shape so, later in the year, Vnukovo Airlines was acquired

which resulted in Siberia Airlines instantly doubling in size but most importantly getting good access to Moscow.

As a result of the quality of service Siberia Airlines has been presented with a number of awards and became the number two Russian airline.

In October 2001 Siberia Airlines lost one of its Tu-154s with the loss of 78 lives during a flight from Tel Aviv to Novosibirsk. Initially, it was a mystery as the plane broke up over the Black Sea without any radio message from the crew. It transpired that the Ukranian Army had been firing anti-aircraft missiles and, although it was initially denied, one of these missiles had strayed and accidentally hit the airliner.

New domestic and international routes were added to the Siberia Airlines network with hubs established at Moscow and Irkutsk in addition to Novosibirsk and the passenger levels continued to rise.

Siberia Airlines entered into a series of co-operation agreements with Armavia that included some code sharing. As a result an A320 was leased by Armavia and is jointly operated by both airlines. Armavia supplying the cabin crew while Siberia Airlines provides the pilots and servicing.

In October 2002, the first jointly operated service with the A320 was flown from Yerevan to Moscow,

Singapore Airlines/SIA

Registered name: Singapore Airlines Ltd

Country: Singapore

Region: Asia

Address: Airline House

25 Airline Road

Singapore 81929

Tel: 0065 65 41 58 80

Fax: 0065 45 80 83

Web site: www.singaporeair.com.sg

Main operational base: Singapore (Changi)

STATUS

IATA scheduled international carrier

National Flag Carrier

Employees: 14,499

Passengers per year: 14,765,000 (2001)

ICAO code: SIA

IATA code: SQ

SERVICES

International / Regional / Passenger Cargo

International routes: Australia, Bangladesh, Belgium, Brunei, Canada, China, Denmark, Egypt, France, Germany, Greece, India, Indonesia, Italy, Japan, Malaysia, Maldives, Mauritius, Netherlands, New Zealand, Pakistan, Philippines, Saudi Arabia, Singapore, South Africa, South

Korea, Spain, Sri Lanka, Switzerland, Taiwan, Thailand, Turkey, UAE, UK, USA, Vietnam

ALLIANCES/CODE SHARES

Star Alliance / Air-India, American A/l, Asiana A/l, Delta A/l, Vietnam A/l, Virgin Atlantic Aw

OWNED SUBSIDIARY AIRLINES

Silkair, Singapore Airlines Cargo

FLEET

A310-300 - 10, A340-300E - 6, 747-400 - 39, 747-400F - 11 operated by SIA Cargo, 777-

200 - 22, 777-200ER - 10, 777-300 - 7
On order: A340-300E - 2, A340-500 - 5 for delivery 10/2003 to 3/2004, A380-800 - 10 for delivery 2006 to 2011, 777-200 - 15, 777-200ER - 3, 777-300 - 1

The origins of Singapore Airlines (SIA) can be traced back to 1947 when Malayan Airways Ltd was formed. Domestic operations commenced with an Airspeed Consul on May 1st.

With the introduction of the DC-3, longer range routes were added including some international services. These expanded further during the 1950s and 1960s as aircraft performance improved. Airlines operated included the DC-4, Viscount, Super Constellation, Britannia, Comet 4 and F-27 Friendship.

The Federation of Malaysia was formed in September 1963 and the airline was renamed Malaysian Airways Ltd. The name changed again in May 1966 to Malaysia-Singapore Airlines (MSA) following the separation of Singapore from the Federation.

MSA entered the jet age with the arrival of the first of its own 737s in 1969.

Following a decision by the governments of Malaysia and Singapore in 1971, MSA was split into two separate airlines with Singapore Airlines (SIA) being formed on January 28th, 1972.

Concentrating on international services, new aircraft were steadily added to the SIA fleet with the first 747s arriving in 1973. These have been, and continue to be, the backbone of the fleet. These were followed by the 727s in 1977 and the DC-10s in 1978.

Tradewinds was formed as a subsidiary in 1976 to operate the charter operations with aircraft obtained from SIA as required. In 1989 it commenced operating as a regional airline and was subsequently renamed SilkAir.

The wide-body 747s and DC-10s were used to service the rapidly expanding international network which had already reached as far as London in 1971.

ABOVE: *Singapore Airlines A340-313X (Airbus)*

A Concorde was operated by SIA from 1977 on a jointly operated route with British Airways. As a result it was painted with BA colours on one side and SIA on the other. This service ended in 1980.

SIA continued to expand its fleet with the A300s which entered service in February 1981 and the first 'Big Top' 747s in May 1983 with the stretched upper deck (SUD).

1988 saw the arrival of yet more 747s with the first of the long range -400 models.

BELOW: *Singapore Airlines 747-412 (Jeremy Flack/ API)*

Singapore Airlines/SIA

A massive order for 77 aircraft was placed in November 1995 which included 61 777s. The balance of 16 aircraft was for the Singapore Aircraft Leasing Enterprise (SALE) - its leasing associate.

SIA acquired a 49% stake in Virgin Atlantic in December 1999 and 25% of Air New Zealand in April 2000.

In October 2000, an SIA 747 was involved in an accident when it attempted to take-off on the wrong runway and struck runway maintenance equipment. The aircraft exploded killing 83 passengers.

In February 2001, SIA announced a firm order for 20 777s plus options on a further

10. These aircraft will be used to replace existing A310s as well as providing additional capacity following the planned delivery between 2003 and 2009.

As the competition for the more lucrative business class increased, SIA introduced what it claimed to be the longest business class bed, measuring 1.98m long and 0.69m wide. This was part of a revamp programme to its Raffles Class.

SIA had been showing an interest in making a bid for Air-India which was moving towards privatisation. However, after receiving hostile opposition from various quarters it decided not to proceed and gave its

ABOVE: *Singapore Airlines 777-212ER (Singapore Airlines)*

attention to troubled Air New Zealand.

More recently, reports show SIA to be interested in reviving Ansett to provide a domestic Australian service that would compete with Qantas.

A new route, that was inaugurated towards the end of 2002, was Hong Kong to Las Vegas. Using a 777, this is one of the world's longest routes.

SIA will become the first operator of the Airbus A380 when it enters service around 2006.

SkyEurope Airlines

Registered name: SkyEurope Airlines as
Country: Slovakia
Region: Europe
Address: Ivansk cesta 26
               PO Box 24, 820 01 Bratislava 21
Tel: 00421 2 48 50 11 11
Fax: 00421 2 48 50 10 00
Web site: www.skyeurope.com
Main operational base: Bratislava

STATUS
Low-cost regional carrier
National Flag Carrier
Employees: 82
ICAO code: ESK
IATA code: NE

SERVICES
Regional / Domestic / Passenger
Cargo
International routes: Croatia, Czech, Germany, Italy, Switzerland

FLEET
EMB-120ER Brasilia - 2, 737-300 - 1
On order: EMB-120ER Brasilia - 4

SkyEurope Airlines was formed on September 6th, 2001, by Christian Mandl as the first low-cost airline in central Europe.

Mandl, who was an investment consultant in Bratislava, had noticed the impact that Ryanair and easyJet were having on the industry and decided that he could take it one step further by taking advantage of the

lower overheads in Slovakia. Equipped with a pair of the Brazilian-built 30-seat Brasilia regional airliners, a pricing strategy has been developed enabling competitive prices with trains and coaches and considerably cheaper than other airlines.

Bratislava Airport is only 50km from Vienna and SkyEurope tickets cost around one third of standard fares - these can be further reduced by 50% by purchasing the ticket a couple of weeks in advance. As a result it is hoped that a substantial portion of the 12 million passengers that use Vienna Airport can be attracted to the low-cost carrier. In one survey carried out for Bratislava Airport it was discovered that some 600,000 of the passengers using Vienna Airport were actually Slovaks!

SkyEurope commenced a domestic service in February 2002 shortly followed by international routes to various destinations in Europe. Additional routes to Venice, Zadar and Split were operated in 2002 as a 'summer service'. This will be repeated in 2003 together with Dubrovnik.

Such is the success of SkyEurope that, in the first seven months, they carried 30,900 passengers and accounted for almost 50% share of the scheduled market. In that short time it has established itself as a major player within Slovakia.

With the arrival of its 737s further expan-

ABOVE: *SkyEurope EMB-120RT, OM-SKY (C/n 175) Sky Europe)*

sion of the routes are planned to include London, Paris, Brussels and Amsterdam.

SN Brussels Airlines

Registered name: SN Brussels Airlines
Country: Belgium
Region: Europe
Address: The Corporate Village
Da Vincilaan 9
B-1930 Zaventem
Tel: 0032 2 754 19 00
Fax: 0032 2 754 19 99
Web site: www.brussels-airlines.com
Stockholder: SN Airholding NV
Main operational base: Brussels

STATUS

Scheduled and charter carrier
Employees: 1,031
Passengers per year: 3,300,000 (2000)
ICAO code: DAT
IATA code: QG

SERVICES

International / Regional / Passenger

International routes: Angola, Austria, Belgium, Cameroon, Congo Dem Rep, Denmark, Gambia, Germany, Guinea, Finland, France, Italy, Kenya, Liberia, Norway, Poland, Rwanda, Senegal, Spain, Sweden, Switzerland, Uganda, UK

ALLIANCES/CODE SHARES

BA, Finnair, VLM A/1

FLEET

A319 - 3, A330-300 - 3, BAe 146-200 - 6, RJ85 - 14, RJ100 - 12

SN Brussels Airlines was originally formed in 1966 as Delta Air Transport NV. It commenced operations with some light aircraft and DC-3s as an air taxi and charter service.

As it became established, it began operating scheduled services from its bases at Antwerp and Brussels to Amsterdam.

In 1970 DAT was acquired by the Compagnie Maritime Belge.

By 1977 DAT had become an all Friendship operator with four ex-Ozark US Fairchild built variants of the Fokker F-27 and later a F-28 Fellowship was added.

SABENA took a 49% stake in DAT in 1990 along with KLM who took 33%

Following the bankruptcy of SABENA in 2001, which had become the 100% owner of DAT by then, the airline was relinquished by the administrators as DAT Plus and acquired by SN Airholding NV.

In February 2002 DAT was re-named SN Brussels Airlines and re-launched with some of the old SABENA routes.

While needing to move ahead, the new airline retains some of its ancestry with the SABENA 'S' retained on the tail and the 'SN' being the old SABENA / DAT IATA code. The 'Brussels' immediately identifies its base.

South African Airways/SAA

Registered name: South African Airways (Pty) Ltd
Country: South Africa
Region: Africa
Address: Airways Park
Jones Road, Private Bag X13
Johannesburg International Airport
1627
Tel: 0027 11 978 11 27
Fax: 0027 11 978 11 26
Web site: www.saa.co.za
Main operational base: Johannesburg

STATUS

IATA scheduled international carrier
National Flag Carrier
Employees: 10,310
Passengers per year: 6,100,000 (2001)
ICAO code: SAA
IATA code: SA

SERVICES

International / Regional / Domestic
Passenger / Cargo
International routes: Angola, Brazil, Cape
Verde, China, Comoro Islands, Congo
Democratic Republic, Cote D'Ivoire,
France, Germany, Ghana, India, Israel,
Kenya, Malawi, Mauritius, Mozambique,
Namibia, Nigeria, Rwanda, Switzerland,
Tanzania, Thailand, Uganda, UK, USA,
Zambia, Zimbabwe

ALLIANCES/CODE SHARES

Air France, BMI, Cathay Pacific, Delta A/l,
El Al, Emirates, Ghana Aw, Lufthansa,
Nigeria Aw, Qantas, South African Express
Aw, Thai Int Aw, VARIG

FLEET

A330-200 - 2 (on lease from BMI), A340-
600 - 3, 737-200F - 2, 737-200 Adv - 17, 737-
800 -14, 747-200B - 5, 747-300 - 6, 747-400 -
8, 747SP - 2, 767-200ER- 2
On Order: A319 - 11 (to replace 737-200s),
A320 - 15 (to replace 737-800s), A340-300 -
6, A340-600 - 6

South African Airways (SAA) was formed
on February 1st, 1934 when the government took over the assets and liabilities of

the private airline - Union Airways (formed
1929). Initial domestic operations were
operated using Junkers F.13s and W.34s.
These were later augmented with Ju-52s
and later by Ju-86s.

South West African Airways (formed in
1932), which had already established routes
to Kenya and Uganda, was acquired in
February 1935.

The first international SAA route was
flown to the UK in November 1945. Known
as the Springbok service, it used an Avro
York in co-operation with BOAC and was
later replaced by a DC-4.

Over the next few years a number of
other aircraft types were operated including Constellation DC-3s, Doves, Lodestars
and Vikings.

Jet operations commenced with a Comet
I leased from BOAC in 1953. When fatigue
problems were discovered in the Comet,
the service returned to Constellations
which were replaced with DC-7s in 1956.

The Vickers Viscount entered service in
November 1958 for domestic and regional
service and the 707 was used for SAA for
services to various European routes from
1960 including London. In 1962 they
began to be operated as non-stop schedules.

The 727s arrived in 1965 for domestic
and regional operations along with the
Viscounts and the 747s introduced wide

ABOVE: *South African Airways A320-231 (Airbus)*

body operations from December 1971.

A new route to the Far East was established when Hong Kong was inaugurated in
1973. The USA was added to the SAA network in December 1982 when a 747SP flew
to Houston.

The imposition of sanctions against
South Africa during the 1980s for its policy
of apartheid meant the suspension of many
international routes.

The USA was returned to the SAA network in November 1991 when New York
flights were re-introduced following suspension in November 1986. Australia followed
in January 1992.

In November 1999, Swissair took a 20%
stake in SAA from Transnet with a value of
R1, 4 billion.

In April 1990, SAA announced an undertaking to donate a portion of the revenue
from every international ticket sale to the
SAA's African Wildlife Heritage Trust to
help boost endangered wildlife.

An order for 21 737NGs was placed in
February 2000.

The demise of Swissair with its 20% stake
caused SAA problems when the SAir Group
was forced to sell all of its interests as part of
the debt recovery. As a result, Transnet - the
state holding company, bought the state

85% of the shares value. Following the depressed market after September 11th it was felt that another buyer would be unlikely and serious financial damage could be inflicted on SAA. The resulting renationalisation of SAA was against the government's privatisation strategy but it was felt that there was little alternative.

The events of September 11th caused SAA to reduce its US service and reduce a substantial portion of the managerial structure amongst other cost-saving measures. Despite a significant drop in passenger levels it benefited from the Rand / Dollar exchange rate and SAA was managed a profit.

At the end of 2001, SAA were discussing the merger of South African Express Airways - owned by Transnet - and South African Airlink of which SAA already owned 10%.

SAA announced a large order with Airbus in February 2002 for a new fleet of aircraft. Potentially worth US$3.5 billion, the order was for the lease or purchase of 11 A319s, 15 A320s, 12 A340s with deliveries spread from 2002 through to 2011. These will replace the older 747s, 767s and 737s including the 737-800s which had only been ordered the previous year.

SAA withdrew from the joint venture Johannesburg - Lagos - New York route in

March 2002 due to substantial losses being incurred with falling passenger levels after only one year of operation. Subsequent discussions were on going for a resumption of this route.

In October 2002, the Tanzanian Government approved the SAA bid of US$20 million for a 49% stake in Air Tanzania - SAAs first acquisition outside of South Africa. This would be used to provide an East African hub as part of its network strategy.

SAA concluded an agreement with Air Sénégal for a joint venture service to New York and the first service commenced at the beginning of 2003.

Southwest Airlines

Registered name: Southwest Airlines Co

Country: USA

Region: North America

Address: 2702 Love Field Drive
PO Box 36611
Dallas, Texas 75235-1611

Tel: 001 214 792 42 00

Fax: 001 214 792 42 11

Web site: www.southwest.com

Main operational base: Dallas - Forth Worth

STATUS

Scheduled domestic carrier

Employees: 34,000

Passengers per year: 64,447,000 (2001)

ICAO code: SWA

IATA code: WN

SERVICES

Regional / Domestic / Passenger
Cargo

International routes: Domestic only

FLEET

737-200 - 27, 737-300 - 194, 737-500 - 25, 737-700 -124

On order: 737-700 - 116

Originally formed as Air Southwest in 1967, Southwest Airlines was renamed and commenced operations on 18th June 1971 with 737s operating between Dallas, Houston and San Antonio.

Being the first low-fare airline proved difficult with legal battles from the established airlines. As business grew, a fourth new 737 was purchased in the September. To make best use of this capacity it had been decided to offer out-of-state charter flights. However, a legal challenge was successfully awarded against Southwest Airlines denying it the rights to operate charters outside Texas. Without this income it was impossi-

ble to operate the new 737 as so it had to be sold.

The loss of this 737 created problems for the scheduled operation which was already stretched. As a result a huge effort was made by the staff team to turn around the flights in just ten minutes. As a result the airline managed to pull through that difficult period and has since grown from strength to strength while a number of the less efficient competitors of the time have fallen by the wayside.

Routes were added as well as the RUSH Cargo service and by 1974 the 1 millionth passenger had been carried. Routes contin-

RIGHT: *Southwest Airlines 737-2H4, N102SW (C/n 23108) (Jeremy Flack/API)*

Southwest Airlines

ued to be added to various locations around Texas.

By 1976 Southwest had taken delivery of its sixth 737, it then carried the 5 millionth passenger the following year and was listed on the New York Stock Exchange.

Despite the early difficulties, by 1980 Southwest had taken delivery of its 22nd 737 but it wasn't stopping there. By concentrat-

ing on customer service and making the whole experience fun plus keeping fares low, passenger numbers have continued to grow at an impressive rate. In May 1988 Southwest became the first airline to win the Triple Crown for a month. For this they had to achieve best on-time record, best baggage handling and fewest customer complaints. Not only has it won this on numerous other

occasions, it also won the annual Triple Crown five times during the 1990s.

Southwest Airlines now reaches some 60 destinations across the southwest USA and operates a fleet of 355 737s. With passenger levels in excess of 64 million per year Southwest has become the fourth largest US airline and it is the only major US airline to be operating with a profit.

Spanair

**S
P
A
N
A
I
R**

Registered name: Spanair
Country: Spain
Region: Europe
Address: Palma de Mallorca Airport
PO Box 50086
Palma de Mallorca
E-07000
Tel: 0034 971 74 50 20
Fax: 0034 971 49 25 53
Web site: www.spanair.com
Main operational base: Palma

STATUS

Scheduled and charter passenger + cargo carrier
Employees: 3,200
Passengers per year: 8,128,000 (2001)
ICAO code: JKK
IATA code: JK

SERVICES

International / Regional / Domestic Passenger / Charter / Cargo
International routes: Denmark, Equatorial Guinea, France, Germany, Italy, Portugal, Spain, Sweden

ALLIANCES/CODE SHARES

Air Canada, Austrian A/l, Cubana, Ecuatorial Guinea, Lufthansa, Portugalia, Regional A/l, SAS, United A/l, VARIG

FLEET

A320-200 - 6, A321-100 - 3, 717 - 4, MD-82 - 11, MD-83 - 23, MD-87 -3
On order: A320-200 - 26, A321-100 - 2, 717 -11
Spanair was formed in December 1986 although operations didn't start until March 1988.

It was run as a charter airline carrying passengers to and from the Canary Islands and Mallorca with leased MD-83s.

Some 767s were added to the fleet in 1992 enabling services to Cuba, Dominican Republic and Mexico.

Spanair commenced scheduled services in February 1994 within Spain. Afterwards, it gradually added European routes.

Intercontinental scheduled services to North and South America commenced, with 767s, to Washington-Dulles. This was followed by Madrid to São Paulo, Rio de Janeiro, Buenos Aires and Havana.

Spanair was not particularly hit by the events of September 11th. This may well be due to new agreements with Austrian

BELOW: *Spanair A320-232, EC-HRP (C/n 1349) with Airbus test registration F-WWBD (Airbus)*

Airlines and Portugalia that helped keep the passenger numbers increasing although the cargo operation was down.

While intercontinental services were suspended in March 2002 more new code-share agreements were signed with Air Canada and Aerolineas Argentinas.

Currently, Spanair operations are split roughly 74% scheduled and 26% charter.

RIGHT: *Spanair MD-83, EC-FTS (C/n 49621) (Jane's)*

SriLankan Airlines

Registered name: SriLankan Airlines
Country: Sri Lanka
Region: Asia
Address: 22-01 East Tower
World Trade Center
Echelon Square
Colombo 1
Tel: 0094 73 16 17
Fax: 0094 73 56 12
Web site: www.srilankan.lk
Main operational base: Katunayake (Colombo)

STATUS

IATA scheduled international passenger carrier
National Flag Carrier
Employees: 4,112
Passengers per year: 1,719,000 (2001)
ICAO code: ALK
IATA code: UL

SERVICES

International / Regional
Passenger / Charter / Cargo
International routes: Bahrain, China, France, Germany, India, Indonesia, Japan, Jordan, Kuwait, Malaysia, Maldives, Oman, Saudi Arabia, Singapore, Switzerland, Thailand, UAE, UK

ALLIANCES/CODE SHARES

Emirates, Indian A/l, Malaysia A/l, Oman Air, Royal Jordanian, Swiss

FLEET

A320-200 - 1, A330-200 - 4, A340-300 - 3

SriLankan Airlines was originally formed as Sri Lanka International Airlines on January 10th, 1979, by the government to succeed Air Ceylon (formed 1948). However, the name was changed to Air Lanka before operations commenced.

Operations commenced in September 1979 with two leased 707s from Singapore Airlines which also provides managerial and technical assistance. These were joined by a leased 737 a couple of months later.

New routes were quickly established, not only to major destinations in Asia, but through the Middle East and Europe.

The first of a number of Lockheed Tristars arrived in August 1982 followed by 747s in June 1984.

Air Lanka underwent a restructuring in 1998 that resulted in the name being changed to SriLankan Airlines the following year. This was part of the government's plan to move the airline towards privatisation.

In July 2001, SriLankan Airlines suffered a major blow when terrorists attacked Katunayake airport and destroyed four of its 12 Airbus airliners and damaged a further two.

As a result of the threat, SriLankan Airlines commenced services operating direct to the Maldives from various points including London, Tokyo and Zurich thus avoiding the trouble spot. This was appreciated by the Government of Maldives who rely heavily on tourism for the islands economy especially as Air Maldives had ceased operating.

BELOW: *SriLankan Airlines A330-243, 4R - ALA (C/n 303) with Airbus test registration F-WWYH (Airbus)*

Sudan Airways

ABOVE: *Sudan Airways A30B4-622R, F-OIHA (C/n 530) with Airbus test registration F-WHPI) (Airbus)*

Registered name: Sudan Airways
Country: Sudan
Region: Africa
Address: 4th Floor, SDC Building No 3
New Extension Street 19
PO Box 253
Khartoum
Tel: 00249 11 47 24 51
Fax: 00249 11 47 23 77
Web site: www.sudanair.com
Main operational base: Khartoum

STATUS

IATA scheduled passenger + cargo carrier
National Flag Carrier
Employees: 1,784
Passengers per year: 431,000 (2001)
ICAO code: SUD
IATA code: SD

SERVICES

International / Regional / Domestic
Passenger / Charter / Cargo
International routes: Central African
Republic, Chad, Egypt, Jordan, Kenya,
Nigeria, Oman, Saudi Arabia, Syria, Turkey,
UAE, UK, Yemen

ALLIANCES/CODE SHARES

Royal Jordanian

FLEET

A300-600R - 3, 707-300C - 3, 737-200 - 2,
F-27 - 1, Il-18 - 2, Yak-42D - 1

Sudan Airways was formed in 1946 by the
Sudanese Government with assistance from
Airwork. Operations commenced in July
1947 with a pair of de Havilland Doves.
Early aircraft also included a number of
DC-3s.

A Vickers Viscount was delivered in June
1959 and used to operate international
routes, including London.

The first F-27 Friendships arrived in
January 1962 and were followed by the
Comet 4. In June 1974 a pair of 707s
replaced the Comets.

In 1983, the President decided to sell
Sudan Airways and dismissed the management. With no interested takers, proposals
were made to rename the airline Nile Air.
However, before this happened the
President was deposed and his successor
reinstated the airline.

The arrival of the A310s in the early
1990s replaced the 707s in the passenger
role although some still remain as
freighters.

In 1994 a Special Flights Services Unit
was established with two King Airs and an F-
27 to provide charter flights as well as an air
ambulance service.

With the discovery of oil and mineral
deposits there is the potential for a healthy
airline operation with some investment.
Although government owned, no investment has come from that direction for
many years due to fighting. What cash is
raised is used to make payments on the
country's massive debts. Steps are in hand
to move Sudan Airways towards privatisation which it sees as the best way for the airline to develop.

Surinam Airways

Registered name: Surinaamse Luchtvaart Maatschappij
Country: Surinam
Region: South America
Address: PO Box 2029
Coppenamestraat 136
Paramaribo
Tel: 00597 46 57 00
Fax: 00597 49 12 13
Web site: www.slm.firm.sr
Main operational base: Paramaribo

STATUS

Scheduled and charter carrier
National Flag Carrier
Employees: 567
Passengers per year: 236,000 (2001)
ICAO code: SLM
IATA code: PY

SERVICES

International / Regional / Domestic
Passenger / Charter / Cargo
International routes: Aruba, Barbados, Brazil, French Guiana, Netherlands, Netherlands Antilles, Surinam, Trinidad & Tobago, USA

ALLIANCES/CODE SHARES

Air ALM, KLM

FLEET

DHC-6 Twin Otter 300 - 2, DHC-8 Dash 8-300 - 1, MD-87 - 1

The origins of Surinam Airways can be traced back to 1955 when the Surinamse government decided to provide a domestic service with light aircraft.

On August 20th, 1962 Surinaamese Luchtvaart Maatschappij (SLM) was formed. Bell 47G helicopters were acquired for agricultural use and were even chartered for spraying in Guyana.

DHC-6 Twin Otters were operated to provide a domestic scheduled service. So successful were they that two of the newer models remain currently in service.

In 1964 SLM entered into a pool agreement with KLM and Antillean Airlines (ALM) to operate a route between Paramaribo, Surinam and Curacao, Netherlands Antilles via Georgetown, Guyana and Port of Spain, Trinidad & Tobago.

When ALM became an independent airline, KLM withdrew from the agreement but the other two continued. Initially, SLM just provided the cabin crew and managed marketing in Guyana. Later, some flights were crewed by SLM.

In 1975, at the same time as the independence of Suriname, SLM leased a DC-8 from KLM. This enabled the airline to be able to operate routes that rapidly increased in number stretching as far as Miami.

In 1993 a transatlantic route was established to Amsterdam as a joint venture with KLM.

SLM continues to maintain its co-operation agreement and operates routes to Curacao and Miami together.

Swiss

Registered name: Swiss International Air Lines Ltd
Country: Switzerland
Region: Europe
Address: PO Box
CH-4002 Basel
Tel: 0041 61 582 00 00
Fax: 0041 61 582 35 54
Web site: www.swiss.com
Main operational base: Zurich

STATUS

IATA scheduled passenger and cargo carrier
National Flag Carrier
Employees: 11,400
Passengers per year: 11,600,000 (2002)
ICAO code: CRX
IATA code: LX

SERVICES

International / Regional / Domestic
Passenger / Charter / Cargo
International routes: Albania, Argentina, Austria, Belgium, Bosnia Herzegovina, Brazil, Bulgaria, Cameroon, Canada, China, Croatia, Czech, Denmark, Egypt, Equatorial Guinea, Finland, France, Gabon, Germany, Ghana, Greece, Hungary, Pakistan, Iran, Ireland, Israel, Italy, Japan, Kenya, Kosovo, Libya, Luxembourg, Macedonia, Morocco,

RIGHT: *Swiss A320-214, HB-IJP (C/n (681) (Airbus)*

Swiss

Netherlands, Nigeria, Norway, Oman, Pakistan, Philippines, Poland, Portugal, Romania, Russia, Saudi Arabia, Serbia, Singapore, Slovenia, South Africa, Spain, Sweden, Tanzania, Thailand, Tunisia, Turkey, UAE, UK, Ukraine, USA

ALLIANCES / CODE SHARES

Air France, Air-India, American A/l, BA, Finnair, Malev, Tunisair

SUBSIDIARY A/L

Loganair

FLEET

A319-100 - 7, A320-200 - 11, A321-100 - 8, A330-200 - 13, RJ100 - 15, RJ85 - 4, ERJ-145 - 25, MD-11 - 12 (to be replaced by A340-300), MD-83 - 8, Saab 2000 - 28

On order: A320-200 - 4 for delivery 2003 - 2004, A340-300 - 12 for delivery 6/2003 - 8/2004, ERJ-170 - 30 for deliver from autumn 2003, ERJ-190-200 - 30 for delivery from early 2004, ERJ-170 / 190 - 100 options

Swiss was initially formed as Swiss Air by the renaming of Crossair as the new national airline of Switzerland on March 31st, 2002. This followed the bankruptcy of Swissair (formed 1931).

Due to objections from the Swissair Group administrator and to avoid any legal problems, it was announced in April 2002 that the airline name would change from the planned Swiss Air Lines Ltd to Swiss International Air Lines Ltd.

Crossair was originally formed as Business-Flyers Basel Ltd on February 14th, 1975, as an air taxi and charter carrier using various small light aircraft - mainly Cessnas.

The name was changed to Crossair on November 14th, 1978 and in July 1979 it commenced scheduled operations with Swearingen Metroliners.

The light aircraft were disposed of as a fleet of SAAB 340s began delivery in 1984 for scheduled services. Crossair was the launch customer for this new Swedish twin-engined turboprop 30-seat airliner.

As the business developed, it was seen by the national airline - Swissair - that Crossair was providing an increasing amount of business for it. Many of the Crossair passengers were using the small airline as a feeder to catch Swissair flights. As a result, Swissair acquired a 69% stake in the airline and handed over its MD-80 fleet to Crossair to operate its regional services.

Fokker 50s were added to the fleet in 1990 followed by a total of 26 RJ85 / RJ100s. Crossair was the launch customer for the SAAB 2000 that was developed from the 340. First deliveries commenced in 1994.

Crossair performance continued to grow and in 1997 4.7 million passengers were carried.

During 1999, Crossair announced that it would replace the entire 340 / 2000 and RJ85 / 100 fleet with a range of Embraer aircraft.

Sadly, in January 2000, Crossair lost one of its 340s with all 10 on board following what was thought to be crew disorientation during landing approach at night. An RJ100 was also lost in November 2001 with 24 of the 33 on board killed, the survivors all being in the tail section that broke off. Mobile phone use during flight was men-

RIGHT: *Swiss A321-111, HB-IOC (C/n 520) (Jeremy Flack/API)*

tioned as a possible contributing factor in both accidents.

In December 2000 plans were announced to replace the MD82 / 83s with A320s.

The Swissair fleet was grounded on October 2nd, 2001, due to having insufficient funds even to pay for fuel. This sent shock waves through the whole Swiss population. The Swiss Government arranged sufficient finance to keep the airline to the end of the month to enable stranded passengers to return home. Such was the country's resolve that through a referendum, together with local and national government and private industry support, an urgent plan was put together.

In the meantime Crossair maintained some of the Swissair routes. Two Swiss banks agreed to invest the necessary funds (SF258.8 million) to enable Crossair to acquire the SAir Group 70.4% stockholding

in Crossair and enable it to remain a successful airline rather than being pulled under with the sinking SAir Group.

In an apparent leadership disagreement with the steering committee, the entire board of Crossair resigned in December 2001.

In March 2002, Swiss announced that it had suffered a loss of SF 314 million of which it attributed SF 290 million to the collapse of Swissair. However, in the last quarter of its operation as Crossair, passenger

levels had increased by 66.6% over the previous year with March 2002 achieving 79.3% increase.

On 31st March, 2002, the name of Crossair was replaced by Swiss.

In November 2002, Swiss announced that despite the earlier passenger figures, it had lost SF 583 million in the first nine months. As a result 300 air and ground crew jobs were cut although 200 technical and IT staff were being sought. Some routes were suspended along with the grounding of eight aircraft.

Syrianair

Registered name: Syrian Arab Airlines
Country: Syria
Region: Middle East
Address: Youssef Al-azmeh Square
PO Box 417
Damascus
Tel: 00963 11 223 31 74 ext 167
Fax: 00963 11 221 49 23
Web site: www.syriaonline.com/syrair/
Main operational base: Damascus

ABOVE: *Syrian A320-232, YK-AKF (C/n 1117) with Airbus test registration F-WWBN (Airbus)*

STATUS

IATA scheduled carrier
National Flag Carrier
Employees: 5,264
Passengers per year: 761,000 (2001)
ICAO code: SYR
IATA code: RB

SERVICES

International / Regional / Domestic

Passenger / Cargo
International routes: Algeria, Armenia, Austria, Bahrain, Bulgaria, Cyprus, Egypt, France, Germany, Hungary, India, Iran,

Italy, Kuwait, Lebanon, Libya, Morocco, Netherlands, Oman, Pakistan, Romania, Russia, Saudi Arabia, Spain, Sudan, Sweden, Tunisia, Turkey, UAE, UK, Yemen

Syrianair

ALLIANCES / CODE SHARES

Cyprus Aw, Iberia, Royal Jordanian

FLEET

A320-200 - 6, An-24 - 1, An-26 - 5, 727-200Adv - 6, 747SP - 2, Il-76M - 4, Tu-134B-3 - 4, Tu-154M - 1, Yak-40 - 6

The origins of Syrian Arab Airlines date back to December 21st, 1946, when Syrian Airways was formed. Aircraft operated included DC-3s, DC-4s and DC-6s.

Syria became a member of the United Arab Airlines in 1958 and incorporated its airline operation. Due to the turbulent political situation in various parts of the Middle East the association was terminated and the Syrian element withdrawn to form Syrian Arab Airlines in 1961 and continued operating the DC-4s and DC-6s as a domestic airline with some services to neighbouring Middle Eastern countries.

In 1963 the route network was expanded to include Athens, Munich and Rome. The Caravelle took the Syrian airline into the jet age with the first delivery in June 1966 and two more in 1971 which enabled the network to develop further.

Two 747SPs were delivered in 1976 along with a pair of 727s. The following year the airline took on a new image with the name Syrianair painted on its aircraft.

Tu-154s began to partially replace the Tu-134s during the 1980s.

The newest aircraft to join the Syrianair fleet was the A320 and the last of the six ordered was received at the end of 1999. This enabled new routes to be established to Beirut, Marseilles, Vienna as well as Yerevan.

TAAG - Angola Airlines

Registered name: Linhas Aereas de Angola
Country: Angola
Region: Africa
Address: Rua Da Missao 123
             PO Box 79, Luanda
Tel: 00244 2 33 09 64/7
Fax: 00244 2 39 22 29
Web site: www.taag-airlines.com
Main operational base: Luanda

Passengers per year: 193,000 (2001)
ICAO code: DTA
IATA code: DT

SERVICES

International / Regional / Domestic Passenger / Charter / Cargo
International routes: Brazil, Cape Verde, Congo, Cuba, Democratic Republic of Congo, France, Mozambique, Namibia, Portugal, Sao Tome & Principe, South Africa, Zambia, Zimbabwe

ALLIANCES / CODE SHARES

Air France, Air Namibia

OWNED SUBSIDIARY AIRLINES

Angola Air Cargo, Sociedade De Aviaçáo Ligeira

FLEET

An-26 - 4 (operated by Angola Air Cargo), 727 - 3 (operated by Angola Air Cargo), 737-200 - 5, 747-300 (SCD) - 1, F-27 Mk.200 - 1, F-27 Mk.400 - 1, F-27 Mk.500 - 1, F-27 Mk.600 - 2, Il-62M - 1, Il-76 - 2 (operated by Angola Air Cargo)

TAAG - Angola Airlines was originally formed in September 1938 as the Divisão de Exploração dos Transportes Aéreos de

STATUS

IATA scheduled passenger carrier
National Flag Carrier
Employees: 4,553

Angola (DTA) and commenced operations with three de Havilland Dragon Rapides.

DTA commenced operating scheduled services in 1940 with the Dragon Rapides together with Leopard Moth and a Klemm. In 1948 a DC-3 joined the fleet.

DTA underwent a partial privatisation in 1973 with TAP taking a 30% stake and the title changed to TAAG - Angola Airlines. The first of a fleet of F-27 Friendships were delivered and used to established domestic and regional services.

Following the independence of Angola in November 1975, TAAG was nationalised and returned to state control as the national flag carrier. Discussions with TAP resulted in a jointly operated Luanda - Lisbon service with a TAP 747 and partly manned with TAAG cabin crew.

TAAG entered the jet age proper with the delivery of its own 737 in March 1976 followed by its first 707 in October 1977. As more of these aircraft were delivered TAAG services rapidly expanded. Domestic passenger figures for 1977 were 230,000. This rose to 795,947 for the following year and by 1986 it broke the million mark for the first time.

Angola had been the scene of conflict since the early 1960s but during the mid-1980s the situation was such that the fighting between the MPLA, FNLA and UNITA made it extremely difficult to travel by road or rail. As a result TAAG found it almost impossible to keep up with demand for air travel that was mostly operating at nearly 100% load. This was despite the fact that a TAAG Yak-40 was shot down in June 1980 and a 737 in November 1983.

Two TAAG subsidiaries were formed in 1991. Sociedade De Aviação Ligeira to provide an air taxi and a crop spraying service as well as general aviation and Anglo Air Charter.

A new route to Harare was launched in 1993 which was followed by one to Johannesburg the next year. In 1995 the schedule to Lusaka was restored.

In July 1997, TAAG took delivery of the first of a pair of 747s which was named 'Cidade do Kuito' in memory of the massacred people of that city. In November the Paris service returned to the schedule.

Tajikistan Airlines

Registered name: Tajikistan Airlines
Country: Tajikistan
Region: Asia
Address: 31/2 Titov St
Dushanbe Airport
734006
Tel: 007 992 372 21 22 47
Fax: 007 992 372 51 00 41
Web site: www.tajikistanairlines.com
Main operational base: Dushanbe

STATUS
Scheduled and charter carrier
National Flag Carrier
Employees: 1,655
Passengers per year: 289,000 (2001)
ICAO code: TZK
IATA code: 7J

SERVICES
International / Regional / Domestic
Passenger / Charter / Cargo
International routes: France, Germany, India, Iran, Kyrgyzstan, Pakistan, Russia, Saudi Arabia, Thailand, Turkey, Turkmenistan, UAE, UK, USA

FLEET
An-24 -1, An-26 - 1, Tu-134 - 4, Tu-154B, Tu-154M, Yak-40 - 6

The origins of Tajikistan Airlines date back to 1924 with the formation of Bukhara-Dushanbe Airline that commenced operations on September 3rd with a Junkers F-13.

Middle Asia Airways was formed in 1930. Crop spraying and aerial photography services were undertaken in addition to the scheduled operations. The first five-seat Stal-2 was delivered in June 1933.

The Tajik Territorial Civil Air Fleet Department (TCAFD) was formed in 1940 as part of Aeroflot.

With the war over, ex-military Ju-52s and Li-2s were added to the fleet in 1945. New aircraft arrived in December 1950 in the form of the An-2 which entered service the following spring.

The first Ilyushin Il-12 arrived in 1954 followed by the Il-14 in 1956. The supercharged An-6 variant of the An-2 was delivered in 1958 to provide a better performance at the higher altitudes and in 1960 the first of the turboprop Il-18s were delivered.

A Mil Mi-4 was delivered in 1964 and on completion of crew training a mountain rescue service was formed. In 1968 more crew training was undertaken. This training was for the An-24 which was capable of carrying cargo or passengers, and in August the first one was delivered. Operations commenced in November followed by the Yak-40 in 1969.

The Tu-134 jet airliner entered service in 1974 and followed by the larger Tu-154 in 1978. The first An-26 was delivered in 1979. During the year Il-18s were used to fly a humanitarian mission to Afghanistan.

Following the breakdown of the Soviet Union, and the splitting up of the Aeroflot Divisions, the TCAFD was formed into the Dushanbe Airline in 1988. In 1990 preparations were made to receive its first Il-76 transport while the improved Tu-154M was delivered the following year.

Tajik Air was formed on March 1st, 1992 with a single aircraft leased from the United Airlines but failed after only a few months due to lack of financial support.

Tajikistan Airlines was formed in 1995 as a joint venture with TAP to replace Tajik Air. Services commenced to Afghanistan, Germany, India and Pakistan in 1995 followed by China, Saudi Arabia and Turkey in 1996.

TAM/Transportes Aéreos Meridionais

Registered name: TAM Linhas Aéreas SA
Country: Brazil
Region: South America
Address: Rua Monsenhor Antonio Pepe
94 Jardim Aeroporto
Sao Paulo
04357-08
Tel: 0055 11 55 82 88 11
Fax: 0055 11 578 59 46
Web site: www.tam.com.br
Stockholder: TAM Holding
Main operational base: Sao Paulo

STATUS

Scheduled international and domestic carrier
Employees: 4,118
Passengers per year: 13,030,000 (2001)
ICAO code: TAM
IATA code: KK

SERVICES

International / Regional / Domestic
Passenger / Charter / Cargo
International routes: France*, Germany*, Paraguay, Spain*, USA (*Code shares)

ALLIANCES / CODE SHARES

Air France, American A/l, Iberia, Lufthansa

OWNED SUBSIDIARY AIRLINES

TAM Express, TAM Mercosur

FLEET

A319-100 - 13, A320-200 - 34, A330-200 - 10, 208A Caravan 1 - 6 (operated by TAM Express), 208B Grand Caravan - 32 (operated by TAM Express), 550 Citation Ultra - 5, F-27 Mk.500 - 3, Fokker 50 - 9, Fokker 100 - 42
On Order: A319-100 - 5, A330-200 - 3

The origins of TAM (Transportes Aéreos Meridionais) lay with the establishment of the Táxi Aéreo Maríla (TAM) on February 7th, 1961. It was formed by a number of individual pilots initially operating a Cessna Skyhawk. A number of small single and twin-engined aircraft were added to carry passengers and cargo between the north and south of Brazil.

TAM-Transportes Aéreos Regionais was established as an airline jointly with VASP and Táxi Aéreo Maríla on May 12th, 1976 and commenced operations in July as a domestic carrier. EMB-110 Bandeirantes had been acquired to provide the main fleet although a variety of other aircraft continued to be operated from the original TAM fleet.

TAM accepted delivery of its first F-27 Friendship in 1979 and this commenced a long association with the Fokker airliners.

Votec - a domestic airline formed in 1966 and operating in the northern and central west regions of Brazil - was acquired in 1986. It was initially renamed Brasil Central but later that year became TAM Meridional following some route expansion.

TAM entered the jet age with the delivery of the Fokker F-28 Fellowship in September 1990.

TAM Linhas Aéreas acquired LAPSA Air Paraguay in 1996 which was renamed TAM Mercosur. It acted as a subsidiary to operate South American services from Asuncion, Paraguay, and later expanded into USA and Europe.

BELOW: *TAM A320-232, PT-MZG (C/n 1143) with Airbus test registration F-WWBG (Airbus)*

ABOVE: *TAM A330-223, PT-MVE (C/n 361) (Airbus)*

TAM ordered five A330s in October 1997 together with options for a further five. The delivery of the first A330 at the end of 1998 enabled them to commence a new route to Miami that was followed by an expansion of services into Europe. These commenced with code-shared scheduled services to Paris with Air France followed by Frankfurt via Zurich with Lufthansa.

During the late 1990s, the airline invested in establishing the TAM Ticketless travel system which helped to speed up the booking in of passengers.

TAM Linhas Aéreas was formed following the absorption of TAM Transportes Aéreos Regionais S.A. into TAM Transportes Aéreos Meridionais S.A.

Passenger service has always been the priority for TAM. A red carpet is laid out for the passengers walking out to the aircraft where the captain waits to greet them. The red carpet has become an important image for the airline and the aircraft colours are now all red to carry this image through.

The passenger numbers dropped below an economic level on some routes following the events of September 11th and a number of these were suspended in March 2002. While the overall passenger numbers have increased, the effects of its economics have not been so good due to the poor state of South American economies and a substantial amount of its business being in US dollars.

TAME / Linea Aerea del Ecuador

Registered name: Transportes Aereos Militares Ecuatorianas
Country: Ecuador
Region: South America
Address: PO Box 8736
              Avenue Amazonas 1354 y Colon
              Quito
Tel: 00593 2 50 93 92
Fax: 00593 2 50 95 94
Web site: www.tame.com.ec
Main operational base: Quito

STATUS

Scheduled and charter carrier
National Flag Carrier
Employees: 730
Passengers per year: 1,175,000 (2001)

ICAO code: TAE
IATA code: EQ

SERVICES

International / Regional / Domestic
Passenger / Charter / Cargo
International routes: Colombia, Cuba

FLEET

727-100 - 2, 727-200ADV - 5, F-28
Fellowship - 2

TAME was formed on December 17th, 1962, as an 'airline' within the Ecuadorian Air Force. Its role was to provide a civilian domestic air service to assist the development of the most remote cities where no commercial service existed.

A variety of aircraft has been operated by TAME including the DC-3, DC-6, Electra, HS748, DHC-7 Buffalo, DHC-6 Twin Otter, 727 and C-130 Hercules.

In 1992 TAME commenced international service with schedules to Cali in Colombia followed by Santiago in Chile and Panama City and Havana by 1996.

In January 2002 a TAME 727 was lost with all 92 passengers and crew when it flew into a volcano.

TAME currently carries about 3,000 passengers a day. It is hoping to be able to modernise its fleet before long and hopes to establish new alliances with other airlines to enable more international routes to be operated.

TAP Air Portugal

Registered name: TAP Air Portugal, S.A.
Country: Portugal
Region: Europe
Address: Aeroporto de Lisboa
                 Apartado 50194
                 P-1704-801 Lisbon Codex
Tel: 00351 21 841 50 00
Fax: 00351 21 841 57 74
Web site: www.tap.pt
Main operational base: Lisbon

STATUS

IATA scheduled passenger + cargo carrier
National Flag Carrier
Employees: 8.763
Passengers per year: 5,388,000 (2001)
ICAO code: TAP
IATA code: TP

SERVICES

International / Regional / Domestic
Passenger / Charter / Cargo
International routes: Angola, Belgium,
Brazil, Cape Verde, Cuba, Denmark,
France, Germany, Guinea-Bissau, Italy,
Luxembourg, Mozambique, Netherlands,
Sao Tome, Senegal, South Africa, Spain,
Sweden, Switzerland, UK, USA, Venezuela

ALLIANCES / CODE SHARES

American A/l, BMI, Finnair, Iberia, LAM,
Olympic, Portugalia, SATA Air Azores,
TACV

OWNED SUBSIDIARY AIRLINES

Air São Tomè, São Tomè Airlines

FLEET

A310-300 - 5, A319-100 - 16, A320-200 - 9,
A321-200 - 3, A340-300 - 4

Transportes Aéreos Portugueses (TAP) was
formed on March 14th, 1945, but its first DC-
3 was not purchased until 1946. The first
scheduled service - Lisbon-Madrid - commenced on September 19th. On December
31st a route designated the "Imperial Line"
was inaugurated to Luanda in what was the
Portuguese colony of Angola. The flight by
DC-3 included 12 night stops.

A Douglas C-54 - an ex-military version of
the DC-4 - entered service in 1947 to fly the
African route. In 1955 the first two Super
Constellations arrived and reduced the
flight to Angola to just 22 hours.

In 1953, TAP became a private company
although the majority shareholding was
held by the state.

ABOVE: *TAP Air Portugal A319-111, CS-TTA (C/n 750) (TAP Air Portugal)*

In 1959 the DC-3s were retired and in
1961 three Caravelles were ordered with
the first jet-scheduled service in August the
following year. In 1963 707s were ordered
and the first was delivered in December
1965.

In the meantime the scheduled route
continued to expand not only across
Europe but also to Brazil and the 707s
enabled the African route to extend to
Johannesburg.

Delivery of the 727 in March 1967 was
closely followed by the withdrawal of the
last of the piston-powered types and the
operation of an all-jet fleet.

TAP took delivery of a pair of 747s in
1972 and ordered two more. In 1975, it
reverted to becoming a state-owned company once more.

In 1979 TAP underwent a corporate
image change that included a new logo,
uniforms, fleet colour scheme and the
name was amended to TAP Air Portugal.

In 1982 a plan was commenced to phase
out the older 707s and 727s as well as the
747s that were proving difficult to fill. 737s

and Tristars entered service the following year on the medium and long-haul routes.

Achieving FAA recognition in 1983 as a repair station enabled the achievement of a contract to maintain and modify 35 727s for Federal Express.

As part of TAP's 40th anniversary celebrations in 1985, a museum was opened to preserve and display its history. In the same year Air Atlantis was established to operate the charter operation and LAR (Linhas Aéreas Regionais) for the domestic services.

Orders for the A310 and 737 were placed in 1987 and, following satisfactory return of the 35th 727 to Federal Express, a new contract was signed for more work including DC-10s which was added to their fleet the following year.

While deliveries increased the fleet size, two more aircraft were ordered in the form of the long-range A340s in 1989 plus two options. These were followed by additional examples of the A310s and 737s the following year to cope with the increasing annual passenger levels which were passing the three million mark.

By 1994 TAP had delivered the 150th aircraft to Federal Express and the first of the A340s arrived. The following year, Project TAP 2000 was launched, to modernise the company.

ABOVE: *TAP Air Portugal A320-211, CS-TNB (C/n 191) (Jerremy Flack/API)*

A decision was made in 1996 to renew the medium-haul fleet which led to the initial ordering of 22 A319 and A320 airliners from Airbus, of which the first of 16 A319s arrived in December 1997 together with a simulator.

During January 2000 TAP announced the formation of Yes - a charter company to replace Air Atlantis which had failed in 1993. In February, the Portuguese Government - TAPs current owner - announced that the airline was to be privatised following an agreement with the SAir Group. At the end of the year TAP stated that it had carried over 5 million passengers for the first time.

In February 2001 the SAir Group pulled out of the agreement in which they were going to acquire a 34% stake of TAP for US$139 million.

The events of September 11 did not greatly affect TAP, which although it made a loss for 2001, had more than halved the amount of the loss from the previous year.

TAP has completed its modernisation programme including establishing an all Airbus fleet. This has left it in a strong position for the future. However, it is still looking towards privatisation in the future.

BELOW: *TAP Air Portugal A340-312, CS-TOA (C/n 041) (Airbus)*

TAROM

ABOVE: *TAROM ATR 42-512, YR-ATA, (C/n 566) (ATR)*

Registered name: Romanian Air Transport SA

Country: Romania

Region: Europe

Address: Sos Bucuresti-Ploiesti km16.5
Bucharest 11152

Tel: 0040 1 201 47 05

Fax: 0040 1 201 47 61

Web site: www.tarom.digiro.net

Main operational base: Bucharest

STATUS

International and domestic carrier

National Flag Carrier

Employees: 2,686

Passengers per year: 1,126,000 (2001)

ICAO code: ROT

IATA code: RO

SERVICES

International / Regional / Domestic

Passenger / Charter / Cargo

International routes: Austria, Belgium, Bulgaria, China, Cyprus, Czech, Denmark, France, Germany, Greece, Hungary, Italy, Moldova, Netherlands, Poland, Russia, Spain, Switzerland, Turkey, UK

ALLIANCES / CODE SHARES

Aeroflot, Air France, Alitalia, Austrian A/l, CSA, Iberia, LOT, Malev

FLEET

A310-300 - 2, ATR 42-500 - 7, 737-300 - 7, 737-700 - 2

The Franco-Romanian Company for Air Navigation (CFRNA) was founded in 1920 to establish the first Romanian civil passenger and cargo airline. It offered a Paris to Bucharest service via Strasbourg, Prague, and Vienna, and as such, was the world's first trans-continental airline.

In 1946 Transporturi Aeriene Romana Sovietica (TARS) was formed as a joint Romanian / Soviet carrier operating Li-2s. The Romanian Government took over the Soviet 50% and on September 18th, 1954, the airline was renamed TAROM (Transporturile Aeriene Romane).

Il-14s were acquired and growth was remarkably quick with services to most European countries within six years. Il-18s entered service in 1962.

In 1966 TAROM made it's first transatlantic flight. This led to a scheduled route to New York in 1974. Around the same time another was inaugurated to Beijing while locally the An-24 was introduced for domestic routes to replace the Il-14s.

In 1968 BAC 1-11s were received to take TAROM into the jet age. These were followed by Il-62s, which were used mainly for charter operations, and 707s in 1974.

At that time, an unusual agreement was signed in 1979 between the British BAC and Romanian CNIAR for licence production of the BAC 1-11 of which a number were delivered to TAROM.

In 1992, two A310s were ordered following a decision at TAROM to modernise its fleet to ensure its ability to compete with Western airlines which were already routing to Bucharest.

This order was followed by another for two 737s in 1993 and a further three in 1994. These numbers have steadily increased and the ATR 42 has been added for the short-haul routes.

Towards the end of 2001, TAROM reduced the number of routes and suspended the one to Montreal.

Thai Airways International

Registered name: Thai Airways International plc
Country: Thailand
Region: Asia
Address: 89 Vibhavadi Rangsit Rd
PO Box 1075, Bangkok 10900
Tel: 0066 2 513 01 21
Fax: 0066 2 545 38 91
Web site: www.thaiair.com
Main operational base: Don Muang - Bangkok

STATUS

IATA scheduled international carrier
National Flag Carrier
Employees: 25,860
Passengers per year: 18,619,000 (2001)
ICAO code: THA
IATA code: TG

SERVICES

International / Regional / Domestic
Passenger / Cargo
International routes: Australia, Bangladesh,
Brunei, China, France, Germany, Greece,
India, Indonesia, Italy, Japan, Kuwait, Laos,
Malaysia, Myanmar, Nepal, Oman,
Pakistan, Philippines, Singapore, South
Korea, Spain, Sri Lanka, Sweden,
Switzerland, Taiwan, UAE, UK, USA,
Vietnam

ALLIANCES / CODE SHARES

ATAR / Air Andaman, Air-India, El Al,
Emirates, Japan A/l, PB Air, SAA, Vietnam
A/l

FLEET

A300-600 - 21, A330-300 - 12, ATR 72-201 -
2, 737-400 - 10, 747-300 - 2, 747-400 - 16,
777-200 - 8, 777-300 - 6, MD-11 - 4

Thai Airways International was formed on
August 24th, 1959. This was a joint agree-
ment between SAS (30%) and Thai Airways
Company (70%). The latter is Government
owned and this new airline was established
to take over the international routes.
Operations commenced in May 1960 with
DC-6s leased from SAS.

Routes were soon established to major
cities around the region and during 1962 a
pair of Convair 990 jet airliners was leased
from SAS. These were soon replaced with
the Caravelle of which the first was delivered in March 1964.

Two leased DC-9s were delivered by SAS
in January 1970 followed by two DC-8s in
April. The DC-8s were mainly leased from
SAS. Some of the later deliveries included
the stretched -63 model and by the time the
last ones arrived in 1977 a total of 13 had
been operated.

The first wide-body DC-10 arrived in
March 1975 followed by A300s in 1977 and
747s in 1979.

The intention with Thai Airways
International was that it should become
independent as soon as practical. With that
in mind SAS provided the necessary training and management and gradually Thai
nationals moved up within the company. In
1977, the Thai Government bought the

ABOVE: *Thai A300-622R, HS-TAM (C/n 577) with
Airbus test registration F-WWAG (Airbus)*

remaining SAS 15% stake.

Thai Airways International continued to
grow and on April 1st, 1988, the airline was
merged with Thai Airways Company under
the International name with that company
being responsible for the whole.

In June 1995, Thai Airways International
was listed on the Thai Stock Exchange and
made its first issue of 100 million shares.

The Thai Government is keen for Thai to
be privatised but the airline has substantial
debts of over US$2 billion plus a short-term
debt of nearly US$500 million. Passenger
levels are improving and profits were
returning in 2002.

BELOW: *Thai 777-3D7, HS-TKD (C/n 29212) (Jane's)*

Thomas Cook

Registered name: Thomas Cook Ltd
Country: UK
Region: Europe
Address: Commonwealth House
Chicago Avenue
Manchester Airport
M90 3FL
Tel: 0044 161 489 57 57
Fax: 0044 161 489 57 58
Web site: www.thomascook.info
Main operational base: Manchester

ABOVE: *Thomas Cook 757-28A, G-FCLF (C/n 288835) (Thomas Cook)*

STATUS

Charter carrier
Employees: 2,200
Passengers per year: 5,969,000 (2001)
ICAO code: JMC
IATA code: MT

SERVICES

International / Regional / Passenger
Charter
International routes: Bahamas, Cuba,
Cyprus, Dominican Republic, Egypt,
Gambia, Greece, India, Malta, Mexico,
Portugal, Tunisia, Turkey, USA

FLEET

A320 - 22, A330-200 - 2, 737-300 - 1 (leased
from Lufthansa), 737-700 - 2, 737-800 - 5,
757-200 - 30 (2 leased to Dutch Bird), 757-
300 - 15, 767-300 - 9

JMC Airlines commenced operations as
Flying Colours Airlines in March 1997 to fly
leisure passengers for inclusive tour companies.

Flying Colours also operated scheduled
routes to Florida and the Caribbean on
behalf of British Airways. This was under a
joint company - Airline Management Ltd.

The Thomas Cook Group acquired the
Flying Colours Leisure Group in 1998 and
later that year merged it's own Airworld

Airline into Flying Colours.

In September 1999, it was announced
that Flying Colours and Caledonian Airways
would be merged to form JMC airlines and
commence operations from March 2000.
The initials JMC stand for John Mason
Cook - the son of Thomas Cook.

In May 2002, Thomas Cook announced
the rebranding of its global fleet (JMC - 24
aircraft, Condor - 50, Sun Express - 7 and
Thomas Cook Belgium - 5) with a new logo.
With 86 owned aircraft in the Thomas Cook
fleet this now becomes the largest holiday
airline.

Transavia Airlines

Registered name: Transavia Airlines CV
Country: Netherlands
Region: Europe
Address: PO Box 7777
NL 1118 ZM Schipol Airport
Tel: 0031 20 604 62 32
Fax: 0031 20 604 65 45
Web site: www.transavia.nl
Main operational base: Amsterdam - Schiphol

ICAO code: TRA
IATA code: HV

SERVICES

International /Regional / Passenger
Charter
International routes: Greece, Italy, Morocco,
Nepal, Netherlands, Portugal, Spain, UAE

ALLIANCES / CODE SHARES

Continental A/l, KLM, Northwest A/l

FLEET

737-700 - 5, 737-800 - 17, 757-200 - 4
On order: 737-800 - 2 (for delivery from
2004)

STATUS

IATA scheduled and charter carrier
Employees: 1,540
Passengers per year: 3,661,000*
(2002)*includes charter pax

Transavia was formed in 1965 and commenced operations in November 1966 as
Transavia (Limburg) NV with DC-6s to fly
charter services.

The name was changed to Transavia
Holland in 1967 and in the following
March the first of five 707s arrived. These
were used to carry an ever-increasing por-
tion of the Dutch IT market that Transavia
was attracting for holidays to Europe and
North Africa. Additional subcontract work
was also carried out for Aerolineas
Argentinas, British Airways and Saudia
Arabian Airlines.

Transavia took delivery of its first

Caravelle in 1969 and built up a fleet of 14 of which the bulk were ex-Alitalia, Swissair and United Airlines. The delivery in June 1974, of its first 737 saw the demise of the Caravelle as the airline standardised on the US-built airliner.

An Airbus A300 was leased for a while in 1976 but was returned the following year.

The name changed once more in 1986. This time it was to Transavia International.

In October it commenced its first scheduled service to London / Gatwick. More schedules followed to Greece and Spain including the Balearic and Canary Islands.

Basiq Air was launched in December 2000 by Transavia, as a subsidiary, to operate as a new budget airline. The aircraft and crew it uses are from Transavia and operate in Transavia colours. Basiq Air has taken on a number of Transavia's scheduled routes.

Transavia is 80% owned by KLM but operates independently. In addition to its carrier services it also leases airliners to other carriers. Although its profits dropped slightly for the year 2001, it was the 24th year running that Transavia has shown a profit. It will be returning to an all 737 fleet shortly.

Tunisair

Registered name: Societe Tunisienne de l'air
Nationality: Tunisia
Region: Africa
Address: Boulevard du 7 Novembre 1987
Airport Tunis Carthage
2035 Tunis
Tel: 00216 71 70 01 00
Fax: 00216 71 70 00 08
Web site: www.tunisair.com.tn
Main operational base: Carthage

STATUS

IATA scheduled and charter carrier
National Flag Carrier
Employees: 7,230
Passengers per year: 3,562,000 (2001)
ICAO code: TAR
IATA code: TU

SERVICES

International / Regional / Domestic
Passenger / Charter / Cargo
International routes: Algeria, Austria, Belgium, Czech, Denmark, Egypt, France, Germany, Greece, Hungary, Italy, Libya, Jordan, Lebanon, Luxembourg, Mauritania, Morocco, Netherlands, Poland, Portugal, Saudi Arabia, Senegal, Spain, Syria, Turkey, Sweden, Switzerland, UK.

ALLIANCES / CODE SHARES

Air France, Royal Air Maroc, Swiss.

FLEET

A300-600 - 3, A300B4-203 - 1, A319-100 - 3, A320-200 - 12, 737-200Adv - 3, 737-200CAdv - 1, 737-500 - 4, 737-600 - 7, 737-800- 1.
On order: 737-600 - 7.

ABOVE: *Tunisair A320-211, TS-IMB (C/n 119) (Airbus)*

Tunisair was founded in 1948 as a joint venture between the Tunisian Government, Air France and some private investors. It commenced operations with DC-3s operating the Air France route structure. DC-4s were later added.

Following Tunisia's independence from France in 1957, the government took a 51% controlling stake in the airline, which was later increased to 87%. The balance being held by Air France.

Tunisair entered the jet age when their first Caravelle was delivered in August 1961. Three more followed and they remained in service through the mid-70s and enabled a number of new routes to be established.

Tunisair

A Nord 262 was acquired in April 1969 for domestic services.

The first of 10 727s were received in February 1972 and enabled more new routes, Jeddah and Luxembourg being added later that year and London the following year.

In 1982 an Airbus A300 was introduced into the Tunisair fleet with a further eight A320s from the early 1990s. Gradually a number of 737s was added, resulting in the current mixed fleet.

Tunisair retains its connections with Air France which owns 49% of the shares, the balance being held by the Tunisian Government.

The general drop in airline business resulted in a US$24.3 million loss being recorded for 2000 but, despite the events of the following year, this was reduced to US$18.1 with more recent trends improving.

ABOVE: *Tunisair 737-2H3, TS-IOE (C/n 22624) (Jeremy Flack/API)*

Turkish Airlines/THY

Registered name: Türk Hava Yollari AO
Country: Turkey
Region: Europe
Address: Ataturk Airport
 Yesilkoy
 Istanbul
Tel: 0090 212 663 47 40
Fax: 0090 212I 663 47 63
Web site: www.turkishairlines.com
Main operational base: Ankara and Istanbul

STATUS

Scheduled and charter passenger + cargo carrier
National Flag Carrier
Employees: 8,621
Passengers per year: 10,277,000 (2001)
ICAO code: THY
IATA code: TK

SERVICES

International / Regional / Domestic Passenger / Charter / Cargo
International routes: Albania, Algeria, Austria, Azerbaijan, Bahrain, Belgium, Bosnia Herzegovina, Bulgaria, China, Croatia, Czech, Denmark, Egypt, France, Georgia, Germany, Greece, Hungary, Iran, Israel, Italy, Japan, Jordan, Kazakhstan, Kuwait, Kyrgyzstan, Lebanon, Libya, Macedonia, Malaysia, Netherlands, Pakistan, Poland, Romania, Saudi Arabia, Singapore, South Africa, South Korea, Spain, Sweden, Switzerland, Syria, Thailand, Tunisia, Turkmenistan, UAE, UK, Ukraine, USA, Uzbekistan

ALLIANCES / CODE SHARES

American A/l, Asiana, Cathay Pacific, Croatia A/l, CSA, JAL

FLEET

A310-300 - 5, A340-300 - 7, 737-400 - 14, 737-500 - 2, 737-800 - 26, RJ70 - 3, RJ100 - 6

The origins of Turkish Airlines (THY) can be traced back to Turkiye Devlet Hava Yollari (DHY) that was formed on May 20th, 1933 as part of the Ministry of National Defence. Operations commenced later that year between Ankara and Istanbul. Various aircraft were flown including the de Havilland Express and Rapide and Junkers F-13.

BELOW: *Turksih Airlines A310-304ET, TC-JDC (C/n 537) (Airbus)*

In June 1938 control of DHY was transferred to the Ministry of Transport and the airline became known as the General Directorate of State Airways.

After the war, DC-3s were acquired and the first international route to Athens established. By the early 1950s the airline was operating 32 DC-3s as well as six Rapides. The first of seven de Havilland Herons were added to the fleet in February 1955.

The Turkish Government formed a new corporation to take over the civil airline operation on March 1st, 1956, named Türk Hava Yollari AO (THY). The government held a 51% stake and BOAC took 6.5%.

Five Vickers Viscounts were ordered and deliveries commenced in January 1958. These were followed by five F-27 Friendships in 1960.

THY entered the jet age with the DC-9 of which the first of 11 was delivered in August 1967 and the last in 1976. Four ex-Pan Am 707s were the next type to be operated following delivery of the first in 1971.

The DC-10 introduced THY to wide-body airliners with the first of three being delivered in December 1972 for long-haul routes. The following month saw the first of six F-28 Fellowships being delivered over that year for domestic services, to replace the F-27s.

The A310 was introduced during the mid-1980s followed by the 737. A service to New York, which was routed via Brussels, was inaugurated in July 1988.

The first delivery of an A340-300 to THY was in July 1993. This was followed by the RJ100 during the following month. September saw the merging of its domestic subsidiary - Turkish Air Transport (THT) - into THY.

1994 saw the registered capital level rise to 5.5 trillion Turkish Lira (TL) during January and in July the New York service commenced flying direct. During September the DC-9s were retired and the following month the registered capital was increased to six trillion TL.

ABOVE: *Turkish Airlines A340-311, TC-JDC (C/n023) (Airbus)*

The first A319 was delivered in February 1995 and was used to introduce their First Class service. The following month the registered capital was nearly doubled when the level was taken to ten trillion TL. Later that year, three of the 727s were withdrawn from passenger service and converted for the purely cargo role.

During 1996, the first of four smaller RJ70s joined the RJ100s while four 727s

BELOW: *Turkish Airlines 737-32J, TC-JEA (C/n 27143) (Jeremy Flack/API)*

Turkish Airlines/THY

were retired. During December the registered capital was raised to 50 Trillion TL.

Block space agreements were signed during 1997/8 with Austrian Airlines, Croatia Airlines, JAL and Swissair. In addition THY became a member of 'The Qualifyer Group'. The first of 26 new generation 737s was delivered in November.

A further nine 737NGs were delivered in 1999 along with the 6th A340. A code share agreement was signed with Malaysian Airlines and in November the registered capital was raised again. This time it was to a staggering 175 Trillion TL.

A new service to Sydney was inaugurated in September 2000 for the Olympic games. The signing of an agreement with American Airlines in February led to code sharing on ten domestic services in the

USA. The agreements with Austrian and Malaysian Airlines came to an end but further signings were made with Cathay, CSA and LOT.

Two more 737NGs were delivered during 2001 but six of the older A310s were sold to Iran Air. The Turkish Government had been hoping to sell up to 24% of THY to a foreign carrier. As there were no interested buyers in the current climate it has been decided to shelve privatisation plans for the time being. A code share agreement was signed with Sun Express and a new route was inaugurated linking Ankara and Sabiha Gokcen. When the 2000 figures were published THY was shown to have recorded a loss of US$52 million.

THY managed to make a profit of US $ 6.1 million for 2001. However the events of

September 11th did cause a loss of approximately one third of passengers. As a result some 1,000 staff were laid off and pay reduced for the rest. A number of the older aircraft were also retired although all of the 26 737NGs ordered were delivered. The cuts and the entry into service of more efficient aircraft had the right effect as THY recorded its highest ever profit for the first nine months of 2002.

One new route was started to Pristina in April 2002. However, services to Kuala Lumpur were suspended in September, along with several other airlines, due to poor passenger levels. A new service to Hong Kong will be operated instead.

In January 2003 an RJ100 was lost while attempting to land at Diyarbakir airport in thick fog; 5 of the 75 on board survived.

Tyrolean Airways

Registered name: Tiroler Luftfahrt AG
Country: Austria
Region: Europe
Address: Furstenweg 176
PO Box 98
A6026 Innsbruck
Tel: 0043 512 2222 12 20
Fax: 0043 512 22 22 90 05
Web site: www.tyrolean.at
Stockholder: Austrian Airlines Group
Main operational base: Innsbruck

STATUS

Scheduled and charter carrier
National Flag Carrier
Employees: 1,024
Passengers per year: 2,166,000 (2001)
ICAO code: TYR
IATA code: VO

SERVICES

Regional / Domestic / Passenger
Charter / Cargo
International routes: Austria, Belgium, Bosnia Herzegovina, Croatia, Czech, Finland, Germany, Hungary, Ireland, Italy, Kosovo, Luxembourg, Moldova, Norway, Poland, Romania, Slovakia, Slovenia, Spain, Sweden, Ukraine

ALLIANCES / CODE SHARES

Star Alliance / Air France, Lufthansa

FLEET

CRJ200 - 12, DHC-8 Dash 8-100 - 1, DHC-8 Dash 8-Q300A - 10, DHC-8 Dash 8-Q400 - 6, ERJ145 - 3, Fokker 70 - 6
On order: DHC-8 Dash 8-Q400 - 2

ABOVE: *Tyrolean DHC-8 Dash 8-100 (Bombardier)*

Tyrolean Airways was formed in 1958 as Aircraft Innsbruck to provide air-ambulance, air-taxi and charter services.

Gernot Langes-Swarovski and Christian Schwemberger acquired Aircraft Innsbruck in 1978.

In 1979, the fixed wing of Air Innsbruck was renamed Tyrolean Airways. Equipped

with Citations and a DHC-7, it commenced scheduled services from Innsbruck to Zurich and Vienna in April 1980 with the DHC-7. A total of 35,000 passengers was carried in its first year of operation.

Tyrolean Jet Service was formed in December 1984 to provide a charter service using the Citations to which another Citation plus a Falcon 50 and a Turbo-Porter were added.

A 37-seat DHC-8 Dash 8 was acquired in 1985 and in 1987 the services were extended to other destinations including Frankfurt and Graz.

Tyrolean became a public limited company in March 1988 with Gernot Langes-Swarovski holding 92% of the shares.

In 1994 Austrian Airlines took a 42.85% stake in Tyrolean, then withdrew its domestic services in favour of Tyrolean.

A Fokker 70 was delivered in 1995 to which the first three Bombardier CRJ200s were added in 1996 taking Tyrolean into the jet age. It was awarded the 'Regional Airline of the Year 1997-1998' by the European Regions Airline Association (ERA). This was the first of a number of similar awards that were presented to the airline over the following years by various organisations.

Austrian Airways bought out Gernot Langes-Swarovski's 42.85% and Leipnik-Lundenburger Industrie AG's 14.30% stake in Tyrolean to become the 100% owner. Tyrolean Airways was voted "Regional Airline of the Year 1998" by Air Transport World. Such has been the growth of passenger levels for Tyrolean that since its alignment with Austrian Airlines it has had to increase the size of its fleet from 16 to 31 aircraft.

A total of over 2 million passengers was

ABOVE: *Tyrolean DHC-8 Q401, OE-LGA (C/n 4041) (Bombardier)*

carried in 1999. This was the first time such a level had been reached in Tyrolean's history.

Tyrolean became a member of the Star Alliance along with Austrian Airlines and Lauda Air in March 2000. An order for six of the Q400 variant of the Dash 8s was placed with Bombardier and the first four entered service before the end of the year.

Following the appointment of a new board in 2001 a new relationship between Austrian Airlines and Tyrolean was formed. With effect from January 1st 2002 Austrian Airline purchased all of Tyrolean's flight capacity. As a result, all the market-oriented planning and management functions for Austrian Airlines Group scheduled services are also integrated into Austrian Airlines.

Ukraine International Airlines

Registered name: Mizhnarodni avialinii Ukrainy
Nationality: Ukraine
Region: Europe
Address: 14 Peremohy Avenue
                01135 Kiev
Tel: 00380 44 461 56 56
Fax: 00380 44 216 79 94
Web site: www.ukraine-international.com
Main operational base: Kiev - Borispol

STATUS
IATA scheduled carrier
National Flag Carrier
Employees: 700
Passengers per year: 300,000
ICAO code: UIA
IATA code: PS

SERVICES
Regional / Domestic / Passenger
Charter / Cargo
International routes: Austria*, Belgium, Denmark, Finland, France, Germany, Italy*, Netherlands*, Portugal, Spain, Switzerland, UK. *codeshare.

Ukraine International Airlines

ABOVE: *Ukraine International Airlines 737-247, UR-GAC (C/n 23188) (Ukraine International Airlines)*

ALLIANCES / CODE SHARES

Austrian A/l, Blue Panorama, Finnair, Iberia, KLM, Swiss Int A/l.

FLEET

737-200Adv - 1, 737-300 - 3, 737-400 - 1, 737-500 - 2.
On Order: 737-700 - 1.

Ukraine International Airlines was originally formed as Air Ukraine International in October 1992 as a joint venture between Air Ukraine (88.2%) and GPA plc (11.8%). Established to operate flights into Europe , the name was changed to Ukraine International Airlines to avoid confusion with Air Ukraine which operated domestic routes only.

Initial equipment was the 737-400 which was leased but this was replaced with the-200 model due to overcapacity.

In 1996, the SAir Group and Austrian Airlines took a US$9 million stake in Ukraine International Airlines. This was followed in 2001 by the European Bank for Reconstruction and Development which took a US$5.4 million stake.

As passenger levels have risen the fleet has expanded with newer models of the 737. By November 2002, Ukraine International Airlines had carried its 2 millionth passenger and over 10,000 tonnes of cargo.

United Air Lines

Registered name: United Air Lines, Inc
Nationality: USA
Region: North America
Address: P.O. Box 66100
Chicago
IL 60666
Tel: 001 847 700 40 00
Fax: 001 847 700 69 47
Web site: www.united.com
Stockholder: UAL Corporation
Main operational base: Chicago O'Hare, Denver, San Francisco, Los Angeles and Washington-Dulles

STATUS

IATA scheduled international and domestic carrier
Employees: 101,758
Passengers per year: 75,457,000 (2001)
ICAO code: UAL
IATA code: UA

SERVICES

International / Regional / Domestic Passenger / Cargo
International routes: Argentina, Aruba, Australia, Bahamas, Belgium, Brazil, Cayman Is, Chile, China, Costa Rica, El Salvador, France, Germany, Guatemala, India, Italy, Japan, Netherlands, New Zealand, Mexico, Puerto Rica, Singapore, South Korea, Spain*, Portugal*, Taiwan, Thailand, Trinidad & Tobago, UK, Uruguay, Venezuela, Virgin Is.

ALLIANCES / CODE SHARES

Star Alliance / Air New Zealand, Air Wisconsin A/l, Aloha A/l, Atlantic Coast A/l, BWIA, Emirates, Great Lakes A/l, Gulfstream Int A/l, Skywest A/l, Spanair, US Airways, Virgin Blue.

OWNED SUBSIDIARY AIRLINES

Biz Jet Charter Biz Jet Fractional Biz Jet Services

FLEET

A319-100 - 55, A320-200 - 98, 737-300 - 101, 737-500 - 57, 747-400 - 35, 757-200 - 97, 767 - 200 / 200ER - 18, 767-300ER - 23, 767-300ER - 14, 777-200 - 22 (6 operated as two-class), 777-200ER - 38
On order: A319 - 21, A320 - 21, 777-200ER - 1.

The origins of United Air Lines can be traced back to April 6th, 1926, when Walter

ABOVE: *United Air Lines A320-232 (Rolls Royce)*

T. Varney launched a contract mail service between Pasco and Elko via Boise. This marked the beginning of US commercial transport and the birth of United Airlines.

On October 30th 1928 the Boeing Airplane & Transport Corp. (BATC) was incorporated and acquired Boeing Air Transport (BAT), National Air Transport (NAT) and Pacific Air Transport (PAT). Each of the members had won a sector contract and subsequently operated various aircraft as a subsidiary to BATC. BAT used a variety of aircraft and in the first two years carried some 6,000 passengers in addition to the 1,300 tons of mail on the Chicago-San Fancisco sector. NAT flew the New York-Chicago sector while PAT flew the Los Angeles-San Francisco-Seattle sector.

On February 1st 1929 BATC was renamed United Airlines and the Boeing 247 was introduced in the early 30s and DC-3 in 1937.

In 1934 BATC was formed into United Air Lines Transport Corporation (UALTC) and in 1943 the name was modified to United Air Lines, Inc. (UAL).

During the Second World War United's overhaul base at Cheyenne, Wyo., became a modification center for B-17 bombers under a contract with the US War Department. The airliners were contracted

to fly troops and supplies.

In 1947 a Douglas DC-6 service commenced featuring full-cabin pressurisation and reducing US coast-to-coast travel time to 10 hours.

The Boeing 377 Stratocruiser joined United's fleet in 1950 and was operated on the San Francisco-Honolulu route.

In July conflict reared its head again and United started its US military airlift to support the Korean War effort which lasted until October 1952. Convair 340 was introduced in May.

In 1953 United introduced "Executive Flights" for men only. This featured complimentary cocktail, steaks, business publications and cigars. This proved popular and continued until January 1970.

The Douglas DC-7 entered service in 1954 and was used on the New-York-San Francisco-Honolulu route. The following year saw the introduction of a weather radar developed by United and the Radio Corporation of America. It also became the first US domestic airline to order the jet-powered DC-8 while the old radial powered DC-3 was finally retired in 1956.

In September 1959 United launched its DC-8 on the New York-San Francisco route and in July 1960 the 720 entered service.

On June 1st 1961 United acquired

ABOVE: *United Air Lines 767-422, N189UA (C/n 26878) (United Air Lines)*

Capital Airlines. With 7,000 new employees and all of Capital's routes UAL became the world's largest commercial airline.

United introduced the three-engined 727 on its Chicago-Denver-San Francisco route in 1964. The following June saw the airline launching a military airlift once more, this time to support US operations in Vietnam.

1965 saw United become the first airline to qualify for the Federal Aviation Administration's (FAA's) all-weather program. This allowed DC-8s to land at specified airports with as little as 100-foot ceilings and quarter-mile visibility - greatly improving operations in poorer weather.

In February 1966 United applied to the US CAB to extend its US Mainland-Hawaii routes to new destinations in the Far East. This represented United's first major move toward international operations. The following year a Chicago-Toronto commenced representing a further development of its international expansion.

In August 1968 United became the first airline to launch the 737 into service. In November United dropped its long standing "no marriage" rule for stewardesses.

United stockholders approved the forma-

United Air Lines

tion of UAL, Inc. as a holding company, with United as a wholly owned subsidiary, which became effective on August 1st, 1969.

With airliner ranges constantly increasing, United launched a non-stop Chicago-Honolulu service with Douglas DC-8-62 aircraft in August 1969. Two months later a similar service was offered from New York and at 4,979 miles it was the longest US domestic air route.

In September 1974 United adopted a new corporate identity programme featuring a stylized "U" logo, new color scheme and a two-word signature (United Airlines), marking the company's first departure from the three-word name which had been adopted in 1931.

On April 1st, 1983, United launched Seattle-Tokyo service, its first transpacific route.

In Februaury 1986 United began a service to 13 Pacific cities after purchasing Pan American Airways' Pacific Division for US$715 million. This was followed by the acquisition of its European facilities in 1990 and the Latin American Division in 1991.

On April 30th 1987 the holding company - UAL Inc - had its name changed to Allegis Corporation, however, just over a year later this was dropped in favour UAL Corporation.

In 1989 an international service was inaugurated between San Francisco and Mexico City and the following year more routes fol-lowed. This time they were United's first transatlantic service routeing to Frankfurt from Chicago and Washington DC.

1990 saw yet another airlift. This time United participated in the Civil Reserve Air Fleet (CRAF) operations and flew in support of US troops participating in Operation 'Desert Storm'.

In 1991 United launched its first scheduled services to London departing from Miami, New York, Washington DC and San Francisco.

On December 9th 1991 Pan American Airways went out of business and United acquired its American operations for US$135 million. That year UAL Corp reported a loss of US$332 million.

In January 1992 United launched its first scheduled service to Latin America with flights to sixteen different destinations. However, UAL Corp reported a loss for the second year running - this time of US$957 million.

United adopted a new gray, navy blue and red color scheme in 1993 to reflect the global nature of its operations. 15 of the 17 flight meal kitchens were sold to Dobbs International in September 1993 which brought to an end this in-house service which had been operating since 1936.

In November 1993 United took delivery of its first A320.

The following March a new maintenance facility was dedicated by United in Indianapolis. The same year, UAL provided for a 55% employee ownership in exchange for various working practices and became the largest employee-owned company in the world.

On October 1st, 1994, United launched its low-cost, no-frills "Shuttle by United" service on the US West Coast.

In June 1995 United became the first airline to fly the 777 on a scheduled service when it was flown on the Washington DC-London route. 1995 concluded as United's most profitable year ever as it reported US$662 million in net profits.

United launched the longest commercial route in its history in June 1996 with the start of a seasonal Chicago-Hong Kong non-stop service. In August an order was announced for 24 Airbus A319 aircraft while end of year profits soared to over US$1billion maintaining United as the largest US passenger / freight carrier.

In May 1997 UAL became a founder member of the Star Alliance with Air Canada, Lufthansa, SAS, Thai International and Varig. On July 1st United became the first US carrier to take delivery of the A319. Days later an order was placed for eight 767s. The end of the year brought more good news with the recording of the third year of record profits.

1998 saw a series of major orders being announced with 20 A320s and 10 A319s in March. This was followed by one other 747, six 767 and 16 777s. In July a further 12 A320s and 10 A319s were ordered.

In December 1998 United signed a 10-year contract with Atlantic Coast Airlines. This ensured that ACA remained its primary US East Coast United Express carrier and enabled continued expansion of the regional jet service by ACA.

The end of year figures were affected by the Asian economic downturn but United still managed its second highest profit for 20 years.

In March 1999 the airline announced plans to build its new World Headquarters at Chicago's O'Hare International Airport.

In October 1999 UAL and Lufthansa bought C$230 million of Air Canada newly issued perpetual convertible preferred stock which was part of the Canadian airline's restructuring and strengthened its place in the Star Alliance. In May 2000 US Airways agreed to a merger with UAL for US$4.3 million.

In 2000 United ordered 44 Airbus airliners followed by a further seven A319s and eight A320s in February 2001. This took total deliveries / orders for Airbus up to 192.

United restored its London - Delhi service in April 2001 after a six year break. As a result the airline became the only airline to be able to offer a true around the world service which could be achieved in 40 hours.

After 16 months of protracted negotiations with US Airways, the merger plans were abandoned.

September 11th is a day that few people will forget. It has also left a lasting scar on most airlines throughout the world. United suffered two horrific hijackings - 767, UA175, took off from Boston just before 8am local time, the hijackers took control and then crashed it into the World Trade Centre 46 minutes later. Just after 8am, 757, UA093, took off from Newark. The aircraft

was bound for San Francisco and headed in that direction for about an hour. It then turned back and, according to the cellphone messages, an attempt was made to overcome the hijackers and the aircraft crashed near Pittsburgh.

At the same time, two American Airlines aircraft were also hijacked - one being crashed into the World Trade Centre and the other into the Pentagon.

The impact on UAL was immediate. Within a week announcements were made of 11,000 staff to be laid off and a flight capacity reduction of 23%.

End of year figures showed a loss of US$2.1 billion for 2001.

In November, United announced plans to commence non-stop flights from US to China and the following month commenced Los Angeles-Melbourne.

ABOVE: United Express 328-120. N329MX (C/n 3049) operated by Mountain Air Express (Dornier)

In June 2002 UAL filed for a US$2bn loan of which 90% would be guaranteed by the US Government ATSB (Air Transportation Safety and System Stabilization Act) provisions. However, this was not approved leaving the airline in severe difficulties. The mid-year figures showed a US$851 million loss for the first half of 2002.

Following on from the abandoned merger, United and US Air were given US DoT approval in 2002 to enter into a code-sharing agreement.

United Air Lines filed for bankruptcy protection in December 2002.

RIGHT: United Express CRJ200ER, N65BR (C/n 7500) operated by Atlantic Coast Airlines (Jane's)

US Airways

Registered name: US Airways Inc
Country: USA
Region: North America
Address: 2345 Crystal Drive
Crystal Park Four
Arlington
Virginia 22227
Tel: 001 703 872 70 00
Fax: 001 703 872 51 00
Web site: www.usairways.com
Stockholder: US Airways Group Inc
Main operational base: Charlotte, Pittsburgh and Winston Salem.

STATUS

IATA scheduled international and domestic carrier
Employees: 41,260
Passengers per year: 56,114,000 (2001)
ICAO code: USA
IATA code: US

SERVICES

International / Regional / Domestic
Passenger / Cargo

International routes: Antigua & Barbuda, Aruba, Barbados, Belgium, Bermuda, Canada, Cayman Islands, Dominican Republic, France, Germany, Italy, Jamaica, Mexico, Netherlands, Netherlands Antilles, Spain, UK, Virgin Islands

ALLIANCES / CODE SHARES

Deutsche BA, United A/l

OWNED SUBSIDIARY AIRLINES

Allegheny Airlines, MidAtlantic Airways, Piedmont Airlines, PSA Airlines, US Airways Shuttle

FLEET

A319-100 - 66, A320-200 - 24, A321 - 28, A330-300 - 9, 737-300 - 48, 737-300LR - 37, 737-400 - 22, 737-400LR - 32, 757-200 -34, 767-200ER - 11
On order: A319-100 - 6, A320-200 - 45, A321 - 41, A330-300 - 1 for delivery in 2007

The origins of US Airways can be traced back to March 5th, 1937, with the formation of All American Aviation which commenced flying mail from remote communities in 1937.

During the immediate post-war period a number of DC-3 / C-47s was acquired. The name was changed to All American Airways in 1949 when it commenced passenger-carrying services. It changed name again in 1953 to Allegheny Airlines from when the DC-3s began being replaced by Convair 340s, 440s and Martin 2-0-2s.

Convair 540s and F-27 Friendship turbo-prop airliners entered service during the early- to mid-1960s and the first pure jets arrived with the delivery of the first leased DC-9 in 1966. British BAC 1-11s were operated from the fleet of Mohawk when it was merged in 1967 followed by Lake Central Airlines in 1968. During the late 1960s and early 1970 a substantial fleet of DC-9s was accumulated - partly with new aircraft together with some second-hand.

Following US deregulation in 1978, the name was changed to USAir. PSA (formed 1949) was acquired in May 1987 and fully merged the following year. Ever hungry, USAir continued with Piedmont (formed 1940). At the time this was the largest ever airline merger and gave USAir not only the hubs at Charlotte, Baltimore, Dayton and Syracuse but also its international routes and with them its first wide-body airliners the 767s. USAir Shuttle was inaugurated in conjunction with Trump Shuttle in 1992.

In 1992 a merger with British Airways was proposed and declined as was another with American and United in 1989.

The USAir services to Europe expanded over the next few years with new schedules to Frankfurt, London, Madrid, Munich, Paris and Rome. In 1994, USAir expanded access to South America by becoming the sole US domestic airline partner of Latin Pass with 14 South American airline members.

In 1996, USAir placed a massive order with Airbus that, together with options, was potentially worth US$18 billion. This was for 120 of the A320 family and options for a

ABOVE: *US Airways A321-211, N165US (C/n 1431) with Airbus test registration D-AVZB (Airbus)*

further 280 for delivery from 1998 to 2009. This order was to replace the 390 existing F-28, DC-9 and MD-80 airliners.

In 1997, the name of USAir was changed to US Airways and the US Air Shuttle became a wholly owned subsidiary. In 1998, MetroJet was launched to provide a low-cost carrier competitor in the eastern USA, with 727s.

The first of the A320s was delivered in 1999 and entered service on the Philadelphia - Los Angeles schedule. By the end of the year a total of 40 A319 / A320s had been delivered and the 727s began to be retired the following year.

The US airline business was having a difficult time when the terrorist attack struck on September 11th. With passenger levels at an all-time low, routes were rationalised as was the fleet and engineering programmes, staff levels were then reduced by some 9,000. However this all took time and the extended closure of Reagan Washington National Airport did not help and resulted in the closure of MetroJet. When the figures were released, US Airways made a net loss of nearly US$2 billion in 2001.

US Airlines resurrected proposals with United Airlines regarding their possible takeover. However, United was also suffering and gave warning of greater difficulties to come and needed to drastically reduce its own costs. With the merger solution gone, US Airways asked for US government backing of a US$1 billion loan and entered into a crash programme to cut US$1.3 billion from its annual costs. Attempts to reduce wage bills were fraught, with union negotiations that took nearly a year to resolve.

On August 11th 2002 the US Airways Group and some of the subsidiaries, including US Airways Inc, filed for bankruptcy protection with losses put at over US$2.1 billion. Under its Chapter 11 status the airline continues to operate while attempts are made to reorganise the business and make a return to financial stability.

US Airways continues to operate while a longer-term solution is sought. During mid-

ABOVE: *US Airways A330-323X, N67US (C/n 370) with Airbus test registration F-WWKH (Airbus)*

2002 the airline discussed a code-share agreement with United by which the airlines could sell tickets on each others flights as the two airlines complement each other - US Airways concentrating on the east coast and United centred on Chicago.

In August, US Airways announced that it had entered into an agreement with the Retirement Systems of Alabama to provide US$500 million of debtor-in-possession financing with a US$240 million investment in new equity on emergence from Chapter 11.

Despite its problems, US Airways announced a planned expansion of the regional operations using the Potomac identity created during the proposed merger with United Airlines. Potomac was formed in late 2000 and operated out of Ronald Reagan Washington National Airport but ceased operations in October 2001 after the closure of the airport. Plans for MidAtlantic Airways were to commence operations towards the end of 2002. The creation of this new subsidiary was seen to be an important part of US Airways recovery through the smaller airline structure with lower overheads at the important airport of Washington DC.

In the meantime, US Airways and United were given the go-ahead for a formal code-share agreement by the US DoT and Midway joined the US Airways Express

operation in October 2002. This took the number of US Airways Express operators to eleven, operating a combined fleet of 283 aircraft operating from 158 airports and fly over 2,000 trips per day.

The US Airways Express operation comprises Air Midwest Airlines, (CCAIR ceased trading in November 2002), and Mesa Airlines, which are subsidiaries of the Mesa Air Group. Allegheny Airlines, Piedmont Airlines and PSA Airlines are wholly owned subsidiaries of US Airways Group plus the recently formed MidAtlantic. The remaining four - Chautauqua Airlines, Colgan Air, Shuttle America, and Trans States Airlines remain independent operators.

The three existing wholly owned US Airways Express operators - Allegheny Airlines Inc, Piedmont Airlines Inc, and PSA Inc - all recorded rising passenger levels during 2002 although these were still slightly below those for 2000.

Sadly, bad news continued into 2003 with the loss of an Air Midwest Beechcraft 1900 with 21 aboard which was operated by the Mesa Group on behalf of US Airways Express.

GE Capital has offered immediate and post-Chapter 11 financing totalling US$830 million helping US Airways towards recovery.

Uzbekistan Airways

Registered name: Uzbekistan Havo Jullary

Country: Uzbekistan

Region: Asia

Address: Movarounakhr Str 41
Tashkent
700060

Tel: 007 3711 33 70 36

Fax: 007 3711 33 18 85

Web site: www.airways.uz

Main operational base: Tashkent

ABOVE: *Uzbekistan A310-324, UK-31003 (C/n 706) with Airbus test registration F-WWCM (Airbus)*

STATUS

Scheduled carrier

National Flag Carrier

Passengers per year: 2,000,000

ICAO code: UZB

IATA code: HY

SERVICES

International / Domestic / Passenger
Cargo

International routes: Azerbaijan,
Bangladesh, Bulgaria, China, Germany,
Greece, India, Israel, Istanbul, Kazakhstan,
Kyrgyzstan, Malaysia, Netherlands, Russia,
Saudi Arabia, South Korea, Thailand,
Turkmenistan, UAE, UK, Ukraine, USA

ALLIANCES / CODE SHARES

Alitalia, Asiana, Malaysia A/l

FLEET

A310-300 - 3, An-24 - 23, 757-200 - 2, 767-
300ER - 2, RJ85 - 3, Il-62M - 8, Il-76TD - 15,
Il-86 - 10, Tu-154B - 21, Tu-154M - 3,
Yak-40 - 25

On order: 757-200 – 1

Uzbekistan Airways was formed on January
28th 1992 by the new Government of
Uzbekistan from what had been the
Uzbekistan division of Aeroflot.
Commercial aviation interests were previously served by Aeroflot prior to the break-
up of the Soviet Union. Uzbekistan Airways
was established to continue this service and
initially operated purely ex-Aeroflot aircraft

such as the An-24 and Tu-154.

With the need to attract Western passengers Uzbekistan Airways initially leased a
couple of Airbus A310s. These were joined
by 767s and RJ85s were ordered for domestic use.

Gradually Uzbekistan Airways has built
up its scheduled service and this national
airline now operates a number of routes to
Asia, Middle East and Europe.

The events of September 11th caused
Uzbekistan Airways to suspend some of its
services but most were resumed in 2002.

VARIG

Registered name: Viacao Aerea Rio-Grandense SA

Country: Brazil

Region: South America

Address: Avenue Almirante Silvo de Noronha 365
Rio de Janeiro 20021-01

Tel: 0055 21 814 50 00

Fax: 0055 21 814 57 00

Web site: www.varig.com.br

Main operational base: Rio de Janeiro

Employees: 16,065

Passengers per year: 10,487,000 (2001)

ICAO code: VRG

IATA code: RG

SERVICES

International / Regional / Domestic
Passenger / Cargo

International routes: Argentina, Bolivia,
Chile, Colombia, Denmark, France,
Germany, Italy, Japan, Mexico, Paraguay,
Peru, Portugal, Spain, Uruguay, UK, USA,
Venezuela

ALLIANCES / CODE SHARES

Star / Alitalia, SAA, Spanair

FLEET

727-100C - 4, 727-100C - 1, 737-200Adv -16,
737-300 - 33, 737-700 - 5, 737-800 - 10, 747-
300 - 3, 747-300 (SCD) - 2, 767-200ER - 6,
767-300ER - 10, 777-200ER - 2, DC-10-30 -
5, DC-10-30F (CF) - 2, MD-11 - 12

On order: 737-700 - 11 options, 737-800 –
10

VARIG dates back to May 7th 1927 when
this air service was set up by various German
interests, including Deutsche Lufthansa.
Initial aircraft were all German built and
included such types as the Dornier Wal that
were later joined by the Junkers 50 and Ju-
52.

STATUS

IATA scheduled international and domestic
carrier

National Flag Carrier

After the war VARIG re-equipped its fleet with surplus military aircraft including the Catalina, C-46 and C-47 flown on domestic routes.

In 1951, VARIG acquired Aero Geral, which gave it assess to routes north of Rio de Janeiro. Gradually the network expanded reaching as far as New York in 1955 using Super Constellations.

The jet age brought VARIG the Caravelle in 1959 and the 707 the following year. However in 1961, VARIG obtained a controlling interest in the REAL Aerovias consortium. REAL had built up an extensive network and had become the largest airline in South America. Gradually this network was merged into VARIG.

In 1962 VARIG bought a number of surplus Electras from American Airlines to replace the older aircraft on its domestic routes.

In 1965 VARIG took over the bankrupt Panair do Brasil giving it additional routes and aircraft including three of its DC-8s. That year VARIG leased a 748, which proved popular, and as a result ten were purchased of which the first was delivered in November 1967.

VARIG took delivery of the first of a num-

ber of DC-10s in May 1974 that enabled improved international services.

While VARIG had been going from strength to strength, 1994 saw financial problems come to a head resulting in the cancellation of orders and a general restructuring need.

Despite various plans, VARIG has continued to run at a loss. Competition for international and domestic carriers has reduced its share of the market. TAM has now taken over as the recognized Brazilian leader.

Having lost a further US$329 million in the first half of 2002, VARIG underwent fur-

ABOVE: *Varig MD-11, PP-VPJ (C/n 48404) (Jeremy Flack/API)*

ther radical restructuring in an attempt to raise US$300 in a new share issue. Since September 11th it had shed 10% of its workforce and 20 aircraft that were on lease.

VARIG was still trying to renegotiate its US$900 million debt at the end of 2002. The situation had been exasperated by the continued fall in value of Brazil's currency that resulted in higher fuel, leasing and spares costs.

VASP

Registered name: Viacao Aerea Sao Paulo SA
Country: Brazil
Region: South America
Address: Praca Comandante Lineu Gomes s/n
Edificio Sede VASP
Aeroporto de Congonhas
04626-910 São Paulo
Tel: 0055 11 532 30 00
Fax: 0055 11 542 08 80
Web site: www.vasp.com.br
Main operational base: Sao Paulo - Congonhas

STATUS

IATA scheduled international and domestic and charter carrier
National Flag Carrier
Employees: 4,458

Passengers per year: 4,222,000 (2001)
ICAO code: VSP
IATA code: VP

ABOVE: *VASP A300B2-203, P-SNL (C/n 202) with Airbus registration F-WZMJ (Airbus)*

VASP

SERVICES

International / Regional / Domestic
Passenger / Charter / Cargo
International routes: Argentina, Aruba,
Belgium, Canada, Germany, Greece, Japan,
South Korea, Spain, Switzerland, USA

ALLIANCES / CODE SHARES

Continental A/l

FLEET

A300B2-200 - 3, 727-200FAdv - 1, 727-
200FAdv - 1, 737-200 - 6, 737-200Adv - 14,
737-200CAdv - 2, 737-300 - 4

VASP was formed on November 11th, 1933,
by local government and banks and commenced operations with a three-seat
Monospar ST.4. These aircraft were joined
later by de Havilland Rapide and Ju-52s.

A fleet of DC-3s was built up after the war
that was augmented by five SAAB Scandias

during the early 1950s with a further four
DC-4s and C-46s added later. VASP took
delivery of the first of its batch of six new
Vickers Viscounts in October 1958, followed by a further 11 ex-BEA models during the early 1960s.

Loide Aerea Nacional and Navegacao
Aerea Brazileira (NAB) were merged into
VASP in 1962 as part of the nationalisation
of air services in Brazil.

The jet age reached VASP in December
1967 with the arrival of a pair of BAC 1-11s.
YS-11s were added from late 1968 to replace
the Viscounts. The first 737 was delivered in
July 1969 and it has gradually become the
backbone of VASP operations with a fleet
that has remained strong ever since.

727s joined the fleet in April 1977 and
Bandeirantes were added shortly after for
short-haul feeder services. Three A300s
were added during the early 1980s.
Subsequently, DC-10s have been leased for

short periods.

During the early 1990s VASP encountered ever-increasing financial difficulties
that left the management with little option
other than to suspend international services and cut many unprofitable domestic
routes. The cuts also hit the workforce
badly and about half have been shed.

VASP managed to survive a number of
difficult years and, having undergone a
restructuring programme, was looking at
reviewing its short-haul and medium range
aircraft.

In 1996, VASP acquired a 50.5% stake in
Loyd Aero Boliviano but this was later sold
to a Bolivian enterprise in November 2001.

A 41% stake in the airline was made
available to investors. This has provided sufficient funds to re-open some of the suspended domestic and international routes.

Vietnam Airlines

Registered name: Vietnam Airline Corporation
Nationality: Vietnam
Region: Asia
Address: Gialam Airport
               Hanoi 10000
Tel: 0084 4 827 16 43
Fax: 0084 4 827 22 91
Web site: www.vietnamair.com.vn
Main operational base: Hanoi

STATUS

Scheduled passenger carrier
National Flag Carrier
Employees: 1,499
Passengers per year: 3,386,152 (2001)
ICAO code: HVN
IATA code: VN

SERVICES

International / Regional / Domestic
Passenger / Charter / Cargo
International routes: Australia, Austria,
Cambodia, China, France, Germany, Japan,
Laos, Malaysia, Netherlands, Philippines,

Russia, Singapore, South Korea, Taiwan,
Thailand, UAE, USA.

ALLIANCES / CODE SHARES

China A/l, China Southen A/l, Malaysia
A/l, Qantas, Singapore A/l, Thai Aw Int.

FLEET

A320-200 - 10, A321-100 - 2 , ATR 72-202 - 6,
ATR 72-500 - 3, 767-300ER - 3, 777-200ER -
4, Fokker 70 - 2.
On order: A321 - 5 (for delivery between
2003 and 2005).

ABOVE: *Vietnam Airlines ATR 72-202, VN-B208 (C/n
416) (ATR)*

The origins of Vietnam Airlines date back
to 1956 with the establishment of the
General Civil Aviation Administration of
Viet-Nam (CAAV), which operated in conjunction with the military, with five small
aircraft.

In 1976 the airline was named Hang
Khong Vietnam following the reunification
of North and South Vietnam. Aircraft operated included the Il-18, Tu-134 and Yak-40.

The airline was established as a state enterprise in 1989 and renamed Vietnam Airlines. Region Air arranged a package for the charter of an A310 on behalf of Vietnam Airlines in October 1991 which included service and the training of cabin crew. This was followed by another Region Air package to operate and maintain three 767s in 1996, lasting three years. A short lease of an A310 was also made in 2000.

In 1996 the Vietnam Airlines Corporation was formed as overall management of the airline and a number of associated service companies. Western aircraft began to be ordered to replace the older Soviet types, including ATR 72 and 767s.

During the 90s the scheduled network expanded throughout the region and in 2001 a Ho Chi Minh to San Francisco route was established in conjunction with China Airlines.

Vietnam Airlines has been successfully

ABOVE: *Vietnam Airlines A320-214 (Airbus)*

increasing its passenger levels in recent years and in 2001, placed an order for four 777s to replace the leased 767s.

Vietnam Airlines announced its 10-year plan in which it expects to increase the size of its fleet to 46 aircraft by 2010. This resulted in an order for the purchase of an additional five A321s in addition to the 10 A320s and two A321s which had already been leased.

Virgin Atlantic Airways

Registered name: Virgin Atlantic Airways Ltd
Country: UK
Region: Europe
Address: The Office
Crawley Business Quarter
Manor Royal
Crawley, RH10 9NU
Tel: 0044 1293 56 23 45
Fax: 0044 1293 56 17 21
Web site: www.virgin-atlantic.com

STATUS

IATA scheduled carrier
Employees: 7,027
Passengers per year: 4,105,000 (2001)
ICAO code: VIR
IATA code: VS

SERVICES

International / Passenger / Cargo
International routes: Antigua & Barbuda, China, Japan, Nigeria, St Lucia, South Africa, USA

ALLIANCES / CODE SHARES

Air-India, BMI, Continental A/l, Hawaiian A/l, Malaysia A/l, Nationwide, Singapore A/l

FLEET

A320-200 - 1, A340-300 - 10, A340-600 - 4, 747-400 - 12
On order: A340-600 - 6, A380-800 - 6 (for delivery from) 2006, 747-400 - 1

ABOVE: *Virgin 747-Q8, G-VFAB (C/n 24958) (Virgin)*

Virgin Atlantic Airways was formed in 1984 by Richard Branson and commenced operations in June as a low cost carrier with a 747.

Virgin Atlantic's first route was between London / Gatwick and New York / Newark with a starting single fare of £99. A second

Virgin Atlantic Airways

747 was added in 1986 that operated on a new route to Miami. In 1989 two more 747s were acquired and a Tokyo schedule commenced. A further two 747s were added to the fleet in 1990 and two more the following year.

In 1994, Virgin leased an A320 to operate on its Gatwick - Athens route. Previously this had been operated by a Greek carrier, South East European Airways (SEEA), with a 737 as a franchise agreement. When SEEA failed to keep up the leasing payments Virgin took up the lease to continue the service.

Three of the 747s were retired in 1998/9 and replaced with a further five similar -200 models. The additional aircraft enabled new services to be operated to the Caribbean.

Virgin took delivery of the first two of an initial order of ten Airbus A340s in 1993. These were operated on the increased schedules to Tokyo as well as a service to Johannesburg.

A new schedule to Shanghai was inaugurated in May 1999.

In June 1999 Virgin underwent a corporate image change ready to take it into the new millennium. The new colours utilised a new commercial aviation pearlescent paint technology. This new image was to represent a return to the glamour and romance of the golden age of flying in the 1930s.

Included in the new image is an overhaul of the upper class cabin with new seating that can be opened out into full-length beds. Twin seats are also available which

open out into the first double bed in airline service. Besides improvements to the audio-visual entertainment, a new dedicated beauty area enables it to provide an ever-improved service.

In December 1999, an agreement was reached with Singapore Airlines to take a 49% stake in Virgin for £600 million that included a £49 million cash injection into the airline.

New scheduled services to Las Vegas and Delhi commenced in June and July 2000. Another to Toronto was inaugurated in June 2001, followed by a further one to Lagos in July when the Nigerian Government wished to break the British Airways monopoly on the route.

Towards the end of 2000, Richard Branson made the proud announcement that Virgin had ordered six of the A380 (A3XX as it was then) plus a further six options.

ABOVE: *Virgin A340-642, G-VSHY (C/n 83) (Virgin)*

In 2002 Virgin announced its first loss since 1990 that was as a direct consequence of the 11th September atrocities. About 1,200 staff were laid-off, the older 747-200s retired and routes to Chicago, Toronto and Athens halted. However, as with most other transatlantic operators, it had been impossible to reduce capacity as quickly as the demand although Virgin reacted quicker than many. The pre-tax loss of £92m was less than expected.

During the second half of 2002 passenger numbers were steadily rising and staff were being recruited once again and routes being re-instated.

BELOW: *Virgin A340-311, G-VHOL (C/n 002) (Virgin)*

Virgin Express

Registered name: Virgin Express plc

Country: Belgium

Region: Europe

Address: Building 116

B-1820 Meisbroek

Brussels Airport

Tel: 0032 2 752 05 11

Fax: 0032 2 752 05 06

Web site: www.virgin-express.com

Main operational base: Brussels

STATUS

Scheduled and charter passenger carrier

Employees: 740

Passengers per year: 2,423,000 (2001)

ICAO code: VEX

IATA code: TV

SERVICES

Regional / Passenger / Charter

International routes: Denmark, Italy, Portugal, Greece, Spain, Sweden, UK

ALLIANCES / CODE SHARES

SB Brussels A/1

FLEET

737-300 - 7, 737-400 - 8 (1 leased to Virgin Blue in Australia)

Virgin Express was originally formed as EuroBelgian Airlines (EBA) in November 1992 as a charter carrier by the City Hotels group. It commenced operations in November 1994 with the 737.

A scheduled service commenced in November 1994 as EuroBelgian Express and established several routes to destinations in Europe.

The Virgin Group acquired a 90% holding in EBA in April 1996 and the name was changed to Virgin Express. Advantage was taken of the deregulation of the airline business to move emphasis from charter to scheduled services.

By keeping costs to a minimum and aircraft utilisation high, Virgin Express offered lower fares. However, margins were tight.

Sabena was struggling to maintain its Brussels-Heathrow route despite the losses that it was accumulating. Virgin pulled off a deal in which it would operate the slots with Sabena taking a block of seats.

A subsidiary - Virgin Express Ireland - was established in 1998 to compete with AB Airlines on a Shannon-Brussels route. However when AB failed, Cityflyer and Ryanair competed with their low-priced fares, and margins were then insufficient to create a profit.

In autumn 2000, Virgin Express withdrew its operations from Stanstead and moved them to Gatwick enabling better connections with its other services.

Virgin Express completed a restructuring programme in 2001 that left it more efficient enabling it to compete more strongly over the difficult times. This resulted in a number of unprofitable routes being sus-

ABOVE: *Virgin Express 737-36M, OO-VEA (C/n 28332) (Jeremy Flack/API)*

pended, the fleet size reduced and Virgin Express Ireland closed down. However, some new routes were opened from its Brussels hub.

The financial results show the success of the programme with cost-cut by 40%. An operating profit was generated in 2001 of US$1.36 million compared to the US$55 million loss of the previous year.

SN Brussels took over the Sabena Heathrow slots when it went under but in October 2002 they were sold, leaving Virgin Express which had been operating them on its behalf, without access to Heathrow.

A planned expansion into the German market was abandoned in 2002 as Lufthansa and TUI announced their low-cost travel plans. With easyJet, Ryanair, Deutsche BA and Air Berlin already operating, it was felt that there was already market saturation. As a result Virgin Express is looking at other markets to establish a new hub.

As 2002 progressed, Virgin Express was showing increasing passenger levels, which was good news for the airline. Besides the increased numbers, prior to SABENA's bankruptcy in November 2001, 50% of passengers carried were booked through SABENA. As a further bonus, the percentage of customers booking through the internet was also increasing.

Widerøe

Registered name: Widerøe's Flyveselskap AS
Country: Norway
Region: Europe
Address: Langstranda
PO Box 247
N-8001 Bodo
Tel: 0047 75 51 35 00
Fax: 0047 75 51 35 82
Web site: www.wideroe.no
Main operational base: Bodo

STATUS

IATA scheduled international and domestic passenger carrier
Employees: 1,248
Passengers per year: 1,409,000
ICAO code: WIF
IATA code: WF

SERVICES

Regional / Domestic / Passenger
International routes: Denmark, Germany, Sweden, UK

FLEET

DHC-8 Dash 8-103B - 17, DHC-8 Dash 8-300 - 9, DHC-8 Dash 8-Q400 - 3

Wideroe was formed on February 19th, 1934, by the aviation pioneer Viggo Widerøe as a domestic carrier and it is the oldest Norwegian airline still in existence.

Initial operations were air taxi and ambulance together with training and photography using Lockheed 14s.

After the war a scheduled seaplane service was operated with a Republic Seabee. Norseman and Otters were used to provide some land-based services.

During the latter 1960s the Norwegian Government reacted to public demand for improved services and established a number of small airfields from which Short Take Off and Landing (STOL) aircraft could operate. Widerøe took delivery of some DHC-6 Twin Otters and inaugurated a service between Trondheim and Bodo.

RIGHT: *Widerøe*DHC-8 Q402, LN-WDB (C/n 4070) (Bombardier)

ABOVE: *Widerøe* DHC-8 Q402, LN-WDB (C/n 4070) (Bombardier)

Widerøe was reorganised to enable it to play the leading role in providing this valuable service to the, often remote, communities.

With fresh capital Widerøe was re-established as a scheduled airline and the network quickly expanded. The Twin Otters that had, by the end of the 1980s, provided virtually the whole fleet were gradually replaced by the DHC-7. This aircraft had greater space and comfort for the passengers and extra capacity as the routes developed and numbers increased.

The DHC-7 was added to the fleet in the early 1980s and replaced by the improved DHC-8 Dash 8. Initial deliveries were for the 37-seat -100 Series model that is the largest-sized aircraft to be able to operate the STOL network. Some of the larger 50-seat -300 Series variant were subsequently ordered.

In June 2001, Widerøe placed an order with Bombardier for three of the 72-seat DHC-8 Dash 8 Q400s. With their better operating costs, the Q400s are used on services in southern Norway and international routes where runway length is not a problem.

Wideøe provides a scheduled service to over 30 destinations within Norway in addition to its regional schedules.

Virtually unaffected by the events of the preceding September, Widerøe announced its best ever half yearly figures in August 2002 with a pre-tax profit of NKr 57.2 million - up NKr 2.1 million on the same period in 2001.

During 2002, SAS acquired a further 33.1% of the Wideøe shares for NKr 131.2 million taking it to 96.4%. In October it was awarded the silver prize for being 'Europe's best Regional Airline'.

Yemenia - Yemen Airways

Registered name: Yemenia
Nationality: Rep. of Yemen
Region: Middle East
Address: PO Box 1183
                  Sana'a
Tel: 00967 1 23 23 80
Fax: 00967 1 25 29 82
Web site: www.yemenia.com.ye
Main operational base: Sana'a

STATUS

IATA scheduled international and
domestic carrier
National Flag Carrier
Employees: 3,800
Passengers per year: 841,000 (2001)
ICAO code: IYE
IATA code: IY

SERVICES

International / Regional / Domestic
Passenger / Charter / Cargo
International routes: Bahrain, Comoros Is,
Djibouti, Egypt, Eritrea, Ethiopia, France,
Germany, India, Indonesia, Italy, Jordan,
Lebanon, Malaysia, Pakistan, Qatar, Saudia
Arabia, Sudan, Syria, Tanzania, UAE, UK.

FLEET

A310-300 - 4, 727-200Adv - 2, 737-200Adv -
1, 737-800 - 3, 747SP - 1 (operated for the
Government), DHC-7 Dash 7 - 3, Il-76TD -
2.

The history of Yemen Airways can be traced
back to 1949 when the Government of
Yemen purchased two DC-3s. They were primarily used to fly government officials and
mail in Yemen although they were occasionally used to transport businessmen.

On August 4th 1961 the Yemen Airways
Company was formed as the national airline
and the two DC-3s transferred ownership.

In 1965 an additional four DC-3s were
purchased enabling an expansion of the
domestic network. Following a co-operative
agreement with United Arab Airlines (UAA
- now Egypt Air) two DC-6s were added to
the fleet in 1967. These enabled an international route to be operated for the first
time and established a link to Cairo. A further two DC-6s were added in 1970 following another co-operative agreement with
Saudi Arabia.

In 1972 the name was changed to Yemen
Airways following nationalisation and a
reorganisation. Chartered Caravelles were
operated to increase capacity to Jeddah
when required.

Leased 737s were also operated for several years until Yemen Airways took delivery
of its own in 1976.

The current title of Yemenia was intro-

ABOVE: *Yemen Airways A310-324 (Airbus)*

duced on July 1st 1978 following the joint
restructuring and ownership by the Yemen
Arab Republic (51%) and the Saudi
Arabian Government (49%).

In 1979 Yemenia took delivery of four
727s and two DHC-7s in 1980.

In May 1996 a historic step was taken
when Alyemen from South Yemen was
merged with Yemenia from North Yemen to
form a single national airline for the whole
country.

Two more 737s and two DHC-7s were
ordered in 1996 and the passenger levels
continued to grow.

In 2002 a total of 17,555 pilgrims was
flown by Yemenia to and from Saudi Arabia
during the Hajj.

Yemenia has added a total of four A310 to
its fleet. As a matter of course, Airbus monitors the aircraft performance with the customer. Yemenia has been operating these
aircraft without foreign support (apart
from the Airbus customer support manager) and managed a 100% despatch rate in
the last six months of 1999 while the rate
for the whole year was 'just' 99.4%.

Negotiations for a fifth A310 have been
undertaken.

AIRLINERS

Aerospatiale/BAC Concorde

Four-engined supersonic airliner

BAA

Design of Concorde commenced in the mid 50's. The prototype first flew on March 2nd, 1969 and entered service on January 21st 1976. Despite a number of initial orders from various airlines it only served with Air France and British Airways. A disastrous accident for this unique Mach 2 airliner in 2000 saw it grounded. Following extensive safety modifications which included kevlar / rubber fuel tank liners and new tyres, Concorde returned to the sky in November 2001.

Production of the Concorde ended in 1979 with a total of 20 built including two prototypes and two pre-production aircraft.

VARIANTS

Concorde Series 200: Initial production model

Airbus A300

Twin-turbofan medium-haul airline

Jeremy Flack/API

The A300 programme was launched in 1969. The prototype A300 first flew on

October 28th, 1972 and entered service in November 1974. The first product of the European Airbus consortium, has remained in production through many variants and many retired passenger airliners are seeing a life extension through conversion to freighters.

The A300-600 is the current production model which first flew in 1983 and delivered in in March 1984. It has increased fuel plus maximum weight and a greater range than the earlier variants utilising the A310 rear fuselage / tail.

The -600R offers extended range with an increased Maximum Take Off Weight (MTOW). It features a fuel trim tank in the tail.

Orders for the A300 stood at 583 at the end of 2002 with 517 delivered.

VARIANTS

A300B1: Initial production model
A300B2: Basic production model
A300B4: Extended range, increased MTOW model of B1
A300B4-200: Increased MTOW + Krüger flaps
A300B4-200F: Cargo model
A300-600: Advanced A300B4-200 with A310 rear
A300-600R: Increased range + max weight
A300-600 Convertible: Passenger/cargo model of -200
A300-600F: Cargo model
Beluga: Modified super freighter

Airbus A310

Twin-turbofan short/medium-haul airliner

Jeremy Flack/API

The A310 was launched in July 1978 as part

of the A300 family and is based on the A300B4. It has a shorter fuselage and a smaller, more advanced wing. The prototype first flew April 3rd, 1982 and entered service in 1983.

The A310-300 was the first commercial airliner to feature a drag-reducing wingtip. Orders for the A310 stood at 260 at the end of 2002 with 255 delivered.

VARIANTS

A310-200: Initial production model
A310-200F: Freighter conversion
A310-300: Extended range model with wingtip fences

Airbus A318

Twin-turbofan short-haul airliner

Airbus

The A318 is the latest and smallest member of the A320 family. The prototype first flew on January 15th, 2002.

The A318 is derived from the A319 with a 2.4m shorter fuselage but a slightly higher fin and rudder. It features a new generation Cabin Intercommunication Data System (CIDS) which will give an improved flexibility to accommodate customer options. Inflight entertainment includes an 'in-seat' video.

Laser welding of panels is a new manufacturing technique introduced on the A318 which is lighter than traditional riveting as well as reducing corrosion.

At the end of 2002, the order book for the A318 stood at 84 with deliveries to commence in 2003.

Airliners

VARIANTS
A318-100: Initial production model

Airbus A319
Twin-turbofan short-haul airliner

Jeremy Flack/API

The A319 was launched in June 1993. This reduced length A320 first flew on August 29th, 1995 and deliveries commenced the following April.

Orders for the A319 stood at 856 at the end of 2002 including the recent order for 120 by easyjet. 492 had been delivered.

VARIANTS
A319-100: Base production model
A319-ACJ: Airbus Corporate Airliner

Airbus A320
Twin-turbofan short-haul airliner

Jeremy Flack/API

The A320 was launched in March 1984 and the prototype first flew on February 22nd, 1987. Deliveries commenced in March 1988.

The A320 was the first airliner to operate with fly-by-wire systems and a side-stick controller. This significantly reduced the weight of the conventional hydraulic system enabling a greater range.

The A320 is also the first subsonic commercial airliner it incorporate composite materials in major structures to further reduce weight.

In 1998, Airbus began testing a laminar-flow tail which featured small holes in its leading edge to suck air in and release it at the rear of the fin to reduce drag.

Orders for the A330 stood at 1,597 at the end of 2002 with 1,128 delivered.

VARIANTS
A320-100: Initial production model
A320-200: Standard production model with wingtip fences

Airbus A321
Twin-turbofan short-haul airliner

Jeremy Flack/API

The A321 is the increased length A320 model and was launched in November 1989. The prototype first flew on March 11th, 1993 and deliveries commenced in January 1994.

The fuselage is lengthened with the addition of a 4.27m plug immediately forward of the wing and a 2.67m aft. Additional 2,900 lt of fuel is carried in an additional centre tank and the undercarriage has been uprated for the increased weight.

Orders for the A321 stood at 421 at the end of 2002 with 256 delivered.

VARIANTS
A321-100: Initial production model
A321-200: Extended range model with increased MTOW and fuel

Airbus A330
Twin-turbofan medium/long-haul airliner

Jeremy Flack/API

The A330 was developed in conjunction with the A340 to become the medium/long range family with models to suit the airlines requirements. The prototype first flew on November 2nd, 1992 and entered service in December 1993.

The A330 construction is common to the A340 with identical fuselage and wings. They are easily differentiated in that the A330 has two engines compared to four on the A340.

The fuselage design is such that it has a large underfloor hold capacity. This can take substantial quantities of cargo as well as optional crew rest areas, galleys, lounges and/or washroom areas to provide extra cabin space.

The A330-200 features a shorter (59m) length fuselage with 50 less seats for medium ranges.

At the end of 2002, the order book for the A330 stood at 419 with 251 delivered.

VARIANTS
A330-200: Extended range/short fuselage model
A330-300: Base model

Airbus A340
Four-turbofan long-haul airlin

Jeremy Flack/API

The A340 is the long range four engined model in the A330 / A340 Airbus family. They were jointly launched in June 1987. The first model made its initial flight on October 25th, 1991 and the first delivery was made in January 1993.

The cockpit layout remains identical with all other Airbus airliners which all have similar handling characteristics.The identical fuselage and wings with the A330 enables aircrew type conversion from one type to another to be reduced from 25 to 3 days while conversion from the A320 family can be achieved in 8/9 days.

The A340 range of models covers 295 to 380 seats and at ranges of up to 16,050 kms. The 500 and 600 variants are fitted with the more powerful RR Trent.

The A340 features a tailplane trim tank which uses fuel to adjust the trim more efficiently reducing drag and therefore the quantity of fuel burnt.

At the end of 2002, the A340 order book stood at 317 with 228 delivered.

VARIANTS

A340-200: Reduced length fuselage model
A340-300: Standard production model
A340-500: Increased length, power + capacity
A340-600: Further increased power + capacity

Airtech (CASA) CN-235

Twin-turboprop short-haul airliner

Jeremy Flack/API

Design of the CN-235 commenced in 1980 and the prototype first flew on November 11th, 1983. The first delivery was made in December 1986.

All work is conducted jointly by CASA of Spain and IPTN of Indonesia who subsequently jointly formed Airtech to continue development and production.

The CN-235 orders have been primarily for military operators but is also successfully flown by some airlines. 208 CN-235/CN295s had been built by the end of 2002 with a further 14 orders outstanding.

VARIANTS

CN-235-10: Initial production model
CN-235-100: Re engined with CT7C
CN-235-110: Indonesian model of 100
CN-235-200: Strengthened + increased range
CN-235-220: Indonesian model of 200
CN-235-330: Military transport model
CN-235-AEW: Military AEW model
CN-235M: Military transport model
CN-235MP: Military maritime patrol model
CN-235QC: Quick change (cargo/passenger)
CN-295: Stretched CN-235M

Antonov An-24/26

Twin-turboprop short-haul airliner

Jeremy Flack/API

The An-24 was designed in the late 50's and first flew in April 1960. It entered service in September 1963 with Aeroflot.

The An-24 saw extensive service with civil and military operators with in the region of 1,200 built by 1979.

Production continued with the An-26 of which over 1,400 were built mainly for freight/military operators. Further production continued with the increased power An-32 with a similar role.

VARIANTS

An-24: Initial production model
An-24V: Improved power model
An-24V Seriiny II: Increased wing area model
An-24T: Freighter model of Seriiny II
An-24RT: Freighter with auxiliary Ru-19 turbojet
An-24P: Specialised fire fighting model
An-26: Redesigned rear fuselage with beaver-tail door.
An-32: High-lift wing + higher mounted engines

Avions Transport Regional ATR 42

Twin-turboprop regional airliner

Jeremy Flack/API

The ATR 42 was launched by Aerospatiale and Aeritalia in October 1981 and the prototype first flew on August 16th, 1984. Delivery commenced in December 1984. Production commenced with the -300 model of which 285 were ordered and built before production was phased out in 1996 in favour of the -400 and -500 models. The -400 is fitted with six-bladed Hamilton Sundstrand propellers.

At the end of 2002 370 ATR 42s had been ordered of which 369 had been delivered.

VARIANTS

ATR 42-300: Initial production model
ATR 42-320: PW121 powered -300 for hot/high performance
ATR 42-400: PW121A powered with 6-bladed propellers
ATR 42-500: Increased power/weight with ATR 72-210 fin

ATR 42F: Freighter with cargo/airdrop door
ATR Calibration/42MP/SAR 42 - Special
purpose models
ATR 42L: Freighter with lateral cargo door

Avions Transport Regional ATR 72

Twin-turboprop regional airliner

Jeremy Flack/API

The ATR 72 is basically a 4.5m stretched model 42 with new wings outboard of the engines and an all composite tail. The first development aircraft flew on October 27th, 1988. Deliveries commenced in October 1989.

The -500 model is fitted with six-bladed Hamilton Sundstrand propellers.

At the end of 2002 306 ATR 72s had been ordered of which 285 had been delivered.

VARIANTS

ATR 72-200: Initial production model
ATR 72-210: PW127 powered + with composite propellers
ATR-72-500: PW127F powered with 6-bladed propellers
ATR 52C: Rear loading cargo model

BAe 146/Avro RJ

Four-turbofan short-haul regional airliner

The Avro RJ and BAe146 family of airliners began with the Hawker Siddeley HS.146 which was launched in 1973. As a result of a recession, this project was cancelled the following year. In 1978 the project resurfaced with BAe of which

Jeremy Flack/API

Hawker Siddeley was now a part.

The prototype BAe.146 first flew on September 3rd, 1981 and entered service in May 1983.

The unusual four engine configuration for this size of aircraft resulted in it being very quiet and quickly earned the name "Whisper Jet". This feature was quickly exploited resulting many successful sales.

Further development of the BAe.146 by Avro led to the RJ series with uprated engines and all digital-avionics. The RJ85 first flew in March 1992 and replaced the BAe.146 on the production line. The RJ70 was the shortest for 70/82 passengers while the RJ100 & RJ115 were longer with 100/116 & 116/128 capacity. As the orders slowed down a decision was taken to halt development of the RJX and cancel the outstanding orders.

BAe built a total of 389 of the 146/RJ family (219 BAe146s and 170 RJs).

VARIANTS

BAe.146-100: Initial production model
BAe.146-200: Increased length model
BAe.146-300: Further increased length model
BAe.146QT: Freighter
RJ70: Shortened fuselage for 70-94 passengers
RJ85: Lengthened fuselage for 85 to 112 passengers
RJ100: Lengthened fuselage for 100 to 116 passengers
RJ115: Increased max weight RJ100 for 116 to 128 passengers
RJX-85: Project cancelled during development flying

BAe Jetstream

Twin-turboprop commuter airline

Jeremy Flack/API

The Jetstream was originally designed by Handley Page in the mid 60's as an 8/18 seat transport. The prototype first flew on August 18th, 1967.

Handley Page ceased operating in 1970. The Jetstream passed through the hands of Jetstream Aircraft Ltd and Scottish Aviation with only a small number built. In 1978 the Jestream 31 was successfully launched by British Aerospace with TPE331-10 replacing the unpopular Astazou XIV engines.

A 4.9m stretched Jetstream 41 was launched in 1989. Although not put into production the Jetstream 61 was in fact the renamed ATP.

When production finally ended in 1998, 386 Jetstream 31/32s had been built plus 99 Jetstream 41s.

VARIANTS

Jetstream T.1: Military trainer for RAF
Jetstream T.2: Military trainer for Royal Navy
Jetstream 31: TPE331 powered base model
Jetstream 32: Improved performance model
Jetstream 32EP: Enhanced Performance model
Jetstream 41: Stretched 29 seat model

Boeing 707

Four-engined medium/long-haul airliner

The origin of the 707 commenced in the early 50's with the prototype Model 367-80 first flown on July 15th, 1954. Some 745 Model 717s (not the newer 717 airliner)

Jeremy Flack/API

were ordered for the USAF as C-135/KC-135 transports and tankers plus some special missions. Civil orders were placed for a variant which had a 10cm larger diameter fuselage designated 707. It entered service in October 1958.

The 707 saw widescale operation with civil airlines in various configurations. The 707-320 served in the largest numbers with 482 built. A major sub-variant was the 720 which was smaller and lighter.

Most were fitted with noisy turbojets or early turbofans and noise regulations for most western airports have banned their use. With around 100 still flying, they have either had their engines replaced or had hushkits fitted. The majority of these survivors operate in the cargo role.

When production ended in 1994, 1,010 707 / 720s had been delivered.

VARIANTS

707-120: Initial basic production model
707-120B: JT3D turbofan powered -120 model
707-220: JT4 turbojet powered -120 model
707-320: Increased size and intercontinental range
707-320B: Increased power -320 model
707-320C: Convertible cargo / passenger model
707-320C Freighter: All cargo model
707-420: RR Conway powered 320 model
720: Basic model
720B: JT3D tubofan powered 720 model

Boeing 717
Twin-turbofan short-haul airliner

The 717 is the re-branded McDonnell

Jeremy Flack/API

Douglas MD-95 which was announced in 1991. Initial development was with a modified DC-9-30. A prototype was subsequently built and first flew on September 2nd, 1998 with deliveries commencing the following year.

Orders have been slow and although plans were made for a stretched and reduced length variants they have not been proceeded with.

At the end of 2002 a total of 115 717s had been delivered.

VARIANTS

717-100: Proposed shortened 80 seat model
717-200: Initial basic production model
717-200 HGW: Higher Gross Weight model
717-300: Proposed stretched 130 seat model

Boeing 727
Three-turbofan short-haul airliner

Jeremy Flack/API

Design of the 727 commenced in 1959 and the prototype first flew on February 9th, 1963.

Two of the -100 models could be used to carry cargo with either the convertible or Quick Change which enables seats to be taken out in blocks.

As with all of the early jet airliners, the Chapter 3 noise restrictions require hushkits to be fitted. With the numbers built, a substantial number continue to operate although these restrictions will hasten the demise of many of them.

When production of the 727 ended in 1984, a total of 1,831 had been delivered.

VARIANTS

727-100: Initial production model
727-100C: Convertible model
727-100QC: Quich change model
727-200: Stretched model
727-200Adv: Improved model with noise reduced interior
727-200F: Freighter

Boeing 737-100/200
Twin-turbofan short-haul airliner

Jeremy Flack/API

The decision to proceed with the 737 was taken in 1964. The prototype first flew on April 9th, 1967 and the first delivery on December 29th, 1967.

Competing with the rear engined US DC-9 and British 1-11, the 737 was a conventional design which continued to use the 707 fuselage design.

When production of the -100 / -200 series ended in 1988 a total of 1,144 had been delivered.

VARIANTS

737-100: Initial production model
737-200: Increased length & capacity
737-200C: Side cargo door
737-200Adv: Improved performance & reverse thrust
T-43A: Military navigation trainer for USAF

Airliners

Boeing 737-300/400/500
Twin-turbofan short-haul airliner

Jeremy Flack/API

The 737-300 represented a step up in this family of airliners which entered production in 1981. The first example flew on February 24th, 1984 with deliveries commencing in November 1984.

The 737-300 incorporated a 2.64m longer fuselage over the -200 for a 129 / 149 capacity. This was achieved with a plug fore and aft of the wing. It also featured increased tail dimensions plus improvements to the wing including new flaps and slats as well as overall span.

The -400 model increased the length by a further 2.39m and featured a tail bumper while the -500 was 2.39m shorter and carried 108 / 138 passengers.

Production for the -300, -400 and -500 totalled 1988 when the last example was delivered in February 2000.

VARIANTS
737-300: Basic production model
737-400: Extended fuselage + strengthened wing model
737-500: Shorter fuselage model

Boeing 737-600/700/800/900
Twin-turbofan short-haul airliner

The Next Generation 737s were launched as the 737X in November 1993 and the prototype -700 first flew on February 9th, 1997. The first delivery followed in December 1997.

The 737NGs offer a modern cockpit with

Jeremy Flack/API

large flat panel display technology with optional display formats. They also feature an advanced wing with increased, span, performance and fuel capacity to give a greater range. Then also have an increased span and height tail.

The 31.24m -600 is the shortest in this group and carried 108/132 passengers. The -800 is stretched to 39.47m for 162/189 passengers while the -900 is even longer at 42.11m for 177/189 passengers.

Orders at the end of 2002 stood at 2046 of which 1257 had been delivered.

VARIANTS
737-600: Short length, 108/132 seat model
737-700: Next Generation basic model
737-700IGW: Increased Gross Weight model
737-800: Increased length 162/189 model
737-900: Further stretched 177/189 seat model
737-BBJ: Corporate jet with -700 fuselage + -800 wings
C-40: Military model of -700 for US Navy

Boeing 747-100/200/SP/300
Four-turbofan long-haul airliner

Jeremy Flack/API

The 747 programme was launched in 1966 and the prototype was first flown on February 9th, 1969. The first entered service in January 1970.

An increasing number of these older 747s are being concerted for use as freighters.

A total of 769 of this 747 Classic family were delivered before their production ended in 1991.

VARIANTS
747-100: Initial production model
747-100B: Increased MTOW
747-100SF: Cargo conversion with cargo door
747SP: Short length, long range model
747SR: Short range, high cycle model
747-200B: Increased MTOW & engine power
747-200F: Freighter
747-300: Extended upper deck standard
747-300M: Combi with rear port-side cargo door
747-300SR: Short range with extra windows
E-4: Military model

Boeing 747- 400
Four-turbofan long-haul airliner

Jeremy Flack/API

The 747-400 is the advanced long range model which was originally announced in 1985. The prototype first flew on April 29th, 1988 and the first delivered in January 1989.

The 747-400 combines the -300 fuselage with the Stretched Upper Deck (SUD) with a two crew digital flightdeck together with an increased span wing incorporating

winglets and redesigned wing/body fairings.

The 747-400 is the only 747 model marketed and in production.

At the end of 2002 a total of 595 747-400s had been delivered with orders of 648.

VARIANTS

747-400: Extended wings + winglets
747-400F: Freighter with -200F fuselage + -400 wings
747-400: Combi with rear port-side cargo door
747-400: Domestic - High density model with five extra upper deck window + no winglets
747-400ER: Increased MTOW and range
747-400X: Quiet Long Range model
C-19/AL-1: Military models

Boeing 757
Twin-turbofan medium-haul airliner

Jeremy Flack/API

The 757 had been designed to replace the 707, 727 and early 737s and was announced in 1978. The prototype first flew on February 19th, 1982 and deliveries commenced in August 1982.

The 757 retains the basic fuselage width of the 707 but incorporates a new cockpit and new wings.

The -200SF is fitted with a side cargo door and was designed and built to meet a specific requirement for DHL. It is similar to the -200PF for UPS. The -300 has a 7.1m longer fuselage.

The 757 has seen orders low down, in fact none were placed in 2002. This is due to the development of the 737-800 and -

900 which offers similar performance as well as competition from Airbus.

At the end of 2002 a total of 983 757s had been delivered against orders of 1049.

VARIANTS

757-200: Initial production model
757-200PF: Package Freighter with cargo door
757-200SF: Freighter with cargo door
757-200M: Combination
757-200F: Freighter
757-300: Stretched model
C-32: Military model

Boeing 767
Twin-turbofan medium-haul airliner

Jeremy Flack/API

The 767 was launched in 1978 and the prototype first flew on September 26th 1981.

The 767 fuselage is 1.22m wider than the earlier single isle models based on the 707. This enables twin isles with around 224 seats in the -200.

The stretched -300 featured a plug fore and aft of the wing plus strengthened undercarriage and some lower skin thickening. The -300ER had some strengthening which enabled increased gross weight for additional fuel in the centre section.

Besides the AWACS model, the 767 is being considered as a tanker to replace the KC-135 for the USAF as well as other Air Forces.

At the end of 2002 a total of 686 orders had been received of which 632 had been delivered.

VARIANTS

767-200: Initial production model
767-200ER: Extended Range with extra fuel in centre tanks
767-300: 6.42m stretched fuselage
767-300ER: Extended Range with extra fuel in centre tanks
767-300F: Freighter - forward port cargo door - no windows
767 AWACS: Military model

Boeing 777
Twin-turbofan long-haul airliner

SAS

The 777 was launched in 1989. First flight was on June 12, 1994 and deliveries commenced in May 1995.

The 777 features a new larger fuselage which can accommodate up to 10 abreast seating for tourist/economy class. The -300 variant is 10.13m longer fuselage than the earlier -200 model

A substantial amount of composite materials are use to reduce weight and improve performance.

At the end of 2002 a total 543 deliveries have been made against 619 orders

VARIANTS

777-200 Initial production model
777-300: Increased length, reinforced fuselage & increased MTOW
777-300ER: Extended range model
777-300LR: Longer range model

Boeing (McDD) MD-11
Three-turbofan long-haul airliner

The MD-11 is the continued development of the DC-10. The prototype first flew on

Jeremy Flack/API

January 10th, 1990 and deliveries commenced in December 1990.

Closely resembling the DC-10, the MD-11 is slightly larger and is fitted with winglets. The passenger and freighter models were both offered from the outset. Nearly a third of those bought new were freighters and a number more have been converted subsequently.

When production ended in 2000 and the 200th MD-11 was delivered in 2001.

VARIANTS

MD-11: Initial production model
MD-11F: Freighter

Boeing (McDD) MD-80
Twin-turbofan short-haul airliner

Jeremy Flack/API

The MD-80 is the continued development of the DC-9-80 of which the prototype first flew on October 18th, 1979. Deliveries commenced in October 1980.

The -80 is a series number of which there are a number of variants.

A total of 1191 MD-80 were delivered by the time production ended in April 1998.

VARIANTS

MD-81: Basic model
MD-82: Improved power model

MD-83: Increased fuel and power model
MD-87: Reduced length fuselage
MD-88: Increased power and updated avionics

Boeing (McDD) MD-90
Twin-turbofan short-haul airliner

SAS

The MD-90 is the stretched follow on series from the MD-80 / DC-9. The prototype first flew on February 22nd, 1993. The first example was delivered in February 1995.

The 1.37m longer fuselage of the -30 and -50 enable an additional 10 passengers.

An assembly line was established in Shanghai using US supplied kits.

A total of 113 were delivered

VARIANTS

MD-90-30: Initial production model
MD-90-30ER: Extended range model with optional extra fuel tank
MD-90-50: Further extended model
MD-90-55: Similar to -50 with extra doors

Bombardier (Canadair) CRJ-100/200
Twin-turbofan regional airliner

Bombardier

Design studies of the CRJ-100 commenced in 1987 based on the CL-600 Challenger. The first development aircraft made its maiden flight on May 10th, 1991. Deliveries commenced in October 1992.

Production commenced with the 100 model before transferring to the improved 200.

The CRJ440 utilises the 200 fuselage but with reduced 44-seat capacity for the US market. This is to enable it to conform with the pilot unions' restrictions.

Orders for the CRJ100, 200 and 440 are approaching 1000.

VARIANTS

100ER: Initial production model
100LR: Extended range model
200: Standard production model
200ER: Extended range model
200LR: Long range model
400: Reduced weight 200 for US market

Bombardier (Canadair) CRJ-700/900
Twin-turbofan regional airliner

Bombardier

The CRJ-700 was originally designated CRJ-X when initial design commenced in 1995. The prototype first flew on May 27th, 1999 and deliveries commenced in 2000.

The CRJ700 is the 70 seat variant of the Bombardier family of regional jets. It features a plug fore and aft of the wing to give it the 4.72m longer fuselage.

The CRJ900 further stretched with an extra 3,89m over the CRJ700 enabling an 86 seat capacity. As with the CRJ700, the

CRJ900 features a 1.89m (6ft 2.25in) headroom in the cabin as well as repositioned windows and overhead bins.

Orders for the CRJ700 and CRJ900 exceed 200.

VARIANTS

700: Basic 68 seat + ER option
701: 70 seat model + ER option
702: 72/78 seat model + ER option
900: Stretched 700

Bombardier (DHC) DHC-6 Twin Otter

Twin-turboprop commuter airliner

Jeremy Flack/API

The DHC-6 Twin Otter was developed from the DHC-6 Otter with a greater wingspan and increased length fuselage incorporating a new nose and tail. The prototype flew for the first time on May 20th, 1965 and entered service in July 1966.

The first two models were powered by the PT-6A-6 turboprops but the more powerful Series 300 could carry an additional 454kgs. With an impressive STOL performance, the Twin Otter was used by many airlines on difficult routes and could also be seen operating with skis and floats.

When production ended in 1988 a total of 844 had been built.

VARIANTS

Series 100: Initial production model
Series 200: Increased baggage capacity in larger nose
Series 300: Increased power and MTOW.

Series 300M:/MR/UV-18 - Military models
Series 400: Improved STOL model for inner city airports

Bombardier (DHC) DHC-7 Dash 7

Twin-turboprop regional airliner

Jeremy Flack/API

Construction of the Dash 7 commenced in 1972 and the prototype first flew on March 27th 1975. The Dash 7 entered service in March 1978.

The Dash 7 was designed to meet a need for an aircraft that could operate safely from small rough strips to link town and cities. The Short Take Off and Landing (STOL) performance was therefore important as was its quiet operation.

Orders came from a variety of customers with many requirements including providing mountain and island services.

A total of 113 had been built when production ended in 1988.

VARIANTS

Dash-7-100: Basic production model
Dash-7-101: Combi model with forward freight door
Dash-7-150: Increased fuel/MTOW and range
Dash-7-151: Combi model of 150
Dash-7-IR Ranger: Ice reconnaissance model

Bombardier (DHC) DHC-8 Dash 8

Twin-turboprop regional airliner

The Dash 8 was launched in 1980 and the prototype first flown on June 20th 1983.

Jeremy Flack/API

Deliveries commenced in October 1984.

The Dash 8 comprise a range of STOL aircraft with capacity from 36 to 78. It is a short haul airliner / feeder liner capable of flying in and out of confined airstrips / airports.

The Dash 8 has proved popular and over 600 have been ordered

VARIANTS

Dash 8-100: Initial production model
Dash 8-100A: Restyled interior
Dash 8-Q100B: Improved performance with PW120A
Dash 8-200A: Improved performance with PW123C
Dash 8-200B: 200A with PW123D
Dash 8-Q200: Q100 with PW123C/D
Dash 8M: Military model
Dash 8-Q300: Stretched 200
Dash 8-Q400: Stretched Q300

CASA C.212

Twin-turboprop commuter airliner

Jeremy Flack/API

Design of the C.212 Aviocar commenced in 1964 as a light utility transport aircraft for the Spanish AF. The prototype made its first flight on March 26th, 1971.

Besides the military role, the C.212C was marketed as a 19-seat airliner. An agreement concluded with IPTN initially to

assemble then build C.212s in Indonesia.

At the end of 2002, 430 C.212s had been built of which one third were for civil operators.

VARIANTS

C.212-100: Initial production model
C.212CA: Initial civil model
C.212-200: Increased performance with TPE-331-10 engines
C.212-300: Revised nose, tail + winglets
C.212-300: A number of military models
C.212-400: Increased performance with TPE331-JR engines

Dornier Do 228

Twin-turboprop commuter airliner

Jeremy Flack/API

The Dornier Do 228 was first publicly displayed in 1981 having first flown on March 28th, 1981.

The Do 228 is a STOL general purpose transport incorporating Dornier's new technology wing. The -100 and -200 were are similar although the -200 is 1.52m longer and an additional four seats. As the maximum weight for both was similar, the -200 had a 620km shorter range.

Dornier built a total of 240 Do 228s when their production ended in 1996. However HAL obtained a licence to built up to 150 in India.

VARIANTS

Do 228-100: Initial production model
Do 228-101: Strengthened model
Do 228-200: As -100 with longer fuselage
Do 228-201: Indian produced model
Do 228-212: Longer increased capacity model
Do 228: Military models

Embraer EMB-120 Brasilia

Twin-turboprop commuter airliner

Jeremy Flack/API

Design of the EMB-120 Brasilia commenced in 1979. The prototype first flew on July 27th, 1983. Deliveries commenced in June 1985.

Standard production commenced with the EMB-120 and quickly changed to the PW118 powered EMB-120RT. In 1994 it changed to the increased MTOW EMB-120ER.

352 Brasilias have been built.

VARIANTS

EMB-120: Launch production model
EMB-120T: Reduced Take-off Initial production model
EMB-120ER: Extended Range, Standard production model
EMB-120: Cargo - ER Freighter
EMB-120: Combi - Mixed passenger / cargo
EMB-120QC: Quick Change convertible
VC-97 - Military model

Embraer ERJ-135/ 140/145

Twin-turbofan regional airliner

Jeremy Flack/API

Plans for the EMB-145 were originally revealed in 1989 and re-designated ERJ-145 in 1997. The prototype first flew on August 11th, 1995 and deliveries commenced in December 1996.

The EJR-145 is based on a stretched EMB120 fuselage with a new tail and wings. The ERJ-135 has a 3.54m shorter fuselage and was launched in September 1997. Two of the development ERJ-145s were modified as prototypes and the first flight was made on July 4th 1998. Deliveries of this 37 seat model commenced in 1999.

The 44-seat ERJ-140 is 1.54 shorter than the ERJ-145 was built for an American requirement.

The Legacy executive jet is the most recent model of the ERJ-135 which has winglets.

Order at the end of 2002 stood at 122 ERJ-135s of which 91 had been delivered. 174 ERJ-140s of which 58 had been delivered. 583 ERJ-145s with 301 options of which 474 had been delivered.

VARIANTS

ERJ-145ER: Initial production model
ERJ-145LR: Increased MTOW and range
ERJ-135: Reduced length fuselage
ERJ-140: Mid sized model for US market
Lagacy: Executive model of ERJ-135

Fairchild Dornier 328JET

Twin-turbofan regional airliner

Jeremy Flack/API

The original design of the 328 commenced in the mid '80s as a turboprop powered aircraft which first flew on December 6th, 1991.The turbofan powered model was launched in 1997. A prototype was built by converting the second turboprop

prototype. It made its first flight in the new configuration on January 20th, 1998.

Fairchild Dornier were facing financial difficulties and in 2002 they had to halt production at 106 although they still had some orders outstanding.

VARIANTS

328Jet: Initial production model
Envoy: Corporate model

Fairchild (Swearingen) Metro/Merlin

Twin-turboprop commuter airliner

Jeremy Flack/API

The Merlin development evolved from the Beech Queen Air. This led to the Merlin II and III. This led in turn to the stretched Metro 23. The prototype Metro first flew on August 26th, 1969.

By the time production ended in 1999 a total of 1,053 of all Metro / Merlins had been built

VARIANTS

Merlin II: Initial production model
Merlin III: Slightly longer fuselage + new tail
Metro III: Stretched Merlin + new wings
Metro 23: Increased MTOW
C-26: Military model

Fokker F-27/FH-227 Friendship

Twin-turboprop short-haul airliner

The F-27 Friendship prototype first flew on November 24th, 1955. Deliveries

Jeremy Flack/API

commenced during November 1958.

The F-27 was designed to be a DC-3 / C-47 replacement and managed to sell it quite successfully. Fairchild arranged a licence to allow it to undertake production in the USA.

When production of the F-27 ended in 1985, a total of 787 had been built.

VARIANTS

F-27-100: Initial production model
F-27-200: Improved power with Dart R.Da.7 Mk.528
F-27-300: Freighter with cargo door
F-27-400: -300 with Dart R.Da.7 Mk.528
F-27-500: Lengthened fuselage + cargo door
F-27-600: Quick change variant
F-27M: Military model of -400
FH-227: Fairchild built

Fokker 50/60

Twin-turboprop short-haul airliner

Jeremy Flack/API

The Fokker 50 was the follow on from the F-27 Friendship based on the -500. The prototype was first flown on December 28th, 1985 and deliveries commenced in August 1987.

The 50 featured a new digital flightdeck, six bladed composite propellers, and a twin nose wheel. A Fokker 50 was the Fokker aircraft built before all production ceased with its delivery in May 1997.

The 60 is a utility model of the 50 which incorporated a 1.62m fuselage increase

A total of 212 Fokker 50s and 60s were built before the lines were shut down due to financial difficulties.

VARIANTS

50: Initial production model
50: High Performance - Fitted with PW127B
50: Utility - Multipurpose model
50: Maritime, Enforcer, Kingbird, Black Crow - military models
60 - 50: with 1.62 fuselage strength

Fokker F-28 Fellowship

Twin-turbofan regional airliner

Jeremy Flack/API

The F-28 Fellowship was announced in 1962. The prototype was first flown on May 9th, 1967 and delivery commenced in February 1969.

A total of 212 had been delivered when production ended in 1997.

VARIANTS

F-28: Fellowship 1000 - Initial production model
F-28: Fellowship 2000 - Stretched fuselage
F-28: Fellowship 5000 - 1000 with larger wings + increased power
F-28: Fellowship 6000 - 2000 with larger wings + increased power

Fokker 70/100
Twin-turbofan regional airliner

Jeremy Flack/API

The Fokker 100 was launched in November 1983 at the same time as the 50. The prototype first flew on November 30th, 1986 and deliveries commenced in February 1988.

The Fokker 100 featured the longest fuselage, new wings and a digital cockpit.

The 4.62m shorter Fokker 70 prototype was built by modifying the second 100 prototype. It took to the again on April 2nd, 1993 with deliveries commencing in October 1994.

Production the last Fokker 100 ended with the last delivery in April 1997.

VARIANTS
70: Initial production model
Executive Jet 70
Executive Jet 70ER
100: Initial production model
100QC: Quick Change model

Ilyushin Il-62
Four-turbofan long-haul airliner

Jeremy Flack/API

The Il-62 was first flown on January 3rd, 1963 and entered service in 1967.

Initial production powered by the Kuznetsov NK8

Production of the Il-62 has been completed and 289 were built.

VARIANTS
Il-62: Initial production model
Il-62M: Increased capacity & power
Il-62MK: Strengthened wing & increased capacity

Ilyushin Il-86
Four-turbofan medium-haul airliner

Jeremy Flack/API

The Il-86 was Russia's first wide-body airliner. The prototype first flew on December 22nd 1976 and it entered service in 1981.

The 130.5 kN Kuznetsov NK8 powered Il-86 proved to be not only underpowered but also noisy. As a result they didn't pass the Cat 3 restrictions. A planned to re-engine has stumbled over funding

Production ended in 1994 with 104 delivered

VARIANTS
Il-86: Initial production model

Ilyushin Il-96
Four-turbofan long-haul airliner

Although it looks similar to the Il-86, the Il-96 a significantly new design with new more efficient wings including winglets and longer fuselage.

Initially the design was referred to as the Il-96-350 then changed to Il-96M. The prototype first flew on April 6th, 1993.

Jeremy Flack/API

Deliveries followed in 1996. It is planned that later production models will be fitted with the Aviadvigatel PS-90P when available.

Orders and production have suffered as a result of the Russian economy. As a result orders for the Il-96 are 27 with 11 having been delivered.

VARIANTS
Il-96-300: Initial production model
Il-96M: Upgraded with western avionics & engines
Il-96PU: Presidential VIP model
Il-96T: Freighter

Lockheed L.1011 Tristar
Three-turbofan long-haul airliner

Jeremy Flack/API

Lockheed commenced a study for a new airliner in 1966 which resulted in the Tristar. The prototype first flew on November 16th, 1970. Deliveries commenced in April 1972.

The Rolls Royce RB.211 was selected as the powerplant. Part way through the development, Rolls Royce were declared bankrupt which delayed the whole project and let the DC-10 gain the lead in sales.

Tristar production ended in 1983 by which time a total of 249 had been delivered.

VARIANTS

Tristar: Initial production model

Tristar 50: Converted initial model with higher MTOW

Tristar 100: Higher MTOW & fuel capacity

Tristar 150: Conversion on initial model to increase range

Tristar 200: Uprated engines + higher MTOW

Tristar 250: Re-engined initial model

Tristar 500: Short fuselage with long-range

McDonnell Douglas DC-8

Four-engined medium/long-haul airliner

Jeremy Flack/API

Design of the DC-8 commenced in 1955. The prototype first flew on May 30th, 1958 and deliveries commenced the following year.

Most of the DC-8 variants differed mainly with just powerplant and performance. However the - 60 series which resulted in significantly varying fuselage length of which the -63 was the longest. In addition, some had wingspan increases. A number had their early turbojets replaced by quieter more efficient turbofans. Those that did not were required to fit hushkits to operate at most airports following introduction of the Chapter 3 noise restrictions. Most operate as freighters.

When production ended in May 1972, a total of 556 had been built

VARIANTS

DC-8-10: Initial production model with JT3Cs

DC-8-20: Increased MTOW powered by JT4As

DC-8-30: Long range with JT4As

DC-8-40: Long range with Conway turbofans

DC-8-50: Long range with JT3D turbofans

DC-8-60: Stretched model with JT3D turbofans

McDonnell Douglas DC-9

Twin-turbofan short/medium-haul airliner

Jeremy Flack/API

Initial design studies for the DC-9 commenced in 1962. The prototype first flew in February 25th, 1965 and entered service in the December.

Each of the variants were offered as DC-9F freighter, DC-9CF convertible or DC-9RC rapid change. Each of these feature a cargo door.

Surviving DC-9s have required modifying and hushkits fitted to comply with current airport noise restrictions.

Development continued with the MD-80.

When production of the DC-9 ended a total of 976 had been built.

VARIANTS

DC-9-10: Initial production model

DC-9-15: Increased power and MTOW

DC-9-20: Increased wingspan, power & short fuselage

DC-9-30: Increased wingspan, fuselage length and power

DC-9-40: Further increased fuselage length & power

DC-9-50: High density, further increased fuselage length model

C-9: Military model

McDonnell Douglas DC-10

Three-turbofan medium/long-haul airliner

Jeremy Flack/API

The DC-10 came into being as a result of a specification for a new aircraft issued by American Airlines in 1966. A design was agreed and an order placed for 25. When United Air Lines placed an order for 30, production was authorised.

The prototype was first flown on August 29th, 1970 and the DC-10 entered service in August 1971.

The initial DC-10-10 model was designed for short to medium domestic routes (480 - 5,795kms). The -20 was re-designated -40. The -30 and -40 are equipped with an additional central undercarriage. The convertible CF models feature a large cargo door towards the front.

When DC-10 production ended in 1989 a total of 446 DC-10s had been built including 60 as KC-10s for the USAF.

VARIANTS

DC-10-10: Initial production model

DC-10-15: Increased power model

DC-10-10CF: Cargo/passenger convertible

DC-10-20: Increased MTOW and range (to -40)

DC-10-30: Longer, extended range model

DC-10-30ER: Further extended range model

DC-10-30CF: Cargo/passenger convertible

DC-10-40: Originally -20, then re-designated

KC-10: Military model

Raytheon (Beech) 1900

Twin-turboprop commuter airliner

The 1900 was developed from the Super King Air and the prototype first flew on September 3rd, 1982.

Jeremy Flack/API

The 1900 has been popular with commuter airlines and has seen a number ordered as corporate transports. A military variant serves with the US Army and Air Force as the C-12J

Manufacture of the 1900C continued until 1991 with 248 built. Production continues with the 1900D.

VARIANTS

1900C: Initial production model
1900C1: Increased fuel with wet wing
1900D: Increased headroom model of 1900C
C-12J: Military transport

Saab 340

Twin-turboprop regional airliner

Jeremy Flack/API

The 340 commenced as a joint venture by SAAB with Fairchild which was launched in 1980. Fairchild subsequently withdrew to become a subcontractor. The prototype was first flown on January 25th, 1983, Deliveries commenced in 1985.

The 340B had a better hot and high performance which then became the standard production model. It featured an increased span tailplane.

The 340BPlus introduced various improvements that led to the 2000 including optional extended wingtips.

When production ended in 1999 a total of 459 SAAB 340s had been built

VARIANTS

340A: Initial production model
340B: Improved performance model
340AEW/S100B: Military model
340BPlus: Improved interior and performance

Saab 2000

Twin-turboprop regional airliner

Photo; Saab

The SAAB 2000 was a development of the 340 with a larger wing and new engines. Launched in 1988, the prototype was first flown on March 26th, 1992. Deliveries commenced in August 1994.

The 2000 incorporated the improvements of the 340BPlus with an increased length fuselage and extended wings on which the engines were moved outwards to improve noise reduction.

Although the 2000 was fast and gave good economy with its turboprops, unfortunately for SAAB, the market sought jets.

As orders slowed down a decision was made to halt production. When the last 2000 was delivered in 1999 SAAB had built a total of 53.

VARIANTS

2000: Production model

Tupolev Tu-134

Two-turbofan short-haul airliner

The Tu-134 was developed from the Tu-124 and details were first released in 1964

Jeremy Flack/API

shortly after its first flight. Commercial operations commenced in 1967.

The initial production model could carry up to 72 passengers. This was followed by the stretched Tu-134A which was 2.10m longer and could take up to 80 passengers.

When production ended, over 850 Tu-134s had been built

VARIANTS

Tu-134: Initial production model
Tu-134A: Stretched model with increased MTOW and capacity
Tu-134A-3: Increased power engines
Tu-134B: Spoilers fitted
Tu-134B-1: Internal improvements
Tu-134B-3: Further improvements + increased seating

Tupolev Tu-154

Two-turbofan medium-haul airliner

Jeremy Flack/API

The Tu-154 was originally announced in 1966 and the prototype first flown on October 4th, 1968. It entered service in 1972.

Designed to replace the Il-18 and Tu-104, some 600 examples were delivered of the earlier models.

The Tu-154M replaced the earlier models on the production line during the mid 80's.

Some modifications and fitting of silencers have enabled some Tu-154Ms to continue operating into European airports.

Although production has now ended several incomplete airframes remain after a total of 930 have been delivered.

VARIANTS

Tu-154A: Initial production model
Tu-154B: Improved model
Tu-154B-2: With western avionics
Tu-154C: Freighter
Tu-154M: New engines + increased MTOW & range

Tupolev Tu-204/214
Twin-turbofan medium-haul airliner

Jeremy Flack/API

Development of the Tu-204 to replace the Tu-154 and Il-62 was announced in 1983. The prototype first flew on January 2nd, 1989. Initial commercial operations were as freighters from 1995 and commenced passenger services the following year.

A number of proposed models have been proposed for various purposes. A dual fuel Tu-206 or natural gas powered Tu-216 may be built.

Orders and production have moved slowly with approximately 30 delivered by the end on 1992.

VARIANTS

Tu-204: Initial production model
Tu-204-100: Extended range model with increased MTOW
Tu-204-120: Powered by RB211s

Tu-204-120C: Cargo model of -120
Tu-204-300: 164 passenger, 9,000km range model
Tu-214: Increased weight and range model
Tu-214C: Combi model

XAC Y-7/MA60
Twin-turboprop short-haul airliner

Jeremy Flack/API

The Y-7 is a Chinese reverse engineered version of the Antonov An-24. The prototype was first flown on December 25th, 1970 and entered service in January 1984.

Production is well in excess of 100 with the majority used by civilian operators.

VARIANTS

Y-7: Initial production model
Y-7: Freighter - All cargo model
Y-7-100: Improved model with winglets
Y-7-200: Westernised with PW127 turboprops
Y-7H: Military models
MA60: Further westernised including avionics

Yakovlev Yak-40
Three-turbofan regional airliner

Jeremy Flack/API

Design of the Yak-40 commenced in the mid 60's to replace the Li-2 (Russian built DC-3). The prototype first flew on October 21st, 1966 and it entered service in September 1968.

It has proved to be highly successful to the extent that when production ended in 1985 a total of 1011 had been built.

VARIANTS

Yak-40: Basic production model

Yakovlev Yak-42
Three-turbofan short/medium-haul airliner

Jeremy Flack/API

The Yak-42 was designed to replace the Tu-134 in the early 70's. The prototype first flew on March 7th, 1975.

Western avionics incorporated in the Yak-42 to increase its appeal and became the standard production model. A 6.03m stretched model has been proposed as the -200 with a 150 capacity.

Production totals approach 200.

VARIANTS

Yak-42: Initial production model
Yak-42A: Re-designated Yak-42D
Yak-42B: Re-designated Yak-42D-100
Yak-42D: Increased fuel/range + western avionics
Yak-42D-100: Improved spoilers/flaps/avionics
Yak-42-200: Stretched model with increased MTOW
Yak-42T: Freighter

Specifications

Dimensions have been rounded up or down to one decimal place.

Aircraft type	Seats	Engine
Aerospatiale/BAC Concorde	128	4 x 17,260kg st Olympus 593 Mk.602 turbojet
Airbus A300-600R	2 + 266/361	2 x 274kN CF6-80C2A5 or PW4158 turbofan
Airbus A310-300	2 + 210/280	2 x 238+kN CF6-80C2 or PW4152/6A turbofan
Airbus A318-100	2 + 107/129	2 x 98.3+kN PW6122 or PW6124 turbofan
Airbus A319-100	2 + 124/145	2 x 97.9+kN CFM56-5A/B/P or V2522/4-A5 turbofan
Airbus A320-200	2 + 152/180	2 x 111.2+kN CFM56-5. V2500-A1 or V2527-A5 turbofan
Airbus A321-100	2 + 185/220	2 x 133.4+kN CFM56-5B/P, V2530-A5 or CFM56-5B2 turbofan
Airbus A330-300	2 + 335/440	2 x 300+kN CF6-80E, PW4164 or Trent 768 turbofan
Airbus A340-300	2 + 295/440	4 x 151.2kN CFM CFM56-5C4 turbofan
Airtech (CASA) CN-235-200	2 + 46	2 x 1,305kN GE CT7-9C turboprop
Antonov An-24V	3 + 44/50	2 x 2,148kW Ivencko Ai-24 turboprop
Avions Transport Regional ATR 42-500	2 + 42/50	2 x 1,610kW P&WC PW127E turboprop
Avions Transport Regional ATR 72-200	2 + 64/74	2 x 1,611kW P&WC PW124B turboprop
Avro RJ85	2 + 85/112	4 x 31.1kN Allied Signal LF.507 turbofan
BAe Jetstream 31	2 + 19	2 x 761kW Allied Signal TPE331-12UAR turboprop
Boeing 707-320B	3 + 219	4 x 75.7kN P&W JT3D turbofan
Boeing 717-200	2 + 106/117	2 x 82.3kN BMW RR BR715-A1-30 turbofan
Boeing 727-200	3 + 163/189	3 x 72kN P&W JT8D-17R turbofan
Boeing 737-200A	2 + 115/130	2 x 71kN P&W JT8D-15A turbofan
Boeing 737-400	2 + 146/168	2 x 97.9+kN CFM CFM56-3B2 or -3C turbofan
Boeing 737-700	2 + 126/149	2 x 97.9kN CFM CFM56-7B turbofan
Boeing 747-200B	3 + 385/500	4 x 222+kN RB211-524. CF6-50 or JT9D-7R turbofan
Boeing 747-400	2 + 416/568	4 x 252+kN PW4056, CF6-80C or RB211-524 turbofan
Boeing 757-200	2 + 178/239	2 x 169.9+kN PW2037, RR 535E4 or PW2040 turbofan
Boeing 767-300ER	2 + 269/350	2 x 222+kN CF6-80, PW400 or BR211-524 turbofan
Boeing 777-300	2 + 368/550	2 x 409+kN GE90-92B, Trent 892, PW4090 or 8 turbofan
Boeing (McDD) MD-11ER	2 + 250/410	3 x 267+kN PW4460, PW4462 or CF6-80 turbofan
Boeing (McDD) MD-82	2 + 172	2 x 93.4kN P&W JT8D-217 turbofan
Boeing (McDD) MD-90-30	2 + 172	2 x 111.2kN IAE V2525-D5 turbofan
Bombardier (Canadair) CRJ-200ER	2 + 50/52	2 x 41kN GE CF-34-3B1 turbofan
Bombardier (Canadair) CRJ-700ER	2 + 70	2 x 56.4kN GE CF34-8C1 turbofan
Bombardier (DHC) DHC-6 Twin Otter 300	2 + 20	2 x 462kW P&W PT6A-27 turboprop
Bombardier (DHC) DHC-7 Dash 7-100	2 + 48	4 x 857kW PT6A-50 turboprop
Bombardier (DHC) DHC-8 Dash 8-Q300	2 + 50/56	2 x 1,864 kW P&WC PW123B turboprop
CASA C.212-200	2 + 24	2 x 671 kW Allied Signal TPE331-10R turboprop
Dornier Do 228-212	2 + 19	2 x 578.7kW AS TPE331-5-252D or -10 turboprop
Embraer EMB-120ER Brasilia	2 + 30	2 x 1,342kW P&WC PW118 or PW118A turboprop
Embraer ERJ-145ER	2 + 50	2 x 31.3kN Allison Ae3007A turbofan
Fairchild Dornier 328JET	2 + 32/34	2 x 26.9kN P&WC PW306/9 turbofan
Fairchild (Swearingen) Metro 23	2 + 19	2 x 746kW Allied Signal TPE331-11U-612G turboprop
Fokker F27-500	2 + 52/56	2 x 1,730kW RR Dart 536-7R turboprop
Fokker 50-100	2 + 46/58	2 x 1,865 kW P&WC PW125B turboprop
Fokker F28 Fellowship 4000	2 + 85	2 x 44kN RR RB183-2 Mk.555-15p turbofan
Fokker 100	2 + 107/122	2 x 61.6kN RR Tay Mk.620 turbofan
Ilyushin Il-62M	5 + 198	4 x 107.9kN Solviev D-30KU turbofan
Ilyushin Il-86	3 + 316/350	4 x 164.6kN P&W PW2337 turbofan
Ilyushin Il-96M	3 + 312/375	4 x 164.6kN P&W PW2337 turbofan
Lockheed L.1011 TriStar-500	3 + 330	3 x 222kN RR RB211-524B turbofan
McDonnell Douglas DC-8-63	3 + 259	4 x 76kN P&W JT3D-1 turbofan
McDonnell Douglas DC-9-50	2 + 139	2 x 68.9+ P&W JT8D-15 or -17 turbofan
McDonnell Douglas DC-10-30	3 + 255/380	3 x 234kN GE CF6-50C2 turbofan
Raytheon (Beech) 1900D	2 + 19	2 x 954kW P&WC PT6A 67D turboprop
Saab 340B	2 + 35/37	2 x 1,395kW GE CT7-9B turboprop
Saab 2000	2 + 50/58	2 x 3,096kW Allison AE 2100A turboprop
Tupolev Tu-134A	3 + 76/80	2 x 66.75kN Soloviev D-30-II turbofan
Tupolev Tu-154M	3 + 148/166	3 x 104kN Aviadvigatel D-30KU-154-II turbofan
Tupolev Tu-214	3 + 184/212	3 x 191.7kN RR RB-211-535 or Aviadvigatel PS-90 turbofan
XAC MA60	2 + 60	2 x 2051kW P&W PW127 turboprop
Yakovlev Yak-40	2 + 27/32	3 x 14.7kN Ivchenko AI-25 turbofan
Yakovlev Yak-42D	2 + 120	3 x 63.4kN ZMKB Progress D-36 turbofan

Wingspan	Length	Height	Max Speed	Range
25.6m (83ft 10in)	62.1m (203ft 9in)	12.2m (40ft)	M2.05 (1,176kt; 2,179km/h)	3,450nm (6,390km)
44.8m (147ft 1in)	54.1m (177ft 5in)	16.5m (54ft 3in)	M0.82 (484kt; 897km/h)	4,160nm (7,700km)
43.9m (144ft 0in)	46.7m (153ft 1in)	15.8m (51ft 10in)	M0.82 (484kt; 897km/h)	4,350nm (8,050km)
34.1m (111ft 10in)	31.5m (103ft 3in)	12.6m (41ft 3in)	M0.82 (470kt; 870km/h)	1,500nm (2,778km)
34.1m (111ft 10in)	33.8m (111ft 0in)	11.8m (38ft 7in)	M0.82 (470kt; 870km/h)	3,697nm (6,846km)
34.1m (111ft 10in)	37.6m (123ft 3in)	11.8m (38ft 7in)	M0.82 (470kt; 870km/h)	2,800nm (5,185km)
34.1m (111ft 10in)	44.5m (146ft 0in)	11.8m (38ft 9in)	M0.82 (470kt; 870km/h)	2,325nm (4,306km)
60.3m (197ft 10in)	63.7m (208ft 11in)	16.8m (55ft 3in)	M0.86 (493kt; 912km/h)	5,500nm (10,186km)
60.3m (197ft 10in)	63.6m (208ft 8in)	16.8m (55ft 3in)	M0.86 (493kt; 912km/h)	7,100nm (13,150km)
25.8m (84ft 8in)	21.4m (70ft 3in)	8.20m (26ft 10in)	240kt (445km/h)	957nm (1,773km)
29.2m (95ft 10in)	23.5m (77ft 3in)	8.3m (27ft 4in)	243kt (450km/h)	1,293nm (2,400km)
24.6m (80ft 8in)	22.7m (74ft 5in)	7.6m (24ft 11in)	306kt (563km/h)	1,000nm (1,852km)
27.1m (88ft 9in)	27.2m (89ft 2in)	7.7m (25ft 2in)	284kt (526km/h)	910nm (1,685km)
26.2m (86ft)	28.6m (93ft 10in)	8.6m (28ft 2in)	300kt (555km/h)	1,600nm (2,963km)
15.6m (52ft)	14.4m (47ft 2in)	8.6m (28ft 2in)	263kt (488km/h)	419nm (778km)
44.4m (145ft 9in)	46.6m (152ft 11in)	12.9m (42ft 5in)	M0.95 (548kt; 1,014km/h)	5,420nm (10,040km)
28.5m (93ft 6in)	37.8m (124ft)	8.9m (29ft 1in)	M0.76 (438kt; 811km/h)	1,730nm (3,204km)
32.9m (108ft)	46.7m (153ft 2in)	10.4m (34ft 0in)	M0.95 (548kt; 1,014km/h)	2,370nm (4,392km)
28.4m (93ft 0in)	30.5m (100ft 2in)	11.3m (37ft 0in)	M0.84 (481kt; 890km/h)	2,060nm (3,815km)
28.9m (94ft 9in)	36.5m (119ft 7in)	11.1m (36ft 6in)	M0.84 (481kt; 890km/h)	1,960nm (3,629km)
34.3m (112ft 7in)	33.6m (110ft 4in)	12.6m (41ft 3in)	M0.82 (470kt; 870km/h)	3,245nm (6,009km)
59.6m (195ft 8in)	70.5m (231ft 4in)	19.3m (63ft 5in)	M0.92 (525kt; 973km/h)	5,400nm (12,223km)
64.4m (211ft 5in)	70.7m (231ft 5in)	19.4m (63ft 8in)	M0.88 (507kt; 938km/h)	7,284nm (13,445km)
38.1m (124ft 10in)	47.3m (155ft 3in)	13.6m (44ft 6in)	M0.86 (493kt; 919km/h)	3,030nm (7,270km)
47.6m (156ft 1in)	54.9m (180ft 1in)	15.9m (52ft 0in)	M0.86 (493kt; 912km/h)	5,505nm (10,195km)
60.9m (199ft 11in)	73.9m (242ft 4in)	18.5m (60ft 9in)	M0.89 (510kt; 944km/h)	5,720nm (10,593km)
51.7m (169ft 5in)	61.6m (202ft 2in)	17.6m (57ft 8in)	M0.945 (542kt; 1,003km/h)	7,240nm (13,408km)
32.9m (107ft 10in)	45.1m (147ft 10in)	9.00m (29ft 6in)	M0.87 (500kt; 925km/h)	2,050nm (3,798km)
32.8m (107ft 8in)	46.5m (152ft 7in)	9.33m (30ft 7in)	M0.76 (437kt; 809km/h)	2,085nm (3,862km)
21.2m (69ft 7in)	26.8m (87ft 10in)	6.2m (20ft 5in)	M0.81 (465kt; 860km/h)	1,645nm (3,046km)
23.2m (76ft 3in)	32.5m (106ft 8in)	7.6m (24ft 10in)	M0.83 (475kt; 879km/h)	2,032nm (3,763km)
19.8m (65ft 0in)	15.8m (51ft 9in)	5.7m (18ft 8in)	182kt (338km/h)	700nm (1,297km)
28.4m (93ft 0in)	24.5m (80ft 6in)	8.0m (26ft 2in)	239kt (443km/h)	1,190nm (2,204km)
27.4m (95ft 0in)	25.6m (84ft 3in)	9.5m (24ft 7in)	285kt (528km/h)	800nm (1,483km)
27.4m (90ft 0in)	25.7m (84ft 3in)	7.5m (24ft 7in)	208kt (386km/h)	410nm (760km)
17.0m (55ft 8in)	16.6m (54ft 4in)	4.9m (16ft 0in)	255kt (428km/h)	560nm (1,038km)
19.8m (64ft 11in)	20.1m (65ft 11in)	6.4m (20ft 10in)	327kt (606km/h)	800nm (1,482km)
20.0m (65ft 9in)	29.9m (98ft 0in)	6.8m (22ft 2in)	M0.78 (450kt; 833km/h)	1,320nm (2,444km)
21.0m (68ft 10in)	21.3m (69ft 10in)	7.2m (23ft 9in)	335kt (620km/h)	1,000nm (1,852km)
17.4m (57ft 0in)	18.1m (59ft 5in)	5.1m (16ft 8in)	290kt (537km/h)	1,115nm (2,065km)
29.0m (95ft 2in)	25.1m (82ft 3in)	8.7m (28ft 7in)	259kt (480km/h)	935nm (1,741km)
29.0m (95ft 2in)	25.3m (82ft 10in)	8.3m (27ft 3in)	290kt (537km/h)	1,665nm (2,678km)
25.1m (82ft 3in)	29.6m (97ft 2in)	8.5m (27ft 10in)	M0.75 (430kt; 795km/h)	1,025nm (1,900km)
28.1m (92ft 2in)	35.5m (116ft 6in)	8.5m (27ft 10in)	M0.77 (441kt; 816km/h)	1,550nm (2,870km)
43.2m (141ft 9in)	53.1m (174ft 9in)	12.4m (40ft 7in)	M0.85 (486kt; 900km/h)	4,210nm (7,800km)
48.1m (157ft 9in)	59.5m (195ft 4in)	15.8m (51ft 10in)	M0.89 (512kt; 950km/h)	1,944nm (3,600km)
60.1m (197ft 3in)	64.7m (212ft 3in)	15.7m (51ft 7in)	M0.86 (493kt; 912km/h)	6,195nm (11,482km)
47.3m (155ft 4in)	50.1m (164ft 3in)	16.9m (55ft 4in)	M0.84 (481kt; 890km/h)	5,297nm (9,815km)
45.2m (148ft 5in)	57.1m (187ft 5in)	12.9m (42ft 5in)	M0.91 (521kt; 965km/h)	4,000nm (7,400km)
28.5m (93ft 5in)	40.7m (133ft 7in)	8.5m (28ft 0in)	M0.87 (500kt; 926km/h)	2,195nm (4,066km)
50.4m (165ft 5in)	55.5m (182ft 1in)	17.7m (58ft 1in)	M0.88 (505kt; 934km/h)	3,800nm (7,040km)
17.7m (58ft 0in)	17.6m (57ft 10in)	4.7m (15ft 6in)	283kt (524km/h)	1,476nm (2,736km)
21.4m (70ft 4in)	19.7m (64ft 8in)	6.97m (22ft 11in)	250kt (463km/h)	910nm (1,685km)
24.7m (81ft 3in)	27.3m (89ft 6in)	7.73m (25ft 4in)	270kt (500km/h)	1,549nm (2,868km)
29.0m (95ft 2in)	37.1m (121ft 7in)	9.1m (30ft 0in)	M0.85 (485kt; 897km/h)	1,630nm (3,020km)
37.6m (123ft 3in)	47.9m (157ft 2in)	11.4m (37ft 5in)	M0.90 (515kt; 953km/h)	3,723nm (6,900km)
41.8m (137ft 2in)	46.1m (151ft 3in)	13.4m (45ft 7in)	M0.80 (459kt; 850km/h)	2,591nm (4,800km)
29.2m (95ft 10in)	24.7m (81ft 0in)	8.9m (29ft 1in)	248kt (460km/h)	1,325nm (2,450km)
25.0m (82ft 0in)	20.4m (66ft 10in)	6.5m (21ft 4in)	M0.70 (401kt; 742km/h)	971nm (1,800km)
34.9m (114ft 6in)	36.2m (118ft 10in)	9.8m (32ft 3in)	M0.76 (437kt; 810km/h)	1,240nm (2,300km)

Index

Index